the Alphabet

RON SILLIMAN

the Alphabet

The University of Alabama Press
Tuscaloosa

The University of Alabama Press
Tuscaloosa, Alabama 35487-0380

Manufactured in the United States of America

Designer: Michele Myatt Quinn
Typeface: AGaramond

The paper on which this book is printed meets the minimum requirements of American National Standard for Information Sciences-Permanence of Paper for Printed Library Materials, ANSI Z39.48-1984.

Library of Congress Cataloging-in-Publication Data

Silliman, Ronald, 1946–
The alphabet / Ron Silliman.
p. cm. — (Modern and contemporary poetics)
Includes bibliographical references and index.
ISBN 978-0-8173-1618-1 (cloth: alk. paper) —ISBN 978-0-8173-0 (pbk. : alk. paper) 1. Experimental poetry. I. Title.
PS3569.I445A78 2008
811'.54—dc22 2007038309

For Krishna Evans

Contents

the Alphabet

ALBANY

for Cliff Silliman

If the function of writing is to "express the world." My father withheld child support, forcing my mother to live with her parents, my brother and I to be raised together in a small room. Grandfather called them niggers. I can't afford an automobile. Far across the calm bay stood a complex of long yellow buildings, a prison. A line is the distance between. They circled the seafood restaurant, singing "We shall not be moved." My turn to cook. It was hard to adjust my sleeping to those hours when the sun was up. The event was nothing like their report of it. How concerned was I over her failure to have orgasms? Mondale's speech was drowned by jeers. Ye wretched. She introduces herself as a rape survivor. Yet his best friend was Hispanic. I decided not to escape to Canada. Revenue enhancement. Competition and spectacle. kinds of drugs. If it demonstrates form some people won't read it. Television unifies conversation. Died in action. If a man is a player, he will have no job. Becoming prepared to live with less space. Live ammunition. Secondary boycott. My crime is parole violation. Now that the piecards have control. Rubin feared McClure would read Ghost Tantras at the teach-in. This form is the study group. The sparts are impeccable, though filled with deceit. A benefit reading. He seduced me. AFT, local 1352. Enslavement is permitted as punishment for crime. Her husband broke both of her eardrums. I used my grant to fix my teeth. They speak in Farsi at the comer store. YPSL. The national question. I look forward to old age with some excitement. 42 years for Fibreboard Products. Food is a weapon. Yet the sight of people making love is deeply moving. Music is essential. The cops wear shields that serve as masks. Her lungs heavy with asbestos. Two weeks too old to collect orphan's benefits. A woman on the train asks Angela Davis for an autograph. You get read your Miranda. As if a correct line would somehow solve the future. They murdered his parents just to make the point. It's not easy if your audience doesn't identify as readers. Mastectomies are done by men. Our pets live at whim. Net income is down 13%. Those distant sirens down in the valley signal great hinges in the lives of strangers. A phone tree. The landlord's control of terror is implicit. Not just a party but a culture. Copayment. He held the Magnum with both hands and ordered me to stop. The garden is a luxury (a civilization of snail and spider). They call their clubs batons. They call their committees clubs. Her friendships with women are different. Talking so much is oppressive. Outplacement. A shadowy locked facility using drugs and doublecelling (a rest home). That was the Sunday Henry's father murdered his wife on the front porch. If it demonstrates form they can't read it. If it demonstrates mercy they have something worse in mind. Twice, carelessness has led to abortion. To own a basement. Nor is the sky any less constructed. The design of a department store is intended to leave you fragmented, off-balance. A lit drop. They photograph Habermas to hide the hairlip. The verb to *be* admits the assertion. The body is a prison. a garden. In kind. Client populations (cross the tundra). Off the books. The whole neighborhood is empty in the daytime. Children form lines at the end of each recess. Eminent domain. Rotating chair. The history of Poland in 90 seconds. Flaming pintos. There is no such place as the economy, the self. That bird demonstrates the sky. Our home, we were told, had been broken, but who were these people we lived with? Clubbed in the stomach, she miscarried. There were bayonets on campus. cows in India, people shoplifting books. I just want to make it to lunch time. Uncritical of nationalist movements in the Third World. Letting the dishes sit for a week. Macho culture of convicts. With a shotgun and "in defense" the officer shot him in the face. Here, for a moment, we are joined. The want-ads lie strewn on the table.

BLUE

for Gil Ott

The Marchioness went out at five o'clock. The sky was blue yet tinged with pink over the white spires which broke up the east horizon. The smell of the afternoon's brief shower was still evident and small pools of clear water collected in the tilt of the gutters, leaves and tiny curling scraps of paper drifting in the miniature tides which nonetheless caught and reflected the swollen sun, giving the boulevard its jeweled expression.

Government was therefore an attitude. Dour, the camel pushed with his nose against the cyclone fence. The smell of damp eucalyptus is everything! You stare at your car before you get in.

From here we can see the sex. They are folding the flyers before stuffing them into envelopes. Badminton is nothing to be ashamed of. Grease and old tire marks streak the road. From here we can tell the sex.

Rust designs that old truck door. The number of objects is limited. Some leaves on the fern are more yellow. Sooner or later you will have to get up to change the record. That buzz is the dryer.

Longer ones demand a new approach: there's not enough water for a second cup. These crystals are useless on a sunless day. More than that, the fence is apt to give, pulling free of its posts. Tell me the one about the fellaheen again.

It's a trap: they want you to think that light is Venus. Under a microscope we see them absorb their elders. A spider plant is only one design. I took the message.

At dusk, very little is neutral. The corner merchant, a quiet Persian, nods to her as she waits for a break in the traffic. Those who are not consigned to the prolonged concentration of driving have already fallen asleep. At the intersection the sidewalks are rounded.

The flower closes slowly about the unsuspecting fly. The thickness of the gum limits the rhythm of his chewing. Wasn't he happy here, viewing clip after clip of that old successful launch? The glove compartment never held a glove, nor I.

So you go faster, hunched over, avoiding the headlines in the boxes. The taller buildings suck the wind. That butter only appears to be firm, the hood never will quite shut. Between what were once squares of concrete, anonymous weeds bunch & spread.

If challenged, its first response is to spit. This took place at the museum. Wires slope from the pole to the house, where they gather, entering a narrow pipe along its side. This conveys motion. I am writing in shadows. Don't you worry about accessibility too?

Mother simply likes to have the books. Like a serenade, only earlier. He lets the clay on his hands begin to dry. Fuchsia blossoms stain the walk, the doorknob strangled by rubber bands. Another thing, pepper is not a corn.

So what is despair? The cyclist trapped inside her helmet? The girl sent to the grocer for milk? The moment before? The mops on the old porch have begun to dissolve. Don't turn the light on till you get the shade. Atop a small house, the cartoon dog types away. Turn the page.

Shorter is. The fern sits, its clay pot in a pool of water. In doubles, that's called poaching. The back of the television faces the window. From here you can smell the sex. Give those socks a little more time. More narrow.

At the arched door of the restaurant she checks her watch, a delicate gold bracelet dangling from her wrist. Bands of a deep orange streak a near purple sky, the brisk air shuddering in the small trees, slender branches bending back. Children begin to gather up their toys; lights on, their homes begin to glow. The host, recognizing the Marchioness, invites her in.

CARBON

for Erica Hunt

I

But this is a false tart, the trap door insecurely latched, a tear in the velvet curtain. Yet the tear was but a drop of glycerin sliding down her cheek. Nonetheless skin is not porcelain, however it spots.

But the display of sugar bowls shaped like cabbage continued to draw its crowd, ears wired to rented cassettes, milling. So the cowboy slowly unfolded the napkin and, with a ballpoint, began to draw his gun. Yet relative to what sleep is a lap defined?

So the animals of the wood gathered round the spreading princess, small animal noses twitching in the dusky pine-scented air. But what chest of drawers is not the violence of number? And then went down to the chips, set wheel to gambit, forth in the Reno night.

Yet a chair is not avoidable. Nonetheless a V of shingles turned upside down is not a roof any more than the glaze in a potter's eye, which is blue compared to the ocean's olive gray. So there's a vacuum just for the car.

But a point *is* reached implying distance, implicating even the Slinky's progress across the clipped lawn in the face of a berating rooster. So the scar tissue of definition settles, forming the crust of syntax. Yet the sprinkler is a portable fountain.

Later, there's no more coffee in the hollow of the cup, merely a brown stain, while an impatient audience waits in the dark, starting to whistle and stamp. But but. Thus purple is a trademark and this violet is red.

Therefore the semicolon is but a hiccup in the line. Yet the narrative of shadow crosses the garden, cool and damp. Nonetheless, those two guys in that parked Buick have just got to be narcs.

II

A simple message staples the sleeping, gaseous, known for his alludic (dip) fleece.

Gravity evaporates the eye's cushion.

Heroic scrubpads, red-yellow, stalk the slate, suck knobs, scud.

The ranch glows in the postcard, jeeps waddling thru sage, fridge shudder, sun seen, registered dianetics.

Arrows in the heart of blintz, straw with a bend, stutters the pickup's direct-to-disc shag.

Paprika mascara, tuna with a reason, tender is the hobby, sees in Elko the plantains.

Inverted bulb snaps mouth.

III

Invented blob snips north: stanza shuts the kiddygate; So a body sags with the age of reason.

Biopsy finagles closure: art-broom viewed as multilith, rolodex, sky. Therefore cannabis unequals fingers against the slate.

Harmony mops the auditorium: pink as Texas deferred, doors adjoined index perpendicular wall. So this is where the emotion is, spotted.

Glass pistol worn as box: do not feed the numbers. But alcohol is its own remark.

Pentagon of tot-finder blooms: earwig turns at thunder's linen. Yet principle of housing projects across axis of traffic at twilight.

Steady drizzle of connotation: push-pull with deckled lip. However canvas tablets start to fade on mesa.

Nextness is wetter and I want hard: sponge of state with echo in place. But then the radio begins to ring.

IV

Damp, like the sandwich of reason. Second, because I always have. A fish named for a figure in Shakespeare: a politician or outlaw portrayed by Robert Redford. This proves conjunction, jet trails dotting 'i's in the mountains, cat licking its penis. Look at the city through a microscope. These fingers refer back to the previous sentence. The smell of burning leaves clogs the air.

Yet down the hill is In Town. A plastic pumpkin into which to put candies. Thereby disputing the chimes of my lexicon, vacant, blooming, spotted, terry cloth band about its wrist. Stand there real natural like: rhyme with the shape of pancreas. A taxidermist backorders horns, smell of chicken, while the streetlamps pop on. Little pyramids atop each taxi shimmer. Coming soon to a paragraph near you.

So there's always a drain in the floor of a tavern john. Each word starting to bloom at the heat of your approach: a sculpture from which to hang the fern of a satisfaction. Nor am I the only person in this room speaking aloud to myself, occupational hazard. Rope-a-dope to justified margin, form of command. Bluster of espresso machine, long levers, drowning taped guitar, exact depiction of incorrect answer: as yet. Cigars do not float above Utah moonscape. Therefore tropics.

V

The necessity of this writing is.

Exhaustion completes the thought

"pangs traced upon nard"

Burden's theory was Abuse the performance. Drip of Marioni at base of palm. Thumb of cocoanut in sea of syrup, corridors in shape of Fox.

Then small girl applied to kitty: plane's shadow explodes before we touch down.
First invent the bottle: cat insists on lap ergo sum.
Between saxophones strike a syntax: do you mark the space at the page top?

Sequence of loop shades into angst
Steam up shower window before chart
Enjambed by brigands on a voyage to

Lubricated afternoons all topless: the space of the shadow contracts, tho it fills our descending field of vision.

Demonstrate the jade tree: therefore coffee rooted in the cup.

A discount despair (to spare): brilliant C of brick, waves of sand through wind exporting.

Sharp hawk of Skratz laugh against perfect all-over surface pressure of flattened Hall fills planetarium. Oil of Aylon, what money Beuys. Ghettobox meditation, pillows without cases, Tepper ware to loss of dividend in word Acconci.

Because heliocentric, therefore asymmetric.

Solder iron sound source

blue cusp

VI

1) Aspics of the theory of mulch (tone) pamper thought (rewriting its will).

2) Embolism of adverb corrodes the noun modeled on the small intestine.

3) No such thing as a phrase.

4) Sentences join, softly weeping amid the sway of lily stalks.

5) Prose is a maize.

6) Echoes gather, later to be removed by Q-tip.

7) Geiger counter sweeps, then blinks.

VII

We, the mind, rain storm, five card stud, settle, setting doves adrift in the air above the volley. But pigeon's mode's debris, deuce. Atari tacked to cauliflower starts to walk. Jacks scuff along the surface of the plaza, face up. Bulldog in a derby closes the lone eye with a doubloon. Tint the world, fore of clubs, amber of bourbon. Therefore tree's bad as its bark.

Prosody alone now, brisk later days, Y framed by drizzle so cobbled, lurch, lurk, look, the page curling into brown, the spotted eye, our hero is the porch, bland and leafy, creamed. Nor any gravel to shade the queen, stalk scraped by air. Thou dumb-born rook, song fails to cattle. Scorch pan to hard, face rang herd pores together. Solo nostril flares (pulse), illumines the mushroomed forest pink. Feet first, toward the punctuation, stones giving way. The dove hang-glides through the fog.

Smell of rot, salt, the moth ball, testicle or sea. Brain grinds to caffeinated loop (shudder), the long blades bend on the lawn, chips gather while stuntmen swing silently between channels to score chalkscrape chorus. Breasts are not twins. I see you (and raise you one). But take notes to demonstrate fractal unity of rain against sprinkler patterned storm or saddle the vice-president. I've already breathed this air. The sedan goes straight to pool's bottom.

I can understand your frustration but. Zeroism dictates rectangularity in art, by confab. Trowel caked in peat sinks into toasties. Slowly a flamingo looks about. The air is ribbed with radar. Bare gleaming shoulder. Next.

Reichian macromusic vs. dog on the porch, unanimous in its foliage, a short-cut, centers on votive cactus, sparking liquids in the prime rate. Nervous energy registers for drift: three of doves. So what is the outside? Massive molar points to jaw, crushing Buicks warm in their primer coats. Tanker kindles on the bay. Pinesol cologne baked in onions, pasted and stapled, wasted in maple, basted in apple in triplicate. It is not the signal that's busy.

Coathangers dangle from a brass floor lamp, a wind chime, a breeze so slight that chopper high over 280 might be the cause. Intent on flowering commerce (royal flush), a theory of porch has eluded the more honed mind. Thoughts are like suction to the starfish which goes rigid in the gift shop. It is not the elimination of constraints but their shapely abuse: the arctic bunny hopped over the retort, moss at the base of dwarf cypress. Torch panda hard, fangs laced to leather. Ink in the ballpoint clots. Rose wilt models direction of time, a syntax.

A century (a surgeon) requires patience (their stickers). Doves have criticized our monuments: I know a little tune (number means less than chips). But one step in each direction nor any. Invited Bob slaps moth: clouds beflag stadium of sky, vend flocks. Knit cap surrounds ears – a command is felt for shifts. Effect of ground cover hedged in rhyme, snail bait, extends preserve to galvanized steps. A rain begins with drops.

DEMO

for Kit Robinson

This is a test.

The hammer of birds (rabbits) secure in the deficit garden, fog along the coast.

Water hammer, rock board – recurrence as key in phlegmatic analysis (fellaheen hurdling custard pie into the face of Bette Midler).

Friends are perpetually "going to get it together," jobwise: the coast is altered one quarter inch.

Just like that.

The window conceived as a form of torture, through which a century is expressed (blue hands, the chartreuse of a tennis ball): dobermans of delight crowd the sun.

Met against metaphor (I want white rooms): the cast is clear.

Up against the woolite, desire for narrative condemns millions – French bread hard as a rock.

Nouns aver facts (pinched nerve at base of neck): a terrycloth sweatband is an insufficient monument (dress for excess), specific as the smell of chalk.

Words row.

The sun, backlighting your blouse, reveals all, newlyweds at a Grateful Dead concert, birthmark of the surgeon general.

Birthright of way: foghorns and a rooster counterpoint hazy morning.

The outer wall of the prison is yellow, the inner one green (old paperback bought at a garage sale).

Verb is the eye of the sentence (world stylized for efficiency's sake): dogs bark.

Dog barks – there is another way to compute the tides.

Eminent ptomaine.

Poets propose sky, only to fall back on cannibalism (downhill on a skateboard).

Crudely mechanical, an adjective grinds meaning from a noun forming the perfect countenance of Elvis on black velvet.

My pockets are a jungle.

High heels grind pavement into paste (memory of color scheme popular in past war) – the construction is *not* parallel (taster's choice), pruned tree's new sprouts.

My hand on your thigh in a dream (not expected): if critics had ethics . . . a suburb without sidewalks.

Flat country with clear conscience.

Vajra banking: the nosebleed is slight but lasts for days (lesbianism seen as a preference for clarity).

A plainness so extreme it makes her striking – pain articulates the spine.

That's poet talk, the door ajar (donation requested).

Going back, crossing out articles (baker's ponytail kept under hat), gradually features widen into flaws, humor mistaken for humor, the mouse beneath the counter, color postcard of the airport, parchmint chicken.

Pulling staples from a pizza, untitled, I rise from the water of the bubble bath: duotone landscape.

A fat lawyer with a hippie wife (an architect).

The next step is not automatic, drawn curtain: sun's glare reflected renders window opaque.

A swamp (the MLA) is reputed to have devoured the children – line break in the trail of crumbs.

Old men walking small dogs (I crouch against a wall to write), the sun in no hurry, jazz penis, the smell of hot pretzels from the far end of the bar – windows of the burnt-out apartment boarded up.

Lipstick stain on wax paper cup (double canzone), tugboat in harbor honks, uh huh, long wasp neck tattooed as if an earring (slender is the nut) – the letters are buglike.

Ceramic teapot imitates cabbage.

New work.

Poetry's not the boiler room of history (in the forest trees unfold), but the discrepancy in scale (nuclear explosion on the cover of *Mushroom Cookbook*) calls dawn itself to attention (this switch for fog).

"Stanza strophe, stanza strophe," taunts the young girl at her still younger brother, a cocker spaniel.

Space farts.

Morning is toxic (sun shines in green sky), red bandana round blonde hair, veins bursting in the eye.

The shape of the day a figure eight, smell of mustard (how those light stockings tint the leg): it's a wrap.

Ears as hooks for glasses (57 words for deduction): roto-reader spins on gerund.

Stop continental drift.

Generic dawn (chromatic rooster) yawns over eastern hills, wreath of flowers atop the hearse, thumbnail longer than the rest.

Here and now.

Here and now.

Here and now.

Ning mind.

A man in a blue bathrobe walks to the corner store (a model of physics, a church) – gestures are quotable (he's wearing thongs) . . .

Aka zoris, the mark of: piglike snoot on small white dog (flesh-coloured hearing-aid), TL, kitchen full of poets.

Take a number, your description is coming.

And with the blade of his pen carved his initials, LZ, into the forehead of the critic.

True shed.

Red brick hospital run by nuns (bowling alley vacant, for lease), ethnographic study of go-carts.

People's heads turn to watch a funeral procession.

Birds march up the slope of the hill, pecking at the cut grass (one's relation to an audience is historical): the wind sends dead leaves skittering (rhymes with punt).

Standing around in the air of an old fart, apricots fading (politics), into changing a lightbulb in the ceiling of a dark room (weather) – balance insinuates order (our books will not be read).

On the hottest day of the year, this small, aged woman is wearing a raincoat (the young man wears a Walkman in a holster).

The shadow of a butterfly.

The park breaks up the sky (a small triangle of cloth covering the nipple of each breast), sun blanched thought.

Busdriver's keychain dangles from his belt (form as a ridged cut seeks to fit), neo-Victorian (from the mind of Minolta).

Ancient, her dog Sadie falls over each time it attempts to scratch (a series of small thuds in the kitchen).

Terms of enjambment.

The fog returns: cop with a toupee appears strangely vulnerable (we wait for the light to change).

Does the work present its sense of space (more art history than art): under the pile of elm leaves (there are no elm leaves) he found his voice.

The sun in a stark sky (red loop, gold loop), shelf life of a mind (this morning my lip is blistered), shining beetle-god scans her universe.

Lap is shown not to exist . . . the blinds are drawn is drawn.

Biography of the senses drying on the blotter.

Sleep's burden is dawn's laboring list (angle of pen to page) . . . job limits personality, vanpool of synapse, styrofoam cup.

A week's growth, the beard seemed tentative, a hint of itself.

Chicken Dachau, Eggs McMassacre, a beautiful woman hauling bags of laundry home in the fog (associations witness structure), smell of rain in pit of summer . . . letting your hair dry on the busride into work.

Aging, faces cave in (super slomo), necks swell, then sag – skull emerges through field of hair.

On the bus, children like to sit apart from their parents, feigning independence.

Fog devoured the hill.

All bleeds toward the gutter only.
Plastic sequence of holes and bumps at rear of one-size-fits-all baseball cap (rubber finger, "we're number one").
Her breasts formed a narrative.

Rounded – rounded first and held up as the cutoff man took the throw from left field.

High heels on a hardwood floor (as they come closer, I realize those two teenagers are signing) . . . parked motorcycles clutter sidewalk.

Elements are gathered (punctuation forms a low wall) – trying to decide before my name is called whether to answer "present" or "here."

Crows cluster in the park at dawn.

Predicated on no more than their clothes, their hairstyles, the expressions on their faces, I give each boarding bus passenger a narrative all their own (this one lets his hand rest knowingly against that woman's ass).

Four-color butterfly.

She's braless beneath her Garfield "I hate Mondays" muscle shirt.

Clothes tattered, the nomadic homeless mentally ill begin to show up in the malls (seniors in wheelchairs in a paratransit minivan).

The cyst as big as her nose (the new plastic supermarket shopping bags harder to stand upright on the sidewalk while waiting for the bus) – this is understood as persona.

Each small city has its band of nostalgic dadaists (just waiting for a show of postcard art) . . . after 4 years the campus leaves you stranded, philosophy listed under Home Ec.

Barefoot on her toes across the kitchen floor.

Bright sun in the long shadows of early morning (I wear dark glasses to shield my eyes from the wind): light is something to read by, a wheelbarrow red without reason.

Proceeding from market study to ground lease, a career move (single again and turning 30).

The discourse of Marxism obscures the state's monopolization of capital within the form of the state (them): the discourse of individual liberty and democratic choice obscures capital's ability to predetermine desire through mass market technology (us) – socialism (economic democracy) nowhere exists.

Green glass shards in the gutter, ground halfway into sand (an airplane glistens reflecting the light of the sun, causing one to see it far out over the bay).

Antinuclear themes in Latino graffiti . . . cherrybomb in a mailbox.

Construction workers in the financial district huddle together for lunch, whistling at women in pantsuits to express fear at the larger tribe.

This causes people to identify with capital as if it were in their interest.

Cartoon advertising painted on the windows of the mattress warehouse ("when do you find the time to write?").

Men touching their girlfriends in public to display power . . . they go to a reading and sit separately (once on a nude beach I watched a woman fondle her lover's balls – every man within eyesight went hard).

Three women escorting 40 seven year olds onto the bus (taste you can count on) . . . it's 9:00 a.m. and the "nickel whores" are already out in front of the Town Pump.

At this point in the work I still haven't settled on the title, posters decaying on the boarded-up windows of the old milk bottling plant.

In the assessor's office, make a list of all property owners on City Block 1254 (a stretch limo parked in front of the officers' club), experience a helicopter overhead as the pulse of its blades.

New park bench all metal and plastic feels wrong.

I notice beercaps and peanut shells at the foot of the gnarled cypress – wind in the palm tree sounds more harsh than that in the eucalyptus.

Lick my balls narrative sequence, tugboats in the discontinuous bay.

A woman in blue shorts (I can describe anything), fog over the far hill.

There is no New York School, 70% of all poetry in the hands of creative writing students (I only slept with Auden out of respect).

I only slept in Arden out of respect: the Cubs at last (bone marrow transplant), what in the morning gets to be written.

Helicopters and maps to chart all the joggers at dawn (an overweight white woman is used to portray the oppressive prison warden in the video of Jermaine Jackson's *Dynamite*).

Poetry fever – catch it!
The bus smells of curry . . . beginnings of smog smear the downtown sky (that our youth lack a sense of history is not their fault): don't Laos me up.

Becoming an old man with too many combs and pens in my pocket (fog predicts sky), the way horses in slow motion are understood to mean something else.

Morning's chatter (chattel), the city symphonic, rattles the windows on the 33rd floor, jostling across the intersection.

Hunker down: morning *is* everywhere, a break in the fog (a break in the dog) . . . I can still taste last night's wine.

From Mission Street we could see the car on the overpass consumed in flames, but later could find no mention of the event on TV or in the papers.

The plot gets sicker.

Smell of the roofers after season's first storm (trashcan my escritoire): her dress (blue vertical stripes) is but a long shirt with a matching belt.

A euphoria on the brink of despair . . . paper-covered wire used to seal trashbags . . . white sox above high heels.

To Do list: that jogger's step is but a half skip (smash pumpkin time).

But used in place of *just* lingers an old reading – let's wait for the next stanza.

Sweet strained feeling in the scrotum later (I used the bacon grease for the scrambled eggs), desire for coffee is nearly erotic.

Monday mornings the guys in the back of the bus discuss yesterday's football (the child wants to be the one to put the quarter in the newspaper rack), blackbird hopping in the gutter at my feet.

The crowd danced to the "space music" as tho feigning a slow motion backstroke.

Notion of quantity defines a plot, is given a name, fingerprints (he do the poh-leese in diff'rent vices), yes m'am, just the facts . . . clang, Mark VII.

"How do you make friends – by talking to people, right?" asks the boy behind me of his mother (she grunts).

New role for pockets in this fall's fashions (surfboard on sawhorse used for ironing), deep gray sky.

Form is passion.

Organic brain syndrome prefers end-rhyme . . . after 3 days of torrential storm, people walk in the new sunshine in raincoats and galoshes . . . trope or treat.

Dr. Stanza I presume (your tires low on air), bag-over-head dramatic monologue: my one vice, my other. . . .

Unmediated, unmedicated.

Through the hole in the knee of the punk rocker's jeans I see his long johns, ribbed white cotton: pools in the parking lot after the rain.

Crime personified by a bloodhound in a trenchcoat fails to acknowledge pervasive absence of economic justice (big breasted woman dripping wet in a t-shirt which reads "Jamaica"), automobile named for endangered species.

Father was an absence a post-structuralist might have use for, music piped into the aquarium.

Vanguard wheelchair more like a golf cart, the proposition of a hat (tone of a smashed wax-paper milk carton kicked down the street).

Switch shoes to alter pressure points on feet (note rhyme), kids repainting rental unit.

Photo of mother dressed as lion for Halloween, 1935 (absence of articles making language poetic), deposit main verb here.

Car double-parked in front of the church, orange window stickers reading 'funeral' . . . res hotel fire escape landing is used as a natural refrigerator at window (milk carton, eggs), perfectly visible from sidewalk tho hotplates are illegal.

The word (round, shining) jets into view (style), the small professors quoting loudly for their kibbles: the lawn sprinkler's sweep forms the perfect trap (see my new gesture).

Samoan shifters join the police.

The hard, smooth surface conceals the watery, incomplete mind (shooting from the foul line): the poems were discreet, each book arriving at a three year interval.

To as in today . . . interliberary loan (the new watch with the leather watchband).

It has been twenty years since the Democratic Party carried a majority of the white vote in a Presidential election (the docents in white coats), my mother says of the cutbacks at Bechtel, "I'm only one-third nuclear now."

One hears only fragments of a talk (the skyline is not to be inferred), umbrella held as a club.

A poetry of the cities vs. a poetry of the campus (women's *needs*, not women's knees), the slow, exaggerated enunciation of the children's TV cartoon hero.

Their eyes shut, each face an index of stress and pain, evening rush hour subway commute (woman in a tweed suit reads the Wall Street Journal).

This focus group suggests a greater attention to the tone-leading of vowels in future rewrites.

The low spray of the mechanical street sweeper, the bald, bearded man all dressed up in black leather and studs (she has a ruby nose pin).

A man cynical so young is apt to grow bitter, a daughter is a dance frozen upon water later in laughter and after we slaughter the pink pet pig we smoke it: pass me the roach.

The problem of problems is the model of the problem imposed upon heaving tissue, such a glass imprisons water, champagne, hours (what is an hour?), sand's form determinate on the beach, a point spread.

The oil atop the peanut butter when one opens a new jar is my index of resistance, homeboy.

This curious half-light or life, the sky muted to admit stars, porch lights on, teenage girls trudging uphill carrying bags of groceries.

To sleep is to read and to read is to wet loom star by a davy-lamp or thread, old v-neck t-shirt through which to see your breasts.

This is a fundamentally serious art.

Giggling (on the defensive), a generation of actualists forgets to breed, we only call the binding perfect.

A decor specific to a small town beauty salon, your eyes draw gauze curtains across the sun setting in my smile: it's not the right that's ragged.

My instinct is to sprint across the street (nomad is an island).

Sushi-roshi: you are what you it, it are what you see meant . . . morning as a state of light elusive in winter, versus the arbitrary quantification of abstracted time (morning as a social contract).

Last night I saw my 11th grade English teacher for the first time in 18 years, I scramble the eggs with sour cream and season with dill and basil.

Are we there yet?

Bus vs. subway, who rides is a political question, the way your galoshes stretch to fit over new jogging shoes, the date feature on the watch has never worked.

An inference engine governs the new politics of stasis (22 line stanzas), money the signifier, credit the signified.

Pen and notebook direct to hardcopy . . . just to sit next to him, he smells of cigars.

Redhead, "thin as a rail," bent over now, glaucoma spreading blindness from the center out (in her wedding dress, 1920, she stares at the photographer, pensive, nervous).

Behind the shade, see curtains.

Man with a large head and feminine face, the microwave oven buzzes "done."

Hats on a cold day (her work at this point more hopeful than formed) . . . poets in the corner talking software.

Each stanza is a poem, each word . . . the tiny body given breadth by the wheelchair (what is found within a wall).

Prose is the distance between (two-prong plug in three-hole socket), the trouble with depiction when attached to an object is, punctuation in the manner of Cassius Clay.

Mood elevator: change notebooks.

Happy face with band aid sells health plan.

First winter run, faking it (knot in my right thigh vs. knot in my lungs).

Birds beneath these deep gray clouds are what give it that sense of distance (in the back of that old white Volvo, between the two babyseats, a ten gallon hat).

In the projects on Christmas eve, I notice how twice as many homes here have their windows decorated with strings of colored lights (attempt to tell a home from a unit).

Is it racist of me to feel sad watching three teenage Latina women walking down 22nd Street pushing strollers (kids and middle-aged men playing softball under the trees in St. Mary's Park, artless lunging after that image of grace)?

On the exercycle, reading the morning paper.

Old tin drum, cut in half, used as a trash can (closed grip reverse lat pull) . . . he finally achieved his perfect imitation of Olson, only to discover that no one cared: at least the cabbies have tenure.

How pink one gets, rising from a hot bath, how limp!

At this hour planes are but lights passing in a black sky . . . one by one, the windows in the houses on the hill go dark.

The man is in handcuffs, his car wedged in by two black-and-whites (by her outfit I see that she works in a donut shop), the glass fogged by the sheer difference between the heat indoors and out.

The sheer presence of the military apparent in any airport (the rhythm of a dulled patience, the tolerance of exhaustion, or of tedium), able to cross a vast lobby, passing hundreds of others, without one look into anyone's eyes (hearing a question to which you know the answer, but remaining silent), 64 cents for a cup of tea.

Two tablets of Pepto-Bismol and a decongestant yield a thick black coat upon the tongue (metaphor for technique).

String X is the sound sequence of a Polaroid camera, not-X that of the color white, the feature "wide" applied here in its aspect of the liquid (the cylinder white to indicate salt, but gray to indicate rain), recurrence violating the laws of distribution, the way 5 daughters (grown now) recast their parents features (false closure has its grand-dad's eyes, their color white).

Men don't stand before urinals but lean into them . . . old habit: at the end of leak, tug on foreskin.

O Bananarama
Our life is full of drama,
But you are surely keen
My little dramamine.

Anti-telos, grown men in 49er T-shirts, the low whirr of motorcycle engines up Mission Street, people in line outside the automated teller (wearing headphones around her neck like a collar), bulldog in back of pick-up.

Any guy who's been driving cab night shift for 35 years (raw goat cheese is now available), bright colors of the used car lot.

Listeners at a talk: how the hands are placed indicates what is/is not being heard (alternate codes: legs, spines) . . . a man pinches the bridge of his nose, eyes shut tight.

A contemporary vampire spends his afternoons in Market Street cinemas, watching horror flicks (whether the ears are revealed by the hair, hidden, half-hidden).

Two details develop a relation: gas stove settles slowly into green waves of forest, sputter of the straw in the now empty glass.

Auntie Telos: ladder as model of knowledge, tapioca prosody, mirror in the palm of my hand.

In the *Tractatus* numbered statements argue an economy of logic, but in the *Investigations* reflect fragmentations of a partial knowing (arrange noses in a room according to shape).

Blue veins map the back of your hand, the mystery in a woman's purse.

A symbol is any signified which functions as a signifier.

Small children on the bus often sit or stand on their seats backwards, ignoring the passing streets in favor of that larger puzzle, the society of the bus.

Jai ram, jai jai ram, "emotional science project," lights flicker, the reed without the horn, phone it in, small holes in the wall where once tacks stuck, grammar modifies prosody, consonants keep the vowels from leaking (chewing on one pen, writing with the other), a child struggling pull her sweater off, the blank space inaudible at the start of a text, old enough to hold his head up, sucking on mother's blouse, "duck tape," that billboards existed at all said more than one needed to of their social system, the idea of continuity between numbers, letters glued into words, the way velcro shoe straps begin to curl up after awhile, flowers etched on the mouth of the sax, a narrative of clouds low over the sea, bend in the fern as it turns toward the ground, a "catch" in my throat, trousers will gradually dimple at the knees until in the early 60's an entirely new sequence of men's hairstyles began to show up which continues to this day, only now the older ones never quite go away (nehru jacket in the rear of closet), the way "b/w" means one thing in a description in a film catalog and another in one of 45 rpm records, errors here, revisions, delete word right, he always thinks of the window seat in the second row facing front on the right hand side of the LRV as "his" seat (waiting for the fog to clear), sport coat with the collar turned up, wobbling on a rented 3-speed thru the park to the windmills, the horse' name is Foxfire, tiny Deadheads encamped in doorways on Haight Street (where have all the flowers gone – west Marin), so that one might survive, suit and tie, making movies (kino-eye), kemo sabe, yo no say, at the lawn's early blight, a round of poodles (playing) bark, on the first day of 22 cent stamps I stand in a long line at the dark branch office on 29th Street, a.m. radio music on low in the background, the sound of change, of adding machines, the customers (mostly seniors, mostly philippino) grunt or laugh or curse, seeing the line as they enter, already I'm far away, having stopped at a bakery to grab some rolls – and caught the bus to work.

Tin sun, one broom.

On the freeway traffic inches forward, the low hill throwing its shadow to the west (the big trucks stick out).

How write poetry amid such chatter, but *listen to it.*

Doing your homework on the way to class . . . the wind blows his tie back over his shoulder like a short scarf.

What he liked most about the National Enquirer was its use of drop-out type in headlines and crowded layout . . . like architecture, poetry was a fundamentally conservative art (some men thought of auto maintenance as a hobby).

A supermarket shopping cart stood abandoned in the gutter, filled to overflowing with broken chips of cement; some women tip their head down when taking a drag on a cigaret, others tilt their head up (assign according to class).

Emotion is only an ideological commitment stated (felt) irrationally – irrational because overdetermined (there's a conflict), I pluck these strings and the sun rises to the platin.

A dog in a muzzle might receive tenure (note please how this joke exploits caninism (note please how this line, following two iambs and the twist of the trochee turns on the single syllable *might*)).

On March 4, 1985, I killed my father and slept with my mother (it's February 26th).

Punk rock sunglasses frame Mrs. Reagan's face . . . diaphragm of the vowel expands and contracts.

The logic of morning (is no logic) is complete.

Big ol' red setter, blue leash chains you to your master, woman in a green down parka.

That was just sylabbles, this repetitive, obsessive counting, letters in an absurd chorus, strangers on a chain.

A foot is to kick with (Vegas-style), arthritis in my big toe (stereo blaster roars mediocre rap funk from the back of the bus).

White Wolf vodka brand, distributor's truck forms a sign (little wagon's plates read "Tuumba").

Stone escarpment: waterfall over granite (snowmelt), yellowgreen lichen, all these stones the size of homes shape the river.

River in snow in mist, still pool, a fine rain . . . moss-covered pines form verticals.

White noise, bad boys, no toys.

Old red Beetle shell left on the street (an injury to one is an injury to all), roomful of costumed Masons singing "Louie Louie," a bird in the hand will make a nest.

Willie: the pure products of America never were (what was most beautiful was neither the catch nor the throw, but the long high arc of the ball off Vic Wertz' bat).

I rush to write these wrongs (songs heard in dream clashing . . .).

Marx train: gnosis bunker (so fond we are of the old runes), white whale beached in Lilliput, number of fingers per hand is the puzzle, length and width of nose is the clue, circumcised at the nostrils, flaring and snorting, horse head stylized by flame, winged centaur harpooned to the old man, cetacean rising or writhing, waist-deep in the water (devoid of form and color) in the harbor at Gloucester or Tyre.

On March 21st, the last (one hopes) Christmas tree of the season, so dry and dead it's half-brown, needles shedding like cat hair, turns up, abandoned on the corner . . . by the next day, the trunk now cracked, it's moved into the gutter half a block down.

East Bay hills barely visible, half-silhouette in the red-brown morning air.

Random curd, that which is merely personal shall soon appear in APR, we've been practicing (reciting from memory, eyes closed), the real money's in conferences, metaphor of anyone's parents carved in accents.

My thumb instead of a dildo: serbo-martian exile pens essay in plain style.

Staples pock a phone-poll, rear of housepainter's pickup demonstrates meticulous order: sun's head fuels pen.

Jellyfish begin to appear in catchbasin of the City's sewers (the go-carts of Westciv sputter).

Off-tune, by headphones hidden in the hair, I, Minnie Mouse, squeak: old orange plastic breadwrap, the big trucks in the lot down at the dairy (like ships they are, literally docked), the young Latino boy sits on his daypack like a stone, reading a bible, waiting for the bus.

Temporary as morning, these words like shadows fall across the page, the value *is* the inversion, an old woman in the park recalling her childhood in Taiwan.

You're telling me something urgent, but I'm only counting the syllables as you speak.

Painters' scaffolding frames the house (yet behind that bay window stands an easel), red fruit of the peppertree.

"Meaning is use," but use without context conceals power (the perfectibility of the system is predicated first upon its continuity, and thus the permanence of internal relations and rankings): his didacticism was felt to be "anti-art," an irritant, scratching on the blackboard of their heroic-tragic monologues of suburban family grief.

Chicken in the comfrey (fascinates orange cat), Spanish ballad from an open window, cardinals atop the plum tree – breeze on a hot day.

The larger the crowd the narrower the assumptions one might then make attempting to speak to it (Foucault's laugh conceived as a flag): the bunting about the panel's table hides more than their legs.

Will your needs be met, simple notebook?

Jogging a different route just to see these streets again (car without wheels up on blocks in a front yard, lawn crushed into mud).

Sound of dog or hammer barely audible only because we so will it, foreground against the shush of valley traffic (jet's arc like the strain of a violin), white cat with black collar, bright pink ears and nose.

Clothespin clips playing card against bicycle spokes – number makes a poor defense, baby's fist pulling on your lip, jar more visible for having cracked.

Breakfast nook: these forms are imposed (imagine the family that has no father), mop on the porch left to dry (subtract the *r*), you don't greet your peers so much as stalk them.

Old theatre carved into thirds, the letters on your marquee are so much more crowded, small billboard mounted against apartment house wall.

The point at which a wide yawn will shut sound out: don't point your saxophone at me.

Think of horn as big straw (simile when you say that), polyvocalic want a closure?

Little windows (edit valley) . . . now the chicken's chasing the cat.

Curb cut: capitals at the margin require setback (if they write about language, there's a reason), voicing the slash in s/he (if they write about language, there's a cause): the indigo of the Iowa delta erodes, wounded buffalo in perfect binding.

O knife of theory in fog of tenure: that this day, converted into art, might be again transformed (computer paper scotch-taped over a bathroom window for privacy), loosened by steam . . . I sit, heart beating fast, on the fourth bus I've been on in just 12 minutes, route to the job.

1985: I notice the gang of roofers (tossing old shingles from a housetop into the back of a red dumptruck, slender wrists fitting into large, grey gloves) are speaking Vietnamese.

Blond god, all muscle in loincloth, slays blue dragon with sword, image painted on the side of an RV.

Tiny orange clip-on Garfield fixed to the brake grip of the cop's chopper (or stuff towel between windows to block draft), an 8 year old's day pack: placement of For Sale signs against vacancy rate defines city.

Old barber alone in storefront shop sits in his raised chair, reading racing forms.

Writing, rhythms writhe: stylized grain forms a watermark.

Long fingers press on closed eyes, then bridge of the nose (red spots from years of glasses, nearly indentations): where, deep in the head, does voice focus?

Poets pose either as visual artists or rock stars, but novelists mime nerds, plastic pocket insert full of pens (trying to guess women's vocations by their earrings less reliable than by their shoes): watch as bracelet versus watch as cuff.

Start to study Stein: see or saw or was at sea with oars, without (shoulders and soldiers, soldiers and shoulders), never let show what you don't know.

Ah posh gush (dear Kush, dear tush), the air one hears is there in Chinese verse.

Counterclockwise, the asymmetry of baseball is the key to its narrative (funk anthem), bottle gang on a park bench, double-dipper: Enver Hoxha is dead.

We're in the caffein reaction faction: now mean this: the colon is swollen (semi) – she's got it . . . he sees it (better book reviews): Dennis Wilson (Natalie Wood) steps into space (the sea), just the tip of the Iceman (rises).

Counterthoughtwise, the words are stenciled on a glass door (light above the elevator, when lit, means "in use"), this is a test (sign in please), little pickup nearly buried under a load of old mattresses, half-athletic, all day.

Insertions, against the false silence of the City, voiced comma: the cat just stares at the fearless hen, hissing.

New plums weight old branches down into shape, another generation has discovered water balloons off rooftops, junkyard dog tears at raw beef, syntax appears straight forward waiting for the ambulance to arrive.

Young man with shoulder-length hair seems now old-fashioned, green parrot loose in the back yard, cat white as the steps on which it sleeps, a world in which Chris Martinez never dies in Vietnam nor Marion Dale Cook inside the walls of San Quentin nor Fay Stender, confined to a wheelchair, swallowing pills in Hong Kong.

That names are not words is evident to any: over decades the small house becomes its modifications, its repairs – you sit in the sun with your eyes shut, sensing the breeze against the hair on your arms, 13th of April.

Ink sinks into the paper, then spreads: thus the light around the body extends down from a gun tower, while three young women have joined hands, sitting on the train tracks, halting the shipment of troops.

People treat stairs with due caution, traffic in the valley feels endless, the day effortlessly slips into dusk.

The next page is another country, the moment a pop fly hovers before dropping back to earth.

The sun itself demands no explanation, but this cargo cult of nouns sings its own song, its own name, again and again.

ENGINES

with Rae Armantrout

A herd of wild helicopters scuds in the night. Syllabics penetrate the red mulch of values, skeletons bloom at the rear of the lab so recently repainted a pale green. Fingers curl slowly in sleep. The logic of ambition is to seem a straight line. In the butcher shops of the North End blood stains the flesh of skinned rabbits. Style is its own mark. Electrical storms in the skull cloud the eye. The volley maintained nears orgasm. Narcs prefer down vests, the low cut in the rear concealing both gun and handcuffs. The smell of curry in the corridor of the small hotel. You stand in the glass booth, pretending conversation. Under the back stairs cobwebs define the spiders' hunt. The noise of the fan cooling the slide projector is punctuated with clicks. The cosmos is a purple flower.

Unable to reply, melodrama skips ahead. "I think something happens in the end." Her face, like her mother's, is tense. One death had sent an unidentifiable pulse of dread across three unborn generations. "How will I know when I make a mistake?" Pinpointing errors, I know where I am. A yellow 'sea' or 'field' of vinyl tufts. Glamor makes sense of the creature. So they laid her in a glass coffin The spirits whom we call angels were never at any time or in any way darkness. The eucalyptus only seems to shrug. Light flicks over those leaves in complete silence. That is a slippery tongue. Do we suggest relations we aren't willing to declare?

For this paragraph, attach separate form 1040-ES. His face, like his mother's, was dense. Instinctively we crouched, disembarking the Sikorsky, darting swiftly in a bent-over manner beyond the wide sweep of the blade (which only became visible as it slowed to a stop). The red spot on the beak of the male gull is thought 'beautiful.' Her one idea provokes disaster. He came in from behind. There are several ways in which this can be taken, but we prefer air freight. In a magazine, store ammo. The body distills poisons. Something longer and more languid perhaps, convoluted, looking simultaneously over its shoulder and between its legs, saddened by the very idea of girth, wearing a saxophone like a medal or sunglasses after dark. I chance this sentence at the point of max conflict. Thank you Saint Jude. Over several months he domesticated the rat, making a pet of it. Melodrama *skips?*

Skeletons *bloom?* Animated by a sense of unreality and a love of measurement. It needs to be shown that no mistake is possible. A radio projects an arc of interlocking squares onto the otherwise soft morning. He attempts a series of irrefutable statements. "An angel equals his traits. Vertical red lines distinguish the horsefly's snout. What anybody might call head." Unsure where the danger ends, we remain crouched. It is more difficult to believe that the holy angels are now unaware of their eternal blessedness. Playing the lecher, someone strikes a simple pose and thus hopes to escape notice. We are happy to leave the beach, begin a segmented evening. So accustomed am I to spinning that reappearance seems a moral good. Maybe waggling leaves won't work.

But a fern is not intended. This is a redo. The metaphor of person lurks in the work. Great numerical hysteria is numbed by words. The angel was not as we had expected, but moody and violent. Bats weep in the shadows of the foundry. He found hair flattened to the leg by the scrim of nylon intensely erotic. Number makes the simple marriage. The radio speaks to the kitchen. 66. Huge, well-hung, balls of type. We putter about the desert. The large child disassembled the crib. They take on the countenance of helicopters, shuttling from the clouds.

For the sake of argument, one point has been elevated. A pinhead. Often invoked, seldom identified. Hi, Mom. After a 'peak experience' the poor monster dies happy I won't die, for then I wouldn't grow in your enlarging appraisal. Pleasure detaches from the stroke and spreads. I recognize the soft jolt as a car door closing in the street. In heaven it would not arise. One grows more individual - uniquely marred and indescribably attired, unable to join the talk. You must be the angel, Gabriel. You must be the color red. I wanted each sentence to leave a question in mind - a sense of puzzlement - vague, at first, but capable of being formulated. Pressure fills the channel nicely, not exactly wet.

More gentle than the art of pushing is the desire slowly to withdraw. The head is both swollen and mottled. The angel steps under a streetlamp to light a cigarette. Only the policemen's horses appear neutral to the sight of so much blood. The next slide is of an invoice. Their wings are like blades. This is inserted to test your response. It has the look and feel of milky eggwhite. Thanksgiving is marked by a fire at the hotel. His fear was of scale. By themselves, they are silent. The unit for gum is the stick. You must be the window. The clouds go red at twilight.

You are the void from which the angels create the archangels. The massless particle created in Beta decay is not, in fact, the neutrino. The semblance of existence lurks in the verb. A group is a band or host. Sustained in euphoria by the statements of their clothes. Dialogue excuses the creature. Pearls perch on crinkled lobes. At daybreak the old palm looks reptilian. Razor backed, then sabertoothed. Though a burning log does form a *strange* landscape, nothing that glows can be called desolate. Metatron is called the scribe of heaven. Recorded song refers to dreams. This blasted backlot is of no account. Then she caught sight of something not exhausted by its name.

A helicopter. Style is the fiber in description which shrinks at the first wash. His argument that flight was discontinuous only made them more nervous, stare more intently at the three-panel, four-color plastic *Emergency* instructions, whose universality was marked by the total lack of text. The angels stand in the front of the cabin and indicate how to place the mask against your face, in the event it "drops" from a compartment next to the irritating jets of air. I stood on the beach of a small island, watching all of that pass from the surface. Narrative suppresses immediate attention. The sky is blue by agreement, however not today. The collie howling over the figure of the fallen settler in the snow is frozen on the wall of my grandmother's diningroom, which does not exist. The opposite of memory is nostalgia. An old billiard table is no longer an exact surface. Blood gels on the instant of contact. Take a deep breath. Some conversation is not a come-on. I mean: *stampedes* in the night.

Static emblems in the train of thought. In America we are wistful about horses. The plural is restful and suggestive. Unwilling to surrender their role, the congratulatory party went to photograph the encased newborn surrounded by monitors. Is there an exact instance? Is she the lady of the house? Light bounds toward her drugged eyes unparried (unparalleled). Out there gigantic fronds sidle. She likes to think that time passes. He infers the existence of an engine and a track. They're en route to Los Angeles when the collision occurs. But that was a special case. The hawk's dive is one fell swoop. Victims are designated "reactoids."

At the base of their neck, each wears the small scar of tenure. In public, wishing not to be conspicuous, they fold their wings, creating the image of a cape. The patient is the battery that runs the machines. Plurals are abstract, is abstract. A more difficult problem is the tail, which wants to twitch. In the heat of an explosion, body fluids boil. Dr. Davidson's tastes run to Latin flavors. So Thurber drew a fat example. In *Dallas,* capitalism and the family are the same thing, and no scene need last more than 90 seconds. I put in my thumb and you start to writhe. Bride, bridle, bridge. Dead leaves of a coleus. Between the towers the pilot and his mount glide smoothly, invisible to those on the ground but for what appears to be the reflection of the sun where no sun exists. In the distance the shadow of a man in the caboose waves slowly.

Seeing blown leaves, the toddler puckers. To understand is to 'follow.' Driven from the lips, tension gathers round the eye. A point of pride. He attempts a series of irrefutable *movements.* By style marked. Genghis Khan Antiques, Godfather's Restaurant. Years of carrying the heavy tray leave one shoulder lower than the other. I know now what I'd like to order. Am I also convinced that the earth exists? Protons, Pions, Dominions, Thrones. Above Fashion Valley they're building Fashion Hills. Minus continual impact the creature freezes. Twiddling shadows of late afternoon mix drowsiness with infinity's mystique.

Your paragraph. Pride is the plural. I put my tongue to the button. The mark of an attorney is contempt for the law. Theory is a place. Verbs never suit the frame. An angel named Mustang with blades of steel. Only part of the tree blows in the wind. Pistons contain the engagement. Cropped wide lawns and three models of homes to choose from. At this distance the skyline becomes sculpture. With the tower silent, each is left to his own devices, and some become human. As if being pulled through a tunnel toward a globe of light. In the ashtray, the cigarette burns to the filter.

You twist your key in the ignition. A woman mumbles and shakes. Fucking as if to stimulate an ideal reader. "A figure in white hovered at the end of this passage." So death-bed dreams are not incomparable. How am I supposed to feel? I mean: *licks* over those leaves. To master a branch of study. In dreams one floats from room to room. Dressed to match vinyl booths, the young waitress hums absently. Content seems increasingly prescribed. Michael heals. Uriel descends in a chariot of fire. Elsewise, do nothing.

FORCE

for Bob Perelman

The audients of politics
in the -torium sounds
eye is for fours
is thus tragedy first
then farce, majestic speech
muttered under morning's breath
while brushing. Against news, noise. Against toys, few respectable chariots, blue as cribbage, ocker as in Rx, Delaware's a warning. No-load, after a long illness or preventive strike, thunder allegro in the woodwinds converts the spare, hiring from within, primer coat. Inservice flea-flicker absent deicing refunds the smoking entitlement. How teacher
taught himself unthoughtfully spoken
toward the sake of
particulars, few nouns breaking
predawn stillness but songs
from red garbagetruck's hydraulics
haul history into landfill
(moist pulp become book). Aftertaste of bauhaus warms a canvas at the tollgate. Stet fish. Up against the whiteout, a woman on a porch curses her daughters' sluggishness as they drag cartons of pampers up the stairs in the rain, registered trademark (LVN). You roll a finger around in all that wetness.
I rose at 5
to type these words
swords heard in dream
clashing long after strong
seams sighted the writing
as scaffold to building
reveals little within, tents
to attentive eyes, child's

circus peek yields pitch
of memory years after. Prime rate or chuck, dehydrated syntax in the garden of arrows, thoroughly misgiven, perfects a hub within. Next scene the cabinet is on the telephone, but the key grip offers a line of blow to Best Boy, not what they mean by Greek. Thus to the pipeline of steaming prunes the resin of critique is so much KY if the budgie's lost in a chandelier, our deficit climbing. At Smith-Barney we make money the old-fashioned way, we steal it.
Sirens
throb in troubled sleep
nightsweat curdling twisted sheet
before dawn's quiet rescue
repeats robin's elm admonition
'seek only immediate necessity
worm/twig/wind/sun'
warm in breezy solitude
book's leaves, deckled, turning
(unnoticed) over in lap
first desk, best desk
who in silence sat
writing on back deck
in black ink set
ideas to motion, frozen
as white line rising above cumulus is wrapped
by seatbelt's strap down. Federalism of the bulldozer's yawn into the street, curling and marketed, recursive and choking, gathers venom of the asphalt (San Andreas), aired out with a touch of sugar, but slimy to the kiss. Small curd nickel defense fidgets with the lilies. Axiomatic, but with its pulse stable, the paper glider swoons by, so unlike the Heimlich mode of rapture. Uno!
This fix not visible
nonetheless real has chosen
or not such fate
as was available words
to you. Interim autumn ate 'em. The width of the week is white at the knees.

This is completely serious. Greens gouge into the daylight's grayness, but the lone tree is a fine pine. Plate burning images
positive cannot imagine not
turning reverse & back
to verse as farce
making phases what lack
phrasing's strict consonant cluster
chattering thought's distraction retracting
tongue's audible actuality brought
or bought off on
bay bobbing boat cough
phlegm to geyser up
chuck the sought clear
clean salt water seen
solving drought. Get this: mood of undress, each book left in its cage (always with the front cover missing) against the trill of a distant clarinet in a nation of small lakes and even smaller cars. Let's wax, then wane. Dad's name (is) (is not) Floyd. The Prosoids hang out at the corner. Blue raft is
my sail red soil
speechless to spring sings
caught in the throat
out loud, rings rock
of moon below glass
* to NASA masks
MX to Exxon an
essential connection, can act
flat onto forklift fits
death to its market. Intestinal shrinkwrap holds lunch, actual victuals, while swirls of grease design the coffee, designate awareness, ignite the mind, Juan Valdez. The medical abstracts start to flower, an IV in every trunk, the red-cap in the plum tree. Thus perceived as Bambi's fear of Soviet aggression, golf is the appropriate monument. Drain the pool to the very last drop. Yet clouds
on my title yield

capital punishment by taxes
deferred as a field
harbors mole & worm
warm in earth's night
seeking food below graze
of roan bull alone
amid domestic herd bred
to die wrapped red fluorescing
cellophane glare, universal product code
sings light line by weight-
shaded theory. The carnage erupted at about 3:45 p.m. in the offices of Mission Insurance Co. on the 18th floor of the 43-story office tower on the waterfront at the foot of Market Street. Tinker's palace defoliated cupped in the palm or paw of a more difficult muzak, aftertaste of gasoline, siphons the people's will to itemize deductions. Borderlines sit on the fountain, passing the joint. A career of thought disorders stretches the canvas, what any cop thinks to see a young man in blue jeans and a Levi shirt. Participles of the coleus need to be stripped, hot phlox, corrugating the wind tunnel's sun roof to the tinkle of ice melting in a glass. Sun centered speaker sets own demand
known to any, one gets
to be taken, bets cloud
against heat to seed's future
hedged by irrigation. The attaché's pit-bull rhetoric in the vocabulary of cowboys echoes in newsprint half the week. The waxer, the wainscot, intravenous as the IRA (IRS), number 2 pencil, blisters in the museum alcove: the messenger's bicycle's yellow. Tubed blueprints roll on the sidewalk. Feed, seed and farm needs. Imperial rosebush clad in seersucker sips Cinzano, disproves the surreal. Convey
bitter young jobless to rasta
(no punk dreams future) OJTs
no say he learn trade
who mock time in class
but earn against teaching's struggle
to be not laid off
leads a cynic logic asking

zero sum morning lesson over
tea or wrought he who
in the street fields bullets
slumps into feeling's last dissolve
(grim stat) rotting fame's swell
corpse blue in Guyana sun
amid many one & one
composts memory, friends (are none
when gone), facts *stun,* faces
at the newsstand stare, block
letters **SLAIN BY WACKO** con
whosoever listens, sell fear, sex
image of the body, blown
thru videology's dotted line down
to new proportion. Wordless as the pun of a green stain on dry grass, mighty stalks of hair start to bloom as the shade of an eye is drawn. Along the phone banks, by a new clump of commercial paper, multiples regurgitate in the palm and dogs paddle listlessly amid the carrots of the soup. Lenin was wrong. Modals do twitch at the seams, causing geometry or red, an ultrasound waterpik, but the yeast of judgment demands each primary color accept the monosyllabic. Against the rigid frame of the boxspring, set the curling mattress down. Fiduciary conduit phase
projects shortfall back
seedtime & startup
vs. train's leadtime
hard to predict
erosion by profit
provides cash transit
against static worth's
D line rumble
anticipating light's onset
deep in tunnel
announcing arrival – yours
(to so write
in The Ramble

of Olmsted's sight,
snow-covered brambles bend
to precipitation's weight
white artifice forest
cast against height
midtown Manhattan) rate
ambition to anger
possible motives, make
of sense statements
meant to change
states. Death and Texas, prepositional to the wall, blitz neomodern cafe: check. Can you curl your tongue? Ear's goblet (draining) (driving), ausland-ish, calls a halt.

GARFIELD

for Alto

The tropic treacle tripped over the derivation causing Lit. Blue and slides. Old webs are a shading on the shed sill. She accounts the complaint as failure. Unlike a cat, you have to walk it in the rain. Because therefore if I only knew then what I I I seem to be saying. Linebreak as breath-unit can only mark neurosis. The spiral jetty has begun to jell. Word fossil of intention. Dropped fork foretells a visit. The idea of ownership becomes foreign. Deckled vs. wisps. But the Decembrists were a spark. I sat on the stoop in the cool sun. Sweet corn of Maryland. The Boston Bees became the Braves, but later moved to Milwaukee. But I don't know if I can ever love you enough (the room is still and you notice the sound of distant traffic in the rain). Dear Ron – basically, the sky most anywhere in Manhattan is comprised of staggered trapezoids perspecting off in one cardinal direction or other (the percentage filling the frame tells me where I am). Chop the vegetables coarsely. The elevator's just an old metal cage. "Speak up!" shouts the woman with the walker.

I don't mean to presume uh if you could it seems that is I only intended apples and oranges more steep than every boy needs his if its not too inconvenient sleep. The sun is draped. Its ears went flat as it growled. Any word beginning with a vowel seems incomplete. Spider plant's new shoot seeks a window. Four wings are less efficient than two. Ribbed vs. ochre. Broken windows along the fire escape mean thieves live in the building. Put ingredients in saucepan. Her work is lush and peaceful, measured and textured, as if conflict had never been encountered. Toss spilt salt over left shoulder. The term yoyo dates back only to the 1920's. I was a fussbudget. A house and persons to keep fed and no questions asked. A car trickles in the dark and shapeless (shameless). Her roommate's PL. Butane and propositioned. If you're downtown on Wednesday we could have lunch. Intimate on the telephone in a crowded room. A bicycle for the Whitney. Men in uniform have That Look.

The clouds were relentless. Her kitchen was small but the intense order kept it from ever seeming crowded. Symmetrical letters versus all the rest. I thought the dog's name was Tide. The belly of the spider was flecked with spots. Above the clerk's desk was the checkout time. Arguing that cross-class collaboration equals class betrayal. Spicer's line enjambs predicates (state of perpetual hallucination). Induces maternal guilt in feminized workforce. Filmy and rusting. I heard, I felt, I thought I saw. Stereo koala penetrates breath of math. Misogynists like de Kooning? Narcotic, like a preposition. Stooped sunflower. If I listen to my voice, I cannot think my speech. Dip in milk and dredge in breadcrumbs or seasoned flour. Make change with the pennies first. Beneath the name of each flower was its other name. I turned the cube. Crisis and betrayal (forms of entertainment).

Sparts like to think of 'crazed social democrats.' Snarling, baring its teeth. Glassy and damp. Thought confined to the needs of some corporation. The sky is choked with a brewing storm. The fly mummified in an abandoned web. She wears ant i.d. badge with her photo, color coded as to the degree of clearance. The cactus is known for its patience. Each word wobbles in the mind. Lewitt's cubes market variation. Tunabelly, Fat Boy, Alto. Fallen vs. brass. Sauté onions in a skillet, stirring constantly. I rubbed my knee and longed to be younger. He's worth reading for the vocabulary alone. The outside fork is for salad (unless salad comes last). As though if only, a pounding, a telephone. It had been the Dunloe, Minerva and Taj Mahal, but now it was the Hotel Zee. He spent his time with her alone, preferring solitude to her friends, with none of his own. Questions demand. Turbosnowy and ionic, dewy and sliced, the ostriches of tenure stark as any carrot descend between the calculus of cement.

Who is this woman to me, so wrapped in her silences, thin thin lips set tight? A breeze is "cooling." It wagged its tail. Sometimes I prefer my numbers spelled. Pink of Guston (disgusting grey). Spider is a hunter, setting traps. Barking vs. justified horizon. We support this faction's continued use of the name Unbound Feet. In the lobby is one machine for cigarettes and another for soft drinks. I could see the splinter in my palm just below the skin. This glass is for wine, that for milk. What he saw in her was that she would never need to hurt him. A separatrix is a virgule. Strain the sauce and pour it over the fish. The compliment precedes the demand. If snails eat the tops, the carrots will never grow. Balloon payment. Oiled and buttoned. His stanza concedes defeat. Sox of carbon fidget. Perhaps if you were to why don't you?

Proud and ascared. Think of poem as liquid or prose. Bred to kill. The only television is in the lobby. Machine of the fly. Morandi's bottle recedes into light. Sgt. Pecan of the Prism. Nail clippers vs. the sound of music. Left dry, the fern goes brown in the sun. Stop payment. I hardly, but then would I ever if it already hadn't? Nobody's oleo governs the frost. The clouds are thick, filled with shadow and light. Touch plastic. The name on my first book was Ronald. Combine in a blender. At thirty and still looking for Mr. Right. Mouthing words silently across the crowded bar. She has her hair done each Saturday. I mean.

I let these adjectives worry me, their half-fluorescent distortions. From the perspective of survival the most successful evolutionary design belongs to the cockroach, which has no brain. Don't think of bop ear as limit. The term for this is cornhusking. Asking a question from the rear of the audience, so that everyone must turn their head. On her apron in bold letters is a joke. Above the manager's desk is a list of emergency numbers. Lush vs. too far Picasso's line was manic. Not compared to the RCP on sexuality. Looking both ways before crossing totally empty street. I looked at the mirror but saw only a reversal, the room behind me inside out. A siren sets it barking. Small curd and saddle stitch. Prefer to play with plastic. The sky is receding, rising, drawing back. Add and stir until smooth over low heat. Other than one-night stands, she enjoys long, talky breakfasts with her roommates in the sun room. A potted pine webbed with tinsel. Did you, with him or he, was it, how was it? Sax crested at the margin.

The bathroom is behind the elevator at the end of the hall, and the shower one flight down. Bill's words tend to hover. Squats at the curb. Each an accumulation of hundreds. This is not the sequence of composition. Cups vs. algae. Indigo and shixa. Greedy saucer's hypothesis deferred blankets the playground. She perceives his solicitousness as a kind of tender failure. Neri's people are never fat. Tie the left shoe first. There was Littlebit, talking to Spider, Easy and Boston. I hadn't didn't but I wanted it was. For Xmas he gave her a teddy bear. On the porch the fern cooked, curling. Aerodynamics respects the strophe, brown and thick like a crystal in the gut. The air is moist. The seller will carry a second. Carving shad is a very direct process. I sense my body heat begin to counter the cold. Humor is a shelter. A trade union is not yet an opposition party.

His silence against her overreaching thrusts led a third to assume the center. Flecked and fluid. Random vs. yellow. The lightness of her red hair anticipates my blond. It sits in the back seat as if to protect the car. Stir constantly Who's got the Mao franchise now? That imperial dragon, the snail. Segal's people are never tall. Waiting for the rates to drop. His metaphors compress until they hope to burst. No symmetry to a plum tree. The buckle goes on the left side. There are buckets about the kitchen with which to catch the sky. Expedite or clarify the personality or butcher paper to which priorities or waiver. It's valid that you should have a stomach, fuzzed bulbs, let alone the list of birds to notice, my lobe or the constant patter of a rhomboid conga too big for the sea's decor. Lev, Pero, the pen, becomes Leon, the prophet (harmed). After the fire, the Wentley became the Polk-Sutter Studio Apartments. Your quiet tones increase my attention. I heard it was understood someone said everyone knew I thought you and he. I peered out from deep within the skull, over the waves of sinus.

That work = word salad ballad. Regal and rusted. Frothing, because rabid. Each day a new sky. First the verb. A view of the lightwell. Warrior image of earwig. I seem to be saying, I see myself begin, I, terms bubble at their own inexact, it it is, drupes or goblets, space stations in two point, ink but a trail or squid of. Raised her children in her parents' house, sleeping for twelve years on a sofa bed in the livingroom. But the Freedom Socialists were a Trotskyist splinter transformed by the feminist critique of a particular divorce. The air is cool, discounting rain. Such difficult constructions serve to put me off balance. High-pitched tight farts vs. feigned cough. The cactus' despair. I took the names out. Thick patch of babytears in the damp behind the tree.

Slice the rind away from the meat. Take a bunch of vitamin C. Marketing the Cube without using the name. Because a balance is struck in this decentered freedom and a soft black dog can sleep on the porch. The separateness of the lines in stanza.

The fearsome remains of a potato bug. Day begins, but not before I raise these blinds. At first a word "freezes" at an intersection of meanings, but then it begins to drift. A damp nose, cool to the touch. Hello be thy name, Lyn. Green and sandy. Leafy as the celery seen from above. Weekends spent visiting mama at the rest home. Monochromatic, but a line. The negation of PC = PI. The sky is volatile, testy. The lobby is a cavern, shadowy, filled with overstuffed chairs. Nouns are not friends. Blowing vs. shorn. After work, goes over to put a few hours in getting the unit ready to rent. Each board member listed as to corporation. I saw myself in that photograph. Fold into the batter. Ammons' line's all air. Why don't you fill out this evaluation yourself? I snuck in a last word.

There, it was Tom who freed the line. Asparagus fern goes gangly. It sleeps on the porch it intends to protect. So she designs breeder reactors. The words combine, forming meaning. Spiders waddle forth. Chilled and anxious. The air is dense. State Department Stalinists. Clump is the strength to endure the courage of trees. At a coffeehouse to play chess. On the ground floor, a pawnshop encased in bars. Screen door rust vs. Ovaltine with zwieback. I saw my scalp emerge like an island in the Pacific. The pet food cats ask for by name. I distrust that story of being shot down over the Crimean. Fold the ribs in half. She stopped seeking a father. Examples are a banana. Apply the aloe. Keep the tone even and soothing.

A shudder, because someone has walked on your grave. Only the air is ever "muggy" Sow bug curls into a ball. When August 7th split from Nam, they took the name Solidarity. Poem as non-site. Dripping and fuzzed. Barking to be let in. What the storm did to the fuchsias. Jenkins' abstracts equate beauty with blur. Substituting friends for family at a holiday dinner in a distant city. Then what this not door revolving? Consonants bracket the vowel. Party vs.

the state. No visitors permitted after 10 p m. Arrows of perpetual bathhouse begin to honk. Moonunit. Ironic chuckle seen as putdown. Serve at room temperature. Should a general ledger reflect in-kind donations? I prefer to write at my table. Her favorite dish is zucchini in a cheese sauce.

Education postpones unemployment. Leaves of the jade tree thick as tongues. A meter based on the inflammation of short syllables. The rapid cycling of gulls spells rain. Polarization for later regroupment = disrupt the meeting (paragraph). The syrup of vowels. A quarter century ago one pulled me from a motor scooter, my leg firm in the grip of its teeth. Steaming vs. cancelled. Let thaw. I poked a single to right-center. The germ of a proletarian moment, acrylic and pulleys, rains. A sequence of mirrors by which she can see the front door all the way from the second floor manager's unit. Acconci croissant. There is an F such that F = lightning brilliant (terrible) across the sky (to the next sentence). Sects and insects. Spelled "Neilson" on the sign at one corner and "Nielson" at the next. The slug is not a worm. That's a poor time of month, she said, because reports are due. Reduced negative patient outcome enhancements. When she says won't you that means you will. Her intensity is not personal.

I waited for my eyes to adjust. Between geometry of pine ribbon dharma for practice into transfer and belching duplicates of tempered waver a serene trumpets the joust of cats. In the window a small neon sign blinks rates. Salary history. Here the lone word buzzes its question. Galvanized vs. circling. Fetching Frisbees on the beach. Even without lawns grass erupts from the cracks in the sidewalk. As if in anticipation the blue-black fly rubs its hands. Cut into slices one-half inch thick. Do not kid yourself that his irony is not barbed. At this stage, deletions are shadows that dot the page. The sky is solid, raging. She allows as to how his name is Mel. This was a contraction of Milford. Sailboat and fud. The state capital line on the Soviets. She sought security without intrusion. On the telephone in measured, sweetened, patient tones. Any number of men will distribute themselves at the urinals so as to permit each a maximum of space. Stop by my office if you have a minute.

The speed of the coleus' response to water. Its ears, alert to the presence of danger. The then-Trotskyist SWP. The sun is spread by the cloud layer into a blanket of dull light. The linebreaks of a huge man with bad lungs. She loses two days per month to her migraines. Aphids appear as a stain. To vote as if you would someday own property. The family term is boppo. Phrase cups quiver in industrial juice. Beagle vs. bagel. To friends it looks like bumper cars but they enjoy the energy and neither shows any dents. Management replaces the linen once each week. I need to feel wanted, I said, beginning to cry. That Rothko worked quickly. Let sit for 15 minutes. Greasy and convex. As if each letter were a separate block. Short words stress force. The man on deck gives you the high five. I chew my pen.

Your name here. Theory drips at the edge of a cartoon. Write in the morning, print in the afternoon. The unit of wind is a gust (in the shape of a fist). Horizon the tree palm a by signified, point vanishing right the to migration slow a begins, hats toy in ostriches tamed, surreys fringed, cages tiger bearing wagons pulling dromedaries, circus a, fellaheen of caravan a be to appears him to which, silhouettes, objects of sequence A. Prize terrier registered as Moby Sue. Patel is the leaseholder or master tenant. Moth orbits globe. Any pronoun yolks assumption. Sewer socialist. Tone-leading of pit bull vs. man on the flying trap. Arneson's brick perfect in its containment. Coleus goes red in direct sunlight. Dry copy and business agents. Beat this and return to mixture. You didn't mean to interrupt. I sat against my pack by the side of the trail. Facilitate the workshop. At 55, her bedroom is still just a bed and small table, with no ornamentation. Store coffee in the freezer. She ran off with him to California, where they became buddies.

Hard vs. edgy. The fern, hanging, presents obstruction. They call it The Marathon, but there's no sign outside. The speed of those dark clouds is a sign of rain. Vicious because it lacks the concept of malice, cropped tail. Brown-eyed and propositional. Working as a nurse or cabbie, studying anthropology (art). Andre's sculptures are lists. She took her mother to visit Hawaii. Shachtmanite lament. This is called a Phillips. Such bugs inhabit books. Braiding the newsstand fog for shelter coasts against the mantle. Preheat the oven to 350°. I watched the tweezers gouge into raw flesh, distant from it all. She goes along with his insistence on a three-way. Rigid as a margin. A laugh that turns heads. Speech is just a model, delicious and cold. Meows for the door to open. Would you mind will you would I?

By the time I saw that collie it had already started to spring. The light was crisp and bland. For years she only dated cops. A short sentence is a rhythmic unit. The flower of the violet turns brown. This is the topic. Yo tengo speaks, balloon of thought in carton of bull, a slider or aunt linebreaks in the garden. Depicting the leaders of Solidernośc̀ as "Jew intellectuals." A dentist looks at Bruce Nauman. She picked up the milk account. I brought in the mail. The sky is mute, sullen, waiting. Separate the whites. In the place of her art she inserted a child. Nor am I related to the Silliman who was mayor of San Leandro. Hog vs. diesel. Daddy longlegs red-brown. A tree for the lobby for Christmas. Deafening whisper too close to my ear. You had they did she said I was. Setting the spoons out, even tho we won't need them.

Bring to a boil, cover tightly, and let sit for two hours. House shudders in the gale. Butterfly understood as an insect. Composition by starlight (impeded by fog). A lone bulb is architect to shadows of the lobby. Throws himself, growling, against the fence. On a bookcase are photographs of her parents, her children. Functional resume. Expels the impossiblists. In Lorca, as in Yeats, the background of literature was not necessarily something written down. Sculpture sandwiches the follicles of duty, creamy and sanding, beneath the leafless spine of the trout which flashes all night over the freeway's crotch. I felt the caffeine organize the system. Aging, the wreath dries, losing its scent. Spiral and inky. Was Still's scale "heroic"? The disclaimer embedded in each assertion. Atonal vs. salted. They sat at home, learning Greek. Into as of as when as if however if ever as is as when into into. Which way does the toilet paper turn? The cat's name is Trouble.

In the midst of an argument the ultimate violence is a silent refusal to respond. Butterfly twists in the morning breeze of the garden. Each letter a wedge in the still space of the page. Rub its chest and it goes right to sleep. Such weevil smirks in the farts of them. Brimbody I nothing am. In her work the story is again possible. The kale in the dark. The great Albanian goat-fucker debate. Sun mote vs. wax path of crayon streak, rough and mauve. Stain scraped by spire, cloud quill, Dolby, starter set, between hung crystal and the tinsel echo of lingering trees. His head in her lap on the sand by the sea, eyes shut to center on the heat of the sun, the soft sound of water, smell of salt. She did a house as a piece once but I saw it as all about light. Heat in a heavy skillet. She loves those horrible shag rugs. Stainless and under party discipline. The hail is battering the glass. Elevator door too narrow for the wheelchair. Hair of the dog. Midcareer. I opened the door to the ocean.

HIDDEN

"Lucky"

Is this form? My mother comes home
from her date with both eyes

blackened. The perfectly overcast sky
gives even this glade an indoor feel

like swimming in too-chlorinated water
the way antihistamines clear sinuses

while they cloud the mind. A weaving
pressed against a damp clay dish

will leave a residue of texture
beneath the brown glaze. We roll

when first we wake, and before
we rise. Row houses. I say

this way. The eyes of all
raised to the line fall silent.

In Britain, monarchy is but
a theme park. The thick brush

of the blackboard's eraser
is entirely sensuous – chalk

dust smells sweet. The arc
of park sprinklers, automatic

in a summer rain. T-shirt
beneath linen sport-jacket,

collar up, is this year's fashion
for about six weeks. Realism,

so-called, alienates, by virtue
of the shell posed around objects.

The eye, neither flesh nor hair,
absolutely other, glistens.

The hand squeezes into a fist
about to vote. I wrote that

I write on the bus in a subway,
pleased by the smoother motion, sensations

of speed. Blonde hair turning gray,
a woman in a short skirt

walks in the rain. Further questions:
is recurrence itself sufficient

to state theme? I rest my vase.
Enjambed by brigands, on a

voyage to fetch groceries, that which is
merely accessible soon blots.

Mondo condo: in the epoch of ear cuffs
and jelly bracelets, bowling alleys

decline. Everyone into software
in time to flood the market.

Canned meat. History in slices
fit for xeroxeria.

Argue out of anger into wit
half-way. With a long blue dress

but on roller skates, he glides
not a typo. Redfish in a tank

at Chinese market. When I drive cab
all lives are in danger. Rose

ties Cobb in Ty game with Cubs.
Sun throws billowing clouds

into sharp relief. Hand thrust
into vat of hot tar

on $5 bet. The dependency,
being chemical, is passed on.

At noon a beer would stem the withdrawal.
Drumbeat of iambs in blood. I

will not make fun of the poem
chalked on a black board

500 times. Wipe that slate green,
coin-op. Oil-based, reviews present

mock critique. House at the hilltop
offers generous vista

soon to be blocked by condo.
Nickname fit for a collie,

burned flesh has long since dropped
from your bones. Genetic abstraction

forms a tradition
clumsily. Thick sour smell

by restaurant dumpster. Or
that you would call your clothing concept

Banana Republic, only to sell
out to a chain, and this

The Gap. Stop Muni fare hike!
These are just the facts.

Neo-punk bank officers
form self-help network database.

New wave or no wave – now!
Baby finger roams in nostril

up to the second knuckle. Young man
shoulders bottled water. Another

drives a Toyota with a paintbrush
clenched between his teeth. Land

'o lawns. If you don't mean it
to be a portrait, don't put

me in it. Thus one book follows another,
only partly a corrective, spreading

new errors all its own, and these
are more powerful. Rapt reason is apt

to get you shot, like a carbomb trapped
in rush hour gridlock, with only three

shopping days left before Christmas:
the window displays are stunning,

the muzak seductively familiar
though you barely can hear it.

Bagpipes blare out into the afternoon
from within a dark tavern. Bored cabbie

leans out yellow window. Thrill mixed with terror,
first day of high school. Slip aboard crowded bus

through back door. When I crouch to write
toes of my right foot (always)

firm against the walk, heel up,
on top of which I rest my butt,

left leg turned out, almost perpendicular,
the body a base, my own

best desk. One size fits all
cereal bowl, used now for soup.

The way you shove, to slam shut
car door. "Why so many women

hate sex" is men. Nails once painted
now a chipped purple. Aluminum quad cane

lightweight on purpose. Sign on lifeboat shell:
plastic bouyant apparatus. Wait for light

to read "Walk." Man on subway yawns,
hand over mouth. Gum boots for rain.

I watch people's faces, eyes
filled with alarm, lips tight,

hurrying to the busstops at dawn.
He carries his coffee

in a styrofoam cup
(you gotta stop talkin

in regular rhythms).
New lines for old. The gold band's

design, darkened by oxidation,
curls. Door bashed in on the driver's side

roped shut. Gaunt young men in suits
want to seem sharp (look tacky).

You take this in, certainly no wiser
for having watched the assistant manager

dolly crates of new product
from the truck to the store, your own bus

ten minutes late again, the fog bordering
on mist, recalling without pleasure

how as a young man you once applied
for a job at the airport, or that

your lover's struggle with PMS
has equally become a part

of your own daily accommodation,
the way a novelist thinks, mid-career.

Buddha-belly boards bus, eyes wide.
Mirror's reversal, familiar fiction:

can you curl your tongue? Ears adorned
or otherwise, mere detail, project balance.

Offload by islands
hidden in the traffic, I

de-bus, ah swirl of morning
alive as caffeine, bag ladies

in the plaza, one by one,
huddle in on themselves,

snarling or snoring or dead.
In the middle of the wood,

in a clearing, stood a tall
grey concrete highrise

with redwood balconies and
sliding glass doors, in which

we saw the tall eucalyptus
trees reflected – new condos

"ideal for adult living."
Dry drunk. The face is not the clock.

Empty apartment's open curtains.
Cat's white fur shades into orange.

Poem's black ink fades into white
(not this). A hinge, a bell

signalling recess. Little black girl's
beaded braids (her mom's

dozen bracelets) tipped with aluminum foil.
Fifteen small suns (yellow, yellow-white)

circle the large planet. Giant mouse,
beheaded by the trap, gives a final sigh.

Socialite editrix enlists brownshirt
to mop up scene. Stalin as a

codeword for an unhappy life
is thus assigned random content.

Hard-edged, hair forms frame
about the ear

right after haircut. Personal growth tapes aim
at morning commute auto cassette market.

Tall, broad-shouldered Samoan girl,
maybe 15, followed by thin-faced

freckled Okie woman
with her even more freckled

mulatto son, crowd on bus.
Another white-haired perm

held firm by hairnet
next to tall black teen

in 'coonskin' cap. Boxful
of donuts in woman's lap.

It's all a dream. From petite-bourgeois
to near-lumpen to 'new collar'

in three generations. Men
who lack the capacity

for intimate talk spit,
make sexual jokes about women

just out of reach. Fingering grapes
one by one in your mouth

in the midst of a boycott.
Our monsters are your monsters

says Canadian poet. Buy a pack
of gum with crisp twenty

fresh from automatic teller.
These are not facts. Old guys

in green blazers. Tweed caps
bent into back pockets. Breakfast

yogurt. Red rock over Glen Canyon
covered with brush. Grunting baby

smells of poop. Is this form? Fog
burns off, row houses built over dunes.

The party is not the state. The party
is not the hors d'oeuvres nor tapes

fit for dancing. Can you hear
your own accent? Finger taps throat

to take pulse. In the land of good
Germans, Reagan's a nice man. Disem-

bowel the nets of being? Girl sings vowel
'E' to mother. The breeze is not the tree

it shakes. Homeowner thought
to paint bricks red. Man pushes stroller

uphill, wife carries basketball.
The fog rolls in. Woman in pigtails

at the age of 50. Details
articulate a structure

otherwise not seen. Bombast
feigns axiom. PCs give nerd

further connotation. Nunnery
is to women as military

to men: road out of town.
Sperm spills from a reader's lips,

maybe yours. Man with a cleft chin
in old torn photo. Invert adjectival

order, delete articles – take pride
in your devices. Utility crew

cuts pavement. Serbo-Laotian
Huichol boy. The way mist sits

over still pond. Hooded sweatshirt
under army fieldjacket, denim chaps

and large gray gloves: uniform
of sanitation engineer.

Motorcycle permit parking. Bop
till you flop. Sun in light mist

dissolves into glare. Sawhorse toppled
alongside pothole in street. Where the elite

meet to eat. Man in a three-piece suit
with full beard. Mouth implodes

from absence of teeth. Drivers glance left
at intersection, before turning right.

New wave dial tone. First caulk,
then sand. The fog, once we're into it,

isn't so thick. Rothko-esque swabs of color
cover graffiti on wall. Old defect

carried forward in genes? Theory of
middle name. Recurrent as a nightmare,

paisley's back. Old school bus sits in weeds
of vacant lot. People in mass

cross intersection,
each with a different gait.

Dressed only in hiking boots and kilt,
carrying a huge backpack, head shaved,

the muscular black man approached the depot.
Under the eucalyptus, leaves layered

the earth. Even though you couldn't hear them
you could see in their faces

unresolved anger. Shadows behind dark glass
of stretch limo. C'est moi, Crusader Rabbit.

Pearson's ear's an absolute index.
Perelman's fear: that we are, each one,

responsible for war. Quemoy sabe,
Matsu ball. The public is private

as your own privates have been subject
to much speculation from all your friends.

Thus reading's one-way mirror works
in just the opposite direction.

Still the dead are not perfect
merely to have stopped

committing mistakes. In the family
all cringe together, huddling, exposed.

Say too Rags the Tiger. Where dream
and memory mesh. Curtain-style, linked

fireplace screen, visible as I'm lifted
shoulder-high. I'm still terrified

of falling. The line, like any ankle,
twists. Black bread brackets peanut butter.

By the docks, fog turns to rain.
Hardened vessel fills with blood

as sperm gathers, pulses. Bank
branch manager's desktop sign:

new accounts. News accounts little info
flooded with style – black bra half veils

Madonna's tits. All this and heathen too.
Capital trivializes the cog-

nitive power of the visual arts.
Word "ambulance" on hood spelled backwards.

That each line be created equal
is contra-narrative. And then bashed down

on the cops, dug heel into forehead,
sociopaths of false order: of thee

I sing. Frank O'Hara with no time for lunch.
That mortician placed Davy's cheeks too high.

Pool's water magnifies the diver.
Old stone fence. Red chips of wood

scattered over the terraced hill.
Eyes ache after sleepless night,

body shudders awake over coffee.
In Yemen, in Mocha, people

drink tea. I find an old Irby
in a used book store. The ear hears

ahead of thought. The plan is not
the body, nor brain's design. The rain falls

(or not) throughout the region. Yet
not all have shelter. The mind stops here

even as hand continues. The pay phone
at the corner endlessly ringing.

At dawn, in fog, in the park
two men play tennis.

Condo balcony: hibachi, chairs,
potted plants. In the street, old tin

trash can lid has been flattened
by traffic. Of poetry the editor

the editor wrote to me
cutting my text. Sweating,

I lie naked atop the sheets
half-drugged with sleeplessness.

The penultimate violence is to
fuck with my time. Hot days

of October. I fill my bowl of
Familia to the point of spilling

(coffee sloshes onto my wrist,
soup flows over onto the table),

enacting a ritual of
deprivation I don't

even begin to fathom. The poem
is not what's dug into the cave wall

nor cut on the wrist – it goes deeper.
Lepers want to be known as victims

of Hanson's Disease. Hey, little monkey,
let's get funky. Against the grain of

weather, heat against wind, we lean.
Row houses on treeless streets, where

even a phone pole becomes decoration,
its wires ribbons. Paint flakes

from shingles. In which *from*
is the verb. Lyric's instinct,

in our generation, derives value
from conflict. A thick book for the bus.

4-wheel drive with mag wheels,
gun rack in back, the black truck

is caked with mud. Green, blue, pink
in the pigeon's neck. Behind the last row

of condos, a field of wild anise.
Hearing aid's flesh tint

like a cyst in the ear. On the desk
a cup holds scissors, pencils.

Ring's gold is oxidized (burned)
to yield a rougher finish.

Suspicion in the eyes of
older women: young girls

("scantily clad") crowd out
of the bus at the high school.

She walks the dog at dawn.
It's not the scene that matters

but its lack of variation.
Double play pivot as perfect form.

Small cafe across from the factory,
black doberman asleep at its door.

That anger I cannot be rid of
tho it has no face. Your own eyes shut

fail to smile back. So day
(like the line) breaks. Haze hovers

over the still bay, beyond which
the far hills seem light and flat

(the bay itself would be invisible
but for the reflection of the red sun's glare

pocked by the shadows of waves, against which
the silhouette of a long barge sits). Up

amid eucalyptus and pine
sky's a deep blue. High school

terraced into the hill, long low
buildings, concrete and glass. Cinder track

around astroturf infield, the lights bright
for a night meet. Man with a blue thumbnail.

The world is all (the word is all)
that is the case (is false).

The face grimaces, a forced grin
perfect as celebrity hair,

fresh shaved neck. Gone grey,
dead fronds form a collar

high on the palm tree's trunk.
Six sikhs seek some slick slacks.

Why do I write? An old man
now gone, half-Puerto Rican,

asks me that. God forbid, paisley's back.
Norms of the real (crushed bottlecap

in gutter, lollipop stick
denuded of candy, white, snapped

tip stained pink) present a chain
of associations we read as continuous

yielding life as a solid.
Lone runner along canyon path.

Abandoned gas station becomes
temporary pumpkin fest.

Long arcs of the park sprinklers
refract the sun. Dead pond smells

of human shit. The look she saw
on the driver's face, fighting

to regain control, before
his sports car rolled, hit

and broke his neck. Old surgeon's
slow gait across hospital campus.

Ribbed rim of a dime
shines in my coin purse

amid the darker pennies, thick
nickel, lit (just barely)

by the streetlamp. White leather tie
with bright red Japanese ideogram

logo (against the black shirt).
The question of details, the slope

of your cheek, a down so fine
it's not even visible

until close up, backlit by the sun
(curve of the lip or breast, bump

that shapes bridge of the nose).
Arm bent at elbow hoists a purse.

Earlobes stretched by decades
of heavy earrings, clips to gather

tufts of hair. Boxscore read
for Bach score. Bounce that way mudra.

Black cat with a silver bell
dangling about its neck

darts between houses,
its run a half-crouch.

So the moon is quiet as I am not.
The way the blind walk, their heads seldom turning.

Meat of the carrot a brighter orange
to have just been snapped. Liquid paper.

Carbon reaper. A man in a field
walks a small black dog. This is not

a description. The small table
in the kitchen corner where a man sits

staring into his coffee. Bras exist
(body as site of the state)

as a form of bondage, heels spiked
not to add height but to tighten

calves. Locked ward. Locked word.
Hill half-hidden in fog, neither

speech nor song. Old khaki-colored
canvas covered truck. The point is not

to yield poetry safe for millions
fresh from TV. Emotion

is the opiate of (drugged
against more critical

sensation). . . . My thumb
instead of a nation.

"Newborn girl gives birth
to twin brother." That splendor

can be made to cohere
with enough ovens. Old hotel

vacated by fire, refurbished
for gracious downtown living

upscale studio condo. Doves against fog,
the range of gray. Navy blue sky.

Man in a grey suit with bright red shoes
dances in silence, Walkman headphones on

waiting for the light to change.
It never does. That code's opaque

to the color-blind (was invented
1905). The streets in Europe

too thin for cars. Gloves demand a sacrifice
poor. old. tired. cow. *Miami Vice*

demonstrates the difference
between narrative and plot. Cannot shut

revolving door. Town in which they jog
in thick sweatsuits. Lath and plaster

is not my master. Nor is this
a linebreak. Mandarin canon

false ideal. Don't you wish
you invented Velcro?

Blurred ink and tiny print
of evangelical tracts.

Sun's light dimmed by a scrim
of high clouds. Large dark ships

on the bay (words) surrounded
by the small white sails

of pleasure craft (punctuation).
Time is real as tense is not.

My ears 'pop' at the hilltop.
Stoic half-frown on the man's face

being wheeled up to the ambulance
in blue cotton pajamas. Green dice earrings

and blue sunglasses – the large woman
picks her nose. The cop leans forward

before he spits. It's not a neighborhood
people pass through going to work

or shopping, or to visit a park.
Yellow-brown wall-to-wall carpet,

optometrist's outer office.
Think here: you are reading a poem

– already this defines you. Hyperopic
boy makes good. Off-rhyme by iambs

hidden in the flood. Willingly I'll say
there's been a clear rip-off. No ideas

but in drugs? No teeth, bad back
don't make Ted a bad boy.

Bright pink scarf against turquoise jacket.
Out of print, out of mind. Woman

with pocked cheeks (sequence of alternate details
by which to triangulate image)

pulls up her jeans. Hear the loud chewing
in one's own head. Penis minus bonus.

Dan White is dead also. Sleeping pigeons
atop power line. Tar-heater

like a caboose linked to roofer's truck.
From sacred to salsa: a woman

in nurse whites carries three purses
into her place of work. Truck double-parked

on residential street. Face moved by muscles
of the jawbone as it chews, teeth sliding

side to side. What is the social content
of a poor night's sleep? Between terms

thought moves through a process
of distraction. Syntax slides

over a rough surface. Noses slope
or rise or spread (sometimes twist)

across the face. Hardware wholesale house
next door to machineworks (big sheds

of corrugated metal), since we're clanging anyway
any way we can. Thought into action

divided by social constraint (terms repeat).
Teams don't. Soft earth absorbs the fog,

spongelike, until the sky clears. The air
is not the mind nor a reflection of it.

Ironing board juts out of dumpster.
Refrigerator upright

in the back of a pick-up. Shadows
in a dense fog, headlights barely cutting thru.

Weight is relative to height. Fate
correlates to sight. Each place waits

for the right stress. I thought
in D.C. to head south for a visit

tho what had I to show? Vacant lot
turned into community garden

bulldozed as site for new video mart.
Song: (*oh no*) don't say nothin'

bad about my baby (*oh no*).
Thought replacement technique.

Shag knit sox cover golf clubs
(only the woods). Touch of rouge

to shine up cheeks. Writing by the light
of a kerosene lamp. Stomach rumbles

during group meditation. Pants pockets
are hidden holsters. Cricket buzzes

alone on a deer trail (further,
solitary woodpecker

knocks on a tree) – big horse chestnut
impossible to eat. Even here

in the high chaparral, the shining monarch
lands and is still on a rock amid dry grass.

Blue jay, descending, fans its wings.
Old pine, having fallen, forms both bench and path.

Oh that world, the real one. Potted cactus
oxymoron. North of Calistoga

a car that's rolled and burned: semi-circle
of ambulance and fire trucks (no hope here).

The world is all that is your face
isn't it exactly either. Try to write

as the bus turns (the body pulled
is the body). Lunch or lurch,

which one? Sea and shoe, which
is the foreground, which the rear?

Sky perceived as the object, against which
land's the margin. Who, what, when, where, how

are there also. Trochee's trick (again
twitch): protagonist. I, I, I

take you out on others, old pronoun,
cleft chin. An image (as in a dream)

of being held aloft – that fear
of not falling (which it's since become).

Boredom in the eyes of women
at a laundromat, class specific,

against the restlessness of their children,
men absent, constructs a world.

Neo-moderne, *USA Today*'s
vending machine converted into a kiosk

for graffiti art. Fog's moisture
against my face. Details differ,

thus they mean. As red from the hibiscus spreads
from the teabag at cup's bottom

kitchen radio spiels Twisted Sister.
Car parked in intersection blocks wheelchair:

the guy rolls into the traffic
to the nearest driveway.

Old "defenders of Bataan" t-shirt
half-covers rolling belly.

One size fits all sonnet.
Man on the bus (it's 8 a.m.)

reeks of red wine. Half-purr, half-growl,
ocelot snarls at emu. Lizard skitters

from dirt path into matted grass. The vineyards
turn red-brown in October. Graveyard

is compost with headstones. Unintelligible
roadside carcass with rabbit paw. Hindu son

lights father's pyre. Abandoned truck gone to rust.
Making love, yet watching our reflections'

slow movement in the bedstand mirror,
dawn light through the bamboo curtain,

a kind of silent thrill. To be the verb,
not the noun, is to move beyond syntax

here into the real. There now, I've said it,
and already it's fled into the past

the way light travels. Ich bin ein earthling
forms a border. Memories are barter

in the grammar of emotion, even
(or more so) when absent. First we die

then later we are dead, but it's not the same
nor even connected. Count each breath

just to stop thinking. A young wife,
many months pregnant, rides Greyhound 6 hours

to Santa Rosa, to visit her sister
who lives in Rohnert Park. Two maples

growing so close together you wouldn't think
they're separate trees. As we're not, legs tangled,

our bodies rooted. Sun off the goose pond
ripples on the ceiling. Pool's chlorine

still stings my eyes. Willingly I'll write
your name in this book, long lashes,

deep brown eyes. Your full lower lip
drives me wild. Ritual marks

significant form in one's life:
vision quest of the junior prom.

Men who wear scarves to look European
sip grenadine. Thus an absence of conflict

is not peace. One cannot cleave
Pound from his politics. Convert ovens

into saunas. Meanings are not hidden
save as repressed. From the coast

waves gray as the sea sky churn
into a landward froth.

Inversion styles wrath. The sound of
bird wings rustling in the rafters,

feathery shuffling. Schoolgirls huddle,
whispering heatedly in Spanish.

Woman in over-large sunglasses:
each lens is a mirror is a mask.

Undocumented worker wins lottery
= rich deportee. Big noun seeks verb –

object syntax (nonsmoking preferred).
New grass green under cut grass.

The yellow in dawn light: hot November sun.
Row of milk bottles on a porch

triggers an old loss. In the land where
large lawns announce success, dogs

ornament the family. My other car
is a book. Funk city ditty. Up the stone

path, through the eucalyptus, until
a long flight of wood stairs, several

landings (each with a bench and small clay pots
of moss), at the top of which, in a clearing

stands the white cottage. Mudhens asleep
at the edge of the lake. Soft-core,

by implants hidden in the chest
ich Orpheus tsing. That words are whole

but aren't is what each child learns
reciting the alphabet. Each sentence

(re)states a complete thought
which cannot exist. Colors

compose a wheel but are known
only through contrast. Genes

of eyes I've never seen
stare through my own. O moth

of Sisyphus, thy wings unfold
from a cocoon so heavy

gravity is not bold enough
an explanation. That woman stands

bruised perhaps but filled with power
you cannot own, between whose legs,

still attached, bathed in blood,
like the stone within the oyster's folds

whose shell sits cracked upon the shore
(like metaphor), the infant flesh

unfurls. The world is all that is a vase
thrown against the door. My face reflects

more than mirror can tell. That man is dead
whose life was spent in hell.

INK

Jessie's book

spreads, content centered, then sinks into the fibrous mesh that forms the page. Each strand close up a cylinder, rough about the edges, wrapped in its own web, coated with pigment. Not to defy silence, but to define it. Thus letters shadow space. An invisible barrier is called a margin. A version of marking, any one at all, fills the territory in. The toy monster, dropped into a jar of water, grows vast, but is slime to my touch. The eyes, dotted, remain opaque, vicious.

Slightly palsied loping gait of hippie circular distributor, long blond ponytail but a reddish beard, moving slowly door to door, walking just part way up the steps to each porch, in his own world beneath walkman headphones. Frozen OJ on a stick poses as a dessert. Scuffbearded oily street wino's sidekick a curiously healthy and muscular bulldog. Imagine the mall as a consumer circus. Big Bird, bright yellow on the tube, addresses joint session of congress.

Glimmer of light high over Mount Diablo (silhouette flat across the hot hazy day) would be an airplane. Each truck is a roving sign for the products within. A loose blouse barely buttoned. Influence governs chains of the imaginable. She speaks and the illusion is shattered: she's a reactionary (to which you respond by nodding before moving down the bar). The original lyrics were *tuti fruti. good booty.* Butch gal on her own chopped Harley. I ride the bus. Roofing gang, on a break, crowds into the orange donut shop. More "private" cops than real ones in America today. She uses one crutch as a sort of cane. Next to three Latino youths, each wearing a baseball cap with the bill turned back, catcher-style. O lord, raspberry vanilla ice cream. Old guy, riding the bus for the sake of it. He's 400 lbs. of soft flesh, pink almost, and, even though he's balding, the eyes and mouth of an infant. The driver hops out of the bus and into the corner market for a styrofoam cup of coffee and, while waiting (a tall light-skinned black man with a muscular build, short afro almost red), he relaxes, lets go for a second of that tension, that needing to be in control of his crowd of rowdy passengers as well as the traffic, and his whole body changes, shifts, shoulders slump suddenly rounded, spine curves, until he's a smaller man, no longer young at all. Chances as at slathering.

Bend from the waist, back straight, to pluck the rose from the stage. Cellophane envelopes the dry-cleaned suit. Cardboard box strapped to the little luggage dolly used to wheel the groceries home. Standing passengers brace themselves as the bus lurches to a stop. I think that was a print shop, but now the building's vacant, scars on its surface where the signs were removed. Generations of graffiti give layered effect. Lines of seniors (tiny Filipino women) Queued up outside the storefront travel agent's office, waiting for the bus to Reno. Skimming *Crusoe.* Motel decor: you have to architecturally mark the office. A man who will make a pun would pick a pocket. Ferns Quiver in the light breeze of the open door. Cat's sneeze is muted. Net on a long pole just to rake bugs off the top of pool's water (wasp drowns, fooled by antialgaic chemical additive). Kids on a farm use old Windex bottles as water pistols . . . broom handle becomes light saber. Moments when the filter of memory serves to magnify (grandmother dies). Paying bills is a way to feel anxious. A torch to blister the paint from the wood. A truck that's a press, heating the asphalt gravel until it melts together. Blue car pauses in the intersection, waiting to turn left. Wide brim hat on a hot day makes its own shade. Cash flow management (my kind of fun). I watch a gang of roofers rake the roof. Not by the line but by the ream. An alarm clock in the image of a robot stamps its" feet" at the appointed time. The duck in the lake alone on the water.

The crush: a new paragraph means a new job. Sun rises thru the dissolving fog. On the train, half ride to work with their eyes still closed. People find seats, then snap open their briefcases and pullout a magazine. Thumb and forefinger press down on the bridge of her nose – the pleasure of pressure. Long calves with tiny thighs, plus a long torso that's nonetheless thick about the center: I'm a piece of work alright, virtually random. Dreams recede quickly (I remember there was a fire at hill's bottom, people carrying wicker furniture out into the night fog). I rise, feet bare on the cold linoleum floor. Steam pours from factory vents. Big cranes at the drydock like erector-set horses. Already a forklift empties a truck. David's umbilical cord, big red scab, ready to drop off. The way adults love to dance with infants and toddlers. Brandy billboard reads: B&Behave. Left coast. Small girl shy in her daddy's arms, looks away—over his shoulder—to be introduced (in a way we're all like that all our lives, almost violently intimidated by the shock of a new person, coaxed very slowly out of our cocoons [each new male (if we are male and if we are straight) a potential danger, each new female possible in bed], until gradually we repress our original fearfulness, moving through school and job and the great malled markets with their cool hum of air conditioning as if with confidence, tho the old twinges soon return, say, speaking to a crowd or the anxiety of hitchhiking. Small white tuft of fog settles low over the wide groomed lawns (large white stucco homes) of Saint Francis Wood, the hills above perfectly clear. The first single, a high infield chopper, breaks up the no-hitter end the next swing, a clean rope double down the right field line into the dusty bullpen, ends the shutout, but it's still a laugher, 8-1, end the tension of a great game is gone forever. Dream geography: around the corner from the Tenderloin Clinic you come upon the large porch to your childhood home in Baltimore. The fog here is dry, almost smoky. She holds the sweater over her head like a hood. The familiar flap flap of a pigeon in the eaves. Cars at mid-day, driving with their lights on. The cat's lip curls, whiskers shake, at the sight of the fly. Green-black trash bags filled with their mysterious lumps, bulges, sit atop the lids of the large plastic cans. This bus is a local. Not by the whine, but by the seam. Not by the rhyme but by the theme. Not by the crime but by the cream. Penisilliman. I can see, written right there in your eyebrows, the word *bunkydoodle.* A man on a ladder paints a windowsill white. A fat boy shimmies, to twirl a hula hoop, bright orange-red. *The* first thing you learn at the hospital is to always tell the family that the patient died without pain, the second is that everyone dies in pain, spirit ripped violently from the body. That's true even if it's not. Through the picture window I see the backs of heads, people sitting on a couch. Deep cavern of empty moving van, open, sits out on the street – men in jumpsuits move about the house. Raised toilet of wheelchair accessible john. What I hear is hum of air: breath, breath. Floor made of boards laid over 400 tires. Even down in the basement, one flight below, I recognize the laugh of pleasure. A reading at a suburban community center, red metal chairs (half empty) in a large cold room. Baseball at twilight on the telly looks blue. Slow sweep of the second hand. Jessie's 1920 wedding photo framed in wood on my kitchen wall – I realize, ten days after her death, I haven't look at it once. More words spin past. Mother's ring on Hannah's finger. Plastic lamp base is mock giant whiskey bottle. Red rectangle on wall where Tire extinguisher hangs. Doesn't hold his pen so much as grasps it. Moonlodge. Humus or homos? It's good to live with a bagel.

My new belt is wearing because I've been wearing my belt. Freeway's shadowy lower deck. Morning's message all its own. We watch the 67 bus turn down into the projects, from which it does not re-emerge. Winter light: fog is the world scrim, the unillumined houses half visible on the next hill. Lone teen hits a green ball off the wall of the school gym. No other single expense shapes the quality of life to the degree of rent. Thru the window I see a roomful of books— who lives there? Tennis, stucco: I go back and remove these words. Fresh paved street, loose asphalt scattered on the walk. Thick chain on saloon door before dawn. Little girl wears a patch to cure "lazy eye." Not by the pout but by the glare. Chips in the cookie, some atop it, crisp, others melted deep within. Flock of coots on a "man"-made lake. Yellow-tip overbite of the pelican's beak. Mom's learning Wang. Thru the fog half-visible canyon. Tools in a wheelbarrow define your work. I always attacked my teachers, surrogates for a father that wasn't there. Coot's bill is white, legs yellow-green. City autumn: mock pumpkin patch on a vacant lot. Establish a baseline. On Niepce's table: the spoon is a soup spoon, its ladle deep and wide, tho narrower at the lip, so deep in fact that the handle, which begins broad and rounded, thins rapidly as it rises from the horizontal of the table draped in a plain cloth, shaped metal arching upward until it opens out into this "mouth" or bowl in which, 163 years later, we still find (frozen) light reflected. I don't write these texts so much as shed them, shells left behind that should you find them years later should prove no less opaque to you than to me: who was that masked man? But I remember (often, not always) having written these words – what I recall are my emotions, where I sat, what the weather or light were like, what else was active, charged in my life at that moment – not to be confused with understanding the text. Woman in the seat next to me (we're barreling downtown) inhales the mucous in her sinuses, loud deep gravelly sound. Front page of the *Wall Street Journal* has drawings and graphs, not photos, a 6 column page and seldom a headline more than one column wide (ah, but their verbs, the implicit metaphors of business as war, circus, game, are pure bunk). The young girl looks up at John Wayne and says, "I hear you're a man of true grit." Glare of the sun on the rain-wet asphalt. She already has her nametag on ("Evelyn") on her way to work. I pull the pen's cap from its point with my teeth. Someone's pulled the boards from the windows of the abandoned house – glass cracked, jagged edged, or just missing – so now it sits hollow, empty, shaded in the light rain. Thick bunches of red and green bananas. I don't even see the accident at first (it happened 'fore I got here), crumpled car hood, old sedan angling out of the parked vehicles a block up, until I see the bus I want moving slow to inch around it, but now (from the opposite direction) an ambulance siren approaches fast. You've got a pimple on your nose I'd love to pop. The backs of stores as they open onto a small parking lot, trash cans, empty wood flats, stacks of broken cardboard boxes, jerry-rigged hand-painted signs, but here's one in pink neon. It's not that long, slinky knit dress so much as the oversize yellow rubber rainboots. A canary in a cage sings, hung from my neighbor's porch. I sit on my own back steps and look down at the shed, padlocked, the key missing. Do not write in this space. When the plum tree goes bare in the fall, the small square white house behind us comes into view. Nearby I hear a toddler crying, straining to cry, seeking an effect. The long stem of the begonia twists to reach the sun. So-called rag mop with pale green soft yarn brush. A plant in a pot with a bow on it. They've added a story to the top of that house, giving the new wood a thin coat of primer paint, but never following up. Two doors down, the old woman's crumpled newspapers into plastic bags, piled high atop one another under the corrugated fiberglass awning of the back porch where they've dried, yellowed, cracked, begun to crumble into dust. Old high metal pole gone to rust has clothesline pulleys, nylon lines going off in four directions – on this one a purple towel flaps loudly in the wind while the heavier bathmat next to it hangs still. Nothing is more confusing to the typesetter inexperienced with contemporary poetry than variable spacing. White nylon shorts over sky blue sweatpants, hooded sweatshirt, knit cap pulled low almost over his eyes, the cyclist struggles, pedaling up the steep slope. Under the rafters where the pigeons nest, the station floor is stained light green. By election day, every power pole in town will be thick with posters. Point my finger at my own chest, then, hands shut, cross arms at about the wrists, held close to body, then point finger at you. Three would-be roommates wait outside the apartment house door for the realtor to arrive. By the very foreignness of its name, the phrase *camera lucida* is anything but – the title of Barthes' book, translated literally, is the Clear Chamber. Now that you are gone, reduced to ash, I sit in my livingroom alone listening to your voice, 90 minutes of tape recorded four years ago, an oral history, research my wife (not then my wife) was doing for a paper in college, your high voice thin in the ambient noise of the Highview Convalescent Home, and I'm scribbling notes (with this very pen) from which I will later construct a narrative that in a week I will read to relatives – not one of whom has ever come to hear me read – words that capture nothing, ghosts of fact, when you were born, whom you married, what play you saw on your first date with him, 1919 *(An Eye for an Eye),* as on the tape right now you quarrel with your older sister, who herself died earlier this summer, an old anger unabated, unquenched after nearly 90 years.

The house next to the house on the corner. Black strip of rubber, torn tire, sits in the street. Sound of a jet not visible through fog. Halloween cutouts scotch-taped to the windows. Vow! papercut on back of knuckle stings to bend finger. Imagine myself writing on a bus bench. Jaywalking on crutches? I'm not writing for 'a small circle of friends,' I'm writing to you. A sequence of pockets down each leg of his trousers, a zipper on each. That cheap waxy paper of an old copy machine. A pyramid of dots (.∴). international symbol for "toner out." A man is trying to pull a garden sprinkler without it flipping over or getting too close. Irritation of gum at base of tooth (tongue obsessively rubs against it). Tina, don't stand in the stepwell. Moving through a thick dawn fog, the world feels only half real (over a fence I see the shape of a man, bending to work in his garden). Abandoned gas station covered with campaign signs. Felt tip marker draws a face on the pumpkin. The loud hum (deafening up close) of the rotating brooms of the street sweeping machine. Blackbirds roost on the power line. Strong odor of banana in my briefcase means it got smashed by the sliding books (I'm afraid to look). Tennis racket juts from day pack. I scratch words into being. Used condom decaying on the sidewalk – how does it *get there?* Magnetic resonance imaging. Posthumous music. Trick or trout. The stone I felt in my shoe (which I took off and shook) turned out (once the shoe was back on and laced up) to have been in my sock. The message on my machine is you. O red string net bag, so full of onions. Now the little sun motes have dusted up my glasses. This tie invariably twists. All the potted or hanging plants in these windows, a barricade against the treeless streets. A flat truck with stacks of wallboard. A concrete wall around a densely forested garden, the fence raised higher still by sheets of green fiberglass. The little metal part that holds the eraser to the pencil. After an hour in the hot tub my fingers smell of chlorine. What makes sense? Fog's burned off overhead, but for some reason not yet at the bottom of the hill, just 6 blocks away. What politicized me first was my grandfather's racism (what politicized me first was my resentment that my grandfather, reserved, shy, nearly deaf, would never take the place of my father). He shows emotion only when he's driving – and then only anger, frustration, aggression. A man with a mole on the tip of his nose (cartoon rhino profile). The title sits outside the text, arbitrary. An hour after I depart the sauna, sweat continues spilling from open pores. You lie back and I drag my tongue slowly over the nipple. As any sentence or even a word, when pulled from a text for closer examination, is unable even to fully abide there again. Yet I do not aspire to silence. Chocolate flavored coffee. In the jar on the porch in the sun, red of the hibiscus spreads in the water, becoming tea. The small girl holds the large cat awkwardly, using both arms. I blow on the spiderweb softly, just to see the strands bend, then return again taut. Wasp pauses near my head, almost still in the air, then shoots into the branches of the fuchsia (maroon petals at the center, light pink ones folding back). I'd forgotten about that children's game, Candyland, until I saw it on the neighbor's porch. The setting sun turned the mountain orange as we gathered under the high trees for the service, folding chairs in a semi-circle around a card table, two small candles and a potted yellow flower still wrapped in pink aluminum foil. Trying to force the orange liquid into the baby's mouth with a dropper (fingers pinching its cheeks, to keep it from spitting the antibiotics out). Six blocks away, I'm in a dense fog. Pea green Volkswagen stands out amid the candy-colored cars on the lot. Jiminy Cricket stands as witness to the great events of our time. Even after the funeral I haven't fully managed to cry. Brewers blackbirds hopping over the cut grass. A cat on a couch is a test of civilization. A woman is handing out flyers at the entrance to the station – it's a week to the election. People prefer to "debus" by the front door even though there's a crowd there waiting to board. Threadbare secondhand sportcoat, collar turned UP to reveal brown felt underside, under which he wears baggy army khaki pants, black cowboy boots (he's maybe 18 years old, thin fuzz of first beer). Deep etched eyes stare out at the world, withdrawn and suspicious (I see her at the bus stop almost every day). White woman enters with a black child – the old women roll their eyes, glower, look away. The dog lunges at the limit of its narrow chain. Samsara notes. Lunchpail in one hand, stereo blaster in the other. Little paper packets of sugar in a bowel. Arm in arm, grinning and laughing like a cliché of young love – but they're not young and are in fact blind (she's Latina, he's black and more than a little portly), canes tapping and sweeping ahead of them. The bus rolls over the hot, fresh asphalt (dozens of smell stones of which, thrown into the air) – I love the small. When I see him (it's been months) I recognize the purple spots of Kaposi's sarcoma immediately. Far from any market, three shopping carts rest against a phone pole on this corner. At the edge of the construction site, the little cubicle of the portable john. Ah motherboard. I pour the liquid soap onto the "scrubby" side of the sponge. The ratchet effect: your salary drops before your consumption. Methane muddles Mono fight. Who figured out that shaped wire (staples) would not only pierce paper but could then be bent back in on themselves. His Halloween costume is a trash can, so he must be Oscar the Grouch. Egg carton's built to buffer the egg. Puffing my cheeks out to give the razor a firm surface. Hummingbird high above the barren plum branches, juts. The world is all that floats through space. Porch light on, tho barely visible, middle of the day. "Ah, Mr Trouble," he says to the cat, "you back again?"

A sneeze wells up, uncontrollable, and it feels great, like an oncoming wave, swelling and swelling – when will it crest? Sitting on the stairs, I'm three steps up so the toes of my feet hang off the edge of the first step. Upstairs, the kitchen door is open to let in the sun and warm November air. It's quiet here, in the back, but out front on the street the blasters blare funk city. Hey, bro', wanna buy a watch? She uses a shopping cart to go from trash can to trash can on Mission, retrieving aluminum cans. North beach is a battle zone, alcohol-engraved neuron receptors. Old ladies who bunch their hair under string nets. Is it different when it's a short Latino wearing the ten gallon hat? Now the music's drifting back through the open houses. Shouts mark a touchdown. For example, do I indicate if the person is white if that's what they are? A white butterfly, in among the fuchsias. Ink jink, kink link. Unk junk, kunk lunk. Suddenly the parrot begins to scree. A jet flies into the sun. The freeway is quiet, nearly empty. Odd to see a dragonfly this near the coast. I sat cross-legged in front of the pelican and showed him his picture from the field guide. Long green toes of the white-billed coot. By the shape of its head, this is a lesser scaup. Old white men carrying bags of crumbs to feed the geese. Mother times her biscuits. Val gal invents a game (she's only two): climbing on a stool, she throws herself atop me or really just leans forward, arms out wide, letting herself drop, great wild joy in her eyes at the instant her balance is breached, control abandoned, the fall! But it's tough to carry the baby atop your shoulders if their diapers are poopy. Library's name rubber stamped across the page tops, legible only when the book is shut. By nature, I'll crouch if writing at a bus stop. Awake at 4:30, I realize by five I'm not going back to sleep. I let the 67 go by in order to catch the 10, which I see just a few blocks down the hill, but which, when it arrives, is jammed, no light visible through that swarm of bodies, so that its driver refuses to stop and it slowly pulls on by. His office is his breadtruck. Each morning she put the little metal basket out on the porch, full of empty milk bottles, a note stuck in one of them with the day's order (the tiny bottles were for cream). We gathered in the livingroom as the Jewel Tee representative opened his case to display this week's offerings. She's wearing an understated grey tweed suit and when she snaps open her briefcase I see, next to the *Wall Street Journal,* a copy of *Dianetics.* Already to have written these words is to have gone past them, *through them,* unable in any real sense ever to return (save possibly as one does to an old photograph of a dead parent). Old VW bug, stripped of its fenders, hunched open wide, high mag wheels: a dune buggy. My name is not Blood. From the el you can look down into people's yards, but not just any yards, only those of people who've learned how to live near the el. Here's where the tracks run parallel thru beds of gravel. Do not place tongue on third rail. Try to look inconspicuous wearing a lemon yellow jumpsuit. No, actually it's a two piece outfit with a Keith Haring design. He pulls off the backpack and sits down, hugging it to express sheer exhaustion. Next to me sits an old man holding a saxophone. It's disturbing when someone your own age dies of a disease you also have. Darrell's eyes red under puffy flesh appear to squint. At dusk, the street lamps flash or in a sequence, row after row of lights on the next hill coming on. The stillness of the ride home at 5:00 pm – the train is crowded, but people appear listless, stunned. But this long thing that was inside of me, which I shat (dark, curling spiral sinking to the bottom of the bowl), is not me. The trouble with rice cakes is the way they break apart. On the street, walking past the too-sweet smell of the donut shop. Full-length mirror abandoned in the low grass at the edge of the park, shattered but holding tenuously in its frame: a sign inauspicious to the superstitious. He's the King of Rap, there is none higher, CBS execs all call him Sire. Pigeons peck at scraps of crust. In the dream, we're in bed when the earthquake hits, the towering bookcases starting to topple, books sliding spine forward, into the air, tumbling, but I can't move, I can't even shout. [brackets] [here] [inform] [place] Pen in the shape of a dart. The band binds the watch to my wrist. Irritable, narratible. I dig my thumbnail at the small red tear in my flesh, edge of a knuckle, until the black speck of a wood splinter rises up, then out. The chapter on friction. They sit on the bus silently, neither reading, looking out the window, nor even watching other passengers. not wearing headphones, eyes open, thoroughly contained, each in their own world. By the SP Yard, a lot full of containers, red, blue, yellow, stacked one upon the other, teller even than the surrounding buildings, a pyramid. Her body, long and lanky, is very nearly a boy's, small breasts barely noticeable under the Izod shirt, yet it fits her delicateness perfectly – she gets off the train and I never see her again. Machinists on a picket outside a red brick building, half the signs leaned up against the wall as guys smoke or sip from steaming styrofoam cups. Deep blue metal finish of mailbox is perfect background for fluorescent graffiti spray. A lone coot in a still pond. Already they're putting the wire fencing up. soon to be xmas tree lot. I read Butterick's review of *Paradise* and feel so flattered I can't write straight for three days. Even before they start drinking, the alcoholic's liver is different. She sits with her knees tipped together. Monkey Street. Once we're under the bay heeding east, the mob on the train thins out, he finds a seat and the small plastic case is revealed to be a laptop typewriter, upon which he begins banging away. Ships white in the drydock. Harsh light of the dawn sun – horizontal. That odd square collar almost a mini-cape, on the sailor's shirt. That period of true dusk, less than 20 minutes, when the sun's set but it's not yet dark, red-orange haze in the low sky, the bay a still gray, lights in the City just now becoming visible, half moon rising – later, down by the port, interior lights illumine factories, warehouse, flat blue fluorescent hue. Burst of citrus – nothing here even vaguely natural – cough drop dissolves. Five employees huddle by an office door, waiting for the one with the key. The escalator steps chewed into my shoe before I could yank free, series of teeth marks gouged into the rubber. Woman with a rep of a nympho, no longer young – what needs, I wonder, are thus displaced? Half empty train: people sit scattered to give one another space. His briefcase contains just the morning paper and lunch. Oft-heard, by iambs hidden in the head, words warp eyes' gestalt Wrecking yard directly under the freeway, the corrugated buildings lone ship spews steam out in the harbor. She's at the age where chins begin to multiply, making the transition to a new body. Cars inch up the on-ramp, waiting to merge. Solitary house on that empty block, old wood frame Victorian (you can still see where the foundations of the others stood, in among the high weeds) has been gutted by fire. Out of the tunnel, city's fog turns into East Bay's haze, glare of a diffuse sun. Night of the living chairs. It don't make no never mind. What's great about a fireworks display isn't the pyrotechnics but the crowd. This store is not for rent. Unreal brilliance of a gas station after dark. Banter of people punning. That instant when gravity starts to alter, train pulling forward. The finger seems huge, wrapped in the cast. In a used bookstore, the poetry section tends to be small and to the rear – I read the titles like a social map: what got purchased, what discarded, what the used book dealer thought might sell again (here, next to Leonard Nimoy, sit 5 crisp copies of a saddlestitch chapbook, a local street poet long since dropped away). Who remembers Bill Deemer now? Pigeon-toed gait of a palsied man. Are the cheerless mercenaries of the financial district any less deluded than the prideful faculty of the research university? Teardrop tattoo. Trying to think through anger (is like losing syntax): heart's muscle clinched tight as a fist. Dear "Beware of dog" sign, I believe you. It's the exceptional that gets defined as news, the parolee in a thousand who fucks up royal allover the front page, the lottery winner whose family rushes onto the stage to crush her with hugs, yet the mind, that reading beacon, seeks for patterns even among such factoids, design more powerful than any politician's rap – thus the public sphere is inherently unreal. Man at a pay phone half-whispers. It's a later train and the people on it aren't just going to the financial district, therefore dress with variety and color. Long vertical column of short lines, each enclosed in quotation marks: shape of dialog in paperback novel. Sartre's translator arrives at the publisher's, where a secretary buzzes her up to the editor, saying into the intercom, "the typist is here." Bright damp mound of dogshit piled high on the edge of the walk, red, red-brown, almost steaming. At night you can see the rodents in the streetlamps' shadows, scurrying, following the concrete wall of the gutter. Here's a beetle the size of my fist. These daypacks seem huge on the backs of children. Just six blocks away we come into deep fog. One foot leaves the skateboard, dragging on the street as a brake. That moment in history when mailbox rental shops suddenly multiplied. Streetwalkers with their high cheekbones, gaunt heroin air. It's hard to walk down a long flight of steps with the sun right in your eyes, I thought, tumbling end over end. "I'm a goner," she said to me, that term, in fact, being literal. Commas began to breed. Refrigerator door as kitchen kiosk. It's Sunday morning and I'm squatting atop the roof of the house, checking out the repair work in the gutters. He inserted the long needle directly into her vagina, drawing fluid from the cyst from within the abdominal cavity. Having grown up with a typewriter keyboard, I have a bad attitude toward this device called a mouse. The train stalls in the tunnel. I squint to read the letters through the shadows of my hand. A new program means a new idea. Three day week. He was a terribly think young man, so gaunt as to appear frail. It's not the knees torn out of the jeans but the longjohns beneath that creates the effect. A tendency to jut his tongue out when he concentrates to write. She coughs and you hear the fluid in her lungs. Mouse scurries from behind the stove. A woman at dawn standing at the telephone kiosk on the corner, long wool coat over flannel nightgown. After the funeral we went back to my mother's apartment and ordered a pizza. Freckles on my nephew's nose. Green glass beer bottles litter that roof top. The traffic copter sinks into the bay. Sox and tennies worn over her dark stockings. Two quarts of I.V. fluid to rehydrate the patient, bringing the blood pressure back to normal. I slept in a chair in the Emergency Room waiting area, that brief period between when the TV stations sign off the air and when the Saturday cartoons come on (I saw the fall of Pompeii in black and white). All play and no work makes dull Jack a boy. Give the cat a tonic. Write the cat a strophe. This notebook cover (leatherette) cold to the touch. Now I'm on hands and knees on the livingroom floor spraying clear glass lacquer on color photos. There's a black mole like a dot punctuating the lobe of his ear. This pen is dying: black ink fades to gray. People rub their foreheads more than you would think. Book is for to read now. Hot coffee to jumpstart the brain. Krishna, people stumble over your name or presume you took it in response to a religious conversion (once somebody asked me, "oh, you married a woman born in 1966?"). Blue leather binding: a law book. Built on small square lots right after World War 2, these boxy houses (low ceilings with the swirled cement look) were thought to be "ranch style" – three speed bike dominates small foyer. Big "A" in a circle more prominent these days. Ballpoint pen attached by cord (curled and plastic) to the clipboard. Train roaring in the opposite direction suddenly shuts my view. Old familiar: red and white Coke truck. The forklifts are yellow, sitting in the yard. Flexing fingers, popping knuckles (thin calfskin gloves manufactured in the Philippines). From above, the oiled tracks of the railyard glisten in the early sun. A civil war soldier's cap, but made of leather (this was before they thought of helmets). Two kinds of barbed wire atop the chainlink fence. The power generators behind the hospital. A sneeze trapped up in my sinus cavity waiting to happen. Try writing with your gloves on. Mattress on a sidewalk becomes impromptu trampoline. His theory of poetry is that it should have no theory. Map of rivers, veins stand out (up) on the back one's hand (a fine down covers the flesh, so light you hardly notice). Try to guess at which stop other passengers will get off, based on their clothes. Hip to wear high top tennies with the laces untied. Before ears "pop" you feel the pressure build. Crow seems huge, standing amid the pigeons. Under the freeway, in shadows, the highway department maintains a staging area (infrastructure of the infrastructure). A desire for stanzas. Her eyes seem large, but that's only the contacts. Old wood frame house appears to sag, a small building virtually swallowed by its own additions (porch, closed in, breeds a porch). Buddhists call the buddhologists spiritual nerds. I have 30 seconds after the door's open to reach the alarm box and punch out the code. Shadows in front of curtains: the lives of strangers. El Taco Loco. A large, older woman, jowls and neck folding into one another until there is no jaw line. I shut my eyes and feel the stress and pressure points in my body, shape of this seat, the pull of the train as it plunges through the tunnel at the bottom of the bay. Freight line warehouse: row of raised loading docks. I watch the bag lady meticulously fold her red blanket, putting it back into the crowded shopping cart. It gets hard to type when fingernails grow long. Ahmal and the day sleepers. "Bad Pun, bad Pun," she said, scolding her dog. She's wearing that short, pleated parochial school skirt, but with longjohns beneath. The pen streaks across the page, leaving stains of thought. I pick up the morning paper to read the latest lies. One way to cross your legs is with one knee directly atop the other (hands cupped atop), another, broader and more triangular, is for the ankle of one leg to rest upon the knee of the other. You depart the train, walking slowly up the smooth escalator, while I remain aboard, squinting into this notebook, and in minutes we're miles apart. There's no view in the tunnel but the flash of passing lights. Laser cut means not cut at all, five reams' worth accordioned into a single box. The first thing you notice about that building in the projects, green and boxy, is that all the ground floor windows have been boarded up. Narrow vertical window slits of the modern jail. Painted shut years ago, the second floor windows in our livingroom have grown cloudy with dust and grease. The wooden handle of the teapot's smoking, blue gas flame of the' stove too high. First the bed's unmade and then I drop a few books atop it, and later a basket of clothes fresh from the dryer, then a sweater, then a newspaper. I'm the only person left in the entire car of this train – "all passengers must offboard at this location." Trying to remember what this neighborhood looked like before the freeway. Finally, nine weeks after my grandmother's death, I'm able to cry. Reviewing flesh cards, preparing for the test. Now that I own a car I'd better learn to drive. In this ad, the Marlboro man's a in a yellow rain slicker, looking to his right, our left, cigarette in profile, his horse in soft focus just behind. Thumbnail pushing my cuticles back. Play on the cliché. There's a guy in Berkeley who thinks he can prove Stephen King shot John Lennon and that Mark David Chapman's just a lookalike scapegoat. The idea of spreadsheet function. Blackbird struggling with an orange peel. Cradle the phone receiver between ear and shoulder. Next to me on the train a little white-haired man is reading a pamphlet, *Tips on Getting Published.* Day so cold ink's half-frozen in the pen. Ambuvan. Alcohol's isolation: Darrell dead in his room for a week before anyone noticed. Electrical flashes to colored lights make a sign. Surprised, coming out of the long tunnel, that the sun's out. Cheap orange plastic *of* the road gang's vests – they trudge along the tracks. Someone's left a coffeecup atop the mailbox. This is about my emotions. Silhouettes of gulls backlit by the sun (bay invisible thru the polluted air). Motorcyclist on the sidewalk – how come, in the cold air, her breath doesn't fog up her face shield? The sign reads "Ikaros Private Club." Theory is the sex of academic intercourse. Writing in airports is basica1ly weird – is this what Whitman meant (is this why Whitman wept)? A tractor that's no more than a conveyor belt on wheels rolls up to the baggage bay. He wears a painter's cap with the visor in back. Men in business suits, especially if overweight, often look like adolescents playing dress-up. We will begin preboarding at this time. Increased informationalization in the NATO/OECD zone-regime brings rising colonization to the lifeworld of its subject-objects. Finally, we're above the clouds into the pure night. Next to me, two men speak of "leveraging power." Far out over the Pacific, streaks of red deepen (yet above the clouds the sky's a pale, colorless blue). Earth reduced to veins of lights. When this you see (cup of tea). One sits in the sun because where else, man? A small tree still stands, dense roots clinching earth, tho its clay pot has cracked and fallen away. Baby bottle bags. That metallic sound specific to the lid of dumpsters. When I see that dog has chewed the buttons off my good jacket and shredded my checkbook I go into a state of shock, laughing because what else can I do? We glide over the low clouds like skaters over ice. Mountain that tears through the soft cloud flesh. As we descend our shadow rushes to meet us. I leave the reading to go off with some "non-literary" friends, glad to be released from that world. Trudging up the slope of the hilltop, one leg bent, the other stretched. With her child in her left arm she has to reach across her body (half standing) past another passenger to pull the cord to stop the bus. Verbs vibrate in the bowels of nouns. The way a coat stretches across a huge-bellied man. Sikh in a suit, beard white as his turban. This dude's combing something medicinal into his hair, dipping the teeth of the comb into a small bottle, camphor fumes choking the air of the cafe. Ah tenderness in the muscles of the neck. Rail yards this morning virtually empty. Clouds cling to the low hills. I yawn and my body shivers. Acquisition of capital obtained through issuing stock underwrites new expansion. Odd to see pickles and lettuce strewn on the walk. This train is bound for Concord, this train. Telephone booth smells of piss. Brothers in the rain remain indoors. The streets are stained with water, glistening yellow under streetlamps. Steam from a factory vent roils up, lit in the night air. I watch a woman stick her gum almost delicately between the pages of a trade journal, then yawn. A tall young black man in a beautiful skirt. Polyester girl, something of a churl. New grafts for a decision tree (thought is a hybrid impression). Legs ache from strain of day – it's barely dawn. The bus in the mist. Full moon lights my room: coleus casts its shadow. Suppository like a hard wax bullet. That's not a yellow ribbon in her hair but a shoelace. Fission Street. Roses wrappt in wax paper. Safety pin as earring, a teen's goatee. Imagine learning to walk in heels. A young Latino man watches me intently, distrustfully, as I write. This woman on the train sits back, throwing her long wool coat over herself like a blanket. Stickpin closes collar tight around the tie – school colors. Pigeons flying in and out of burned out apartment. I watched the young man, huddled into his seat on the crowded bus, trying to write amid the hollering into a notebook. Get another sandwich! O shadows of tunnels! Concrete pillars to support a freeway. Ivy to clothe barbed wire. Shadows of trucks pass. Cowboy boots beneath tie-dye skirt! Exclamation point for the joy of it. Lettuce and pickles and carrots. How exactly does one corn beef? Sherlock Homes and Gardens. My neck feels stiff from a sleepless night, my eyes sting. Just say North. A woman's knit cap meant to look like a seashell. Take note of individuals whose hairstyle is mixed, ambiguous, schizoid – for example, the man with short hair greased back and big bushy sideburns. She meets an old acquaintance from City College on the train and they agree on a date. Full-sized, the billboard (a canvas in the shape of a truck) dwarfs the stucco building to which it's attached. Thoughts flicker, sputtering in the mind. Two rows back, a woman sneezes again and again. All economy ultimately resolves to an economy of time. The headphones and dark glasses give her the "walled-off" look. Tendency days. A newspaper's blown off somebody's porch and has completely disassembled, gray-white sheets billowing in the street. Coat hanger twisted straight lying in the gutter means someone was locked out of their car here once. Hands too cold to hold. Trying to keep both hands steady, staring into the small mirror of the compact case, applying eye shadow on a moving train. This brain is bound to story, this brain. The loneliness of the long-distance programmer. Long deep coffee belch. The car is under a sheetlike tarp which, in the rain, clings tight. She in that taut white skirt, olive skin, hurrying to get under cover, the whole world able to see the outline of her panties. "Rock and roll, brother," says the drunk (white) to the driver (black) . . . gin in one hand, orange soda in the other, the small man shambling off into the rain. Sand dollars hang onto gold loops that cling to each ear – she's beautiful precisely because her eyes are red. Feel of your teeth against the edge of my cock. Low sky's a great grey wall. Silhouette of a woman on a mountain top, just lighting a cigarette at dusk, beneath which, in small print, the surgeon general's warning. Dust of the rail yard gone to mud. Lone wisp of hair, isolate on the pink skull reflected back down at me from the dish-shaped mirror of the corner store. Hummingbird hovers around my head like a giant wasp. On the freeway in the rain, driving with their brights on. The hills in fog Cause the mind to bog. Plastic cover over unfinished roof. The weightlifter wavers under the shadow of the bar. Nameism. Boarded windows of an abandoned school postered over. A sock on the floor by the door. Houses shoehorned into tiny lots. Green triangle with red dots: child's crayon drawing of a Xmas tree (ornaments look like measles). Trees that turn color even in California. I shut my eyes and want to drift back into sleep. A man in a wheelchair pauses before the steps. Ballad of the body reduced to ash. Mysterious little concrete house (no windows!) amid the tracks. A man is wearing a tweed cap over a knit one. Cars whip past. Asa, age two, screams just to hear his voice. Echo of helicopter bounces off valley walls. Out beyond where there are street signs. Surrounded by factories, a brief three block commercial strip, a row of residential hotels and one dark bar (crowded in the afternoon) that calls itself a social club. Unused in a back yard, paint-splattered ladder leans against a porch. The circling gull peers down at its valley. He leaves the phone unplugged, but the answering machine on. The pear tree is barren. A parrot in a cage on a wooden perch. Lunch or lurch, which one?

Lounge! Three robins in a bare tree. Soft-bore at targets hidden in the head, fools and piecards, I, erroneous, aim. Mr. Banana Breath, Dr. Truth Decay.

Electron micrographs of chronic alcoholics' liver cells depict an eerie battleground: the mitochondria are scattered haphazardly, some grotesquely misshapen, others with gaping holes in their membranes, end still others white and vacant, bled dry of everything inside. A break between words. The point where Chinatown and Nob Hill imperceptibly weave together. Someone's puked into the discarded Frito bag. Clausewitz on art administration. Will Build To Suit. Fourth day of a bad cold: you no longer remember what it feels like "to be normal." The non-materiality of a year is what makes it so difficult to get the date right on one's checks for the first few days each January. The yellow paper of a Mexican book. This isn't a subway stop where you'd expect to see a young woman ell flashed up like that in the middle of the day. Eighth day of the same cold (stuffed heed, hacking cough) and I head out just to keep from dying of cabin fever. Men who wear dark glasses underground. Hand cramps to push the pen, what then? The man sitting next to me, wearing an Italian suit, has a single tiny silver ear post in the design of a swastika. I sense the fever in my cheeks, my hands, my neck (I don't sniffle, I snuffle). That fire engine's chartreuse. The sense of detail to those hills on the first day after e long rein. Glass of shattered bottle forms a pattern on the tracks. I want a new form (ah won't, a new foam). By pause and pitch, I recognize that conversation to be in Chinese . . . Mandarin or Cantonese I cannot say. The cast turned his hand into a large white club. Bespectacled, freckled little man, red heir gone to fuzz over the bald crown. Why do I recognize that voice over the intercom as black? That yellow should be the middle light between red and green. A man in hip boots on a sunny day. Grandfather tumbling in the air, felling three storeys from a mountain of old newspapers at the pulping plant (wrists end ankles shatter on impact). Leather shoes with the toes soaked through. He likes to wear what he cells college ties. Two new books in a single week (double word score). Cheek resting on one hand, eyes shut, she looks glum. Bright stripes of a yuppie umbrella. But leg warmers over high heels? My father, blown by the explosion four storeys into the air, third degree burns over eighty percent of his body. Coming out of the tunnel, the rein's stopped, the sky half clear. If you hadn't celled at sunset, I'd've spent the entire day without speaking. No peeking. A shop in which they make architectural models, city of smell dolls. Idly drums his fingers on the briefcase. It's a rainy afternoon in Berkeley and suddenly I feel 7 years old again, darting amid puddles past leaf littered lawn. The snorting breath of anyone with clogged sinuses. Halley's comment. Who is served by this discourse (the question implies: discourse serves)? The Vietnam Vets' Center is closed now, the space for lease. Tiny curtained storefront for AA. The snot had dried in the cold air, clinging to the heirs of his nostril. Privileged aesthetic communication. One of the things David Salle's work is not "about" is irony. White cat chases black cat. The bus is crowded and she's got the seat so he puts the beg of groceries (old fashioned brown paper) in her lap. After opening the can, I drain the water before pouring out the peas. Velcro snap to canvas briefcase. Brittle as an old man's toenail. As market culture expands in order to create through absorption a single world ideological system, there remain two basic varieties of aesthetic form which continue, however fitfully, to subsist on the outside: pre-market cultural genres, predominantly rural, peripheral even in the context of the Third World, and those market modes which openly contest the primacy of capital, at the one end forms which previously were associated with feudal courts, the historic avant-gardes, end at the other the militant nostalgia of "folk art." Walking, with each step I feel the cramp in my calf. There is no "third person." It's cold enough to make me curse, grey car looms through fog, headlights dulled by the smoky air. The voice cool and soft over the intercom, "Fremont train approaching Glen Park," then repeated. Watching her change from tennies to heels right there in the station feels inordinately intimate. Teens jogging up the down escalator, laughing, making little progress. Conjugate, coagulate. Little metal hand device with which to curl lashes. The train. a cubist slug, slithers into the tunnel. I press your nipple between thumb and forefinger. Man in TV commercial sticks out tongue at mirror, which talks back. Men in airport bar gather to watch NFL playoff game. screen filled with snow. *Dressage & CT* is a publication with 6,000 subscribers. At quarter to five everyone in the office gets the giggles. Two deaf persons signing to one another simultaneously. Trying to write with my gloves on, letters are large and loopy. It's not often you see a woman urinating in an alley. An odd elegance, man sipping a cup of coffee with a cast on his baby finger. Wide-eyed lady of the highlands. Cheap chandeliers in lighting store window. An expression that stern has anger to burn. Coming down the escalator after the train's already begun to pull away, faces reflect frustration, fury, resignation, regret – laughter, shouts, curses still audible as the tunnel sucks us in. Tiny piroshki, twist of sour cream. Your firm here: we've got what it takes. A novel begins with a description of place. People of the past unite (black cat slithers through traffic). He steps on the heel of his skateboard and up-tilts the front so he can pick it up. Notice how mottled old gum stains render any square of city cement. Divestiture of the past, alas. Anti-apartheid activist from Australia comes to visit, I swear, holding a teddy bear. Those white boots with fuzzy lining look like a pair of high heel casts. Speed's creed: power steering. What is beef but embodied corn? Choose your world (walls against war). Out behind the Oakland hills, pale and pointed stands Mt. Diablo. Gulls sweep past, coasting on their wings, curved arcs, never a straight line. Shattered glass beadlike in the cracks of the walk. Neighbors gather, children in their arms, laughing, telling stories, as all day the men stir a huge pot, a two-by-four as their spoon, boiling, raised upon stones over an open pit, wood smoke and the thick smell of chunks of pork (later we watch them slice and slice and the next day, hanging from three clotheslines, strips of entrails and flesh, slowly drying, turning bacon dark). Sitting next to me a thin man in e gray suit, but with green socks, is reading a xeroxed copy of a crime report, stamped in red "Defense Copy." The thick gold loop hangs from a narrow wire running through the ear. As the wolfhound stops and turns toward us, my chest tightens with instinctive fears. I want to turn the page and it to be gone. Bright red beacon of a zit on the tip of my nose, not ready yet to pop. Train emerges from the tunnel like a long slow worm. There is a poem, mother, very far away and very long, toward which I am climbing in the dark. Skin flaking in the inner ear, flesh coiled about tufts of hair. The nostril, a trumpet, widens. What's the deliverability on that connotation? Kurds in the way / Olaf Palme did slay. Content is never more then e form of extension. Whole earth excess. Pimple on my forehead (the unicorn factor). Pencil sharpener juts out from the wall. Oinks: double income, no kids. As if all the silent 'e's began again to be voiced. Fecund, sickened. Not this. Since when? Off-white leather tennies gone scuffed end dark. The tray rolled up to their table filled with small plates of nameless pastries, pork-centered here, shrimp there. Poor. Old. New. College. The shirt was a cotton blend (leather tips at either end of the white-striped belt). Atop the old ladder in the dark room, I fumble about in the ceiling fixture until, having unscrewed the "dead" bulb, I hold it beside my ear and shake it. I thought of it because I was speaking. Two modes of irony, one thoroughly cynical. Tall red-cheeked blonde licks her lips, as she reads the morning paper, tongue passing slowly to moisten the flesh. Poetry is like a spoon but with a serrated edge. People chuckle at the idea of seven pens in my pocket. A woman vamped up enough to be a drag queen (it's the freckled through the rouge above the day-glo pink lipstick, red-blonde hair stringy over dark eyebrows). Handkerchief still neatly folded, man mops his brow. They rush to crowd the entrance of the escalator like grain in a funnel. In the dream, the cat's speaking to me, asking me not to leave it behind. Predestination creates salvation anxiety. Just Squeezed Grapefruit Juice (round pink sticker on the bottom of the skateboard). I get to the bottom of the escalator just in time to see the train's red lights disappearing into the tunnel (trains in both directions create a great wind effect). Fake leather chair, legless, sits glistening in the rein on the walk. Odd duck speed reader uses e knitting needle to guide his eye down the page of the *Wall Street Journal.* The train is empty now, end of the line, newspapers strewn about the car et one end of which, strewn on the pale yellow rug, stepped on, a bag of potato chips. I love to stand on the porch in brisk rein, shielded (sheltered) yet feeling *in it.* Here's an old vacant lot become a lake. Your transfer spot for the Fremont line. A huge, rotund man, he never tucked in his shirts which hung free and loose over the great shelf of belly, but wore ties that seemed dwarfed against that landscape. It's not the sun's glare reflected off the windows of that train passing in the opposite direction which bothers me so I turn my head, but the flicker effect I caused by its motion, strobe in broad daylight. Facts form acts to bracket lacks – don't ask! An ache around the eyes like a band pulled tight breaks my concentration. A book in the mind is want to grind. Art *is not* a distraction. Paragraph *is* plural. Buppy mofos of the night, ignite – what have you to lose but your subscription to *Jet*? A better door than a window. All of Acker's work might be read as a meditation, sometimes coded, on the sexual abuse of children. If my subject be broken, who then is the agent of this intention? The small old woman (my grandmother) chased me around the house with a knife. The wine label through the bottle of wine – lines of glue cling to the glass in horizontal rows. Tho level, the beer's horizon defines the brown bottle's slant (slope of the table). Sex is not a drive, not even neutral, let's call it park. Let's breathe in a recently painted room. The grain in that voice is corn. Here's a small white bowl, smaller than a cup, filled with a hot sauce. Lean forward and let your elbows rest upon the podium. Hair is to hear as tear is to tear. Here the lace is tied in a double-knot. The small rough legs of the calamari. The color of this ashtray is limestone. To be a poet is as specific an identity as being 'queer,' but this is particular only to this period and place. The iron weights bang against the gym's cement floor. Entropy is inherent (no sentence *needs* a period). He sits at the ballet, watching not the dancer but the dancer's breasts. This next poem began days ago, perfect couplets bound like an old woman's feet. The hair on the back of his hands not uniform, but thicker along the base of the baby finger. Think of the incinerator burning in the alley as a space heater. Gag me with a loom. The name had just three letters, two of which were identical. The accent and lisp blend perfectly. The small hand grasps the long spine of the glass. The black dot in the raspberry soda was not a seed but an ant. He did not experience his head falling away from the guillotine as the loss of consciousness, but as a sense of imbalance accompanied by a tremendous chill, the eyes of the spectators still fixed on the blade. The tease of a plot. I slipped the ring from my finger and examined the smooth, indented flesh. A cold morning, conscious of each arthritic bone in my foot. Roly-poly, drinking Stoly. I wake up filled with an unidentified despair, almost giddy with emotion. Trains roar Past in both directions. People who merely stand on the escalator versus people who rush down. A small stone caught in my sock right at the heel. The price you pay to have been born into a family that couldn't deal with anger. When I'm anxious I monolog. I read to myself half aloud even in public. She's wearing old comfy leather sandals, but with stockings. But when I say I, it's you I mean. Morphine no longer muted cancer's pain. I rotate my wrist slowly just to hear the bones crack. By the door to the kitchen, three tiny metal ant stakes had tipped over. Slice of a pitted olive, like a miniature donut. No yelp whatsoever. Dream recedes to a child's voice – I don't wake so much as admit to waking. Haitian Creole in a Boston suburb echoes French. Preschool abstract expressionism taped to refrigerator door. A slender economist with big brown eyes. Red brick hospital appears still in the snowy field. The dog whines at the door. Poor little jade plant, you've been overwatered, pot's dirt gone to mud on the bathroom floor. Then, on the bus heading downtown, a golf course in the snow. Wood frame funeral home. Then gravestones, grey against white. In a children's playground large silhouettes of animals in bright pastel colors, each with a capital letter, E for elephant, D for duck. D for dunk. Express yourself explicitly on the problem of operationalizing the dependent variable. In the dream I see the face of an infant I recognize as my own. Tapdancing cartoon critters sing my song. Page 1 headline of *USA Today,* Friday the 13th of February, 1987: "ABC's 'Amerika': See It or Leave It." Cold swirling wind rises up off of Boston Common. In the next room, same dream, people from the Institute, from every Job I've ever worked, were calling my name, even honking horns, imploring me to get back to some meeting, but instead I rushed ahead to you as the baby started to spit its milk up allover your sweater and you shouted for me to grab a towel, to see that it didn't get on the blue Christmas stocking. The Charles River appears frozen but deep down we know it's not. Our family style was denial: I felt so guilty at having broken up the family home, having forced my own mother to move out of her parents' house, so disconsolate for the lack of love, that I was sucker for the first beautiful woman who wanted to bed me, so long as she was as intense and crazy as my grandmother – thus I was married at age 19. O bare birch trees of New England. She's reading the latest issue of *Contact Lens Spectrum.* Horses wearing blankets stand in the snow. Port's piers notched into bay's water. Fuck everything, said not as a curse. Hot as a purse. Plastic sailfish on tavern wall, lightbulb in eye. Urban skyscrape flattened by reptilian footprint. The nose as a sequence of curves. Inner swirl *of* the ear. The cup on the table is full of small paper bags of sugar and sugar twin. Who put the chill in chillun'? Eating lukewarm scrambled eggs with a plastic fork off a styrofoam plate. Outline on my leg of a residue adhesive, exact shape of a band-aid. Custer's analysand. Sentences I forgot: she shoves the stroller out into the street at the driveway so as not to wrestle with the curb. First coffee in two days and I'm wire. Fingernails feel overlong. Mixed message: camouflage pants (big pockets!) and lavender shirt (running uphill with a soccer ball tucked in his arms). We cracked the gasket. Businesslike on the train, a woman consults with her daughter over a spelling lesson. Machine hurtles through the tunnel. The biker and the analyst are the same person. Infant's t-shirt as expensive as an adult's, but with bears on it. The specificity *of* the avant-garde audience is sociological. O henna dreadlocks. Rhetorical flourish worthy of any porch banister. Momento mort: I see a young woman I recall having met as a child. Who remembers Ferris Fain? Sky settles into darkness. What if night is the norm and day *its* other? Already your ankles have thickened. Wino's green bottle is no kinda wand. Loud funk rhythm in the too-bright falafel shop, red formica table top. First Hunan Restaurant Vegetarian Seafood. Her stride down that dark street suggests experience with the martial arts. The dream dissolves at the instant of the alarm and, try as I might, I can't remember why I woke upset. An old woman, bones bent, white hair still reflecting an earlier red, turns her head. How can anything end with a question?

JONES

Homage to Bromige

Socks on the floor by the door. After the rain the sidewalk dries unevenly. Pyramid of cans in a corner of the yard, waiting to be crushed by a hammer, then piled into a plastic bag (bags of cans stacked high against the fence). Yellow thorny weed that rises between the cracks in the cement. Small grey dead bird, crushed, feathers matted, nearly unidentifiable in the rain beside the sturdy motorcycle chained to the phone pole, glistening. Little yogurt cup wedged into the catch basin at the corner – shreds of old newspaper dissolve into pulp. Christmas tree discarded on the walk, still dressed in tinsel. Think of parked cars as gigantic litter. Little rectangle cut in the asphalt (layer of wet cement) guarded by a lone sawhorse, not a horse at all, while on the corner, bundled in plastic, papers await the paper boy (not a boy at all). Because the basement is paved, the cellar floor is cold and damp. A dumpster, full, forms a cornucopia. Cracks in the asphalt veined as the earth. Orange rinds scattered and flattened by the traffic, a pair of white plastic bags of trash, neatly tied shut, sit on the catchbasin. Exhaust from the auto warming up billows out over the walk (old wad of gum hardens into a kind of stone). The trashman's can is special, larger, on wheels . . . this one's decorated with blue and orange bumper stickers for a TV station (jingle: *We've got more of what you're looking for – TV 20*). Spotted dog, alone, patrols the middle of the street, blocks away a car approaches. Underneath the sink (old porcelain stand) is a plastic watering can and bottle of plant food. Beneath the bed, blowing about like sagebrush in a sandstorm, balls of dust tumble – up close, they're galaxies, worlds. Cracks in the sidewalk at the peppertree's root. But the sidewalk's in squares, chipped and veined, birthmark of an oil drip. The freeway follows the valley's contours. Black patches of fresh asphalt (you can tell how old it is just by how pale it's gotten). Streets cling to the globe like the web of a net stocking (funny little Chinese diary to write this in: page of pale purple lines bordered with a scene: ducks, wings open wide, settle into bamboo, while beneath something like a catfish leaps from the sea). Up off the floor maybe two feet, the height of your bed, mattress on a home-made wood frame, what I see below are your undies, black cotton, twisted and dropped on the old green rug. Next to the yellow-flowered scotch broom, planted in a ragged hole in the walk at the foot of the steps, a dry but pungent Christmas tree, still with a few strands of tinsel. Dense fog diffuses a dim light – no horizon – color's an effect of the sun (that objects are pointless evident to any) – worm stretches past a small stone. A scrap of paper (a subscription form from a magazine) blows about the gutter, limp from fog's damp. Torn and broken, a dark mattress smolders in the half-paved alley. Black coffee in the soil to keep it acidic. One reason the street looks darker when it rains is all the little slips of paper dissolve. Sawdust spills from a workbench – bird sings back at the saw (spiders amid the dead leaves under the shade of the strawberry).

Loose fluffs of cat fur, gray-white in the parsley, suggest an old fight – on the walk, a scrap of roofing shingle, through which sticks a rusted nail. Headlights' reflections stretch out atop the rain-slick asphalt – illumined nightworld in mid-morning. Pale brown tip of a crushed cigarette butt – blind fibers (mashed) jut out. The leaves at the tree's base – on the walk in front of each house, full and waiting, sit garbage cans. Discarded newspaper headline: the death of Liberace – blackbirds in the crosswalk flock. Somedays, today, I don't see it at all, yet last night under the glow of the streetlamps I could tell that the walk there was cut in a zigzag design, every second Z mixed with a reflecting glitter, aesthetics of the mall displaced here in the ghetto, guys hanging out even in the night fog, leaning into the open windows of parked cars (visibility of the informal economy) – she drops her McNugget, catsup side down, and walks away (a pigeon drops from a phone wire and waddles up). Thick-soled, the heavy black shoes of police officers (inside a rough square formed by yellow tape tied around a busstop sign, a trash can and two trees), the mottled, mixed shoes (cheap, old, graying) of the bystanders – inside, by itself, untouched, lies a purple poplin jacked filled to overflowing with thick, red blood. On the porch, an old aluminum pot is half-full of rain water – cat sleeps, its chin hanging over the edge of the step. The ground defined by my relation to it (the ground defied by my relation to it): highway 280 snakes out of the San Bruno mountains, the bay before me met by the rain's low sky, gray against gray, roadway's lighter gray (false river cutting down) leading to the industrial horizon of the airport – lobby's wall-to-wall carpeting shifts from brown to a dull orange to articulate a false wall between corridor and gate 83. Crystalline glitter where the sun hits the snow, a clean drift pocked by a dog's prints, parallel – lump of white on the strap of a swing seat (sways in the breeze), the shadow of its chains sharp against the snow. In the playground, the shining spiral slide descends right into the snow – having shoveled the rest, he scrapes the last icy layer, half-brown from the walk. The dog leaves snowprints on the hardwood floor – cord winds from the wall to the small TV stand. Shuffle of an old man (but he's not an old man) across the checkered linoleum of the bus depot floor – in the gutter slush has hardened into ice. Seeds and crumbs gather on the floor at Zabar's – outside, snowflakes swirl but never land on the dark cement. The neutrality of the museum's carpet – muddy footprints in the water at the base of the urinal. The only snow that remains is on the cemetery's brown grass – or a view from which the surface is no surface at all, but an endless, soft, off-white layering of cloud. Dog poop and spittle – a black pigeon (pink legs) hops. A banana peel, deep brown, and a black canvas belt with a brass buckle – smashed styrofoam cup. Newspaper scattered under the seat of the bus – shoes (in this case grey tennies). Insist on what's present (broken glass, nearly powdered) – a drunken man, half-sleeping, at the feet of two cops. Crushed plastic orange juice bottle – there's no horizon in a tunnel. Little nameless plants that grow at the edge of gardens – the way old gum leaves its spotted shadow on the cement until the walk itself is thoroughly freckled. What mortar between the grooves of these bricks – rubber casing lines subway's third rail. On the freeway, rain spins out from under the wheel of a truck – hailstones (like small salt rocks) give the street texture. Gradually, cracks in the sidewalk add up, cement squares gone to rubble – still smouldering, cigarette in the gutter is pure ash. An old truck up on blocks – no stains yet on the new asphalt. Throw-away newspapers wrapped in a red rubber band, one on every porch – building's mural continues, painted on the walk. Fresh white paint (STOP) on the new asphalt – petals, also white, surround the base of the tree.

Tracks, trees, streets, tiny houses (trees jut up to mark a park), valleys where the tribe has settled. Asphalt cracked until it's begun to dissolve (pothole at the gutter retains muddy rainwater), red paint of the curb pale and chipped. Lone waterbug miniscule crossing the great plain of the mall lot (blue-grey, the water on the bay is still), green-white stain of pigeon shit atop the polished brick. Goldfinch settles at pruned apple tree's base (lines to articulate a plan for parking), islands of ground cover at the rim of the mall. Pothole in asphalt as if the earth below has been sucked away (thick rubbery cushion under the carpet) or asphalt so fresh you can still see the lines from its roller. Here the walk's have been patched with a different shade of cement (blackbirds on the mall, what gall), loud frogs in the bushes at dawn after a hard rain. What could seem smaller, more still, than a dead mouse, huddled fetal-like on the curb's edge (green-painted wood of the busstop bench too damp to sit on), old gray dumpster alone in the lot. Article in the newspaper about a man who photographs manhole covers (perspective from which these bunched clouds are the surface), amber glass reflectors in the center of the street. A rose petal, pink, perfectly formed, has dropped onto the walk (corridors of the mall hosed down at dawn) alongside the brown, round wrapper of a Reese's peanut butter cup. A metal door in the sidewalk for access to the store's basement (white marble stoop of a Baltimore porch), pushed by the wind a blue napkin skitters across the lot. Red tile squares cut a path to the street (by the school yard green pots for small plants, each with a number on its side (painted white)) – after the rain snails cross the damp walk. Brown beer bottle, tipped on its side (in the distance, steam rises from factory vents in the flatlands), a lead slug, exact size of a quarter. Red-tail squirrel dashes for the phone pole (path through the brambles leads to the creek), ants swarm about the green-brown mash of a crushed snail. Before they freeze together, snowflakes rest lightly on one another (at night, I was unable to see the thin film of ice on the driveway and so went sliding down onto my hands and knees), difficult to tell under all that white just how far down the earth really is. Because it is carpeted indoors, one walks barefoot (an icicle drops into the snow, sinks immediately from sight), a string of cars beside the road, drivers crawling underneath the wheels, chains in hand. Dark dead bug foregrounded against the brilliant sunlit snow (duck down feather clings to the rug's fiber as the vacuum passes overhead), mountain chickadee small next to the red-breasted nuthatch. Sprinkler's pipes jut through the dry earth (stump of a felled tree, the cut still fresh), welcome mat of astroturf. Grease on the rainslicked pavement forms a discolored rainbow (thick gum sole of a cop's shoe), dark gum stains of the train's carpet. Round cement trash receptacle with removable plastic bag (squirrel's tail not as red as the shingles of the A-frame on which it sits), condos gouged into the terraced hill. Peach pit crushed by the weight of the truck's tires (trowel digs into the crack in the walk, uprooting a milkweed), mop juts out of a bucket on wheels. Soap granules dust the laundromat floor (impossible to tell that that cloud is moving save by watching the rub of the horizon), large checkered squares of cafe's linoleum. People, of course, and lots of them all the time (wires just to brace the phone pole), streetsign at the corner is angled, index of an old accident. Baseball card (stat side face up) gone to pulp in the rain, a late winter. Trail made of grass crushed by feet (I slip an "ant stake" sideways on the floor behind the toilet), tunnel burrows path under the city. A bottle gang sits on the sidewalk day after day, moving around the corner when the sun slides into the west (earth in the planterbox dry and lifeless), teeth barely rooted into gums that bleed at the lightest touch. Large see-thru plastic shopping bag (yellow handles, painted yellow flowers), someone's discarded an issue of Awake. A boat on the horizon enters the gate (rubberband, alone, lies on the walk – impossible to tell what it was used for), crushed cigarette butt, the tobacco flat, but the filter still with some body. Blue-flowered ground cover (the soil, being damp, is soft and penetrable), I remember, as a boy, being hired to "spike" an old man's lawn. Smoke rising out of the valley, yellow-brown, where no smoke ought to be (pale pink plastic dildo, cut into slices, lies in the street), just watching her from behind you can tell her walk is agitated, off-center, angry. Big bright yellow-green snake slides across the path (young doe pauses to watch me before leaping into the brush), far below, down the trailside past the lake a faint calliope sings. As dusk falls, cool and shadowless, we begin to see the lights of the far hills, streets and houses, at first a faint glitter, then brighter as the sky darkens until these points are all that remains (I was raised by that clump of trees yonder), what once were mudflats we now call the wetlands.

lines of red brick
staggered form a locking
insensitive to the mortar,
demanded by the eye

at walk's edge weed
spurts, jagged, sweet, unnamed
spreading land's cracked vent
gills for surfaced soil

white fungus on stump
soft coral, ground soft
being needle of pine
red-brown in the rain

dove overhead hovering coos
whose shadow is cast
far to the east
red sun horizontal light

white clover amid thin
low cut grass alive
with bees, ladybug's wings
spread out to fly

slug wet in mud
little rivulet forming deerpath
amid shredding eucalyptus bark
mallard atop still pond

noise skitters through underbrush
index of the not-seen
one person: 20 birds
here they are now

stones between cross-ties black
with oil Howard Beach
concrete TWA terminal shaped
like a non-existent bird

the world as imagined
room without windows – rug
carpets hardwood floor – air
lay still without vent

men lean to chat
against a police car
styrofoam cups steaming sit
atop the blue hood

constraints of the sun
street half in shadow
trees half in bloom
trash can sits empty

grate in the floor
is a drain in
case of rain in
center of men's room

finch in Little Italy
amid debris tossed up
by street excavation finds
mound of fresh earth

couch on the rug
on the floor between
walls straight down into
cement dirt sand rock

ants in a row
on the tile sink
think to swarm onto
sweet old honey jar

hills half haze hidden
bright pink gum wad
against concrete's dull gray
this rose is yellow

furrows of cut grass
visible as stripes form
field's concentric circles ready
for a baseball game

leaves gather in gutter
edge of shed's roof
dry, gnarled, twig twisted
but here's a rhododendron

berries on the casket
to sweeten the loam
soft red rich soil
makes a new home

beer bottle set down
carefully at gutter's edge
still there at dawn
beside can of V-8

imagine jackhammer as adz
cracking the earth's shell
hardened soil dry skin
exposes vein of pipe

an orange cat crosses
street at the light
armored waterbug wanders forward
shadow of a weed

train cuts thru fog
sky a dull glare
the damp trees shudder
the lights on inside

spots on the walk
soon fade to grey
burned bush edges mall's
vast scar of parkinglot

maps reduce detail, trace
curved surface as plane
index populations by grid
folded into coat's pocket

film of what content
collects in tile's cracks –
gray mortar's abrasive surface
is apt to cling

ill-lit, the dark realm
wind-filled, gusting, echoes whistles
train's rattle hums on
the perfectly empty tracks

city in miniature as
background to these houses
near to the eye
shimmering, solid, almost touchable

mallards on the promenade
stale river, barefoot girl
is running to class
against the joggers' flow

trees surround the field
divided by a river
leaves yellow as grown
over the darker water

Hours after flowers by virtue of light's path (cloud darkens ground) – red ant scrambles crosswise over the walk, weighted by a crumb . . . man in a wheelchair, his lap is his desk – ladybug spreads her wings . . . rounded turn to curb's rim. A lone weed defines the lawn – their names come later . . . gum soles press down, lift up at the heel, push into air (children on the "people mover," the wrong way walking), layer of rainwater darkens the long asphalt of the airport runway. Texture of rugs is related to sweaters (pressure point of high heels)(broom herds paper scraps toward dustpan's tilted lip), spilled cola, like bead of oil, resists absorption (whole of world enclosed). Dried pigeon doodoo provides texture to the too-smooth tiles of the mall walk . . . before the train arrives, everyone's watching, a five dollar bill blowing loose around the third rail (sawdust drifts about the lumberyard) – the rails dark with grease . . . there lies a cluster of crushed M&Ms. The wide brush of the janitor's mop . . . smell of stale sewer, rotting in the heat . . . sky amber on the horizon, smog on the bay . . . homes are blisters on earth's surface, inflamed by light . . . between two lawns, perfectly groomed, lies a third not trimmed at all. Skateboard slips down the long slope of street (bricks mesh to form a walk)—fresh chalk marks out a cinder track . . . trees bunch up behind houses . . . as the train emerges from the tunnel, station's sudden glare. Filled with shadows, diffuse in the dispersed light – scuffed shoes wrap ankles, themselves wrapped in scrim of stocking – sun's glare in a crushed can – leaves crackling in the dry heat – smouldering skeleton of car. Clouds mock the air's light: hard porous surface, dry ground (bee's weight bends the leaf) – train never free of its tracks, Oh line of loose caulk. Wet wood streaks as it dries, growing lighter . . . mockingbird atop brick chimney sings . . . water in the clay pot sinks into the soil (roses by the fence shaded by the house) – glimmer of old snail trail across the deck. Spider that lives in a cord of wood (empty wood barrel that once was a planter) – gradually shade crosses the garden – flat rooves (means snow is rare) gather leaves. Bodyweight shifts forward as, at the top, escalator levels out – hazy green hills, dew steaming off in the sun – richer, darker green of the weeds – condos on a hillside affect the layered look – spider drops down from the brim of my hat (!). Someone's thrown birdseed onto the tracks – pigeons leap straight up to escape from our path = sand congeals, sealing the planet in (boards between sawhorses to shut us out), soft light filters through the curtain. Threads, stitching, nets (out in the plains states, where small towns rest atop hard soil like dry scabs, where states' boundaries merely trace a river's erosion, taut twisting of the earth's skin to stretch over a round (not really round) center) – thin, yellow municipal carpet, passive in the lobby – or trees as spears, piercing its flesh . . . unnamed (solely because I don't know that jargon) concrete risers hold the overpass aloft. Space as fathomable as the sea (hard rock molecules merely packed closer together) – who knows what a fact is, solid ground . . . versus, say, drip grind in the rain forest . . . versus, say, verses. Wires encased in rubber taped to concrete floor . . . grid designs on shoe soles, worn down, dusty . . . tack stuck into the heel . . . shining metal taps (!) . . . wires twist and knot in the corner. Somehow leaves blow inside . . . pigeon dead in the men's room, beneath the white sink . . . lean-tos behind houses offer sheltered storage . . . stains on the floor at the stove's base . . . windowsill's thin film of dust. Rug tacked down . . . from the damp bushes at dusk, frogs sing . . . yellow haze of streetlamp on a starless night . . . cut grass dry atop the green lawn . . . thin red curl of dog stool. What is a site (planet's skin thick as the rind of a tangelo, thin as that of a potato, or all skin, layer within layer, like flesh, like an onion) . . . waves not only dense with life but debris . . . whole neighborhoods built upon sand dunes . . . beneath them, hidden rivers drain to the sea. Mole squints into the morning light – clouds drag along coastal hills, are ripped apart – sun's light not external to the leaf – drops pearl up on each sharp blade of glass – massive foil wrapper (a "stick" of gum in the form of a sheet) rolls across the high rim of the gutter. After the shower the vast paved lot doesn't seem so flat, pools formed in the cracked valleys of asphalt . . . the white rows of painted stripes are an abstraction, do not relate to the contours of the land . . . sign here indicates the border between two ranches, neither of which have existed for a century. . . . Soaked, even this old egg carton loses its shape . . . but not, however, this styrofoam cup. Robins in the cut grass, piles of raw board stacked in the lumberyard (graffiti glows on tunnel walls) – a gray so even you aren't aware of the depth of those clouds – parking lot in which, years ago, Phil Laponovich, surrounded by cops, shot himself in the head – the way an old newspaper blows into single sheets. Juniper makes a hedge (ice cubes melting in the porcelain sink), earwig discovers new world atop picnic blanket . . . the way aphids shade a leaf . . . ants in the bathroom, seeking new resources, new markets. Stillness of the pigeon's corpse sunlit on the tracks . . . here's another, mashed to abstraction (broken feathers) – orange cones divide the street . . . shoelaces in a double knot. Jogger alone on the empty street, small houses, small trees – one lawn neatly trimmed but entirely dry and dead – bottle gang on Jones Street, opposite the market, still alive enough to wolf-whistle a woman (she turns back, gives him the finger, then walks on, half-dragging her daughter) – bland brown towhee hops amid gutter debris. Half-burned-off, last tuft of fog tugs at the ragged rim of the hills – sun's glimmer before it emerges over the horizon (later light falls in strips thru the Levolor blinds onto the cream-colored rug) – not looking at the men, but merely the rows of shoes under the cafeteria table . . . the way a wallboard is punctured with sockets. Deep in the toaster's belly, where all the burnt crumbs are – an abandoned building (a school), roof mysteriously covered with large shards of broken glass . . . gravel as fill around the ties of the track – *sightation* – gap of an inch between train's car and the platform. Head down, one finds pennies . . . trashcans encased in boxes of concrete – forklifts behind a cyclone fence – a roll of roofing felt on its side on the sidewalk . . . cars parked at angles with the edge of the lot. Tree's trunk sunk into a square of dirt cut from the lawn . . . pier over a small pond, now entirely drained . . . pipes stacked into a pyramid by the loading dock . . . a small three-sided fence, to surround the "man" hole when it's open and occupied . . . from the yawning basement grate of the store came the familiar strains of *Louie Louie.* It's not that the spots on the linoleum are "shapeless" but that each is so irregular that to name or define it (let alone generalizing to the entire group) falls back on some analogy to the organic . . . not even a stain exactly but a place where the hard smooth surface has eroded (been eroded), yielding the rougher uneven texture beneath . . . dead leaves at the base of the jade tree . . . oil's dark shadow on the light cement . . . the grass

dry and yellow between the tall green eucalyptus trees. Dust on the sill – on
the rug's surface a fine layer of broken fibers – behind the juniper, hose
coiled like a python – spider stomped into the grain of the wood – you
lift your shoe and stare at the dog poop. Three cars parked with their
right wheels up on the curb . . . bars of the heating grate in the living-
room floor . . . rows of brick in front of the fireplace . . . records leaning
up against the side of the speaker . . . soft web of shadows on the street
from the power lines. Breeze waves leaves' shadows – tall stalks of
weeds shoot through low ground cover – fly's path, walking, is not a
straight line – the way new planks cross-hatch a hole in the base of the
fence. These leaves newly fallen are yellow . . . those (older) are brown . . .
stone footpath barely visible through the growth . . . dense as a forest,
shuddering in the hot wind . . . tiny vireo hops on the walk.

Sour cornucopia: trash can tipped asunder.
Far corner of the lot, where the shopping carts stand abandoned.
Fire crew milling around the false alarm.
Offshore, fog sits on the water.
Under the bird feeder, blades of alfalfa sprout through the dry soil.
Beneath the seats in the theater, cola dries into a hard gum.
Gravel in the grass where the sidewalk ends.
Piles of cardboard cartons, mashed flat, tied up by wire, out by the loading
dock.
Trains slide past in opposite directions, liquid motion.
It's at the base of trees that trash collects.
Yo, faint paint of the crosswalk, arrows vanishing in the imaginary
corridors of the mall lot.
Tricolor imitation topsiders, pale pastels, worn with socks.
Pine needles, leaves gather in the gutter.
Meaning not clear of a coathanger on the sidewalk, twisted wire.
Sloping rooves for the most part shingled, flat ones gravel over tar.
Patch of white quartz makes a mock garden.
Late twilight, past the sun's set, the hillside is muted, shadowless.
Road markers, orange plastic cones stacked one onto another, rise.
Cut grass, drying, mixes with the shorn grass that remains.

Ferns front up under the tree.
An idea that a walk is raised makes curbs.
Bridge gone in the dawn haze.
Grease stains in the gutter shimmer with the morning sun.
What's in that sack, sticking out beneath the bush?
Ink runs in the gutter, downhill to the margin.
Unmaintained, an old asphalt path returns to dirt and gravel.
Coils of ice plant dry by the roadside (lone hubcap crushed and bent).
Point at which leaves gather in the gutter.
Sharp spray of water pushing dog stools from the walk.
Ankles tense from tilt of high heels.

Pale ink, pale writer: this is the way the path wends, in (oh woman on the bus, your fists clenched tight), the line a horizon, a kind of ground. Inset rectangle where once a lawn grew, bounded by house, sidewalk, driveway and path, later held a bed of colored stones, but now even these are gone. An edge to the curb where it meets the squares of the walk . . . tufts of weeds grow in the crack (now it is "man" that includes nature, not the other way around). A child's gravestone sunken into the dry grass, bees among the clover. In back of the small school we come across two women sitting on the concrete in the shade, carving up a vast red watermelon, reaching out to offer us thick, dripping slices jeweled with black seeds. Between buildings in the mall, the walk is paved in large squares, perhaps ten feet in each direction, which after 30 years have begun to warp, sink and crack, returning to the shape of the earth beneath. Sun's heat shimmers up off the pavement (the scraping sweep of the blind woman's stick), drunk asleep in his own piss gives a deep dreamy sigh. Pages are quiet: the tiniest leaf, dried and curled, blows slowly over the street, breeze so light those grains of dust, lacking aerodynamic form, fail to stir. Living high on the food chain, mosquito makes a home on my arm. Lying flat on my back, I see overhead the white-striped wings of a mockingbird sail past. On the sidewalk, an old open suitcase displays plastic bracelets, cheap dark sunglasses. In North Beach and the Financial District, parts of the city are constructed upon the hulls of old ships, gambling parlors, taverns, the small homes of men returned from the gold fields, the even smaller crowded cribs of the brothels, over which the street forms a hollow crust. Here the houses are built over what were long sloping sand dunes leading down to the sea. The textures of cement various as the hand (here a path of polished stones). Them that prefer ground cover versus them that prefer lawn, oh paved patio with your little redwood deck. Now that the hills are yellow, dry midsummer morning, what's missing (tho we never saw it) is the blue in the grass. Fragility of this grid of paths not evident here in the city, streets that extend in all directions . . . tho here some end at the frontage road by the landfill at bay's edge . . . yet from the sky high over mountains only one or two narrow roads snake through reaching the plains to the "next place." Fresh dark earth of a gopher's excavation against the pale dry dirt of the ground. Dandelion's bright against the dull weeds. Theory fertilizes a seed of intuition. Path C:\DOS; C:\MSWORD is one way to get there, the way a woodpecker's ground is likewise vertical, the sound of a keyboard like rats in the eaves, pecking towards babylon (surge protector's light glows orange in the dark room). In Baltimore, where I am not, there's an exhibit near the aquarium, the Visible Street (or something like that), a cross section, layered as flesh is layered, pipes, tubing, wires beneath the dark meat of asphalt (not only hokey but false: skin's dead layer flakes away, while here, in Baltimore, not Berkeley, it's simply piled on, the newest flesh is at the outer edge, tender, alive with root and worm). Open-ended as in free-falling, in search of punctuation or an object, the way a child might be out of doors and far from home long after dark, even syntax seeks only shelter. Something startled forward out of the bush at my feet, a cat I thought at first in the yellow glimmer of the street lamp, then a rat, seeing the long thin tail, if not hairless at least without fur, then, it pausing to stare back up at me before scuttling down the cement steps behind the last row of houses at the edge of the woods, I realized, no, here's our friend the rabid possum. There's a damp, almost oily quality to fresh blacktop, which grows dry and pale as it ages, revealing the rubbed streaks of scraped tires. Beneath the hanging birdfeeder, seeds lay scattered on the dark soil. She unfurls a large towel before she lies down to bathe in the sun. Imagine each paragraph as a maze (every sentence presents a possible wrong turn). A young man with a hoe standing beside a pile of dry ivy ripped from the strong soil. At night the mall lot is dark, a vast black plain (lunar surface) punctuated by the yellow glow of tall lamp poles, its only sounds the scraping of a plastic bag tumbling in the wind across the asphalt and, somewhere, the song of a displaced cricket. What comes next, one wonders, as the path nears a turn. The jet of water on the hot cement instantly turns to steam.

A new paragraph means a new month: scrub jay in the jade tree, small green anna's hummingbird hovers by. Red and checked tile leads to the walk, too short and shallow to call a porch or path – oh bright orange monarch against the yellow-green fern, against your own black trim (lost in the middle of a dense forest, remember this: walk in any direction in a straight line and you will arrive at the edge, but no path is harder than to define a path), I see from their shadows in the street that our four finches weight the line. So pry into the primal scene: soft worm curls back into damp soil (high above, fledgling herons still fear to fly, cautiously stalking, pacing the tree's top branches (point at which the adults simply stop feeding them, until hunger drives them into the air)). One imagines paths inexorable as a train rail when the better analogy would be that of the man on the raft with no sail, the sea still, no land in sight, a half-bland, half-ominous cloud layer the full expanse of the sky (no sun, no stars), food long since consumed, with a lone gull circling overhead. The way these leaves gather even in summer, brittle ellipsoids, smooth-edged, more yellow than brown when they dry, names not known to me, little forestation at the rim of the bank lot. An image in the mind of a body sprawled, broken upon Houston Street (grey sky, brick walls), young woman struck by a motorcycle (an image in the mind – you cannot shake it), crowds gather wild as animals, sirens begin to emerge in the distance, an image in the mind the sky mixed with blood, the unyielding concrete, sirens so loud they burst my ears, an image in the mind of Kate Berrigan. A man in shorts rakes cut grass from a lawn (yellow dots of a pumpkin patch seen from the air), the entire horizon dulled by the colorless sky. Imagine the path not as circular, but a spiral, gradual arc of 'progress' without that sense of forward. A hill so slight you're not even conscious of it until you look back, down at the valley. The blind woman has made a pallet of old cardboard boxes on the sidewalk, upon which she sits cross-legged playing a moanful accordion. Blow-ins from magazines litter the floor of the crowded news shop (always it's the free newspapers that are stacked up on the linoleum): one might simply gauge or catalog the various shoes that pause here. Empty, snail shells lie strewn about the poisoned garden. A line of ants curls about the base of the garden faucet, path leading back to a crack at the edge of the house. The number of rubber bands discarded, rotting on the tracks or between them at the platform is an index of the commuters who arrive each morning at the station with their newspapers still rolled up. Old dead skunk in the road no longer smells (black and white and red all over). Dark strip of wet sand at the edge of the beach, etched with foot and paw prints (high up on the ridge the path, winding line of crushed grass, has a sign – "unmaintained trail"). Willets in the marsh at low tide jab at the mud for food. Fruit mashed into the sidewalk (impossible to tell what it was): plastic bus shelter with its roof and half the walls missing, graffiti scratched into the plastic. Small polished stones embedded in the pale cement. Comb rakes through last wisps of hair (there is no ground without a theory of the ground): do earthworms squint? A jay (not visible) harps repeatedly in the tree, but what I see instead are the epaulettes of the red-wing blackbird. Wild pennyroyal, little blue flowers, amid the dry grass. Underneath her stocking she's wearing a small golden ankle bracelet. Big dark plastic trash bag of dried grass leans against the stucco house. The lines in 'closed' letters stenciled here on the asphalt slate of the mall lot, fat, white, spray-painted strokes, are broken (from above, from the sky, the painted corridors and parking slots must look like oddly orderly abstractions (Sol LeWitt portrait of a feather, skeleton of a fish)). The way feathers curl, fuzz at the base of the stem, blowing across the red polished brick – and here are the leaves of the eucalyptus. Hosed down at dawn, the walk in front of the department store is slippery (is there an oil in this cement?). How do maxipads end up on the sidewalk? Empty, the beer can juts from the paper sack behind the cyclone fence (through whose links wood slats form a screen): before you see the train you hear the train. Coke can in the weeds, familiar design caked in mud. Repetition flags the theme: finch at dawn hunts among weeds (seeds fall to the surface).

Repetition flogs the theme
    the intent thickens
        as the cement hardens

heel and ankle rise
toes form a base
with the ball of the foot

two seagulls pull apart
abandoned box of
Kentucky Fried

sky orange-brown with fire
ash settles into the mulch
squirrel upright, frozen with alertness

the ground itself is unfirm
crusted over steaming springs
cracked rock spitting and hissing

oh scratching-foot
skeeters gnaw at ankles
welt beneath this light fur

the sufficiency of nature
like this hand towel rotting in the gutter
the narrative implicit, indeterminate,
complete

steady drop of pine cones
punctuates the ground
vast against the fine mist

mystery grates dot these walks
meters, sewers, trap doors
beneath which the lights are shining

objects dropped are gradually flattened
rhythm of the gait in the blackbird's walk
lines of cars parked at an angle

that's a new brand of beer can
here in the gutter
one I've not seen before

boulders of stone rubble
where just last week
stood the boarded-up house

old man is rolling home produce
in that otherwise empty
kiddie stroller

empty plastic trashcans stacked three deep
wire shopping cart, abandoned, tipped on its
side
hand tool combines forklift and dolly

one imagines the necessary (soil,
air, light) coming here together
brook by the bridge

bale of crushed cardboard wrapped in wire
out by the loading dock
next to the bright yellow dumpster

yellow eyes of a blackbird
no taller than these dandelions
at the base of this pine

on the still porch
beneath the white lawn chair
ants swarm about a dead finch

bright glare on the street
broken by dawn's sharp shadows
articulates a shimmering ground

paper wrappers that once held straws
flattened on the black asphalt
catsup stains dry and dark

bicycle rider glides down the light slope
leaning into his turn
butt high, spine parallel to the ground

upright and alone on the stone step
a brass nozzle, small column
far from any garden hose

gravel strewn about the sidewalk
no clues as to source
leaves of an unravelled cigarette

layer of moisture once the fog burns off
contracts into round drops
little rivulets begin to stream

images of labor
as a parking lot
filled with cars, unpeopled

sun's light refracted
up off the glistening rooves
or the steamed-up bay windows

one aims even at a distance
to step upon
a styrofoam cup

some cross their legs
while others plant them firmly
sitting on the bus

paper scraps carried by the wind
herded along these gutters
first rain under a deep sky

"Oh my . . . OH MY . . . it's happening again . . . down in Louisiana the ground don't do this," Will Clark, 23, in a telephone interview from his hotel room during the L.A. quake, people trapped in elevators screaming, October 1, 1987. The way gravel spreads from the edge of a stone garden or the way the tractor-driven rake evens out the dirt on the basepath (automatic lawn sprinkler turns the morning paper to a pulpy mush, damp swollen log). Not a straight line but like the logic of chess, each move (each word) opens entire sequences, others shut forever (train plunges into the tunnel) and reversing your steps can never take you back. Slowly, the skateboarder snakes downhill (it's the janitor who raises the flag at the high school), gulls picking at paper bags in an empty lot. Hitting the pothole with bad shocks. As the train pulls into the underground station, the waiting crowd rises from its benches and starts to surge forward. Outside the laundromat the white dust of detergent blows about the sidewalk, caking into the cracks. Two-headed arrow stenciled to indicate options (left turn, straight ahead) available from this lane. The street itself is a collage of dozens of greys, from deep oil stains to sunbleached paved squares of the sidewalk, the road itself arched, sloping down to either gutter. The trail of crumbs leads back to the margin: the origin of the paragraph a blank space of no apparent cause (capital needed to break it), dust on the horizon in two-point perspective, runners at the corners with nobody out. The light here is indirect, refracted from the sides of buildings, off the towering eucalyptus, the twisted jade, filtered with children's voices, the topsoil damp where the groundcover has yet to spread. Red spiked heels, but her ankle's in an ace bandage (gulls this far inland foretell rain), train's third rail is raised up higher (has a safety cover). What's visible in back yards: garage nearly a lean-to, patio with a paved surface, gathering of mops. Here the old sidewalk is so patched it's turned into a motley (tall stacks of recycled lumber streaked and stained beside the raw orange-buff of fresh-cut boards). Signs that a road crew will be here soon: arrows, lines, circles, and Xs are painted on the asphalt, words such as "gas" and "water." After the leaf falls, it flattens (brown rounded edges rolled over or stepped upon), cracking, then shedding, until finally the wind whisks the fine powder away. Ice cube trays grow old and brittle, why not the earth likewise (fissures in the cubes themselves, white lines, clouds like cataracts), dew steaming off the grass in the morning sun sucking the dirt dry (he means the soil), squirrel makes its way up the ancient flaking phone pole, nut in mouth, then across the insulated wire that runs through the trees. Fly at your ear sounds loud (mysterious bird peeps in the bush), a creek and only barely that cutting through this rock, ability of moss to cling. A swimming pool, still blue water, shines in the dull fog – the anxiety of train riders queueing up, jostling into line at the ticket gate. A stack of plastic laundry baskets in bright primary colors (plus green, plus brown) up against the door of an old-fashioned five-and-dime, beside the bright stack of galvanized trash cans. At the top of the narrow escalator, where there was no room to turn around, commuters crowding their way up, the janitors hose had burst, suddenly trapping all. The street's oily after fall's first rain, blotches of it broken into dull milky rainbows (sullen spectra). Warning: severe tire damage – in the early morning before the stenciled parking grids fill, cars take the shortcut, zipping diagonally across the vast lot . . . small wren perched atop the squat hydrant, an old man walking a tiny, pug-nosed Chinese dog. Diamonds cut into the walk where once trees were planted, harbor only rubbish, and here a great burst of yellow-headed weeds through the cracks in the walks. Pressure nozzle on the hose, jets of water crash against red brick walk (he's wearing black knee-high rubbers), ricochet spray that fills the air. The stairs empty but the escalator full. At the window, watching the driving rain, lakes forming in the gutters, the far hills abolished, even these trees half-hidden, the border between indoors and out is absolute. Pigeons cooing in the station's eaves, shaking their rain-soaked feathers, while here, under the awning people refold umbrellas (blazers that serve as lining for their greatcoats). Shoots sprout up in the soft soil, little blades of the unintended, miniature clover – the earth this damp is sticky, almost gummy. Lake in the garden fed by a waterfall from up on the roof where the drainpipe must be stuck. Flowering jade: what's smaller than a hummingbird darting in the fuchsias unless this spider hanging from its own web? Pushing the plastic basket of laundry across the concrete floor to the frontloading washer ("porthole" open) with a foot encased in a high-heeled, sharp-toed boot. Uprooted, the cement twists and cracks, leading the eye back to where the thick trunk of a pepper tree juts skyward. Under the long shadow of the el, par course and footpath come to a small wooden bridge, the creek beneath a bare trickle, beside which three high school boys and one girl with flowing blonde hair share a morning joint. In the dream, it's not solid at all, but cloudlike, musky, giving away at each step so that I'm sinking in, ankles cold and damp, cuffs already soaked, until I simply stop trying and relax, giving in, which must make me lighter because I immediately begin to drift up, as the breeze blown, rising out of and then over it, not able to determine direction but moving very slowly, rooftops drop away, people are staring or not even noticing, going about their small business as I begin to glimpse the entire landscape, sun setting far over the curve of the horizon, fog bank a mere pink-orange smear out over the ocean. Storm clouds lower the sky, spreading the land out, streets flattened, houses hunched, braced for rain (visible already against the hills, houses turned to shadows, blotches of trees where the park should be). What's under the table, chairs, bureaus, beds – here's the stuffed toy bunny without any nose (and here a mysterious mound of wadded, used tissues). Rutherford Hills: blue smoke spirals up from the floor of the valley, the hills behind silhouetted by the sun – this long view holds me, quiet and rare, a sense of scale I'm not certain I believe in (six-year-old Kelsey, her pockets full of acorns, hunts in the fall leaves for more). One layer of clouds high over the hills and beneath it, clinging to the trees, another, tiny and intensely white. After the second week of rain, a brilliant yellow-green begins to emerge over the brown hills (which we Californians like to call "golden"). Name of the cement contractor etched into the walk. Bright bright sunlight blanches everything but the shadows under cars, even the yellow-eyed blackbird (fresh odors drift up from the edges of lawns, warm damp puppy poop oddly familiar and nice). Here the driveway's been widened into a paved ramp on which, on a trailer, sits a small yacht (here, in the back yard, under the pine a plaster horse rears up on its hind legs). Lakes in the lot in the driving rain. These trees heavy with water (under awnings, cars, dry spots on the cement as if a form of shadow). Dark-skinned woman in white stockings: amber effect. We sat on the cement base to the huge Lions Club cross atop the small hill, the valley I grew up in is oddly still. The BART track itself is three storeys high, wall effect in this neighborhood of one and two story houses (textural detail of gravel roofs). The dew thick on the bus bench, these three highschoolers perch instead atop the thin strip of its back, feet planted on the seat. Short grass glistens with the morning mist. Trying, mid-crosswalk, blinded by the rain, to fathom, already sweating in down jacket, hood snapped tight, sunglasses fogged (no sight of sun), fathom where best to leap over the swirling lake between me and the curb (gutters are rivers but the catchbasin too small, too clogged to cope) – in the middle of the well-cropped highschool football field hundreds of seagulls have settled in to wait it out. L-shaped mini-mall constructed around its parking. Grass at the tree's base is longer, uneven, an index of the mower's reach. Without garbage to weight it down, trash can topples at wind's push. Face so familiar, I imagine this young man, asleep hunched in the doorway of this empty storefront, might be the son of a childhood friend. The mall expresses 'the suburban' through its oversized display windows that begin only inches above the sidewalk (here a boutique has solved a design problem with a giant stuffed panda, besides which stands a mannequin in fall fashion). The slow, even, from-the-shoulder walk of the black-and-grey-striped cat through the cactus garden. The pavement speckled with pigeon shit, but here by the lawn chair, killed by a collision with the Bay window, is a tiny gold-crowned sparrow. Small clay flowerpot, blown over by the wind. Ten days ago this hard rain was a typhoon over the Philippines, dozens swept away, whereas at Tahoe they look forward to a good start to the ski season. High over the dry grass the black-shouldered kite, a small hawk that looks like a gull, flutters, hovering to spot rodents below. Dropped into a puddle, an unsmoked cigarette begins to unravel, tangled strands of weed. A place where the brick walk's given way, earth's crust over hollow center. Day after the rains, pools of water linger. Sun's glare against the still damp walk. The morning paper right in a pile of dog poop. The ground surround. At the end of this path, let's kneel and, crouching, speak to pigeons. Sound of a portable saw, crew slicing fallen branches (a severe storm) into moveable pieces. See-thru rubber rainboots, beneath which white tennies look foggy. Drive, he said (forgetting, parked on a steep slope, to put my left foot on the brake before shifting into "drive," the car begins to roll backwards so I push down hard on the accelerator, the little car lurching forward with screech and shudder), for Christ's sake, watch out where you're going. Dry leaves twirl in the roiling wind. Boxy boats fade at the horizon, backlit by sunset, bridge reduced to a silhouette of the bridge.

Underneath molten magma heated to 2,000 degrees. Hypothermia kills an old man on a park bench, undetected until sprinklers fail to arouse him. The cord to the table lamp lies underneath the table, coiled (even knotted) – all that wire is simply potential. I hear the pigeons flap and coo, huddled under the eaves, rain driven sideways by the hard wind, but I can't see them until one settles by my feet, strutting, feathers soaked and matted, its own feet bright pink with long white what? nails? claws? (what is a road but drainage, a city but an encrustation of debris, latching onto itself, growing, coral or guano?). . . . One imagines morning (abstractly), hummingbirds punctuating the fuchsias, glare of the first sun in several days, cement taking forever to dry. The man with the gas-powered leaf blower, huge protective ear muffs, appears small under the elms. Over the bay, not thick enough to be called a cloud, a translucent layer of haze. Smashed and flattened on the sidewalk, styrofoam burger boxes are color-coded (yellow to indicate cheese) – they don't crumple so much as shatter. I pass by this corner each morning (brown beer bottle, after a week, has been knocked over and broken, rusting shopping cart has disappeared). Sun at this hour, low, just over the horizon, impossible to stare into – eerie clarity of a cloudless sky, the frozen air. In the lot, three white gulls and as large, a loud crow. Streetlamps glisten, reflected in the puddles of a recent rain. Old Victorian house, outlined with winking Christmas tree lights. The awning stretches entirely around the department store. The cuffs of my trousers damp from the rain. Wind shaking water from the trees. From the bowling alley, even at dawn, the rolling clatter of pins. A cyclist pedalling madly in the wrong gear. In the gutter, leaves and cigarette butts, pink gum gone hard and gray, the plastic case of a ballpoint pen, snapped in half, drippings from parked cars even though it's a red zone, and here, grinning wildly, the yellow rubber duck.

KETJAK2: CARAVAN OF AFFECT

for Rae Armantrout

Revolving door. Revolting odor. Slivers or sofa, splinters or couch. Curious at that face (your own) in the old photo (no sense of recognition whatsoever). The deer swim in the clear lake. Begin again, in again. The east is rad, the west is rotting. I didn't say that. In a hang glider, hovering, suspended over farm fields, watching workers, silent, bending. Grease spots on the train window. Memories of underdevelopment. I won't even meet you for another three years. As you push at last through lobby after lobby, **voices** ebbing, the soft light of the grand concourse, there is nothing (finally) to turn you aside, the crowd's **momentum** become your own. For each and every sentence an equal but opposite sentence. Now I am in Death Valley, now on the **moon**. This desk is an ordered sequence of stacks of papers, files, books, **mounds** of chaos barely contained. Dry blood. When I saw this notebook, I **knew** it would be a poem. The tenor's sex is a tool. The furnace shudders when it lights. **Stretching** the canvas, the text. **Behind** the desk is a filing cabinet turned sideways, its outer wall covered with notes, schedules, **numbers**. This is a hypothesis, no more than haltingly proposed. The gendered text (is a kind of hex). **T'ai** chi like a pitcher's kick—Spahn, Marichal—but in slomo. The movie I wan see, dude, is *Psycho Ward*, man, that's gonna be so *icy*, the **reviews** are *boomin'*. Serial number. Bright blue winter coat with an **equally** bright yellow umbrella. As the coffee steeps, say, raising the shade, a morning habit, each day's particulars conjoined. Reiteration **hidden**. Ideo-radiology. Past sunset, the sky nearly colorless, about to go dark. Smashing bottles, chewing cabbage discards, **chorus** of the trash collectors from beneath the bedroom window, the odor from the cud of their great truck. There's lots of free food in this job. Locked-in, projects that **will** not resolve eventually empty into a lonely logic, endless consequence of equation, terms providing terms, until final factors ("in the last instance") **fail** to cancel out. Rods from which to hang sweaters in a track-lit display window. You are not sure which constant **to** hold as real. He's running through the frigid dawn, bundled, mittened, jogging. Clay fear signifies change with no significant modification. The too-formal wear of limo drivers at the airport. The oncoming traffic brought out gradually from about the **turn**, elongated motion, emotion slowed him. The yellow eyes of a cat (staring at me from atop the hood of a car). Laura, say, **to** have stopped writing, Riding, poems not complete until old act back into print. Not available in any store. Where the truck hit fibers, trunk of the palm snapped about. Remove what is **precisely** most visible about the text. Distribution of questions here. A throat so **swollen** I almost faint to swallow. Figs of the seed. Red sky at night—toxin's delight. Language as value or where these are the same, economics or speech. The **nude** formalists. If we are limning the true and ultimate structure of reality, the **canonical** scheme for us is the austere scheme that knows no quotation but direct quotation and no propositional attitudes but only the physical constitution and behavior of **organisms**. I want to write the letter "Z" simply to fashion that **shape** with my hand. We are preparing to start over and start over and have started over. What's new? Kareem and the sky hook. Tanks, of all things, rolling across the mall lot, **helicopters** overhead crowd the sky. Mossback of the morning. You knew the reading was important: Ashbery not only **showed** up to introduce Schuyler but appeared to be **stone** cold sober. That the thing which you thought **possible** is not, which, having once made the assumption, governed your days until the fault this morning showed, the wall's weak rock, which, although it has **not** made itself felt, shall, is **not**, since you now carry it to its conclusion, rubble, to be acknowledged (a month before the election, Dukakis knows he's doomed). As the train accelerates, people on the platform blur into the past. The **skaters** were a kind of solution (counter clockwise). Verbs **vanish**. Your hand as I shake it, fleshy palm, pudgy fingers, is not my imagination (how will I know when I make a mistake?). His hair is but **a few wisps** atop a freckled skull. The yellow concern of civic rose. A good fart takes the pressure off. Act upon ladders propped **against** the walls. The unreadable. Disturbed that your approvers seem oblique to the intention, unaware that the **concentric** circles expanding about the stone thrown into the lake will extend to the shore, that the flute's **vibrations** form an act that yet others will be consequent to, as your own presence was predicated upon the pine odor in the air, you **turn** the orders of your attention to your fingers in their **relation to** the stops along the bamboo shaft, a fix on **precision**, aware without saying so that evasive action cannot solve it. This was **implicit** all along. Alice and the sky boat. A **cavern** of sudden silence as the stereo shuts itself off (threshold shift in the wake of loud noise). Tonto gives notice: life is hard, pard. Anorexics of the **dance**, advance. Definition itself is a form of Manhattan. Sun's down, but the **horizon** a bright red. As we loitered, waiting for the bus, I overheard her whispering to herself, a **furious** conversation. Small hunchbacked blind girl with a hair lip. Representness. Emotional response to **roadkill**. Nurse of cities. Conscientious objectors to the war on drugs commit civil disobedience. The limit is the eye. Yawn's **pressure** on the Eustachian tube: roar fills the skull, inaudible to others. Stenographer of cities. A kinder, more gentle deconstruction. First day of July. Goes to the video store to get *Lord of the Rings* for his nine-year-old son, comes back with *Lord of the Flies*. **Subtext** at Division Street. Does the shrimp stop here? Only way he could know what would be the thought in their heads would be to put words down in a sequence. The **whale** that ate Liberty Valence. City of administrative assistants, of bus boys. At the onset of flu, consciousness **pulsates**, alternating between an almost **euphoric** lucidity and total **disorientation**—which is this? Moment at which the old bar of soap disappears. Logic, the Other. Here is this: this word is **used** like an empirical fact. In military standing, ease is the opposite of attention. The curious vacated meaning of literal. I remember **when** everything was a western. As he stood waiting for the light to **change**, we stared at the bruises on the young Persian's face. Here was the petition in repetition. His obsession with boundaries, of the shift in an instant within the irrevocable, trigger's hammer **exploding** the powder, dissolve of the space shuttle before the eyes of millions, **driven** by the clarity of closure. When flossing, stand as far back from the **mirror** as possible. Conference of corn flakes, kind of the birds. Great tray holding boxes of packs of gum tilted at an angle across from the cash register. Wind in the chimney would **scatter** ashes back into the room. The ants not only discovered the bar of soap, they discovered they *liked* it. Here the **vast** moraine is terminal (in the last paragraph a key term is misspelled). What was the first consumer object but a book? The **unfinished** business before he died left her with a taste of half-formed friendship. I said, Hey, big boy, what's her name, *She's about a mover*, Hey, Hey. The unrevealing mass of effort **to force** this to cease its absolute self-existing quality. As the pass rush bursts in, quarterback drops into **fetal** position. Chess board for a penny game, doubling square by square. Dental **dams** now come in vanilla flavor. This is the town that never went to the city, and this the lagoon. A new magazine is a new idea. Plain C. With full deployment of line **scanner** registers at every chain supermarket checkout stand, combined with the more recent advent of ATM linkage for payment, it becomes **possible** at last to correlate every individual in the land with the objects and **brands** of their consumption, an ongoing social census of habit entirely open to centralized monitoring and management, to the compilation of lists, say, of **compulsive** buyers of Robitussin, say, or of Dristan Nasal Mist, lists that might be utilized to target market **segments**, of, worse, individuals at risk. Time dislodges oranges. Under the oak tree, a cow lay dead, brown and **bloated**, but not yet starting to smell. In the attic, ontic antics. Across the room and by itself, the VCR switches on. Dialectic of the **adventures**. Mutant teenage ninja turtle. The garbage barge at the bridge. Leafless as the apple in December. List this. Spiral staircase situated oddly in the middle of an asphalt schoolyard. Brushing dead leaves off dry poets. As snow geese escape, **bursting** into the air, coyote pauses at reservoir's edge, freezing the instant it sees us. A woman to polka dressed. Bing's Big Burger is now Richie's Choice Meats. These analytics count only **against** hoping (to base isomorphism of propositions on some sort of intensional synonymy derived from the broad sort of **identity** which is interdefinable with sentence reflection). On the bus in the **rain, reiterate** the old refrain. It was Heisenberg causing me to hear these blacks in the cafe discuss my racism. Little bean (you know what I mean). **Scratches** his fingers, then sniffs his ass. If you don't like that sentence, here's another. Syntax of dinner in the vocabulary of my mouth. Iconoclastistic. I tugged at the plug to **coax** the cord from its socket. The slow, arduous construction of a box, but then it's not exactly a box, is it? He rose from our table, then suddenly left. Waved **over** the window, the bar code triggers beep as the price is registered. Writing would be as tho **speech** nailed to the wall. Excavation pit **as site** of former gas station. As September nears Berkeley. To stop the invasion of ants about the sink, we build little **barricades** of Vaseline. We watched him repeatedly butt the garage door, **slowly**, head down, the blunt precision. Antarctica has no legal time. Drain words. Learn the burn. Deepen the dream. At a poetry **reading**, we readers at least find ourselves, even if silent, that chasm between words at a reading, frozen into our chairs, our thoughts emerging, weaving into the text itself, that deepest silence of all. Who put the ram in the Baba Ram Dass? Albino pit bull gallops up in my direction. In a **red** sport coat, red trousers, white shoes, stands the Japanese floor manager. This **chair and** that table are not just pieces of furniture, having been built many years ago by my roommate Elliott, the carpentry plain, square, blocky things, **elegant** in their ugliness, what **remains** for me a decade after his death. Seven headed sign of the cobra. Sad celery. Veins of the foot, the bones. Interactive trailer camp beetle. Resolve this. 1926: Lemon Jefferson is led through the **crowded** juke joint by his friend Huddie Ledbetter. Cold coffee. Naked lunch poems. Read would I this? A large Asian bird that has nonetheless established itself in the Ruby **Mountains** of northeastern Nevada, the Himalayan snowcock flies downslope over the rugged terrain early in the day, and feeds on tubers and plants as it walks slowly back uphill. If our objective is not an **austere** canonical form for the system of the world. The scare bears. I was trapped, I felt, within the restaurant, **moving** from table to table, rising and sitting, to write this sentence, that one, this one. Sane day service. Those **mean** rural boys are bulky what get called the Bulls. The superego, he mutters, it all coheres. Not art is not not art. First as tracheotomy, then as face. The predators of calculus. Instead of traveling to, and implanting in, the uterine wall, the fertilized egg sticks instead in the fallopian tube, typically at the site of an old scar, the wall of which, as the egg grows, **ruptures**. It has the particular turnings, springs, shutters, the weavings and one riding away. Aubade of birds. The inexpensive **reproduction** of prints on the wall alter order. First moments of dusk, when you start **to notice** cars driving with their lights on. The trash of treasure. Who was that masked text? Vienna is thinking about stone. The first shot is **morphine** to kill the pain, the second is something else to kill the nausea of the morphine. Attitudes of **introjection** toward past **periods**, interest in the past, the historical attitude, histories, annals, time as used in physics, time graphs, time wages, clocks, chronologies, calendars, dating, **exact** interest in inverse sequence. Worm-eating warbler wanders west. **Throb** in the wrist or knee-joint (did I anticipate then, as I know now, the fact of arthritis). Cream of mystery soup. Wide range **of practice** in ideation. Don't necessarily could afford it this month. Procrastination drinks quadruplicity. Sun **explodes** into the low clouds. Limit is the history of **con-**

fidence. For each and every sentence there is an equal but opposite syntax. Cheapo keeno. Instead of stitches we now use staples. Ungazed fix. We've stayed young **by virtue** of an incredible immaturity. Simplicity of the don't-care is a major source of tolerance. Anti-shock trousers (see-thru plastic) strapped about bare legs and abdomen, held by Velcro, inflated to force your blood pressure up, to keep you alive until we can get you to surgery. Pints of weather. Give a noun its verb. We **climbed** through three flights of stairs, slope of a eucalyptus grove, to arrive at the rounded wood door, then two narrow flights **up** through dark rooms of loud, throbbing disco, shadow dance shuffle, and thru finally to the back porch, old boards holding couch and rocker, for **to** view the City **from** that great height gave the night sky place or weight, veils of fog wedged in **amid** shingled rooves, but still the clear view, Orion. The flan is **the body**. If a lion could speak, it would mumble. Root is the money of all evil. A single unpartitioned universe of values of bound variables, a simple grammar of prediction which admits general terms all on an equal footing, but with holes in the toes. Pooh-heart. As tho one were **searching** for an object in a room, opening a drawer and not finding it, closing the drawer, waiting, opening it again, closing, waits. Crack's not a drug, it's a **marketing** strategy. Burn the news to keep warm. The post-card rack in the drugstore is dusty and many of its wire slots are empty. Neckerchief. Necker cube. The type of old man who wears his white hair in a crew cut, who keeps small, fat dogs, who prefers short sleeve shirts and a string tie. Like larvae, the homeless in doorways in **sleeping** bags. The pressure artist and the pressured. Today's dimple, tomorrow's jowl. **Domains** fix terms. Eigner's sigh. Don't try to cold me up on this bridge now. Same day service. Art **as** a habit merges with the renewal of solutions that constitute it. The tires **tread** lightly over the ice-ridden road. Tier-tender's tale. Thick stitches **over** the autopsied skull. It was only when the trash bag crashed into the middle of the kitchen that we realized it bore the weight of ants. Daypack's **smaller** pocket. Perception traces, day erases. Put statements in **positive** form. Terms whose deep objects are learned only in **context**. One ground cuckoo, the roadrunner, is still zygodactyl. The gradual but sustained failure of the mails. Familiar half-forgotten tone of a **rotary** phone. Mass murder meridian. Corduroy's ribbing starts to **dissolve**. Brown-blue. Use the proper case of pronoun. By positing intermediary subjective objects of apprehension **anterior** to the physical objects overtly alleged in the spoken sentences themselves (this sentence could never be "**spoken**"), intervening neural activity goes on (snap, **crackle**, pop—they never knew what hit them) but the claim is (as if a claim might be an agent without an actor) that nothing is clarified, **nothing** but baggage is added (the train ceaselessly **invents** the station, but what we notice here is the **compulsion** at the heart of the impulse, when, as we look up, the light at the end of the tunnel **quickly** recedes until it is no more than a pinprick, and then goes out). April galleons bring May scallions. Antagonism toward personal art. Gas in one's stomach like clouds in the sky. Old odor of **orange** in compost. Self life. The children of culture (hi Asa, hi Emma). Invalid as invalid. Pot **unwashed**. Red cell pack. Directed attention to attention **directed**. Cormorant dark as its silhouette. Earth science. On Sunday, January 15th, I nearly lose you. Carbonated water. Scale is all. Soap dish. Doves in a **hurry**. Fastidious women have unwanted hair removed. White plaid shirt on a large belly. Speed basic law. Avoid a succession of loose **sentences**. Now explain six into eight by page size. As we (think we) know. Terms of proofhood. Adam's autumn. Short gray pile of indeterminate undershirts. Half-moon **blur** over the field of vision. This tapestry concerns the mass **capture** of rabbits. Make the paragraph the unit of composition. Er plat rock form. Back slash. The description of operators can be reduced to class abstraction, and quantifiers to description. Quadrant of three-prong **sockets** stares out of the wall, face defined by plastic mount. **Groan** in my bones awakens ache. Pastafarian. Because my room faces east I watch the sun set in the windows of those far hills. Astronomy **reconjugates** taxonomy. We have made the turn now by far. Big bull clip. This sentence has four spaces. Insects don't see red. She my baby has no **shoes**. Can't have no rainbow without no rain. Corridor of fire escapes, loading docks, dumpsters—steam pours from alley sewers. The blot chickens. Two rocks ducked in. Storm of intention. I confused seeing history and resentment natured at every turn. The **cursor** calls. Leather yellow vest. Every ink has its genre. Soup sky. Tea seeps from the bag, **clouding** the bottom of the lukewarm cup. Bond of too fondage. Public spear. This day's proposition: flower in the lemon tree, warm sun dissolving **amid** the fog to the porch, each conclusion an **eternal** return to dawn. Lucy in the sky with **macros**. Now April. Turquoise tie is a muted paisley. Watching her quiet sleep, capable of sitting in this chair for hours. I'm writing this in Milwaukee, in a house **overlooking** the river. Greeks in the pinball cafe. Tab, the one soft drink named for a typewriter key. Tone of a squeal in the clothesline pulley. In **direct** mail, the envelope is more crucial than the letter inside. Gases force the presence of the stool in the tract out. Seaside **smell** of salt in the air. Memory emulsified. Clouds in a row prefigure snow. Was what I saw in her awakening or merely my own true deterioration. Others, authors. **Now** and again unswayed by **wishful** thinking, reflective persons can themselves have **cause** to **wonder** what, if anything, they are talking about. No apostrophe to Macys. Where fire is literally herself, earth itself is inorganic. **Burning** sphere. Their goal was first to separate the workers from their means of production. Out in the yard, thinkin' hard. Waking in the year's slide, so more in the dark each day. A game we play in the dream, night after night. Mind and Body against Number. The truth shall make you work. The corrective **function** in the partial touch. Silhouette of a freighter on the water's horizon. You come at last, down the **spiral** hardwood staircase and across the carpeted lobby, into the realization as into a banquet room, **white** shirts and black trousers of the catering staff, domed perhaps but with chandeliers distributed evenly across the high ceiling, each **divisible** into a concentric series of rings, the small yellow bulbs with their too-brilliant cumulative effect, that a **lush** ordering of events, like the glitter sprinkled over the row of freckles that dot a **bosom** jutting from the low-cut gown, is no different than any other, the mix of perfumes in the air blending then **blurring**, so that one might as well (and why not?) eat squid as tripe or plums, preferring after all the minuscule tentacles for their **texture** and subtle taste, dressed in the regalia of tennis, although perceiving in the punchbowl reflection a costume as clownish as it is offensive. Little grid of the notebook page, how familiar you've become. Here is what. Shoes buffer feet. Red eye. Today's dimple, tomorrow's vowel. The right has no light. Whitefolks Bay, Lox Point. Musical **process**, notational juncture. But there is no "last" sentence, last paragraph, last word. Do not denigrate the **solitude** of history. Let them eat tech. That object positing fails to share the pattern of our language. Watching the kitten stalk its mother. But trees are not orderly. **Vanpools** of the night, ignite. Propose how to release the fly from its bottle. A man no longer comfortable with his eyes. Bigger—to serve you better. After ten years clean and sober, he begins to show **symptoms** of cirrhosis. The moth that destroyed Detroit. A pigeon with red-brown wings. Close cover before striking. I feel that **pressure** in my chest, index of a state that would be easy to trigger—toggle?—into a burst of hysteria. No hassle, no hurry. A **participial** phrase at the beginning of a sentence must refer to the grammatical subject. Only a thorough historical-materialist analysis can hope to disentangle the snarl of tendencies and counter-tendencies, forces, influences, convictions and opinions, drives and resistances which **account** for the pattern of economic and social development, but, in so doing, this strategy leaves its own deposits (confidence in the gravity of the material) that gradually alter the course of perception, building a city of certainty alongside (in place of) the drifting **semi**-autonomous ensemble of the real, castles of **narrative** behind which the homeless (invisible) **huddle** around the flames of alleyway incinerators. **Song** that could only be a redwing blackbird. Reshaping houses on the hill's other peak, heat **ripples** the air rising from the street. Tall dark plume of smoke, fire across the bay. Each **meaning** has a word. Tracklighting for highlights in the department store. Honeydew head, bean sprout hair. Menopause is not an illness. Related to a **prior** decision, knowledge comes out here. Grainy **surface** of forehead's pores. Subvention of the usual capital **outlay** process. Much sausage. Waterways of Marin. Poultry? I too despise it. Labyrinth is a thot. The muscle "catches" (hooks) on the **bone**. This process is due. Express coordinate ideas in similar form. Amid dryers, **atop** washers, the boys play at war. Here, reading, *these* **words** upon *this* page, you find yourself **separate**, apart from the world, isolate. Diphtheria of the larynx. The way two **bodies** coil, sleeping, to shut out winter cold. Shelves of neatly folded linen. Jumbo scallop, marshmallow of the sea. Californica. I **began** to write at the age of ten as a means (and a good one) of **making** a safe place for myself in a house ruled by **madness**. Her roommate remarked pointedly that she could tell when he had stayed the night—the toilet seat would be **vertical** in the morning. Before you can **hear** the train, you see its lights, stars deep in the **tunnel's** dark. Hobo oboe. Psychoanalysis understood as **interior** design. Aiming from the window, **silent**, not alone, he bears a resemblance to Lee Harvey Oswald. (M)orality. That is about that. Tho the TV's off, the VCR is taping. Duck and run, **whipped** at by branches. In experimental theater, word reveal **displaced** intention. Badwater. Liquid soap sits in rounded plastic container.

Why do you do? These **corridors** are spokes, the mall a wheel at whose **center** sits a softwater fountain. Is seriousness **boredom** coming of age? Pants **leg** jammed into hiking boot. Dump the beautiful truck. Certain solid sounds. Sky at red night. Cops and jobbers. *Poem for Michael Palmer beginning "Dear George. . . ."* When you get a value judgment, that's all you get. Strophe to apostrophe. Miles are alike. Sometimes I can tell you everything I need to **just** with my eyes. May you **remember**. Bone barrettes. Eggs use. But where is the field of knowledge? Nothing was substantive but **authenticity**, and so authenticity became the very life of my senses. Place the emphatic words of a sentence at the end. Tea as an iced system. Anticipation of the need to sneeze. Called metabolic **imbalance** a cold. Some day service. Hap glands. Were the letters of the alphabet fingers on a hand, then the **blank** space, that pause, would be the opposable **thumb**. "If you are heading for the present," as if that were not everywhere outdoors. Sentences to go before I weep. Amid silence, could write of shouting and not disbelieve it. **Unmistakable** odor of root beer fills the air of the subway **john**. Time state. Eggs for Apollinaire. Wild dog packs root at the dumpsters in that part of the city. The **minerals** in the mineral water have turned to rust. Ask. Form the possessive singular of nouns by adding *'s*. **Insert** erotic. Put an otter in your gas tank. The quality of consumer **research** in writing might only be another form of concern. Pick a sentence, any sentence. Rum scent with a **lather** for shaving. Now this means something different. Fast karma orange. Download that font. The **child** who saw me write that, asking what it was, is today an adult. What's under reconstruction at the Lenin Museum is Lenin. Starvation **against** personal strategy. The rain falls quite suddenly, before you can even **smell** it in the air. Mold of poetry: writing that grows out of itself. "Donald Wesling, he is my pen friend." Tooth that will drop out of fear. Another plate of boiled beef. Sill or dusty wainscot. **Female** country singer by the name of C.D. Backslash. Such as **percussion**. Portrait of the artist raised by wolves. Drawing of a Balinese spirit with its face in its stomach. Horns of the Aurora. Standing on the porch, dog **would not permit** us to pass. I clip my photo ID card to my belt. You would know if this were **prose**. I can in my imagination trace the shape of your wrist, so thin. Broken blade of the scissors. Yet the alphabet too is only part of a poem. Ives' hives. I sit in a chair in a frail house, writing, the sun **filling** the window to my back as it sets. My in**tent**ions are clear. Keep related words together. That the **homes** together weave the **wives** (is false). Micro to mainframe: when this you feel, stop and kneel. First day of September, viewed from a **distance** of fifteen years and 11 days. If I still **drank**, we would have slept together, and this explains—perhaps better than anything—why it is best that I don't. Behind the sculpted temple the sun rose, undetected in the humid air of the eucalyptus grove, out over the Mormon Temple and the Greek Orthodox Church. We're talking through an **interpreter**, but looking into one another's eyes. Great **sinus** swell. James will say this is unreadable. Stretch **marks** across the text. O crowds of Nevsky Prospekt! There has been a **hierarchy** of languages (not this) headed by the "direct readout from the object" language (what then?), which has served (I started over & over) as the creative **core**, and then various support languages (last week I cld barely hold this pen) acting as explicative and elucidatory tools (this morning my lip is **blistered**) to the central creative core. Shklovsky lived in this house, and for a time the Briks also. The words are **bells**. Christo's Berlin. Copyright is theft: I steal. Painting has its **prosody** also. Positing intermediary sentences in the **image** of facts for as what is. Instinctively, she reaches into her **blouse** to pull up a strap. On why a poem is this. At dawn, the lone swimmer doing laps in the pool. This wider arc is more gradual. Touch me first. Outside a **society** of language users, a form of art could not maintain itself. Pull up AppleLink and take a **look**. About the pen, the hard press of her **fingers** (rough-edged and calloused) as she **write**s into her diary and I watch. The old woman had been a ballerina with the Kirov, but now, held gently by her great niece—the same **blue** eyes!—she stares out as if from some deep **private** place of an inner silence at these noisy intellectuals from America, Poland, and France, then slowly **raises** her glass forward so all can **touch** it (this small flat once a torture house for the KGB), glasses clinking quietly, sketches and portraits of **dancers** crowding the dull walls, a toast here to survival. Merely specify the poetry component. **Beneath** you, the ground suddenly rolls about like a **liquid**, sloshing. Torn tendon. Bad fat. Black burro. We're standing in the rainstorm having a **terrific** conversation about the role of word-of-mouth publicity in our two countries, Ilya translating as fast as he can, **contact** with your blue eyes all the real communication we can really ever have, and I not even knowing yet that your husband is "in hospital" with a heart attack. **Folk** art is vandalism. Amiable, am I able? Something **forbidden** becomes a mistake as a result. When the **pain** starts, it's as if the entire sector of my **mouth, gums, lip** and cracked lingering hollow fragment of tooth has been flushed with acid, an involuntary secretion. Portrait of the best worker in Auto Plant 7. Last night I dreamed my infant's death again, oh neverborn. The **essence** of **doubt** belongs to the absence of the language game. Secretly conscious of huge pimple under my beard. Flowering **milkweed** through the cracks in the sidewalk, around which to draw stars in colored chalk. The mall, them all. Acknowledgment in the end is based on **knowledge**. Raspberries in the pitcher of water to **sweeten** the taste. Leave your emotional options open. At the **edge** of the pine barrens. As I am dreaming, this remark is dreamed as well, as I dream these words whispering meaning to you. Like a dog or cat, I wander about the office when I **arrive** in the morning, a trip to Mr. Coffee being more than it appears. Balloons, having gotten loose from the hands of children, would rise up **steadily**, yellow disks diminishing on a blue plane. If I don't write this now, I might not live to write it later. Art language. Fountains of the financial district do not **spout** in a drought. Literally a soy milk product intended as a dietary frozen dessert for dogs, called Frosty Paws. Untying shoelace, **removing** shoe, like undoing the knot in a balloon. "Votive housing set," says Clark. Half-asleep on the **slope** of the hill, blanket **amid** clover, the breeze passes over this part of my **body**, then that one. I saw the best minds of my generation trying to figure out why the network crashed each time they tried to log on. Trumpet friendship fade-out. Ten years later, still discovering new positions, new rhythms, new ways to insert my tongue. Rise up—sun at six threatens day. I don't think of myself as a thief of language, but as a **value-added** remarketeer. Barnwood hisses, pops, as it burns in the fireplace. Deep notebook. This after, this before. Goethe's pen was an old bone. Is discourse **jazz**? Alongside Malyavin, Tadeusz is smashed, staggering, singing *Mellow Yellow* (the tune of which he does not remember). Repeating on paper this **stanza** one hundred times, each with a new pen, watching how the width of the ink's black path shifts the weight and intention of reference, shadow of nuance, from act to act. You cannot step into the same line twice. Mathematical piano. Under the **crushed** layers of freeway, they not only have to amputate the small boy's leg to free him from the mashed car, they have to cut **through** the body of his mother just to reach him (later, reading in the paper on her way into work, that "he didn't even cry," my wife **begins** to sob in the subway). He stood over them all, alternately shouting and drinking from the bottle of bourbon. Imagine Helsinki as a kind of Oakland, then **imagine** Oakland as the capital of a vast nation, fourth largest in all of **Europe** (aware how unfair this is). Intention garden. Dry cleaner **refuses** to admit he's lost my shirts. The enormous farce of the image **imposed** on the emotion of the peasant's bent shoulders. Down the server. The **being** toward which these signs spill over is neither more nor less than the being of thought. Time **without** shadows. Theory as the geometry of relative **position**. In Leningrad, half of all police calls are for domestic violence in communal flats. In Berlin, the stanza falls. Conference at which they're not **speaking** my language. Grow, thumbnails of my little moon. Passive-aggressive feminist men. The torch bulb holder—connected to two **stiff** wires and inserted in a test tube that serves as a handle. The moment within the quake I realize I won't be able to stay on my feet much longer, it's time to get under a desk. Writing in public as a form of **performance**, on buses, say, or here amid sunbathers, **not** paid attention to, looking up myself to watch the jugglers. Chestnuts roasting over an open wound. You have no adequate lines of **force** to deal with such things as ordinary terminology. First we conquer AIDS, then we locate parking in Berkeley. These were true events. Kit stands **to read** aloud and I still have a cookie in my mouth, so fear to bite down for the loud sound of chewing, letting my saliva dissolve the hardened dough. How these words, this sentence could **open** to comment upon itself, first swelled with written intention, **spilled** meaning later to have become so opaque certain terms expanded, first modifiers of the redistributed purpose, overtook value. One imagines the world as round when it is in fact **deeply** furrowed like a brow or lines about the eye that smiles to realize, by the thin yellow stripe along the red epaulet, that this red-wing **blackbird** is in actuality tri-colored. This used to be a nice place. My night at Alexy's. The conditions of production corresponding to this specific, historically determined, **mode** of production have a specific passing character (now I would call this the SSA, Social Structure of Accumulation). *Im Waschraum nicht rauchen.* Darrell's tale (bleached-out poet trotting thru a throng of mourners of an evangelical bishop to a black church) brings to mind that **young** blonde woman I see each morning, jogging in a green sweatsuit, trailed by her four small dogs. Don't mourn, Galvanize! Poon tang. As if a race of **giants** had disappeared and this new species, ourselves, struggled to eke out a survival in the ruins. Each morning I rise to praise these faces. Your name in Russian means 'crystal.' The **desire** to fix the point at which doubt and belief **bleed** into one another. Because this text is in print, the meaning of separating these sentences even further apart is different. A controlled burn **blackens** the hill. Shadow RAM. Funereal disease. "I," the dream is not of necessity. Bending forward, to clip my toenails while standing. Ilya is exhausted by all this translation. Ideology defined as the unmoving (unspoken) foundation of any language-game. From here the Germans could see Leningrad, and **waited**, and waited, and waited. In a far room of the apartment I can hear a **hammer** and music. What I cannot explain is this enormous sadness that has settled like the fine **ash** dust from a distant volcano. Paratactics. Flying north at dusk the sun sets to our left in the west, then, our having now crossed the North Pole, so **flying** south, it rises again in the east, which is now to our left also. Whether to speak of indifferent objects as by-passed or reconstrued is a **matter** of geometry. Carpool tunnel syndrome. Universal (coordinated) time. Write once, read many (WORM). Poem takes the form of the Glass Age. Hot spares spur top sale. It is a wall that closes and does not. When I ask you how your husband is, you almost start to sob, **choking** it back, shrugging, and I read an answer in your eyes. Often, **elimination** can be allowed the gentler air of explication. You're in the City and the bridge is down. It **repeats** and repeats, adding new lines without apparent relation, building with great visual and **mental** invention a tremendous formal beauty that carries no **cargo** at all. In those days, *Poetry Flash* was a single mimeographed sheet of paper. The wall of bricks falls so **suddenly** on the passers by that their bodies are decapitated before they hit the ground. The asymmetry in any face. In Oakland, in the neighborhood where my grandmother was born, people scurry over the vast, **twisted** concrete of the collapsed freeway, crawling, inching between sections through broken glass and gasoline, calling, searching for voices, movement, anything—in Berlin, thousands **dance** atop the graffiti-thick concrete wall, using hammers and chisels to pick away at their own imprisonment. Speech is, words do. Now you've become a logo. **Sperm** count. Art gecko. **Oral** Balinese form. Next morning I'm sitting atop the rubble at the edge of

Ulitsa Gercena—Herzen Street—**eating** a tiny summer apple, when I hear you call my name. Fat man at the bus stop. At 43 I've learned that it's not necessary to sleep with you for you to become a part of my life forever. Reality makes its appearance—**X** marks the spot. "She's eating my brains out," Arkadii says, laughing, "telling me how strong you are, how **masculine**." Morning in the gauzy curtains. As a boy after dinner I would **carry** the heavy black metal typewriter from my grandfather's desk in the dining room to the table in the kitchen nook, where for hours I would **bang** at the keys "being a writer." Bear likes a **body**. Towhees on the lawn before dawn, exact imitation of an alarm clock. To give the sky **weight**. One of those days when you want to **urinate** constantly, a teaspoon at a time. The so-called noble gases: neon and xenon. **Shallow** sleep of the homeless. Remarking on its admiration of the great Watts Towers, tho it had never visited them, the poem spoke of itself here, casual **dissembling**, feigned. Dairy products in the afternoon. How is doubt? Why Vanna **claps** while the wheel is spinning. Light night. Others' otters' altars. September days are warmest. This key came **with** computers and is called Escape. To set our drinks upon while we gaze at the divers' half-gainers (spirals backlit by the Hawaiian sun), a metal table, round, whose center is a large beach umbrella rooted in a coffee can filled with **concrete**. Demo to ink. Space allocation. Teeth exert pressure on surface of lozenge until it cracks. Sunday service. Layers of bandage about the ankle itch. Life occurs at home. Edible complexion. People are **starving** (in Leningrad, famished after the reading, we ducked into the restaurant on Ultisa Gercena only discover that it had no food). Sentences to go before they're lost. Carpenter composing corporeal music. Rational anthem. **Anchovy**. Purpose of poetry is not to find your voice but to lose it. The gift of the shirt in the right size. The hummingbird's song is a **kiss**, kiss. How will I know if this is page or wall? The TV's on but the day room's empty. Works at the cement. No tad poles in the tide pool. The bear flag in the black **marble** plaza of the bank. Boot from a floppy. We held **sparklers** on the porch or about the back yard's pine. Hours are ours. Rainbows of TP, hand lotions, **bandages**. Shagbark hickory. Face cloth green brocade. Had he lived in America, Beckett might have called it *Waiting for the Mail*. From Japan, straw shoes. Each **cartoon** strip reduces narrative to four distinct stages: context, setup, conflict and closure or release. Without constants, sight itself is **prelogical**. Eye strain to the point of pain. Bus routes constitute a **sculpture**, with density of lines, frequency of units, the pleasure to be taken in **slashed** seats. Backing up is hard to do. Now denim hat—white, wide-brimmed (fourteen years later, my memory of this object is of the gray, **shapeless** mass it almost immediately became and I have no memory at all of when or how it exited from my life). Motorcyclist calls helmet his brain bucket. An ideal roundness is embodied in the **nostril**: let me kiss your nose. Alack and alas, this has no élan; I could make it rhyme, but I can't make it scan. Debts hover like the **permanent** threat of war or those high, dense clouds settled in off the coast. Remember to wear brass **knuckles** (rough edged) when fist-fucking Jesse Helms. Transfer points. Seminary cemetery: priests' stones face in the opposite direction from those of the **nuns**. Write this down in a yellow notebook. In the interest of time. The aardwolf. Hardware **functions** must be accessed via calls to the kernel. Memories tend of be remains not of past sensations but past verbalizations. Dream you. The external is **plagiarized** and this is called learning. I recognize the brand of your sox. Pick up stix. Lamp shade **aslant** the lamp. White bowl of split pea soup is set upon the table. The **state** invokes history as a monument to itself. Ballad of the ice cream vendor. Writing is an aid to friendship. The yellow **house**, the beige house, the blue house, the block (on the far corner, a house in a **godawful** purple). Like the small chamber closing in on Flash Gordon (Buster Crabbe), threatening to **crush** him, the shoe shrinks to crowd the foot. Towel like summer wrapped **around** a poem. In Houston the creeks are called bayous. Saturday evening (Krishna asleep on the couch). How much information is too much? This piece is directed at you. Well, suture my **discourse**. Monday morning on Joe's steps, filling in the notebook. At night, precipitation forms atop the car. Great white belch. Sirens at dawn / A life is gone. It's cold. Cash register's wand is a sort of **metallic** pen. You don't learn that books or chairs exist, but to fetch or sit in them. Having never before seen a lobster boiled alive, Ilya Kutik says a **prayer**. Muslims milling before the mosque. Cataract redacts. Language did not emerge from ratiocination. In the men's room, the large stall is for the disabled. Patterns of possibility come together, **intersect**, disperse. The puzzle is the body, the puzzle is the body, the puzzle is the body. Page or **day** at a time. You make me Lizzy, Miss Dizzy. Dream of a great air tragedy, the neighborhood **smoldering**, lit by floodlights atop police cars and firetrucks, damp night fog, everybody **dazed** on their porches, the odor of meat. "No," says Fred, "I didn't like *Pierrot le Fou* this time as much as I did twenty years ago, but then no one could like a film as much as I liked *Pierrot* twenty years ago." Bus ride right to the ocean. A long warm **wormy** stool, yellow as a baby's. Rapid transit information. Politics is a process, not a project. Soup **repair**. Stand by your LAN. One knows how to receive this because it is a poem, **because** it bears that family resemblance, this assertion, because one gradually understood how to receive the last one, and the one prior, because one has learned how to receive them in general without seeming **conspicuous**. Does Habermas cross against the light? How many times have you read this? I sing the body eccentric. My childhood **passed** in contemplation of Ichabod Crane. How co- can you go? Why should a language game rest upon **knowledge**? Finland silence. Dreams shatter sleep. We manage to hold a conversation at last without translators by merely **pointing** to objects—table/*stohl*, chair/*stool*, fork/*vielka*, glass/*stakan*—with only our smallest fragments of German to hold these **two** other languages together. Meringue, like a wedge of fog on the bay. First I boot up, then I **log** in. Doors open, footsteps, faucets: people are rising. "Have some watermelon," says Dmitri, handing me the **casaba**. What if these words don't mean what I believe they do? A long day of **popping** bubble wrap. Crash city. What a piece of man is work? It is or is not your cup of tea. The King of Spahn. This used to be a nice **place**. She's the eros of Arbutus, the thrill of Catonsville—you really can't refute us and you know you never will. The conditions of production **corresponding** to this specific, historically determined mode of production have a specific, historical **passing** character. If Tom Clark didn't exist, I'd have to invent **him**. Feel the stress in day's recesses (error admitted is permitted to stay). Iraqi monetary unit (the sentence). Anticipation specifically an extension of memory, so that one **salt flat cracked** into pentagonal patterns will generate the next (desert understood as a construct). Those **curtains** which I like above the kitchen sink no longer exist. Upon the completion of *Eighty Flowers*, Louis Zukofsky had **begun** *Ninety Trees* when he died, leaving behind notes for yet a third series, *101 Dalmatians*. Reading a page of print I see **through** the paper to words inverted on the far side, become conscious of the **margin**, begin to anticipate new paragraphs, etc. Lets get demographic. Beeswax mixed with paraffin. Herons in the **nest**, far west. I is a predicate. Little

Patti Post-it. Imagining, we posit lives in these **passing** bungalows, counting (with another part of the same **mind**, uninterrupted) phone poles. Technician, install thyself. Wide brown rim about the tit. Raster Ops. Wasp adheres to flesh (flash!). Syncopation **somewhere** of light rain against the surface. Contempt that, as children, we **felt** for any other forced to have his/her mother present just to cross the street. A second, more exhilarating **force** than speed is acceleration. I stood there broke and rapidly becoming hungry, **staring** at nickels and pennies at the fountain's bottom. Amazing, incredible, fantastic, terrible intensifiers. Lemon ice, soft pretzel. *Poem for Michael Davidson beginning "Dear Robert. . . ."* A walk through the rail yards, rainbow out of gray-brown. The **horned** owl glides through the white beech wood, furious crow in close pursuit. Particular discourse. The blue light of the gas flame flowers beneath the tiny pot. Dear Quine, sentences are not synonymous when they mean the same proposition—not even when repeated. The way rain **stains** old stucco. Analgesic. Would the subaltern recognize her name? Kids with nothing better to do than to ride **around** in an old car shining flashlights in the eyes of night drivers. Shadow sleep of the **homeless**. Advent of winter hinted. My mother stops to watch the filming of M.C. Hammer's latest **video**. How the heel rises and the ankle bends to carry the body from one stair to the next. The Czech is in the mall. A decision not to permit his work to **change**, year after year, several times each month to write the same poem, not **copying** but each time working his way back through the identical process. Dizzy with anticipation at the letter carrier's **advance**. The feminine way men hold their hands when, say, they ride the bus. The tocks are clicking. Humidity of the laundromat. Each of the plug's **twin** prongs has, quite near its end, a hole. This page is slower than. Logo violation. **Able** to sunbathe in winter. This drive is semi-intelligent. Old hotels for single men. My night at Aleksie's. I want a form to cancel form. On a panel—in a forum—under the gun. Outside first thing: forced to purchase food for one's breakfast. The long **twilight** over Ulitsa Gercena began at five and lasted nearly to midnight, making the dark tones of the brick buildings appear even deeper and more somber. In fact a fact. Lunch is one plate of **parsley**, one plate of curds, all washed down with a pitcher of mint-flavored water. Each solution is a sentence. "You are brave," the woman said to me after the reading, "too brave," and I wondered what to make of that. A specific form of **practice** is called theory. The leading cigarette is Opal, a Bulgarian brand, the best wines come from Georgia. The even keel, the overhaul. Clouds sweep over the moonscape of Houston. The monkey **hordes** come to the aid of Prince Rama, again and again. It's dawn: do you know where your text is? The fight is going on quietly in the **back** of the bus, barely noticed. Black V on the **breast** of the western meadowlark. Cupcake corral. Ashes to **ashes**, DOS to DOS. Chalk **dust**. The night belongs to politics. Either I will do this thing or I will not. To write this next sentence **means** something completely different from what it **meant** 16 years ago. We walked through the financial district at midnight, the street deep between these buildings, a film crew working down an alley, **artificial** twilight, pausing as we passed to stare at great **tapestries** in bank lobbies. Stand by your gland. Now I will ask the reverse questions. Fifteen cent stamp should be small—space on a postcard is precious. Write and sunbathe at the **same** time, or ride the bus, or eat dry cereal in a bowl of **milk** on the up-ended cable spool we use for a table. Grossed-out surgeon vomits into patient's wound. Golden rain in dawn of world. Pat, the cat. Great whistling anus. A playground for toddlers inside the McDonald's. Sits on a stage behind a **panel** of instruments and begins to read. The gecko will starve if the food doesn't move. Hunker down **against** a cyclone fence to write words in a **sequence** concerning the movement of a chair to a room's center for the purpose of changing the light bulb. How can you expect your dog to **behave** if you don't? Skycycle. Smell of coffee **steeping** (now that I've given it up). What if it were cancer? He's one of those radical **geographer** types. The evil king Ravana. Chestnuts roasting over an open pyre. Cigarette butt in clovered grass. Unity, **unity**, all is unity, pull down thy unity, pull down. It cannot be rushed, it must be steady. Fordism is bunk. Morning of the middle. Red sky **at night** (write by that light). The history of all hitherto existing society (is)(is not) the history of domination. Above the simple latch, long **since** painted over, frozen open, welt on the wood over the **door** handle, a polished new lock, brass yellow, **juts** forward, solid. The coffee for desire. Ballad of the flattened affect. Personal destiny is directly proportional to temporal bandwidth. In the **dream** people are eating at a feast, going back for seconds, even thirds, until I can no longer eat any **further**, while others return for more and I ask "How can they keep on eating?" to which he answers, "You were hungry, so you ate and are now full, but they are obsessed with the idea of hunger, so they can never be satisfied." Designate art **words** here. There is no 'front' to the mall and therefore within it no hierarchy of location. Sign **oriented** verbal behavior. In the next room, beyond the Gaugin, the tomb of Alexander Nevsky. Ships, arriving or **leaving** the harbor, stir water, leave wakes as we also, walking a trail to the hilltop, **displace** the air. We crowded into the room, more than a **dozen** of us, because it was the one room in the flat that was really hers, a bed, a desk and a dresser around a **central** table, and she went down the corridor to **fetch** her great aunt. Reported speech is speech within speech (not this), message within message (what then?), and, at the same time (I started over and over), also speech about **speech**, message about message, voices you can almost hear (but not quite) through the static of the line. Enlarge your footprint. Kill what you eat. Watch two **women** hold an animated conversation out the window on the street (they're oblivious to the **drizzle** of this coastal low fog, tho one's cotton dress increasingly clings to her body) unable to hear a word they say. Gum bichromate. I mow **lawns** the way some men make war: to exercise my faculties at large. Lighting the bus because it will make the cigarette come. Crosswalk's faded. Half **invisible**. Suspicious in a garden of flowers. Avecless. Banana in the bruise. Scratch the paper, find a sentence. When I speak these words (as I do not) you do not hear them (tho you do, later, when in your head you find their spaces, shadows **formed** and growing. When the pipe bursts above the ceiling it starts to rain. Prairie bomb, cherry **fire**. Time Zone Hoo-Ha in Kansas Pits. Sunburnt kneecap. I can tell the oystercatcher by its bright orange bill. The **cranes** in the gray dawn fog hover over the holds of the boats. Site license: a new **cadence** means a new upgrade. Subjection of nature's forces to humankind, machinery, application of **chemistry** to industry and agriculture, steam navigation, railways, electric telegraphs, **clearing** of whole continents for cultivation, terraced hills, **canalization** of rivers, whole populations conjured out of the ground (domestic swans **stock** artificial lake in business park). **Breastfeeding** your baby while interviewing me for the job was a kind of dare, but never even blinked nor once mentioned that lone soft hair curling up from the brown **flesh** circle that disappeared into the infant's mouth. Animal crackers in my soup. The two toughs crowded about our table, their thick English just **good** enough to say, "We kill Jew guys, yes, Jew guys, commies, blacks, people with black hair, yes." Anything I say, anything I do. The Composers Union was **next** to the apartments in which Nabokov had been born, and half a block **down** from the Architect's Union, but the street itself had been **torn** up, turning into a swamp in the almost daily bursts of rain. Left in the bowl of salad oil, leaves of lettuce lose their form. Relics of the Czars **hardened** into the shell of this city, coral of elaborate design through which now swims a civilization of the truly poor. Pleonasm's spasm. Trill the "r" when you say my name. Drums **accelerate**, bells begin, then flutes and I am walking on the **dusty** forest floor, wearing trousers held by suspenders, bare of foot and chest, searching **again** for my hat (my father) where caterpillars weave homes upon its white, wide brim. The end of the line is Finland Station. Like an old lady **misplacing** constantly spectacles or keys, so I words their **meanings**. "Allergic," I say, trying to explain in one word to the Russians why I no longer drink. Dylan liner notes (no such thing as **liner** notes in the age of the CD). I'd almost imagine you as **anorexic**, but the way you wear your hair and the padded shoulders in your jacket contradict the thinner-than-thou effect. Does go for **collecting** as it does for **knowing**? Full moon emerges over the bland modernist architecture of the **building** of the KGB. The young man with the long eyelashes. Nation in which the factories don't have **parking** lots. I hear the fire reels charming out of the guard house. We must cut the salami one **slice** at a time as we climb the ladder of today's technology. Swarm of carpenters within the burned-out house. Emotion both **cramps** and explodes, like a muscle, like fireworks. Breathing asleep with my mouth open. Compsurf your driver. Imbalance in the body compass. One feels the roadway as a pulse. Rise up **before** dawn, the whole hill still dark, wash, eyes adjusting, as colors begin to open up. They sit on their front steps in the dark, listening to a **transistor** radio, wondering how much of the City's burning. We were well within the **made** place. Nameplate—"Bill Hess"—flies off the desk, first **sign** of how strong this quake will be. I will circle you now as you move slowly **round** our friend, X, as he walks an arc across the field, so as to **explain** to ourselves more completely the motions of **solar** system. Blood **blister**. The tenor sax is a toy. The Eros of Arbutus. Trystero. TLA (three-letter acronym). The deeper, slower heat of August. Ohio is a wait state. We **camped** that night in a field so that when day broke a whole **valley** lay before us. Product awareness (intent to shop). Three teeth in a pill bottle kept on the mantle. Center of Discourse Control. The **language** in which knowledge does not exist. Look for the Jungian **label**. Pores are eyes as they open, nostrils breathing in (the whole body **dilates**, contracts). Rosabel at dog school: she came, she sat, she lay. Sky carved into cubes of air. Outside the ranch-style **suburban** motel, yellow police tape roped off the parking lot and patio outside the room in which the recently dismissed employee had **murdered** his coworkers, barely visible from the freeway on which the rush-hour traffic hurls past, far **enough** from the city to have already begun thinning out, sun setting in the red sky. Felt thought. She never left Tucson and now, at thirty-seven, works as an editor for a trade book company and has a twelve-year old **daughter**. Next to me on the bus, woman **pretends** not to see what is written. Tie conceived as a silk chain. Xerox days. Chocolate ilk. Waylaid by brigands on a **voyage** to get millions. Irony, Silliman. It's all the same principle, sparklers or incense. People get ready, there's a **brain** a-comin'. Dark rain on the gray bay. The controller is **autoconfigured**. White or gray or white-gray, cream call it, fade **away**. When, in the 1930s, the first tour of Chinese nightclub acts arrived in the **deep** south, they discovered the public restrooms labeled "black" and "white," the **women** instinctively choosing to use the white **facilities**, the men those reserved for blacks. There is always the danger of wanting to find an expression's meaning by contemplating the expression itself, and the frame of mind in which one uses it, instead of always thinking of the practice. Stand by your flan. Watching her **hand** to see if there is a ring amid long, thin fingers. Make it neo-. Feel of fever **spread** evenly throughout the body. Let's get infra. The possibility of terms like rooms in a house, huge Hillsborough home, doors of **syntax**, windows of nuance, a long, carpeted hallway lined with Persian mirror, doors ajar through which you see (a guest in this place tho not thoroughly welcome) the furniture **of** usage. Fingerprints barcode the body. This is taking longer than I **thought**. Papermint petty. Piano clusters. Danto's Comedy: philosophy becomes art criticism (Mary Boone assigns value). Please send please very much. All the world's a mall, Jamal, and we are but **shoppers searching** for an angry fix at dawn, that release of anxiety we just know the next purchase will bring (register's ring releases endorphins). The Cessna's propellers, its song. An old man with a **gentle** face, vertical lines over his shrunken upper lip, wears a white hat with a narrow **brim**. What do you mean, justify margins? The good shape lollipop. Putting my shoes on last, then standing dressed. Microarchitecture. It must nestle itself **everywhere**, settle everywhere, establish connections everywhere. Even bracketed, deconstructive terminology is always already **jargon**. This is or is not an object. "You want to buy rubles?" she asked, mere child on the elevator. Now and then the workers are victorious, but only for a time. Arkadii's industrial-strength slingshot, just for the gray-winged **ravens** the size of cats. Blood Thursday. Having seen a revolution and two world wars, the old woman's **eyes** were drained of emotion. A musical composition is what the mind immediately reconstructs of the experience from the score or while **listening**, and by memory the whole effect of the experience, an intellectually reconstituted esthetic consistency, which may **differ** in almost every way from the composer's intentions, and which may be supplemented by related and in many cases unrelated events that occur **externally** to the reading or performance, or by imagination or reverie while listening or **remembering**. Was that Quine? Kill what you eat. The **restaurant** was open but had run out of food. A similar movement is going on before our own eyes. The **wine** had come from the Little Birch Tree, the hard currency shop. Snow is remarkable to one not **accustomed** to it. When you took out photos of a friend, a leading avant-garde theater director who models his looks after Jim Morrison and his lifestyle **after** Fassbinder, Hocquard and DeLuy leaned forward while Barrett squeezed back up into the corner (all this in a bedroom) trying to get **distance** sufficient to take a photograph. What else does the **history** of ideas prove than that intellectual production changes in character in proportion as material production is changed? One thing I've learned is how to use this notebook. A sign within the diesel's **whine**. Bowling Green is our own Siberia. The acoustics of **emotion**. I proceed through the page like a **swimmer**, just below the surface. To view the whole bay from the porch was not the point but to stand there, mineral **water** in hand, perceiving oneself in relation to all visible lives each in the midst of a personal navigation, so that this interlude was itself a form of carrying **forward**, was what it meant. Much like the pine ride. This is logic. Artificial waterfall over the sculpted rocks between these two hotel towers is **listed** on the lobby map as Water Mall. Piss **smell** of eggs. Exhausted by the long night of dreaming. Revolving door! No bad disks. The gentle **knocking** of a sock filled with sand on my forehead. Shoes, hoes. How will I know when I make a mistake? The audience **stalks** not only the speaker during the question-and-answer period (visible target) but one another as well. Just the **way** I wrote when I was twelve years old. Paint brush with bristles cut on a slant. Garbage barge at the **bridge**. A priest incorrect on gospel music is an erroneous monk. Each term **bares** its purpose. This is a paragraph and you're not. Throb in the wrist. Meet my bid box. Reduplication, extension, modification, addition: the form itself is a model of the city. Was ist ein Satz? Earth **science**. Ears are arrows, gyros, compass—I think it's that way. Gives names to his typewriter, car, chairs. I live to see Nelson Mandela with my own eyes, a tall, **frail** figure at the center of this rally of 60,000. The first goal was to separate workers from the **means** of production—the land. After dark two women sit alone in the Chinese diner in the only chairs not turned over onto tables, each holding her **legs** pulled up, knee to chin, the shining, just washed linoleum floor drying under the fluorescent light. (1) Sound of an electric saw from the (temporarily) closed-off gallery, or (2) sound of a film projector rewinding. If I never bought **another** book, I would still never be able to read those I already **own**, even if I live another 60 years, but yet each new volume, in the mail or shining under **top** lighting in a store window, represents for me a potential of a further, vital, still-to-be-seen **horizon**. He bears a resemblance. First botch, best **botch**. Terrorism courts respect (I imagine, looking backward, that this sentence must first have been a newspaper headline). Winning is an aid to **memory**. A drawing of a Balinese spirit with a face in its **stomach**. Shrill call of the killdeer here thirty miles from the ocean, north edge of the **drainage** ditch. Writes better when he wears his hat. Backlit by the sun, the no-smoking decal on the lobby window casts a **shadow** on the blue **striped** carpet. Fountains of the financial district spout **soft** water in a hard wind, afternoon without sunlight between these tall buildings. Call Mo **before** the water boils. We want coherence because, as **infants**, it's what we thought our parents had. Just say Yo! In a far room of the apartment I can hear **music** and a hammer. Hawaiian punchline. An expensive sundae carefully constructed around three mounds of French vanilla, entitled Hobo. I was on my way to meet my ex-wife for lunch. The bear flag in the black marble plaza. It's **dusk** in the suburbs now—late because it's the first week of summer—and two homeless men (one black, one white) **slowly** move up different sides of what passes here for the main street, checking through each concrete encased trashcan for returnable bottles, aluminum cans. Epic of doodling. One if by LAN, two if by fax. Rapid transit. Black England. The page is only the documentation (ink shadows the hand) or the page is more, the field, resistance (in the dream Creeley **wheezes** "The plan is the margin, the plan is the margin, the plan . . . "). The god in you isn't going to be Zeus, it's going to be one of those **limited** pantheon goddesses. How the heel rises and the ankle bends to carry the body from one stair to the next: portrait of Anna at a party. Smell of gasoline **on** my fingers. She was a unit in a bum space, she was a damaged child sitting in her rocker by the window. Tell a grackle from a **starling** by the color of its beak. The desire for coffee ultimately is not desire. Bear's Knee. This emptying out of interiority to the benefit of its exterior signs (my book has a spine), this exhaustion of content by form, life by life, is the **point**, sort of. The ironing board has become a desk. The tenor sax is an add-on. Chronotrope. Carry, if you can, the proposition **to** its limit. You can lead a horticulture but you can't make it thick. One is remarkable to snow accustomed to it. Cancer rots Tom Clark's jaw. The particularly **thick** nail of the big toe. Two crow. She was a unit in a bum space (this is not repetition), she was a damaged child (this is not recitation), **sitting** in her rocker by the window. The syringe **beckons** as the doobie beckoned. Yellowing gauze curtains. In this city, at least, not very many people **seem** to work hard at their jobs but then put **enormous** energy into coping with problems generated by a collapsed economy (later, 10,000 miles away, Ilya says the **difference** of *glasnost* is that "we used to have time to write, but now everybody's starting magazines, book collectives, reading series, so there's no time, but it's crazy **because** there's hardly any paper"). The formal beauty of a back porch. The dream of phonemes. Waking, **sleeping**, days **bleed** one into the others, so that it is this unrelenting need to rest breeds discontinuity, **line**, cycle, circle, line. The three of us crowded **under** the one umbrella. I'm unable to find just the right straw hat. Katya tells me of your husband, himself a former dancer with the Kirov, ten years your senior, a "funny guy." Listening to **seals** on the dark beach, not able to see them. I'd not imagined the sultry summer warmth of Frankfort. He hit the bricks, took a vacation, got rolled up, popped, as they say. Floss shreds between these **rough** teeth. Listening patiently, until you hear the one watch in the far corner of the **room**, the sound magnified, etched by the absence of others. Buildings don't just sit there, but actively resist the pull of **gravity**, each **roof**, every wall a struggle. The fishermen's cormorants wear **rings** around their necks to keep them from swallowing, to force them to surrender their catch. This is the title sentence. The plain highway **raised** through the flood. Watch is a man's bracelet. She had only the slightest **pubic** hair, light brown and trimmed at the edges to the shape of what must have been a bathing suit. Warning: invalid semaphore sent to the **kernel**. Each time this path is taken, distances shift. Finally I'm wearing the right straw hat, writing in the **hot** sun so pen's point traces through hand's **shadow** impossible to see into against the glare of the page. We drove through **fields** of artichokes. Stand by your sand. We came upon the god of the starfish. After the revolution, NPR sends Andrei back to the town of his childhood, tape recorder in hand, walking **down** streets dreamlike in their familiarity, speaking for one last time with an uncle who'd had to resign his post in the army for having **married** a Jew, his wife so old now she doesn't even know of the revolution, Andrei's voice **cracking** with emotion: "Romanian words are flooding me." Feet, do your stuff. Boot locally, print globally. We bring to the encounter what we choose to see, so that of all the terms picked to **describe** the dog, only one (proper name, so-called) defines a category that has but one member yet, not knowing it, the **next** time we see him, we would recognize, we would greet him, we would be correct. How competitive am I as a driver? Dark **brown** houseboats beached at the point of **low** tide—men atop their cabin roofs, idle, play a **dobro**, a jaw's harp, a 12-string guitar—only to **float** again when the sunset is reflected red-orange in the water of Richardson Bay. In a West-End Dallas Mall conspiracy **theorists** operate assassination theater and **gift** shop. White wings of a magpie. The first winter there was still food in storage and people got through in spite of the shelling and bombing; the second winter they were dying in the streets, their bodies **hurried** away to be buried; but by the third winter the bodies simply froze where they dropped. Frying yellow squash in the wok. How many wait states **between** nuance and response? Great jolt of travel. As he pulls himself from the pool, I realize that he's missing half a leg. Write this down in a green notebook. Press space bar for **more** selections. At possibility's edge occurs **limit**. Who will read me (who are you)? Television in the 1950s (Jay Ward's first cartoon,

Crusader Rabbit). "How was it for you?" Kit asks of the Quake. Each day as I lay here, lie, I hear her rise and wash. Those sides of me that know ambition. Silverfish, potato bugs. Armadillo ranch. Formal beauty of a **back** porch. Product mammal. We stopped for hot **chocolate** topped with whipped cream and to discuss the Sicilian Defense. I'm in a crowd. and someone **introduces** me tho he doesn't know me, so it must be a reading, but I'm barefoot or rather wearing just one **sock** and have brought no texts as I begin to search around for them **wildly**. Spider bites. I imagine hours extending infinitely to years (ears' lobes looped). A tenor sax is a weapon. A very good son is on the radio. A learned solitude, in the **head** looking out, constantly waking, new day. When she turns her head, the **flesh** on the neck folds. The Main Library was a grey weight in a white rain. I'm alone in the car in the parking lot at Coit Tower, sun to the west about to set, the last tourists **hanging** around in clusters, t-shirt vendor breaking down his stand, while on the radio Bill King's voice describes Dave Steward of the Oakland A's in Toronto pitching his way through the ninth inning of a no-hitter and I'm sobbing like an infant and cannot stop. One's age is best seen in the **back** of one's hand. Please irrigate that cornea. What I want is the grey-blue grain of Western summer. Radio and television playing at the same time, he puts a tape in the deck, saying "I like a **layered** effect." Void is what's left when the cosmos **breaks** down as the interesting evidence of order. The leg restraints are from the days of ether-drop anesthesiology, when there was a moment of involuntary excitement prior to rest. Subtitles lower your focus. My not drinking makes other people nervous. Sentiment is memory **fused** with desire. The dream beckons because it's real. Mention **sex**, fruit, the nine deer we saw in the sand dunes at Asilomar. Simultaneous conversation in three languages. Mexican blue hammock to write in. The foil-wrapped pads of butter have begun to melt. Drip **candles** kept atop old, empty bottles of wine. Grenier reads each sentence as though it were a question. Fuchsias **fall** and stick to the walk. The feel of metal in the eye is abstract—I can't quite tell where it is. The young nurse in yellow sunglasses, by a subtle redistribution of weight, gravity's center, moves in front of the black-sweatered student of Oriental porcelain in order to more **rapidly** board the bus—which is in fact not a bus at all but an LRV, **before** all the seats are taken. Orange cat sits atop **plastic** bus in dawn fog. Wind chimes. The active voice invokes the passive reader.

Are pears form. The Sikh tucks his turban in at the back. That he was not **brutal** enough for her confused him. Don't pick at that cold sore if you don't want your lower lip to turn into a bloody mess. Awake but still in **bed**, I listen to cars pass, doors, birds, children are day's first voices. Intuition has no conscience. Across the empty states to Chicago if at all possible. Kestrels **mating**. Eventually scratches become scabs. The light at the end of the eyeball. Red shingle roof. This is the topic sentence. A cardboard box of wool sweaters on top of the bookcase to indicate Home. Sunlight **through** the trees in this breeze gives the page before me a strobe effect. The **naval** airbase across the still bay water, behind which the hills rise, houses crowding the lower slopes, deluxe condos lining the top: United States. Lift that cornea, **please**. At first, Bedlingtons were bred to hunt rats in coal mines. Tune in, turn on, log out. Waiting for the phone to ring at the far end, for her to pick it up, I hear voices, whole **muted** conversations. Big dog on a short chain. Attention is all. The legitimation of the polymorphous **structure** of legal performance, "internally" noncoherent and open at both ends, through a binary vision, is the narrative codification I offer as an example of epistemic performance. Jack rabbit's fatal dive **across** the blacktop. A finished good is just a marketing tool for a service contract. He knew how to hold an adz, an Uzi. The value in waiting is not rushing the **emotion**. I'm unable to find just the right straw hat. Just seven international flights per day for a city of five million and three of these are to Gdansk. A day of rain in the middle of June. Push the green button. Slept by the roadside to **wake** in a vast flat space—we'd found our way to the floor of Death Valley. Two slicks and a spiff. The gamelan is not **simple**. I want to talk to you about that second **Louie**. Tuba booms. I've been doin' some hard copy, I thought you knowed, I've been doin' some hard copy, time to download, hard copy, grammar's sloppy, wording's vague, disks are floppy, I've been doin' some hard copy, lord. Modal rounders. "Everyone in Moscow **thinks** capitalism means Hollywood," Kagarlitsky argues (we're eating whoppers at Burger King), "but I think it means Mexico." A slope filled with soldiers **sifting** through the large charred green debris, explosion of a helicopter, Vallejo, 1974. Not swallowing the cock so much as cheeking it. A sequence of objects, silhouettes backlit by a setting sun (the rising moon), which to him appears to be a **caravan** of fellaheen, a circus, dromedaries pulling wagons bearing tiger cages, dogs **dragging** Eskimos in sleds over the sand, the sound, **fringed** surreys with tricolored bunting, tamed ostriches in toy hats, the real ghost of Babe Ruth, the **Elvis** Presley float, begins a slow migration—we think we can hear the didgeridoo—to the right **vanishing** point on the horizon line. Decimal decibel. Primal **soup**. Eat pillow, Mommy scum. Slag iron. Grackle at Dealey Plaza. Red sky above dry land. Clip art. The power implicit within the ability to draw a single, vertical straight line. In the middle of the mall is an ice rink, children racing as their parents **wobble** over the glassy surface that serves as a giant ice cube, sparing them all from the Texas heat. Forms from nouns are known. Across the Neva **floats** a ship on which, 72 years ago, the fate of a revolution turned as it turned its guns on the Winter Palace. That was when my nose began to peel. She **brought** out a box of old chocolates, although only four pieces remained for the 16 of us, because it was **what** there was to offer. Red dirt hills. I remember reading. Look at that room filled with **fleshy** babies, incubating. My eyes have seen the **glare** of the coming of the cursor—they started out as bad and now they're getting worser. Pineapple **chunks**. Too much verbiage in that diet. A tall glass of tawny port would prove my undoing. One-legged man uses his hand to brace and **balance** himself as he stands in the shower. Nevada into Utah as though through conditions of the **mind**. Once-white shoes have discolored unevenly, dark gray at the toes. We ate them. The dog days of August are **woofing** on my Giants. Agents, he noticed, once removed from their jobs, were the **dullest** ones of all. Noting shifts in the fly's path by the alterations of **tone**. Wants to know what revision means. Teach-in on the **politics** of content. Day's first **sky** was blue fan. The cars are clustered, knotting traffic, then one in the left lane **pulls** forward and the white sports car behind it **spurts** out of the pack while on the right one, two, three, each slowing, pull off at the exit, one other joining from the on-ramp that soon follows, a little **red** roadster, top down, catching up from behind but by now the entire left lane's spread out and a blue truck's moved over from lane **number** two so that the sense of density, of formation, rapidly dissolves as some speed ahead while others **lag** on the four lanes that ribbon the base of the Oakland hills. Motown, O Town. I can't tell the point at which the **old** lens is sucked from my eye through the hypodermic needle. Extra paper money was kept in the **closet**, rolled by my grandmother into the amber shade of the small window there, behind the coathanger **heavy** with ties. Through

rough slough. Now you are **here**. We are flying directly into the sun as if into a target, so that as it moves **lower** our flight path does also. Writing, riding, ridden. It becomes **fixed** as a narrative so that anyone alive then in the U.S. knows the phrases grassy knoll, Dealey Plaza or Texas School Book Depository, while very **few** outside the Dallas region recognize the corner of Elm and Houston. Graffitus. Don't believe your own reviews. Said of her organization that it was the **third** largest tendency, but the only one to follow the correct line. Starving neon artist repairs **broken** windows. Fish, fishes. Benjamin on Krauss: "He passes **by** night among the sentence constructions." From the house where Trotsky died **they** caught a ride with a man who worked for the World Bank. You relate to objects as if they were **plentiful** whereas we do not, therefore it does not occur to us to think of the word as an **object**. Increments of the familiar. Get me the forceps, please. He hit the bricks, took a vacation, got rolled up, **popped** so they say. Caustic accounting. Nearer and father. Pixels of light, left to right. You read this sentence before. My instinct is to **shut** the good eye to star out at the simplified world of fuzzed shadows. New bulge. Montana is the Bolinas of Hollywood. Bulky **tail**, pointless as it is long. Not a **typo**. Vacancies. Two jets in tandem mean it's military. The **true** sign of agriculture is the small plane. I don't have an audience for broccoli. This will be hell to **type**. One of those inexorably hot Arizona days when a soda over ice will quench your **thirst** only for a moment. Luggage. Snow in summer. It's all over, paperclips. Waiting **ten** years to get a phone (to see even if your application **to** obtain a phone was properly filled out). Where ranch hands wander in at dawn for coffee or eggs. Now lose consciousness. See how sane this is. Red **streak** in the eye marks stitches. It's not as tho our lives bear meaning, but that gather about us like **fallen** leaves someone has failed to sweep away. A salad bar salad, **salad** of many salads lumped **atop** one another, hot bacon dressing dripping **down** through the alfalfa sprouts onto the garbanzo-crested cottage cheese. What is the meaning **of** a single sentence? Not a man who can take a joke, but one who can take a pun. Occasionally, a dirt road will **curl** out of the mountains to come up to the freeway, tho you never know what fact it extends **from**—house, mine, town, farm. Phlegm at eleven. Before after (but after before). Stand by your brand. A **blue** flame. What did the elephant say to the naked man? This is a **test**. Rooftop mothers meet. Drop City. White-haired **woman** under five feet tall, back bent, shuffles slowly **down** the street, huge boom box in hand. All this only **lately** translated from the Korean. Bears on the grass **alas**. All talk. Loosely scalped penis. Face of the clown colored in. Did I mention that the lady with the **boom** box is Swedish? On holiday, I read Barthes' "The Writer on Holiday." Out of the airless afternoon Arizona heat onto the cool shaded bus **bursts** a dozen developmentally disabled adults with **two** stoic attendants, chattering, laughing to themselves, one speaking to the social worker **in** sign language, the bus is suddenly bright, crowded, a circus, **until** it stops in front of the frozen yogurt shop **and** they scramble down much more **slowly** now, shimmering burst of heat while the door's held open, **one** helper shouting out numbers until all are **accounted** for, the bus again (and just as suddenly) cool and quiet. The function of the paragraph is visual (virtual), to break the page into units, **prelogical** intent. More women trust their cars to JiffyLube. Western movies. Drink tea and **pee**. Disembedding. When this you see, meat and three. We are, each of us, given to realization of the potential of disaster, but when the slowed traffic took us **around the curve** into view of the scattered, shattered remains of the helicopter, engine strangely whole at road's edge, blade knifed into the side of the hill, no **other** part larger than the palm of my hand, our car **inching** through the crowd of soldiers, police, hearses, the traffic pushing us immediately onward, away, it was an image we saw, no mas. Gag reflex **at** the center of the tongue. Got this from a fortune cookie. Prim versus prime, **slim** versus. . . . I quote unquote hate quote unquote speech quote unquote. Trash bag to garbage can is in**verse** prophylactic. Geomagnetic, iron filings at the North Pole. Flying over Amarillo, I'm unable to see Smithson's ramp. Child's form. Search globally, **replace** locally. This is not a new sentence. It's dawn in Denver on a Sunday morning: the first **workers** downtown yawning their ways slowly across the square—Writers Square!—to the shops at Tabor Center, three floors of t-shirt boutiques. The fisherman's cormorants wear rings around their necks to keep them **from** swallowing, to force them to surrender their catch. Ring of water from a glass of ice stains hardwood floor. They're good in all the violent spaces. Willie was pickin' **cotton** over by Fayette when she got married at 15, and now, just 61, she's already a great grandma. House of the art **historian** Panovsky, room in the attic, sloping ceiling—breeze off Lake Michigan turned this page. Kestrel fans its tail out, hovering kite-like over the thistle-thick field, searching out rodents. A doubt without an end is not even a doubt. Fried **catfish**, hoppin' john and a baked tomato, followed by a slice of peanut butter pie. Tales from the **crypt**. "A telephone rings in an empty room and by now we both know what to do"—message on Gayatri Spivak's answering machine. There's a difference between a mistake for which a place is **prepared** in the game and a complete irregularity that happens as an exception. The way an old woman **cups** her eye to shade it from the blue light of the television, the dayroom otherwise empty and dark. House of red brick. Remote diagnostics. We might **speak** of fundamental principles of human inquiry. This hat will hold these thoughts until I catch them. Monday morning. Rotator cuff. Even if his dream were actually connected with the **noise** of the rain. OPM (opium): other people's **money**. Cowbell doorbell. Fanny, when you're living at the edge of society, are you closer to the era past? Memory **not** well. The pure products of America are introduced by Ed McMahon. In the fog I saw the great **grass** boats floating toward the delta. The metal patch is to guard the eye while I sleep. The first ring of the **phone** is short, abrupt, an intrusion, and, though we hear it, we feel frozen, fixed in place, unable to **act**. Poem conceived as a marathon, a life. The burned truck, now, at road's edge, glowed merely. The limits of morning visible over the water, **boats**, gulls, pelicans disappearing into the fog (need for an horizon that is not there). He adds no figure to the atlas of the impossible. You're feeling hyper. The word I **want** is Shampoo. Tyranny of the toilet seat (up or down). To destroy syntax in advance. Boards beneath the linoleum fail to meet, leaving a **dimple** in the floor. Friends of the young children of the wife of my friend's brother. One never **buttons** one's shirt at the top button first, but the one just below, proceeding downward, then turning one's arms up at the elbows, one cuff and then the next, before returning at last to the throat. A **multiplicity** of tiny, fragmented regions in which nameless resemblances agglutinate things into **unconnected** islets. "This isn't interesting," Viktor Mazin says, refusing to translate Yulia's talk on the mythology of Stalinism, meaning not her talk but the question of Stalin per se. Procedure by which they stick a **metal** device up one's prick. "What good is money" Alyosha asks, "when there's nothing to buy?" Superimposing different criteria. Mickey Mouse cartoons taped off Finnish television and dubbed into Russian—who has all this **equipment**?—both soundtracks (the other is English) running simultaneously, Finnish subtitles in the lower left corner, are popular at the moment on the **black** market. How the roads wrap around the town. **Doorknob** thick with rubber bands. Detention garden. Up against the Woolite. Cat **sleeps** on hood of the parked car. This is the sentence in which you begin to **suspect** that the author is no longer in control of the writing. Why order exists in general, what universal "laws" it **obeys**—or finds too trivial to transgress—what principle can account for it (or be superimposed to do so), and why **this** particular explanation has been established and not some other. Relation of hula to t'ai chi. Italian aubade played on the **accordion**. You must remember this—to dis is just to dis. Implies, employs. A hot bath before bed, then a shower when I rise. Linear accelerator: now here's a **method**. Morbidity is skewed demographically. As the ambulance passes, everyone stares to see if there's anyone in it. People in the country go to the **city** for the weekend. If for every window there were a person. Trying to write without my glasses, **force** letters onto the line. Twenty-first century full of **dumpy** houses. Intense yellow of mustard in old-time **fast** food joint. She had only the slightest **pubic** hair, light brown, and when I put my **tongue** there, however lightly, she moaned. Words at the end of a decade (this hand is your hand). Riding buses on the weekend. Subtle as a puddle. At home **amid** engineers, on a patio, with chicken and gin and tonic. Debby Gibson, factoid. Next-to-the-last page in the green book now, deep in the yellow. Body **language** of listeners at a reading. What if one killed one, never to be caught, constantly alive with that information? The crisp look of a new shoe. These conditions of constant change demand the weapon **of theory**. See vineyard as poison farm. Large, evenly hard beds. Pearls of wisdom drop from the **wrong** end of the horse. The meaning of this sentence resides in no one word. Moist Maoist. I **swim** in a clear pool. Carpal tunnel. Moth patiently **beating** its wings on the glass. Meaning skips between words like static **electricity**. Here also are buried the soldiers killed at the Battle of Lake Erie, 1813. On one corner of the box is a large printed square with a caption that reads "label here." Not **urban** but metropolitan culture now, city and suburb single web. Voice mail says, "This is a general **distribution** broadcast." What does it mean to know, sleeping, that you sleep in Idaho? That's in **beta** now. Seismograph and thermostat in display case, gallery of imperial theft, painted porcelain, jade. **History** teaches: eat your peaches. The fountain forms a geometry of the particular, five water **falls**, six spouts, all of which arrive in the general pool. Ding dong, Baghwan's gone. Ozone Park. Wake up and smell the copy. Playing with the **pilot** light. Meet your macro. Asleep in spurts, awake in **starts**. Awaken sparts. Each event will be its own name. The **idea** that a box will have a patent. Fabulous flab. The Specific Islands. A clear thing. If the. Visitation Valley. Good morning, banana breath. This is the fable **of** objects. "I wanted a blend, not a blond," she said. As if by special procedures at the pinball machines, free games without tilting, **weeping** and half-singing, he could speak directly to that force he called the giants. I've got a **giant**, I've got a giant latitude. Infinite expansion. Works written to be read sitting down. Animalism of the **garbage** trucks. The camera's "snap" is in fact a series of whirrs and clicks. Sulfur, the hanged man, I swing between realms. The pressure of the **text**. Stem of steam from a kettle, cream in a small white cup. Calling an impromptu meeting, Kit says, "The company's been reorganized, but our department hasn't been **touched**." She threw her legs back up over my shoulders, **wincing** slightly as, with my ass, I shoved in, then pulled back slowly until just the tip rested against the red lips of her vagina. Two male hooded orioles, heads **bobbing**, face off for control of the bush. That winter there were zeppelin alarms. Getting down on her **knees**, still dressed in the most prim of business suits, blouse topped with an oversized blue bow, she said, "I want you to urinate on my hair and face, **and** in my mouth, and not to stop." This line **written** in Windsor, once the way out, as, say, Guatemala **now** is, sitting on a park bench, river's edge, facing Detroit. How I changed my **mind**. The **migration** of oranges. In Tucson they don't even attempt lawns, although grass is permitted as if by accident between the cacti. We drove **through** fields of artichokes. You're stitching my eye and I know it. A great many notions that intersect, overlap, reinforce or limit one another on the **surface** of thought. Because you are an American, you are sent to buy the wine. Green water, gray sky. In one week, all **of** this will have been a dream. Plants that grow in the antlers of stags. This **mineral** water is in fact heavy metal—if I leave the cap off, it rusts. Primed canvas. Because you could no longer find it in public places, people had taken to carrying their toilet paper with them everywhere they went. Early memory of sensation, being picked up by father, held aloft overhead, first recognition of **height**, absorbed now into dreams where I just **float** off the earth's surface, slow uncontrollable weightless flight. Three thousand books but only three book cases presents an inherent **structural** problem. Canadian cactus. Angular, vertical great blue heron, utterly still in the small lagoon. Demons can **travel** only in a straight line. Everyone talks of the quake. One does not shiver here, one shudders. Through rue slough. Prose **of** the world. The clamp on my finger measures oxygen saturation in **body's** extremities. They invented logic and classification. Threw rue slew. Confrontation of **resemblances** across space. Feel of the surgeon's hands on my forehead and cheek. A key ring raps on the glass. We're rushing to **catch** the bus, to get over the river before the bridges go up. Inca flute. I sip at the tea, hoping it wouldn't keep me **awake** all night. Form is to seize (size) the time. Redwood in parquet floor comes from Viet Nam. Of adjacencies, of **bonds** and joints. The fun part of moving is the unpacking, the designing of rooms. Women, smelling of ammonia, **board** the bus. Dissolving, fog filters these islands. Stalactite or storm. In the sign of the garbage can that says, "THANK YOU," who speaks? Form is the tame cat, asleep atop the fence much narrower than its **body**. Voices in the steep airwell overecho and thereby muffle themselves—one hears not words, but tones. Gunsel, styler, heavy-duty lowrider. Truck **whose** sides are a sequence of rising, corrugated metal doors. Throat, hearing the toilet flush, invariably swallows. Between a pillow and a soft place. A made tunnel, for **trains**, beneath the bay. Fog scrapes across the low sky. Form is the **minute** hand. Retrobulvar block. These **emotions** have been proposed. Academic migrant. His veins great rivers, his **bladder** the sea. Jaywalk the line. Form is the structure of character, what? She **pedals** the fat-tired bike from laundromat to laundromat, scanning each bulletin board, searching the three-by-five cards, hunting for a **share** rental, the cheapest way to live. Strike opponents' **ears** with both fists. We knew which jars of jam we would buy, but let her offer us **samplings** of the rest. Manifest destiny—this sentence is a command. Shops are **filled** with brightly colored, useless objects. Through sky cannon. Your sentences are altered by the book you are reading. BFTP **of** the Apes. Smell of the Xmas tree. Hands over the keyboard as though a dredging motion (dreading **motion**). Marksmen (snipers), to maximize contrast in the visual field, wear yellow-tinted sunglasses. Feet, do your **stuff**. Eyes rotate in skull, looking inward. In need of a new needle. Words wend to send **message**, never knowing what gets heard.

Wanted no limits, only possibility. Just making the appointment to see the eye surgeon was stress enough for me. When uses of the morning rush do **pass**, I stare from my seat into eyes of those who go other ways. Watch television with the sound off and describe the **plots**. Woman new to the building seemed interesting, until the night she brought home the man who clearly was not. High, thin cloud smears the sun. At certain hours whole neighborhoods will drain or fill with people. Syrup forms **pools** in the sunken squares of a waffle. Table with a black top. A long walk in a new city, taking care to keep sight of landmarks (golden dome of the state capitol), each **block** in this direction cuts off many alternatives (it's a decision tree), quiet low-grade commercial strip, used book store with no poetry section, then, half a block down, an extensive used record shop, **musty** odor of old LP jackets, across the street a MacDonalds recessed deep in its own parking lot in front of which, on a bus bench, two small very alcoholic-looking Native American men are talking with a very burly female cop under a sky with fast-moving clouds that threaten thunder over these Rocky Mountains. Language is my given. When the patch is lifted, light floods in, **brilliant**, shimmering. Green tint to the shit. Identifying Phil Spector tune on the muzak. Wrote on the wall its word until I would learn it. Sunday brunchtime divides world into exercisers and eaters. **Filling** the yellow cup with coffee. Pushing Patagonia. Once each day my small cigar. Sun-dried brains. Water in the pipes doesn't wake me, but keeps me from sleep, unable to determine the source, the user, the time of night. The plane backs away from the accordion tubing of the gate only to queue in an interminable line of planes inching along the runway toward take-off. Bok choy, bok-fu. When my brother has his **fourth** child, I realize that I will be the one, years hence, who cares for our mother in her final years. A sentence begun on the green page is completed on the yellow, then **repeated** on white. The poetics of political form. Ants would attempt to escape from the heat by crawling into the **freezer** only to die from it, black ring around its door. I'm with stupid. On the reparsing of names. The day without eyes. Bent bell mat. A Russian without a cigarette is like. . . . Sat in the Ford World Headquarters lobby, reading Olson. Suddenly, we're above this high thin **webbing** of cloud, the top of which lit brilliantly by the setting sun. Grew up, she said, able to hear firing squads by the river at dawn. A point in life where the writing becomes **more private**. The boy was abundant. Because film itself is in some sense European, the films of Leningrad we'd seen made it appear much more European than we found it. Dark glasses on the white desk cast a blue shadow. The one **vegetable** we ate growing up that was neither carved nor frozen was carrots, except two or three times each year, corn on the cob or an artichoke. Class wart. At least this time the elevator **breaks** down, I'm not inside it, I think, beginning the trek down 28 flights of stairs. Instances return, thought to have been lost. Conan the librarian: open empty **dumpster** on a sunny day. Cars arrive or drive off in the dark. 1990: the favorite word of ten-year-old boys is *dude.* To kill the clock. Sweatshirt stand outside Coit Tower: duck-assed woman aims minicam out over **bay**. We bring our little silver spoons. Index of American Jacket Notes, Blurbs, Prefaces, Introductions and Afterwords, vol. XVII. Waking wasted. Leadbelly dies of Lou Gehrig Disease. Friends, kindred, days, estate, good-fame, **plans**, credit. Old water stain high on a wall over the door forms implicit narrative. Assertion, not journal, in a four-bathroom house on a two-acre lot. Relaxed Wanderer **stagnant** liver oil. To him who in the love of nature holds communion with her visible **forms**, she speaks a various language. Think of *thus* as plural of *thu.* Dark red-and-brown houseboats beached in the mud at low tide—men atop their cabin roofs, shirtless and in overalls, idle, play a **dobro**, a jaw's harp, a 12-string guitar, while a lone woman in pigtails frets a banjo, red kerchief about her **neck**, freckles on her nose—only to float again, anchored, when the sun is reflected in Richardson Bay. Jet **tilts** up, off of the runway. Postures of plenty. Where we say "gesundheit," you say "scat." The particular, the particular. When her car flipped over into the small puddle of **rainwater**, the famous newswoman, trapped by a jammed seatbelt, drowned. Attention to objects *out there* in the **material** world is constantly subverted by memory's demands. At that age finally that when you stop to ask my age, I have to stop and subtract. Words in a line pass time. Going to a lot of **truffle**. Willful concentration is constantly dissolving into involuntary association. I hear Thom Gunn "introduce" Bob Perelman. Auto-gyro. Blue light pressed up against the **eye**, behind which an optometrist (a hippie) stares. I've got silence on the radio. His shirt has pockets with snapping flaps, the corners of which **curl** up. One wants a place to locate mind's events. Comes to the end of her poem, only to learn it **continues**. Funky Kingston. A paragraph in the life. If you wider, deeper (if you see Carolina in the morning). This is not emotion recollected in tranquillity, but emotion itself. Burn Sienna. Cardboard stands on which to display books. Tourists **from** Taiwan. In/dict/ment. Somewhere between the retina and the visual cortex, the information signals are modified to provide information that is always already linked to a learned response. On the **motel** billboard is the name of the employee of the **month**. Later they send for their wives. If the rug has a pattern, identify the unit and count it. We thought we were getting ride of ownership, substituting use. Make it neo-. Prose is like a garden. Yuppie thai yin yang, get a long **little** fogey. Winter comes to spacetime. Condom that stays **hard** if you don't. Globe is the lower. Raw broccoli **florets** stick on/between teeth. Vertical law, horizontal **justice**. Little echoing birdcall I don't recognize somewhere up high in that palm tree. Diminishing word where the head dwells, **avoidance** of which is the test—I don't remember what I was thinking when I wrote that, but 16 years later it **sounds** rather depressed. Think of the ways Steve Benson models forthrightness in writing. You understand this because of the **common** social convention that is language. The eight-year-old in the seat next to me is taking her first flight, animated, **fascinated**—"Are those clouds?"—on her first voyage to Disneyland. A light that I saw, that **mountain** road, that passed. It is more dangerous to walk down the mountain than to walk up. Idiot size spaces out nature. One kind of racism just for foreigners. Solid object. It's not the radiation from the TV set **and computer** screen that frightens me, it's the magnetism. How, between tongue and lips, she took my foreskin, licking. "A co-op matrix in advance of the kit," said Kit. Alone in a stranger's house. Each stanza is broken out and **carries** a separate P&L. Autobiography of precision. Crushed and splintered, the sawhorse lay in the street, orange lantern still flashing. She makes **constructions** to sit in, whose common form implies the electric chair. The foley editor rumples a paper sack. This indulgence. Pigeon's **waddle**, blackbird's hop. Only in the flats is the fat of the green gone. Am I a low tenor or a high baritone? Jokes **replace** form—this is called Actualism. Not the **weight** program, the paint program. Frying yellow squash in the wok, with string beans, bell peppers, tofu cakes crumpled up, and mung bean sprouts. The hotel stairwell is undecorated, **pure** concrete but for the metal banister, each floor **identical** until we get down to the high-ceilinged **bottom** two floors. Between body and destiny lay mirrors and attractions. The level at which my father was himself the victim of a dysfunctional family cost him his life. **Intermittent** as it is, the process of refrigeration sets up a **hum** in the wall, non-specific, not to be avoided, not precisely heard, felt rather by the wake in the belly's fluids. The light's so bright I can't tell if my eye is still open. The **grammar** of being is an exegesis of things. What I'm **aware** of missing most, nine days apart from you with no **hope** ever of phoning, is the warmth and weight of you next to me in bed at night, or those moments on the couch when we talk and I softly rub your feet. Bone bruise. Exact point in temperature at which one is too cold without a sweater, but too hot with. Possibly words on a page are the language sleeping, waiting to be moved by eyes that sweep left to right. One could be a room if only the question of **doors** would keep shut. Rose of china **embedded** in the **lamp**. She follows her two large dogs down the street, a small shovel in one hand. Memory in search of a mind. I go to Moscow the way I'd gone to Denver, touching down at the airport, never leaving the plane. An old spool for cable made into a table, made home for a garden in an old wine jug. The first course is veal, the second steak, a **combination** of beef and beef only a Texan could think of. Aesthetic derision. This has too much negative **twist**. The alimentary life. The idea of lines upon paper, superimposition of what's already there. A real, tho not popular, instance of discourse. Caffeine junkie deep in withdrawal. Each morning geese **circle** the lake until they refind day's forms. A neighborhood one sees from the freeway. Lost in the **rain** in Juarez. His trousers hang baggily because the legs beneath have atrophied through years of disuse. Feta cheese. Hours from now jugglers on unicycles will fill the square, the sun high over the executive suites atop the tall glass **and** brick highrises, tourists pausing impressed or not, **but** now it's so quiet that the fountain drowns out the **faint** first traffic of day, house sparrows loud in the **lollipop** trees of the plaza where I sit in a plastic chair by a metal table outside an outdoor café that has yet to open. Dog star boy. Sun sets into these clouds, deckled horizon. Normal discourse. Giant truck has black rubber flaps as mudguards extending from its fenders. Equivocation, **synonyms** and etymologies, differences, form and **description**, anatomy, nature and habits, temperament, **coitus** and generation, voice, movements, places, diet, physiognomy, antipathy, sympathy, modes of capture, death and wounds, modes and signs of poisoning, remedies, epithets, denominations, prodigies and presages, monsters, mythology, gods to which it is dedicated, fables, allegories and mysteries, hieroglyphics, emblems and symbols, **proverbs**, coinage, miracles, riddles, devices, heraldic **signs**, historical facts, dreams, simulacra and statues, uses in human diet, uses in medicine, miscellaneous uses. Cypress structure or Cypress *super*structure? You are not the most complicated of men eating an English muffin. Crust that forms over the scrape. Resented for favors asked. Uncolored seltzer, cherry-flavored. What in the well **whistles**. Light metal grid holds acoustic tile **of false** ceiling in place. A poor good-man tell-clock. The chronic depression that haunted her must have appeared early on, for she had left school after the ninth grade like all her seven sisters before her to work, yet by 17 had already left the labor **force**, returning to it only briefly just twice, although they were always modest of means and she lived another 72 years. Exploration in closure. He turns the **ignition** and an antenna rises silently from the hood of the car. Blind to the alternate. In passing the manuscript to one another, so that **nobody** at any moment had all of it in hand, we **reduplicated** the conditions by which knowledge could be possessed in Russia. Prefers instruments of **percussion**, for discreteness. Refer reefer. Way in which winter wanders in. The felt **tip** pen in your pocket has come loose from its cap. Fat **dimpled** thighs. Warning: the following sentence contains language. The nice guy. More violins in Beirut. Raw mushrooms. Focus my eyes at a distance just to prove to myself that I can. Soap root. Soup route. The waitress, Nora, looms over the counter, **pot** of coffee in hand. College radio: rubber band music. Assuming there is steadily less to **be** said. Each **bird** is an accomplishment of nature (but that implies a will). Write this **down** in a green notebook. Up to your old matrix. Could it bee seen **as** – turn page here – the single act, which took months to **do**. Stand by your bland. Regular geometry of the tiles, the plane of floor held level stories **above** the ground, which flows under the black metal door in this cubicle of the john. Ted and **Alice** versus Gertrude and Alice. Free, white and forty-five. In this mini-mall, each awning's **overhang** ends in a sign, but not every title signifies the current tenant. Salary, celery. In the circle of fifths. In the **head** head. From here I see cars, vans, big trucks inching across the bridge, the sky **behind** green-brown from smog. Autiodactyl dream (what do that mean?). Degrees **of** light, yellow, **white**, shade and glare. Hair as it dries weighs less on the brain. I'm only two rows from the reader, but there's **fuzz** in the loudspeakers—he seems **distant**, hard to discern. Piano man. There were few **wild** flowers because of the drought. I said a **maximum** of shit last night. Are you here to see my new **baby** sister, Mr. Walker? He gave the impression that very many cities **rubbed** him smooth. Now **code** the prototype. Pleasant tense. Local politics on the telly in a new town demonstrates formulaic gestures—city manager shows grave concern. **Almonds**. Half-asleep, I dream of my friend Scott who's been dead 27 years. Was this the topic sentence? Ed Kemp has lived on this block for 70 years, first in the cottage at 1818 which his parents **bought** in 1920 while his father build Ed's current house with his own hands, neighborhood of Finns all in the construction trades—"We were as clannish as the Chinese." The warm blood of rain. O let that **staple** be unbroken, by and by, Lord, by and by. Place holder (say such image **proposes** an aesthetic). Pacing and waiting, waiting and **pacing**. Power curtain. Facts, also called *unit clauses*, are declarations of attributes of objects or of relations **among objects** that are by definition true. An afternoon **nap** becomes sculpture. The people **united** shall never be completed. I woke in a castle (or rather its inner court) whose walls of yellow and brown brick supported twisting vines of ivy, standing slowly, **shaking** off dead leaves and the stiffness in my bones, I see into the windows discovering there classrooms, boys and **girls** in rows within who, having been reading aloud in unison, now stop, staring at me, the horror in their eyes **marked** by sudden silence. The tomb of the unknown pharaoh. Early winter sun. Apricot papercut. Each day **new** vistas become possible, yesterday's earlobe, today's **toenail**, the radio on a mantle one had forgotten to think of, a flashlight small enough to fit in a **pocket**. Between reference and refinement. Videography. Bulletize your thinking here. Would pour pigment directly onto parchment, then manipulate that. Ice **cubes** having melted together. Sleep's weight still heavy on flesh of face. Trekking through yak muck. Interest is something you impose. Mudman cometh. It may be a form of semiotic analysis, whose validity does not depend **solely** on the multi-permutations of application but on the interrelated observance of the field of propositional formats. Call me E-mail. Endless possibility, drifting from campus to campus, hanging out. Thesaurus rex. Never fear, chandelier. Kingbirds play tug-of-war with **a** struggling orange **butterfly**. Cohn's loans. In the hallway, the anesthesiologist is screaming at the surgeon. The hair in the ear or nostril. Ripped cream. So muggy it seemed there was no oxygen in the air, how was it that the cigar burned all by itself **untended** in the ashtray, sizzling and snapping. Reading with my new eye. Since there is a term "poem," many assume there is an entity "poem." Cursing the feeder on the Xerox **machine**. Television in the 1950s. A skyscraper by itself, alone in the desert. Demonstration forest ahead. My sentence, my self. The mountains, visible more by **darkness** than their own size. The rattling noise a flagpole **makes** in the wind. Scrawl. Aaron's eyes. Could you trace this to its source, particular, iridescent, useful only as it disappears? Italian **proverb**: There's no place like Rome. No reason to read this, to read it now. He goes to Nordstrom's to **write**. Lone Star Hotel. A plague in vogue is offered a **vague** plaque as testament to their anxiety. Painter as **banker** or bandit. A value is given (who by, white man?). An harbor, Ann Arbor. What I took to be the gold dome at Georgia State turns out **not** to be that at all, but the state capitol, kitty-corner from City Hall, the **site** where once General Sherman stood and **ordered** the city razed. Assertions, substantives, attributes, relations. Adam's Apple, serpent's Mac IIfx. Evolution of the mailbox, professionalism of cops. This brand is your brand, this brand is my brand. Soft tones, light tunes, late in the day's air. In front **of me**, a small truck pukes black smoke. A poem as long as California, as summer. Womb **of** the unknown baby. The nation of significant sequence versus the nation of synonymy. Bubbles pass back up the **esophagus**. Until I myself became trapped in the Bermuda Triangle of the heart. Push zero. Marsupial. MARTA: humid afternoon, exit the hotel and descend one escalator, then another (the second as long as any I remember), Vivaldi **piped** in, it's Saturday at Peachtree Center, the train to Five Points crowded **and**, not knowing the system, I exit one door to confront an Eastbound sign (not my plan), so spin and push **right** through the train to exit on the far side, then ascend a flight of steps only to realize I could have done it the other way (memory of confusion **at** the train station in Frankfurt), there are no benches at Five Points (no other white people either, or rather just **one** other – do I know what I'm doing?), the first **two** stations westbound are underground, then we emerge, descend, emerge, descend – tho in fact entailing no descent at all, it's the earth that's **rising** —what scenery I see in those bursts of air **instantly** visible as the lush foliage of the South (it's September and earlier, still at the conference, a trainer from IBM told me this would all be gone in another month), now we're past West Lake **alongside** a freeway, a gas plant to our right, then we're at Hightower, end of the line, the crowd funnels down a **narrow** flight of stairs but only I cross the wide **lobby** (is that the right term?) to the escalator up on the **far** side, there's music here also (an electric piano?) **but not** piped in loud enough to hear, the parking lot outside is empty, but many are waiting – there are concrete benches but no room to sit – and now the same train returns, I board, have a seat to myself, see a red brick church with a white cross, the tops of what might be factories, realize there are **no** windows at the West Lake stop, **continue**, hear behind me two women, a distinct slow drawl, a baseball field perfectly groomed but empty, then we're **rapidly** back into the sequence of tunnel and air, they also have an Ashby Station, it's a tiny system **really**, at least by the standards of BART, glimpse of a red brick complex that could only be a college, it's a black world here but I don't sense the tension I recognize at home, many young people have to stand when we get to Omni Station, then it all **but** empties back at Five Points, transfer hub for these two short lines, yellow brick dome of Georgia State, low rows of warehouses topped with **barbed** wire, somebody's laughing to the point of **hysteria** but I can't tell who, a humongous cemetery of **ornate** white stones, then a railroad parking lot full of containers, Inman Park makes me think of Peter, we're still beside the train tracks, houses built of wood, now a train beside is moving in the same direction, only slower, who lives out here on Howard Street, simple wood duplexes, an architecture without ornament, all right edges, I'm painfully conscious of all I don't know, east of East Lake we again descend, then emerge briefly to a view of Decatur, I smell cigarettes, a station with murals, is this a colonial sentence, at Arondale I depart only to realize I can stay aboard, so return, **facing** now in another direction (that slow freight train is finally passing by), is this the moment of farce, the view from above hollowed out by absence of **context** or with the context opaque, brick store painted a deep red-purple, the train pulls us forward, cumulative architecture of the older homes, a sleeping man with eyes squeezed tight, sweat **covers** his broad black brow, so I narrativize a full day of labor consistent with what appears to be an auto mechanic's uniform, I don't see a lot of **people** on these streets, Employee-of-the-Month sign is vacant, I wanted to see Atlanta, peachtree tropicals, blonde woman sits in front of me smelling distinctly of meatloaf, burned-out building with its roof caved in, by King Memorial it begins to feel urban, rows of brick projects, Grady Memorial Hospital of vast yellow brick, return to Five Points and **escape** the meatloaf lady with her green halter top and belly full of freckles, already there's a familiarity here and the crowd at the Northbound platform is, for the first time, forty percent white, between trains you can here the Muzak, a woman is **kissing** a man old enough to be her father but it's ambiguous to see that as paternal affection, I wanted to glimpse Atlanta, I can tell which way the train will come by the way people turn their heads (and I'm right), foot-high flat-top very popular here, a man brings his daughter aboard his shoulders, a **couple** in matching Michael Jordan sportswear, red and black, little girl with a balloon in the shape of a fish has a **congested** cough, daddy ties the balloon to her fanny pack, all the way to midtown underground, it's a **giggle** to do this, I'm enjoying myself to the limit, then we emerge suddenly at an overpass **crossing** a freeway, skyscrapers ahead in the distance, you can't see the commercial streets from here, here's a tiny river, strange new **weeds**, an armored car lot (mostly empty), a road crew working on Saturday (it's a non-union state), high-tone condos with lots of trees, Lenox Station is an urban center all its own, voice of the driver announces this is a northbound train on the **southbound** track and people scramble both off and on (as if direction were not a clue), there's a little lake behind those trees (and, everywhere but downtown, trees are abundant), out there **now** a middle-class world, brick buildings are recent construction, Diet Center, Package Store (meaning here liquor sales to go), more new pastel townhouse apartments (I'll return only to Five Points, I've **known** this from the beginning), I don't have stories to tell about these buildings (but I'll tell them just the same), train struggling now to go **forwards** stops and lurches, I'd heard that Marta was the most advanced rail system in the country but, **other** than the frequency of trains even on a weekend, I can't see it, more than a few brick buildings get **painted** pink or mauve, again the train jerks and stops just north of Lenox, doors between cars only to be used in emergency, man behind me telling his friend that she'll have to transfer at Five **Points** and that the suburbs to the north are resisting extension of the system, we're still stuck as a northbound slowly **passes**, then we **push** forward, then halt again, white-haired man with thick handle-bar mustache may be only five years older than I, now we're moving

smoothly, half-finished apartments with skeletal rooves, this is the white world, a geography of race, am I telling too much, a long train of open cars filled with sand stands still in the rail yard (at first I wrote rainyard tho it's a sunny day), I've been writing (riding) for over two hours, many depart at Arts Center Station, I turn to who's speaking with such a thick drawl, an orange-haired girl in pigtails, I'm fast **approaching** the end and exhausted, fingers aching, cramp in the back of my hand, only two stops to Five Points, so underground again all the way to the Underground, a low-end mall that smells of old popcorn, knowing that **one** day this will become what I did in Atlanta, conference forgotten, escalators up again, Peachtree Street here I am. Technographic typography. Ich bin ein Iraqi. Because it is not normal, this text is apt to be art, tho abnormality is not a sufficient condition for art, tho a tradition exists of abnormal art texts into which this sentence, this paragraph might fit. As in "we can't craterize all of Iraq." As in a calculated refusal to perform the normal chores of verse. Nouns **swarm** into traffic, onto bridges, **in** protest. The "what" is an achievement term. Trim the oleander, plant the rose. From the barracks of Wilcox Mansion where I take the oath of office, I see now only the offices of doctors. Under the lid, the discarded eyelash **scrapes** across the retina. Sea-sick sea serpent. I imagine hours extending infinitely to years (ears' lobes looped). Xenophones. The truth-valued object in the predicate logic is the *atomic formula.* Think of you in terms of masses evolving and erupting, re-shaping yourselves, succeeding one another and **vanishing** – versus think of you as you, the specific **gendered** individual you are. What causes capitalism? Mountain View Cemetery equal to Central Park. Sparrows in the eaves, falling leaves. One hears in **reality** only aggregations of terms at various registers, tangled lines whose macroscopic effect is that of an unreasoned and fortuitous dispersion of meanings throughout the entire frequency-spectrum, **mere** surface and mass, a contradiction inherent in the polyphony which will disappear as soon as the words become totally independent. Number makes a **margin**. A kick in the coccyx for good luck. Mudman leaveth the shower in an unbelievable state. Stochastic, apocalystatic. Milking the golden goose. The way the open hands, palms down, hang **limp** at the wrists, elbows out as he jogs. Low-level format this. Thick days of sun in the late September. Motorcycle coughs into motion. The day's reaches feature **peaches**. Do I dare to eat a pear? A walkway, which **arches** over several systems of roadway, from which a broad view of the light industrial district, vacant now, **half-abandoned**, awaiting the inevitable onslaught of little townhouse condos. I always expected the microsurgeon to be **short**. That jay imitates the cricket. The word *Tattoo* in neon. Looking back from rock atop water, I can see how **boats** cluster below the bridge, few choosing to leave the sanctuary of the bay. Piss like a butterfly, shit like a bee. Silverfish morning, bedbug afternoon. In 1936, Robert Johnson invents rock-n-roll. A large hot-air balloon drifts **over** the center of the city, shadow passing over canyons of the financial district. Rhyme **stories**. From the verandah of a mansion over the Russian River, the home of a young quadriplegic whose name I remember only as Jack, I first heard this music **in** 1972, his attendant (my lover) pulling out a Nonesuch album called *Golden Rain*, putting it on the **stereo** at his request. Orphans of Iraq, alack! In the faded tapestry, small animals called ferrets chase rabbits into the peasants' nets. Covered, **contained**, the muffled sneeze explodes harmlessly in the head. The proposition "Everybody balls everybody, eventually, and nothing changes" turns out to be false on **two** counts. Grammar is always autobiographical. At the edge of *October*, of *Representations*. Tho it is still up, fully visible, the low sun no longer illumines this landscape. Wept, swept, slept. December 21, 1990—2,197 days since I last had a drink (make that a meaning, poem written long ago). A room of table tops. As I begin to slip I reach out for the wall of the shower but grasp the curtain instead, which tears as I fall right through it, nearly knocking the sink from its **fixtures** as I crash to the tile-patterned linoleum. Deliberate sentimentalism perceived as description. Armadillo ramp? I'm tremblin' for my boy, tremblin', tremblin' for a lot things I can't control. Who remembers Pinkville? Dense red meat. Norma writes "sugar dada." No individual sentence given particular attention. In the dream I know she's naked but can only make out **details** of face and hair. Calling out, as though after a large dog. The meaning **united** shall never be repeated. Stumbled, the two of them, out of the bar, a little country roadhouse no fancier than a garage, one of them face and hand already cut, the other continuing cutting. The hour is an invention of the thirteenth century, minutes **arriving** four centuries later. Antelope bites, watermelon **fever**. Core today, peripheral tomorrow. The wall is cooler than the floor. When I think of all my **unanswered** mail, panic grasps my chest. His friend forgot her sandals. Aha, the ruddy turnstone. Full moon in the **morning**. The analysand on the couch cannot see the analyst cry. There the drab girl sat, spacegun hairdryer in her lap, awaiting the airport limousine. Watching a play through a mirror gives it the **flatness** of video. At times thought these cuts he gave himself, shaving, were intentional. Apache fog. The nap is not the territory. Switch from pen to **crayon** and draw a conclusion. Generally speaking, what does it mean, not being able to continue thinking a certain thought. You stand wearing only a **camisole**, trying on different earrings before the small bedroom mirror, neck tilted, ear towards the glass, one foot flat, the other gently raised so that dimple forms at the base of your butt, while I pause in the hallway watching, silent, still in awe of you after all these years. Does it **contradict** action? Theory of kiosk. Fried knuckle crimes. Even though it takes half an hour the first time, once you i.d. the **ruddy turnstone**, it seems immediately recognizable. Tiger balm. For me, reading is only slightly removed writing – a good text will send me to my notebook again and again, almost never to simply cite quotations – and the two together form the deepest mode of introspection. Patched in just to alter Tibetan bells. Variorum sedition. Sheet lightning in Michigan hills. (C)lip art. To change the wave shape or size of the window. A 4MB memory board comes fully populated. Man on the bus, scavenger, sips cough medicine. Running head (Medusa perm). Woke to **find** mice in my hair, scurriers. We had to eat the **cookies** in order to save them. Of gobbled space, speed **as** experience. What in Watten whitens water. Varieties of pretrial detention. He sits on a stool, watching x-rays of luggage pass by in black and white. We stopped for hot **chocolate** topped with whipped cream and to discuss the Sicilian Defense. A fool aloof in the leaves. Days of doors. On his knees, Dan Quayle coughs, **choking** on the president's cum. Motion is a vertical **disorder**. Natchrel sunshine killin' me by degrees. Under the cuticle, below layers of thumbnail. The impulse **to** not write as strong as the impulse to write – which to obey? Day's light precedes heat: bugs of the soil waken, wiggling to surfaces, shivering about their business. Son of suffix. First rain of winter **woke** me in the dark, sound of water on the sill by **my** head. The mother of all discounts. The nice man. My brother's oldest boy, at nine, already an obsessive reader (an echo of genetics). Compare psychological profiles of those on the train facing forward versus those facing the rear. One urinal always **shorter** than the rest. Book of short poems to be called *Spare Parts* (the genre is logistics). A **finch** on the fence is worth two in the text. Thought becomes troubled as it contemplates itself, jettisoning familiar forms. A desert woof. The private lives of kindergarten teachers, a party **about** the clubhouse of an apartment complex in Livonia, one who by the pool shows the young woman an appropriate way to drive a golf ball, or **strangers** stare confusedly at the sauna, read instructions, implies to the strangers engaged now in a contest of pocket billiards, chalking his cue in that harder light, high-beamed rough redwood ceiling, **aligning** in the mind ball to pocket, a world of repose, of a **stasis** (July's end, 1974) that includes activity, sailboats decked in a garage, as – what is the word, he can't find it – as *something* as the light which each night is turned upon the garden. Kit Robinson **is** a long man. Where is JFK's brain? Radical drag in a suburban mall ("say Hi, y'all"). Yonder. Pound's dyslexia. The **distinction** between measure and order. Keypad on the wall means burglar alarm. History is not a good bourgeois. Since cholera broke out in Peru, I look at grapes and go "oooh." The absolute character in what is simple **concerns** not the being of things but rather the manner in which they can be known. This one's self-centeredness doesn't mean she doesn't care – she does, the loyalty of a pit bull disguised as a passion for gossip – but the teasing, the ironies, the rounded pink tip of her **tit** flashed at him in front of her own husband, undercut instantly by a mock-cruel remark and the demand that he read her poems left him dizzy often afterwards, refrigerators empty **but** for a can of Coke, as we note, all four of us in this conversation, that in twenty years of marriage they'd never bought towels. The oil in skin, **odor** in towels. Amateur hour at the White House. Write this down in a red notebook. The inner harbor, like the inner self. Repress behavior: a small grin over gin and tonic. The speed at which Helena **dies** of cancer. Permit me to speak of evil. Background color values for use with the graphics predicate. Exorcise your monkey. In Tuscaloosa, Jack is busted **as** a peeping tom. This mute sentence is a mark. Check the owl ball for bones. The abruptness of **seafood**. The episodic subway. Because the mind analyzes, the sign appears. The dark **spots** on the ultrasound screen are follicles developing in the ovary. Early morning mental system. When you're running AFP over TCP/IP. At dawn in the eucalyptus grove I watched him perform **sequences** of the martial arts. A bar at page bottom between footnote and text. Doors here are **more** complex, framed panes of glass interlocking with one **vibrating** in a windless room. Panhandle. At dusk **near** Times Square I watched her perform sequences of the marital arts. The poem as a form **sensed** prior to the writing, as the act thereof, as a **text** fixed upon paper, as the act of reading, as the memory of any of the above, as a unit in a larger discourse of power. It's morning again in Saudi Arabia. The fine, sharp **rim** of autumn. Students are cutting class struggle. The usual dead people most parents are. Hotdog relish lingers in mustache. I like to walk thru the glade as the fog burns off, in the growing glare **of** that **diffused** light. A day at the traces. The tenor sax is a weapon, but oh the sopranino! If Jesus is Lord, then Madonna is Lassie. Gradually the **absence** of milk trucks. Messages along the ethernet backbone decay into tasks. Our lives **in** the mineral world. When I was a cowboy out on the **western** range, I went a cow-cow yippee, cow-cow yippie yippie yay. Sing tonight of the Wipe Out Gang, Pugo and Yazov and the coup that couldn't think straight. Sodfather III. Posits of new information not like cars recently attached to a train (Whoo-ooo!), but like memory (say wha?), embedded in the presences. ROM wasn't built in a day. You presuppose a determinate form in our **consciousness**. It is not enough, it is just a rabbit. Pleistocene statements. Minstrel shows, such as Silas Green of New Orleans, survived into the 1950s. Meaning cannot be more (yazzir) than the totality of signs arranged in their progression (yazzir, Mistah Benny). T for Tech Show, T for Tennessee. We stood or sat on the deck, breaking oranges into slices, watching the four-masted prison ship glide across the bay. The bar plays a muzak version of "The Night They Drove Ol' Dixie Down," then a version of "Heart of Gold." The mechanics of image in time. The hunt haunts us. A tractor necessary to care for this lawn. Floss like a butterfly, brush like a bee. Blood blister. What does the fetus think when the mother has an orgasm? Her sense of the distance within families is American, **but**, beyond that, Chinese. Homeless man carrying a clarinet as tho it were a baton, reed missing. Green **urine**. Hallmark is the largest manufacturer of greeting cards and social expression products. Assembling the beginnings of a new phenomenology. Tomorrow I will more than likely in the afternoon be here. Certain dreams, because they **purge** deep illusions, bring great rest. Rooftop tennis court atop a highrise Hyatt empty in the long humid dusk of Kansas City on the last day of May. Linoleum Story. I **link** therefore I am. Thunder is real. The sky car of Berkeley. Void **in**, void out. Plastic spatula melts in the hot pot. One seeks for the middle point, where the object (if it is an object) is the reality of the intention, knowing the intention to be the reality of the object. Chairs for bears. Men eating burgers in **silence** under the fluorescent light over the drugstore counter, wearing t-shirts and short hair, staring **at** their food. Three-pronged plugs mimic old civil defense signs. Do not piss in the sink. Ear's awl pries thought from words, all heard. Greased lady. Shakespeare's Discordance. This city has different **systems**. Some of us suffer spells, others suffer grammar. Bob's bitter days. Trapped by her seatbelt in the **overturned** car in the ditch on a rainy night, Jessica Savitch drowns in a puddle of water two feet deep. It was not language as definition, but language as language, a larger circle. A crap that large ought to be in the circus. The last dance, the end of dancing. Sourdough bastard. I rode with Ocean in the back of the **truck**. Finches in the frost, all is lost. The bottle of white wine is empty. When I come close **to** its nest in the abandoned gopher hole, its **mate** still inside, the burrowing owl hisses, imitating a rattle snake. How can **you** hope to penetrate personal style? Scud Lite: no matter how much you drink, it never hits the spot. Force the eyes to focus. Methods for assigning a confidence factor **to** a rule. Porkpie hat. If he reached out to her, she struck back, whereas later with someone else his same **gesture** invoked a flinch, followed by the stiffening of her spine, but it would take years to see these movements as the ushering of defense, a form itself of communication, **and** so at last to begin to wonder what his own original message had been. The Main Library was a grey weight in a white rain, its steps **shelter** to a dozen of the sleeping homeless. Running shoe whose tongue invariably slips to the right. Swollen fingers. She's more shy as a reader than as a person. Against the hearth leans a line drawing encased in glass, in which the apple tree with its too-small fruit is reflected, **whipped** by what must soon become rain. At the break in the workshop, several attendees reach into their briefcases to fetch their cellular phones. Tho I left the bus, my umbrella continued the journey. A white jeep on the sand spit – three **horsemen** galloping along the shore. He sat under the kitchen table, writing **furiously** into a notebook every word we said, Emily scolding, the bright light of a bare bulb on dark painted walls, the Kelly green fridge, the rest of us talking or smoking dope, but it **was** his kitchen. "I'll try to keep channel 9 tuned to local radio," the pilot's voice disembodied over the intercom, "so you can listen to the war." Tally. Patrick Ewing **born** the day Marilyn Monroe commits suicide. The competition of these realities, as tho any of us were **a mobile**, spinning, each point one view to be taking in the rotating geometry. This is not a metaphor for anything. The day's claims **decline** in winter. Products for donut, teaser on air. What is to be taken as no information, decisions made each time we cross the street. Rain on the skylight overhead – indoor drumming. Beginning to notice the bathroom habits of your new friend. I'd surely give a fish to a cat who'd wash a dish. Gradually these pages fill, an intentionality like moss or like shadows across the hillside. Miscarriage is the emotional inverse of abortion – a sense of overwhelming loss **surrounds** an absence outsiders never recognize. The existence of language is both **obvious** and unobtrusive (mark here of a claim I'd never make). Nobody bogged down in the second half and they hit they **shots**. Mucous membrane. Hat hatches hatchet. Her eyes wide **with** indignation. Berlin Wall crumbles into sand blowing across the bones of Kuwait. Cool **clouded** sanity. I keep coupons in my notebook, having torn them out of newspapers, **magazines**, but I never remember to use them. She sat in the car in the shut garage, letting the engine run. Counting the seconds **between** lightning and thunder. The knot is not the rope. Teabag's second cup. Tenth day of October. Post-its form a tourniquet. Amelia naps. The shortstop is in **love** with the second baseman. Truth, precision, appropriateness. Grill's stripes streak the sausage. The signs sing. The border left blank becomes a margin. The seriousness **and** quiet in the eyes of people who ride the bus to work. Hotel **lobby** seeks the effect of a mall. The afternoon curls about me or I wrap myself in it, **folds** of attention aired with movement to a pot of coffee or to the john. Echo of chewing inside your head. This is to thought and signs as algebra to **geometry**. Wrong old filament. Lots of exercise, little thought. You can get graffiti off the tile, but not off the grout. Green slugs in grass, cut by the mower. The Big Vowel State. Twang in the rope, what holds the new apple tree **to** such wind as this. The actors in the porn orgy scene seem curiously bored, **index** of the lack of intimacy. Words I lost because I did not write them down soon enough. Blood bursting, spurting from his own aorta, the boy ran blindly down the hall, dead even before he reached the arms of his teachers, his footsteps echoing off the metal lockers the only sound anyone would remember, no other students present but for one young woman still holding a pair of scissors. These roofs, their angles, give the hill texture, houses packed tight, cramped yards, kids on porches, dog growls, mowers, yelps, web **of** clothesline. On Broadway, what remains of the original community of Nashville are the **pawnshops**. The chair at my desk after years gave out, which now creates a tension whenever I sit in this new one: dual expectations as to the seat I'll find, the body progressively taken by gravity, small half-instant of fear until the sensations resolve. Romancing the bone. Eye as sponge to day's light. It's **not** a shoe, it's a machine. The work in thought – **progressive** labor. The quick brown sauce jumped over the lazy **pasta**. What I want is the grey-blue grain of Western summer. Often I'm permitted to return to a mantra. Years over the hot plate, making breakfast **before** dawn. Destination churches, of which there are at least 300 in the United States, have at least 2,000 **worshippers** each week, are typically Baptist, and often house such facilities as health clubs, some taking over entire old shopping centers **with** their vast lots of parking and easy freeway access. Attempted (without success) to confront her explosion at my own diffidence, but did not, could not transfer the smell, the mould in the meat about whoever might ski or skate, **white bread** world she herself was **so** circled by. Your **breasts** have arrived. This sequence presents simultaneity. "I love the smell **of** napalm in the morning," the waitress said. Yellow beach, pink sky, pink beach, yellow sky. The **chicken** smokes, smolders, but is it cooking or is **dripping** fat merely setting the briquettes into a last sizzle of remembered warmth? This alphabet of **ants**. Big Tiny Gang, Kampuchean teenage gunsels from the land of Pol Pot, loose in the streets of Long Beach. Eye is spine. The instant, even **before** I feel it, of orgasm, my come running out of your **mouth** and through your fingers, each of us staring into the other's eyes. Interior of time, exterior of speech. Flavor of aspirin as it dissolves on my tongue. Sea cucumber. Neck broken by the plane wreck, Thurman Munson, already a quadriplegic, **shouts** to his passengers to get out before the flames explode, burning him alive. Rat-like function of wild dogs in a ghetto. Felt-tip pen clipped **into** the collar of his t-shirt. Air more active, clouds piling, folding into **themselves**, rolling. Flap-flap **of** his sandals as he walks across the concrete floor. Talking to you on the phone when what I really want to do is to ball you. A bottle of WAN. Burma Shave parataxis.

Sound of a man erasing pencil with an eraser worn below its **metal** cup, scraping the word from the page. I got up before **dawn** and went down to the park. Respect and obey your matrix. Who needs not a lover but a tennis partner. Spontaneity is best (spontaneity is stress). Aerial perception of traffic flow. In the dream, my grandparents are alive again, all the old conflicts forgotten. In the **beach** night, campfires illumine the city of dune buggies, surfboards pitched vertically into the sand, a presence as of clan shields. I call this driving meditation, you call it white line fever. Likes to sit in the glade and practice his trumpet. The ill-wrought **worm**. As if these words not written remain **forever** locked in ink. Keep the sheep. Familiar odor of the dentist's Gruff old white-haired woman **sits** on the busstop bench to smoke a cigarette which she mostly lets burn down between discolored fingers, **then**, done, rises and walks off. How the flood of detail, the first time you walk down a new street, cannot be repeated (will never be defeated). InfoMonkey. There is only the verb "to be." New fingernail moon. Quills or crackers, **jewels** and miracles. Can I get a whatness? The words will possess **more** force is you use a crayola. I like icon. For example, one propose the inclusion of anything. Disposable thumb. Extraordinary mouth session. This message will be deleted when you hang up. Cigar shaped object hovers near the highway, then quickly **flies** away. Trio of T-squares hangs from wainscot as the draftsman leans over his table under a small, long-armed lamp. These words **frighten** me to write them. The 400-lb. man envelops **his** Harley as he moves down the freeway. With such attention the mind can follow the act of her washing in the next room, knowing hands from **neck** from cheeks. May your stools be **as** soft as the flesh of your **thighs**. I have a time problem. An iceberg twice the size of Rhode Island threatens shipping off the Falklands and is named AZ4. Haul ass, kitten. What's hot and what's not. Existence is an attribute. Inner organs of the rich and famous. Subtitles lower your **focus**. The metal point **pricks** the flesh, then the vein, the tube filling a deep red until it is full again, pen ready **to** write. White tribe, the golfers migrate up the tailored slope. As, nine months ago, we met others who were themselves "fertility challenged," no we suddenly – everywhere – meet twins, the parents of twins, their siblings, cousins, lovers, neighbors, someone who's sister's boyfriend's uncle's manager on the night shift seven years ago used to date the great aunt of twins, though they'd never met and never will. Of such, of suchness. We were supposed to be landing in twenty minutes and yet that barren landscape could only be Nevada. She liked to **lower** herself on top of him. The word *homeless* **permits** us to accept them as an identity, to airbrush out the conditions through which they exist. The first person to remove himself, as Zukofsky debuted Reich's *Violin Phase* to the west, Mario Savio. Surrounded **by** the race teams of the Baja 1000, we note two types of roadies in these crews – one **imitating** the astronaut technician, the other more a beach- or ski-bum outlaw artisan – each a variant of warrior. Palace of the Legion of Honor. Someone else is speaking. Yoyo's alibi, the way back. In slow motion, in black and white over and over we see the **assassins** rise up from the military parade, firing in forward and reverse, Anwar Sadat toppling back over a folding chair on the suddenly empty platform, then rising again, then toppling. Balling on the beach, as tho some places are **so** public one's privacy cannot be breached. Bubbles rise up the esophagus from the depths of the swamp. Old **sentences** heard new carry a different purpose. Please seat to be weighted. The eaters of wheat. Canary dead in Plato's cave. Weight in the **line**. The system is down, as is the economy, tho airline discounts have risen to combat falling margins, the stewardesses **upon** them, their calves exhausted in spite of flat shoes, offering cream for our tea. Gullies really, **pathways** that trickle down the side of the cliff, down **which** we half-climb, half-slide, to arrive at a beach of large rounded rocks, there to spread out a big towel and slip out of our clothes, sails at a great distance, not even gulls to **disturb** us. Quit as a synonym for exit. Tourmaline, rhodochrosite. The universal American article of clothing is not blue jeans, not a Stetson, not a T-shirt nor tennies, but the one-size-fits-all plastic-snap-in-the-back baseball cap. Conjugations: no term is single, but **a complex**. Frank Robinson, not the baseball player, but an employee of the Pemberton Chemical Company, created both the name and logo of Pemberton's most successful product, Coca-Cola. Motor City Farewell. Herbie Hancock first learns of **rap** from a record by Malcom McLaren. Sentences sent hence. Describe the day not by its colors or sounds, but by the breezes it makes, warm and just **gusty** enough to shake the magnolia on which that grackle sits. You wake in waves, each new day's tides of attention. Each table top seeks its own debris. Secret joy **at** the little residual pains of exertion, **muscle** segments declaring themselves newly self-aware. Pine-scented poison sinks into the **twitching** wasp. The road, the rug, fading dawn moon. I return to BART like an alcoholic to the bottle. Empty milk carton in which to place a wick, then cubes of ice, over which to pour hot wax, becomes **at last** a candle by which to write of the folk arts of the 1960s. You don't get blintzes in New Mexico. Analysanda and their analysantia. Insect incest. To **circumambulate** the planet on my exercycle. Outside each hospital bedroom, bright yellow plastic bag with big red letters: Infectious Linen. A field of corn, green, in a plain of dry grass. Tale of two **fishermen** wading for Godot. Sweet wake-up. My twins have nicknames (Dweezle and Noodle) before they have names. Such poems are **like** keystrokes in search of a monument. Giant is the **brand** and Butte is the model. Crude **rotation**, this life. I am in these words, inextricable, **and** if you look close – or listen – surely you will **find** me. Learn the art of seizing control. Walking **under** the plum tree at night, my face pushes against a **spider's** still unfinished web, fine as mist. Dawn's brink. Seeds of an apple are **toxic** and a cup of them would be lethal. Barnwood ash. Repacketize that. Need in the abstract (need *for* the abstract). Poems of the past form a vast plain filled with both pain and promise. They live in condos. Runrate of words in the **text** hints at the crisis in flooring. Crime against nurture. Birds of the west, go **nest**. Mention sex, futures, fruit, bar codes, candy, slasher flicks, exchange value, hang time, cities, self-rewind, securities, black-crowned night herons, books **yellowing** in acidic paper (the words are on fire), realtime, the wheel, nostalgia for eight track, the cinema, violets in a white vase, land forms, Central Asian Republics, sky. Passing **by** the chapel just as the pallbearers start down the stairs, you notice how small the coffin is. To be **eaten** by the situation of your own sentiment. Farting fleas. Happy faces atop water towers. The quick brown tooth jumped over the lazy tongue. A million **threads** of forward motion in the social explosion **of** our times, ours to untangle and engage. The body gets a phone call. The air in its **fair** layers (invisible grid of microwave transmissions). Predictable **contents** of any used bookstore poetry section: Auden, Dante, Stevens, Merwin, Strand, one volume of letters from Olson to Creeley. This means recognizing that revolution is a lifetime of fighting and transformation, a risky business, and ultimately a decisive struggle against the forces of death. What pleases in applause is the permission given. Between clouds, **jet** trails disperse. One fluttering dove **overwhelms** the scale of sparrows in the plum tree. The

connection between geography and character. To alternate pressure points, never wear the same pair **of** shoes two days in a row. Necrotizing laryngotracheobronchitis, consequent of a **chemical** irritant, CS (no mention here that the tear gas canister, fired from a specifically fitted gun from a **distance** of less than eight feet, shattered his Adam's apple **on** contact, nor that he was dragged down several **flights** of metal stairs on route to the prison hospital **by** his ankles, head **bouncing**, hitting every stair). Panting is such sweet sorrow. You have here a dichotomous key. At first the tan absorbs the **freckles** but then the freckles re-emerge stronger than ever. Not the sick, strict, slick legalisms. Tres bland mousse. Some combination of fungus and algae. Between Bing's Liquor **on** San Pablo and the Taco Bell four blocks away on University, a street person in **camouflage** has established a daily territory, his range, beyond which he will not venture. Employment gainful of what? I chart the feeding and digestion of each twin. Allied Gardens. As the audience ages, the **type** grows larger. Iowa clay, that slight planes (plains) do sculpt place, the rest west horizon bearing night. A spreadsheet way of knowledge. Helicopter hovers lower over backyards, glass in the houses' windows **shuddering**, dust rising into the clothes drying on the line. Coup people. Glossed lines (embossed minds). Box juice. Listening to the record repeatedly until I learn it. P for pizza, P for paparazzi. I am meat in motion only, all other is construct, Pinto heading west (social formalism). The other of all **battles**. Write now in the dark. Rainbow truth. Special weapons and tactics. On Broadway, what remains of the original community of Nashville are its pawnshops. A state of identity instead of entity. He **gives** good blurb. The signifier is empty, the sign is full. "Race you to the grave," says he. When the moon goes down, it comes up again behind my eyes. It is **cold** outdoors so one wears a jacket, but warm indoors so one sweats. Passed ball. Send in the **clones**. My fate: **to** rise late. The weight and frame of my glasses. Eroded mesa. Bird watching on the slough of despond. Cloudy urine. Send in the **cloves**. Weary **of** waking, talking, faking it. The instant I get the hang of umbilical cord care, the **black** raisin on my son's navel drops off. A kick in the **brain** brings rain. New radio donut. Night rodeo. Wait **states** happen. It was then that my real work began. Vomiting vireos. Drip candle kept **atop** old empty wine bottles, coffee can full of pennies. I want to lie naked next to you, your head on my shoulder or mine on yours, talking quietly about **any-**

thing at all, the world drifting absently out the window, nothing **sexual** in this image, an impulse instead for total relaxation, an intimacy **in** our conversation neither of us will ever know with anyone else, bed in the center of this small room, no light at all, talking almost at a whisper, **time** seeming have disappeared. A bath with **bubbles**. Is this ComputerLand or is it poetry? Mountain lightning (up close and personal as we spin through these hairpin turns). People – by the hundreds – are somber, quiet, as they board the train heading for the first mass antiwar march in a generation. Hobo, so-called, possibly drunk, had fallen from a freight car, head caked with still red blood as we found him stumbling by the road. Gutter slush. The strictures against propositions apply equally to attributes and relations. On stage, Bruce Springsteen and band lean into their mikes, singing "cataract, cataract." For whom all music is an expression of percussion. Between oneness and Tunis. The man lurched suddenly in front of our car, blood already flowing from the **torn** scalp. Green sky at night, bombers' delight. A return **to** standard time. Barrel of Texas intermediate crude. Tuesday noon Wednesday, 2:15 AM). Aldebaran is yellow, southpaw and a flake. Eye grows back over the **plastic** lens. Somehow fog on the desert floor. Table of remaindered art books. Bones in my hand. Sport bra. Nails that glow in burning wood. Jays colonize the eucalyptus. Warm early autumn. Wooden spoons float in dishwater. Myth is a language. Homeless woman with a thickly **bandaged** foot is searching through a pile of collapsed cardboard boxes. A bar into which come women who wish to sing opera. Waitress making small **talk** in her second language. A clock talks ticking. In the dream I know you're naked **but** can only make out details of face and hair. A long correspondence over why had I not yet begun to receive my subscription. street person at dawn walks with a **blanket** over his/her head thru foggy intersection **against** the light. In the Great Salt Desert one is the **vertical**, located. No talking in the courtroom – be seated and be silent. A thing you had not expected to find. Theoretical arugula. From what they did, he will not recover. Time capsule of **prose**. Sudden as the change in governments. One urinal **always** shorter than the rest. Morning moon over mountains. In the park, a woman **in** jogging clothes does **stretches** against a tree. The form is too clear. Moog stops Montreal as Bruins advance to semis. Eggshells in the flowerbed for calcium. Sunday at dusk, everyone remembers **to** go to the laundromat at once.

This is the fifth meaning of glass. What pleases in applause is the ritual itself. The road a **line**, to define a canvas. Yet **on** the next step I sink knee deep into the mud. Amazed to find all that **sand** in her crotch. A furniture store called Freedom. Consumption of word by fire. Looking for an FSH (follicle-stimulating hormone) level of 19 or less. Desire to spite. Poem: insert text here. Because my **name** is lion. What to say to a truck full of hay? An argument over kitchen tile. Old RVs and lean-tos on a desert hillside form a Baja town. The **young** nurse, strawberry blonde in blue sunglasses that accentuate the roundness of her **eyes**, by a subtle redistribution of weight, shift of gravity's center from one leg **to** the next, moves in front of the lanky African-American graduate student (ABD) of Oriental porcelain, in **order** to move more rapidly aboard the bus, before all of the seats are taken, so that she may choose someone, anyone nonthreatening **next** to which to sit, such as this old Latina in a cloth coat reading the Bible, but just as she settles onto the **hard** plastic seat she notices, sticking out of the woman's blue leatherette handbag, the handle of a gun. Next morning we **slice** the unused baked russet potatoes and fry them for breakfast. Big **black** desk. Ears are amber, hair ochre, sienna eyes. Watched, each day as we traveled west, the moon dissolve. Small eye on the door recognizes the chip in my security **badge**, not me. A year in the white room. Margin and point size fix the length of a paragraph – a page the **size** of an entire wall so that paragraphs are revealed as lines at last (*Moby Dick* as free verse). Three days **of** July rain. After the C-section, penetration prohibited for another six weeks (after 14 weeks of **bed** rest with orgasm itself verboten), I move my hand over your panties, finger pressed lightly **over** clitoris as you move and writhe in the dark, bassinet within five feet of us, until at last you gasp, then begin to sob with relief. Memory of brick was the Midwest. Lemon Kurdistan. Reassert **older** orders. Eat cake for the frosting. Causality. Rhyme reporter. Mould forms in old coffee. The **verb** is not what you think. Standard images, feet **in** the ceiling, etc. Mother is the necessity of invention. The bells return. The sky is not falling, Chicken Little – we pushed it. Two ducks rock in: one, **long** fingered and bespectacled, with shoulder-length straight, stringy hair, says, "Write in any **state** of mind, Alabama." Blue chalk for the pool cue. As the heat of the hand will draw leaves up to it, so thought's pressure folds the flower. This is my epigraph. Words on the page age. Sound **of** a child running flat-footed end to end thru the flat upstairs. Andy has leukemia, needs blood. Down low, jump shot, Hardaway! Previously specified rate of words per minute. Mall kiosk empty in **melting** snow. Urinary habits of Dr. Williams What place could be emptier than an empty airport? A pattern of speech elsewhere in the house that could come from the television. Armada of chopped Harleys glide through the pine **wood**, on each a bearded, helmetless man wearing a blue kerchief headband, a woman in a tank top and black Levis hanging on behind, procession moving too quickly to read any of the tattoos. The flat **on** Missouri Street was empty, lights on, dishes in the sink, books about the floor, the shower torn to pieces. In a **standard** read non-burst mode, access 64 bits. It is not the night that tires. A point in life when ideas return so frequently I begin to discern their orbits. I thought somehow to copy Rodia not having seen the work. Ye who meditate is **moss**. Thus Berkeley became the past. Spots of snow on these far peaks even at the tail end of August. Today's embraces. Gas station, abandoned, transformed into a mountain of earth covered **by** sheets of black plastic behind a chain link fence, Robert Smithson dead and gone. Hot piroshki smothered in **sour** cream (the mean inside crumbles from my fork). Initiate customer profiling, using standard **methodology**, to elicit and articulate strategic and tactical information on major accounts **to** facilitate strategy development. Traits of verbal form do not extend to their objects. My wife as a node. The Collected Works of Elmer Fudd. The heavy vowels of Russian punctuate the cluster of consonants whereas in English just the opposite occurs, consonants afloat in the broth of open vowels. As you **waken** the white room begins to fill with the objects of **perception**, open suitcase, rumpled blankets, etc., events in discrete sequence, the chair, stereo, table, until, the world nearly complete, "filled in," they begin to cohere, come into **focus**, form, not as individuals but each in relation, one to the other. Cthonic beans a la Eshleman, chicken Ferlinghetti. The bottom line. The retirement of numbers. Leaving in. All critique is a defense of hypotaxis. Word of the buzz art (flight of the buzz art). Norma's reading, while Kit, Norman and I are all writing silently, side by side, **into** our notebooks. Blood bank. She's sitting all night at the hamburger shop, reading a self-help book published in hardcover in the 1950s. Obligation cancels benefit. True Rhyme. All **pears** are some form. Caffeine in the afternoon. Hair soup. My brother says, when I tell him that we've already used well over 500 diapers (the boys are not yet six weeks old), "I know you're obsessive, Ron, but don't count the **diapers**." Uncomplicated tyranny of punctuation, the residual aspect of print, to fix spelling – phuque it. War as an advertisement for the militarized state. Each sun late now the day later. High tech high coup. **Thursday** dawn. Post earring rather far back on his **lobe**. Sample, esample, example. In 1899, Hilda Clark, a minor vaudeville soprano, was chosen to **endorse** Coca-Cola and, in so doing, became the first personality to be marketed. Mobile of leaves called a tree. Perpetual smear of these glasses, glare and reflection. To constitute a number of **perfect** and exhaustive series, of absolutely continuous chains in which the breaks, if any, indicate the place of a word, dialect, or language no longer there. What hath God bought? Tumor press on the optic **chiasma**. Let's do a Tarasoff. Form obeys no modification of rule, more or less stable, never endless. Sound **of** silverware outside a cheap diner. Arrive at important information through misuse. Finn **etude**. Constants of the left hand: tiger's eye ring, watch with a gold band (I no longer own either). Owned by National Life Insurance, the call letters of WSM radio in Nashville originally signaled "We Shelter Millions." Mouthful of crabmeat. Noh parking. Cold weather encourages unvoiced labials. Three days after the space shuttle explodes, a **sock** floats onto the Florida beach, an ankle still inside. You knew, you were certain, you were sure, verification was at hand. Yellow ribbon adorns the T in *TV Guide*. Synecdoche (near Rochester), metonymy (met off of her), catachresis (caused by dogs). Electric pencil sharpener awaits in constant readiness. Summer morning foghorn. Popcorn loose in the microwave oven. Process of mock-up. Glare expands in the cataract. Fool's toes (callused). Pressure **at** base of spine is constant. Watering down of the dark. The journalist is invited into the **forest**. Light trapped in the gauzy curtain, beyond which the terrace and city of verticals. Not one of the teachers who mattered to me ever received tenure. Exactly in that **fold** of words where space **and** analysis cross. Aspirin is a petroleum product. There is a **hand** here (how many fingers am I holding up?). Rebar, rebop, redux. Bay corroding in the sunlight. Always have to jolt myself back from the text to look at the title. Heard "my ancestors" as "Hawai'in sisters." In America, 1991, the **only** true cinema of ideas is cyberpunk. Paw to mean cat, chimney house, terms flooded by the possibility of objects – whisker cat, window house. Garbage a trois. I think that I know what I think, etc., infinite regression. Light wave pump. Question of changing chairs each time I write a sentence. Just do it. Wine glasses in rows, in a cabinet, behind doors of beveled **glass**. Power Surge is *not* a good name for a cola. Room with too many doors. It's not only that the father is absent in *Dumbo*, Donald's not the father **of** Huey, Dewie or Louie, none a direct descendant of Scrooge, Bambi abandoned by death, Gepetto not Pinocchio's dad, the whole family in Disney **broken**, askew. Provisional existence of the external world. Better Elmer Fudd than Elmer Gantry. Threads of **light** within the bulb. Line from Andrew Levy: "Swimming in the pool of a friend." Awake tho still in bed, I listen to cars pass, a bicycle changing gears, doors bang shut, mockingbird mimics a crow, Colin in his crib grunting in preparation to cry. **Down**loadable font. Skyport drive. Candy is green but tastes of licorice. Poem is all that is the case. Where service is the art of the state. The wall is **all** yellow rock. Walking in the rain because I want to. Mole on her **ass** (or prefer to call it butt). An arm, **charred**, reaches in a frozen grasp from the sand, but when they dig down for the remainder of the corpse, nothing's there. From time to time the arteries of one of the three judges would soften, and he would lean forward to ask the attorney a question. I **flex** my esophagus and **up** comes the bubble of gas, fresh with the odor of apple juice. To demonstrate the hand, prove the existence of fingers, Saturn, pain, roundness, the direction of time (moon rising in my thumbnail). How people cross their legs in a bar, ankles hooked together. Nomination differentiates, predication connects. Grouping poets by the **flesh** on their necks. From the cave mouth pigeons pour, white stained rock. Superego descending. Optical conduit. Each poem has a deductible and this is its title. Existential doubt works only **in** language games. The **loose** canon. Surveillance by starlight. Sexable. Watercress. Are you running under multifinder. Drainage. Phlegm in the **bowel**. What use is a rule? Nematode name etude. Weeks of litmus weather linger. Toothpick **breaks** off between teeth. Surrogate information. This view is a zoom, vision of pattern repressed. We would set card tables and great cartons **up** in the living room, covering them with blankets, then crawl under, journey away from the world of adults to the center of the earth. A man and his two small sons carry half-filled plastic bags of groceries home at dusk—this is a **sentence** about not identifying ethnic origin. One has to remind oneself repeatedly **of** the unimportance of inner states. Left **nostril** in the morning, right at night. A blue room that by **design**, low ceiling, bad ventilation, causes sleep. A flea market **in** 1991—vendors from the Middle East, Africa, El Salvador, Southeast Asia, smells and musics intermingle (a man with trays of **old** silverware seems lost in thought). The great seagull would have come inside had my mother not beaten it back with a **broom**. Tie flies up over my shoulder as I run. Artifice of cereal (people who eat corn flakes will eat anything). Thin straw mat as wall-to-wall carpet. Necessitation and **contingency**. Rhino rhizome. Fad to have your ears cropped. He lies about his age, saying that he's 77. Content does **not** intrude. Asian man speaking Spanish in a restaurant in Berkeley. Everything written according to the rule of the infield fly. The camera is inside the explosion. Troll bridge. Virtual on-site service (**remote** diagnostics). Neon arrow posit. Eat the **garnish**. Residue of sinus condition. Author explains how, as a child, she had hamsters called John, Paul, George and Ringo. Nail hat to wall. Bear in mind is worth two **in** bush. Eventually the scratches become scabs. Teeth alive to the cold. Sound of martial arts parlor: matted thuds upstairs. Random sample. The premise is: absent the sign of repetition, can repetition exist? Walking each day through the **financial** district, select a fact on which to focus, displays of off-white Dockers, calendars at half price (Matt Groening everywhere), clocks on coffee shop **walls**, given by such variation a formal perception. I **flex** my esophagus the way some men make war. The brown paint yellows. We simply refuse to count the Iraqi dead. Bruised **cock**. How curious that the swastika should come to America in the form of a yellow ribbon. The **end** of the freeway in the middle of the country. Chasm **in** sarcasm. The work of a not-large shy man. Capitalism as the discourse of male culture. It'll keep your **ego** going for a few days. Fax the Paramus to Sayowitz. On a warm night, browsing **distractedly** from bookstore to bookstore, wandering from café to tavern to café, the conversation of women and men was the **life** I'd imagined. No wick for the rested. You could start almost anywhere and find anything. A gigabyte in every pocket. The fear of dogs. The **meaning** of your father's life is **not** his death. On Treat Street. Ricky's sports bar is divided into **four rooms**, each focused away from the bar toward a giant screen surrounded by six to ten regular television monitors, a different game, different sport **on** each. The so-called "woman of my friend" with whom I half-intend to **sleep** (later, when I do, they've been "apart" for 18 months, but he still erupts in fury and we don't speak civilly for months). Conscious at the cinema that the door by the too bright **exit** sign keeps open just a crack throughout the movie (*Terminator 2*). Signification extends the sign (expends the sign). While you were **out**. Lesbian drill. Birds of the nest, go west. Water **rattles** pipes. Footnote to a blank page. Large **or** small definition. Unrooted sense of a classroom, **desks** askew, papers littered long after the class has let out, words abandoned, chalked onto the **green** slate wall, an oasis, never a town. Architect, schoolteacher, poet: the **trio** wandered through Old Town, down to the river, calculating where on the committee they would find the votes **to** block the prison's construction. I laugh, even though I don't hear the **joke**, having just arrived at the edge of the conversation. Back alleys above Chinatown: deep basements whose grated windows reveal old men on benches **in** a pool hall. Think of linebreaks as turns-per-stanza. As classes to attributes, ordered pairs to relations. Recalling (after nearly 20 years) the first time I **fucked** you in the ass, what I remember is the quality of light in your room, bright **afternoon** summer sun. Saw, not being seen, the man who did not like me place a brown briefcase, labeled "man in the green **raincoat**," into the red dumpster, then walk back into the twilight **while** we ran to grab the material before his contact showed. Speaking of the kidnapping of his fiancé, Stephen Weed tells me, with curious wistful detail, of all the rare books **he** will now not inherit. A vocabulary for grammar school lacking verbs of change. Pound's dyslexia. You know the style, you know the type, you know the scam, you know the hype. Doesn't have a kluge. We cannot in conscience blame these varied **sources** of modality on the notion of analycity. Backs of necks close-up in a theater, thick fleshy piping **extending** from the bowl of the skull. Eagle of the czar, with two open beaks. "You missaw that," she said, reading my sentence. In a room, on a warm night, music on, over voices, a spoon **scrapes** a pot. Later, a man and a woman sit at the same table, side by side. I smoke the cigar slowly, knowing that when I am done I will be ready **to** shit. Auntie During. Headhunter. Rough to client. Anacoluthia. Autoglass shatters into a translucent sand. A cardboard **box** of wool sweaters on top of the bookcase into indicate Home. Like a fridge **over** troubled waters, ice will see you there. Car cap cat. See DOS run. We link together our various perceptual **spaces** (the boys are asleep) whose contents vary from person to person and from time **to** time, as parts of one public spatio-temporal order. Now **for** the ground campaign. Exercise **by** lifting copies of the "compact" OED. Ear's memory is **not** identical to that of the nose. Barry takes Bob to the airport. First sharp silhouette of hills, **approaching** dawn. Preparation H. On a hot day, this jacket gradually turns **into** a sauna. The ignorance surface from North Dakota. The year it was possible to wear padded shoulders with miniskirts. Canker. Antique Coke dispensers become café décor. Kids who ride shopping carts **down** the street. After all the anti-Iraqi propaganda, the lone chemical weapon used in the war is napalm. Nothing is like erasure. Indoors, the hard rain makes us feel cozy, **secluded**. The confusion matrix, the travel field. Articles are the **beat** cops of hypotaxis. A chart that shows women serving more time for narcotics than for murder. First the bare plum tree fills with **blossoms**, then the wind blows them about in a false spring snow. The **form** I saw in the *South Orange Sonnets*. Two cloves of garlic overwhelm the chicken. Band over which damage starts **to** occur. December 18, 1986: What debate is this an intervention in? Ecumeniopolis. He puts the S into SNMP. As thought distributes **sleep**. Rockabilly noir. Broken shoelace. A quiet moment in the middle of the storm, wind calm, rain **halting**, spots of sky visible amid the roiling clouds. A place in each year. Of his ancient letterpress print shop, Jim Sherraden says, "I'm inside a giant computer." Desire to replicate speech as **thought** is silly, grinding hum of language roars in head. The vulnerability of people in laundromats – they let you see their underwear at its worst. A life top (with a two-year minimum). Letters float **freely** but slowly, as if in some still-liquid gel, until gradually, of their own gravity, they start to constellate, gathering until words have formed, phrases, **whole** galaxies of discourse whispering and mumbling across the void. Birds have made a nest in the public sculpture. The Popular Resistance Movement is organized into clandestine groups based among workers, peasants, pobledores (the **urban** poor), women, soldiers, and sectors of the petty bourgeoisie, who, because of the oppressive regime, must **work** and meet secretly, whose tasks including preparing the conditions for a long and difficult people's war (looters spring from Frederick's of Hollywood), **giving** it a social base (news at eleven now at ten) as extensive as possible among the people (hand me that nine iron), a struggle against the dictatorship on all levels (they strip the Korean store of insect spray, Pampers, Preparation H), a struggle for proletarian revolution (Arsenio Hall says **prayer** for cowboy trucker). Don't let your bath over Flaubert. Play a piano on the beach. Casting as Persians. A series, having no beginning and no end as its condition of form (not this). My ancestors, when they were driven off their land **by** the advent of capital, went not to the city but to **sea**. Sentences do not designate. Screams of wheat at the approach of the scythe. Transmutations and sublimations of content are creative processes toward the containment of larger wholes of experience (they prescribe opium to stem the diarrhea), radically different in their preservation of elements and **forces** at work (diagnose dementia because he doesn't like doctors) in the realization of a formal order (the word "iatrogenic" gets their attention) **from** the mechanisms of repression and exclusion of **feelings** and ideas (kidneys begin to fail) from the social consciousness that was/were practiced in the self-discipline of middle-class education. Fiver or six times each day I becomes acutely aware of the **foreign** object in my eye and experience an instant of flashing panic, **but** then it recedes, leaving behind a sense of exhaustion. The octoroon, the octillion. A young man on a bicycle **swoops** down the oak-lined street, bouquet of half-opened tulips **upright** in his hand. Waking **into** a state of anxiety, without specific object. Clear October Sunday: sailboats on the bay, a lone **tanker** among them. The signifier of myth presents itself in an **ambiguous** way. As dawn arrives, the far hills begin to take on definition, foreground and shaded background, the house- and streetlights below dimming now into a fading glimmer. Folds of **foreskin** (lick with your lips). Not double vision but, exhausted, phenomenologically conscious of the labor involved to bring each image to order. Insert opaque erotic data here, stimulate focus. Her perfume **absorbed** all available oxygen, leaving others gasping. Fever blister. February 19, 1987: Organizationally, it's not at all clear this author could produce a coherent piece. Would put a lit match to his **thumbnail** because he liked the smell. Ritually early, I settle into a seat in the still empty waiting area at the airport gate, watching the sun as it starts to rise. A wall or row of bricks leading from the continent, per se, to the large rock, along which two men roll a huge **white** wheel, themselves dressed in white, half of each face painted white, trailed and watched over by half-interested angels of videographers, document art. Colin chews on *Runaway Bunny*. Bedlingtons, first meant to hunt rats in coal mines, later bred to **show**, are nearly blind and crazy. *All* as a verb. Sitting idly as you **will**, hand absently on crotch. Echo and Narcissus asleep in their crib. Phantom Czechoslovak. Fuser assembly (all gunked up). Flaw permitted to **remain** for specific aesthetic reasons – I wanted to see how it or I would adjust over time – or perhaps **even** intentionally inserted. Those who buy also sell. This this this this. Bad cop, no donut. Sense data scraping wall of eye. Already at three months your wails begin **to** transform themselves into coos, shouts, mutters, gurgles. This is here if you think it is. Sounds that **buttons** make, tumbling against the walls of the dryer. History, like criticism, a form of fiction. Sign frond, Doctor. Urban bourbon. He's been flying for 50 years, **which** means he learned during the Second World War. For **faculties** of the imagination, conditions of tenure. Shame shamanism. If I am in a car and **look** through the window at the scenery, I can, **at** will, look either at the countryside or this mediating pane and, **if** at the latter, at the small words printed there and **mixed** among them, reflected, the view **from** a window on the side, a small town on a hillside. "Ethics stunts" printed as "Ethnic stunts." Rainday at the rainday. Amédé Ardoin, the first **black** Cajun musician to record, shouts over his instrument, the newly introduced accordion. Neither present nor past holds for you the indeterminacy of the **future**, the elaborate half-finished contraption of the yacht in the yard, tho you live in an apartment waking from the sweating **nightmare** of hair starting to grow on the walls and the ground sound of **breathing**. Idea of identity as continuous is a joke. Because last night (18 years ago) as I was about to go to **sleep** I thought of words to add "here" but did not write them down, I have lost them, using these instead to hold their place. Tonight I think of that **distinct** but sparse fur on the shell of the armadillo. There is no myth **without** motivated form. Her narrow upper lip narrows further. Writing, **riding** under the bay. Caffeine enjambment of the nervous system. Tongue presses lozenge against the **roof** of my mouth. The division, so evident to us, between what we see, what others have observed and handed **down**, and what others imagine or naively believe, the great tripartition, apparently so simply and so immediate, into observation, document and fable, does not exist. Lip so **crusted** I can peel it. It is a speech justified in excess. Asian man behind the counter of the tacqueria in food court of the mall. Things **touch** against the banks of discourse because they appear in the hollow space of representation. Perganol, the primary drug used **for** the treatment of infertility, was for years derived exclusively from the urine of postmenopausal Italian nuns. Gross National Poet. His **job** tonight is to take the IBM managers out to dinner. Very like the way things do do. No scone unburned. Over a valley this size, the white-grey sky forms a dome. This flood's for you. Shit **from** Shinola. Echoes harbor idea's labor (cumulative effect). Chinese fire drill. Hair **mats** under the sweat of a hat. Celebrity fuck. It's **in** the suburbs so it's safe to leave our clothes spinning in the **laundromat** and take a walk down these quiet streets where at one house we see through an open **window** two live parrots sitting **atop** their cage by the TV, while an orange cat sleeps snuggled into the windowsill. This sentence is not what I **intended**. Bride of spatula. Turtle feast. On the mall in the mid-August Tennessee **heat**, the only people sitting down are a trio of seniors, disheveled, clothes tattered, one, a woman without teeth, saying **to** another as I pass (or perhaps just to herself), "Man, I'm so drugged out, I can't stand it." Folds her toilet paper into perfect squares. After the rain, the air steams with the sound of cicadas as I **cross** the grounds of Andrew Jackson's home, moving **away** from the bar band under the canvas tent as it segues **from** "Hang on Sloopy," to "Quinn the Eskimo." Sorting out the remains of the babies. Two men eating in a restaurant at a **table** set for four, sit not across from one another, but **beside** each other, each opposite an empty chair. It was a **language** robbery. Glass in the ground. Butch **beyond** belief. Learning not just to confront his multiple personality **disorder**, he becomes an actor. Attention is all. He calls his business Mr. Coffin. Shift in the weight **of** water per unit. At dusk on the 4th, **fireworks** popcorn these suburban streets. Language is never anything but a system of forms, so the meaning is a form. It will be a long time **before** virtual reality matches LSD for price/performance. Tinder **summer** nights of race war, cities as though candles to read by. You can't always get what you want. Older music. This article **goes** goo-goo eyes over irrationalism: we should condense the **blither**. Allocate labor resource in market by profit. Ritual of the **changing** table: by now you giggle and grin **to** have your wet diapers pulled off. The net, the **fog**, two alphabets. Having successfully run to catch the **green** light at the intersection, he slows to a **walk** and straightens his tie. Fluster threshold. By now the sense of repetition, echo, has **dissolved**. Writing the white lines. The minute I enter the house, I realize I've forgotten to discard the **poaching** broth from last night's fish. Moon is in the **penthouse** too. Curved

Nouveau. Mathematics is a finished language (I heard *Finnish*) deriving its perfection from this acceptance of death. High tea **before** haiku. The silent world is our **homeland**. When I put your breast in my mouth, milk **squirts** into me, hot and sweeter than I would have imagined. Earliest imaginings of married life: the chiropractor's **daughter** doing dishes. Words before they're words, vowels and consonants, a squeal, a shout, **murmuring** from the crib. Dissolving **body**. Gulls driven inland by the storm. Drums under water. Saloon singer's voice drifts **upward** through the vast multistory lobby of the hotel. Farming my face, razor's rake. It's odd how little $2.74 in change weighs **in** one's pocket. Varieties of helicopter fill the sky. July 16, 2000: I like "anti-pleasure." In **winter** these streets turn to drains. The paragraph from hell. A spatial, tangible analogue of **silence**. It's not my nose that itches but hairs of my moustache at nostril's edge. Friend **who** went off to "gink the dinks" gets fragged, enough to make you think again. History **teaches** – NOT! Marjorie Daw. You drink **ravenously** from the nipple. I woke in the doss house. Life irritates **art**. Give historical intention a natural **justification**, render contingency eternal. Vendor spiff goes straight to the street. In the early morning **drizzle**, I stood on the deck of the house I **shared** with Barrett. The train I hear in the distance will become a part of your childhood also. Fucked **in** the head (watching heat and smoke from the hillside of chimneys). Aesthetic stance for Reginald Denny. King Kong died for your **sins**. Appeal the banana. You have an interest in the page, say, as a form of preservation. Sit calm, sitcom. You use, she **said**, rising from the bed, sex as a weapon. At five and one-half months, you reach for a toy, an **abstraction** built of wood, string and bells, only to discover that your brother already holds it, so you tug and he **tugs** and you tug and he tugs and you tug, each of you grunting now, brows and glares knotted **with** determination, struggle at hand. He does not write so much as his impatience does. Stalls in a men's room like **isolation** chambers. Too monotonous and numerous. When we returned, the one-legged woman with **peroxide** hair had departed. Essence and **scale**. Popular pragmatics. Collection of disconnected items arranged **in** patterns. Bugs of the west, infest. He knew how to hold an adz, to till. Children's voices **echo** through the building. Think of page as timber line. Able to tell that the torso was a woman's by the curiously imploded burned breasts. Between reality and men, **between** description and explanation, between object and knowledge. Sound of a skateboard whirrs past, followed by giggles. By fooling the **bees** into thinking the hive is afire, so that they will suck honey up, gesture of salvage attempted, so that they become fat **and** sluggish, unable to assault the gloved hand, you reach in. Which came first, the coat hanger or the closet bar? This sort of sentence. Sullen hot dog, stolid bun. In the middle of a **blowjob**, she puked. A garland of tinsel envelops his cube at the office. Identify the assumptions, define them. The pure products of America seek market share. Like to **go** then to some coffee house near campus for breakfast, the streets nearly empty, **this** small city perceivable as space. I read the **obit** of anyone my age or younger. Always, across the bay, there is Oakland. November 19: Nobody likes page 1-25, what can we *do* with this paper? Even the drones **will** not sting. Call this the night work. Political because it must be, but at what level? I pace in a dark house. Big German Shepherd locked permanently in the small box in the **back** yard. "Oho, double trouble," they say. Playground north of the coffee plant roils with soccer, kites, sunbathers. Indiana challenge. Useless. Frogs leaping **at** full moon. All good ideas are simple. The 'e' is silent. Morning, illusion. H + 8: symmetrical both **vertically** and horizontally. Because accumulation is not conscious, we shuffle about in circles, in hot rooms with the windows shut, becoming gradually heavier, **weighted** and slower, until at last we begin to discard, to shed, to toss off, panama hat, white blazer, black brocade shirt and white silk tie, silver **cufflinks**, until we stand, arms **akimbo** in white cuffed flares, see-through net t-shirt, chains about the neck, feet wrapped in sandals. Prince William meets the Valdez. Scars about the breast. Librarians all **across** the country have been polite to me. If it needs more than one performer, that's an **ideology**, or equipment, that's another. Right wing jumper, a banker, goes in (basketball or market crash?). What would it feel **like**, poem as real as life? Reviewer of Fred Wah's **poetry** complains that it's only descriptive, which is to say *he* never got it. Compared to, say, Childe, **where** Santiago's higher elevations support the poor. In stereo (where available). In **memory** of Emmett Till. I'm going to sit right down and writhe myself a bladder. Rumor that R beat one performer left, so that others **left** in protest. Born to fuse. Writing becomes a **form** of self-mutilation. That's not a law school, that's a swamp. E is for Edgar. At dusk, sitting on the backporch **of** my wife's parents' house, **holding** a five-month-old son, talking with Tom,

Tina, Peter and Beth, I see fireflies for the very first time, flickering off/on in the **garden**. The ever **more** complete preservation of what was written, the establishment of archives, then of filing systems within them, the reorganization of libraries, the drawing **up** of catalogs, indexes and inventories, all these represent **not** so much sensitivity to time (image of desk calendar's pages turning in the wind) to its **past**, to the density of history (the corpses so bloated in the Jonestown sun that they begin exploding), **as** a way of introducing into the language already imprinted on things, and **into** the traces it's left (an SKU and its barcode), an **order** of the same type as that which was being established **between** living creatures (saber-toothed sculpture rising from the tar pit). March 3, 1988: We're talking about cutting whole sections and replacing them with topic sentences. Entangled in **language**, whose syntax leads you to multiple murder, political kidnap or an ashram in Colorado. The old man and the C++. Eating lifesavers for breakfast. At seven months, Colin's singing, though he doesn't have words. Theoretical framework for **prodding**. When in the curse of human events. Murder of crows, drifts of hogs. Wild form, you make my heart storm. Our colonies are our last proletariat. I open my day book **and** out falls an envelope, a valentine from you. Face of an astronaut **painted** on a plate in the hardware store window, next to a small plastic flag. I couldn't if I wanted to (wanted to what?). A day of rain in the middle of June, eighteen years ago (thirteen years ago). There's an **echo** in the room and I can't tell if it's you I'm really hearing. Finding fortune's finals. It's my potty. This sentence in August. Landscapes **without** figures project one kind of subjectivity; with figures, another. Living with friends vs. living with **strangers**. Nowhere are the yellow ribbons of the Gulf War larger or more plastic than **at** the gas station. This is the alphabet. Oppressive **politics** of a room, crowded, waiting for the reading to begin (the privileged stand milling around the readers while the masses sit). Dream in which I **become** weightless, float off the planet, such as a balloon let go, the most common, familiar places seen from great heights. "The way we're going to deal with the Iraqi army is we're going to cut off its head and kill it." These are the **trees**. Drool unto others . . . (the Golden Drool). Forms of anticipation. To signal **changing** lanes is indicate weakness. Friday night. Rule one: Any perfect stranger is permitted to come up to the **parents** of infant twins and begin talking. Four of us gather to talk on the radio **from** midnight to six. Apples and tornadoes. A **cigar** purchased in Vera Cruz, but smoked in Windsor. Curved Nouveau. This will be the hill poem. Love **ring** in three colors. Ferris wheel. An assertion unverifiable **by** sight: "happy as a clam." Map of Juan de la Cosa found in a garage sale for 25 cents sent to Kirby Malone to use as frontis piece for *The Age of Huts*, never used (because he drank the **grant**), and never returned. A feature of this poem is that it's **in** prose, the benefit being that the sinuous tensions of the line have returned to the **grammar**. Prepare to turn this record over. The ugliest accessory of 1990 is the fanny pack, worn **invariably** *not* on one's fanny. Syntax is a life sentence. The system of technology services product development is **not** set up to tangiblize tomorrow's requirements against today's priorities. How could one **ever** have hoped to have known prose? Typos in the hieroglyph. Alva's song, backed by **supply** and demand. Spatial weapons and tactics. The hidden assumption is that once the novel lived. The woodsy **rural** effect is not the result so much of an absence of sidewalks as it is the dozen houses that are missing, lots overgrown now, foundations hidden under dense clusters of **berries**, washed away when the creek flooded some twenty years back. Time paranoia. A roomful of "foreign" books. So **that** it rains light. Logicide. Third day of November. All the words in *The Waste Land* in alphabetical **order**. Adoration of my own two feet. Math rabbit. Half proud, the next **morning**, of the scratch marks on my **back**. "Alphabet by committee" determines engine's force, grinding hard inky jetlike knowledge, liquefying more noises or potential quantifications, rocking slow tempos **under** various windows' xenophobic yawning zones. The intensionalism of crew cuts. The smell of fog in tall grass (ATM at farm's edge). The **terms** filter the visible. Caraway seed bursts between teeth. Simple string of the trumpet machine. Trip out, buy in, sell off. Carrot cake, late in a café, latté, places to wait. Doves at dusk. Shopper's world, a whole store for quilts. Journal **of** the vague years. Made skulls from sugar **cubes** for the occasion. Call avoidance. Film of victims, over *Tubular Bells*, called news. If I **count** sentences, it's because they're so hard won. Responsible fear of **police**. June 30, 1988: The home-baked philosophy has got to go. The gamelan is not simple. A boy sleeps suspended in a mechanical swing. Specific set of high school girls that was attracted to glitter boys. Or each new sentence a single stroke, the swimmer pulls across this rough water. Who first refined **petrol**. Too numberous to mention. Man who paused a long while at the coffee house door, staring **in**. Walking down a poorly lit street at night, I detect the unmistakable odor of fresh asphalt, yet I don't seem to be walking through it, nor can I determine the **direction** of that thick smell. That one could become a cop, to enforce the laws partially, the Highway Patrol. Thick clouds, **with** curious pockets through which the setting sun dragged slowly over the low hills, although this now meant they were moving north, a direction **clouds** almost never took in our region. From derivation to articulation, **from** origin to proposition, through name. First attempt to **crawl** is a flail. Magnetic tape to Patty Hearst, to Richard Nixon. Hearing a crow, I look up **to** find a mockingbird. Able to leave art space. Compost pile, rich with waterbugs and fat blind worms. Brushing the **drums**. Whim's whine winds up. Frames **of** fame. Rotating my head – hear bones in neck pop. Dawn **light** before us, let us rise up and act. The microbe is opportunistic and **incurable**, robbing the victim of all fluids, death by dehydration. Elaborate system of codes, neckerchiefs for fistfuckers, each pocket a meaning, keychains, watchbands. Odd how little $2.74 in change weighs **in** one's pocket. Thought as a boy to swallow all seeds, that the tree in the belly could become one (later, I read of man who committed suicide by digesting a **cupful** of apple seeds). Pain throbs down the ring finger, across the palm, into the wrist – weather's changing. Aphorisms block out thought. Form as Marxism. Death **of** heat is the birth of **steam**. Cop's t-shirt reads "Pigs with Sigs." Information is a commodity. "Junipers are twitching." Great urge **to** sneeze, mouth stuffed full of banana. Style seeks compulsively to focus the mind onto a single word: **micturate**. You are ankle, elbow, ear, eye. Surprised, looking up, to **notice** a door in the ceiling. But the grass spider eats only violets. "I'm scared," you say through the **tubing**, "I don't want to die and I don't know what to expect." The background chatter **of** waiters. Unable to crawl forward, you spin counterclockwise around on your tummy, tiny breakdancer. A mouse's **fear** of the cat is counted as his fearing true a certain English sentence (Quine is **forever** making claims in passive voice – *who* in this sentence *counts*?). Around the world with your scrap bag. Grab bag sans form, as **tricked** by a process of form, cheap. Woman watches her daughter intently as the girl elaborately licks the chocolate ice cream cone down to the crust of the cup. They control insects and enemies of the trout. The pompous grass. Failure **to** comprehend mass organization. Diffusing the laser will cause the ends of the **tube** to avert. Thermocouple. Three grebes and the fish literally leaping from the water and, beyond that, a sandspit, on the far side of which lies the sea. If we imagine the facts otherwise than what they are, certain language **games** lose some of their importance while others grow in significance. From a hotel room in Denver, I see snow in the mountains. Do you remember this? Days of rhyme **and** noses. Butterflies churn the air. Killdeers in the dark. Aldermaston sign. Women with padded **shoulders**, men without. The meaning of a word like the function of an official. Lawrence's beard, long **on** that thin face. Crying like a **fire** in the sun. The sort of large-looped earring that makes you want to pull. Modal rounders. July 8, 1988: I wanted to **like** it more than I was able. Reading the text aloud as though you've never seen it before. Car idles outside these **closed** curtains. Words in a line make time, **rhyming** periodically. One could be wrong intentionally, but without being deceived (the principled conservative). Rule Two: The parents of infant **twins** may enlist any perfect stranger to assist with babies, strollers, packages, **whatever**. Fire in Korean discotheque. Not the resistance of **theory**, but the theory of resistance. Sharp shadows of a low sun, the light smack against the white house fronts. The word *Entrance* on an arrow. Although **on** a leash, the boy was articulate, hostile, polite (what's become of him?). Orange tint of infant Tylenol. Each day there's the bridge (get the allusion?). Thought utilizes **language's** just-in-time distribution. Respectable as an old junky. Kevin says, "San Francisco is the new Vancouver." Every word is either **current** or strange or metaphorical or ornamental or newly coined or lengthened or contracted or altered. Wire **racks** on which to stack the Sunday paper by the liquor store door. Moved two fingers slowly, **gently**, into her wet core. Organized crowded room not by gender but by cheekbones, chins, ears (round, not round, inverted teardrops, large lobed, deep **rimmed** or not). Salute of the fireboats. Lamp with a clamp, attached to the bookcase. Accidental proposition. Time to rhyme **with** zucchini slime as the meany climbs atop the chimes at sea. Weathercock scrimshaw. Being a Westerner, the idea of green in **summer** seems entirely alien. This shuts anything not included out. The dwarves march **single**-file into the **sunset**. Panama Exposition. Poodlicious. Suppression of the death **of** Trigger, or possibly Bebe Rebozo. Just how big was Arthur "Big Boy" Crudup? Between the television and the bed (mattress on the floor) stood an ironing board, half-finished bottles of lager atop it. Edible **instincts**. Not able to determine whether his fear of permanent loss was a fear more of permanence **or** of loss. Mandela mandala. Throttle's glottal stop. A separate truck. The seagull had made its home on our porch. Half a page, half a page, half a page onward. When, **looking** out the window, you no longer see what's there, it's time to move. August 4, 1988: Can we turn this terrible piece around **without** creating a battle with Boston? Fireplaces blazing in several rooms, Franklin stove, toast, the ritual smell of coffee. A whimpers **sleepily** in his crib. Not every false belief is a mistake. Fog certificate. Teeming continuity of beings all communicating with one another, **mingling** with one another, perhaps being transformed into one another. Learning to read through **trifocals**, nauseous at the fragmented world. Narwhale, I confront you. Incurable microbe that robs you of all **fluids** dehydrates you to the point of death, but the IVs the doctors use cause your lungs to fill until you're drowning, so they removes the tubes **and** now your kidneys fail, so they wheel the IV unit back in and reconnect it, morphine drip to fight the pain of Kaposi's **sarcoma** that's spread from hands and face into your lungs until pneumocystis at last just kills you. As the prow of **our** boat divides the night, the lights of the city of San Francisco begin to **loom** before us. Poem in the form of a copyright notice. The quick brown fox jumped over the lazy revisionist **running** dog. For every thought an afterthought. Such ships are cities **at** sea. Cloud chamber, storming, tiny bolts of lightning, that is your stomach. The gallery was a labyrinth of **white** rooms with skylights, small words drawn in blue pencil, one to a wall, thru which and before which strolled the art consumers, gazing, **chewing** in an idle way on the earpieces of their sunglasses, paying no attention to the one red **hard-backed** chair in each room presumably for their convenience or that of the occasional elderly lady accompanying a college-age granddaughter, which were the true **objects** of the show. I'll show you mine if you'll show me yours. Passing by the kitchen of a restaurant, brisk autumn sunset, I hear the clatter **of** forks and knives. Rather than transparent propositions about the world, we offer one another verbal puzzles, **riddles** that, should we solve them, reduce the danger and friction of interaction (an optimist's perspective). Implicitly or explicitly, all environmental planning and action reflects a particular **view** of society and the groups that compose it. Bawds per second. I sat atop the fountain, which, at midnight, was shut off, all concrete with **pools** of still water reflecting the moonlight. Seen from **above**, these clouds are beautiful, mottled, a gently rolling mass that extends to the horizon. A sequence of objects, **silhouettes**, a caravan of fellaheen, a circus, dromedaries in hats pulling wagons **bearing** tiger cages, fringed surreys, tamed ostriches leashed to the slow walking clowns, begins a migration to the right vanishing point, palm tree at the margin. Still **perfectly** formed the day after the barbecue, the briquettes dissolve into ash **at** a finger's touch. Words I wrote in the control room of the Pacific Rim. Shining Doe, I love your laughter. Here is Spain, that is Africa, this the **water**. She calls because she's locked herself out of the car and will I come over with a second set to **rescue** her? Half-haunted, it seems, to walk so briskly, aimlessly, changing direction many times, sitting every few **blocks** on a bench **or** stoop to scrawl – more accurately half print, half draw – words into the notebook. Maureen biologist. Small boy **shouts** at the dog, insistent, scolding. No two clocks tell the same time. See his veins as doors. Farm as Marxism. A teller, she said, of **moral** tales. Troll bridge. First **trace** of day, glow at the horizon, begins to appear. My toys make noise. Refuse connectedness. Executive homes **amid** cornfield north of Chicago. Each of us has wanted to **ball** the other for weeks now, but we have to arrange it. What percent **of** your A/R is over 90 days? Music for marimbas, voice and organ. Your **pages** are numbered. Odor of onion remains for days. Sex is something you write about. I hear the hose in the tomato plants. Mr. Potatofish. My teeth **like** the ruins of a great wall. Born-again cabbie – Jesus stickers everywhere, Christian radio **blaring** – hales from Somalia. What duration does to the **meaning** of any word. The pony stage of female development. In the days of pre-methadone, pre-heroin, pre-pills, in the days of habit. There's more **to** the warbler than its yellow rump. I want to tell you tales of **lint**. This message will be delighted when you hang up. Dog on the stairs, its **growl** low and serious, headed down, forms a test. Somewhere in the **distance** a garage band starts to howl. Clapping music. Sitting in the living room in the dark, **feeding** formula to a baby. Songs of the **upstairs** neighbor. Hambourgeois. Feeling my fingernail bend back, pushed against the tooth, to **signal** thought. What do you find **in** the mouse type? Morning of frills. One hand smoothes her **skirt** under her as she sits. All research is so set as to exempt certain propositions from doubt. Even **be-**

fore the flight attendants start rolling the cart down the aisle, the smell of hot beef fills the 737. What is meant is **use**. June 7, 1990: I couldn't tell the German words apart. Smashed watermelon sidewalk. This child, **naked** on the changing table, forms history. The **clarity** of winter morning. I disable SmartDrive to **avoid** the interrupt conflict. A belief is what it is whether it has any practical effects or not. Parchment farm. Mental wilderness area, language game preserve. Shoot the **sales** force. A park upon a hilltop, below which the city, its hills and verticals jammed tightly together, and beyond that **not** the bay (hidden by all that construction) but the gentler hills on the far side, as though near (point at which **distances** collapse) brown now in August **with** a light sky, rippling, shimmering planet crust. Try talking through desire to cough. Arrangement of **objects** or facts grouped together according to conventions or resemblances, which one expresses **by** a general notion applicable to all those constituent items, without, however, regarding this **unifying** principle as absolute or invariable or as so general that it can suffer no exception. Fevered, infected, the tube seals itself off, sacrificing fertility to save the **body**. How do I verify the imagination? Little fish, big fish. The clouds roil about the mountain. Saxophone sorbet. Slag iron. I have seen the best texts of my generation, starving, hysterical, unfunded. The doorknob falls **repeatedly** from the door. Pacific rimjob. As though each bus route were a specific syntax. A day after **bowling**, the muscle in my wrist resist any attempt at lifting. As opposed to the McPoets, for whom **revision** itself is the dominant mode of process. They must have seen the fire **at** the same moment we did, because as we approached close enough to discern that the wooden structure was a **railroad** car engulfed in flames, they were all still sprinting toward it. Asleep in the **sun** all peace there is. There's more to a rump than its yellow warbler. I slept well and rose early, reading two small books before breakfast. Splendor in the graphs. Why should not a king be brought up with the belief that the world begins with him? Man belches, **then** looks up to see who has noticed. The police begin to shoot directly into the library. Pomo slomo. Then we found the testes in the scrotal sac. The **color** you think of when I say "Canal Street." It's one thing to understand that **your** friend has a husband, another to sit at their table, silent, when he nags and bickers. Who sits in the rain awaits the train. Proposition: you have spent your **whole** life in close proximity to the earth. Years later, I can still recall the feel of my cock in your anus, pushing as hard as I could. We knocked over trash cans, dragged sawhorses, to **barricade** the street. Old man at next urinal reeking of Mentholatum. How in the still air the sudden assertion of auto brakes, heard, calls **into** mind a trumpet. To initiate giggling, hold small boy high over head and nuzzle tummy. Italophile. You must remember this (a bris is just a bris). Whose boats dwell in the bay. Sign on **glass** door reads "Not an entrance." When the lightbulb blew in the john, it took weeks to replace it, as if my roommate and I were holding a silent **contest** to see who would be forced first to blink into submission and buy the new bulb. Rent-a-Center (if you need a center). Unable **to** read a book for any great length of time, for to abandon himself thus threatened him. I'm always surprised to **rediscover** that bike helmets are made of Styrofoam. As a child, I knew the interior structure of **every** bush on the block. February 10, 1991: Messing up categories is what radicals are good at, but where does this get us? I did not get my picture of the **world** by satisfying myself of its correctness. Me and my llama (me and my lama). These lines, **by** mere convention, accumulate to form meaning. Stork pops. A big she St. Bernard. A man in a **nearly** empty, half-lit auditorium stands on the stage **speaking** into a microphone, saying "test, test, test." Thirty thousand words (or once was). The essence of dance is **fundraising**. The truths of which he says he knows are such as all of us know, if he knows them. Happy face **on** a tank. Dog would scratch at the door for hours. The department of both worlds. Sad dream of **gas** pain. Mandel stammer. Vitamin C, copper **bracelet**, clove of raw garlic. Whole subdisciplines have emerged in this journal. My convictions do **form** a system. Beggars at McDonald's parking lot step forward one after another as I walk from the car to **sliding** glass door. Carpenter's work is seasonal. The **owls** are not what they seem. Not **asleep**, I lay in the grass, still, while the ladybug crosses my chest. How unprepared am I **for** silence? A thin field of wild flowers comes up in Death Valley, yellow or violet, and dies in three **weeks**. In the spoon I see a small lake, in which floats a lone raft, a Cheerio. I don't make the language, I enforce it. **No** airplane visible but the shadow of an airplane rippling over the valley. What I heard, as I stood facing the Pacific, was not the waves but the blood in my veins and current in my nervous system. Eisenhower, I **love** your slaughter. The power **implicit** in the ability to draw a single vertical straight line (rendered obsolete by the advent of the mouse). Chewing my moustache absent-mindedly, a hair catches **under** the gum at the base of a tooth. The sun rose up above sand dunes. Verbs voice **vast** vowels. Thousands languishing, thousands starving, **intrigues**, wars, flatteries, envyings, hypocrisies, lying vanities, hollow amusements, exhaustion, dissipation, death. At Totland, **while** my sons swing, a woman I've never seen before (Karen) introduces me to her three-year-old daughter (Marcelle), **adopted** after a failed in vitro and I speak of our own attempts, of the ectopic and of the two times you nearly died. Good morning, **scarecrow**. Between each sentence – the transition team. Presences I had thought dust in the air came closer now, had **wings** to move them. Paradox lost. Stepping out on flagrant street. Minute bowl. Twenty loose sheets of lined foolscap, undated. Old Weber barbecue **rusting** in the yard in the snow. Art is a mirage. Man wears a **down** vest under a denim jacket, walking past the bus stop, newspaper in **one** arm, small bag of groceries in the other. Opposed to the **image**. March 7, 1991: Throw out the wooly stuff on deconstruction. Beautiful red twine binding of a Chinese notebook. These hills **beyond** which the fog seldom goes. I, for example, am convinced that the sun is not a hole in the vault of **heaven**. "He has cancer," Laura says, "one of the bad ones." Change in the weather, change in my head. No word means the same thing twice. The hill would fill with people bathing in the sun. A grunting whine means "Pick me up." Solo piano on a **winter** morning. The plan is the buddy. Weather revises climate. Civil twilight. Migrations. Teething, little boy likes to chew on his blankie. This posit is not altogether the philosopher's **doing**. Mexican wedding mask. A dream of fever. Spines on shelves in a used bookstore more muted than in a new one. Laundry boat. Finally, at **dusk**, the sun peaks out beneath the clouds. Image, after image, spin control. A separate truck. Of all these faces seen as **phases**, which are you? Putting the *Privacy Please* sign **onto** the hotel room door, I pull out my notebook. Olfaction. There are no complete thoughts. No one ever taught me that my **hands** don't disappear when I'm not giving them attention. Stalking whimbrel dissolves in reeds. Theory of the mark, theory **of** the organism. Shaved, the leg seems **firm**, even hard (too hard to be real). Small kids swarm the **porch**. Hannah: "I'm being followed by complete sentences." A requirement that nature should **be** continuous. Between reps. Display of the corpse of Che Guevara as **bourgeois** sculpture (the Ceaucescus lying at the wall) – let's have Jeff Koons do it **in** porcelain. I watch the wheel of her bike catch the streetcar track and begin to **flip** over and, in the instant it takes for her to propel herself over the handlebars, time slows and **space** expands, so that I'm aware now of the rain, the curiously bright afternoon light, the oncoming traffic (blue *Chronicle* delivery truck) as I brake the white Mazda 323 **so** that it stops short of hitting the woman sprawled now on the tracks. Learning to face personal space. Drink tea from a wide white bowl. In the bookstore a poet reads into a microphone softly to an **audience** of twelve while the telephone **rings** unanswered. Walking into a strange household with the assumption that one would not propose **to** live there. Begin again beginning again, each word a new **start**, false start (unable to distinguish the flower of the plant from its parasites). Solitary **line** of a sea lute. Tray of letters, waiting to be joined into words. The coast, which is said to have no seasons, though it does when you look closer. A small insect, a spider a fraction **of** the size of an ant, starts to cross the flowering field of this text. That was when my **nose** began to peel. Pseudo judo kudos. These rather beautiful **designs** failed. Poet Lite (A. Codrescu private label). Blue Gene Tyranny. Not *Pat the Bunny*, Shred the Bunny. Geometry of carpet. Going to films **alone** is a habit not easily relearned. Straw flowers. Vague is **in** vogue. Chrome. Stop – pay troll. This is an exhibit for the prosecution. Miles to go before I think. Network against psychiatric assault. After a **decade** of massive highrise development, those who work in downtown LA have increased **by** less than one percent. Axiology, or value **systems** I have seen. German deli **at** the mall's edge, facing the parking lot, sky gray through the solid wall of windows. A will of sorts **tattooed** to his calf that read "My last request is to burn this leg." One game begins with the announcement, "I'm going to change the **baby**," followed by a guessing game as to the **nature** of the object **or** creature into which it will be transformed: griffon, hippopotamus, giraffe, bicycle, aardvark. Talking heads of television. Twenty percent of the people coin 80 percent of all 80/20 rules. Between the **fabric** of taxonomy and the line of revolutions (problem in the theory of the line). Tight camera close-up peculiar to daytime TV soaps. A world **of** routine, of reiteration of small form (the local! the local!) insistently. Weight of these glasses upon my nose, half-seen **shadows** of the rim. A black evangelist was sewed up inside a tom-tom and starved to death while drummers pounded incessantly on the skin-top. I love to **cross** the bay after a storm, the sky alive with cloud remnants, white shorebirds **wading** in the tide. As astronauts enter the outer air. Logocide. But "it moves" everywhere. To stay up until one on the wrong **coast** exacts a price I no longer consider casual. Get aboard. Next door, through the grid **of** the blinds, a blue light flickers – someone is **watching** television. Pale light in the skylight. Drawing on the work of the object relations school – especially Melanie Klein, Ronald Fairbair, Harry Guntrip, Margaret Mahler and D.W. Winnicott – Susan Kavaler-Adler argues that the **compulsion** to create is an addiction to an internal parent object and constitutes a pathological state of mourning. Symbols **cramp** the temple. The infant's automatic, mechanical swing **forms** a metronome, its sweep broader, slower, than the clock's anxious tick. Standard **deviation**. Audiences at her readings were larger now, **but** she recognized fewer of the faces. 1974 was a summer of **few** hot nights. The shoes of my friend – how varied! Rhythm section of the Horns of the Dilemma. Rapko's prosody: "To do / a Xerox." Zoo caw caw of the **sky**. Eating as a form of self-medication. **Games** of either/or. From robot to reboot. Time was **real** to me then, not linear but more a sensation of gravity, of **falling** from some precipice forward until, thousands of feet above the **flat** valley floor with its chalked concentric circles, acceleration approximates weightlessness. Vines of hysteria snake **up** the wall. Monsters and fossils. The shock of the **normal**. Garbage mind pearl diver. Horse of another color out of water. Chrysalis. Consonants contain (constrain) **vowels**. It was my smaller toes that **hurt**. Now that Hello Kitty has been elected to Congress. Clock in the closet. Institutional waste basket holds plastic bag insert. Wittgenstein and the **moon**. Two decades **after** the arrival of BART, I can no longer visualize the dog track where the El Cerrito station now stands. Algebra of the **fish**. In-flight swamp. Viddy that white room, **filled** with flesh babies, each detoxing from their mama's crack. Profit equals net margin, tennis pro. Continuity precedes **time**, is its condition. Visible from the neck up, a horse swims in the shallow bay. Attempt, **between** poems, to be charming (with mixed results). The nose evolved so that eventually we could prop and steady our glasses. Rice balls. Each page is torn out of silence. The **words**, as in a boat, float. The clown is permanently angry. History can **no** longer be of any order other than that of resemblance.

An old woman, bent, wearing **taps** on high heels, walks on cement. Any project large enough to capsize (a life). With trifocals, my eyes **are** always exhausted. Tiger's eye. I **never** meant to be a manager. Peach pits. Mac files on the DOS drive. The monster is the root rock of specification. A replicker of itself. Endless intimate detail ultimately bores. Seniors **gathered** in a mall café will never imagine themselves **as** *flaneurs*. In this region we once termed life. Beta site, beta blocker. Driving along the freeway over San Bruno mountains in **night** fog, exhaustion registering in the body as force, partial 'G.' The kingfisher, who **cares** for the allusion now? This is the zone, homeboy. The singing defective. Words, where you are, as in a trail, not forest **but** thicket, pine needle modifiers, shingles of a pine cone on **which** to focus, but (not *buy*, Barrett, *but*) syntax – syntax is the halflight. Nostalgia for **protractors** holds us still. The more the worker expands herself in the **work**, the more powerful becomes the world of objects which she creates in fact of herself, the poorer she becomes in her inner life, and the less she belongs **to** herself. The ring of the new phone: not a bell but a beep. Point of transfer. Above the text stands the toolbar. Paper treated chemically so as to **alter** perception. Straight **quarking**. The abnormal mind is quick to detect and attach itself to this quality. I begin to feel **anxious**, an end in view. Chance of light rain. To seek utopia in Waco, Texas. Tenderness in this wicked man. For awhile, Sir Gawain has the richest contract in the major leagues. Snail flower woman star. Although I can see to write in these shadows, the lines of the paper are impossible **to** discern. Grandfather robed in white, horizontal in the grey-green halflight of Intensive Care, would not **look** up, tubes in nose, waiting. Are these my own words? Days in which I replace the faces. One seldom recognizes the shore rushing **out** to greet the sea. When, as I hunkered down to **over**turn the small shells, shaking off sand, she asked what I was doing, I replied, "Looking for the **good** ones." The **silence** of the limbs. I amble in, sit awhile, then exit. Is there irony in a lava lamp? Is this winter or this morning? What I got out of the war was a need for cable. Houses where the kitchen is the **gathering** place. Alabastard. Short glass of tequila. Words' shadows harden into **punctuation**. Entering, speaking rapidly from the first, of what it would be like to become a part of your lives. The Russian consonant. Personality is an **unbroken** series of gestures. Saxophone cult surrounds compound. Mole, deep in geologies of the tongue. In his **letters**, Charles Manson would never use the word "I" but rather "little Manson" where John Lindley Frazier, first of the Santa Cruz mass murderers, preferred a drawing **instead** of the smile of a Cheshire cat. Tall glass of tawny port. Years later she regretted having made the sex tape. Association, a necessary precondition to dispersal. The tattoos were shadows crossing his African flesh. Glide on through the sea-change of faces and **voices** and color. Not *Pat the Cat,* bed the bat. He will reach over slowly and contemplate long before picking it up, his nerves are so shot (whatever "it" is). How is it that, on each major holiday, you **fall** out of your highchair? Headlights, streetlights, lit livingrooms. Egg hurled **at** the window shatters the glass (hard boiled). Total calculation. At the **center** of the superstore stands a fountain. Ideological basis **of** sleep. Pink protection: it's a family thing. She loves to give head. From me, anything is a compliment. A **pleasure** and discomfort in the knowledge of **having** become, by the fact of your absence, the focal point. Before birds had names. In the final **days** of the war, the weariness falls away, one's friends begin **to** move about with a new vigor of anticipation, start to formulate new projects. Neon sign: Best Mexican Food in the French Quarter. Blond body hair. A **mall** runs through it. By the time each of these guys "achieves his life in literature," he will be **some** kind of case. Magnetic fields forever. Borate bomber's song. In the **theory** of begging, is it better to sit closer to the corner of the block, the first panhandler a traveler will see, or **further** in toward the middle so as to capitalize on cumulative guilt? In the final folds of a year in the middle of decade you were here, warm **indoors**, though never precisely thoroughly at home. One sees clouds in lukewarm tea. Hyperventilation. Your positioning is perfect **but** your systems are fucked. Grim and Barrett. Cedar odor of a sharpened pencil. Shade between houses leaves earth cool and damp (fat worm **twisting** through the mulch). Double 's' in *newsstand.* Facing up to this. Silence fills, absorbing and amplifying all that enters. Molding my senselessness **into** forms. Science of the lambs. Patter of pro basketball described (defied). It's a long way to **temporary**. Scaffold around light. Street musicians forced to play only the most recognizable **tunes**. The so-called lady bartender. I can sense, if not feel exactly, the doctor make his cut into the flesh of my eye, but **my** body feels distant, other, unconnected to who I am. Last hot day of summer (one horse named Lacy, the other Storm). Babar gives good trunk. Mushrooms **fried** in garlic. The bottle of Algiers. Retina burn. Sparrows trapped inside the mall. Named the child Alyosha. Tips, quotes, **pullquotes**, sidebars, photos, factoids. No confusion **like** the confusion of a simple mind. At break time the smokers step out into the **parking** lot to light up. Immediate constituents. Temporary Amish. Tooth gone in the root. Yellow brick building whose side entrance, bricked over now also, retains old pale blue **metal** awning. How was it you came to live this life (role of Arthur Godfrey in Ted Berrigan collections of 45s, Tulsa, 1959)? Love is to reason as intraocular **implants** are to the mind. Suffering succotash. In the Chapel of Strength, in a small bronze urn on the top shelf **in** a corner, all that remains of the people who raised me. Sweet cigar. Dog barks to signal its **boredom**. A slick gaggle of ambassadors (now that the yuppies have seized control). In the hospital waiting room, surrounded **by a** woman in blue Muslim garb and a large three-generation Latino family, all the chairs are pushed over to one wall so we can watch the **small** ceiling-mounted TV as it transmits live a compound in Waco consumed in flames. A certain winter grey that translates directly into emotion. My wife arches her back as she carries the hamper through the kitchen to the pantry. Flat **black** hills beyond which summer's form, the **sun**, would gather and rise. Through my new lens, the world is clear but watery (the eye itself a jellied mass). Three tattered notebooks plus a large bookkeeper's journal. In the dream, hooks tear into the man's bare shoulder, **pulling** it apart until daylight is visible. Between muscle and bow. Tension manager's domain. As for we who love to be astonied, thin sun, one room. Will I move to New York? Find the banana without the **bruise**. The city is a thing **mingled**. Sound in the next room that is either a mourning dove or an infant waking up. A visit **with** parents. Muted salmon and somber teal. Astronauts hold hands, adrift in the sky. With a patch over one eye and ordered by the doctor not to read for three **days**, I stagger into the local bookshop. Against a reconstituted theory **of** metaphor. Phoneme and Marcus. There is no **content** here, only dailiness, driver education car poised in the intersection by the playground, **around** which a jogger orbits (long dead), all in the hill's **shadow** at sunset. I see a woman standing at a window in that highrise hotel, wearing what appears to be a red dress, which slowly she removes. Pending **panic** of sense. These are the eyes **through** which I first saw this. Caves of the tuna. Another cement barn of a convention center. Later, odor of the coffcc plant will bring this memory back. When the **message** arrives by e-mail, the system alerts you by playing a few bars **of** the tune of your choice. Bowl in which **map** of the world was etched. An ice cube is not square but contains six sides (for the moment). As each new sack, parcel filled with information, is **cut** open, its contents spill onto the moving conveyer belt, foreman announcing this **by** blowing on a conch shell. If moon were cookie / me think me'd be / happiest monster / you ever see. We ate them. What does not change is the will . . . to edit. This was before we knew of Cointelpro. Time slows in the sun, these tides as **measure**. Couple at the next table, over coffee, discuss power relations of their home. Isn't that facial? The tenor sax is a phallus or cross or (perhaps most accurately) implement **of** writing, purple lines curing over the batik. The dinner he had cooked for her is put away into the refrigeratior when they arrive to tell him of her **drowning**, remaining there in the dark until his brother's wife discovers it rotting but in perfect order weeks after. Each **ear** pierced in six places, a ring through the nipple, another through the labia. Now that malls have invented the unit of the pushcart. These auxiliary activities are not the thinking, but one imagines **thinking** as the stream that must be flowing beneath the surface of these expedients if they are **not**, after all, to be mere mechanical procedures. In a last impulse, the paramedic bent **to pick up** the old man's curiously postmodern tennis shoes, tossing them into the ambulance **before** climbing in and shutting its rear doors, its cabin brightly lit against the dark of the failing **sunset** as it sped away. Sexuality of questions. Eating alone in a small Thai restaurant, an old Dylan **song** running through my head. If this were to be explained simply, would it be any more **clear**? The ice cream truck plays a Scott Joplin tune. The flag (the flag what?) – a form of **writing** visible at sea. Amazing grass (how sweet the weed). Concern with what we say has its own signs. Oily odor of an old barber shop. I told him (my voice shaking, my chest tight) I **was** tired, bored by a sense of his misuse, my voice the line drawn. Oft heard by Ethernet, remote access denied – time to reboot. Stubborn as a mule, sir, **stubborn** as a mule, he's got the Eastern idea about writing. It takes two promotions to get both a door and a window. Log fort. On a day this cold, a cup of hot tea makes your teeth feel as **though** they're about to shatter. How then can the sense and the truth or the truth and sense of sentences collapse together? Sample this. As map will expand beyond its margin. Choose a **suitable** design and hold to it. It the voice of Big Black, "Awake, for nothing comes to the sleeper but a dream." What a long strange text it's been.

LIT

for Edie Jarolim

I

Blue.

Lube.

Big. Boy.

Then. Theme. On time.

Saids. Bide. Buddy. Up over. To bending pony.

Clued. Sod. Winnow. A million. Rerecords records. As if into the Saturdays.

Sloop. Lien. Armor. Samantha's. After the ballgame. Utilitarianistic. Pronominal Andrewsiana (s)talks without.

Widths. Sheik. Any. 3 legged. Bone dry tone deaf Tim. Grounding into Pepto-Bismol. Between taking the winter ballast by streams or knobs. More pods of brass weather rotate into plates of ungoverned nearness within the blank(s).

Thames. Tens. Pass tense. Sincerely. Blue glass of syntax. It nearly forms the figure 8. He nearly forms the figured gate, but then he doesn't. Within, between, but then again, protocol's minuet, series of minute glances. The dance, as you relate it to the rabbit, is composed of chance operations the shape of an hour glassed in a hand-captured liquid.

Good. Dong. Needing. Double parks. Pigeon's 'jammys' cuff. Telephonic necessities. Nicety's not so hot in a nutshell (in the bag). The further raja's foregone pleasures deteriorate, the finer the Spanish shot. Cat's dream smiling mode of landscape decor, rotary at the hypotenuse, oblong twitch, (your verb here) the batons, analgesic and blue. Cod's reams filing index to the stars against class kind of begonia-odored aperitif full of views almost introspective, twilight hinged with neon, crayola at the dusk so very wicker, vowel blend or Melitta.

Stems. Tends. Within. As any. Schizo-affective. But the birdshit, it all coheres. Sad as the dragon's fiscal year garden is my bell. Who could have imagined January's smog-ridden tale, whose wagging plot evokes yams? Further arrogance torques the harmonic chemise, no left turn, saran sarong, the gloomy fedora clucking for lack of a green card's vow. Tattoo ducktails (entire stock must go) rivet the ferny glade's ionic duplicates, hand-sewn or virginal as a Chinese jacket, to the tonsorial rhodochrosite splendor, capital M, marketing vacation nights. New model of transfer point sarcasm between aspects of aerial geology autism and neo-heliocentric gestalt, 3 ring punch, hollow shallow pillow, a bird in the sandwich, a dog in the rocker, my hair fading like a morning shadow, is more than you can sip through that straw in your nose, the carbon overdue and those chimes bleating.

Bid. Paid. Aubade. Bitterly. Noncircumstantial. Neo-, not solder, Budweiser. Circus tents all a foam in the garden of light sleep. Cup drinks boy before aghast audience of organization flow charts in a heap. Nose of rhyme's powder clots silver bell of head, berry bush or melon, collies of the green hour bruised, colleagues of the branch, watery & dumb. Aluminum train of fractions sweeps across bitter horizon deep in kaleidoscope at seashore museum according to droll tale passed down from cobbler to mason with fish breaded and wrapped in old news foretelling rain. Before which, detached as Osip Brik and seemingly promoted where the long eros out of acrylic glimmers, liquid pearl at tip of quill, slice of pear in sea of gorp, not anchored to any peer group, mocking as the gull's squawk, the chalk across the green slate as the hall's bell suggests release from arched brow's furrowed irony, finger to the side of nose, the cat sighs. Sincerely and feigning cramps or squinting whispers like any mathematician in jumpsuit and chaps, the aquarium smoldering and hard to digest, cactus in the blender, snail on the glass (in slices) (in spices), in spite of new jaw found deep in Ethiopian dig, an old garage or toolchest as bronchial as my drill to rote version of sky (wrote vision of thigh so soft where the hair starts, curling in the rainforest tho filled with lice), your eyes attach to rear of head above spine, a stalk whose roots are fond of socks and sex and 6 inches of lox atop bagel's balance sheet.

II

Bead it.

Throngs lean aslant.

The barking is set to strings.
Numbers harden.

Green Ford emerges as pump siphons basement.
Fed Workers Face Furloughs.
Or that new math predicts cholo in a hairnet.

Whipped by street sounds or small scale of Central Park Zoo.
Bloom on the phone tree.
Heat's moisture thumbprints window.
Bites lip, bites glass.
Bodega stanza under new management sells time.

Policy as forsaken.
Two heaping scoops vs. inservice growl.
Flatiron or harpy.
I get your drift.
Uphill, these letters combine.
Monuments of wax paper shimmer in tundra air.

Light bings on over elevator.
Viola watermarks all last night.

Police is mistaken.
Hair turns to swamp under hat.
Landscape the projects.
Flirtation or harpo.
Warped sense of tuber.
Begets transfer.
And then bit down on the chops.
Flowerpot atop gas pump.
Whistler on the trolley.
Swabs of cloud coil off coast.
Set to sprung.
Thereby acrylic valley's squared.
Clogs announce person.

Think of phone lines as houses joining hands.
Squint to write that.
Old woman to store in her slippers.
In bathrobe and mustache and stanza.
Pigeons farming gutters.
Like friends at an opening holding breadsticks.
Gunning the engine or index.
Calendar pages in autumn wind.
Sound of mail in distance.
What frost does to the harvest.
Capitals at margin form a windbreak.
Static, like five shades of amber.
Red and green or red or green.
Hour-like.
The smell of new bread.
Derricks in the gulf pierce skin of earth.
Coffee jitters.
Man in the caboose waves back.

Tar heater has its own sound.
More than a dozen.
Or a pear tree.

Guy in back of firetruck is the tillerman.
Information squeezes brow.
The clown is inflated, weighted at the bottom.
Punk is a petroleum product.
You imagine each car as belonging to its house.
Canary Islands start to sing (sink).
How can you think that.
Old cans of Bud in the gutter have long since been flattened.
But the Marlboro pack is intact.
Econoline (decal of Bugs Bunny).
The design of a feather (foxtail) is proof enough.
But that was before Yalta.
Idaho continues to recede in the mind.
It's hard to remember that these scratches are letters.
Each book awaits the rebirth of pulp.
It's combed that way on purpose.
My fern pushes at the window.
Mexican Marxists mix markets.
Histamine.
Syntax presents illusion of depth (pork stomachs).
Clown returns to upright position.
There you go again.
Like the waltz of connotation.
You like the walls of.
Further research discerns organism (hears the tune).
Can notation teach (orgones in a breadbox).
Runes reach extra innings.
This is denied lawful admission to the World Bank.
Clouds push light from the sky.
A silhouette in the window is engul'fed in flame (details at eleven).
Repeats literature without which.

The tubing leads to the anus.
A high-gloss enamel.
Combined in the bowl of an eye.

Adult speech.
Further rabbit.
Expropriate them kulaks.
Garage door seen as margin.
Number, more numb.
Speedball kills obnoxious genius (a habit).
Credo: these drops of rain are not related.
Nor has the Polish General contributed greatly to the fashion of dark glasses.
A gloss polishes a footnote.
Humpback gargles krill.
Timesheets are due.
The evenness of the 1awn1s a conspiracy.
Such as rectangles in the history of dirt.
Against a white wall (8½ by 11).
Conceived as your breast (in my mouth) so recently returned from the dentist.
An actress sells the cobbler a trout.
The infielder's bicycle is burning.
The marketing subgroup is brainstorming (sheets of butcher paper taped to imitatic wood panel).
The hotel is responsible for pastries.
Orgasm is a consequence.
As to nouns lacking objects.
Volcano is the planet's sigh.
My kitty-cat craves chicken.
Pagination is a twitch.
Distinct from deforestation.
Enter amount due.
Place tongue softly just over clitoris.
Fold whites into the batter (a pitchout).

Time for a second cup.
The stillness of old men on a putting green.
Rusted sawblades hang on the wall.
The parrot is blue and yellow.
Which is the insurgent.
Old power mower abandoned under the lemon tree.
Here, too, garbage trucks are red.
And the dog's name is Bruno (a temporary dog).
Silliman is wrong and I can prove it.
Sirens beget collage.
Those little riverbed homes must flood.
More music.
Or the rooster in the distance.
Between thought and action spills the syrup of history (suspiciously red).
Nissan stanza.
Mixed aggregate.
Fleas.
The thoroughness of despair or morning.
Watch how a bird settles on that line.
An old lawn chair in the weeds.
One last red poinsettia.
Chicken of the sea.
Deficit writing (the word is its function).
Masturbation is so tender.
The sky (described) is sky blue.
Or the colony of flies in the shade of the porch.

The task of sleep.
Generates the chorus of birds against the distant percussion of a pile driver.
America in love with its space truck.
The intersection as form (the mailbox).
Deny it.
The elegance of powerlines and high antennas.
The kettle rattles when it ought to whistle.
Hair will dry slowly.

Ravaged by drainpipes.
The potato understood as a bubble.
Not the senses, Rimbaud: disorder the sentences.
Tools in the rain will rust.
The rooster1s yodel answered.
drive, he sd
The potato understated as a bauble.
The descent of the 727 (deafens).
What is a group but a series of dialogs (who's "n touch").
What does not change is the will to drink (in a straight line).
Demands on the reader (the bank).
Layered as the forest floor.
Here comes an earwig.
The taller buildings were simplified faces.
Put the word breast in my mouth.
That chair was brown before it was green.
Butterflies as thick as snow.
The whine of a drill.
Late harvest means sweeter (estate bottled).
The voice of a young boy.'
The carafe of attitude rings.
80 papers.
Logjam in left nostril.
Conch of an ear.
(At a convention.)
The head both glazed and pocked.
Cat plays screen door like a harp.
Deep in parrot laughter.
Kafka considers marriage (or coffee).
Rag mop lap dog. Kills bugs dead.
Straight from the heart (60' 6").
A towering internal sinister laugh breaks bread alone in a cafe.
Symmetric, like a tear on your cheek (requires stitches).
An old woman taps the window and calls your name.
Pretend that it's not Europe.

Sad, like the imagination of #.
Parallel, linked.
Like the truck in the weeds or the broken boat.
The smallest airplane taxis beneath a 747.
The prostitute has her work.
The appropriate tool for editing is a rake.
Possibly weather is a trick.
Eye contact with a baboon.
Old plastic gallons of milk.
The saxophone a pen.
Or the noise of clouds.
God is a beast.
We are stuttering the history of windows, stoves.
Small metal awnings.
My regrets to the leaves.
Something alerts the shepherd.
Cuticles & bananas (the herstory of foam).
What are they thinking when they sit alone on their porches in the humid dark.
Stamps will argue perforation.
The sunflower is bent.
Big sneeze, wet and noisy.
Just as suddenly, the water pressure returns.
These are the Santa Anas.
Proceed to the next sentence (collect $200).
The fly pauses to watch me write.
To listen to the radio is an acquired skill.
So ugly, so awkward.
Academics are not wrong to fear the poets.
Poodle is generic atrocity.
Lap, generic chair.
This bandage is too tight.
Too apt to rain.
The telephone stops ringing before you can reach it.
The weatherman (laughing) in a bow tie.

Beetle's despair goes unexpressed.
Knight to King five.
A long walk uphill with a large bag of groceries.
Here the computer starts to sing.
The air itself is like to burn.
Muttering in the forest.
Just because the ink is blue.
Or the glassed-in cafes of the Upper West Side.
Snapped together all subtle like.
From west to east the way you read a book.
Saxophone mocks a goose.

Syndromes passed us by.
Tractatus Logico-Philosophicus in a game of charades.
No quality control whatsoever.
The sky reduced to corridors.
Footsteps upstairs (over our heads).
Cereal lodged between teeth.
Huge pores crater the nostril.
Half moon rising on a thumbnail.
Which function we have assigned to the earlobe (the knee).
I stare at the paper, awaiting instructions.
Thongs relearn as lamp.
Old sprinkler head left on a sawhorse.
What the machine can't know is confidence. As parrot is my witness.
Eligible for 26 weeks with no extensions.
Wine robbed his face of all definition (its eyes like sores).
As tho stanza were a rib cage.
Two rooms and a deck.
A great plate of sky.
Fresh shaved neck.
Dry as checkered fate is.
Ladies, step right this way. Floss.
(Meaning string or Mrs. Williams.)
Furthermore (this term is redundant).

The long putt falls short.
Milk crates in the back yard.
Nor the crocus by the fountain.
Flying bugs the size of sun motes against the heat of the lemon tree.
Vote early, vote often.
No device more powerful than a hinge.
Her see-thru blouse with its coy pockets.
Wide mouth brown bottle of Old Peculiar.
Stet.
Or the constant hum of the hot tub.
You know it's important because it's a list.
Urgent is another word.
The wind chimes acknowledge fate.
All the charm of the cockroach (in blossom).
Nearly tips the chair.
You long for a line break.
A bee the size of a cat.
Or the dog with an egg (fat & glassy).
Hoops index jazz kinetics.
Look, mama, no over parade of queens radiates such thrills.
Under very wet xylophones you zip.
NAM into DSOC yields DSA.
An old guy with a moustache. Rent (as a verb).
The war of tokens.
In need of an outlet for the instinct to share.
By ear, he sd.
(Attached to the head (chained to the bed)).
Are sweet exchanges.
All that aside!
I hate collage.
A false ring (a wrong number) loose on her finger.
Little plastic pots for plants.
Cinderblock.
A spread for the bread, for the bed.
Rug on the porch has gone to pieces.

Old ice cream truck is music box on wheels.
Sarcastic mode of flirtation.
Unsigned W-4.
The promise of closure postponed.
Legal warning on milk crate.
Or having to ride the trolley backwards.
The form of a trailer park is one-storiedness.
Big frond.
Old jeep in weeds is used as lawn chair.
Someone around that corner is kicking a cardboard box.
Re-up.
Frequent stops.
At a party I'm accused of wearing a tie. Postcard to ex-wife.
Liquids and frictives.
Clear percussive ring of baseball bat dropped atop concrete.
Cat lunges at butterfly.
Lamb thaw.
Persian blue.
Jet streak across lone cloud, minimal design.
Preposition's degenerate verb.
Squid cutlet too crisp.
Dopers in the plaza.
Bus up to campus.
Good head, delicate bouquet.
Count the Harleys.
Narrative thread.
Form crust (children's voices).
Fulltimers savor lunch.
Yeats in despair.
Thru the trees, you never see more than the corner of that house.
Based in fact (breaded).
Pelicans on the water.
The calculus of twilight, shimmering, in the corridors of Sears.
Settling.
Those orange trash bags belong to the city.

Luke Skywalker, meet David Antin.
A chance construction.
On the road to employment.
Decompensates (on the borderline), clearing one's throat.
The rooster.
From which you are cut and placed on waivers.
Seeking plasma.
Out of print.
But in collusion.
A view of the mesa and geometry of new towns.
4 houses on Boardwalk.
Who'd've.
Thought the Navy was so full of boys.
Aerosol and climbing.
The Marias offering Spearmint.
Stripes painted on the donkey.
Branch bending.
On reserve.
Sex perceived as sharing.
The rose stem.
A new line.
The white jeep.
Sky King.
Just because I prefer the Malvinas.
Such glands.
Little penguin's baritone wail.
Sax perceived as shearing.
Cardigan over plaid.
Old Prussian blue licks a paw.
Chew a torta.
Canned soda, Tecate in a bottle.
By the numbers.
Thus a garden.
As if the tide.
Farts of the city.

Sox perceived as a shaving.
Six received as a halving.
Or have not.
Vats of experience.
So what is a person.
But a stanza.
Arbitrary and intimate (arbitrated and ultimate (are berated and estimate)).
Parental guidance advised.
Prenatal, disguised (and gusted).
San semilla.
Web visible because it reflects the sun.
But to a guest, sponges look alike.

III

Hoagy's busted in San
Salvador & B's skull, bulblike, glows
conspicuous in the hardened dark, hot
tub on a hoist, big jets bloated and wobbling
in a final descent, surface smeared in a syrup of strawbs
or the perpetual fear of genre, the slim cat brown
but with blue eyes, what the night
does to these birds these windows
that your teacher so desired, giggling
with ignorance, a lower card of the same suit but
with two eyes and the hands reversed (thumbs up), holding
a cup from which to sip, such
engines in the distances suggest new maneuvers as the band
tunes to perform a cover, a bee
yellow as the alphabet and as hard
to start over or the primates full of sugar and
sweating in the peach-light by a T-square as tho
these straps about your chest
being tightened led to rhyme, thieves

trapped in the traffic with no choice but to go
a.m., or edit the procedures, the flaking
in the eye and smell of yoghurt is to the parrot's
cautious answer that the phone lines or
propellers forgot to gargle or make of this as
recursive a season to days of the weak and willing
to get on, a new dog but temporary
by which to ascribe the sky
through counting, one box for names
but then what is a garden but
tissue at the bottom which once wrapped shoes
all vowel-like and messy with pride in your nipples
reduced to function in the patio's glare and
whiff of burgers diagrams the diver's splash by
the lawn chair and vice and secretary-treasurer
still to be determined with a signature on
the outside where Pookie's in
the foxtails watching a monarch
comment on the Falklands, those hang-gliders out over
the cliffs (motionless, red-yellow) do not
signify an emotion expressible only in sighs, beach blanket or
tetherball, the sequence of yards each the assertion of
a different grass while the porches are settling
comic or sad, visited by the young postwoman in
government shorts, that cocoa butter smell to the
beaches, air full
of radio and Frisbee, battleship convoy
anchored at the horizon where the inevitability of sunset's
brilliances discounts the morning silence shaped
by birds not visible in the shade of banana trees until
a telephone rings and you step inside
to discover that it must be
some other house, yellow or green or
mint, the little cuplike wrappers dark brown
and pathetic in their emptiness, an afternoon as

long as California, with sprinklers and a small ache
in the lower back when lifting
the dark blue crates of distilled water
twice a week against the music box tune of the ice cream
truck or the claim
that the suburbs were a true past even
to the caesura, the glance, a stuccoed chimney or
the tone of a garbagecan dragged
up steps the new hire, nervous and
polite, shoes shining, his loosened tie
a careful study like knowing
just how far to bend over
at the water fountain or the proper
tone to the pilot light is not
a solution for aphids, the cat in
the jeep in the weeds, peaches
big as a walnut, cement truck
with a bell for backing up, something
to put on your resume or swallow q.i.d. for colors
brighter than bright and expensed, tenured
as an idea or emotion and so in step with
the tunes, bases loaded, twilight thick
with acrylics topped with granola, willow said to be
"weeping" or on appeal, salt crust rings
the rim of the glass and you recall
what you'd set out to do, mornings lost
waiting for the coffee to hit or
two weeks of wildflowers in the Anza-
Borrego and Mr. Johnson
is able to see you now, but down
the corridor a boa sleeps on the Xerox,
coiled and shitlike and a new jet
departs every seven minutes, Balinese
term for monkey, Associate Monkey or
Full, this statement is false, mood elevator

at the zoo, day of no mail if this line is being
remodeled is to the hummingbird
sufficient cause so that your ears pop
and then the knuckles, the pattern
of an old foundation on a vacant lot, jello amid lettuce, the cat
knows to get off the table versus
a spider in the tub, a knot
in the gut compounds
the sentence (fracture),
coffee cans used as planters and all the laces
looped (blue lube, big boy) into center until
you get it, are with it, butterflies
by the mulch trying to avoid that second
transfer unless to an express
meaning, very little units, like knowing
the inventor of the ball typewriter likewise
developed Tang, registered connotation, a tint
of real anger filters all, one jar for gefüllte fish, one
for ceviché as though guilt
by association to the next syllable being
next were any more subtle than your own spousal
rape because "it's easier," the bear deranged
begs for nuts and bananas at the main gate flap
in the late afternoon or siecle as the little orange cars
of the skylift float
toward evening at the harbor & the sound
of drinks and weren't those flamingoes something, a code three
in the distance only requires
that you raise the volume, the reports
are due quarterly and for this
we ask what is
a line and who cares for their feathers now, a fog
that burns off but sets the tone
to the whole day, not enough
imitation mayonnaise or the bulb

in the bathroom's blown, how can you
watch the orange cat spray
allover the University of Pittsburgh Press, dramatic
monologue of a false self, a bloop
single or the run
in your stocking, nothing is
grounded and enjambment smears or
sneers, the old power mower
rusting away, a dull spring in the long
season which like the horsehide
is loaded up, but the parrot screams
in his cage all day long, yellow
and blue, the pilot
lights the big jet onto the runway, the guys
at the roominghouse live on its steps and
someone's been sleeping in the park, that
vomit's dried to the sidewalk, & through
the open door you see
the television running
though the room is empty.

IV

We know who they are, beards flecked with straw, collars buttoned, blood crust under fingernails, the terrible breath, sideways glances, roughing Derrida up in a Czech jail, signatures in triplicate, salt rings round yellow margaritas, jigsaw puzzle in the lobby of La Valencia Hotel, the too-thick sweaters, rich sunsets, Conan in Manganese in translation (in full view of pelicans), voice found at the piano bar, profuse apologies denying tenure, 3 balls per game. Content-centered, the dog threatens to bite. Mouth closes slowly over friendliest of genitals. Deep in the garden flowers harden. A sea of unread faces, a day on the deck. New metaphor of tone in a bowtie. The fact of the wheelbarrow at the event of a porch. Talking to the notebook as I write. Barbwire about auto row. To the margin. She-males out cruising on Broadway, secretaries in the plaza spooning yoghurt, yellow floaters of the tuna fleet's nets. Ought to row/out to the island.

Further days seek silence (sentence). What are you going to do with all those connections (trash bags of smashed cans)? So she lives with her shopping cart and small dog in a doorway. The blue parrot does not refer to Casablanca ("red dog, red cloud"). A partial clearing would be grounds for a party. Bottle of Night Train juts from his pocket. The heat of the coffee thrills my teeth. Urine Plaza. The compost is steaming, filled with allusion. Or that Stendahl = Michael Gottlieb. The loud crowd chanting "Rupe, Rupe!" The parrot is no swan.

Oriole gorging on the peaches. Nor was father apparent (seek senses). Grammarian asleep under cactus regrets dream. Game cartridge to flamingo full of shrimp: the renewed native barbarian naturalist checks notes to corroborate syllogistic activity I (Celsius). Mountain comes to rest on a shot glass. Even the jeep needs time to focus, arms wet & pink climbing out of the side of the pool. 44 board feet at three turns per year. Ten centuries of civilization caps a tooth (cellophane tape on a school). People with two first names. The B side is slower, subject to fits. Limo glides to depiction, enough butterflies to darken the sky. The chairs are having chairs again.

Only realism can boil an egg. Asyndeton than sinned against (seeds salsa). An old man and his dachshund. The problem of givebacks. The slow gait of a camel (its beautiful eyes). Weaves a world (weave me alone). Paragraphic. Autoredact. Try walking away from a good thing without a sense of disaster. They import water from over the border, long lashes, new abstracts. Noonish (Was ist ein Satz?). A short walk from the sea.

Interruption generates summer, supper (an RV on a suburban lawn with the sign "Your tarot read here"). The androgynous economist trademarks lips and tongue. New theory of twilight. After nachos comes sex. Or that Noland is Frankenthaler made neat. The blue parrot jealous of the simplest finch. I still haven't mentioned oranges. Boxes and brigands. Over the overpass to old Pot Hill. An emotion midway between anger and despair. The usual crowd at Taco Palace. The parked cabbie fast asleep.

Take your Prolixin. Everything is syntax (there is no meaning apart from the world). Cats are not children. The old Coke dispenser in the weeds forms a better toolchest. Your mother's image is indelible, reflected in the soup. Machines vend lies. The window is not your friend. The ocean was intended. The image reverts to pink and green. This is a narrative (you will die). The jet sets down in the desert. The sun steams into the sea.

Slower and more elaborate, intentional because I want it, aware of all these birds, the screaming in the trees fused with song, the ice cream truck and the rooster, the many cats, the young man in the next yard who speaks no English and is dying of cancer: verbs scar. Last night on C Street somebody died. Later there's a party, but your eyes are brown and wide (what few teeth I have are yellow). Let's read the Sunday Times instead at the cafe, sipping cappuccino; you can buy these Chinese diaries anywhere. There once was a time when a French actress would let herself be named Miao-Miao. Minnesota is so hard to imagine. For 12 weeks in San Diego I had packed 200 lbs. of books. The yard spoke of long inattention. The ostrich's hat is cocked. He bought his own robe to wear to commencement, bright red. We gradually pushed the hot tub up the flight of stairs. You either have reservations or you make them.

Later you look back into the glare of a calendar, the stare of a cat. My own penis disappears into those wonderful folds of flesh. The pelicans share that spit of land with the laziest of seals. Noise of the kite. Enclosed please find my resume: lagoon. Airplanes look so stiff. His lawn chair rose to an altitude of 16,000 feet. The plastic flamingo on the wood fence is a wind vane. Thus the merit increase is denied, the bank patrolled by an old man too small for his gun, the freeway nearly empty of traffic. She hops through the water to get to the faucet. A tiger sighs. Gulls struggle to fly against the breeze.

Summer! The hills dry. The wind shaking the ripe plums from the tree. The small kids use a tennis ball to play baseball in the schoolyard. I can barely read my own writing. Not one house on the block owned a dog. Tenses were optional, a flight from emotion. Whose turn was it to do the dishes? They fired birdshot into the exercise yard to force the prisoners back into the cell-block. The smoke from the barbeque was intense. Those who knew better weighted the clotheslines with ~ plastic jugs of water. The only music was a distant hammer.

The blood of your period covers my dick like a thick sauce. There are so many positions and no two chairs alike. We lay exhausted, silent, in one another's arms. A funny sad story about an x-rated motel. Large bowl of nachos. Long strip of beach. Gutters is not New York-specific, nor Mick Jagger on a camel. Every bad small museum in America owns one Rauschenberg. Panties dangling from the TV antenna. I'm alone on my porch with a notebook. The planes depart always in the same direction. The parrot chuckling in his cage.

The mould of institutions shades the thought blue, a scarecrow which attracts birds. The small rug on the step turns grey in the rain. A Kantian inscription. of hopelessness learns to count syllables while the peasants of data processing lie drugged in the streets. The smell of ammonia through the open bathroom door. The secretaries run the department. The prairies are soon to be joined by tracts, but the bar itself is crowded so long as on the large screen two black men bleed for our pleasure. Radio demands the commuter and fog settles before sunset. We get a gang of lumpers from the docks and beat him to emeritus. But, in the damp forest shade, mushrooms swell. I don't intend to homogenize my meaning for the sake of an enemy. The directions on the machine at the transfer point are not certain. So we eat pork bows and parchment chicken in the tea room on Hang Ah Place.

Lit, then flickers, whispers, flashes out. The horned owl sits still in the fir tree. The buckram heart, no better than a C+, deflates. Loss is as fixed as the sea. Blisters bubble up on the balls of one's feet. Ink hardens. Seed sinces. The jay could read my thoughts. Those butterflies taste awful. The rose blooms on the light-table, the fish glows in the dark. The man with his pushbroom crosses the bus depot floor. Three pigs got two bros spread-eagled against stucco wall.

V

1
The city of glass is warped!

Still photos of point of impact.

Money reduced to cinders.

2
Twelve blocks to the nearest cup of coffee.

Sunset brilliant with its poisons.

On the doorstep they speak in French.

3
Under brightly colored tents sleeps a village of campers.

Gusts of low fog dampen your face.

The brown mare with one white eye.

4
The mind itself is simple, fluid.

A museum abstracts the duty of the leech.

A zucchini will assume a shape.

5
Between a and the, the children of a thousand grocers grow up, consumed
with sadness.

Small boats seek fish at the edge of the storm.

The dice cup slams against the wood of the bar.

6
Each new page insults the past, only to apply for membership.

The school teacher patrols the yard at recess.

A man in a room hits his forehead with the butt of his hand.

7
A tramp steamer pulls into view.

400 soft focus photos of seaweed.

The dog leaps to catch the stick.

8
Bees are harvesting the clover.

The sky remains grey for weeks.

The tricycle lies abandoned by the steps.

9
The militant syntax of the surrealists has begun to froth.

Friends gather in the kitchen.

Old clay pots that await the return of dirt.

10
The sun shines on this sentence!

Enjambment is like a bunt.

The pelican dives beak first into the waves.

11
She lies awake at night, crazed with retiling the downstairs bath.

This line is the trump.

Bulbs of the fuchsia about to burst.

12
The pushcarts of Orchard Street still vend crap.

The meat of the mango is orange.

That one step has been loose for years.

1
The shades are not raised until sunset.

An old clock recasts day in two circles.

The couple is jogging in identical sweatsuits.

2
Nature abhors a dachshund.

The grape tastes sweeter than imagined.

Try writing in a stiff wind.

3
Style in calculus soon curdles.

The basin designed as an altar.

How the toothpaste gets into the tube.

4
Tamed by Milton, I lie on Mother's head.

The bee was as large as a mouse.

The bush grew against the side of the house, huddled against the wind.

5
Slightly left of Macy's.

The banana had gone bruised and squishy.

The beer can on the sidewalk had been crushed flat.

6
Words out of context will eat your face.

They just hang out at the corner store until dinner.

Have you signed your check?

7
All money is emotional.

The skyline of Pittsburgh at sunset.

Add milk.

8
New fee-for-service sought for poetry of cramps.

The third baseman leans into the stands.

Wave pounds into the shore.

9
All these backyards left uncared for!

The thin gold chain about the base of her neck.

The grass all burned off before summer.

10
We sat beneath an umbrella, eating avocados stuffed with calamari.

The Pinto paused at the intersection, ready to make a left turn.

Knight to King's Bishop three.

11
Handbound, the volume is gorgeous, with no hope for an audience.

So she went to the academy to become a beautician.

Administrators want to act guilty.

12
Nowadays purges are carried out by computer.

They were deprived of their zipcode.

New suns begin to compete for the sky.

1
Their last hope was to wed the daughter to the landlord.

Wet and obscene, like a grapefruit.

But in the drawer was a small knife.

2
The 3 pigs are Aryan, the wolf big and black.

Did he say his name was Al Pesto?

Up pulled Pat Brady in a jeep.

3
Bare arms attacked by the shadow of a bee.

Compound sentence, dependent clause pushed through the flesh.

The flags of three nations oppress the plaza.

4
The simplest thing (a paragraph) has begun to melt.

The house shudders in the turbojet's wake.

The head of a pig as an element of sculpture.

5
The disincentives have begun to bloom.

The President trapped in a stalled elevator at the White House.

The riot squad loosens up, swinging their billy clubs like baseball bats,
doing stretches, bends.

6
People walk with their eyes turned to the sidewalk.

The yoke settles into one half of the shell, the white into the other.

A desire to confront the unimaginable leads to a postcard collection of camels.

7
The unit cost per stanza is a concern to this panel.

But to name your child Donkey Kong?

A bowl of plums alone on the table.

8
Sand blows up from those gray lots.

Teeth lurk behind full lips.

There are two kinds of money: painting (bills), sculpture (coins).

9
The house was cut into flats, so now there's a closet with stairs.

Mom's not looking for a lateral transfer.

The cat plays with the mouse until it stops playing back.

10
This felt less like jail than summer camp.

Jittery with coffee, but wanting to yawn, I close my eyes in the sun.

That tree's capacity for asymmetry is what defeats me.

11
Then a whole generation resented its work.

That woman's son is a street person but visits on Sunday.

The small dog was about to be noxious.

12
The lawnchair represents despair.

Red wine kept in the fridge.

The mower at the garage sale caked with rust.

1
The tyranny of the whole molds its parts.

History leads to the t-shirt.

The finch yodels, ignorant as a plum.

2
Exaggerate the valley to construct the road.

He imitates famous men, industrial sounds, the shapes of chairs.

Deep in the forest the woodpecker knocks.

3
Fresh asphalt is mushy, ground for Melitta.

Disassemble the bikes of short prose!

All these shingled rooftops on the slope of a hill.

4
At Small Press Traffic, the books are divided by sex: men, women, fiction.

So you move to Rochester and look for a job.

I wait for the mail.

5
Even the string for the bean plant presents an idea.

The bath mat out on the porch to dry.

Your back stairs as seen by a sculptor.

6
Modernism sought to construct a mouse.

Later, we had carbons.

The library open only three days per week.

7
The Dane is crowded into the back of the truck.

Overlooking the cove was an old pink hotel.

Thus ice cream cones should be pointed at the bottom.

8
Everyone looks to see which house the cop car pulls up at.

Response to enjambment is one in ten.

The cane is a permanent addition.

9
The rv in the driveway is his other life.

Big plaster cow above the market's marquee.

In the comp light.

10
The round scar on the table from a hot pan.

Ten rooms in a warehouse of unsold books.

Blue-striped toothpaste.

11
The fix is in.

Due to declining enrollments, dissertations on sci-fi are now permissible.

The old campus would be a good site for an industrial park.

12
Your Wittgenstein as played by Bogart is getting stale.

The fuzz of one peach versus all of Larry Bell.

The pelican on the side of the rock.

VI

The region itself is L-shaped, a string of towns down along the coast, then suburbs spilling eastward to the mountains, beyond which lies the desert. In the spring when the jacaranda blooms, the streets are lined with purple. Those young navy boys don't know a drag queen when they see one. At the base of the bridge is Chicano Park. All of the students wore cutoffs. Melvyn suggests a game of charades. My room was painted seven different shades of white. By now their child had acquired language and was giving commands. Your middle name is Brenda. They went to a spa in the desert where she complained of the lack of books. The Padres or Pads or Pods. I began to listen to the radio for the first time in years, relearning its structure. She was on the executive board of AFSCME. The parrot was blue and yellow. That's where they build the cruise missile. Downtown, the main plaza was half torn up, causing the winos, players and preachers to huddle close together. Many buses stop at dusk. I had not lived alone in a decade. The prose class was very male. I had the high score on the Qix game over at Taco Palace. Down by the fence several large marijuana plants were ready for harvest. I can appreciate the compulsive talker. Their pitcher, Lollar, could hit too. Two doors down, the rooming house slouched in disrepair. I went to the junior college library, looking for a typewriter. He was always bringing home a stove or old cameras, or even a Packard bought at an auction. The crossing at the border is a series of ramps. They spend more time at home now, watching the tube. The tap water tastes horrible and leaves a white coat on all the pots. One thousand birds greet the dawn. I went to the bookstore Geoff's dad had owned, its entrance golden, the result of shelves of National Geographic. After the film we went to a bar and talked. They imagined themselves punk but were modest. A constant stream of landing aircraft. I don't write to teach. She's drunk before noon. I sat at the wicker table on the deck, enveloped in bird noise. Ernest Hahn owns this town. The banks close for siesta. A walk on the beach in the dark. In the park before dawn, you can hear the lions. He wants to play with the poets. With that big blonde grin she said, "I've never experienced guilt in my life." I was jogging four, five miles each day. It was a lesbian-run coffee house, but open to men. The bed was three foam mats which piled into a couch. Antin kept promising to "get together," but never called. Kaprow was silent. The part-timers are the only ones who ever make sense. She tried to sleep with her student, but he was too frightened. His come-on was overwhelming, an inverted shyness. Up at the cove weld find pelicans. Nowhere else can you get margaritas by the pitcher. I took the manuscript to be xeroxed. The largest porn shop on Fifth Street is in a building owned by the son of President Ford. She tried to fix me up with the law student who lived upstairs. What will you remember most? The little old wino actually lived in that horse trailer parked on the street. This name: Heatherbell Fong. The adolescent narratives were virtually identical, but with men were ironic tales of lost love, and with women stories of sexism and alienation. That's the hotel in Chandler's *Playback.* The museum's view was better than its art. His new wife shook my hand, nearly breaking three fingers. The hoist got the hot tub halfway up the stairs, but we had to build a platform to take it up the rest. She spoke matter-of-factly of how, if necessary, she would bury her husband and son. She's blonde and skittish, a good writer, but terribly unread. When we cross that border, penis and vagina, nothing will ever be the same. The film was shot in Beirut. The canyon in the park had been stripped to build a hospital. Everyone has a story about the plane crash. I made her a cup of coffee to sober her up. The entire dining room table, filled with food and bottles, simply collapsed. His localism was admirable, although a dead end. I never got to the archive. She makes the best flan. The sailors love to bus up to the nude beach. I come over to watch "Hill Street." Her affair with Bob was intense. At the zoo a seal bullies a penguin. I like my coffee so thick it's bitter. We order a bowl of nachos. You can see Mexico from the deck. You were married once, and are an aunt. Kathy was in a mood. The poet decontextualized by his job. The cat's name is Turkey. He let you know that he was a vet. We sat in the dark, drinking beer, while upstairs Reagan and Peter were preparing supper. When the coals went out he started them with a blow torch. The red robe means he went to Harvard. The concussion fucked up her balance. Only one integrated neighborhood in a town of one million. You rolled over and we did it again. Where are my structures? Landing, the planes filled the sky over my house. The Siamese sleeps in the bathroom sink. He opened the bottle of Green Rooster. Walking down the street I'm apt to stumble. The piano player at the Turf Club's named Tiny. A gingerbread Victorian in the barrio where they have readings once a month. So we got stuck in the sand in the desert. Tempy was Fergie's 3000th K. My tongue there, where it does the most good. The firetruck parked at the track, while its crew jogged a few miles, one member left to attend the radio in the cab. The spring scandal was who had not been given tenure. The night after his mother died we went to the game. The donkey's stripes are just shoe polish. I flew to San Francisco for the weekend. We were just up the hill from downtown. "Count your sentences," I would say over and over. The Double Happiness is near Jerry's. Large brown eyes with long lashes. On the official campus map, Che Cafe is Coffee Hut. The high desert is different. A web of shopping centers interspersed with industrial parks. A tall bottle of Corona. A small boxlike apartment, one half block from the ocean. Emotionally, we were both much needier than we'd expected. She said she had some-thing to confess. Barrett taught Aaron to fetch. Your mother's livingroom walls are filled with small religious paintings. What if I hadn't met you on the bus? What if Willie McGee hadn't broken Juan Bonilla's wrist? By the junior college was the inevitable Militant Bookstore. The Vietnamese food here is nothing special. At dawn, I'd see men wander out of the park with their sleeping bags. The kitchen window is always open. A small case of rug burn contracted while fucking. The bay thick with military boats. In her notebook were 52 alternatives for one word in her text. Even wearing a dog collar he looked sort of preppy. He'd been a student in her Spanish class ten years before. Pressure had to be kept on the State Department or Hoagy might just disappear. The Vice-Chairman wandered about the department like a large rabbit. She would show up at office-hour and sit there and not say a word. DiPalma's not getting his mail. I missed the last bus and walked three miles home. More than anything, it was solitude. Rupe circled under the high fly. Ivy grew up the base of the palm. The Mexican women took the bus up to their jobs in the homes of La Jolla. On the floor in two dissertation binders were the collected poems of Paul Blackburn. Each campus has its name and this is Motel 6. In the dark we open the champagne and watch the waves.

VII

Literal transfer. Blows about the face and neck. I don't mean to be the plum tree, but to care
deeply, where the pus starts. The false soccer ball is large among the boys, their green sky acrylic
and the shortfall growing. Somewhere a shower runs. In the white bowl the cereal has gone soggy, but
the milk is sweeter. Indian print bedspreads are not adequate curtains. In a double-play this motion is
the pivot. The driver makes the old woman step from the curb into the gutter before she can pull
herself aboard the bus. How will this look typed? The henna will wash out. The parrot is want
to bite. The old vents are rusted. Cinder blocks built one civilization, then fog. A thick sentence

is scratched out. Under the ocotillo the scar of an old camp fire forms a perfect circle, against
which the pale camouflage of a lizard fails to work. He sits in his dark garage all afternoon every
day. This line is for foodstamps. Into the history of miniatures steps an idea. You cannot sweep glass up
quietly. The cat offers its belly for a rub. Within the forest the smell of fresh asphalt gives rise to
fear. Who left the lights on? A dense mist settles over the small white homes on the hill.

New paragraph: old tricks. Dear squeegee, vend hither. Cloves pierce the orange rind, while out
the dusty window a neighbor stands at his mailbox staring at an envelope, a rooster crows, and in
my daypack is a broken telephone. The wind is full in the sheets on the line and the pages must be cut
apart before you begin writing. The cat sniffs at the sausage. A small red metal "glass" in which
toothbrushes and razors are stuffed. Jitterbugging, here we come! The blue one is the creme rinse.
Mike Heath on a pop fly. Floss. 100,000 Indonesian political prisoners have been kept in jail since the coup
17 years ago. Ex-astronaut Seeks Ark. Rock keeps on rollin', thick mountain of demo tapes. Describe
this breeze: little half-warm gusts. Bees hum in the fuchsias. Dog yawn. In the Tenderloin at midnight the streets
are still lively, folks hangin' out in front of their res hotels, the traffic now mostly taxis
and prowl cars, all yellowed by the streetlamps. A contoured sheet of cartoon cats. In tennies. At dawn
she's in the garden, catching snails. White sky. Dry fern. The banana's peel starts to freckle. In the
kitchen two sisters are dancing to the Stones while the calendar on the wall still shows July.

There's a bee on my knee. Spin cycle. Enclosed please find the self-valuable word. A
young Asian man wearing thick glasses watches me write this through the window of the laundromat where
two small boys circle the washers, playing tag. I see the "help wanted" sign in the donut
shop and think twice. You might find anything on the small shelf in a phone booth. The
drink was a deep blue. The jitneys are cramped but quick. By mid-afternoon it's time to give
up on the sun. Nobody's mutter beats Anselm's. My mother still has red hair. Pendleton shirts
become a cholo fad. Hightop tennies. "Say the tone of an afternoon." Between language and thought
stands a cop. The body shop is in the hands of sculptors: their sinewy dogs look vicious with
cropped ears. I work here. The bath mat is always damp. Thus my sentences sing of love. But when
it rains in the summer and the kids are exhibiting "indoor behavior," don't the burritos look thick with
sauce? Designer pocket? Lease with option? An avant-garde is blessed with amnesia. There's enough
life in a single intersection at rush hour to generate tenure by the dozens.

I just came in to get out of the rain, but's a warm day near the margin. The dustpan fits
onto the broom handle and is left in a corner. We bow to the religion of stanzas, totally
oppressed. The dog sleeps in a fenced yard. Cash-on-cash. So pencils are yellow and a hose for the
garden green. Secondary market. How people still rig up their clotheslines. A minor leaguer to be named
Later. Is that the phone? Artbooks. I yield to the gentleman from South Carolina. Once they are

up those big jets fan out in all directions, but today's clouds are thin and
smeared, giving
the sky the feel of a ceiling. The rose has begun to wilt. I hold off until you
start to come. What are the arcs
of association? White butterfly amid thorns. All the ways in which an
ostrich is not a bird. When
the dog wakes the shade has moved. Old web hangs limp, fuzzed string,
straight down from the ceiling. Blue
ink repeats the word: an I stares out, surrounded by syntax, by sinus. That's
the flying
banana chair. The old shed is pleasantly musty on a warm day, the cactus in
its window bearing a red flower, the plum
tree in the yard throwing shadows through the door. The old parrot gives a
squawk.

Words demand mandatory arbitration: drain the lawn. Pulley squeals
perfect pitch. Simple declarations: cargo
argot. Grody to the next and carry to the tens place. Wasps are nesting in
the mouth
of the drainpipe where winter is unthinkable. Send a blind copy to Region
Nine. A host of
flying things no larger than dust above the clover. The limp in Faulkner's
predicates. These spiders
are my friends. Coleus branch sprouts roots in a glass of water. Once a
dancer, then a weaver. Why
8⅛ by 11? Pope's couplets are nonetheless prose. Veal, video, Vichy.
Through the roses I can see
the old brick seminary on the next hill and the tree tops from the park
beyond, while in the valley (hidden)
the distinct sound of a logging truck churns past. Space monsters descend
from the top of the screen. Victoria
Principal? Morning sweat (writing after running). These small flowers are
blue-purple. On the west slope
you feel a sea breeze. Who said this was non-syntactic? In the shade in the
shed is an

old school desk, waxed wood, uncarved upon. I found the clay pot broken
and the cactus on the floor in
a mound of dirt. Thus every third Fibonacci number is even (use it).

The sea cloud is dark, a brooding storm. The RV is brown with an orange
trim. This seat is reserved
for seniors and the disabled. His prose is better skimmed. I'm drinking
milk for good. The hummingbird
taunts the cat. Short and therefore not scarred with style. This layout pro
brings his own waxer. That
next line is a doosie. The Army recruiting desk at the unemployment office.
The lone pink house
amid a row of whites. My ear today hears different. Memories of past lovers
not by sight. The
relay from the cutoff man is on the button. That poor fern is baking in the
glassed-in porch. Quantity
itself is one mode of tension. Tall and trim, thick straight hair prematurely
grey, muscles etched
under a dark t-shirt, baggy black rubber pants held up by yellow
suspenders, the fireman hoses off his own
little car in front of the station. Negative termination. Typically, the values
of the board of trustees
are in conflict with the needs of the agency's clients. The parrot is there for
friendship and show. Aid
to the so-called developing nations is intended to reinforce existing power
relations within them. Of 13 tenured professors
twelve are white men. Boycott Coors. The tiger stares through the bars of
her cage.

VIII

"Write often, write upon a thousand themes, rather than long at a time, not trying to turn too many feeble somersets in the air – and so come down upon your head at last. Antaeus-like, be not long absent from the ground.

Those sentences are good and well discharged which are like so many little resiliencies from the spring floor of our life – a distinct fruit and kernel itself, springing from the *terra firma*. Let there be as many distinct plants as the soil and the light can sustain. Take as many bounds in a day as possible. Sentences uttered with your back to the wall."

Henry David Thoreau
November 12, 1851

IX

Wild gesticulations, wide
receivers. To shade
white page glare
just write. Decal
on shirt front
is suspect. Boots
for to take
big hill now.
Butterfly. Porch rail
is saw horse.
Red thorns on
old rose bush.

Hand trim lawn.
Under these stairs
find cool shadows.
Poor stereo lacks
one speaker. Shape
of word one.
On line sheets
form sails. Boy
shoots with his
cheeks, ricochets whisper.

Goggle. Blue lube,
big bad boy.

Sliver. Allergic to
detergent. Sun in
row of hard
to caulk sky
lights. Think about
toilet seat. Elastic
aesthetic governs tenure,
fear. Sad old
comp prof. These
suburban streets never
taught to curve
go right home.

Single sitting, subtle
settling predicts quake.
Insects on neutral
feed. Restart. Pair
of dimes won't
buy paper, three
ring carnie. I is for farce
but mean that.
Brown garbage can,
faded steps. Sky
heats dry streets.

X

Late

Light

I stumble, you sing, they lie in the sun. Now here's an in-service on the DSM-III.

When to not make love demands more
Permanent salsa lunch poem
Shifts into higher gear

The ear is wide
and the word is odd
and and inserts its own
hard tonality:
beep beep beep

I sit on a bench on the edge of the park: descriptions of joggers trot past. Three fat flies lunge at the kitchen window and bounce back. A red rose starts to unfold. The glass doorknob is broken and lies on the floor of the shed. Negative campaign in the race for Lieutenant Grammarian. A plume of white smoke from far over the hill. Writing is eyes. I love the way the flocks compute.

Pen half chawed, the rear
door open but the heat
on as the grey cat
is to the couch, lawn
mower, rain shower, slower to
his vocables in a purse
'd lip, "ho ho caribou,"
sleep tips heat's absence, wit
wobbles, here I am, sun
sets, terrible pink orange sky
gets dark, gets down, gets
laid back at the ranch
around the table at lunch.

So simple
set
to strings
kept hidden –

mere lower limit
– margins mirror
fixed borders,
fate
to be born into
if to write to right
thot ecco's –
Is it words
heard in the hollow
chill of morning
real as
this seat is
cold?
To speak,
speak
the line . . .

Look: the rook in the book in the nook was unable to take a hook. I want a poem real as an allusion. The way people bundle up on a chill day. The heat from the coffee enough to steam the kitchen windows. The decorator mugs feeling heavy. Butter melting into the toast. I want a poem real as an illusion. A row of small clay pots on a fence, awaiting plants. A colony of small bugs dances like motes in the sun. In the paper, description curdles and flattens. Patterns of static construct a radio, sending "please remit" toll-free into the skull, a swollen tomato. You want under? Aliens communicate by code: alligator on sport shirt. As for we who love to be astonished, the doorknob is still on the floor. Is it Bob? These nouns crinkle all yellow and pink. Ling P. Sicat asks for an epilog. An earplug distributes opposite of silence. The antennae of the race have been snapped off by idle youth. Clarinet in a cat fight. Get drunk before you vote. Thus reasons soil. A small girl beckons her kitty. This scene is repeated, intended to charm. In Jonestown, bloated corpses begin to explode in the sun. Thus seasons air. Find the noun. At what moment do you realize that you will always be forced to rent? Her unstated tenacity only becomes evident over time. He starts up conversations with strangers on the bus. These sentences occur in this order. I hate what narrative does to time. The garden's grown into a jungle. The butterfly is orange and black.

Please hold on sudden stops
the steppes of Russia rush
across a split blue screen
screaming locomotive plumes into Munich
Chicago (fat fingers – closeup – drop
nickel into palm for news
Who gets to be Rosebud?
so sad Who gets to
(so said my Cid) be
dead, hand me my head
This at least I read

One in five is lost
so trump the ghost, best
past in the alphabet, bitter
tea, tower case, faces front
as ball is a font
spinning to print which words
harden harping theme, absurd luck
thus to land at Boardwalk's
red hotel (near to Go
so posit verb as noun)
My brother wears the crown

Rich heart, hard stitch, reach
down, each word one thing
covers many, multiplies out, surrounds
clutter of the simplest desk
in town, realtor sells insurance –
drowns, self service station: book

breaks binding, kids leave home
return, look sadder, haunted, stare
over dinner, silent, sticks stalk
almond chicken, shoots, baby corn
stereo choking one thin horn

4th: the count adds up
Dear gem spa, it's 5:15
(aha) what limit to pure
differential clatter (cough) the stuff
of art (thus fart: Life
parts, the river Jordan, marts
of perfect bondage, margins) starts
to get simple: fee fi
phoneme, name it, sit straight
sing "Hail to the Chief,
he's a dirty little thief"

Young and savvy, soft but
savage, to square the root
cherishing procedure, put down these
syllables swollen in the red
corpuscular pressured pump, it said
it says, to the wall
that is turning, paper made,
trust the next, it's this,
the last, it's that, thought
fattens, trapped in the head
abstraction's presence left for dead.

Let's stretch. To write, I sit in the shed
in a storm. She sent
recently her statute of limitations,
"you slime." Plastic yellow bucket
gets my drift. Door slams.

Is the parrot in the rain?
Is the parent the reinforcer
of a painful narcissistic response
say, as men in a porn shop
imagine autonomy in sex? One sits
long at the livingroom table
drafting the twelve page paper
later returned with just a check – Iatrogenic Maladies:
Etiology and Response. Our Friend the Beaver
by Eddie Haskell. Thus gunowners perceive legislation
to prohibit Teflon-coated bullets
as a restriction of their freedom
of speech. Mother calls each Sunday
promptly at ten. The couch
is three foam mats
'neath an Indian print spread.
The beach is down the street. The text,
if permitted, encodes time
inexactly. Erving Goffman
is dead. Plum leaves
are blown from the tree. A scale
is something I don't want to stand on
like tradition. The next hill
no longer in sight is nonetheless possible
by virtue of memory
if only you sober up. Tenure
is terror. What if *your* kid
is beaten, his lunch money taken from him,
your daughter fails to come home?
Your head stops still
so that I sense your teeth gently
right at the instant
of orgasm. Which things
come together? Imagine language
on display at the zoo. At the bar tonight

people are making choices
but in the lobby of the La Valencia
a 50 year old jigsaw
remains incomplete. Two eyes
are the cause of depth. Strawberry preserves
on zucchini bread. Negative adjectives
outweigh their nouns.
Laughter slaughters laughter.
The library from out of space
has no fourth floor, thereby contributing further
to a theory of number, fidelity.
If you don't have something nice to say,
write it down. Rodefer made note
of Levertov's washer not out of disrespect,
but the nuclear movement, if it is to include
the familiar, must confront the problem of One.
Rochelle Silliman. Who said
I was uninterested in fiction? This rain
will live on in literature
for weeks. For once
try simple statements. In here
inhabit the head: half
a loaf. In the doorway
Marcie calls for Emma. We sit
at the head of the steps
to the ocean and sip champagne.
The grammarian thinks to rid
the Department
of poets teaching comp.
The sun rises. The sun rises. The sun
rises. But it's the middle of the afternoon
months later and at night.
The sun rises. The International Dateline
breaks. I want a poem real

as an elusion, taped legs pumping
twist out of the block and deep
into the secondary to await the bomb
lighting up thousands
homes roaring in Utah
deafening as the forest, the self.
These are the simples,
salt in the semen,
two strangers in a Navy town
irrationally fond of camels, off-white
walls, first smell of coffee, a small guy
long dead in a cowboy hat, hot
nachos, Mick's lips, being careful
just to walk down the street
O Miss Margaret Jarvis

The song of abstraction cuts glass, difficult standing up in the boat, ear cupped to the wall, the sun rising or setting or both. Complex phenomena are eaten by snails: escalator clause. Small jars full of art preserves. The CPM for upscale is higher. It wants more toner, but the light says "brew," sunny December, towels almost still on the line, a pink clover, Lopping Shear (reggae band), the pen gives off a cheesy discharge. How often only one wants to be fucking. Erica's a teen now (possible source of criticism). Deep in the swipe file, quantifiable and blue, II are we speaking colors, between houses, jobs. In this simple sentence we share eye contact, but at one remove. Context creates equivalence: you in an examination room at Emergency with a sprained back, the woman in the next one rapidly dying. Coriander. The half-musical clang of pots. Sound is a petroleum product, thought a gas emitted from the skull. The sun causes you to unfold your fist. What are men? I put the penis in my cheek so that I won't gag. Merit increase. The working class rises up only to change the station, one finger deep inside, subtext transfer point. French guys construct a thought. The generic word is "huh." Barry picks me up for lunch. Icy Fist Grips East. At the end of the line, the driver sits alone in his bus, reading the paper, waiting to start his run. Words are not solids. She shoos the dog indoors with a broom Predicate engineer. Thus the white hair against the dark skin gives that old Filipino cowboy a *look.* Tho the lot is vacant. One sees the remains of a service station. The auditors crowd in. The smell of a Christmas wreath fills the bus. It's dawn and the neighborhood is full of joggers. The large pen jutting from the breast pocket of the old man's coat looks foolish. Try stamping out that cigarette with a hole in your shoe. At first the word *with* meant *against*: fight with, argue with (*con*test, *con*flict). Maniac sonata. Two weeks for Xmas. Too weak from punning. Wittgenstein's Milwaukee. My grandmother's moustache (copper red). The truss on the table by the bed. Let it all hang out. Let it all bang out a rhythm and call this logic. The dance of the line in the hand in the head of the man writing. Let's invoke Vico, let's provoke Duncan. Floppy disk. An image of order with a spinal cyst. Parrot's name is Tito. Rule one: never kill your publisher. That small table in the kitchen was once the only furniture I had. In another corner, mop, broom and hamper. Why the cat likes to sleep in doorways. Some people cannot let go without trashing the other. Today the sun was only a diffuse light in the clouds. Michael and Michael stood in the rain. Eventually any poster tacked to the wall will start to sag. A huge bag of Meow Mix atop the fridge. A large plastic spinner to just dry the veggies. Fresh bacon on a paper towel. A street walker will want to make eye contact. It wasn't that the boiler was broken: it didn't exist. This year's media Christmas tale is 3-year-old sex slave returned to her parents. The Cid Corman Tradition. The pot holders were just sort of lying around anywhere they'd been used last. Now the jargon says cognitive deficit. Blue loop, big guy. Pink and white and in between. In a new town you think you see more because you're paying attention. Not Rastafarian, Rodeferian. Dear Cheese, don't be blue. I've got Labriola next to Lacan. Words are not silent, even written in a quiet room. Reality is private, charged with crimes. The lights go out in three states. A gray sweater. The wind knocked the construction worker right off of the I beam. They ran the corner store by flashlight, iron gate closed and locked, taking orders and cash and passing goods through the bars. I go in just to keep the office open. The next morning the air's perfectly still. Then comes the blueline, ready for inspection. Great care in simple words. Buffalo Bob moved his lips, so they never showed him on screen when Howdy was speaking. The light at the end of the pencil (shadows on the wall of the notebook). He's upset that the increases aren't retroactive to the Fall Quarter. The day after, people buy every candle in the state. The cat climbs on the couch. The Giants are a monument to the limits of the imagination. The plum tree is barren, a web of dry branches. Why not declaratives? Time to transplant. You can hear the metal in the oven cooling. Porch light. The tree demonstrates asymmetrical balance. Wait, I thought *you* were the Other (here at home). Sad fern. The screws on those cheap plastic hooks won't hold in old wood well. Poem lacking unity (pour M. Jacob). Two rings around the moon, one narrow, one wide. Stations of the crass. Rabbits cannot remember pain for more than 60 seconds. These straight lines are a yoke I cannot escape. Fever model. Headset. In France the noun is something different altogether. Two young cats play a sort of tag out in the back yard. The grammarian's handkerchief, his cape. Donor Life. To shape to shock once awake in stock and out, out. What was that sentence? Think of form as a sister, cousins, several people eating waffles, fig jam, game played with pegs on a board with holes. In the bathroom the plaster has crumbled. I will never marry a fat man. That jar has been on the floor for weeks. Your resume shall be kept on file for a period of six months. The sod mister. Twelves. Different values get asserted here. Add flour: the plot thickens. New Xmas jogging gear. At dawn the old men stand outside the Cherokee Lounge, waiting for the bar to open. The name of that place is Wash & Dry Coin-Op. Coda, cola. The accountant shows up in purple coordinates. The neon signs burn all night. The cat goes up the steps in a manner you would describe as guilty. The purpose of a sports columnist is to express viciousness toward coaches. What does it mean, personally, to become a paragraph? I'll have the chimichanga. The diver seen as paused, half within the water. The calendar you get from the corner druggist. The pen as a razor, cutting silence. I get dizzy from too much coffee. What a trowel is for. Known for its fleas. Heat a pot of tea. The shadow of Stein crosses the text. Kellog's Topper, Reggie's Mantle. He liked his few small scars, sensing he had earned them. A blue mold on the spine of *The Cantos.* You go into a coma and choke in your sleep. A typeface would betray you. The chill in the shed is merely physical. This was many years ago. We were far away.

XI

Painter's reconstruction of the color white
Clatter of birds' wings crowds the sky
Sighing, declarative sentence makes wrong judgment or none
Sandwich wrap harbors dark nine grain bread
Out the window, fog shuts sky
Rhyme invoked scandal greases new semi-gloss wall
Head in lap speaks with frozen jowl
Lack of yogurt now seen as misplaced caution
Rolls of roofing felt dot concrete yard
Signing, a straight line stifles cough
New hope for pronouns refunded once again
Pink shape of future lit behind frosted glass

Hint of rain renews odor of lemon rind
Renaissance of moth is hardened, blue heart
Foot encased in wool, then leather
Swami firemen climb into smoke ridden sky
My book, my bowl, old grammarian slouches in
That's why new physics emits false sun
Stationary cloud growing darker and more dense
Sis writes Ecstatic unrelated on forehead
Dead leaves silent to plum tree's horror
Old pipes start to strangle the white basin
Big sigh, the way the walls breathe
Big dream face wants to gel

So noon is a self-enforced myth
The status of adjectives tends to cringe
Surrounded, the not high porch offers an inadequate vista
Sex as an idea penetrates an army
No verb will denounce a bias
A statue of mother filling the harbor
Then seven repeats the still bad concept

Automatic cartridge return rising high over U.N. Plaza
The lack of light is its name
Sound certain, sound silly, sound off
Red rover, wind in the clover, over
Sailor boy pays to dance with naked lady

Cat gut, rain is its own rupture, rapture
Brain's a hardened cream of mushroom soup
Insert jellied finger deep into anus
Insist "What a good boy am I"
Two armed duck hunters enter the stock exchange
Ardent aliens harden in coat of light
A cat sits, dreaming in its juices
Stoop opens onto shouting in Tagalog
Electronic transfer of whisper or rice cake
It wants to snooze is a bad sign
Curved window reflects sad flock of goose
Forest of vast moss over spider

6-sided house (or seven) falls down
Neon bosom glow is drink my scotch
Rhythm of evasion at program directors' monthly meet
Bite down hard to discover soft penis
Sun rising in pink dawn sky
Coroner's crew unfolds a dark trash bag
Six legged horse, or 7, kneels down
Sausage seals gold deposit is military regime unstable
Dense cloud swarm threatens memory of stanza
Who are you now, little man
Ridge Road rigid load on hell week
An 8-legged hoss swims in dark water

Slant shingle rooves shelter back porches on stilts
Up the canal by speedboat for crackers
Six cities choke on eraser dust

The scientist's beautiful daughter understands his evil
The clear-headed clean-shaven blond young reporter is single
The herd of wooly spiders crossing moss
Fresh hot coffee drips from its filter
The plum tree pink with spring
The new erudition in subway car graffiti
Faded map with foreign countries in wrong colors
Slow rhythm of lone basketball against concrete
Saucer becomes ashtray for old cigar

Gull gang patrols dull urban lake
Too tall antenna on a lone house
One parrot up against the theory of birds
Cost per tea bag equals one noun
Espousing freely into air bag (sic)
Makes too headed a motion rhyme rhyme
That your jackets possess lining, compromise lunch
The watchband cutting into the fat man's wrist
Edit an idea, change channels, insert dime
Assert thyme, ascertain lime's way, limp
Here kitty kitty where shitbrains still govern
Wax melting where the binding nears the sun

Off-white, a narrow sky begins to close in
Soft hyphens fade against the green screen
Half-hidden, nonremarks curtail attributes, crop predicates
Tough blue Stanza Z-80 shuts engine off
Laugh at a chip shot, the long putt
Often unremembered, the face in the mirror
Coughing fears margin & a second cup
After the tap in, insert flag
Overt horizon, slope now to greet fashion
Rough bumps along the road to break line
Suffer motivation, bright red flare of nostril
Draft image, through which seek shadow

Notes crinkle old syntax's loose sway
Rope bridge in monsoon to far noun
Loom foreign to swampgrass curried in hot sauce
Thus Senator Borah says to another bore
Baby corn, button mushroom, bullet vote
Love it or live it, Dear Barrett
It's 5:15 a.m., that world is over
But I just want Yaz to go forever
Two minute warning, four minutes to midnight
Half seven, digits on the readout
Count pulse, court passing sums, again Sam
An old broom standing proud in one corner

New nouns for old, no noons for ought
Caffeine multiplies the thought into red image
The plum tree is snowing petals
The tall porch landing was her stage
Waiting to load transient program, dog bites parrot
For a general, Ike was so femme
The formalist variation on a double play
Sends Europe south into North Africa
Where to punctuate was mother's next question
Get Out The Vote, capital of South Dakota
Dog bites paragraph parachutes over moldy buckram
Sun disk accesses into driven sky

A broken old pen scratched this
Big wooly spider climbs the stoop step
Months of steady rain silences an urban populace
I squint right at the phosphor screen
Now the sun at the margin
To have what are called good hands
The car backfires and the valley echoes
Depositing ink in swirls to code these phonemes
My state of mind is New Hampshire

Light is but the shadow's absence
A fresh cadence marks a new crime
The lines upon paper state the social contract

Blue parrot sips slowly from an amaretto glass
Jigsaw puzzle down to last dozen pieces
The grammarian's palm begins to bleed
House full of bad pens, bad puns
One year ago tomorrow I went down south
Symbols quest for an impossible full morning
A clerk hosing down the produce shelf
Cabbie's view through the interior mirror
Static, like a postcard from your childhood
Too yellow, too green, the pinks too bright
To mean anything, to mourn anything, two
People terrified to speak of love

XII

Words wiggle, tickle, setting cat's whiskery nostrils atwitch, rooster's yodel, breeze in tall grass (little spider), grasses, is as/was is (fuzzy), a blue prick bleeds & what remains (flock of gulls) means, O new Spring (!), rhythm is its own plagiarism, doo wop, vowel's valence splitting the diphthong and beneath the kale a thousand snails still in the damp shade, quiet morning, wasp got into the john, bird's call like a gargled whistle, bang, snap, crack, hid in the flowering leaves of the plum, phlegm's but the solids of sleep caught in the throat, the moat, remote, we crossed in the boat, like a bat out of Philly. Folly to count and hope, however fewer, the fix & feel of a clean edge, eye lid, three lies, loafs settle steaming on a hot board (bed), bid 2 Junior Gilliams for a Lew Burdette, get set, said, sad, smell of ripe mulch is sour, our match made of volleys, sulphur, so for how long is that yellow caterpillar set to sit atop hot wet fresh steaming asphalt? Leopards in leotards, hot sauce, spotted cat on the shed roof, blue-gray flicker on the small screen, radios is hard, bad news, how the heat drops when the sun goes, cup of tea, fog tint, hollerin' in the hallway while the desk clerk snores. Later the sun rises but you have to jam the door shut, ear full of wax, car full of vexed doggies yapping in supermarket lot real loud. Lone Viking in longboat seeks land across page from crosswords, folded in the old man's lap. Each of many lives seems simple, full of repeats. One job I wouldn't mind losing. After the reading. Referent. Bypass. Bid. Call.

Sought. Sweet. Saw it. Sweat it out. Sad Sultan of Swat. At dusk, the blue-pink horizon. The way you hear sirens deepen when they slow and stop. Swaggering though they don't mean it, a heavy slow grace, the elephants cross the roadway. Head of the snail rears up, horns extended, king of this leaf, leaving its trail glistening, to see the grey jet descend, yard shuddering after. The tongue is thick in the head of lettuce on bread, a lattice said to weave lotus leaves along the wrong path to a single meaning, mining half shades of nuance to mime the world, blue swirl, solid object bigger than a breadbox. Gravity is its own absence nor is balloon racing a sport of the poor, pearls in the sky high over a meadow hover, while below rafters in white water rush, rivers too curl from view, hushed where puppies carry hunters to the fox, boxed in by snapping death, bad breath of a rifle muzzling kin of dog, digs image cut by line from a wood block, inked and then stamped. Thus the blisters of history whisper pus, lives pissed to no higher purpose than poverty's trust in service dense as the surface of a jungle served up under jelly flambé, India my Indiana, say that particulars do not fade nor rust consumed in their own dust, or that memory's fair, an old funeral barely the scene of thought's return, my own father flattened into a photo, false smile no knowing could ever fill, fall becomes autumn but never spring, negative my nugget, if we ever got it, that new syntax equal to the living could just as well lie.

Count friends few just as lovers many, money enters in, plot the poem all lit by reams of writing's trace against the face of one who, were it you, is eye alone at home in the head just as the large bed of the past seduces, the feel of what tongue, wet, widens and hardens what is, just as is wills was its future by being, so a small scar spreads into a canyon from which there is no turning back, only demolition, given that entropy is not perfect rest, even as the debris blossoms each mote of dust bloating into a rotten whole swells so fast that syntax starts to sweat. Hot noon on the sloping steps of an old porch, smell of tar: down in the valley between the tops of trees autos pass, over which the sound of a big truck bearing lumber, but the rustle of wind in the plum branch is louder because more near, I hear the sleeves of shirts slap on the line, all tangled (old white gallon bleach jugs full of water weight nylon, bobbing in the air). Garden orders forest or meadow, the park bares design, clay pot to trap roots, hard edge to the hedge, long rose in a slim vase, knife slicing thru torso of zucchini, steamed carrot growing limp, teeth ripping thru leaf of lettuce, gone. A big cool dumb easy fox gets his index jogged kindly, light moan not of pit quiet roar seeking time under vexed waxy xenon yellow zit. Sun sliced through the bamboo shades illumines the room, one window open to let air in. The sound of pots and forks from back inside the kitchen. The curve hits the outside corner. Upside your fat head. Besides that. Siding. Side. Said.

So. Sad. So soft. So sue me. Lofts in SoHo shrink. Rents rise, forcing the poets out. Who remembers the linguist of the Hotel Wentley? White and aimless, cum laude, they have learned which books to purchase, but not which ones to read. The road to Iowa City is paved with good intentions, perfect binding, preferring submission to solicitation, a ragged right. I was not bitter, better, butter being the tiger's fate, finding access where lately excess fought its own fathers to a halt, inhalt, in all the right margins habit sought Rago's white horse, a site for soaring lyric lies. The words are my wife else the mirror break, mere beaked thing worn at the neck, the past is peaked, the page, aging, yellows where black ink hollows out a syntax deep in the stacks of a library not checked out of an infield made of the mind in which spelunkers become fixed by the smell of gas leaking from a pen's tip (tap) along the quay of letters lost, thus thoughts' ruins tossed. Through the print, between the curling graphic spaces, I could see them shitting, grammarians downside up from the rafters in the old hotel, elicans out over the water, the caged parrot, the Tac Squad in snowshoes at the door, the small girl finishing the ancient puzzle and the distinct fartlike odor of nachos until the salt begins to slide from the rim of the margarita and the weeds in between cracked floorboards start to spell out spring's flowering reach, damp garden of seriphs seen from above understood as a rash thing to do, not love but what desire from which I start to sing.

The yard understood as a mixture of motives, porch paint spotting sage and spider, sawdust and old boards killing the lawn, strange bird half yodels in the plum tree against the sound of a garden hose inside a trash can or another bird's higher trill, ears absorb while the eye scans, skin senses the fog's damp, butt upon the step, sound of a broom in which driveway, wind felt in eyebrow's hair, here in the little things (who I am), three flies articulate the sky between porch & tree, poetry is that this, is thought thus, body but a metaphor (who I was) for a medical model of that thing lit. Of late much work, little light, leads humor stuttering home, get the lead out (of the pencil, the penis), the point scratching paper's skin seen to signify mind means the made marks the maker's mask (meet science), ear stitched to side of head, hard wood weds floor to foot (I am not that), float from word to word as if there were a reason, as if there were reason, beyond *a*s and *e*s. "Ease awes," guffaws the talking mule, eyes as corrective to ear's reduction of kitten's seductive vocabulary turned to "mews" is snot enough to lose amid typos the essence of our text beckoning assent. Anxiety of response conducts meaning to lowest denominator, prefaces foreplay plying tongue to punctuation, a setup. "My reputation is in your mouth" is in your mind (read aloud) allows no reading. Speak up or forever hold your piece: this is the place. Word bytes man, and the apple drops. Submit to reading. Now read this. And this. This. This.

Thus. Toss. Tsk, tsk. One gets lost. Lust accounts meter. Made my morning into song sung. Lung got it wrong, tho, stung by redaction: ink is glue. The visible flickers filtered so, selected is neglected, name of the not seen. To construct a clock imagine time seizable in units, sizeable in eunuchs, laggards playing tag to communicate past tense thought. We live in the house that Juan bought, rebuilding steps that spiral up to a meaning over my head rent with practical implication, make it nuance, shade's shift tracking sun's course, cloud muted, the mind is a terrible thing (think). To the bottom, bent pole limits parking, lottery of comprehension to any statement but convention restricts error only narrowly, stop signs vs. stars' names in the night sky, anarchy of house types in town by which to discern home in the dark become regular in the newer tracts, pattern recognition of birds in flight, a walk in the right woods. Words would do it were they real (would they were) but signifieds drain them, hemophiliac meaning, all we can speak of caged in thought insulates action, friction of syntax fought the intention, sparks connotation to belie melody, whomp bop a do bop, pink and green houses, blue glass, the old woman who lives in a shack, kettle's whistle, incomputable smear to greet ear and eye can do nothing but sort, leaving a trail that sought only to lay a track which, sounded, marked a possible present (this), activity grounded in its own proceeding, bleeding store-bought ink onto spongy page.

The abstractions of history, lethal as a foodstamp, clarify the legal real, an all-over texture, the white race to oblivion, the white rice stacked in sacks in a valley town for the displaced Laotian farmer, a frown seen is a sign of displeasure, a fond scene measures the papers' coverage, "human interest" being neither fosters purchase, sculpted tragedy of a playground killing turned into "features" fathers a false remorse (sullen competent cop shakes head), mothers no new insight, the boy just bled 2 pages away from where Garfield contemplates lasagna. Disjunct art-meaning of later collage framed against white gallery wall bends context into content, the difference it makes that the girl rising, mouth open, in horror over the student's dead body in Kent was overweight, message in the politics of appearance not lost on the applicant for what's really a sales job, degree in museum studies. Some do, however, choose education, mechanism by which to lose close connection to the culture of the "working class," whoever that was, solution to my parents' oppression being to change sides (reverse image). Perverse imagination to make equations against scale, as if to sell such small reproductions of thought: no ideas but in context. Form gathers force (my credo) for what purpose but use, source for an assault on habit. Seeming clarity inhibits thought as it ought not. Boy dead because he spoke wrong tongue. Boy George, my hero. You survive. Others. Will. Not.

Now. How. Ever. Buy futures. Bird features feathers. Beard furthers the casual look. Inverse of camouflage, open at the collar: pert. Polo shirt pink pastel backlit in the La Jolla window beside the folded tie. A small wooden box on the dresser in which her father had once kept cufflinks now held only a vial of cocaine and a tiny spoon. The diskettes were kept in what looked like a card file across from the overstuffed easy chair with its faded burgundy brocade upon which lay the sleeping ocelot like any other housepet near the window to the sea. Tennessee fireworks factory goes kerblam, fine rain of body parts, make it noise, red against blue of the news studio, cut to cued dissociation, sailboat silhouetted against vast setting sun, beer glass in foreground rising full until just the slightest foam spills over and this is the sole lamp in the cramped apartment, family of five fresh from Taiwan. Plums too small to eat have begun to drop, the fog if you look closely has its shapes and shadows, the wind in the trees is loud, I can't tell over it if that's a dog barking or the steady squeal of a saw, black beetle on a yellow leaf, parsley gone to seed and the brown cat atop the back fence sniffs the air, too cool to rain, not a fly or bee in sight, the same-ness of any day against another accumulates that sadness which becomes restraint in everyone older feigning wiser, orange cat on the porch turns around and sits, such simple acts set beside each other build.

Hand-held, the image thru the penis lens wobbles as it pans, sweep to right margin, pins sound to paper but the mind adrift hobbles after, gathering few vague echoes of intent, so tend the senses wisely or they tangle, angles frame the object hued by light, hard edged, wedged into an imagined sight but lost, the page turned, the cost of dreaming as you stare at words, birds migrating toward a punctuation, partial truths are all we get, letters home, honed, the bone of thought rings in the head, a sort of bell within a spire, what is higher than sight is heard, hurt, herds these small black beasts of graphics forth. I sit and you set the table, used it and able to do so again (you sit and I set the table, used it and able to do so again): which of us reads, which writes, or writing reads, seeds of a process which binds, not blind to the separateness of different lives, always we find strangers on the bus, but print is a bond we learned by rote, in rows, years ago. Each step taken jars the old porch, beams cracking along the grain, white spots of bird drops speckle the brown paint, the horizontals bowed and perpendiculars slanting, a few nails painted over when they should have been hammered back down. Heat-seeking, the reading eye zooms in on denotation, and old statue gone pale blue in the park with its skirt of broken bottles, dark green. The color chart fused in the eye bears arbitrary borders, blue-green, blue-gray, purple. The globe closes to a focus, or widens and blinks. Thought burdens sight by erasure. The instinct is learned. Blue iris. Brown lash. Yoke. Yolk.

But. Bit. Chewing. Down into. Onto a chunk of. Ontological chocolate. Horizontal on top of it, the sky is not flat. Venn proof by intersection of air into yard or room, such subsets of otherness. A yam what a yam, Ham's syllogism knew Yorick, Powhatten's bridge off coast of Cuba into candied doubt und so max out by the cut. Dive, he sad, for rice flakes, watch what is given (is given back), freedom's just another word, old rooms so silent of their births and deaths, brooms push dust toward a meaning, the moaning wind in the trees thought by some to be their fathers. In the desert once I heard silence, a startling thing, not wind, not even the skitter of a lizard over gravel, until the roar of blood in my head, high pitched, a clear tone, seemed about to deafen and I thought, thinking words, as if to fear a soundless world, still, stillness, knowing even motion to be but an image of time, and that but memory's projection. The idea is to inform all of their layoff at once, at the shift's end, a note on the timecard, telling each to return tomorrow for their severance plus a half-day outplacement clinic, resume skills or retraining: in 1983, the average manufacturing plant lasts just seven years and you can lease the technology out, contracting for the product, keeping capital mobile, wages down, which has its impact on poetry, that writing whose value is not that it has none, but the image presented, craft-centered, of what working could be, the care in the word.

The car in the yard: the ward healers of tenure bicker (suspending Spenser, choosing Chaucer), make it known is such a small demand, not one literate among them in the face of a single syllable sounded, soft and simple, ample enough to sample the whole of the world's thought rounded in the mouth, but curriculum demands division into genre and the vision is gone of a possible writing, sighting the opaque nameless things which fill a garden so hard to fathom, the world at random forcing form is not a farm of hardened meanings, for knowledge cannot be taught. Say that what he wrote were words, heard but never hardened into objects foreign to their making, senses shifting but not to settle (none too subtle), taking out of talk & all that reading a bottled ship not to chase whales in but yourself until the shelf of this impulse swelled and he understood it better – say what he wrote weren't words, that he merely scripted letters. A cat is a stylized wildness chewing grass, blue inhuman eyes over which the sky fills with clouds, white scraps preceding the gray bank that pushes over the houses by the ocean, the garden damp smells stronger, a plum drops. Parrots of the past unite, for what have you to lose but that thru which you live, dream-headed, our own cages more elaborate than any. Voices in the dark, wires tangled, hark to find not an answer but an echo, barking. I know a house of mud and wattles made (no I don't). Gulls circling over the valley. It's the end of May. A hard wind. Thin sun. One. Room.

Roam. Wide. Not build. In it, "A." The el to the Loop. Lit up, writing down: balances. The boys in the binding, the buoys, discipline limits. Ears arc what's harped, I's wide, wade in the foam of, the form is a half shell (my bell), held up. Hurts harden over but are not erased, and in each case I was to what degree guilty, silly centered careless love but an indulgence. In sequins lights shine real serial, un aleph beth, garlanded sin tacks sharp consequence, flex sun's spotted circumstance all Latinate, the lit in it falls to the were, he rows to the sure lea, a lie: thus did we cross the tea. I spy: see shore, 3 masts approaching must broach a new whorl, he, he coming to z'real, breach a broken syntax teaching each a token surreal displacement of the rolling feel of it, eye's wheel, tolling signals rodeo's begun, radio's on, the sun (radiant) fills the air, what hair remains on my head is blowing, the future flowing in off the sea smells sweet. A word wide is deep also heard right, rate of exchange, sides edged by white space placed in a row go forward, knowing only where they've been as possible site to future meaning, hybrid as Marcie's white rose leaning over the fence, name's a neighbor, each a particular as against the typical, person sighted about to cross the street, city mapped in the mind is a grid, greed's a knowledge oddly used, hidden is that you I'd bid to speak with, a letter mailed at random, ladder to the wall's top (edge of the paper) that stops pretending the vision's beyond, left there, mark of an old desire.

MANIFEST

for Barrett Watten

So you're one too. Quantify effect. The kingfisher's blue foregrounds against the yellow-brown of winter forest. The train does not hesitate to penetrate a grass fire, air full of cinders.

Junkies in the snow in Madison Square Park. "So it wasn't his kidneys going off." Songs of a roomful of antique clocks. The first crocus, purple by the fountain.

White cat wends its way between the legs of the chair. Rain centers the body.

Festival of Unfinished Projects. Hybrid as elegant as the First Lady herself. I'm in line for the bathtub next.

One page resume, mid-day nap. Flicker of a big truck behind the pine trees' branches.

Gauze curtains, room full of shadows, mildew in the doilies. She bounds up the stairs, three steps at a time. The elevator settles before it halts.

These leafless trees, brooms stuck in the earth. Rain-soaked clothespins, damp on a line. Sentence is the instant at which integration halts. Spoon scrapes a bowl.

Regressive parallelism intimates mock narrative. Submarine's deck is made of teak.

Cabbie snaps the meter on. Seven is dark orange. In the basement, the washingmachine agitates the dark. A finch is at the feeder.

Natural light of afternoon on the stairwell. Chain from the mailbox to the brick of the porch. Glove's fingers stick from jacket's pocket on the rack.

Just so many leaves desert the tree. Number joins these statements, kneeling on the rug to discuss needlepoint.

Life here on the axis of combination ceases to have been a projection. Her collection of seashells sits upon the keyboard. Coalcars shake thru the forest at sunset.

Post-nasal. Dried leaves of the avocado plant's neglect.

Pre-prerevolutionary. Lexus is our program, calling for the abolition of paralegals.

Abolishment I heard. Attach a rider. Set aperture. Mark.

Any conjunction denotes a caesura. Gulls dip mid-flight into the valley. Big sun sizzles & spits.

My voice appears as an average, new leaves circling the plum tree's branch.

More about this later. Empty suitcases await their return to the cellar. The chalk inscriptions on the blackboard from the previous class are left there to haunt you. My cat comprehends recrimination.

Overt hinging. Bug on the paper with no respect for these lines. Hose nozzle that shoots like a pistol.

Whose intestines reject process. Connect.

Down the street elliptical window locates stairway in the interior of that house. Fragments of Spanish through an open door. Subdivision skylights reflect the sun.

Coal cars share the forest at sunset. Flies encircle thought. New grass registers footstep. Then the dogs go off.

One is to five as light is to X. Black man, red bathrobe, burgundy steps.

Paratransit. Whipped clouds cling to the low mountains. Dull dart bounces from target. Cuticles lie in shreds.

These are facts, buckets. The bread is blue in spots, your eyes red. The shadow on the leaf spells aphids. Music in the water pipes of a distant organ. Shits like pearls grown around kernels of corn.

The light in the bottles on the sill of the bathroom window. Think of veggies as 'storebought.'

Morning in the Mekong. Walking from sun into shadow's temporary blindness, waiting for pupils, stuffed olives amid ice cubes, to grow big. Locomotive approaches detail.

Learning to love the old four-in-hand so foreign to the throat, the goat looks like Groucho. A second cup thru-the old grounds drips slowly. The sputter of event. Pflff.

From the parsley to the spinach is an hour's walk in the life of a spider. The brittleness of morning.

Fishcakes by the dozen. Flies in the dawnlight under the plum tree. The fff-fff shush of a broom.

Impact of gravity on light causing linebreaks, sheep graze on a hillside, ignorant of their despair.

Composition by fly route. That the bird song is near & the baby crying more distant gives space shape. Three clouds linger in the morning air.

Any small-to-medium mall will have a stationery store filled with get-well cards, the toast is served with a miniscule container of jelly.

Non-dairy primate. Wires that steady the antenna. Clothes-lines attached to a crucifix.

Over the horizon the long jet descends into literature, the sea. Fingernails so apt to mutate. Green snake slithers across the path.

Mattress & chairs in a pickup, first day of the month. You size a watchband by removing linkage. Bruise on the heel of foot. Yellow in the ferns.

The women return from shopping & the men come down to meet them. The muffins are burning in a shadowy Kitchen.

Cockroach stuffed with pork & water chestnuts. Markup. Roll of pink toilet paper loose in the street.

Butter flavor. Inflationary expectations discussed as an object. Artificial flower market. Dog glances up from a nap on the porch.

The owner hobbles out of the liquor store, waving a pistol, the ice cream melting down the side of the cone.

Sheet lightning in the linen closet. Tripod. Carbonated appearance of water just before it boils. Foxtails in the cuff.

Varsity apprehension. Fat Japanese Baptists. What is the name for this in ballet? Warranty against downtime. The buff stalks the roof.

Klutts Makes Martinis Mutt Hutt. A fuzz on that side of new loaf. Miniature koala clings to levi pocket.

Articles alter nominative function. The articles alter nominative function.

Can I ask you to stop at the bank? Rooster crows, marking noon. Pushing the bicycle uphill.

Residue of orange juice, crystallizing in a forgotten glass. The page falls from the binding.

New lessons. Record in the sunshine. Disadvantage of the third-born. Shadows of tree's branches flicker in the wind. Pine odor of aerosol.

In sex, it is the women who are realists. Wrecker's jaws gobble bowling alley wall. Five is to three.

Metonymy is not like an afternoon, even against the high ceiling of the bank, small craft bobbing in the waves of the express line, which turns (as in verse), the sun searing more deeply than the video security of the lighthouse, the seals noisily counting out bills.

Good coffee stains the cup.

Next paragraph the submachinegun in the hand of the Secret Service agent is an Uzi. Hands struggle at the rim of a basket, wrists encased in bands of terrycloth. The audience rises to give you a hand. What I hear is a buzzer, presumed innocent.

Daft boy stands in a doorway. The big dog half skips. Certain simple things occur again.

In that I'm not preparing for my talk in Venice, this sentence serves a second purpose. I peered into it.

Tense is precisely described. What will you feel, washing bathmats at a laundromat? This reopens the cut above the eye. What causes the lungs to inflate is the lower pressure in the chest, in comparison with the air. Ball drops fair near the bullpen.

Subvention. It shows sufficiently where it changes, where it ends, where begins, where resumes, without interlacing of words, of conjunctions, or connectives introduced for weak or negligent ears, and without glossing myself.

Fat robin struggling in the wind (disguised as fog). Chicana in high, spiked heels, on her way to work as deputy sheriff.

Femicide. I was right the first time. Day-old rum cake.

Sad flower seeks water. Malted egg, Moosehead Stout. Having to climb the stairs, search the keys out of my pocket, unlock the door, & re-enter the livingroom, now dark, to find the letter I forgot to mail (this poem enclosed).

Talking to 5th graders, they want to know how long an idea takes.

New condo blinds a mural. The bus shivers over rough pavement. Caneiisda lever for that woman on the stairs.

Do you, now? Stalinist in painter's pants. And so equivocates attribution. Corner store called a bodega. Scum forms between the tiles. Stay away from the center of the plate.

Darwin Dias, meet a Patel. The plantains. City scene thru a scrim of rain. The old tanker, passing silently thru the fog, not a soul on deck. A dirk.

Below market rate. Aikido to-do. Dolby.

With a coin, gently rub off all six boxes. Hangover's euphoria, umbrellas in May. That surplus of anger in all that you do. Half the walkers will ignore a drizzle. Connect the dots.

That which is capital intensive (porn) is legal, that which is labor intensive (prostitution) is not. Hygienists dress in white. The most notable thing in the museum is windows.

The tension of conflicting demands puts strain on the ship's bottle. The elevator door opens, but no one is waiting.

Amid the greys of a burned-out wood, seek a new reduction for beauty. Causality poses formalism against structure. What a mailman calls flats. Cylinder filled with sand seeks ash.

Tiger beat. Sitting where the foxtails got cleared away. Over those hills & those, then you come to Petaluma.

The kite glides over a yellowed field, seeking food.

I saw that same butterfly yesterday. An impediment in the left eye, like an impurity in an emulsion, drifts across the visual world. Those trees are like moss in the crevices of these hills. Abandoned tractor. The kite is a type of buzzard.

Beyond even the sound of traffic, civilization reduced to the sight of a distant barn.

L shape cloud (alone in the blue sky). Often in a dream I am weightless, drifting. Abandon the balloon. Pull the cork. Brut is more dry than sec.

The short dog wades in the folds of its own flesh. A tennis ball is chartreuse. An old guy's white beard.

Members only.

Those mailhandlers I worked with are retired now, long afternoons in a cafe nursing chilled coffee, sport pages turned to the horses.

To sweat in the wilderness of monkeys, in parked cars (with no tires), the damp smell of spring onions. Syndicate a shelter based on your easement (air rights). The whole sky vibrates to the tune of a jet.

Pop the bulb on the fuchsia. See who he's running for. Use white-out.

The secret is in finding just where to leave the blanks.

That bright spot on the fence is the sun, mirrored by my watch.

Eyes fully dilated: brain damage beyond repair. Where the sign painter had had his shop, there now was a deli. The center-fielder positioned himself for the ball's bounce off the base of the wall. Backing out of the driveway, the Mazda waited until the oncoming traffic passed.

Gradually webs cocooned unused clothespins on a line. Charles shouts into the telephone to be heard above the siren. On the coffeepot the yellow light comes on.

I want the shovel's sound, hitting the damp earth, or the plastic roar of hot wheels, but the caged song of a canary tames the porch.

I peered into it. Winter left blue spots of mildew on the carton of old books. Pretend as if you're not missing that button.

Rooftop gas pipes all have hoods. Old Sned keeled over. Be sure to get the chili.

The wonders of public transit stop-start herky-jerky in the twilight of the hill beneath this balcony crowded with revelers as you stare dumbly at the stuffed olive drowning at the bottom of a plastic glass, your head pulsing in the balance of chatter, re-focusing, refocusing, or the too-sweet piano of a distant Keith Jarrett type inside the constructivist's spare apartment, while riders spill out of the bus doors half a block short of its next stop, enabling the emptied vehicle to wheeze gradually to the peak.

Turnaround time. Decaf. The shimmer of a hot day's air over concrete. Well drink.

Rear of the coach. Man on the bench practices thrusting his jaw. The bean sprouts heat down in a minute.

More attitude. I went through the garbage bag, uncrumpling each sheet of white paper.

The salesman sees the hood of his car as an office. An old man with a gun. Not valid for return trip. Tripe.

The jackhammers put a hard edge to the noonhour silence. A yellow crane hovers over the shell of an old Chinese building. A woman with a red umbrella on a hot afternoon.

Sheet or leaf. I don't want but. "I've gone off my hormones," said Jerry-Diane. Kentucky Fried. Mixed States. Registers discourse as a competition.

So telekinesis projects across white space. Man steps in front of bus. Snapped q-tip lost in inner ear.

The gate-keepers at each opportunity point tend to discount an undifferentiated cohort by the average characteristics of the group, restricting opportunity for those who are capable and motivated within the cohort, thus magnifying differentials over time.

Phrased out, in turn of, over, over with (width with), the blue sugar in the glass jar, the ducks on the dashboard. Goes off, meaning complete or exploded.

Grackle in the plaza. Burn marks on the spoon. Man's tie is his banner. Old bus jiggles down Mission. Selection & Shreve port.

Clipboards bestow power. Assertion solders value. This year's fashion is one nipple, barely visible between buttons.

A hair caught to pen's tip drags ink through the letters. Lunch in a thermos, on a scaffold, seven floors up.

Paragraphs to go.

The spectacle of the hod-carriers, pre-stressed, remembered. The lumpers gather at the end of the dock. Letters flicker on the green screen. Fica.

Sez the ostrich to the tiger, "This is a fine place," the sun large with departure, the room full of hookahs. You feel the tide through the houseboat's soft rocking, harmonica's low trill swelling the air. Further gestures of closure sell this sweet sadness. These dots connected describe the mouse.

Between architecture and machine lies the frog's involuntary twitch. The metal curtain rolls down over the jeweled display. Two ducks rock in.

NON

for Jackson Mac Low

So then go back
to the old forms
as if they were forms at all

wood frame
of a new structure, a theatre
soon to be covered by stucco
sort of a foam cement

or across the street the small
delicate elderly Korean lady
with her thick
and curiously deep red hair
squats in her garden
so damp that frogs thrive
coming up from the creek

sun to my back
blanches the hillside
each eucalyptus still as a candle
tho we feel the breeze

She rises
wearing green rubber gloves
long stalks
of yellow-headed weeds
in hand

Continuity demands a margin
What is the import of detail?
How do we stake that claim?

Here we fathom connection
each word an accident of letters
ink bleeding into the page

the cage is open
but the canary's dead

Dylanologists who bet on the wrong man

Sam Donaldson shouts
over the copter's din
the prez he home
but nobody in

Little hill shrouded in rain
the way shingled houses streak when wet
or the concrete block apartments
with their bland identical drapes

women my own age
making the transition
away from youth

telling the barber
I part it on the right

fever crowds the brain
its thinking convulsive

porch lights on signal winter dusk

man in a three-piece suit
with a buttoned-down shirt
but the striped tie
hangs loose in two strands

holds his briefcase in his lap
open, a kind of desk

compulsive eye,
mottled world
old friend but an unfamiliar street
too brightly lit
sharpens the dark –
big glimmering headlamps
cars behind them not visible
float past

as the reader turns the page
you glimpse the shape of stanzas

What's the plot of this song?
Be sure to include the quotes

dim blue lights
leave tunnel in shadow
bright burst
arrives the station

one-legged woman
swings on her crutches
onto the escalator's
first step
shining black skin
pulled tight
and through her nose
two gold loops

Imagine light
as a kind of firmament
this small metal lamp

a ground to write by
pen's stiff spine elongated
shadows to swallow letters
merely a shining pole
upon a wide black base standing
on an old walnut dresser
bulb's socket held aloft by a black clip
shade a cheerless plastic
from which hangs an insulated cord

refrigerator's hum
is joined by furnace

the case is made of wicker
and the top is arched
shelves so deep
that in front of the books
stand small framed photos
and a basket

try to write
without shoes on
tight grip of canvas
focus thought

setting the book down
I roll over and kiss you
bumping glasses
up my nose

orange enamel kettle
atop white stove in kitchen
(harsh overhead light)
its wooden handle, tho treated,
has been blackened by flame

small bowls within bigger ones
is the right way to stack them

asleep beside me, you grind your teeth

two needlepoint doves in a circular frame

I hear the rhyme by accident
does not equal
accidental rhyme

earlier
your left hand gripped lightly
the base of my cock
so only the tip
passed your lips

sperm mixed with saliva
spilled onto my belly
you stirred it with your finger
inside my navel

Brilliant postcard of Godzilla downtown

taking my hat off
is sometimes as dramatic
as stepping outdoors

as the play commences
one begins to notice
props on the table
at the rear of the stage

she wears her shirt untucked
to elongate the torso

in Beijing
Col. Sanders' name
translates into
"Elder Head"

the Hac Man with his flap down

Discharge planning

in academic theory
the primary principle
is defensibility

from one letter
generalize an alphabet

add civilization to weeds
yield flowers

What're you doing, asks I
Sucking bear, says she

eggwhite, eyes of the blind

gulls' cries echo
up from the valley floor

after the cold
the bus
hot as a sauna

bread truck's dolly
is in fact
a stack of shelves

silent radio electric kiosk

the particular itself
exemplifies the typical

here disjunction's visible

because spatially figured

just for you

bright blue plastic tarp
atop the unfinished wood frame house
work stopped by the rain

distinct patches
back on the wing
of the black-shouldered kite
small otherwise white hawk
high over the grassland
flapping to hover

road barely visible
thru windows fogged in the rain

Ted's sonnets
mimic Jackson exactly

therefore here
little spasms of light

O parking lot
oh parking lot
I'd give my arm
to find a slot

shattered umbrella

bent

awkwardly as a broken bird

morning markets meaning maybe

old disposable
diapers
tied in knots
atop the black asphalt

almost blue
barely visible
smoke spews
from a red brick chimney

weird social movements

(*save the snails*)

my little chubbette

imagine Nobel laureate in chem.
as political, as pathetic
as those in lit

homeboys in the rain eat brain

After three days solid
indoors
the shock
of the bus

I struggle to keep the shoulder bag from slipping

galoshes
that don't quite stretch
over old loafers

thumb-size
hummingbird
still atop the branch tip
pips

yellow light almost orange
red stained furniture
sun caught in the shades
the gauzy curtains
this door to the livingroom
that to the hall

gaudy rings on the cashier's fingers
undercurrent of banter
half-teasing, half-sexual
between checkers & baggers
I want my wares "double-plastic"

a beard to hide
the wide neck

rough edges
to fresh clipped nails
catch on the sweater

deliberate as the lack of path
is the forward motion
while the gull shakes and flaps

big teeth form a beautiful smile
one man stands on a garage roof
with a small bucket of hot tar
here, closer, another man
pulls a blue collar
up over his sweater
sleeves bunched up to the elbows
or a tall young man in bright yellow pancho
holding a day pack in one hand
grabs a seat
write what you see
but not to privilege sight

fog diminishes the horizon
the biosphere is shut
a man with dark hair on
the back of his hands
the curtains always drawn
on massage parlor windows
ears sting
in crisp air

green plexiglass awning over rear porch
on the highschool football field, the goal posts are rusting
an RV wrapped tight against the elements
woman with a mole at the corner of her mouth

"which section is this?"

"Oh, it's the mess"

I eat a banana
the way some men make war
to exercise my faculties
fully

said the regent
What does not change / is the difficulty
making change, coin vendor
"not in service at this time"

bag of salted
sunflower seeds
corner ripped open
beside the fat
paperback novel
atop one of a row of six
plastic seats
by the laundromat door

businesslike, an informality
that is almost intimate
yet impersonal as a hospital
rolling a cartful of wet underwear
to the wall of large, whirring dryers

everyone's bundled
even indoors
but for the mailman
in his short-sleeve shirt

the sake of a story
an autonomous thing

the whistling banker

random access remote

graffiti
on the walls
deep in subway tunnel

"I am attracted and repelled"
begins the review

I am spatial memory
he wears the kerchief
pirate-style
you raise your hand
into which to cough

Balloon in the shape of a blimp
hangs from a long cord
although "hangs" is the wrong word
for the thick string nearly anchors it
over the brand new Mexican restaurant

you think you're naked
all dressed up in freckles

blanched light of haze preceding rain

pigeon struts
pecks at a cup
composed of styrofoam
containing coffee

brittle rustle of the new
plastic shopping bags

poultry is like a swan
but with a (your pun here) –
railers and oos of the South Pacific
for the most part extinct
women who reread
the Bible on the bus,
the way my knuckles
foretell rain

Off the wall, Motherfucker!

is that how that went?

a new neighborhood
means a new idea

avocets on the mudflats strut

paltry is like a swine
but with a diffidence,
law of supply and DeMan

the folly of labor
on a Friday
seems particularly abundant

that's not how you pronounce that

Budget Bob
offers a zircon pendant
Call Now

(workers of the word unite)

a morning league for seniors
here at the Albany Bowl
already the air blue with smoke

a tiny Chinese couple
quite old, obviously in love
hand in hand with aluminum canes
almost identical deepset eyes

cranberries loom
in muffin's steaming flesh

two old guys in a pet shop
crowded, smelly, full of shadows
guinea pig in a cardboard box
and here on a rack a book on finches
those old color plates of the 1950s

you walk into the post office
and groan to see the line
tall stack of tax guides

a world here of children
means that time will pass

balloons tied to No Parking sign
hair stylist has a grand opening

I offer this sock
to the gods of the laundromat

then I wonder
about the number two

black tipped wings
one million snow geese
startled
thunder into the squawking sky

"Transit Shanties Firebombed"
page one head in the *Trib*
is not even mentioned in the *Chron*
marketplace of ideas

cheap shot
tipped at the rim
drops in

large dead boxer pup
carcass unmangled, not even bruised
still at the shoulder of the road

man on a bus
eating what appears to be
an uncooked hotdog
the way you would a carrot stick

page fills
like a sky with clouds

so tired
even on a Monday
some riders rest
their heads against the glass

imagine space here
as airy, fluid
positions barely (and arbitrarily) fixed
then instead as rigid
etched

pigeons coo on a crossbeam
making me nervous –
the narrative (implicit) slams shut

wad of gum
in the hair of a child
as an act of bullying
decades after
remains intense – tho I've forgotten
just who they were
wondering rather what drove them
what need to establish rank

where elsewhere
was power's absence
felt as need

gull tilts its head back
to cackle old gull-cackle
atop a light pole in the mall lot
glowing in the rain

she twists
her head and
whole upper body
to cast
long hair back over her shoulders
and it takes my breath

light pain behind each eye
almost pushing, almost pleasure
giddiness of too little sleep

woman on the street
to her companion whines
"but I've *heard*
of mutant turtles"

Emma Freud,
Siggy's great grand
daughter tho
by her own
admission's
never read word one
of his, stars
on a British (I think) TV talk show
Pillow Talk
on which the gimmick

is that each interview is conducted
in bed,
she and the celebrity both
wearing PJs

young woman on a park bench in the brisk sun
eyes shut, knees apart, and on each
hand with the palm turned upward
thumb and middle finger lightly touching
international symbol for meditation

older woman here
face a virtual grid of wrinkles
thick white brows, eyes peering out

smokey morning light

a woman's shoe, slipper-like
twisted and bent
abandoned at the busstop

the tops of the buses themselves
bear giant black numbers
intelligible to helicopters
lordly and isolate insects
kin to the dragonfly

small blonde teenage girl
skin so pale her freckles seem red
blows huge pink gum bubble
which disappears
back into her mouth

"Do you do stocks?"
Don't pollute

your commute punctuation understood
as a kind of battle
necessary exactly
an old man as words themselves fail
scribbling hurriedly
into a notebook on a bus

attack of the hard objects

owlish eyes
that sank deeper into gathering jowls
bracketed by cloud puffs of sideburns
the long cape, pale green suit, paisley tie
counting between lines by threes
or eating lunch at Panos'
sun glistening in the glass of white wine
really a pale yellow
I recall being surprised
alongside the stage that night at Glide
when someone (who? Linenthal?)
first brought Oppen up to be introduced
that you didn't already know him
(leaning his wiry, bent frame forward
to say "I want to talk to you
about your open vowels"

willingly we'll say
you were a petulant master

chill air still

This morning the moon is chipped again
almost transparent in the predawn blue
high up over the eucalyptus

in panic
my heart racing
chest tight
not at the choices
but at choice itself
which pair
of cheap sunglasses?

but the page you'll see
is not this page
(light red grid, lines
too close together)

Ain't no toad
but a crow in the road

man sees crow
man writes about crow
man eats crow

clouds cast their shadows
spotting the sea

Each letter conceals
The construction of its narrative
Beginning in fact with the teaser on the envelope,
Through the four-page letter, filled
With bullet-studded (•) lists, curious indents,
Subheads, key phrases underscored (possibly in color),
Leading up to the reply card, dear reader,
Upon which your favorite words (your name)
Are certain to appear
Alongside the word "YES"

yes, she is the most desirable woman
yes, I want you to lie on top of me so that I can
kiss and suck your breasts
yes, let's rub pelvic bones until our pubic hair scratches
or the way my tongue explores the inner curves of your
ear, sweet and waxy

so that she and you must be
and are the same person
even if you the reader is a boy
for what changes here, word to word
is what lurks behind the letter "I"
blur in the mirror, burr in the paw

he never recognized himself in photos
precisely because they didn't
reverse left and right

islands held clouds like a magnet

the plane itself is a shell
abandoned by bodies, filled by bodies
drifting in the currents of air

an alphabet of twelve letters
nearly half of them vowels
two of the consonants 'w' and 'r'
an alphabet without the letter 'r'

hang glider rider

man on a surfboard with a paddle
and his golden lab retriever

an old sugar mill
is being converted to a mall

a tall wooden chair
that to sit fully back in
would leave your legs dangling
so you find yourself invariably
sitting on the edge

mynahs as common as sparrows

double-decker dump truck

an itch under the eyelid

Instinctively
the damp mash of leaves, twigs,
soupy clay beginning
to give way beneath me, I
start to look for
strong roots to grab onto

the descent beckons so slowly
the hill itself collapsing
I watch myself reaching
fraction of a fraction of a second
great nausea of adrenalin
hand locking onto the eucalyptus root
even time to wonder if
it will hold

a bowl of cool sour purple paste

housefinch with a nacho
hops to escape pigeon's rush

several juvenile
black-crowned night herons

share a pond by the airport
with the slender, pink-legged
black necked stilt

floodlights illumine
hotel garden

this page has been deliberately left blank

mongoose skitters across the lawn
like a big stretched-out squirrel

shit stained
black volcanic rock
pounded by the surf
is home
to the black noddy

abandoned jeep
is turned into a planter

zebra dove
much smaller than its mainland cousin
pale blue face

even the endemics
the "native" plants
arrived here
from elsewhere as seeds
in birds' stomachs

now that elsewhere's been lost

the descent beckons
trays returned to their "full upright locked position"

landing gear down
and infants start to cry
their ears popping and
them not knowing what that is

rewinding the tape
people walk backwards with confidence

sox that slide
bunching up
in shoes' bottom

big barf splash
on the window of the bus
upon closer inspection
is the dried yolk of a thrown egg

the children watch their parents
watch the paintings
noting carefully an attitude
they'll learn as art

motorcycle's wheelie
cuts the still air

cigarette's scar
blisters leatherette seat

the 't' in Tahiti

here becomes a 'k'
Kahiki, in Hawaiian
means "land of the fathers"
or did I make that up?

semiotician = failed linguist
oreos not arias
poet = failed second baseman
vireo video Vichy
the rice is white
fender bender parataxis
is there a fish in this text?
industrial occident

on sitcoms
the only prefix is 555-

puns invoke hidden rhymes

a military town
with few longterm locals

gaza stripper
Nonnie Sim

we took the fennel
thru the mountain

first a layer of bright canyon streaks
over which a second solid level
entirely in black
which is then cut into
to reveal the line

a word scratched out
leaves lovely shadow

you can hear a revision

land without roadkill

tort sure
not torch ear

in the utopia of language
so-called, why
are so many meanings homeless

you turn these to paragraphs later?
Tony Vaughan asks

Riding over Oahu
singing

Pineapple fields forever

of the Olympic skater, says
He's so impressed with his gold medal
he's going to have it bronzed

spider plant's web

taking off my hat
releasing weight and pressure
from brow

contiguous: that's a word I seldom use

ambient hearing
like the way the driver
scans the road

fluorescents hum in pairs

yellow light of a shaded table lamp

shrimp feasts on caviar

dog scratches behind locked door

beneath the paint
old sheet
of wallpaper starts of peel

sudden burst
several car horns at once
means intersection's jammed

between that and which

scar in the wall where
once a phone jack

risers you can buy
to alter table lamp's
shade's relation

syllables as a pulse
larynx dilating or gripping shut

great crossbar of 'T'

poem

post-its as labels

pages joined at top and bottom

rust where once
a paperclip held

huge cup of lukewarm tea

leaves him bloated

sun at the margin

water choking
thru pipes in the wall

multiples to go
before I sleep

naughty Liz
not a less
nor a list

technique is a test of domination

grand piano
used as ironing board

Rock solid. Market wise.

The R-Effect

cursors
on the screen
are mean

dull fog
obliterates any background
the hill itself vague
as if hazily airbrushed

Hank calls himself
second-generation
victim of AIDS

I hadn't expected nature
to be so visibly a social construct
volcanic rocks
to which the whole world
has been imported

apple opal poplar dapple
sofa over ortho
grapples oval bother
opiate glover snaps
snits nick wicker wire
waffles after
further global sap wafer
waving gravy clover caps

pleonasts of the past amass

Tricks for modern scouts:
you can tell how long
a cigarette butt on the ground
by the bus bench
has been discarded
by how flattened it's become

letting M&Ms
melt in my mouth
gradually, not biting in
the smooth surface
slowly turns coarse
sugar coating
about to give way

flesh in the ear
curiously dry and flaky

stools
like hard black large rocks

little birds
quarrelling in the tree

in the dictionary
the root of a given word
is subordinated
to its opening letter

I loves you
Monkey-Mix

odd the way a faucet juts
from the side of a stucco wall
overlooking nothing but a sidewalk
with a pole to mark the bus stop

pigeons battling in the rafters

old women
heads wrapped in bandanas
squint
into the harsh wind

string ties
a boxed cake

long green trousers
beneath a white cotton skirt

suburban shopping district
stores mostly closed
on a Sunday

black exhaust spews
from roaring bus

breathing
through this phlegm

large number
red-orange
over which, superimposed
smaller green letters
san-serif
lower case
7-eleven

bulletin board
composed of stretched burlap

trope or trap

in Russia
people sitting at a table
over cheese, tea, bread
chatting, no agenda
is called "shuffling"

bingo form
each letter
factored by fifteen

This is the way the word winds:
blind man's cane
forms a sort of sonar, scraping,
scratching a path across the dull walk
(grim faces await the train), birds
huddled in the pine branches, ache

in the knee; eyes
pressed against swollen sinuses.
Young girls in miniskirts
seem a generic sensuality
upon high school steps. I stop
to retie my shoes. A still
moment in early spring, half
in total bloom. Little metal whirr
of ball bearings in a skateboard.
The way a day pack
crunches a sport coat. The bay
half-visible through the dissolving fog.
Plate embedded in the red cement
is really a door, reads "water."
Train passes sandlot game of hardball,
pitcher in the midst of his wind-up,
leg cocked. Turning the newspaper's pages
in a confined space. Tension throbs
at base of neck. An odd day,
windy enough to demand a sweater,
hot enough to make you sweat.
It's not that the cap is tweed
but the broad green plaid
evokes stares (drinking orange juice
like a wino, tiny bottle
in a paper sack). Marks the margin
as if by magic. I search for scissors
to trim my beard. I heard
you were weird. Loading dock
for pick up, back
of department store. More ways
to pave patios where yards are fenced.
Hence nonsense follows. The truck itself
lifts and tilts the dumpster. Nuts,
caught between teeth,

increase pressure in skull. Hot spell's smog
smears the sky. Eye
of a pumpkin
rotting in the compost.

body heat
steams my own glasses, sweat
band of the hat soaked thru—
sweet salt taste

the bridge rises
out over the bay
the eye sees
dark towers
holding the lanes aloft.

great zoo of my own species
any subway stop

ah hyper rush
a spring day
after hours of squinting
at the amber screen

first whine of the train
as it rushes from the station

first anniversary
of the Grand Opening sign
(bright yellow banner)
of the Cozy
Sheep Skin Seat Cover Shop

Once every six months
like clockwork

I fuck over my root directory
so that I can't boot from the C drive

fat wheels of a motor bike

man in the row behind me
does low, whistling bird calls

Poets R
satellite dish of the race

sun's glare blasts
thru the cracks

so thin
in a down vest
the lollipop effect

sits high
in his wheel chair
like a throne

tho race itself
be a fiction

up close that tweed coat
is a sequence of vertical bars
filled with alternating
diagonal stripes

there is no privilege in an end

hair without gel
looks like
rhymes with
not so

goes to Tahoe
just to play the slots

I turn my neck
and the bones crack

rough streak of stubble
at beard's edge

Proto-mallie: the flaneur.
"The older I get the more
floors I discover
at Macys." Little red
thermos looks like
fire extinguisher. Ants won't cross
trail of
petroleum jelly. Hat
with no bill, cubist
leather beret.
Sore on my tongue, smell
of dung. Voice's choices
sight's relight. In gaol
they make you surrender
your panty hose
to prevent suicide.
The crowd of protesters
approach, chanting
"out of the boutiques
and into the streets."
Seagull brushes
up against my cap.
Rude Work Ahead.
Velcro strap,
reusable cast.

Dog's name
is Cutty.
Eco-Brutalism, Deep
Semiology. Sturgeon
General. Boot failure!
Odd trim
of the ear's rim.
The neck seen
as a tube is
seen incorrectly.
Post-its peeking
from a three-ring binder.
Dog snarls
behind window of
locked Rabbit.
Morning's magic means
make my
daily bread. Ears
put head in
brackets. Hypervariables
in DNA show up
on screen like
bar code
on a cereal box.
Rushed writing.
One is to words
always an outsider,
tho they invade your head,
colonize dreams.
Neither an Aram
nor Omar be.
Picking your teeth versus
picking your nose. Voice
echoes up the lightwell.

Reading to discern liquids
from the bottoms of used cups.
Place mats
map the table.
De Man who shot
liberty: valence.
Blue sparks fly
in the dark tunnel
beneath the train's wheels.
The sound of an egg cracking
against the bowl's edge.
All sirens are narrative.
The brothers hover in the doorway
smokin' their crack.
Powdery sugar
atop apple pancake.
Now that we have computers
liquid paper is doomed.
Pair of grackles
attempt to mate
perched atop
Amtrak arrow logo
till the she-male
jumps into flight.
Water fountain's
cooling motor
hums on.
An odd john:
high urinals
and low basins
hard to tell apart.
Thimbalism. "JWs,"
he sniffed and sniffed he did,
"black Mormons." Yellow stone house

across the way, in which lives
Mrs. Florence Schneider
amid her treasures, rare china,
fine handspun cotton, a garden
of grape hyacinth – that odd
blue purple. Dump truck
pale blue filled with clay
atop which lays a shovel.
Black lores of the red cardinal.
Rounded shovel
is for cutting into
the earth, square ones
for piling it away.
Combination of
the swing and these
new reading glasses
quickly makes me seasick.
Back panel of greeting cards.

Just when you thought it was safe to read: Return to Planet of the Paragraphs. When this you see, justify right for me. Hills of the piedmont act as a track . . . along which the first long finger of oncoming fog is dragged. On the freeway cars cluster, herd instinct. The old man and the bicycle. Sun stuck in a web of cloud. Balconies unused in winter, swimming pool empty in the rain. Fractal tempo: cars rush past. Knowing just how long the "wait" light will blink before it turns to red. Mannish white haired woman echoes husband. Wide arc of bus as it turns. Categorize joggers by how they hold or wave their hands. Hard of darkness. Hanging from the ceiling of the Eyetalian restaurant was a huge plastic octopus. Theme park from hell. Where freckles join to form that small beautiful continent on the small of your back. Blue bursts of veins in the skin of the thigh. Walkers in the night take fright. Open, the briefcase in his lap forms a desk (train's roar echoes in the tunnel): he's using a calculator to balance his checkbook. Belt that missed one of the trouser's loops. Each sentence, dahling, is mahvelous. It's Monday and we're rushing to work – it's almost euphoric. Albino biker gal? Nah, that's just bleached out. Woman like that in spiked heels (briefcase is a Coach bag) running full tilt up the escalator to catch her train, trying to keep the Wall Street Journal from flying out of the crook of her arm. Each one bleach one. Nothing will tell you faster nor more accurately about the sexual allocation of labor in the field of architecture than women's restrooms in public buildings. Am I my brother's beeper? Yellow billed blackbird that I cannot find in the field guide. I turn over in bed and sense my sinuses drift and gradually resettle. Crisp lines of ironing shape the old man's blue jeans. The ice plant in bloom, red, yellow. Hegemony begins at home. Ragged looking plant, the artichoke. Hang gliders over the coast drift past the firing ranges at Fort Ord, almost motionless over the dunes (sand blows across the highway). Without a blink, the clerk pulls out a pair of scissors from under the counter and cuts the woman's credit card in two. Like a vomiter with the dry heaves. Suburban commercial street still empty at nine on a weekday morning. Wheels out of alignment. Abort, ignore, retry? Holding the pen virtually perpendicular to the page, thumb and fingers pinched near the point. Anklets over her stocking before she puts on her tennies. Readable? A cluttered desk is the spatial representation of over-commitment. Porch appears to have a roof, which in fact it does not. Old globe. Waiting for the others to choose their fortune cookies, so that I know that the one which remains contains my "fate." Bush hints at Deukmejian, all-Gemini ticket. Running up the steps, I blossom into a full sweat. Tables turned atop one another, cafe closed, man stands stationary alongside his mop. Anger augers altered ego. Duck into the dime store to buy an umbrella.

words warm
or warn
where meaning wanes

crouch to carve
ink into pages

moan as bus
pulls free of station

Dan Rather
gives me a kiss

"I'd like to buy a vowel"

hot sun
burgundy flowers

balloons on a post
sign for a party
drooping now, losing air

the page, the page
was all the rage
in the age of Olson
mock lung
as the stumble of syllables
plunge
plunges
space reduced
to the details of representation

duet for grackle
and mourning dove

rake on a tractor
smooths the infield

break line at verb

mob scene at station
means the trains are late

simply shifting weight
bones 'pop' in the spine

driver returns to the empty bus
reaching in through the window
for the front door switch

ratty sweater
feels like home

so that linebreaks
are like parsing

when this you see
hold the bus for me

swabs of cloud
in the sunny sky

adults constitute secondary market
for boutique baby food "organic and wholesome"

problem of words
drifting across paper

hawk up
a wad of phlegm

in the park, by the playground
a little old lady, white haired
strums a banjo

symbolism of Uncle Tootie's house
where as a boy I mowed the lawn
overgrown now, gone to seed

a stack
o' flats

radio remote

pen's point feels cracked,
scrapes across the paper

Thick-browed albino
in an expensive suit

try to imagine
pigeons as nature

we just called
that cowboy
Hoppy

Samsonite briefcase
with red gym bag

from gym to gum
hum a hymn

deer body do breed

boy with a perfect
imitation
of a pigeon coo

it's not the tennies
over her stockings
in contrast
to the tweed of her business suit
but those white cotton socks

white haze
of bright dawn
through which
a city rises

pale silhouette
while riders' heads
tilt back
the train asleep
dawn commute
or a man
stares down
into briefcase's cavern
what "e"
is ever silent
to hold
while in motion
styrofoam cup
so perfectly still
large woman
pencil in teeth
crosswise forms
computer imitates bell
soft beep
door closing now
two women
in lace hats
speak German
blind woman's cane
folds up

What's hid (dawn grid): tendons scream in the knee
to ratchet the leg up a flight of stairs

Lazuli bunting's
copper chest
beneath turquoise head
tho brilliant, 's
nothing
paired with its song

drainage pipe
channels creek
to whose mouth, rusted
hummingbirds come to bathe

disavowal
data verb

I thought I'd lost
this notebook till
I picked up your gym bag

lagoon at low tide
rain's loosed anise air
otter's head bobs up
black-crowned night heron
solitary, sits
straw-billed curlew picks
into damp, stony sand
white flecks
of an egrets' rookery
high in the pine
feet in flight
form a sort of rudder
gull pleased to gulp a fish
tilts bill high
soft splash descends my grebe
the brush alive, crinkling
rabbits and lizards
cormorant, rapid
jets right over the water
still, grey – the enclosed sky
asphalt road still wet with fog
birders on the water's edge
binoculars held high

eyes tire
skull's socket
is literal
a fragile thing
vase full of water
on which a flower floats

for a week, for weeks
you seem about to cry

egrets gobble
at their piping young

the way a leaf
falling
spins in the air

I seek simple labor

up against the truck
harlequin duck

anxiety determines the referent

Question:
"Where did I first see
a white-breasted nuthatch?"

Stifle impulse to answer
"In the mirror"

Siren on the freeway
in opposite direction
blurts past

Arm in a sling
worn under
short-sleeved shirt

train grinds
around curve
in tunnel

pigeon drinking from a water dish

"The galleries of the new wing will be entered via a 'Grand Staircase,' leading the visitor to one large and three intermediate sized exhibition spaces, each broken by an interstitial space. From these spaces, there will be windows – tantalizing views out to the Pacific, which give the viewer a taste of the 'real' world before returning to the enclosed purity of the galleries."

delicious
song
mocking
bird

brickwork as lattice

Advance button
on the tape deck

default tab

in a proper linebreak the poet
comes to a complete and discernible stop

lamp holes punched
into auditorium ceiling

flame trees
of PBS

politics of X

giant robot tortoise
shell red and spotted
like a ladybird's wings
saunters forward

pieces & coins
rooms & corners

age has blurred
the old man's tattoos
chemistry is not prosody
Dinnie dear
the lake set deep
atop the higher hills
blue-green stain
inkwell
babies cry
as the plane descends
terrified
not understanding
pressure in the ears
spoon scoops
seeds of the honeydew
my mind
instead of a bunion
factories are not often
many storeys tall
turret vents atop
spinning
he stops

to look at a book
on porn as addiction
springroll
and a sprig of cilantro
bound in lettuce
dipped
in the carrot vinaigrette
my page
instead of opinion
I strum
and the train rises
bicyclist's chain
worn about the neck
you yawn
and the silver flashes
"But I *AM*
Puss in Boots"
said Rae
towhees on the lawn at dawn
cafe over
bluff above the cove
beyond which
swimmers bob in the pale blue
between the shadows
that are reefs
reeves
works not
to read but
to read in
tie worn unlooped
hanging from buttoned-down collar
open at the neck
"pony nails," says Val
meaning the style of her hair
t-shirt under tank top

modesty on a hot day
four store fronts
topped with a row
of apartment gutted by fire
roof missing, interior walls
surrounded now by a scaffold
clouded whites
of the blind man's eye
under the feathered
leather cowboy hat
stone in shoe under arch of foot

End macro. To own a car is to own a carburetor. Black tie on a hot day. The pout of a young girl. Canoe upturned atop a minivan. The hard disk was not a disk at all, at least not in the strict sense, but a pair of disks, shining polished iron oxide, four sides readable beneath the needle's scan. Jai ROM. Utility substation. On the Read. Shopping carts in a parkinglot by the bank. Drums in the dorm. Re bait: rebate. The circle is warped. The dog mopes in the small yard. In the distance somewhere, through the thick rustle of branches, a wind chime gently traces a scale. Hefty sack of potting soil leans against the house. Jay's call a trilled chatter. Thumb's ache after a night of bowling. Arcs and curves in the bee's hovering flight. Dwarf lemon. Wisps of fog so light you need your sunglasses just to see them. Rose twists to find the sun. Sound of a softball against an aluminum bat. Once the small airplane's engine passes, distant traffic fills the air. The two flies are a dark green. Flesh at the elbows revealed an age. Nudity is in fact more mysterious precisely for what it fails to tell. I closed one eye to see the page. That letters beget words is more violent than we've imagined. Towhee in tree peeps at me. O brave new pen! Shadows at the arboretum. Sign on the RV reads Snack Bar. Hard edge of a half moon. Crow amid the blackbirds threatens scale. The benches in the sand under the trees in the grand concourse. The curl of dead leaves. The courage of an awkward, ugly work. The hero with a thousand feces. Realm not of kings but of middle management. Slow belch bottled in the throat. That thing in his pants with a twist-off cap. Fjordism. Rev. Moon's son is "reborn" in the body of an African boy. The Sparts' line on the Afghan invasion is "All Hail Red Army!" A town in which not all cars are yellow. His idea of tennis thoroughly conditioned by overhead highlight shots from the eleven o'clock news. Downhill from the word Go. Lyn hegemony. White trim edges a dove's tail (versus, say, patches on a mockingbird's wings) visible in flight. A sentence bounded by the history of sentences steps forward. Language is not my agent. Aphorisms attack. As plane as the nodes on your face. Flower vendor's shaded stall. First green shoots on a pruned tree. When this you feel, start to squeal. On the lawn under the tree in a bikini. Is a young woman without arms reading a book, bright orange highlight pen gripped between her toes. Mo, whose full name is Maureen, was as a child called Mimi. The sideways "2" shape of a curtain hook. The well-wrought run. The word is all that is your face. Shit, boy, wipe yo' mouth, you got chocolate smeared on your beard like dingleberries on a hairy ass. Sparrow's shadow travels up stucco wall. Problem of drought etiquette: whether or not, at a friend's house, to flush. The Nortonsville dead are for the most part Welsh, recruited to the Black Diamond coal fields of California, suffocating for low grade ore in the 1870s, five towns no longer visible even in abandonment, houses moved elsewhere (to Antioch or Concord), hawk in a low glide over the dry hills, tombstones chipped under a grove of cypress, tho from down the hill, facing north through the valley, you can see the Sacramento River right at the point where the delta ends. The quality of mercy is not strange. Foggy, pronounced "fodgy" – the purpose of intimate nonsense, babytalk amid lovers, is to articulate a space apart. Your turn to have the car today. A form of otherwise vicious habit can become a pol and be named Bruce Babbit. Dull shadowless light of a clouded sky. Each thin braid of these corn rows individually dyed. Lone burst of hair beneath his lower lip can hardly be called a beard. A bird in the hand leaves a mess. From Gilbert and George to Gilbert and Gubar. The task of management is surveillance. Book bagged in polywrap = safe text. At dawn in the distance the compulsive mockingbird riffs trilling spirals. Bee's buzz as a mode of song: volume equals distance. Seamy ontics. Bright rug atop pale carpet. Parsley in a pot. Thin wire mesh of screen before fireplace. Ich bin ein Satz. The opposite field. Desperately seeking Godot. Well, I was hoping you were writing something about this delicious dinner I just cooked you. Digestion recollected in tranquility. Smoke spills from the holes of the barbecue's lid. Dents on my car hood from where crack dealers sit on it during the day time. How spell agapantha? Trimmed tree, as hard-edged as the patio it lines. Unheated pool on a cool day. Mao cap with a logo – this one reads "Tsing Tao." Young man carrying a bicycle up the flight of stairs. What does not charge is the will to charge. Marilyn Monroe had six toes on her left foot. A net sack for thistle seed, intended for finches, hangs empty, swinging in the soft breeze. Hum of a motorscooter's engine as it shifts down to climb the hill.

By the river one sees the homeless
nearly as visible
under Mitterand as Reagan

                    infrastructure of the past is vast

         the beggar with the baboon
                  tourists leaning
                 to photograph its bulging
                        bright red ass
         is at a distinct advantage

                        bananas at a Parisian street market
                        with labels that read Del Monte

        impossible to pop
 pimple with just one hand

          barker at the Greek restaurant
                 breaks plates in the doorway
         to get tourists' attention
          stereotype posed as tradition

 A French woman without a cigarette

 (complete this sentence)

radishes in spiced yogurt

a poet's home
anywhere in the world
visible to the eye

vast fields of sunflowers
and all the cows are white

first there's Raworth's moustache
world renowned
then there's Raworth's hat

in a matter of days
my English decays
struggling with the translation, Francoise
leans forward at the crowded cafe table
to ask "What
is 'giving him head'?"

O crickets of Tarascon!

You speak
the most unintelligible
English I ever
heard, sez Ian to me

Mynah
in the cage in the cafe
knows to whistle

dogs
wander amid the diners
without interest

to read aloud
under the full moon
at a medieval chapel

versus

to shout
facing
into the mistral

once the Nazis governed here

"Les Dents de la Mer"
old familiar poster
in video store window

the flap flap flap
of loose sandals on the walk

brain cells of the past, alas

judge the nation
by the calmness of its dogs

I love prejudice, she said

perch baked in foil
with butter, tomatoes, squash –
and caraway seeds!

if only Eliot Weinberger
had married Carl Andre

How do you say "asshole" in Dutch?

to understand
that inherently you are political
and that politics
is poisoned

From where comes power?

that the middle of the alphabet
should fall
between 'm' and 'n'
gives rise
to a blank space

my mother in Switzerland who served oranges cold

Bar du Siecle Glacier Le Mamba

in Van Gogh's room

versus
Stella at the Pompidou
the perfect site

as if by accident I have done in my life what I set out to do. dark fish form shadows in the stagnant water. the garden is a formal garden; the sky too offers its crystalline structure. the pigeon is our national bird. but I am yet forty-two. the sun sets right in our eyes. on this corner, on August 22nd, 1944, women came into the streets to offer us wine, their lips and themselves, and the men did also. the tapestry dates from the third century: it is impossible to tell which bird is being referred to. the face of the clock is a roulette wheel. this cluster of blacks in the subway turn out to be students from the Ivory Coast, thoroughly bourgeois. people stand in the doorway of the tombs to get out of thc rain. snail rctrcats into the pit of its shell, vain attempt to escape the stone's heat. beware when someone adorns you in basil. a frisbee sails over the wall of the castle.

modelism never sleeps

The world is all that's in your face. Napkins crumpled on the table at meal's end. Horse on a hill. Drill's friction: the smell of burning bone is exact. Apioectomy? Template of an invoice burned into the screen. In the yard of the house behind, the Eskimos' dog yaps up to the fence. Too thick taste of cola. Thick white enamel pain over these metal chairs lends them an air of plastic. Black butterfly, edged in yellow. We both wake to the sound of thunder, sitting up in bed to stare out the window as flashes illumine the shallow valley. I recycle the mosquito on my wrist into the next life. In his last voyage, my grandfather's great-grandfather commanded two ships, the Erebus and the Terror. Winding headphone cord about pocket radio. Two apples bend the slender branch. Fly appears to be "rubbing its hands together." Petals of this purple flower, withered on the deck. The unity effect, being phenomenological, is strictly imposed. Lead-soldered tin cans poisoned the crew: they abandoned their ships trapped in ice, proceeding to march in exactly the wrong direction. For Isotoner, I propose the following ad campaign: a series of videos based on old rock songs, e.g., Gimme Some Gloving and All You Need Is Glove. She paces platform, impatient. Stout puffed neck of the black pigeon. Gradually, over many days, ants devour the sparrow. Woman in the rear view mirror. Dawn frost beads the hood of the car. Vietnamese boy's slender, feminine face, all eyelash and cheekbone. Remove all that seems "characteristic" about your work until the deeper features show through.

Blighted ovum

the black car idles
before the garage door starts

to yawn,
radio inside it
causing windows on the entire block
to vibrate
that way glass hums
or I feel it in my teeth
plugged as they are into bone of jaw
until the vehicle enters
& is swallowed
by the basement
of the green
ranch-style stucco house

chestnut backed
chickadee
no larger than
the hummingbird

shrill burst
of a jay's cackle

transit routes generate
patterns of access
as natural

recombinant corn
taller than anyone
sunset orange with toxins

bulb of a helmet
atop motorscooter rider
bright red

stiff-backed walk
of a tweedy old man

tho the light's against him
no traffic in sight

kid steps on a curb
as if walking a tightrope

Engage the page

we feel your freedom

young woman in laundromat
reading, frowning into the book
Story of O

plastic notches
in the back
of the one-size
fits all
baseball cap

Virginia rail
lives in the reeds
of the weedy marsh,
is larger than a phalarope

rowboat alone
on a small lake
windless day
boom box blasting

Tilted bank of solar panels
atop flat-roofed apartment complex

short stubby handlebars
signifies mountain bike

sweatsuit as formal wear
this must be California

cylinder of ink refill
is a nude pen

that grainy feel
of your shaved legs

folds of flesh
on the bald man's neck

Skyline of a small city:
the highrises are there
but not in such quantity
as to acquire a sense
of their collective shape.
That long last tone
at the end of
a Chinese sentence.
Painter's pants
immaculately pressed.
Oak trees
in the warehouse district.
Mack truck cab
rolling without a bed.
change gears
this high in the mountains.
In the dream the boat
sways in the high sea and
at the far end
is a giant sphere, the ball
rolling in the rough
weather
in your direction

so that you must choose
either to be crushed or to dive

into the impossible water.
Powdery filament tissue
of old spider web.
Floor mats on the sidewalk—
he's cleaning his car.
Yellowing jade
needs a larger pot.
Clutch up on the bat
to quicken the swing.
A film
of the filming
of a feature,
to serve
as filler
for late night
TV. Therefore
conjunctions stitch the seam.
Gracefully disabled.
Thumbingbird.
Unable with that hand
to close a fist
consequent
to a medical experiment
participated in as a student
as easy way
to earn money.
Heavy
pause
on
every
word.
Slaves of

aviation.
Wisp of dust
tumbleweeds
across hardwood floor.
Six-sided solid,
the signified
always
faces the street.
Poem with a shelf life
of just eighteen months.
Double beep of quarter hour.
When suddenly
that part in your hair
widens like a grin.
Medical waste
floats ashore
of increasingly cluttered brain.
My friends,
I am that man.
The flan
is the body.
Titles
are often misleading,
subtitles seldom are.
Checking
out the driver
in the next car
through my rear view mirror
at a stop light
(one never sees
the lower body),
thin ebony man
with a long white beard,
tricolor rasta cap,
high sharp cheekbones

that cause the eyes to recede,
I decide he's a gentle person.
Rolls of roofing
turned upright,
black cylinders atop the gravel.
There comes a moment
whenever
I read my poem when
it is apparent
it is terrible
I'm a fraud,
no one would ever
choose to hear
or to read this,
but then this moment of panic passes.

In *Gargoyle 32/33*, Dan Beaver writes:

> Reading *Paradise* is like trying to put together a jig-saw puzzle of entirely square blocks. There is, no doubt, a proper way to construct the puzzle, but until the perfect solution is stumbled upon, the player will be left confused and angry. *Paradise's* pieces are what the author calls "perfect Silliman sentences." Perhaps, but the paragraphs need a little work.
>
> *Paradise* is too disjointed to work on any level. It is not a novel; there is no plot, no characters, no beginning, no middle, no end. There are, granted, recurring motifs, but they seem to be present only because the author's pen ran dry, and he filled it back up with the first old phrase that came to mind. Perhaps it is intended to be one long, rambling prose poem, with images splashed across the pages like a Jackson Pollock painting. If so, it is too long; the images do not remain consistently interesting to the reader through its length.
>
> The sentences do not hang together and whatever

logic there is behind the book remains hidden in the author's mind. The pastiche style that Silliman employs is mildly interesting for the first three or four pages, but during that time the reader is not given any indication of a sense of movement. If the reader stays around for all 63 pages, he will be just as confused at the end as he is at the beginning.

There are moments, however, of insight, when the sentences almost form a complete thought. For instance: "What is morning/ A cat. Fed. Curls up on a kitchen chair. Sedative sunlight. Gauzy room. All the books written to be read on the way to work." There are other moments when a single sentence stops the reader cold to consider the thought behind it. Perhaps this is enough and all that a writer can hope to accomplish. But there is too much that should be dispensed with. The key to the style of *Paradise* seems to be embodied in a sentence that falls near the end. "If I revised, this wouldn't be here." He is probably right.

moon transparent in the morning sky

antique camera shop's
alarm blurts
as the key turns in the lock

yellow ribbon
around the open pit
reads "caution"

sun's glare diffused
in the scratched plastic
of old bus window

two scarves
make a sling

a stack of pink
ceramic pipe sections
atop the flat bed truck

the way you carry
the bike upstairs
one-handed
hoisted over your shoulder

woman in high heels
turns her foot
to snuff out
cigarette on the walk

tea leaves damp lamp
at the bottom of the bag
on the saucer by
the cup

milky residue
in the soap dish

post contemporary
like a chopped Harley
driven by an older woman

the car pulls
in front of the house
jays cackling high in the eucalyptus
motor running

plastic laundry basket
filled with books—
it's moving day

stucco stripped from the porch
for termite work

Dodgers dish doggy do

the topography of this beach
is not the familiar
gradual incline
smoothed over by high tides
sand fleas thick
over the rotting kelp
cormorant's path
low over the water
but pocked
anemone clenches
to the finger's probe

balloon of blister bursts

self-conscious, chasing
the bus down a busy
downtown street, his run
is a half
skip

Divide wire coat
hangers into
those with cardboard,
those without, those
wrapped in filmy white paper,
whether the hook is formed
by one metal strand or two, design
of the twist at the base
of the neck

what I like most
about the Albany Public Library
is that it smells
the same as when I was six years old

Schizophrenoform

It's not that
there's a dead cat in the gutter but
that it's been there all week

snoodlenook

Little moths under the porchlight,
be with me now
A dog in the distance
barks compulsively
Birds chirp
to greet the early dusk

the landlady lives at the foot of the stairs
that run down the hill beside the house
so wooded you don't even notice them

Dreamlike,
the color TV
thru the neighbor's gauze curtain

ice crackles as it melts

nibbling Cracker Jacks from the palm of my hand
the little man in the blue suit salutes

the runner forgets to run,
so is easily forced at second

as the earth pulls back
dropping away from the rising jet
one sees traffic
recede into patterns
individual cars the colors of candy
slant featherwise
amid the vast black field of parking

Song:
I said over and
over and
over again my friend
I really fear
that we're in the mirror
of production

Soft horizon – the clouds are nearly (but not entirely) unbroken, level at the top, sun-whitened, but here and there: pockets, dimples, canyons. Economy of detail is a value of distance. The way clouds bunch, snagged by the mountains. Pen's tip is hidden by hand's shadow. There are in fact two windows, one inside the other (it feels like a thin plastic). Another jet no more than the sun's glare refracted parallels our own path, but to the south. In a tight housing market, exchange value overwhelms use value, as people purchase homes as part of an explicit strategy of accumulation. Women on the telly tend to wear red. In the dream, there's an ornate dresser with high legs, its wood a polished blonde, beneath which a young man is hiding, trapped, an enemy – how do I know it's an enemy – unable to escape, for on the one side stands Barry and on the other myself and I'm holding the fluid of a huge and heavy egg, shell gone but still within a filmy translucent membrane, so large I can barely keep it from spilling over though I'm using both hands, and I hurl it forwards as though I were a child and it a bowling ball far too large, and the yolks bursts, yellow spreading over the hardwood floor, so that the enemy, young and blonde – I don't think he's myself – has no choice but to crawl through it before coming to confront us, which he does, slowly standing as the rich yolk drips from his arms and clothes. Next to me on the airplane is a woman with a long pair of scissors, cutting coupons she's torn out of old papers, trimming the edges with great exactness, placing them carefully into a box too small to have held shoes which she's placed in the lap of her sleeping husband, while I wonder about the wisdom of sharp objects in a vehicle proceeding at 600 mph. From where the cars exit the park. Emma says to her father, "You're the head of words." A sushi bar with a maitre d' in a black leather tux. "Photography is not permitted," says the sign at the entrance to the Nicholas Nixon exhibit (each sequence in the series of PWAs concludes with a note as to the date of death of the subject). Anselm Kiefer's winged palette: only once in a thousand years does an artist come along who can lead the German people. At a station of the IRT: an apparition of Jack Lemmon crossing the street. In actuality this means a watery yogurt whereas I prefer mine thick as custard. What's better than a new pen? Green-framed dormers of the Dakota. He speaks of the instrumental function of poets in his homeland, Ghana, by which he means funerals, births, weddings. The pigeon picks at the muffin, tossing it in the air, then abandons it to the next in line. He sits cross-legged on the tile circle, directly above its lone word, "Imagine," while his mother squints to focus her camera. I stop at the produce market just to buy a lone banana. Others come up to the tile circle, then step back, careful not to touch the sacramental spot. Oh field of squirrels and brazen sparrows. Leaves gather on the red brick steps: four pairs of rectangles "woven" into a square of eight. Willard Rouse's neo-deco dildo dominates the sky. Pensive people. A police officer with a noticeable limp ambles asymmetrically through the marble lobby of 30th Street Station: flipping sound of Amtrak destination sign. Echo of the subway corridor enhances the beggar's song ("There is a rose that grows in Spanish Harlem"), vowels stretched over the tiny portable organ's chords, while in the distance, from another corridor, I hear the lilt of Peruvian flutes. They're sitting side by side on that bench, but are they sitting together? "I quit the theater to go into politics because I was tired of dealing with huge egos." An old man with cotton plugs in his nostrils and ears. The thick lower lip protrudes over the firm jaw, softened by the spreading neck, the hair above still thick and wavy, tho graying, beneath which shoot the stems of tortoise-shell reading glasses set upon the soft pyramid of nose, long-lobed ears set close to the skull, great thick pale brows balanced by the curiously thin upper lip. Correction: an article on

Nov. 1 about Imelda Marcos' appearance at an arraignment hearing in Manhattan misstated her shoe size in alluding to her reputation for extravagance – the size is 8 and one-half. A Mali ladder on a metal base makes for a narrow, vertical sculpture, and is priced at ten grand. Teardrop pear. The loft quivers, meaning a train in the subway is rushing past. In the middle distance, the Chrysler Building's tower blurs: it's begun to rain uptown. Pear's flesh so hard that my gums bleed. On the cover it reads North Point Press * San Francisco (but it's not San Francisco) and on the press release North Point Press, Berkeley (but it's not Berkeley), the glossy author's photo slipping to the table (collar open to reveal the hair on his chest): it's the small house next to the laundromat, Albany, CA. On the back slope of the cemetery, the stones are smaller, dark and twisted. Detention Windows, says the fading factory sign, For All Your Locked Facility Needs. Red painted tips of two-by-fours, blonde boards stacked high, lumber yard in the rain. I plug one ear with a finger as I shout into a phone at Penn Station, talking to my wife whom I've not seen for a week, asking if she still has all those freckles. Old ties lie by the side of the tracks, black chips. Hello there, Zed heads. Odd intimacy to see women asleep in their seats as I amble back to the dining car (how many are simultaneously wearing headphones?). Autowrecking yard at the edge of the river (which came first?). *Concurrence*, in French, means *competition.* What is the name of this harbor? A field of abandoned buses. Thinking hard for all of us, I honked, and the deer bounded into the wooded dark. Great brick cities of the east. Charlemagne Palestine slaps you in the face, softly, but aggressive enough to mock your commitment to pacifism (Bruce turns to Anne and says "Deck 'im"). Having fallen behind, it feels that we are rushing now to the next station, the next letter, the dawn hidden in the trees like so many raisins amid branflakes, my heart pounding, skin aflame with blood flushing through. Gulls in the sand at shore's end, sun glimmering in the mottled water. Thick web of leafless branches, little ponds of dark water – abrupt hamlet of white wood-framed homes. Interlocking design of townhouse condos. And then went down on her lips, set tongue to tip, forth in the twisting night. Behind the house, a cluster of rusting trucks. Bob is a dog, in fact a bouvier: at this rate of growth, in one year he'll be the world. The papadum is crisp. Three women discuss problems of their cordless phones. The conductor slumps into a chair in the cafe car. Poem waiting versus poem forwarding. Meaning is forever homeless. Jose Canseco twitches his neck. The hang time of telling. Evening is as morning does. Surgeons of the future, suture. *Mais langue n'est pas langage.* Toweling Trades Training Center. Old jet trails diffusing into pencil-thin clouds, beyond which a translucent half moon is already visible in the noon sky, a blue so pale it tends toward yellow at the horizon. Theory of chutney: sweet cuts hot even better than water. Pylons where once bridge stood. Blackbirds over dry fields. You pull your legs up so as to slouch down in the confined space of the train seat. The city is fast approaching. She offers you a slice of pie, but calls it "apple cake." We pass these cars so rapidly they appear to be sliding backwards. Verb tense and sentence length are all you need of narrative. The fly hovers high over the infield. In the distance, clouds break the sun into a brilliant orange-red. I can see this in your eyes.

OZ

for Fred Glass
& Maureen Katz

Forms farm storm's harm.

Imagine a language that worked.

ironic,
euphoric

Medicine is not narrative. Blue trashed sky. Firemen on ladders into the smoking night.

Phlegm fuels cough. Yellow triangle: abstract banana. Money is the aura of art. Consonant etched into vowel. Mexican comic (comment).

Let us go then, I & I,
outward. For
get focus, for
giveness. Enclosed please find
dropcloth wainscot Orion
simmering middle management
Dobermans at racquetball
fine tooth comb

Hum job. Modernism hopes for a lawn. It's hat time. Symmetry in lettuce's system marked by types. Breadstick wedged in the dip. Waiting for Conan. Ponytail in hardhat sells tobacco. Peripherals for my new stanza. Powder detergent. Team meeting. Break-in-the-clouds symbolism. Warrior earwig along garden walk. Sun's warmth on your forehead is different from being smart.

That's mean. That's meaning. Under glass at the deli pigsfeet sit in a pan of pink juices. Laces knotted together, red tennies hang from a power line. Blue bandanna about the pit bull's neck. Analog sky. They seem so lost in thought on the bus on their way to work, still yawning. Chinese shoes of black cotton. White shades appear blue behind tinted glass. Once they pay the driver, their eyes scan the tubelike bus rapidly, searching for a safe seat. Prospect identification. Package of the Year. Ultrasound poetics. Sound of buzzsaw and rooster. Squish of tires over wet streets. Cloud-filtered sun mutes colors amid valley houses. Words scratched out, arrows to new syntax. These vowels my eyes. Lack of trees in all this snow signifies lake Smoke still in the air from a wood fire. Alarm in a locked auto carries through the night.

Theme is trees
them is "-atic"
park verbs auto
versus forest havoc
foot foot foot
Columbia mall moped
on a motto
poetic cheap trick
macho but wounded
stage whisper persona
the too-clean garden
short fat word
perfect for tenure
is the night
constellations an order
connect the dots
to organize sight

Change in fund balance
atomic table water table
your haircut's too political
bison crossing cavern wall

kung fu lunch pail
view of the harbor
additive, but not personal
sometimes a great lotion
pick a dirty penny
soft sound savage sense
fosters apparent cohesion, a
ruse is a ruse
is not the next
allusion, lines are bent
spines against the margin
spin a hardening version
jetlike to the heart

Exit to system. Striped tie divides a great expanse. Pressure sensitive, duplicates purged. Cat sleeps atop car roof. Through a window I see the pocked bottom of an iron atop a tape reflect the red evening sun.

Many sirens: bad news. Such a small old man to be a bank guard. A brown van. Simple syntax yanked them into plot. A bad thing.

Over the fencetop the tip of a bush suggests a richer foliation. Dull scrim of cloud yields colorless day. I let the first bus pass, hoping the next would be less crowded. Each sentence resolves a battle. A title, not a caption.

Pastel acrylic of a flowerpot decorates gallery wall. Chipped cup. Web of powerlines segments sky. Nouns accumulate on the floor of the car. Article is found benign.

At the wheel of the truck I see a nun. Design of the lid of a styrofoam cup. Intense first taste of spring. The question in Hoagy's case is not which side pulled the trigger. An inalienable right to choose nylon.

The asymmetry of your make-up is not intended. Giant tear on cheek of clown. The margin in the mark-up. Big blue truck of the Starvation Army. A mind is a terrible thing to face.

Seven come eleven. These women share a moment, watching their children at the playground. An older lady in sensible shoes. The billboard alters the scale of houses nearby. Flashing yellow lights.

A glass parrot hung in the window. The function of the tiger cub in Michael Jackson's *Thriller*. Blue shading surrounds an almond eye. Small girl skips along. Please pay amount due.

A burning in the bowels. With the window open, the curtains flapped in the breeze. The cord from her headphones led into her purse. A sentence with four strong beats. On the windshield of the car was a sign: For Sale.

I accepted the assignment at scale. Behind the high fence was a tiny boxlike house. This is not syntax. Her red hair glistened copper in the sun. Autos parked on an empty residential street present an image of form.

Caution, frequent stops. The paper has a business section, but never one for labor. The library rebinds its paperbacks. Plaster madonna framed in the window. The half light of the violets.

Ankles away. Parallel function of the I Ching and DSM III. As we age our features turn into caricature. Her stocking reduced the bruise to a shadow. Humor in uniform. Placement is not random. The hacking coo of a pigeon in the lightwell. Brown-white lumps of old snow in the gutter. The rigor of the big trucks. The Eastern Shuttle. Carrying the proofs of Blackburn's Collected downtown on the IRT. Little cubes of frozen carrots. I recall the taste of the tip of your tongue. Under the overpass a group of men huddled around the burning trashcan, their only light its deep orange flame. As Richard Nixon said, "I am not a language poet." Russ & Daughters kosher deli: amber bowl of salmon caviar. Hip-hop, the crews are breaking. We meet by chance at Saint Marks Books and the politeness is awkward. He hands me some poems "for feedback." California boy that I am, the last thing I expected in New York was the stately sound of hoofbeats in the night. The person at the end of the sentence. The radiator hisses and bangs throughout the night. Elbows in, palms upward, spin on heel and toe. Breakers' theory of the shoelace. I'm not responsible for every Jew in New York. I really love you. Words wall emotion in, the verse of a conduit. Not a one of my friends there has a garden, a houseplant or a pet. The mall is a cluster of buildings in the center of a sea of parking. How thin the gravestones seem. Tennis courts empty in the winter. These clouds feel like solid objects suspended from the sky. Memoirs of the Philly Zoo. The "blonde" in the photo hugging Michael Jackson turns out to be Charlie's mother. I dream that I'm trapped in a drug bust with Connie Francis. The large boned dancer stoops. Tricep dip. A thick dal. I can never travel without being aware of the choices I've made. I watched myself telling her that, even under other circumstances, I didn't think we had a future together, feeling distant, nauseous, the disaster coming true, myself to blame. Kansas City but a patch of lights beneath the night sky. Power padded, value added. On the Sufi track. An old news and cigarette stand, single narrow storefront corridor, but they call it Gem Spa. Velcro flaps on the old woman's shoes. Duncan's dialysis. Seniors that wear greatcoats on the hottest of days. Old poster on a phone pole, words missing. Proud of his cute Jeep. Jogging in dawn heat, the soft smells of spring trigger the taste of glue from my Davy Crockett stamp book 27 years before. Ellen Zweig, dyed blonde, her hand on the shoulder of Armand Schwerner. Seeing him dressed in coveralls, paint in his hair, I guessed at his work. memory is not rational. Cuticles of pleasure. Oppen in a rest home. Everyone on the bus is wearing headphones. Spirit disinvents number: lint balls blow across the plane. The new reality is the old one (say it with a smile). The lizard of odds gambles with crisis punctuation (nouns rowdy with substitute clause). Sit down, small bear. Art bean. The files are restless: fluorescent bulb flickers on. Write me a ticket. Ears as hooks from which to hang glasses (batch it): your bra unsnaps in front. Port in the haze silhouette – the East Bay is missing. more elaborate floral arrangements index middle life (no strain, no pain, no gain), airbrushed nudes tacked to shipping clerk's wall: the presidency is just a reflection. Later she will replace that thumb in her mouth with somebody's penis: you probably think this song is about you. An illusion of logic gets you to the job, an architect's drawings by free association, lead deposits in a phone bank, all of religion compressed in a condom, mathematical representation of chaos: the exogamy of want-ads perceived as a face. Pregnancy is the mother of prevention. The ink fades to a monument, visible limp of denotation, flock of adjectives pecking at garbage in a playground. Snort clouds: a black girl shouts, "You walk like a faggot," one size fits all. Stop me before I write again. She visits him in the convalescent home, a kind of prewidowhood. The dark lashes clash against the light, freckled cheek. Details of a universe generalize for consumption, a Sunday stroll through the industrial district (the earring caught on her headphones): the overall's straps pretest gravity. Response device: the dependent clause is not benign (rose's thorn but a form of callous), the circuitry is blissed, an old math abstracts fingers (Trigger stamps out a haiku). Old bottles of beer and gin gathered at the bottom of the phonebooth. Her headphones leaked a drumbeat. The head is on duty (fire), a nervous attachment to hinges (sulfuric), self-confident machine strolling lazily through a field of tall corn, butterflies of all nations, dictionary's illustration of the range of flags (coffee beans in decorator colors): I spy. An astronaut in the bath is worth two on the hood (direct communication), transcendental medication (ears that rhyme never prime), violators towed. Dear Sequence, tar in a ditch (the windowsill is my garden). They call this abstraction person. Rubber stamps made to order, utility substation, bound frond (deliveries made in rear), nearer my Fifth Street to thee. Paper tigger. A sentence is defined as it's defied. Ooze orders snooze. The dream of fact is tuned to a waltz barely sublimated to the silence of this thick forest where light itself is felt as sound. Against this embroidered scrim men are cutting into the asphalt of emotions with a jackhammer. Literature's vertical hold, a belief in the ten's place has begun to flip.

An image of morning in the window
no more than light caught on the fuzzed
flesh of the violet flashes
a memory encoded as odor, cooked
carrots, of a more spectacular kitchen
which is only your grandmother extended
beyond her private language, the weeping
at the sink made song, the erosion
of particulars that renders an old nook
into a fond altar, splinters of its rough grain
more distinct than anyone who ever lived here
which of course we never did.

White against white, birch in the winter forest
photograph in the pharmacy's free calendar
brings January to a wall in May
in a small room, the torn shades

still capable of shutting light
into shadow, the small hands
of the old man rolling tobacco
into cigars in this storefront
halflight are as brown as the
leaves, an image without music
in the hot spring air where now
there stands a parking lot.

Anger as action yields
the danger that factions
wielding power deformed
for the sake of a story
mourned for its climax
as a form of
gloryhole titillation
can only create
the sensations of song,
the beat of the drum,
the round of fiddles
playing rock.

Continuity as a process
with which I am not
familiar (here I
transfer buses), who
speaks, who listens, how
is one, any
one, to speak, to
keep to the same
I without blinking
(pad pun, Mr Old
Song), the stutterer
thinks to sing.

False start, true start, who
hardly harps on a theme
treads the stream's rocky
crossing (stone hinge), bones
impinged on by muscle
stretch: teach verse
in the face of adversity
(get a job), unrehearsed
the hand's search
is its own dance,
my lance spilling ink
in the place of blood.

Ceramic dog, head tilted,
seeks words not heard of
from an invisible master
not heard of, who forms
a model of the not seen
shadowy as static
across the sands of Africa
unfaithful in translation
as any garden image
of a young man, sad,
short hair disheveled,
so loved by Verlaine.

Tea cups in the dream as big
as hot tubs twirl and
dance, we in them (cream
of poets) in our own pants
with the cuffs rolled, cough
to laugh at some
broth of old poems, wilted
profs stirring the roots up

with a spoon so much
smaller at my nostril,
counter-intuitive, like
your simile's big grin.

Rhetor and phlegm, this sham
discourse trims the reader's
excuses, you are not
not permitted, unfit, to respond
nor is this your asylum, this
upper westside wall of words,
syntax my mortar, painted
nouns, a circus
for the faint world, hurry
up please it's time
the echoes of your own war
were heard in the poem.

Pastel, pretty as a needlepoint
seascape, an image forms
which is its own meaning
into which we pour
your ambitions, my regrets,
the shady, busy world
of office afternoons, radio
of the freeway commute, gravy
mix on potato flakes
mashed and scooped into a bloated
wobbling message, wrapped tight
for ease of consumption.

The mind lurches (a ball
of string as large as
the Farallons) forward –

that is, movement itself
creates the illusion
of time (do not
disturb), occupants
as we are to this
perspective, the sky
(blue) joins the sea
(green) off in a distance
that is our own.

MBWA: shoot between
heartbeats, one's eyes
register concentration, the mouth
intensities like the scale of
a thermometer, orange against black
the butterfly's scheme
is its own meaning (beetle's shell),
skull in the museum
with a stupid grin, clarity
(caffeine in the nervous system,
sun on the garden's clover)
is strictly physiological.

When in doubt sit down
is zen's way out, thin sway
of body's logic, laughter's
just steam from an engine
heating, plums rotting
in damp soil, oil siphoned
from a veined earth,
one world I don't understand
but for being (not Bronk's
grim facade nor Ashbery's
cynical lime twist) a hummingbird,
a hummingbird totally out of place.

The symbolist is unable to see the forest for his parents. O tree of life so full of strife, this knife is to carve initials. Slabs of sheetrock by a pink roll of insulation (we are building the alphabet, a pyramid in the desert, a campsite for the caravan, feeding the ostriches, the tiger, bonfires on a dry night). My folks, who are Bengali, were teaching in Uganda when the Second World War broke out. The tunnel is really a tube laid across the bottom of the bay. You hold your arms straight up, waiting for me to lift the blouse off. He said "I sold the novel," verb telling all. The eye, orange-brown, rolled across the floor. Sweetbreads in a light sauce. Spray paint over the marxist-leninist graffiti yields an inadvertent abstraction. If I write more slowly now, it's because I've already said too much. Jerk pulls neck, wins award. Garden party wedding reception. A low fog blurs the ink, each word a stain. A summer in six sentences, ten. market segment. Front yard gone to weeds, the stairs to the blue house lean. Plastic case in which to keep her glasses. Life is detail (steep slope). A man sits on the steps, waiting for a bus. (All that aside!) Fog this thick gives one the sense of forever being indoors. Boarding the bus, she tucks half a donut in her purse. Gary Hart bumperstickers fade to nostalgia. Page numbers date from 1499 (even they have a history, a politics). The dew sits lightly on the short grass, not sinking in. A small front yard, fenced in, full of giant sunflowers. The stores and bars quiet at dawn. The first bus with its few passengers. My penis slips in easily and you pull your shirt off. Upstairs the neighbors are running the shower. The kitchen faucet with its slow, two-beat drip. Ice in the O.J. Romanticism dissolves the poet's marrow (the cells, the selves, reduplicating wildly out of control). The fern on the porch pleased to be getting more water. Jack-off clubs have come into fashion (shoes required). On a hot day the crazies still wear eight layers of clothes. Scratched and dirty, the bus windows dull the brilliance of the sun, glimmering on the boat-crowded bay. Blue pen, black pen. Trying to tell Rich Little from Little Richard. He steps on the glass to complete the ritual (it's wrapped in a napkin provided by the hotel). The dj coos into the microphone. Below, people are playing tennis or splashing about in the intense blue of the pool. The bridge forms a mark, familiar upon the horizon. Your sister in the next room, we fuck slowly, quietly, seeking silence in each orgasm. Andrei Codrescu is his own critique. The old loom sits atop a foot locker. On the windowsill the ceramic elephant in enmeshed in cobwebs, a figure of strength trapped in nets. Beginning the bench press (90 lb. weight), I felt my spine "crack," popping into alignment on the first lift. I shut my eyes and pay attention to my breathing. Refrigerator with no door is used as a bookshelf. We take turns in our movements (sex is a sharing). Imagine two men shopping for food as a thing to do together. Nothing is so reminiscent of childhood as a hot day. Your first lover is now an electrician. An irrational fear of personal vulnerability extends to a national scale and combines with breezy arrogance in the smile of the President. "America's movie . . . *Red Dawn*." Two sisters shout recipe details over the music of Cindy Lauper. On the toothpick, in this sequence, were a slice of red pepper, a scallop, a slice of white onion, a shrimp, and a slice of green pepper. One lives through detail. Wash, pronounced warsh. They listen to Boy George and speak in Tagalog. He sleeps on a beach blanket in a fetal position. On trash day, the Chinese woman from the next block goes house to house, inspecting the garbage, gathering tin cans in a large string net. Things people think to put on their front porch. The plural forms an abstraction. Trousers of golf culture. A generation of humanities professors turn into administrators in order to save their jobs. Fists half-clenched as he walks down the street. The carpenter is writing his dissertation on Thoreau. Little girl skipping to catch the bus. Hello, my name is Mitchell Omerberg and I'm calling tonight from Supervisor Harry Britt's re-election campaign committee. Last week we mailed you a flyer describing Harry's record with a form to fill out if you wish to obtain an absentee ballot and vote by mail. Have you received this yet? List composed of voters who've failed to vote in two of the last four major elections living in buildings of four or more units in liberal neighborhoods, purged of Republicans, landowners and those with no listed telephone for follow-up. In the dream the tattooed woman pulls her head back at the moment of the man's orgasm, sperm splashing on the tip of her nose. Same day service. In breakdancing, this move is called Furious Fish. Crows and rooster marking dawn. In the country the sporadic sounds of traffic comfort. These old hiking boots, never broken in. From the board room on the 51st floor of the Bank of America World Headquarters the entire Bay Area appears in a new scale, Bernal Heights a mere ripple in the topography, a chessboard on which individual lives, consequences, become infinitesimal (directly below, a hole in the ground where once stood the International Hotel). Here, concealed, lie two competing fictions: (1) that the boardroom, facing north, holds no view of Bernal Heights; (2) that, by the power of sheer height, lives might be abstracted, their contents banished. Saying makes it so . . . said the exit poll. Voices in the mosswood. Subtle greens, yellow-greens (the red of poison oak). "How can you write of a bank in the wilderness?" Ah, but that is the wilderness. Gartersnake slithers into the weeds. Horse shoe prints in the mud. She watches pelicans through field glasses from a cliff at coast's edge. This ocean, land at its margins, unyielding text. Where the sun reflects off of the water, the waves are the dark marks. I smell wood smoke. Champagne mimosa. The wild bay leaf. Fresh, the large cowpies are dark, almost black at the crust, a rich, moist green in the middle. Below, a line of reeds wanders through the dry grass of the valley, marking the trail of a brook. In the split-interest trust, the needs of the income beneficiary often conflict with those of the remainderman. Sunflowers growing atop a garage. Strolling into the office 45 minutes late. Turkey vultures circle over the valley. As, at the tip of my tongue, you come, your thighs tighten their grip on my head, your own hips rocking until now they begin to shake. Sliced apple. Bread crumbs and garlic atop the pan-fried oysters. Digging seeds from the watermelon with a spoon. Another Paradigm for Peace. First cold day of autumn, furnace on, the smell of dust burning. Orange plastic cones mark wet paint at a crosswalk. Fluorescent yellow of fastfood mustard. Call Barry. The busdriver's hairpiece. The theosophist's Yamaha (is not a piano). Typed so as to indicate scoring. The page of the manuscript (a vacant lot) is not that of the published text (Wrigley Field). The line drives to the margin. Preparing to write, I touch my cap, hitch up my pants and reach for the bag of resin. Shake off that metaphor. Language parrots the world (with as much understanding). A bench by the window in the study, overlooking the valley's vineyards, a low fog. A flock of small birds descend on one tree. Oz' odds: language was the wizard (not a wall of silence, but a well). Hard rock futon. The wind chimes are still. Footsteps on the stairs, first voices. The hour the most empty, the fullest. At first, pipes in the wall cough and rattle, but now there's a steady shush. By the little orange berry bush Tom (not that Tom) is shading his eyes from the sun's glare on the valley fog. Ten sentences a day does make. My nostrils, tho clear, feel caked with the cold. I feel the pressure points between this chair and these bones. Terrible blue sky. Twenty-two pilgrims walking along a country road. Large, moss-covered boulders. Bluebird as big as a kitten. The discussion heating up, one voice rhythmically insisting, louder than the others, "that's right, that's right." A woman's laughter. Woolworth's, that great trash cornucopia. Black cat sticks its nose into a cup of coffee. Old brick ranch house with a red shingle roof. Buzz of the dragon fly. The heat of the sun on my face versus the breeze in the hair on my arms. The tree's reflection versus the tree's shadow on the surface of the pool. Smell of wood smoke. One can tell by the sound alone that that small plane in the sky is turning, changing course, tracing and retracing the air over the valley. Bird glides into the tree. High up in its branches, one hears the rustling of lives. Thin clouds that appear streaked against the roof of the sky. I draw words, these letters as strange as any, listening to a bird's wings flutter in passing. Footsteps over gravel. The valley layered, its more distant ripples half-misted silhouettes, the vineyards red-brown. Cows moo. Like a lawn sprinkler, a fertilizing machine shoots long green jets out over the field. Out there, the small towns are visible only as lights glistening in the night. At dawn, the one distinct cloud is obviously the trail of a jet, long since passed. Birds in the pine tree chuckle. The tiny lawn "windmill" in the shape of a sunflower begins to spin. Weeks later I'm riding the bus with a new pen (it rains). Glaze of moisture atop the umbrella's surface. This sky is several shades of gray. Baby Fae is dead. Steam spews from behind the old hospital. On days like this I bus into work with no sense of hurry. A young Latino with a spiral snake tattoo is reading Judith Rossner's *August.* Middle-aged Third World man, quiet, works as a rent-a-cop (nothing to do in the bank lobby but stand around). House raised on stilts, awaiting a new foundation. Muscles bulging out of an alligator sport-shirt. I smell hot tar. Differing rhythms of people as they walk. Fists clenched, he runs for the bus. The rocker in the attic small enough for a two year old. One sentence for every reader. Two coils glowing behind a grid of bars, the heater hums. The chamberpot was a plastic bucket. Old farmhouses form a small town, alongside which sits the new mall. The crib in one corner is filled with books. My dear one loves her sleep (I sit and write by the dull light of a grey dawn). That, as it happened, was the central term in their language, gray, the sole word permitted alternate spellings, around which the vast field of other, proper versions, each of them arbitrary, grew. The cup sat atop the glass table, the tea within steaming. It was December and newborn lambs stumbled through the fields. The bar of soap was new, its features perfectly etched. The offshore rocks break the incoming wave. A golden rural schoolhouse where, once, Hitchcock filmed *The Birds*. Sun-dried tomatoes. White wicker couch. I can't find my hat. Thermos of chamomile. Web of wires over an intersection (how we break up the sky). Tiny American flag on the fire engine's cab. Silhouette of a 727, rising slowly headed north, then turning, now sunlit, silver, passing in front of a half moon in the dawn sky. Change your chemistry. A dying custom, plastic manger lit up on the front lawn. She serves as a crossing guard by the schoolyard in the mornings, chain-smoking in her orange reflector vest, accompanied by a black chihuahua. form of the pipe as counterpoint to the shape of the face (his long, white hair half-wild) Chairs upturned upon tables, the cafe is closed. This was history (street numbers broken from the door on the porch). Asleep at the real. Three-sided frame to that woman's walker. December morning, savage in its rhetoric, icy disk of sun striving for a workshop poem effect. A sweep at the veal. A preference for round toothpicks over "flat" ones. Please return trays to the full upright position and fasten your safety belts. Cartoon pig made up as a clown (it starts to rain). Gradually the child's crying recedes, becoming a kind of song. So odd, the deep blue glass of those window panes. Just walking down the street, the cop's body language reflects tension. Chinese windows. The lesson of the moment. Walking in traffic (try to write). The way the cheekbones stand out when he drags on a cigarette. Phone poles jut out at angles, wires sag. No time flat. I chew on the end of the pen till the plastic grows soft. Sports car wrapped in tarpaulin. Big Mack truck in front of produce market. Too easily, the nail sticks into the wall. Idly chew on mustache. Two fingers and thumb to grip the pen. Black pigeon among bird crumbs. Pulling off one glove, fishing for exact change to board the bus. Under that loose chic fur she's a larger woman than she cares to think (bleached blonde with rouged cheeks). Cigarette tucked over his ear like a pen. Flattened bubble-form, styrofoam cup. Bodies on the bus brush together (no meaning). The brown of the bruise in the banana peel. Old red dumpster, overflowing with cardboard. First BART of the day is virtually empty. Already cars pass by on the unfinished freeway. The shamrock is perceptible only from the sky. Grass stains on my chin as I inspect this near horizon. The letters on each blade indicate the patent, the message. That you see words here is a trick. I taught myself to read the clouds.

A new paragraph means a new year. Leading to a direct and further perception: taxes. After Christmas, the white backsides of cut-out paper wreaths hang in the grammar school windows. Extrapolate your theory of the not seen. A stone cherub on one knee holds the flowerpot aloft. Parts is parts. Dried rainwater spots the glass. The watercolor of the doe and her offspring, still in a sunlit glade, the nearby brook fringed with ice, the last clumps of a late snow, is aimed at the viewers' vulnerability, the deep sigh evoking not sentiment, but the memory (half-felt) of the loss of a mother's breast. The transparency of the water in the glass magnifies the goldfish. Dawn but a dilution of the dark. Each solution proposed, gone over in detail. Even the rain is a construct. He was his own name, but to whom?

Leaving the house, I go back and check eight times to see if I've left the heat on, but forget my hat. In sandals and wearing a scarf (scarves?) almost like a turban, the small Laotian woman pulls her shopping cart up the hill, walking in the roadway against the traffic. He wore his pants low, belt about the hips, stomach spilling over. A young woman is carrying a box of vanilla wafers into work. A tube into which one rolls up blueprints. Wearing my Walkman, chewing an apple, far, far from the world viewed. Crouching to read the lead story in today's *New York Times,* I sense the muscles in my thighs stretch tight. That jogger at dawn, first light right behind, is no symbol (is). Genre of the old sailor rides the bus. That freshly-shaved right-behind-the-ears just-from-the-barber look. Dreadlocks on her left side, crew cut on her right. Women coming out of mass from the old stone church. Storefront preschool: the infrastructure redefines space.

Imperfect stranger: these swirls of ink form not a bridge but a barrier, the flask contains but cool tea. Sound, piercing the ears, violates reason, the mirror a reverse of the window. What does it mean, that our national food chain is called Safeway? And then went not down to the ships, old image of conquest. Forth to the shed of the 'hiring office' behind the rusting cyclone fence. Pyrex coffee pot filled with roses. Reba's coffin was larger than the hole they'd dug. Mountain of oranges in the window of the produce mart. Mother and daughter wearing matching daypacks. Distrust the transitions. Billboard of a red bag of fries from McDonald's, with the one word message "YIELD." Motorcycles parked upon sidewalks. Lose mind now, ask me how.

Pigs R Us (horsefeathers!). A jeep in the city, just for the image. Jogging in shorts, but with gloves on. If the self is not writing the poem, who will pay its taxes? It's a cold day, but half the people with gloves are carrying, not wearing, them. A punching bag would scrape your knuckles raw without protection. The conceit fit like a wool knit. The desert relocation village was modeled on a grid like an American suburb, while the Wolof-speaking tribe was polygamous, each wife needing a separate hut equidistant from the central home of the husband, so that when the relief agency evaluation team arrived the buildings were empty, the whole site abandoned, the sands beginning to fill the uncared-for houses, the land itself again in control. What hut? But hat – fat bat cat. The intelligible as a category of itself is perfectly sealed. This is not a diary is not an important distinction, but the omission of the "that" is. Verb in the last place (parallel to what?).

A moustache so thick as to shape the face (nose pointed, eyes deep in the skull). The eyes wide and small, each iris brown-green. The ears virtually without a lobe, set high in the skull. Thick high cheeks pointed outward. The upper lip thin, the lower one full, the two narrow in the round face. The forehead a flat plane, its flesh stretched tightly. Mole on the nostril more red than brown. The flesh at the base of the shell-shaped ear pushes it out, away from the head. Lashes so fine and light, almost impossible to see. Dim sum. Cheese platter. At what point did you become a list (small, crescent-shaped scar below the eye). moon on the horizon stares down.

Lineman strapped high near the top of his vertical. The watchband loose, like a bracelet about the narrow wrist. The past converted into history through redaction. Candy-stripe reflecting strips on the back of the truck. That prosody's different from "the truck's back." How dry the peanut butter gets at the bottom of the jar. Don't weep for me, Union Carbide. Odds, but the g is silent. In the kitchen, the lights out, before dawn: out the window, over the roof tops, the faintest glow gives the sky shape. Most faint. Moist font. Don't sleep for me, Metromedia. But first this word from our sponsors.

12 February: today's heat hints of spring. Young woman on her way to work, hair still wet from the shower. Those apartments have no lobby, merely a stairway behind an iron grating. Half-beauty parlor, half-travel agency. Cafe-deli. Video rentals where previously the Chinese laundry was. Long gray cuff of the garbageman's glove. meter "maid" dwarfed by his own three-wheeler. Fruit drinks packaged in small boxes. Sound of glass echoes as it falls into the large empty drum of the garbage truck. Calling, in his inaugural address, for a "second American revolution," President Ronald Reagan today adopted the platform of the RCP. The idea that the world could be experienced by individuals was that culture's biggest myth. Two boys at play for hours in the shadow of a basketball hoop.

Shape is an issue in the poem. The sky virtually white in the hot still air. Even the asphalt seems to shimmer. That the flood of detail itself thwarts reason. Old white pickup in the driveway is missing its hood, blue plastic tarp laid over the engine. Small ceramic animals decorate condo window. Jogging in place, waiting for the light to change. Where that hill slopes too steep to put houses. Gangs of roofers visible on every street. Inhaling, struggling to find air through the muck in my sinuses. Yet to hold the syntax constant that the rest might vary, Denise, fails to acknowledge that hypotaxis itself replicates the logic of power. Arthritis in my big toe, O variable foot. Young black woman in tank top and cutoffs, dreadlocked hair, sits quietly in the shade of the cypress, reviewing her casebook on torts.

A paragraph in every pot. Black leather tie. Pigtail below ragged crewcut. Rabbit comfit. Simple, sad, savage, soft. The idea that he is not Danny Santiago. The idea that I am not (your name here). Old rolodex sky. Humor is the socially accepted mode of rage. The new first baseman's glove was so stiff as to be immobile. I'm on my back, naked, while you roam over me on your hands and knees, kissing, sniffing, biting, licking, sucking, turning and turning, the room barely lit and virtually forgotten, we're so absorbed in the slow, soft rhythms of this play. Control KD to save text. A>

What is remarkable here in the use of Fibonacci (1, 1,2,3, 5, 8,13 . . . n), the numeric relation found most often "in nature," is not any subliminal assertion of the organic, but precisely the opposite, a form entirely arbitrary and artificial, a shape as inexorable and predictive as a glacier, thoroughly distanced from the conflicting "messages" of content. Was he then no more than a response to his historic condition, a reaction against the attitudes of a previous generation, whose poets had divided on the function of equilibrium in conveying the identity between content and form (between "subject" and "object"), speaking only in terms of tradition, for or against, without anyone ever noting (not even Spicer), the tension, the incommensurable, even shocking discrepancies between the two? I wrote this in longhand to make evident to you that even this Brechtian moment of selfdisclosure, this metacommentary, is itself a mere facade. That I is not the author calls into question here only Creeley, leaving us no closer, the gap between us seemingly unbridgeable. Even as my penis (not circumcised) enters your body (not circumscribed) and we begin again this familiar moving, maintaining eye contact, we remain conscious of the distance, indeed even acknowledge it, taking turns, playing roles, aware of the need for gestures of sharing. Thus blood is thicker than semen due to causality. Musical theme from Bugs Bunny. Think of the shape as a sockful of sand pounded repeatedly against your forehead. Why are you reading this poem? Look out the window (but I didn't say which one). No one will concede ever having thought that Mondale stood a chance. We conceive of suffering because we are stuck on the individual, on the universalization of our own subjectivity into a totem for personhood. That doesn't make it any better.

This can be taken several ways. The fist is to hit with. As if pain (proprioception) were the one true response. The guitar left in the sunlight in the window (an appeal to the image) gets warm, the strings expand, going out of tune. That this is a different paragraph is not obvious. A fistful of linebreaks. I sit in a large chair with my legs drawn up, the back of my right knee serving as a desk. Whoever said syntax was total? An idea of islands forms one state. Acquired Immune Deficiency says it all. Public relations is experienced in private. Just try to change the channel. This buzz isn't static, it's the system.

After staying indoors at home four days with a cold, I'm disoriented back outside: the sense is of extreme vulnerability. Half-awake, the sound of a pre-dawn rain. A woman is rubbing balm on her lips. Their parents put up the down payment. Plastic paperclips never rust. Throwing on my raincoat I discover a pocketful of old gum wrappers. Only down in the projects will you find fathers tending young children on a regular basis. The bicycle wobbles, tilting from side to side, slowly pushing up the steep slope. Flaubert's depiction, though highly visual, is not governed by cinematic tropes. Breathing deeply, listening for a rattle in my lungs. White styrofoam cups, stacked in rows upside down, line the diner's window. The storm served as winter's coda. The infant's small fist felt strong, gripping his beard.

From a schoolyard, children's voices echo up a valley. The wind in the wires. Tiny yellow butterflies. A man sits on his front steps, cleaning little white circles from a three-hole punch. Sheets flap in the light breeze. Gulls swirl, over and over, above the valley. From a backyard one dog barks, then others, until the whole hill is yapping and baying, then it dies back. On the porch, cat sleeps in the shade of a cactus. Against this quiet, all the anger I feel still at never having had a father. Now that I have lived 5 days longer than he ever did. Poor hapless brawler. Big white rooster in a too small yard. Pen's point cutting letters into the page.

Emotional windbreak. Sagging fences. The kitchen was a nook. Smell of the wood of that "bench," within which were kept comics, softball bats, gloves. Until I was tall enough to see better, I thought adults hid things in the sink. My grandfather made all of the formal decisions, against which my grandmother wielded the power of the irrational. I learned to read German before I could English, but I've forgotten every last bit of it, danke. By the back corner of the garage, where the earth was soft and damp, three decades of dead pets had been buried. She was angry, always angry, but it was never clear at whom. Uncle Tootie took me aside to tell me that I had a half-brother, mulatto, mongoloid, dead. Now that my own brother has named his son Danny. Leaving the bank parking lot, gun still in hand, Phil saw that the cops were converging from all directions, so turned the weapon on himself. Skip Casey leapt from the bridge. Joe Eggenberger, the mayor's son, murdered Judy Williamson.

Bright red laces hang from empty hiking boots. That slight electrical hum of the clock. Spinning wheel next to a redwood desk. That such a large, billowing sleeping bag could be stuffed into such a small sack. Theta zed. Where's Fred? Little wicker napkin holder. I metaphor on South Street. Steady drip of fog from the pines, their upper branches iced. At dawn, before the clouds moved in, one could see the mountain. Footprints in the snow grown soft and vague overnight. The flock of Japanese tourists seemed befuddled by the wild deer. I hear the laugh of jays, hidden in the trees.

Too sick to hunt for deer, the coyote looked at the small girl, whose father had brought his BMW to a halt by the side of the road that they might get out to watch this tan, foxlike thing, until it began to approach her with a gait that suggested stalking. The mushrooms were breaded and fried. Empty storefront, shelving stacked against the plate glass doors. The hour at which the city's buses fill the streets, the population shifting downtown from the neighborhoods. Mid-March, the red paper 49er window pennants have faded to a pale pink. From the board room atop the Bank of America building one sees not only the city, but the idea of the city. Pinto with four flat tires is parked on the sidewalk. The coyote stops, too sick even to feign chase. It's the same sun the world around. He came to cherish the commute time over the bridge, often his only solitude for the day. The wildness in the dog startled him, the alertness. Life science. The taste of sweetener in the lozenge.

Excerpt from a review quoted as a jacket blurb, attributing only the journal, cleaves that language from its author, lending it the false air of fact. Even as buildings are not solids. Chained to the stop sign and light pole, newsracks cluster at a corner. With shovels, they pat down hot asphalt into the pothole in the road. Or that a mark in space itself become articulate.

Their cynicism toward all government is the only defense they know. Nickel D. Random curds. That the military itself becomes a projective fetish. Satellite dish. Young women in long wool coats bought second hand. For Sale signs hand lettered in automobile windows. Most of the language we consume is forced upon us involuntarily.

Silhouette of the garbageman, can upon his back, trudging, sun behind him, toward the hilltop. The air so cold I feel it in my teeth. He pauses, straightening, which is when I notice his chaps. RVs by the park in which whole families have spent this winter. Please not to contact citizen of other planet! Swarm of saxophones: cave of alto mirror. Lips on reed, puff cheeks out. Short, fast, fat shout (shod fist fed shed). Shi'ite, muslims – don't make no image here. Old Wonderbread wrapper used as a lunchsack (the ecstasy of rock without the agony of metal): dip knees to mark rhythm. Red sun visor without the crown, terrycloth wrist brace . . . cabin of a Mack truck without the bed (objects of the world indict!). Valley lobster, rag mop lap dog, big plastic trash can all cracked and crushed. Asymmetry of the woman in the park, sunbathing with a cast on her leg.

Latina in a lab coat. One sees, looking out of bus windows, a stain smeared along the glass where, exhausted, so many heads have leaned to rest. O sweet Thai peanut sauce. Bus driver muttering half a song. The primary content of this sentence lies in the sound of its words. Laugh lines about the eye. A typology of persons according to how they decorate that shelf which is the back of their toilets. Cat leaps down from the chair and onto the couch, curling, then going back to sleep. Sauce covers the pasta. Imitation Diebenkorn. Bathtub full of tangelos. You could smell the coffee burning. Junipero, voiced 'J.'

Dot command: muscles needed just to push the spine erect, legs braced, feet against straw mat floor. In tense. Analyze the cellblock through code of family. Looking in, see bus as rolling terrarium. The pure products of America are made in Hong Kong. Ransom of kisses showers together. The answer is, there is no answer. Sketchbook used for spreadsheet. Here we reached the motherboard. Lie back and let my tongue do the work. Sabermetrics comes to OuLiPo. Talking, veins in that long neck pulse. Sitting on a wood bench until Your butt goes numb.

Old shutdown storefront now lived in by hippies Man driving a pickup while pulling a rag wool sweater over his head. Lecard's Stein. Red dumpsters back of the pizzeria. Whom you have never read has sighed. Tinny rock beat leaking from the headphones of that Walkman. Slowly the well dressed old gentleman in the tweed cap on the bus leans forward to let the glob of spit drop in the aisle. She covers her mouth with the napkin to extract small bones from the fish. Four tiny framed paintings of warships decorate a livingroom wall. Better part of a paragraph. Grain reflects: wind weathers woods. Street full of parked cars = industrial waste. You in your blue-green cotton summer suit.

The way milk crates stack outside a corner store. Cardboard boxes of green bananas. The tide of his hair ebbs. Pronunciation of the letter 'H.' Some mornings one feels deep inside one's head, walled in, but on others really "out there," on the surface, brain's raw edge. Recite to yourself, in order, the phone calls to make once you reach the office. Such dark skin for a strawberry blonde. Leather flight jacket on older man, round face thoroughly freckled. Green bags of cement stacked on a flatbed, long truck too large for this part of the city. Young man, shirtless and shoeless in levis, walks down to the stores at dawn, looking to buy day's first pack of cigarettes. 3 stereo blasters on one bus, each bellowing a different brand of funk. Oh silk-flecked summer sport jacket. Two small white-robed nuns at the corner finger their beads.

Renewal notice enclosed. The next generation of writers disappears into private life. That which exists through itself is what is called moaning. Poet, seeking your voice, gargle. Aliens in the form of daypacks accumulate, waiting to achieve critical mass. Swim team. Fingers swell and the knuckles feel puffy. Above, the lineman is strapped to the pole. Hazy sky, blue, blue-white. I gamble, letting the #10 pass, hoping that the 67 will come along so that I'll have to make one less transfer. Guitar growl atop bar band drumbeat. Oh, lune d'Alabama. Spoon of my old trauma.

Paint garage door trim, standing tiptoe on a bucket. Detail wrecks the theory, back alleys present true house fronts. Feet are not symmetrical. Dawn's initiation I get. Silliman too relate I. Heart pounds, thinking I've misplaced this notebook. Trees too differ as to the ideal form of treeness. Now that the chicken's gone. The sight of one's own back is slightly mysterious, islands of freckles. This is not a system. But the history of sentences, encoded here and everywhere, is not forgiving. Imagine the MX as a mode of full stop. Transparent in the sky, high over these houses, playing some small odd stringed folk instrument, the chicken ascends to heaven.

C section. The Chi Squares (barbershop quartet). Statistical significance is not information. Searching for ducks from this double-bind. The el (missing) is not missing. Dark glasses on a cloudy day. You, sloshing almond oil on my dick, rubbing it, say "Now I'm going to let you come." The way a sneeze bubbles to the surface. One cop walks up to the driver's side of the pulled-over Buick, while the other opens her door, standing cautiously behind it, one hand on the radio, the other on her gun. Concrete sidewalk, asphalt road. Big-eyed child stares over his mother's shoulder on the bus, silently watching me write. Only that hawk, looking so small as it sails up against the scrim of gray clouds, gives one the sense of how high the sky. White-haired man, bearded, deep eyes, dressed in black leather.

A man in a wide-brimmed hat is walking, a red-haired dog along the railroad tracks. Fried trout (breaded). Road gang chawing the sidewalk. At this stop the downtown-bound passengers spill off the bus, a cluster of crosstown riders waiting silently for their chance to board. Was what went on in the sentence merely craft? Three Vietnamese school children, wearing daypacks, run at pigeons to set them in flight. Big street cleaning machine wheezes past, driver atop it in a cabin.

I remember the vegematic. Poetics as cluttered as Gem Spa. The burning of Ukes. Neo real. Your reflection in the highway patrolman's sunglasses seems magnified, rounded. Pinhole at the center of styrofoam cup's plastic lid. Wears the same pair of trousers all week long. Houses without setbacks, with electric garage doors, terraced rock gardens sloping down toward the freeway. At 6:30 the donut shop opens, men in windbreakers, JW women in pairs at the doorway, long cloth coats in the fog, silently, cheerlessly displaying copies of *The Watchtower.* Red chard. Down the hill the sun rises above the factories, between the banks of cloud. A jogger, half-sprinting in the drizzle through these wide, lawnless streets, square homes, pastel colors. Small yellow van, new mode of school bus.

The state is not an Other. The shoes (worn canvas loafers) stick out from beneath the sheet in the gutter, one cop pacing off the distance to a now-empty bus, others directing traffic on past. It was an old gym, dusty with resin. I sipped cider at the party and remembered what it felt like to drink. The way the wind burns the eye. Flower of the Bird of Paradise (watercolor on brick office wall). Proceed by addition. The head, devoid of energy, filled with rain. That one feels fever in one's bones, in the muscles of the calf and shoulder. Red spots on a yellow bulb, balloon-like, called ladies' purses – the flowers, fading, flatten. Asa's eyes mime his mother's. In the morning apt to find my shoes anywhere I happened to take them off the night before. Old oak desk.

Colophon's progress. The lineman on the pole leans back, body, wood and safety belt forming a triangle. 9:00 a.m.: there's already a drunk passed out on the bus. For Sale by Owner. Body of the pen too narrow and long to hold comfortably. Little cloud tufts up over the hill. Let us paint a better bird of-paradise. The six functions of poetry: hair on Caruso's chest, cardboard-n-plastic 3-D glasses, q-w-e-r-t, Formula I, when in Roman sublimation, beep beep beep. He parts his hair in the middle, strong jaw jutting forward, making note in public of the flaws of your body. A single idea, properly understood, takes days. A brick on which is imprinted the word "hidden." Sun Yat-Sen. The throat is a thermos that warms the vowels. My head, my hands, my twenty chipped teeth.

Intensifiers of affect, pear-shaped
resume. The edge of fresh
asphalt gives way to dark
gravel. I come not to bury

caesura, but raise you the limit
under the Rent Stabilization Ordinance
allowable (inverse effect). 4-fingered
cartoon hero with ears so
big, bus with its brights on
middle of the day. The evening news
makes you hyper. Make my
danish. Jelly thematics
glaze with meanings
what morning itself
can't offend. An atelier
big as a thimble, above which
parallel *pied a terre*
for two. From here broad vistas
across the lightwell. Phlegmatic
fields. Clouds dim
morning air, red eye's
black dot narrows: big, gray-
haired woman in her fifties
in polyester pantsuit (maroon)
hoses down porch. Please,
whenever possible, network
with affinity clusters – iteration
posed as dundancy, body
gets voiced as limit, floats
in the harbor. Simple strategy:
all-over surface + art gossip
generates response . . . grainy.
But I don't understand
these nylons. Inn of
the misgiving. Your experience
of the Borofsky retrospective
is not separable (2,417,642)
from your cheap sunglasses
(2,417,644) in their blue plastic case

lost in the museum cafe. "Ick,"
sneers the hip writing major,
"line breaks." I hobble
to the station platform, to wait
for the train. Green tea ice cream
leaves a taste. One consciousness,
under stress, indefensible
with royalties and copyright for all.
Thick fog trims the hilltop
visible from here. Counting squares
(diamond shaped) in a chain link fence.
I dream I'm in a Chinese fish shop
where they're laid out unfrozen,
without packages, on wood tables
except for a pair of large rusting barrels
filled with water, in which float
squid and shrimp. Upstairs,
above the liquor store, was a small
res hotel. New keyboard lacks
cents sign, round to the nearest verb.
Beats plot the line, pausing
marks it. Dark buildup caked
under the thumbnail. This,
this is my very own falsetto,
stock rising above previous quotation,
echoes stammer. Spires tear
sky's belly. Young anorexic
takes up marathon running. If you
can read this, no thanks
to the MLA. Biker's brains
spread out over freeway.
Big toe sez storm's over.
Vowels hoot. Clear plastic
piewrap, empty, drifts in the breeze
over asphalt. Weak chin, round

face, will merge with neck
as you age. A once-lit cigarette
hangs bent from his lips, the tip
is smashed. Zone edition. Comp-
osition by objective. Small children
in school playground (parochial), boys
in blue sweaters, girls in red. Down
vests with "fishing pockets" popular
in financial district. How was grease?
Burned out about work. That line
(this one) is about repression
as the heart of narrative
which is why we so love it.
Ambulance without a siren. Hands'
flesh dried out
from having washed so many
dishes. Line break here. How
could father have been shallow,
never having been present?
Shadows in the fog in
the harbor: military boats. Street
sweeper, urban tractor
hums past. Wires fan out
from atop each pole, linking
power to houses. Enjambed
by brigands on a
voyage to fetch munchies,
deputy PD in a cowboy hat.
'Angel of service' motif
to new public works building,
aesthetics of direct mail. That
growl in your stomach sours
your breath. Busdriver with
briefcase and thermos. It's a
spectacle alright, these gaudy slides

projected on the white screen of your
pink belly, smiling faces that warp
into the navel wave
from the Great Wall of China.
A fly is dead in the dust on
the porch wall. A rooster
(offstage) crows. History redacts
populations. A generation of
surfers bearing crosses
from their woodies to the beach.
Dear asparagus fern, do you read me?
What does a horse, stock still
but for twitching tail, brown
skinned, thick-veined (that huge
penis), its mane nearly copper,
alone atop that hill, think?
Consider this lawn a text,
that crabgrass its theme. The purple
outer flower of the columbine.
Epaulets of the red
winged blackbird, breeze
in the cypress. That lichen
is intense. I sense only
sound to connect
that sentence to this. Parallel
bars of a ski-rack in
midsummer bicycles mounted upside
down on the rear of that
Porsche. This is a beach town in
the guise of a text. Two
senior citizens are quarreling,
one of them in tears, in
public so the air feels tragic.
Foxtails are so beautiful when
green. You want to make something

of it? One digests oysters
almost before you swallow them, then
the taste lingers. Large yellow bee
butts its head repeatedly
against the pane. Fog meringue
out over the bay. Vacuous
jabber reduced to trope, bulk
of all talk? Cleft at the heart
of each nipple. The 'windows' narrow
on a cardboard box of tomatoes,
produce stacked by the store front.
Phonetic translation from the original
English, say "Bow wow." Punctuation
ornaments base line. Salsa
horn section, part collie. Cat-
egorize birds into swoopy
and flappy. This idea, that
for each line there is only one
proper break, was itself
historically determined. It is
not symmetry which is
the fundamental fact of
any face but
the opposite I want my
empty V. I want my
Maypo. Safe when taken
as directed. (Less filling!
Tastes great!) Income velocity:
divide the Gross National Product
by the sum total of money
available (M1), to find
number of times per annum
each dollar must circulate to
equal the GNP (current
average 6.7). Formalism

is its own remark: Ninja
throwing star. A brown haze
sits out over the water. On
Divisadero, in front of
the Vietnam-France, I turn
toward you, proposing marriage.
Say that with a little more
conviction. Meanings diverge
for different readers, as well
they should! A weed with a purple flower
fills cracks in the walk. Flossing
versus brushing. Your mind feels
stymied, an old song running endlessly
as if on a broken record. You
never even liked the Everly Bros.
That building mimes its own
I-beams. Like a rationed waterfall
the row of white urinals flushed
continuously. That cop pauses
to adjust his gunbelt. Summer
thunder, rare in the west. I'd
best be going now. Levels of
art, layers of lasagna. Mix-n-
match footwear. Futured hence.
Fruit at the bottom. The people
united . . . will never be
deleted. Ah big calves
jut from miniskirt. Headphones
leaking rhythm track
on bus. Pull in stomach, pull
up pants. New wave fish sauce.
City faces budget gloom. The pause
that represses. Let's privatize
money! Barrio stop subway
platform. Young woman in oversized

men's dress shirt wears bangs. Man in
cotton hooded sweatshirt worn under
leather 'flight' jacket rubs nose
with back of hand. Tri-color
moustache. Years later, aging ex-
big league pitcher George Brunet
still toils in the Mexican League. Detail
conceived as modernist ploy. Black
crewcut modified by long blonde
braid. Lacy half-slip
under see-thru knit. The lips bulge
to accommodate swollen cock,
rhythm of distinct parts, a-
symmetric. Long green sedan
slides into driveway. Diver's arc
high over still pool. Watch water
blossom (equal but opposite). Through
the roof of a burned-out
house . . . clear blue sky. The stripes
on her jump suit's pocket run
the other direction. Seaton says
he remembers having read Blackburn
he thinks. Taste of lemon-grass
tames the beef. Go-bots in window of
Hunan cuisine. Little white-haired
woman strains, reaching to pull cord
to stop bus. Absence of articles
as index of the poetic. Over the park
kites hover. The warm breeze tugs
on my straw hat. An old white
pickup, which has been blanketed
by carnations, which have begun to die. The word
Sold imposed diagonally over that "For Sale" sign
in front of the white house. A banquet
at which half the women wear

hats (low crowns, broad brimmed), sign
of old money. Major Feinstein. The carpenters
are stripped down to their overalls
already, and it's not even 9:00 a.m.
Saddened by syntax, I lay
on the chairman's desk. The release
of the TWA hostages obliterates
media coverage of the Lesbian-
Day Freedom Day parade. Mr.
Rambo's Neighborhood. French-fried parsley
conveys a tang. Hazy hot
breezeless day. Why bees are
yellow. So many old poets fear
the new because they mapped their careers
out against a previous terrain. Bash my
banana. Runner's knees absorb
concrete's shock. Backside of the earring
holds it to the ear. To imply space
of 'suburban leisure,' fast food stand's
architect turns the longside of
the building to the road (discrete sign
triggers memory of commercial). What
there is to say the world itself
stutters. Bound in leatherette. The smoke
from that dock blaze clings to the
bay. The abuse of clarity
in a waste of tame
writing. Rambo in Dogtown. The girl
at the door (is not a girl, is 20)
stands naked, talking with her boyfriend
on the porch as he inspects the potted
violet for aphids. Plums drop
and start to rot. Prewash
spray spot remover. I thought I
ought to let the vowels out

that I might hear them. Row
of identical towels dries on the line.
Pus where the bee stung rises white.
Aesthetic jihad. Gunrack on the back
window of the pickup. Shopping mall
parkinglot touch football.
Chinese elder in cotton PJs
(Sherlock Holmes pipe and walking
cane) wears a knit cap
plus highschool varsity letter jacket,
shuffling in slippers up the block.
Toyota chinook. Upscale deli. High
grass shimmers in the wind. In exact
depiction. Kit's pieced. Butterfly
shrimp. A pole upon which
to string power lines. Webbed sky
of the city. Black dove. Light
mottled thru the dissolving fog. Butcher's
apron's stains. He's carrying two
briefcases and a gym bag. Sometimes a
back porch is built as if
it was part of the indoors. An old
guy with his bus pass pinned
to the front of his shirt. Gums bleed
between teeth. Neon sign blinking
in pizza parlor window, locked tight
an hour before dawn, bright pink.
Red down vest over rag wool
sweater. Bike chained to street sign,
front wheel missing. Dark interior
in armored car. The mind without cause,
noisome thing. Disposable
poetics. Flower vendor's stall,
green buckets of color. Snugglebumps.
Hockett's thesis is that the phoneme *f*

is just 3,000 years old, demanding
mouths shaped by the dental
consequences of higher agriculture.
The knees are not
an organ of prayer. Clouds
open in slomo vortex
to emit beam of light. Vis-
passana (sit still). This is
constant process. Restaurants use tipping
to suppress wages. Cramp in gut
like fist clenches. What
to write. What's
to be written. Child's innertube pool toy
the form of a bright yellow turtle. Wear red
for contrast on the telly. A street full
of trash cans, empty and toppled, after
the garbage truck's passed. You prefer
Le Menu TV dinners for their little plastic
plates. She's going to work with that
just-out-of-the-shower
look (what it does to their
imaginations). One sees dinettes
up against the glass walls
of condos, topped with cheap
table cloths – and a small vase
for straw flowers. Old white stove
abandoned on the walk. But here
the storefronts for lease are tiny,
trashed out. The backs of TVs
stare from apartment windows. T
shirt, bull shi'ite. The word
surrounded forms a ground for
nothing. Even after flossing
(grit teeth at mirror), the residue
of last night's popcorn – an 'okay' flick

– lodged between gum and
permanent bridge. I lie awake
feeling heart pound from sushi bar's
green tea. Not the white meat
of the kernel, but its husk or shell
still topped with "butter flavor."
This one jogs with his fists unclenched,
actually shaking his wrists. Your head
rests on my chest. I rise
and read Bill Berkson's newest book
until the morning paper hits the porch.
Prosody made that civilization. A spool
of ribbon typing black. A bus
with its brights on shines
through thick fog. Peach pits
in the crevices, the grid
of the walk. We want a new
line break, more visible, more irrational
than anything. From the street, through the front
window I see the light of the yard
coming in through the back. A man
without a car puts a dime (I think
it's a dime) into the parking meter.
Teenage girl wearing long johns
beneath a long plaid skirt. Burned-out
house sits vacant for a year. Diaphragm
as metaphor. Soft frisbee. Roofers' mops,
solid with old tar, next to the black encrusted
buckets. Small shards of a broken
bottle held together by the label.
Juxtaposition of Rock Hudson
and the 'killer' bees. Society itself presents
borderline features, as once, eighty years ago,
hysteria reigned. A nurse uses the pin
to her name tag to dig out the crud

from the rim of her glasses. After dinner
the four of us climb back into the Honda
conscious of choosing different seats. Wild
artichoke, blue-purple flower. Alabaster
chesspersons. Room in shadows,
morning light on a rainy day.
It's not my story. Sudden
silence. Then the fridge
roars on with a shudder. Oh
son of Sam, son of Shem, sharp stick.
Hard edge end rhyme. A basket
of bees beats a casket of fleas.
The flask of tea is tinged
with lemon, sugar crystals
(undissolved) sediment
on the bottom. Flat
as the hand turned palm down,
wrist extended, rocking
back and forth, a response
to your question, "Is this
wise?" Wide girl in
black leather pants, neo-orange
henna, walks proud.
'Jelly' bracelets encase wrist.
This is not my home or mother
nor displacement of any other
impulse. Little sedans
cruise the mall, all candy-colored.
Lunchbag tucked into
desk drawer, the thrill of
chilled water. Excess toner.
When I'm mad at you (as,
at this moment, I would seem
to be), it is not (directly)
your actions to which I

react, but how, rather,
I am put back in touch with
this old permanent storm
within. The dream of weather
fogs. A woman walks uphill
arms folded. In the projects
on a hot night, doors and windows
left open reveal
small yellow rooms (perfectly
boxlike) within. What's apt
to clutter a car's
back seat. Trochee's heave
is its own haze. Flag on tip
of sedan's antenna. Had O'Hara
lived, what then? Dog leashed
to stop sign by bakery door
whimpers. Bruises on a ripe pear.
A team of painters, gathered
like birds on their scaffold, transform
the three storey building from
brown to white. She raises
the t-shirt up over her head, arms
extended, torso exposed. The organization
of letters into a single word
always already presumes the line.
Squats flex your quads. A deeper silence
than the fog-chilled air over the little
pastel row houses in the valley
between freeways is the one in the head
swimming in mucous, fever buffer.
The sound a woman makes
scratching an ankle wrapped
in stocking. The glamour of
nuance. That place you say
you've never seen in the small

of your back where freckles
run together, small speckled
continent. Thermos of
sun tea, smell of
hot baked chicken
rising from a paper sack.
A stick in the sand extends
the hand into language, yet
meanings ebb. In the shed
you say yes. O lemon yellow
Continental Mark V, revving
your unmuffled engine, this little Olds
(a deeper yellow) covets
your parking space. Pigeons
alive in the bowels of the
subway station. Stop light
at freeway entrance. Alf
Landon bruised
in fall from bed. Window
edits sun falling
upon table, upon the objects
on the table. I'm from Youngstown
where the body happily is not
the body, cat in hopeless
search for lap, to which we're
connected by modem or
memory as helicopters sweep plane
in ye olde search and destroy.
A half-circle of chairs, empty,
gathers around the VCR. A young man
has an idea, which then hardens
into the bright, new coin of the realm
developed not in the manner of thought
but of land. The Christmas lights, shut off
but left hanging about the trim

of the house year round, form a chain
like speech, each of which conceals
its anchor. Chuckanut Drive.
Any clear thought can scare millions. Me,
I'm merely saying that writing might be
like a sponge and a particularly damp one
what with all the dirty dishes that
have passed thru these hands. But maybe
someone, anyone, thinks they've been fed,
nutrition sucked from these empty calories.
Yet justice is not a placebo. My mom,
alone with two kids, returned
to live with her parents, and did
until she was nearly forty. But
to take a position is to offend
a position. Mr Satellite is a little stick
figure with a happy face in a big blue
roadside dish. Let's switch discourses.
Continuity requires suppression. The swans
of the Gobi desert are an imaginative construct
yet nonetheless real. If a poet could talk
we would not understand her. Line break
applies herewith for its step increase.
Red sun over Elliott Bay: between
two soup kitchens and the Men's Hygiene
Center springs a block of new outdoor
cafes along Pioneer Square. One man
in the crane's glass cage can unload
an entire cargo container, boxes that would
stretch, end to end, seven miles long.
Hammock strung between pear trees, a breeze
in the alley. Dear Credence, that words should not
couple is not possible, unlike the artificial
celibacy of pets. He's pretty bipolar
but she keeps him stable. Clothesline's pole

seems about to topple, old red wood.
Sprinkler's excess leaves a pool in
the gutter, thru which cars whoosh.
Vowels of allegiance. Wooden fire escape
seems a precarious concept. We get out at the border
to wade through customs. A fear of heights
structures an old oedipal conflict. Attack dog charging
throws itself at the link fence. Juniper
tea, herring roe upon kelp, bannock bread dipped
in oolichan grease, with an entree of caribou stew.
Howe Sound: arriving or leaving
the water yields, blue-green dappled, alive
with its weaving of currents (houses
amid fir trees, nestled into the cliffs) –
we rock, carving our own wake. These
are not facts but points in a logic
learned in the living. Old man, your system's toxic.
Irony without relief is its own belief. These islands
(not hidden in the blood) owned by men (not women),
absolute as anything, their roads leading to the shore,
nonetheless shape water. Learn to sing your name
the way a shore bird skims water. I hunt
for vowels. Nor'east of Keats Island but still south
of Anvil, markers like the trail of crumbs
toward a cartographer's reading. Is the waterfall's
cut any cleaner? The body is not
the plan, but the path of its passage,
pure document. Words in sand
fill with tide's water. A family at picnic
waves at the passing train. This must mean what,
to have been rendered in acrylic? Already
we anticipate loss, the end of a journey,
in spite of the tunnels and starless nights.
Lions Gate to Horseshoe Bay. A man in a cafe
leads his small son to the restroom,

passing the culture. Red plastic trays,
food wrapped in foil. Raven is a scavenger
lives in the park. Who is missing? Who
writes the letter I? Camera pans
to the mirror but is not seen. I sit
on a patio in a park, on the bus, in
a plane. The world is not a text
tho we impose one. Robin drunk
on old plums. Cheap signs
in window of used furniture store.
Felt tip talking stick. Skookum
chuck. In the jack pine
spider's web gleams between branches.
Roots like tangled hair grow out
over the cliff face down to the sea.
Clouds out over the coast
backlit by the sun. The way logs
wash up against the sea wall. Two wasps
rend and devour a bee. A bent box
made of cedar. The sun rises
over Fraser Mountain (which is not
a mountain) which to the captains of poetry
or anyone signals time. Houses on the west shore
catch the light. But there are no captains,
the trucks drifting from lane to lane, their cargo
(ourselves) mooing and bleating from the rear.
Here the cat rubs against me, meowing, real
as dry grass. Time itself is a form of fiction
tho demonstrable through fire or any
unilateral process. Pears ripen in summer
when sheet lightning fills the sky. Each poem ends
with the present tense. Crowds move vacantly
through an airport terminal. The afternoon
heats up, smoke souring the indoor air.
The way continuous perspective disperses attention

until you seem to float freely, apart
from your body, attuned instead to the rhythms
of the world, as to the artificial lights
of interior space, subway or mall. Your name
over the intercom entirely without meaning.
Imagine a luggage that walked. Norms calm
form's charm. The cat's lesson is that it's not us.
Stalk to me. Sunflower bends, weary of its own weight.
Don't tell me I'm running to catch the bus! I
avoids rime, the biggest rhyme of all. I
comb my hair and climb the steps to work

PARADISE

for David Melnick

Words slip, does type, hand around the pen a clamp, a clip. Visible breath against constructivist past. The shed crowded, write in a sweat. We celebrate the agreement of a new year, the head shrouded, bright in a knit suit. Loop conceived in a line, the spine with its regions, reasons. On another, sweaters hang by the wrist to dry. The list is sweet. You lie. The eye is met by the season.

Sleep surrounds. Dawn's crack invades dark at the horizon, somersaults underwater, duress. Naturalism is administered, bite-size. The charge is reversed, ticket torn in half. Many await to be one for a time, then two. Cargo cult salute at reef. Nothing in your ear larger than New Hampshire, the oven off. Clouds blot light of the sky.

It's only five, the pleasure of nouns, cat coil, the sky very low today in the cloth. By the pepper grinder a red pen has run dry. Elizabeth Taylor, from pinup to gargoyle. Books slouch on a shelf.

Cheese understood as an action, tending to blue if the clouds part, room temperature. The sound of the shower at the neighbor's house. Morning is a meditation followed by work, pressure sensitive. Little blue book (but blue here is a different hue, too dark). The park parodies a former freedom, a sea wall. A gull in the fog or against it. There are snails in the predicates. This is not a sentence. The words merely crawl across the page, leaving a trail of syntax. It is not the sky we mean, but the past, a non-existent wall. The logic of bottles on the bathroom shelf. Great archetypal coil of an old tube of tooth-paste. The cords head back to the socket. Thermostat set at words per minute. Melody of air in pipes to sink.

Pair of dice is lost. Big old trucks in back of the farmers' market. Black dots on the green meat of the kiwi. Fog filters the hues of the next hill. The tall grass crushed to form a path. Cut plum limb, ragged right. To live in a loft is often to forgo comfort. Casserole. Jade plant in a clay pot. The impulse itself is what thickens.

Spoon scrapes bowl. She speaks of herself as if another, without sentiment, a sentiment in itself. Sparts are a sect. No one was keeping a journal. Tone harbors the hollow of a silence, kindly but sad. Out there, the rain. In here, the body. Light muted by the shade. Response card referred to as the action. Old brass lamp. An etching of three girls from which hangs a cobweb. An inkling or prediction. That the paragraph end.

The month is late and he works as a waiter. The moth is in the light and fate shirks heat. The fakir burps, suffering image creep. Adhesive, suffering connotations to the skull. Old car gets off to a rough start on a cold morn, then another, off-ramps in the valley. On a loading dock on Minna, warehouse-men eat lunch in the shadows. Hog's head smiles in butcher's window. Little nicks in the silence come to a period. Zoned edition of afternoon paper. Folded towel. How the Pyrex plates indict our lives. Eye tracking to center of ad, or scanning to where and how new paragraph begins (reading and thinking at the same time). Tonight I'm the voice of opinion. The cat meows at his bowl. Your nipple hardens to my touch. The butter sits in its dish. Planet spins, heated by a small star.

An ironing board is used as a work table. Trowel caked with dirt. Lined up at the "will call" window. The coffee cool at the bottom of the cup. The pen rests on the side of the middle finger, held there by forefinger and thumb. Technique advances in time of war. Refocusing on the long grass, I feel syntax. Stock characters tumble in a western bar. A parrot from another letter stares in his cage. The diaphragm's jellied spermicide leaves a slightly metallic taste. These short words hammer small meaning. Conspiracy demands agreement in number. A line of red socks dries in the sun. Words situate in newest state of union (shadow text in margin). Diced carrot, warm and soft.

The hat is the form of a demand. The cat paws at your hand. Not all socks are red.

Dawn brakes, pruned fuchsia. These poles from which to string clotheslines slant. Hammer on hollow wood. Window bangs shut. Metal spatula scrapes along iron pan. Typewriter hums, awaiting new paragraph.

Imagine a sinister rooster in the middle of the woods, the fog so thick that under the pine trees it appears to rain. A nagging cough, a sore throat and an earache. A lone plastic rose decorated the windowsill. This is my half birthday. He shared the motel room with a fly. The brevity of life is a given. The sole function of the British monarchy is to attract tourists. He disliked thinking that words such as "do-able" were jargon. At dawn the big trees gradually attain depth and color, the sky clinging. The purpose of the work was the transformation of the worker. The benefit of a light bulb.

The sample of morning. Spoon scoops wet flakes. It is difficult to be frank over sprouts. Upstairs neighbor's shower's on. Crispy crunchy. The low hum of the fridge plus the hiss of the gas oven, door open to heat the room. She sings and combs out her hair.

Half done, half dead, halftone, bidding no trump: "he has give up hope." Cat laps water. First promise of spring, fly unable to tell which window is open. The lone boy hooks the basketball toward the hoop nailed to the side of the garage, but it bounds away. In romance, sexual desire is freed from a relation to power. The real bandit queen of India, Madame Gandhi. Puffball clouds in a blue sky. Simple sentences, again and again. The old sisters walk to the store together, slowly, one wearing bright slippers. Our lives are like this, quiet on a Sunday. Sink full of cups.

Dormer. The smell of your hair fresh from the shower. Asparagus in oyster sauce. Electronically enhanced for stereo. An old chair out back, used only to store a topsoil sack. We rollover and are still, just holding one another in the dark.

Simple span, a sort of faith that whatever's next will finally be there, tollbooth in deco mode, demimonde. How can I read verse with all that singing? Defenseless against kisses. The sky is white, cloud cover so thin you want to discount it (your reflection in that window not clear enough to shave by).

A truth table upon which to set connotation's pizza. Straightforward carpentry of the peach crate. The door on my neighbor's porch opens. David's in the basement, mixing cement, the washer kicks over to the rinse cycle. Define that portion of an hour: carry it over to the reading. That blue ribbed spread takes up half the line. Hose out the bucket. Old ironing board turned into a desk. Further, new books might confuse you, an investment in a tree farm in the path of a volcano. When she's not around, you imagine what it would be like to fuck, part game, part sharing, regardless of the others, but, present, you remember immediately just how quickly that spontaneous brilliance, a carefully honed nuttiness, would begin to grate. Later her children will be taller than you are. Thus clouds part only to reveal a void. You must zip up your trousers and dot the i. The lawn's whole reason is trimming. Once 'famous,' the poet was unable to speak clearly, but was shuttled about wherever plastic cups of white jug wine signaled the occasion. Five words, the spelling of which you will always be forced to look up. The rate at which dishes become dirty allover again.

What diarrhea can do to hemorrhoids.

The sunflower creature with three heads. You can tell where the teapot was glued. Her fingers spread the jelly in the small rubber dish. The wind stills and you sense the storm waiting. I like the feel of a hat, the way it distributes pressure around my head. The older he got, the smaller he seemed. It was old coffee – just to keep them going. The trunk of the plum tree knots upward. I drag the old metal can of trash through the basement, letting it scrape the concrete. The glazed pot tips from the box in his arms and we all watch motionlessly as it floats to the ground, tumbling, drifting until it hits and shatters. Although they also are naked, the two small children stop to watch the crouching woman urinate into the sand on the beach, her eyes meeting theirs with the most serious of contact.

A sentence in the evening. Today the boxscores are green. Tonight the boxcars are groaning in the railyard. The indexical items are not coreferential. Hollywood caenfidential. You made Cheerios number one.

Mock snow: white petals from the plum tree swirl in the wind. I was working on a different poem. The dark patches to the clouds' glare are all we have of depth to this sky. The shudder of laundry down in the basement. A small table in one corner of the kitchen. White petals from the plum tree twirl in the wind. I slip in a pair of diskettes. Don't miss the opportunity to earn Pediatrics Review and Education Program (PREP) credits on an hour-for-hour basis at the plenary sessions as well as Category I credit toward the American Medical Association's Physician Recognition Award. The stapler sits on the table. When in reverse, that car emits an idiot tune. I own not one photograph of my father. The most beautiful of all the carpenter's tools is the level. Becoming identified with an inaccurate but provocative name enabled the Language Poets to rapidly deepen market penetration and increase market share. I turn the muffins over. Dot matrix. The rectangularity of windows is sometimes a shock. Verse is not in crisis, Isis, but only the capacity of academics to comprehend phenomena they cannot predict. Juju use of slide guitar. One less wine glass. Westinghouse is the largest investor in Toshiba. I'm just singing to the muse.

I was working in a different poem. Descriptions of daily life decay. The idea of long words. A glare in the cloud rose, which we thought to be the sun, calling it day. Still the clear memory of my grandmother's icebox. Or that the washing machine with the ringer atop it would spot oil on the linoleum floor. So writing a poem is different from kissing a baby's tush. A complex series of perpendiculars leading to the second floor. Short fat bird in the plum tree whistles. The poem is thinking (white cat chews grass). You only had a bowl of cereal one hour ago. The bruise I don't remember getting. The entropy of later life mocks symmetry. By leasing out the technology and buying back its products for assemblage into full computer systems, IBM avoids any investment in manufacturing plants whatsoever, and is thus free to move its capital as labor market conditions shift. Rhymes with theft. As for we who live to be astonied, basil makes the pesto. Yet as *USA Today* makes clear, condensare is not itself sufficient for dichtung. The shape of the alphabet is itself a system: poem composed in symmetrical letters. Glass in the drying rack turned upside down. Self-gentrification. Orthodox Marxology requires antacid. Adorno escapes Frankfort, locating in Manhattan, whereupon is declared the New York School. Two prostitutes on a day off visit the zoo. An old wicker hamper is repainted green. The female cop tucks her hair beneath her cap. In a crowded department store I get nauseous and disoriented, buying wildly. Peter's criticism gets around. My one goal is a clear mind – right now! Geographic isolation enables the Huichol to resist aculturation into the increasingly Europeanized daily life of modern Mexico. The baby sucks at the full breast. The March sun. The snail clings to the kale leaf. The neighbor's cat bounds from porch to porch like a rabbit. Mountains of clouds from over the sea. First the plum tree blossoms, then come the leaves. Subtlety is not instinctive. At the instant of orgasm you roll your eyes.

The difference between eggs and chairs, fat happy baby, is how the cat sleeps: light drizzle. I lean forward and then the words focus. Beneath the leaf the trunk of the plant stood in the moist earth gathered in a pot atop a saucer on the desk. The point at which you simply start piling books for want of room. Mom sends photos of my brother's new son. The oven is our only heat. A small child runs to the bus in the rain.

Sometimes I come home from work so tired that I don't know whether to cry or throw up or lie on the floor, shaking.

The slope is called the fall line and you proceed up hill with your skis perpendicular to it. In the cabin, the cubicles are like small jail cells composed of wood. The cross country instructor has decided which girl for the weekend. I don't mean woman. Snowblind.

Big slow jet, low over the horizon. Her eyes on me wide and brown. There is no pain equal to the memory of pain. I'm impatient that each word takes so long to write. As when, in the newspaper, an article on how to ride a camel brings tears. All cotton pleated chino twills. My life is not your symbol. Historians eke rhyme from fact. Aka will, verb transitive. Remember the days when Bob smoked dope all the time? Well, Masanori Murakami has been released. You're a commie, too.

When that April with his sure as soot the draft of March has pierced it to the root and bothered every vein in swish liqueur of which virtue engendered is the floor. Damp earth dusts the leaves of a new transplanted violet. Thousands in Denver flee big acid cloud. The bath mat, a deep red, needs shaking. The dresser lacks handles. Big sun wobbles up through branches of the plum tree. Objects repeated take on value. The ostrich is a pretty bird (false). A ceramic jar full of brown sugar. Old bristle brush kept beneath sink. I remove the article. The way an old sponge goes sour. In the valley cars move slowly, crowding into the city. In the papers orchestrated lies compete for space. In the prepositional the temporality of syntax mimes space. Rhyme violates reason: thus I remember.

The street crew hunkers low against the side of the building, passing a pack of cigarettes down the line without comment, safety vests a brilliant orange. A row of robins. Without speech. Eyes fixed upon a passerby. The smoke blue and quickly shapeless in the light breeze. In the gutter a dustbroom lays next to a mound: leaves, paper, glass. This never happened. The world represented is not that world. In one where the wind whips through the eucalyptus, Reagan is never President. The hand is seen jutting from the sleeve. Pain is not questioned. But the moment between sentences. The crowd roars as the rightfielder hurls a strike right to the plate. While from the sideview this is seen as sculpture, smooth, carved, timeless. The gallery's silence is not the garden's. Old trees have been cleared away. Now we use them as benches or as propositions. In that one Gerald Ford is an eternal ideal. Do hummingbirds envy? The organization of dust on a hillside more careful than Chartres. But the moment between sentences, words. Green tables. Are not absent. Count for something.

Plum tree fuller, more green. Two birds, twittering, thrash around in it. In the shade, a chill breeze undercuts the clean blue slate of sky, sun barely above the rooftops. It's yellow, but whitens as it rises. In the blanket of baby-tears at the base of the tree, a snail stretches its full body, crossing toward the shed. I want to call those prongs antlers. The sun shines right through its yellow-green body.

Comp time. Little words inching into syntax, itching into context. The margin of morning. The white space is not silence. The mysterious flea market where all the Deadheads buy their clothes. They lurch out of the doorways with their palms up. Gradually the cereal absorbs the milk. Tiny green plums start to appear. Soon the fuchsia will start to blister. Dull white sun heavy in the sky. This guy calls me Spike. The rotted stairs wobble. A green hamper. Old pipes rise out of the rooves right over the kitchens. To touch them, books in this climate are cool and damp. Countertransference. (the writer doesn't "like" the reader). Cords hang from sockets. The last player to make an unassisted triple play was Ron Hansen, a graduate of Albany High. That key on the latch by the back door is to the lock we never use.

The small children rise in the wind, drifting, long shoelaces tangled all the way back down to the treetops. One corner just to keep brooms in. Simple single syllable. The weight of the dog against the wood of the fence, snarling. The dull distant televised stare of a president.

Words do drift, black on whatever lighter background. Another impulse brightens the face into a silly grin. The script of the neon lettering is florid. No accounting for syllables here. The whole yard brightens into day long before the sun's up. The garbagemen have their own cans, which are larger and on wheels. The ink is an oily film on a metal ball that turns as the pen rolls over the paper. I am not in love with the punctuation. Government enforces new math of binding. In the dream the married woman pulls up her skirt.

All the dogs begin to howl. Pigeon's gray a camouflage for concrete. It's going to be a hot one. All these small, off-white, stucco homes. Sharp smell of ripe banana. The point beyond which poetry is a curse. The leaves of the noun grown too hard and spotted. Teenage girls in white painter's pants. Writing the bus. His face was no longer simple. Old sheets used as curtains, knotted on a sunny day.

New morning, sawdust on the unfinished porch. Follow the machine of the hand up the cables to the wrist. Visible cows. On a day this hot you can smell the sun. Coffee fills the kitchen.

The promise of an old Braxton heard like a chore, sore throat. The whole family, dressed to the nines, piles into the dark car. A week at work. White curtains along the kitchen windows, the high fogged sky behind them just as white.

In the wake of bells. Pose a minute, hand pulling softly at lobe of ear. Yellow dog seems to smile. In the market no one speaks your language. All of human history leading up to a stiff neck. The hanging ferns swing gently to mark the quake. She glances back at you over her shoulder. The plane's approach fills the screen until it rises, passing over. The mode of reading we call doggy-style. The neutrality of the headline is brazen, unreal. What architect planned that shed?

Cat purrs to have tongue tucked in, burrs in gray hair. Light through a curtain fills a room. At the bottom of a gray spoon old coffee has hardened into a brown stain. I love baggy shirts. References provided! upon request. Turned upside down, the cups dry in a rack of dishes by the sink. The refrigerator gives a shudder, then is silent. Even through the curtain one feels the clouds passing in front of the sun. Congruence of images implies a place. We close our consulate in Iowa City. The better galleries are near the larger banks. Western Carloading. Some phrase might haunt you for a decade. The needle arm lifts mechanically off the vinyl disk.

Something beyond ravioli is a cup of hot tea. Wooden squares compose the table. The half shadows of indirect lighting. Another morning is extra. The cat's ear is gouged. The azalea petals seem dry. The kettle rattles when the water boils. It has a wooden handle. The work is "explained" through a description of the social circumstances under which it could have been written. Lately there's been an argument, but it feels like we've been bickering for weeks. Alcohol being merely a slow form of oxidization. A man on the sidewalk clears his throat. I'm not sitting in the desert reading Keats. Once begun, the day is soon over. In her world, OD means organizational development. Like all the swoops and squiggles Pollock ever made.

Where the beer and the cantaloupe play. Because the polling place is at the top of the hill, the old widows at the bottom seldom vote. Blueberries in a white bowl.

Half. In the shade, light's a glare. The letter from Russia with the beautiful stamps. Here comes Mr. Constant Criticism. The dogs gallop down the hill. Couch pillows (and a day pack). Searching through Poetry Flash to find my name. The next door neighbor's car plays a little tune when it's put in reverse that I've grown to loathe. A vision of beauty in the shape of a carrot. The day after a session of lifting weights I can barely comb my hair. The black Volvo pulls up, Smokey Robinson blaring through the sun roof. He wears a ring of keys on the left side of his belt. Hey Fuck, you want to talk or what? Crisp crackers. Now I'm on the other side of the house. Time to put that load in the dryer. High up, that long jet makes a slight sound. Somebody is hosing something out of view. My collar, invariably damp. Never saw a butterfly come indoors like a bee. The echo of sirens down in the valley is strangely beautiful. Don't you find it hard at times to believe that letters form words? Suddenly the screen went blank.

Always stop to talk to a cat. That wasn't his dream, was it? The burned skin bubbled. The song of water rushing through the pipes. The value of sound is that it's outside the rational. The parachutes opened, 1, 2, 3, bursts of orange against the light blue sky.

I overestimated. The small chores, like leaving wine glasses upside down to dry. Aphids drown the azalea. The cat meows to be let in.

O venerable atrophy, apostrophe, catastrophe. Someone is stomping tin cans. The grass dry, the high elastic band leaving a red ring about the waist, a taste of cobwebs in the wind. The legs of the calamari. Patio's white stones begin to scatter throughout the yard. Cat crouches beneath the lawn chair. Shadows shape the light.

Thick smog erases Oakland. All the sunbathers are male. Muscles of the lower back. You can smell the heat. You can sell the meat. Lat pull, bench press. A thin bald man with a white beard is doing yoga. Touch your nose. That boy in a ponytail is a lawyer. In Hinduism the point is to get beyond language. Shaved legs are an abomination. Your perfectly typical Silliman sentence. Blackbirds hunted in the cut grass. Her new name is Ma Prem. That side of the park is cholo turf. I can hear them talking, but not what they say. Stanza conceived as a sitting. Narrative implies progress. No tree mourns a leaf.

In Bromige's attic, a wider range of bird calls. Yellow wood houses on a street of no traffic. How to count the cats. The same books from house to house. Photograph of Anselm. Orange towel placed over the typewriter to keep the dust out. Sawhorse and sawhorse and plywood board make a desk. The continuities of fifteen years from a cramped apartment on Arch Street. A long sentence that seeks to postpone its verb.

You want to describe everything, she said. How many of the men on the nude beach were gay? It hurts to swallow. Being young, the red tail hawk's tail was not yet red. She let him apply the cocoa butter to her breasts.

37, a prime number, a baked salmon. In the jargon of Boontling, much detail is accorded the adolescent view of sex. Growing older, Carla is more modest. White and aimless signals, doers of no good. I bin go walk. The fog thins on the heights. The eyes see what they're trained to.

Dear familiar words: deep pockets, gray sky. Previously it existed only as potential, the next sentence. Closure is lies. Old Butterick sky. I'm writing a letter, ladder. These square yellow brick homes. On each garage a small sign warns "no parking."

Walking down the steps of the house, the woman turns and says to the man shadowed in the doorway, "Draino, bread and cheese?" "Draino, bread and cheese," he replies.

Anger without content (content with his anger). Auto emissions. Although it was a sunny, breezy morning, he felt himself to be still indoors.

Owning a car would alter my scale of the city. This new pen made a fat line. Idle sequence. One fact of traffic is its many colors. The point at which whatever you say next will start a fight. Beneath that skirt her legs seemed so white. Grandmother is blind now. The colors on the telly were too bright. Three of four end in rhyme, a divorce. On 24th Street one is apt to run into poets. The page went by very quickly. I prefer the letters rounded and seriphed. She's jogging with a bag of groceries, hoping to catch the bus.

Passing it on the way to work, the bar is already filled. A Chinese family owned the small diner, getting by by selling cheap meals and expensive cups of coffee. A row of new apartments, modeled to look Victorian. It is a mistake to have considered the idiom in Shakespeare natural. The novels they read on the subway in to work are thick with distraction. Potato chip delivery truck. A new taste in the mouth.

The sway of morning, thick clouds over the cranes of the shipyard. She laid back and closed her eyes, waiting for the trick to finish. Someone in the building is burning toast. The small girl's loud fart drew a frown from her mother. Slowly the cars herded themselves into the city. Old Philippine woman in a red bandana. 2-Rock. You could see dust rise from where the sandblasters worked. The low sun fierce in the clouds.

Mail slot in the garage door. At the foot of the hill I see a bus. Two distinct layers of cloudwork. From this distance, you can't tell that it's a ghetto. She was heading up the slope in high heels, one hand controlling her skirt in the wind. Talking on the phone so long my ear is red. The deeper horn of the big trucks. Amid the cartons of produce on the sidewalk in front of the bodega, three kinds of banana. The dark Buick with Oregon plates. Those dots are called bullets.

Deep in genital soup (a new page). Fiscal to the wall. Metahistorical, the roofers mock up a pulley reaching down to the smoking tar heater. The sidewalk is the sum of its stains. A big dog in a parked car. The relative lope of, different joggers. The penis is not a lollipop. A theory of how you pack foods into a paper bag. Later, a student invokes the principle of insertion. Metahysterical, the woofers fuck up a volley (bleaching down).

"Write in any state of mind," says a poet who doesn't need a job. Letter perfect. Two friends, young Vietnamese women, spent the afternoon going from massage parlor to massage parlor seeking employment. Little amber rectangle – when the cursor falls over a letter, the grapheme is figured in reverse. Your name here. Main frame joystick. The frog arrives safely at the screen top. Korean Air Lines flight 007 is missing and presumed down. A man such as J.D. Tippet. The burns on my father's body. Her lips move as she reads the book. First Max, then Ruben. If this is a narrative, it is driving me wild.

She sits silently during the meeting, addressing envelopes. Pipecutter. Black ant on red ,jellybean on the grey walk. Old coffee cans painted white now are flowerpots in a row on the porch. To try and tell a story is to make a purgatory of the real. A child in one arm while the other drags a wire cart of laundry. The dull half-sun of a partly cloudy morning.

What is morning? A cat. Fed. Curls up on a kitchen chair. Sedative sunlight. Gauzy room. All the books written to be read on the way into work.

These words are no more in your mouth than in my hand. He sat on the steps behind the house. Shed roof stained by the juice of plums. Vowels passive in the face of a consonant. Great torque in a cat spine. Spy against spy: the post-Ted ego stakes heat up. I see her at the reading, head down, eyes shut, each hand clenched in a fist. Bottle of soda water. Even after a revolution struggle would be constant. People forget to read the bulletin board closely. So many drawers in the house are open, cupboard doors ajar. Masturbating, I think of you. I can barely wait to take my shoes off. A small blue dish filled with white sugar. Gradually the fallen leaves settle into dust. Medicated sugarless cough lozenge.

Vowels balance, a form of valence. A characteristic rhythm to the sentence. The asymmetry of one's face. No eyes more foreign than those in the mirror. It's going to be a hot one. Holding my nose, waiting for the sneeze to pass.

The bicyclist lies in the sun on the grass. Nearby, sunbathers lie on towels, listening to cassette players through headphones. In the distance Oakland is smeared in the smog. In a dream we lay naked side by side and were no longer just friends. Paradise is garden. The city in the park. The city in the parking lot. At the reading she said to me, "You look different with your clothes on." A tall black in dreadlocks is carrying an icechest. The bee appeared to be doing battle with the cricket. Image of the plane distorted by the sky it flies through.

The town grew up around a lumber yard in the 1850s, which, as would not happen on the east coast, gives it an air now of being old. A dog stands in the back of a blue pickup. A Japanese woman is breast feeding her son in the front yard, talking with friends. The sidewalk starts at Chestnut Street. It was a hot day but with chill gusts. A glassed-in cafe just like on the Upper West Side. Three teenage boys are racing in the shopping center parking lot. Between the highway and the coast comes Georgia-Pacific. Behind the closed door of Cal's Tavern came the clatter of billiard balls. The name of the bookstore was The Bookstore. The small parade turned out to be some sort of Portuguese holiday celebration, one high school band and four clusters of costumed marchers, moving slowly up what had once been the main street, its sidewalks empty. What looked like an old gym turned out to be City Hall. In the shade of the shack of the bait shop sleeps a yellow dog. An old man alone on the beach sings "Down in the valley, in the valley so low." My feet burn from a long walk. The sound of a foghorn, but no sight of fog. They went into Safeway just to get into the cool conditioned air. Two boys ask the old man what he's doing with a net and a bucket. He throws the empty beer bottle out into the bay. Dressed in black, a silhouette but for the white beard and red flesh. I tossed an onion ring to the seagull and instantly ten others flew up, landing between three and ten feet of my towel in the sand. My name is Captain Graysquirrel and I go which way the wind blows. The bed filled the motel room. At the top of the cliff overlooking the water was a small cemetery with picket fence and a lone tree. Overall, like the pattern of the sun's reflection off the water of the small bay. I was in the navy so I know something, he said. The boys took the bucket to hunt for dry wood. One white sail breaking the horizon. A small hawk out over the beach. The sand caked in the sun lotion and clung to the flesh. The gulls sit facing the water. They built a fire, a narrative. Under the bridge was the poorest trailer park I'd ever seen. It had brown feathers and a black beak. The waves were only the smallest curl of foam, a foot high, rolling up the beach. They had tin cans and cellophane bags which they filled with shells. The small damp stones seemed lovely. They were frightened by the old beach- comber but obeyed his instructions.

The bottom of the page is only a dotted line across the screen. A flock of starlings high over the valley. These are not facts. She stood naked by the window, smoking a cigarette, looking down at the scene at Broadway and Columbus, while her boyfriend behind her slowly pulled on blue trunks and an orange shirt. The thick smell of liver steamed up from his plate. The red letters disappeared into the gray background. The boiler room is referred to as the Chinese basement. These are not facts. This was and now you are constituted in the process of being words, your thought actualizing through the imposition of this syntax. Resistance alone is real (coming distractions). Cross against the light. Leave work to write a poem and not mention the dragonfly. The industrial mower gouged more of the hill than it cut.

The madman stood on the rooftop, silhouetted by the full moon, pulling bricks from the chimney and hurling them into the street. You can tell by how tense their mouths are, the set of the lips, that these bus riders are on their way to work. Yellow tow truck. Long hair streaked blonde.

A noisy band of two dozen poets had taken over the subway station. Her hat was in fact a pizza-sized cracker. A bee had somehow managed to settle in the pocket of his sport coat. I was permitted to hear the work. My lip was swollen, disfigured. The crowd pushed onto the bus.

Like whales moving slowly through the depths of a still sea, the dark clouds pushed silently over the low hills. In the fog the hillside's green deepens. The shingled rooves tilt upward, notching the low sky. The crossing guard wears a red sweater with a yellow sash. Along the side of the house-half-filled garbage cans sit in shadow. An old water heater in the alley. Sidewalk freckled with the residue of gum. I find Melnick eating by himself at Wendy's. A phone poll out of new wood. The sort of cardboard display you find in the window of a third rate travel agent.

Barking is not dead.

Nor that either. First rain. Seating chart. The cranes of the shipyard beyond the arched curve of the freeway. The crows in the grey sky. The crew on the loading dock takes a break. Verbs flutter in a still landscape. An old wad of bright pink gum hard as a stone in the gutter. The bus leapt the curb and ended up wedged firmly in the liquor store wall. The tip of his penis against the back of her throat.

Out behind the diner the empty plastic trash can releases its thick, sour smell into the morning air. Or outside of a bakery at dawn. Running at both ends. I wouldn't return there to live. The weekend storm had cleansed the air. The weakened storm dissolved. A state of perpetual sweating tasted sweet.

The definition of a pencil. Coin Wash and Dry. The fireman in front of the station on a hot day. He searches the aisle for the penny he dropped. A Cross pen you twist to write with (not this). Designs on lace curtains.

The sun shapeless in the muzzy air. The three small clumps of eucalyptus on the top of the hill, where even the City had refused to build more housing projects, reinforced the barren air. Across the bay, where Oakland should have been. But over Glen Park the fog in thick gray slabs. The air in my hair (drying it after a shower). Red feet of a pigeon. The roofers set up their pulley. So hot that she put a towel over the plastic seat before she climbed into the truck in her cutoffs. The truck in her cutoffs. Now one of the lowriders at the gym has made a sauna suit from a trashbag. I set the weight at 90 lbs and do 15 reps. He dresses like a lawyer but works in a thrift shop. She sits up and her breasts settle. The rest of the day is a cinch. I can still make out the logo of the Girl Scouts on that cookie on the side-walk. Then we began to wonder if the bus would ever emerge from the projects. Then it did. Marat's tub was his ship of state. The mailman neglects to close the garden gate. We wander into work a little late. The prose was in the rhythm.

Donor list. The heat of morning, the weight of the sky. Stars fade at dawn rise. The size of the truck by the squeal of its brakes. Spots of brown about the peel of the banana. The luxury of thought. This was a reader-potential sentence. School bus yellow. Stanza's pansies. A break exists between etymology and connotation. The Columbus Day parade marching through China-town. Rolled down, metal curtains simplify store fronts. Must be farsighted by the way she holds that book.

Five minutes down. Boysenberry yogurt. Alternate spelling. The large bowl of his stomach made for a sloping desk. A mean-spiritedness to the humor of the comic poet. Just us chickens, classically trained. Now that she's making 25 thou. A jolting bus impossible to write on. What I wish to say, dear reader, take off your blouse. April, turning toward November. Suggested denotation. An old stuffed chair on the sidewalk in the rain. Caution: frequent stops.

Exhaustion, a kind of freedom, sets in (a new pen). The nose runs, not unlike an engine, a jogger. A complex form of information called a potato. Even the simplest word is sometimes foreign. A balding woman. Trying to look punk, working in a bank. His vowels were dreamlike and indulgent. The cars occur in all colors. Eigner's noun. Dogs dogs dogs. Over the years, counting the little businesses that have gone into that storefront. Limbs off a tree stuffed into a garbage truck. Foundation in the weeds of a vacant lot.

The grass, being damp, is soft. The shoes, being old, are soft. The flesh, being weak. A thick fog had absorbed the haze. That waitress in the coffeeshop is the only one he ever talks to. A thru street (cars push up the hill in waves). & then went down on the ship. With the toddler in her arms, she stands with feet spread apart for balance. The ink dries into the page, shining for one moment in the sun. An idea repeats, then becomes chronic. Lowriding is a state of the imagination.

Any ally on. Any epithet or text. Rages. Strain of tartar sauce. He rides the buses just to talk to the drivers, to have someone to talk to. Means at, not with. You can tell where the tar spilled (without saying a word). An old woman in a heavy coat on a hot day. Now the stuffed chair is in the street. The car backs up, engine hood still open.

Down in the valley, the curves of an on-ramp simplify a landscape. The City, colorless in the first glare of dawn. Empty station wagon, engine running. The dream had exhausted him, and he rose with no sense of rest. There was a fire somewhere just north of 16th Street, dark smoke you could feel with your eyes.

Whatcha up to, dude? I will not participate in that defense. Teaching Reagan to count down from 100 by sevens.

The valley opens in layers, high clouds thinned to a point of utter flatness, below which sit a few lighter puffs. The sun, before it is a sun, light over the mountains. In the gulleys between trees, fog softens the greens. The road to Healdsburg a series of lights. The bottom of the cloud layer catches a pink-orange light (new patterns appear). More yellow in the vineyards in the valley. Above the clouds sky eases into a light blue. Suddenly the red disappears from the clouds and they seem dark and smoky. The hacking laughter of jays. On a balcony two men are talking, half-shouting as though hard of hearing. Five birds do not a flock make, even as they fill the air. Behind a pine windbreak the sun ascends. I sit in a metal lawnchair outside the chapel of the Episcopal bishop's ranch. What is the name of that mountain (let's give it a name). Sky is organized around fix of the sun. Down in the valley, a dog barks.

In singing, feel the point at which the vibration occurs (it moves up and down). Take care not to break the pen tip. Hear the crow. The lawn chairs sit in the rain. Don comes to fetch his zafu. Simple sentences (everyone). Under the window seat I found the baseball bats. The sun frames the page. Plum tree's slant. What does it mean, "tomorrow you would have been married 18 years"? Dunlop Illustrated Encyclopedia of Facts. Before writing, read Chaucer. The valley is such a simple system, waves of earth rolling too slow for the eye to see. One function of chanting is to rid the mind of language. The way a drainpipe extends from the gutter of the roof. In the following year he married a Miss Purden (died 1825), the daughter of an architect and the author of several poetical effusions. Then the harmonium begins to hum. Raj walks past the chapel, sweater slung over his shoulder, toward the dining hall. A squirrel hunts in the leaves.

Motorscooter sputter. Eros of the single life. Visible, nor plausible.

I see by your beeper that you're not a patient. Dropped a skateboard on her big toe. Blue milk crates, stacked empty in front of the corner store. They're painting the steps to their house. Gym bag. Dog in the window is the size of the window. Depends on how you conceive of glass.

Storm on the bay bends light. Write on the way to work. Turkish delight. Sight's fate. Rate an orange. A door hinge wants grease. Peace hoop, green in a white bowl. Owl's aw who calls. Falls: the limits of this writing am.

Owlish, alright: the round face of the cat on the porch. A heavy shower lasting not more than 5 minutes. This is not my report. Sensible shoes. In the narrow cleft above the upper lip the dark old Filipino cowboy had a small white vertical moustache which he rubbed with the back of a leathery hand. See dawn, think disaster. You can tell which unit's vacant just by the curtains. Three pronged plug. Ring of wrought iron.

Language cannot tell the truth. I didn't say that. I didn't "say" that. Window on the bus fails to shut. To write "nyah nyah nyah" and not be ironic. X = X+l. Used cars slouch behind a link fence. At this hour you see children on their way to school. Your fate is to be more like your parents than you'll ever admit. A noticeable limp. He puts the machine to his throat so that he can speak.

Her jacket is supposed to look like leather. As the bus pulls up to the stop they shove and push to make their way to exit the rear door. Although it's early morning, her face reflects exhaustion. An isolate intimacy, the way to work.

Length of sentence. No need to wake the block up. By adding a trim, painters reframe a house. The noise a newspaper box makes when its spring slams the door shut. Long life (short vowel). More old men with full beards.

Standing on the chair, screwing in the lightbulb. The way the muscles of the anus can grip the cock. A chill day. Standing at the busstop on her way to work, hair still soaking wet. Rosenquist's objects, says the sign on the museum wall, must be seen as "nonreferential." Before I even feel it, the first froth of sperm starts to spill from your mouth.

"Oscar," the small boy shouts at the passing bus, gloved hand waving back from the driver's window. Pooh bear tea. Hilltop blurred in a thick rain. Cat asleep at the foot of the bed. I reach out to hug you and see you cringe.

She called her novel Pleasure. Winter receded for a few days, the air cool but clear. Chew into the meat of the banana. At 35, his friends began to find "real" jobs and/or turned to parenting. An ersatz compositional linguist from down under. Applesauce muffins. The clothesline reaches to the kitchen window. Paradigm lost. This pen has a frail tip. Where in the summer plums had dropped, dark pits remained on a stained shingle roof. Why bother simple facts? The shadow of a gull over the back yard. The angle at which a rising jet turns. "I want my next book to have a spine." The cat in the kale. Butterflies in late November. What the years do to a lawnchair. Mom's a stoic. Cop's flashlight long as a baton. Just by its smell, you know that food's Chinese. Engine coughs and turns over. Right to be frightened by the TV set.

When she wears her hair pulled back tight like that, one can see just how thin it is. Clip-on photo security pass. The joggers are beginning to bundle up. A line of newsracks, chained one to the other. He runs for the bus, trying to look casual.

Pleasantly pastoral. All affect. Harmonic disengagement. Writing in the rain. Down in the freeway valley, echoing siren's hollow sound. Something like that. A form of 12s. Stuffed egg, topped with paprika. The heavier the rain, the fewer the pretensions. A baseball cap is not a shelter.

"I" shake hands with Werner Erhard at the Presidio Officer's Club.

Names serve suppository function, insertion of foreign object. People wearing raincoats in spite of a clear sky. My posture, my syntax.

Now Bruce is reading (removed thru amplification). A double knot in my shoelace. Of 50,000 missing children each year, 3,000 are murdered, 8,000 others never seen again. Sleeves rolled up to signify style. Earlobe segmentation. A deformed nationalism roots for the Dodgers. Saké warming on a hotplate. Lover is not user-friendly. Floury stock deemed soup. Sit in the back to indicate diffidence. Her hand drifts onto your knee. Humanist anesthesiology. Interim director. Is your bathroom breeding Bolsheviks? White buttons on black shirt. Stash tea. Sound of a light switch. The middle class is a non-idea. Parolees form a chorus line. Soft outer flesh of cooked tongue. Accredited by the Western Association of Schools and Colleges. When I allude to sex, I mean you. This race was born extinct. All Toyota owners frozen at the height of their leaps. Indirect lighting of back lobby. Charles Olson worked for Alan Cranston. Now she's urinating on his face. Cat cereal. Peckerwood poetics. Boot disk. Seriously ill with a brain tumor, the deputy chief of police was named to the top job for 48 hours. NYR is for those afraid not to be the intelligentsia. If I revised, this wouldn't be here. Freedom is access to two malls. Mick Jagger's bent dick. Post-NEA. A single cigarette stains the air. Revolt of the smurfs. When you wipe your ass, how high off the can do you raise your butt? Soft boiled. Naked brunch. The head too large for its shoulders. Aggressive-fragile. Hear now the news. Lucky Strike means fine tobacco.

An old house boarded up against winter, or strangers. The plum tree returned to its skeleton. An empty flowerpot used as an ashtray. A grand example of the crisis in verse. Militant academics. Only at night does one "see the sky." News is the soup of managed information. Pigeons huddled in the eaves against the rain. I wondered if you were out of my life at last. I struggle just to shuffle the cards.

Spoon in my pocket. I just struggle to shuffle the clouds. Same sentences stuck in head. Tall black teen with a hearing aid. Implicit designation of gender. Underneath old paint observe cracks in stucco. In the dream I wake beside Diana, whom I haven't seen in years, whom I've never slept with. The bus takes the corner, the batter takes the pitch. Of twelves, aerosol icing decorates windows. Christmas shoppers scuttle in the rain.

Postcards to the coast. They're not expecting weather. Pre-emptive first strike the paragraph. Clouds and smoke.

A hill of white houses in a white fog. The unreadable. Traffic bunched and backed up on the freeway. The slouch of old sheds by the railyard. News at the top of the hour (predigital paradigm). Gone off her meds. A procession of old vehicles trails the hearse. Stylish, like painter's pants.

Paris dice. Strategies of the suitcase. An artificial sitting: a setting. A grafting to place. Develop a procedure, then violate. At the edge of the garden sprouting taxis start to honk, large as snails and more yellow. The blimp blossoms over the horizon. At the tip of a highrise, seek pollen. All is scale, bent pianist circumcised into octaves. Life size hologram of a whale in your kitchen. The glasses are spotted. The grasses are spotted, speckled field theory or general (Half track, looking out the window, sees Beetle). Expropriate to the case. Hard shell. Soft shoe. A foot is to trip with. If you don't believe in language, don't speak it. Crumbs in a mustache. A tall woman is jogging, followed by three large dogs. Now the implication is different. When Andrei says that, politically, he can no longer tell the difference between left and right, he means that he no longer chooses to see. My bookcase, my bottle, my Walkman, my shelf.

People move intently through an airport. Images are not sentences. A woman is breast feeding her son. Too sweet smell of a pipe. Hawaiian guitar. Diaper bag. The sun glared on the soft tops of the clouds, a pocked rolling field of white. In the work of Philip Levine, anthropomorphisms express a bitter regret. Below, it is the clusters and rows of dark trees against the cover of snow which give the land shape.

White curs of breath in the air. Blow dryer. Downstairs, voices quarrel over a recipe. The music in the mall. When I was a boy I would go to my room, shut the door, sit on the bed and write in a notebook. Crab lumps. Candied lemon peel for a fruit cake. The content of the tone of voice. Open eyes, hear air in the ears. Side of face resting against knit coverlet. Cooler air of the attic.

Walkman left on fast forward. Inside of the storm window all iced-up. Holiday bells of an older version of radio. Three generations of men silent before football on TV.

Parallel trains. Fingers formed by ice dripping from the palm. Fry bread. Your own head seen from the rear. Your own head seen from the moon. Factory's corrugated tin storm windows. Old stone village built about the mill. Is resuscitated decades later as artsy-craftsy boutique row. The eyes puff right up. Forest of bare trees, iced streams. Down in the cellar the beer stayed cold. Cat's tuna gone dry in the dish. His mode is the sentimental-instructive. Old pendulum clocks with Roman numerals use IIII in place of IV, residue of a monarch that would not stand correction. The train stopped in the middle of the woods. The lobe of the ear as an occasion for art. A flock of green parrots asleep in the mock rain forest. Presentations of ideology in the name of news. As the soft bell rings in the department store, plainclothes security officers sprint for the exit. Pulling the legs, tail and shell from a spicy steamed shrimp. A submarine decorated with Christmas lights. A needlepoint kit with the caption "Darn Me." Antihistamines that leave your tongue khaki-colored in the morning. Cars abandoned on the highway. Age 2, he stands in front of the toilet and pees on the floor. Small islands of ice plant segment a parking lot. Definite article converts abstraction to description. Statue of a general dressed in a toga.

Cul-de-sacs of a housing tract's map. Machines of shelter. Ice in the grass. Heatalator. De moral eyes. Ol' wicker bottom chair. They bought an antique bookcase complete with books. Warmth hummed up through vents in the floor. Then we played Q-Bert. Then we played Clue. The survey crew makes its way through the ice and mud. Frying Pan Park. Mt. Weatherford. Mode of ode. Bridge over troubled otters. I still hitchhiked then. At the side of the cathedral was the tomb of Woodrow Wilson. In her hallway her new Morris Louis still stood on the floor. A coffee house that felt like a soda shop. Past tense to foretell closure. Salt on the roads. The ceiling has that whipped cream look. I asked where in D. C. one went to buy small press books and she said "New York." She calls her doll "Cabbage." As a research institution, you could say we're sleepy. Each branch of the leafless tree was glazed with ice. All he had was a sleeping bag, a bible and a doorway out of the snow. These words scratched my way slowly into existence. Drill-like, the sound of an upstairs vacuum cleaner. Bath salts. I see suffering. Children play touch football in a vacant field. He set himself on fire in the emergency room. The carpenters sat in their shed during lunch. What the red-eyed man carries in his thermos.

Ice on the wing, coffee burns the tongue. I sit at a table in a dark house listening to the dozen clocks. A big wide-mouth jar on the shelf full of butter cookies. Tiger in the next chair stares at me and purrs. Morning Thunder. We drove past the mansion of the vice-president. I took the train in. Tiny row houses with small wood stoves. With her prune colored punk hairdo she seemed out of place in the over-decorated old German restaurant, eating with her parents. As the plane rose, I could see the skyline of Baltimore, Maryland. A thin haze softened the landscape. Narrative is not story, but the joining of words into meaning. You stand there in your red plaid pajamas. I used the bucket to pour hot water over my head. Gingerbread moon. The word for today is "trunkets." Skeptimist. Aliceann'. The two year old likes to slide down the stairs with a thump, thump, thump. "If you put me in your poem, you send it." I've always wanted to go hear Ferlinghetti, she said. I thought of a confused old man I met once in Buffalo. As for we who love to be astonished, isn't that Chicago? Orange juice from concentrate. Cities marked only by the rise of smoke from refineries. The Monongahela. Enclosed mall. Bun Penny. The steward serves what appear to be eggs. Prairie Home Companion. Miso. The woods attempted beauty. Limit the liquid. Whose favorite music is the Axion Esti. Day seen as a turn. In winter, the checkerboard of farms lapses yellow-brown. Sri Ram. What do Marxists think of the spirit? Jai jai ram. Bach's flower remedies. Certified in Reiki. Shiatsu. Product testing. Day's light merely occludes a larger sky. Babe Ruth's birthplace was a dismal brick thing. In winter, Joe Billy's fingers shrink and he wears fewer rings. Try taking the bus. At 20 below, the wind chill factor is no abstraction. Patterson Park was silent. No one reads better than Bromige. They seated what passengers there were by the windows. Yours sober. The descent beckons within the assent (there are sweet exchanges). The page cuts thru thumb's flesh. Am I more like Gregory Corso than Anthony Hecht? Vowels sign ear's track. Beneath the cloud the plain was dark. Those were iambics. Ten days later snow was still on the ground. Death Squads' Politics Trigger U.S. Concern. The middle school was half-constructed. The flight attendant, strapped into her backwards-facing chair for take-off, shuts her eyes, appearing simultaneously exhausted and bored. Next to him slept a boy, a soldier. Official literature demands kitsch. Comforting, like an ice cube against the tongue. Rabbit in gravy. After dinner they would clear off the table and I would bring in my grandfather's massive typewriter and work for hours. At 32, her father still scares her. Your first sentence is "More cookie." I can see through the thin clouds to the shadows they cast on the fields. Verbs vary. He went to the rooming-house bed in his underwear with a bottle of red wine and stayed there for months. That's verse. What's worse, they're militant in this demand. The sky rubs against the land (creates storms). But they're the vestige of an old culture, full of puff and privilege, inherited from the British. I would climb the rocks above Land's End, bringing only my notebook, and stare at the sea. What remains to be done is snow, wax, leather, smoke. A pen just to chew on. The taste of a cold pill and no water. A boy and his seal. A character's an edited list. Creamy mountains. What you didn't do might haunt. A stylized neurosis shapes history. I'm botany. Total Pentax. Utah is a made place. Paper napkins. Others occur in nature like the bicycle. All along Market Street people build campfires in doorways. Spongelike mountains absorb the sea. Tonal index: press release equals one unit of news. Vast plain covered in snow right to the binding. The inadequacy of buses is planned. Listen. Be careful out there.

QUINDECAGON

for Carla Harryman

What does not change is the will:
Jimmy Dodd with his little friends,
their ears vast, round, black,
flickering on the small blue screen
as we sing. A round
reflects its structure, harmony
imposed from above. The pose
of Atlas frozen in stone
conceals his thoughts. Table
proposed as occasion for chairs
holds last night's supper. Boy
groans as he wakes, weighted
with consciousness. Sun
foretells Spring, maple's branch
about to bud. Head's fog

Governed by sinus tides. Friends
must sing before you blow black
candle out. Blitz to thwart screen
pass. "Mouths of the world go round
with the sound" – against forced harmony
the tragedy of war can be posed
as though names etched in stone
mean an end to the fable. *Big Table*
fought *Chi Rev* suppression. Chairs
don't seek endowment. Old boy
network now on cable. Waited
for the rain to stop, the sun
to break through, tears on a branch
allude to Metro. Listen – fog-
horn's warning in the dark will

Edge a path through the black
harbor. Like old slateboard, this screen
is green: mouse clicks on round
circle feature. Harm an "e"
until it becomes long "i" posed
as squeal. Name on stone
more permanent than notebook on table
in coffee house. I arrange chairs
to form circle. Your boy
elongates into manhood, weighted
only by time. Pen skips reason
but continues jotting, lines branch
across page. New med to fog
thinking (I hope) will
open heart to friends

Who seek only to screen
dissonance out. Found object, round
curl of ink forms letter. Harmony
strikes a chord, clustered, posed
as word in language as different as stone
is to water, laughter, caterpillar, table
or night. Stack of lumber possible chairs
if you just stare hard enough. Boy
toys flounce past in beer ad, weighted
less even by conscience than sun
lotion. Predicates, awkward to the tongue, branch
away from verbs into fog
of thought. Will
that dispenses life's trappings to friends
who arrive at cemetery in black,

Surround
pine coffin, voices in harmony
to articulate grief posed
as closure. *Rolling Stone*
by Madonna's *Sex* on coffee table
offsets Saarinen chairs,
elegance mixed with boy.
Even the century waited
for release. Sun
burns hole in sky, branch
-es wither, sap gone to fog
steams high in the pure light of will,
palm held close over candle, friends
to see you home. Man in black
casts silhouette against screen.

Shadowed by stagelight, harmony
deep in organ's chest paused
at end of note. Damp stone
worn smooth in sand sets table
of elements now used as chairs
to form Senate, a boy
thing. Morning, having waited
out the dark, finds a dull sun
dissolving fog off this last branch
of the Mississippi. So fog
's a theme. Thyme's season will
in time will out. Find friends'
names in the morning paper, black
boldface. Little ferry framed on screen
of highrise window swings round

To dock. Ship horns paused
in mist well up the stone
colored river. This table
mocks the sun king, chairs
too ornate for comfort. "Boy,"
says traveler to skycap weighted
by luggage, squinting into airport sun
as cab opens to drive him to branch
office. Deep in chest, fog
bank rolls. Against dawn's will
the true dark lingers, beyond friends'
ability to reframe the black
in brilliant pixels, screen
or scream, which one? Round
up the usual false harmony

Choir, smiles fixed upon stone
gods. Soil's but a text a water table
inscribes. Mysterious circle of chairs
in abandoned house, lone boy
raised by wolves. Articles weighted
that syntax. Oblong sun
offers wavering light. Bend branch
to reverse river. Breath fogs
the window, which a hand later will
wipe off after fingering message to friends
barely visible in the black
night air behind the fine mesh screen
that thwarts summer. Around
here, any slick, sweet harmony
comes off as a pose

Of cousins at restaurant table,
all forced to smile, chairs
pushed tight about the birthday boy
as each in-law waited
for Nikon's artificial sun
to go off. Bench
any batter who can't hit that fog
of a knuckler and you will
forfeit the game. Friends
gather, dressed in black,
to form a screen
around
the pitcher, restoring harmony
even if it's only a pose,
the ball that hit you hard as stone

And more perfect, fans hurling chairs
down onto the field, man and boy
alike. The mob waited
until it got its pitch, big as the sun.
Neck strains in the bench
press. Before *fig* and *fog*
but more vague will
come the clue only friends
are permitted as, say, *black*
also filters, a kind of screen
until the true text goes underground
seeking light. In Harmony,
Texas, should it exist, pause
to contemplate the force this stone
just by being exerts upon table

Until you wonder how any boy
could ever lift what is so weighted
and, turning, hold it to the sun.
Small padded table is the bench
to my press. In search of London fog,
intrepid reporter Kermit will
instead discover such friends
as dog, frog, a curious black
log, dancers who clog. Rhyme screens
the association. The round
hot source of harmony
and light is supposed
to rise but can't, hidden by stone
colored sky. Table
of the seasons. Char-

Ity is something we've waited
for much longer than this sun
that seems to have taken another branch
of the sky, intimidated by fog,
but eventually will
surface, regurgitated by night. Friends
gather in a mood made black
by absence, as if behind some screen,
that if only we could see around
there you'd be, gulping hominy
and grits, sheepish to have imposed
all this emotion. Stone
for text is called a tablet.
This is something we learned to share
reluctantly, as boys

Blinded by the sun
and the thick, foetid stench
of a pond murky as fog
that seeping toward the sewer will
be sucked to sea. Befriend
all difference. A nation of black
aspiration cast upon the screen
is right around
the corner. What new harmony
can be responsibly opposed
out of budgets bare as stone
with wrong number at table's
bottom? My distinguished chair.
My anguished boy,
this science fair's weighted

Against you, governed by bench-
mark of progress. Flog
a dead horse. The will
from the could. Some friends
we'll not see again. Black
is the color of my true love's screen
against that which surrounds,
then closes in. A new harmony
of humble elements proposed
to wring song from stone
above this great drum of table
and the scraping of chairs
pushed by a boy
with difficulty, weighted
as it is by the sun

Dispersing all fog.
That's one end-rhyme will
not return again. Make friends
with words, their fragile black
limbs barely dry upon this screen
cast in the mind. My round
great *O* wobbles in harmony.
Get it? This pose
tho twisted should seem fixed in stone
and as sturdy as a table.
Convention is four chairs.
Thus I found a perfect boy
twinned, for which I'd waited
in search of son,
to whom I extend this branch.

®

for Lyn Hejinian

Touch me first.
There was a young man from Nantucket.
Poem is the practice (corner of forehead in rear view mirror).
Gonna sit right down and write myself a ladder.
Whether it is the dream that is muddy or the memory of the dream.
Syntax sways between the lines, long supple stalks.
Mountain of horseshit steaming in the rain.
First bought, best bought (gag reflex at the OK Corral).
Dan Quayle: "I am not a potted plant."
The pleasure in leisure is the measure displayed.
Shirtless, leaning back in a leather chair on a cold day.
What it means that Lucy was called Lucy and Dezi Ricky.
How, putting on your trousers, the big toe of each foot serves as a probe.
Dimple in the earlobe where it's pierced.
Truck horns a block away index proximity of commerce.
Who is that masked bird – loggerhead shrike (the new farmalism)?
Image of would: grain of condition written in sleep.
Inserting linebreaks fast as I can, cats wrestling like dinosaurs.
The day divided into its bananas.
You touch my text, I break you face.
What makes a deadbolt dead?
Mapplethorpe perfect bound: backlight the mind.
Language itself is in vain or vogue (blacklight the rind).
The rogue nation invades wherever it wants – find out just how absorbant
    new page of history's become.
Wakefulness is its own state of grace (pass the salts).
Left accidently atop a lit burner on the stove, the Pyrex dish explodes
    beneath the steaming pie.
Flock of little bushtits in a leafless tree.
New Theory in Paperback mass mailing tests market saturation.

Wake at dawn with a song in my "heart": "I love what you do to me, Toyota."
Say we only experience our lives as going forward in time and that it's really just the opposite.
Sitting here in the dark, waiting for the dream to recede.
Target boomers now or forever lose thy market (coat on tongue thick as morning snow).
We step into the doorway in order not to be noticed by the comma police.
Rome if you want to (all around, all around this world).
She teaches est to inner city kids.
Patty Hearst hired for role in John Waters film – "we know she takes direction."
Your sentence here.
Swamp thing, you make my heart sink, you make every think Post-X.
Red-orange palette of a toxic sky, thick clouds billowing up off the coast, silhouette of a jet crosses the sun, left to right.
Product mammal prefigures mall glut implosion (thumbs down on digital watch).
Into the byte stream, fog horns before dawn, dove's coo contains its own echo.
Commie alert (kerning off): between Palatino and Times Roman comes a Bembo, multiple aardvarking, discourse fu, three stars, check it out.
Visually, jars of dry goods organize the kitchen counterspace.
Fat with defeat, little nouns shine from the dark, night-ridden text (boats bobbing in the sea, having just escaped the volcanic island).
The neighbors' windchimes in the storm, restless melody.
Fumbling for the lightswitch, then squinting so as not to be overwhelmed by the glare.
I don't think we're in Leningrad anymore, Toto.
A day later, the steamed broccoli lays limp in the pot.
Each chair in the house has been invoked as a coathanger.
I make for myself a picture of great detail.
Asleep, we curl one into the other atop the large mattress, the Big Spoon.
The back porch is a jumble of the unimagined.

Hummingbird on the back birch tree, backlit by the sun, impossible to identify further.
The ascent beckons, using an alarm clock.
Printer without the printer driver.
Pushkin's portrait stamped on a quill pen (which is, in fact, a ballpoint inserted down the shaft of a feather).
Refrigerator door is a kiosk of coming events (alphabet of magnets).
How I place my hand under my head when I lay on my side (balled into a fist).
Burst of cats at war on the fence.
Arise, for the teeming markets of corporate flesh crave your blood.
That moment, waking, when you first recognize the sound of rain.
Naked in the dream, you jump from the steep cliff into the shallow river, hitting the rocks.
One hour augurs how the day flowers.
Concussion from the copter's low blades rattle the house.
Day breaks, fragments everywhere.
Pushing the highlighter over a line of text.
The water is about to boil (the waiter is about to bail out).
Moment when you can see the shape of the highrise (unlit) against the failing night.
Boat-tailed grackles whistle in the trees.
That's not a leather jacket you're wearing, that's an attitude.
Instant at which, imagining this notebook lost on the airplane (or, worse yet, may still be in Dallas or Houston, anywhere), wave of panic, nausea, bathes you.
The dissent bickers as the assent hunkered (memory is a kind of astonishment).
James Brown singing *It's a Man's World* plays endlessly (ironically) in the imagination.
The poetry of memory over the poetry of paper, says Ilya, because "in Russia, it is very hard to buy paper."
Along that side of the kitchen the linoleum rolls up off the floor until it reaches the underside of the counter cabinets.

Caressed by hummingbirds on a voyage to find music (bottom layer pretzels, middle layer Jello, top layer whip cream).
Faucet juts out of concrete wall, nozzle threaded to receive a hose.
Paws, arrows, something on paper.
Endlessly, the pitcher throws to first to keep the runner on.
Song of blackbirds (redwing) rising from the drainage ditch.
Algorithm and blues, boys, invent an old pun.
Today I notice a stain at the edge of the paper, like marbling when the book is shut.
In an old hotel the song of pipes whenever a toilet's flushed.
A party in a loft space, but it's in the desert, so the loft opens out onto an expanse of sand across which a train is moving slowly, crossing bells somewhere in the distance clanging, while she explains to you the meaning of "swamp cooler" and you swallow yet another dip-bathed flower of broccoli.
Having slid into the dry concrete moat between its "environment" and the zoo-goers, the anteater-like coati paces in small, rapid, nervous circles, physical expression of panic.
The sky streaks pink-orange before the sun itself appears: the first shadows are the longest, most stark.
Past, present and suture: dream is enmeshed with memory (the body is heavy with sleep).
Inca dove more tiny than you would expect, the size of a sparrow, amid the rock doves and screeching grackles of the small public park.
Tiny dinosaurs sold alive for pets or food at a flea market (this one bites toothlessly down on my finger, a lovely pressure).
In the dream I have a shouting matching on the telephone with a stranger, but when I turn to go back inside, the door has shrunk to three-feet high and I'm forced to crawl up the interior stairway.
Words whine, behind which the rattle of consonants clutter the thought (adorned by Adorno).
Dream in which my teeth swell (fine wooden fan, each leaf of which contains inlaid a one-word poem the size of a stamp typed onto colored construction paper, each poem containing above it the same word, all in caps, so that this must be the title).

We're the guests in somebody's home in Central Europe, except that it's a crash pad and our hosts are out of town, so we have to negotiate.
If I let my left eye tear up, blood starts to run down my cheek.
A bowl of lemons so old they've shriveled into odd yellow peas.
Blue ink upon gray paper sketches a garden-to-be.
Osprey, high over the mouth of the river, circling with a fish in its claws.
Against the black rock, only the orange beak of the oystercatcher is visible.
In Willits, where is there to eat?
Bananas at dawn: day is on.
Whatever became of (your name here)?
An old Navajo cup becomes a receptacle for toothbrushes next to a trio of pots containing African violets.
The birds begin to sing before dawn itself is visible.
Television on with the sound off, pantomime of a baseball game.
In the dream I've slept in the car overnight and we live in a tiny flat South of Market.
But this one, set in a foreign country suspiciously like Tucson, is a murder mystery, elegantly structured, that I solve through reason.
It was going to be a warm rain, the sky so low and still it appeared a cloudless grey, and these were its very first drops.
The impulse of the sentence is to extend, never to close off.
The electric oven turned up high, door open, to heat the room, its coils a sharp orange, each the shape of the letter M.
L-shaped counter space that ends in the stove (white) next to the refrigerator (yellow).
Then, when the sun at last arrives, the birds settle down, returning nearly to silence.
Overcast sky is never perfectly grey or white, but is mottled, splotched, shadows on the underside of cloud.
Windchime's melody gentle in the rain (where is the social conflict in this poem?).
Sleep's inertia: one wants to continue.
Waking, I remember the dream of an argument, but not who with.
Low-impact aerobics on a vast midwestern plain, tens of thousands of

people in approximately straight lines, a female voice repeating single-digit numbers over and over.

Birdsong at midnight belongs to a bat (sky so clear over Tuscaloosa we stare at the stars in hopes of seeing the nighthawk's silhouette).

Gentleman-banker eats lunch at Manna, the health-food grocery cafe, where his son works as a cook.

In the shadows of the kitchen of the Tin-Top Cafe, the young woman slowly and methodically washes each leaf of the collard greens, pot of okra boiling on the stove.

One bird before dawn sings two-note song over and over, rising and falling, rising and falling, then stops.

The one lens fogged permanently, the world reduced to shapes, masses, lacks a hard edge.

Sweat-soaked shirt, I wake, a song from last night's concert still clear, echoing in the mind.

Sleeping somehow atop my own left arm, I wake with a start, blood flowing back into tingling fingers.

Wake explaining myself (to whom? for what?) to a tune by Neil Young.

Dinner at Limbo: seven old friends sit at a table in the middle of their lives.

Fog's burned off but windchime on the far side of the house picks out a melody.

The cold dawn of what will be a hot day.

A walk through the neighborhood after dark.

The information that the cataract in my right eye will spread as fast as the one in my left and that, without surgery, I will be blind in six months to one year.

A cramp in the muscle in the calf rips me out of the nightmare – vandals hurling rocks thru the windows of our house – so that I twist suddenly out of bed and that frame of mind.

Towhee's song reiterates reiteration, one note over and over, until I realize it's not the clock and curb impulse to throw shoe.

Cat sits with paws tucked under and meows to see me write (this word, that word, this word).

Brilliant light of first sun after several days of cloud overwhelms white paper shade at the head of my bed.

Landscape in dream is plastic and specific only to the degree that it's urgent (each word a parenthesis).
By Wednesday, dirty dishes, pots, pans overflow the small rubber tub in the kitchen sink.
Between *test* and *contest* fall distinctions large enough to construct a civilization.
Infinite cups of tea inside of me all pushing to get out.
I'm at bat and the pitcher's throwing fastballs and sliders not with a baseball, but with cubes of ice.
The five-day-old infant is dreaming, but what about?
Off-center grin enables him to get the toothpick between the rear molars.
How is it I know these are the streets of Chicago?
Not the middle of the morning but the morning of the middle.
Then the alarm goes off, tormentor, old familiar.
Mockingbird in the plum tree in full routine.
Scrunch my nose to push these glasses back up my face.
Addicted to meaning, one could be held prisoner by sentences.
It's a ghetto mall, with anchor tenants like Woolworth's, security guards wearing guns, with seven or eight cheap shoestores, white mannikins in Penney's surrounded by clerks and shoppers who are not.
Ah, swoony, queasy feel as you squeeze, lightly now, my balls.
The strong odor of his own urine.
Standing over an open ditch in the pouring rain, think of the word *gulleywasher*.
My bones are aching and my brain is weak: I think I'm standing on a stubborn streak.
Moment at dawn when the sky has lightened, minute before the sun first appears when all light is true light, every color muted.
Pieces of a music hidden in the mind by memory's collaboration with all other musics emerges again anew in the middle of a dream, every song a new song, each now heard for the first time.
Today I wake with a roaring thirst.
We put the fab in fabric.
All effects are special (you'll wake the birds).
Two weights, twin 25-pound barbells, rest on the rug, implicit challenge.

The roses have grown wild in the corner, rising high over the wire fence.
This compost's a small mountain, out of whose sides weeds arise.
Steam wisps over the lip of the cup, hot tea at the brink of a hot day.
It's summertime, so that after an early evening movie the sun's still out.
The day, crowded with hours, gathers at the horizon.
An intricate dream in which I return to an old job site peopled now by my current co-workers, both moved miraculously to a mining town in the Sierras.
Gentle grip of Ace bandage about ankle (tiny sparrow chases huge vulture high over the freeway, zigzag path, out by the wetlands).
A walkway connects buildings over the street, which, from 12 storeys up, I look down upon.
Old brick buildings of Larimer Square all googawed up, boutiques for tourists that stay open till 9 at night.
What is morning for?
Form sets the reader's expectations, laying the ground for a happy (or unhappy) reading experience.
A sentence lay forgotten under the tree by the reservoir's edge.
Bird in the dark (this morning my lip is blistered).
Weight bends the sunflower (smell of fog).
Imagination seizes power but power buys imagination.
One bad habit is to leave underwear on the scale in the bathroom.
Today a squirrel sits atop the sunflower, pulling seeds out one by one.
Fuchsias open, their pale pink outer petals turned up.
That was a dream, this is not.
I'm not really travelling by submarine to a conference in Europe of paint stores (I'm trying to imagine what it will feel like when the surgeon cuts my eye).
Mockingbird imitates trio of crickets, then quiets once the sun rises.
Standing, the blood rushes to my feet, old familiar river.
Notebooks, phones, forms – the day is warm.
Salt ring's stain circles the shirt.
In her private life, the old actress, now senile, was a surrealist (we pick our way through the cobwebbed residue of her home).
Shower's steam fogs my glasses.

Lift the dead tree stump into the back of the truck.
Quickly the fireworks settle into a terrible sameness.
The way a swarm of connotations settles in once you know the Supposed-to-Mean (in the dream, where do I find it?).
Being a village explainer, I'm always happy to come upon a village.
It's an old bus that travels between these small farm towns so far apart, that I disembark just to run into the store to fetch something to fix the zipper on this shoulder bag, but all my suitcases slow me down and when I get back outside, it's long gone, another not due for days.
Often the dream dissolves instantly as I stumble for the alarm clock and light switch, leaving behind as a residue an emotional tone (I was being threatened or there was a puzzle to solve or I'd been abandoned by a bus).
One difference with waking is that in dream, I see clearly, sharply, I'm never wearing glasses.
The one word I remember is "Chadwick."
It's not the details themselves that are difficult (we're staring off into an amber horizon trying to foretell the weather – is a hurricane coming? – alongside three steamer trunks each of which contains three "bad guys," unconscious, clad only in their skivvies, then I wake up, a Roy Orbison song obsessively in my head) but the linkages between them offer no sensible verb.
Suppress the impulse to name that tune.
The two other people trapped in the elevator are a young man who's been in bed four days with the flu and an older woman who's a receptionist in a doctor's office somewhere in the building.
What spider could have spun a web so thick, so filmy, so strong?
The first horizon of a sore throat.
First burst of light occurs over the bathroom sink, is absorbed, refracted, swelling into the eye.
Wind bends the brambles between the fence and the shed, a sound more like scraping than rustling as a train whistle hoots somewhere to the west.
A solution thick as honey is poured into the eye, then the plastic cylinder inserted, standing upright in this base without actually touching the surface.

A woman I haven't seen in 15 years, haven't thought of in 10, a misshapen thing who'd wrought havoc in our political collective until we expelled her (without, I believe, her even comprehending that that's what we'd done), returns in the dream, as officious and anxious as ever.
Lingamberry cheesecake right before bed enhances the effect.
Nasturtiums as part of the vegetable garden.
The new crown sits tight in the jaw.
A herd of tule elk, 30 of them, sit or stand peacefully in the fog just 20 yards from the road.
Glacial sinus shift as I rise adjusts to verticality.
On Dealey Plaza, I confront memory and grackle, an impossible triangulation.
At night, patterns of light reform the city sky.
Dull, Duller, Dallas.
Point at which the immature guy simply becomes a man without judgement.
High morning: from here on the 28th floor, I can see the parking lot reflected in the black glass-facade building taller even than this one, cars slotted in at an angle, the lone attendant crossing back to his shack in 100 degree heat.
A complex dream in which the present of a t-shirt is intended (do dreams intend?) to underscore a troubling disagreement among friends.
Strength of the smell of urine.
You awake feeling unpoetic.
Often, next to hard running water, I imagine telephone bells.
Lovemaking, we pull the sheet up over ourselves as you say, laughing, "Let's make a tent!"
Weeding understood as an artistic practice, box in the shape of a rabbit.
Oranges are an exception.
Part swap of the eye.
Dream as claustrophobic as a BBC thriller.
Magnetic alphabet on refrigerator door, letters askew, waiting for language.
Somewhere there's a banana that's got your name.
Bears of a feather molt together.

At dawn, I peer out the window to find a giant cat asleep in the fog atop the fence.
Cormorants taken for loons.
I hear the steady ping . . . ping . . . ping of my heartbeat on the monitor as you cut my eye.
I shake myself awake and decide that the brutal sailor in the nightmare must have been my father, then I slip back into the same gore-ridden dream.
The next sentence fits here, as if into a chain of perfect logic.
The Lone Ranger and Tonto provide shopping mall security.
In this dream, my mother's a new executive at ComputerLand.
It's morning, 4:40, and I'm trying to decide whether to get up and write or to roll over and sleep another three hours.
The banana gets pulpy when it gets too ripe.
Gradually, my strength returns and I pay less attention to the stitches in my left eye.
Behind the paper shade a pale light emerges in the advance of dawn.
A room off the kitchen where all manner of oddities are stored, many piled high atop an old washer that has never worked.
Lately, we've abandoned the table crowded into the nook.
Blinking with your eyes shut.
We're taking buses through familiar neighborhoods that, in our waking lives, don't connect this way.
Trying to think of a place name, Jessica says, "I've got a big atlas," but what Melanie hears is "Allis" – "I've got a big Allis."
Hearing the water before it boils.
When you're asleep and I'm walking around, this modest house seems large and silent.
Pages of a calendar turn, visual representation of time.
A block away a dog barks, though here it is barely audible.
Not the dream that lingers on, an afterimage, but the emotion of the dream.
Pitcher glares in to get the sign.
Waking in a panic because I'm not wearing my glasses, then realizing of course not.
The eye also is an output device.
Canary melon, canary island.

Sounding the *L* in tortilla.
What happens now (killdeer and grackle, having gathered by the hundreds at Arroyo de las Positas, suddenly grow silent)?
Will I print the file from her floppy on my laserjet at work?
Poems in magazines in too small a font.
The pollution solution (let's call for revolution).
I wake with this phrase, "night of the long knives," not knowing why or even what it means exactly.
Sun blooms in the crotch of the hills, a flowering of hours in the damp dark.
This time the reorg hits our department square on.
Falling asleep, I begin to recognize my dream before I'm there.
Street people who sell roses individually wrapped, from buckets, stand at each intersection downtown.
A sense (a sentence (a census)) of morning, highrise office tower still on Sunday.
Cream of parrot soup.
Linoleum grid – it's supposed to look like this.
Roar of refrigeration so constant I can't hear it.
The caterer arrives with sandwich trays for the meeting, disdain for these corporate types instantly visible in her eyes.
Before dawn, a train passes, a long one, its intermittent horn fading well before the rumble of cars dies away.
Half awake, I'm still in my dream, Cody's Books devoured by fire, people sorting through bins of smoke- and water-damaged books, wondering if my own are in there.
The dream recurs in which I'm outside a brothel, glitzier and more alluring than any I've ever imagined, plus (how do I know this?) for me it will be free, gratis, but I'm unable to take a step to go inside.
The next morning, the odor of roast duck still hangs in the air.
Craft codger's back, just like ants in rainy weather.
I wake up exhausted.
We're going to war, the enemy has planes (simple ones, no jets), we watch the first bombardment and voluntaristically Charles and I and others are converting an old building into a warehouse – supplies must get

through! – when the old woman who's taken charge insists on first
 teaching us a game called Aces and Eights.
A song in my head of easier banking, of B of A.
In order to apologize to the foxes, the young boy walks into the valley,
 seeking their homes under the rainbow.
The street on which I grew up, with the hill at a different slope.
Stepping outside in the dark, I feel my forehead push against, then break, a
 strand of a spiderweb on the porch.
As the work week advances, each night's sleep feels less and less complete.
Details remain like a memory out of context, say a single word, "kowtow."
A range of possible sentences, theoretically infinite, severely limited by the
 states of mind in which each day I wake.
Hot and sweaty, hot and sweaty, you'd think I was a Tibetan yeti.
Next question.
The sound of the heater, somewhere between a hum and a huff.
The fitful ratchet of the second hand's sweep.
A stack of empty egg cartons under the pantry sink.
Memory decays in an instant – it was a large house and many of my friends
 were there, but that's all I remember.
The voice of A's announcer Bill King, ringing in my ears.
Sentences keep getting clearer, more clear.
I wake in a state of panic over a deadline coming due.
My body still tingles from last night's sweet sex.
Day's light floods these rooms.
The alarm rings, but after three days off I have to think to realize what it
 means.
It's autumn now and chilly before dawn.
Windchime's slow song.
It was someone else's dream I was having.
Your head is on my shoulder as we lie here talking.
Voices outside the house – which neighbors are they?
Furnace gives a whoosh – it'll be warm soon.
Empty of guests at last, this little bungalow feels large.
The sound of water before it boils.
So even if, why not, dreams *are* "neurological junk," the narratives

we impose over them, old parsimony principle, to render each understandable (I was driving into a terrific sunset, thinking "what do whales make of a toxin-red sky?") must be our own, San Jose.

I'm trying to put this jacket on, over and over, my arm bent back, hand seeking for the hole in the sleeve.

Because its height makes it awkward to rinse out, the empty thermos sits on the sink for a week.

The power's out and me with an electric stove.

We're taking the touch costs out of poetry.

I wake because I hear you crying.

Electricity whines and crackles through the walls.

I rise to discover a chill's settled in (a generation of Republican presidents).

Dream of the next war, flesh seared down to my bones.

Dreaming of a database just to keep track of his sweaters.

An unkissed nose is a small tragedy in the middle of a face.

The dish drainer as a form this morning is piled high, bouquet of pots at the very top.

Cold sores swell my tongue.

Later the drain is empty, while to the left of the sink a new stack of dirty dishes, juice-stained glasses, has begun to gather.

Dream in which I'm selling suits and am given a tie as a bonus.

"I'm in an altered state," she says, "and I want you to alter me."

Two horsemen made their way slowly along the beach as a small white dog splashes after godwits in the surf.

Pelican, hunting, flies low over the bay.

Kingbird shakes the struggling butterfly in its beak.

One percent of all the water used in the city of Los Angeles is used to brew Bud.

Back of a chair understood as a coathanger.

Bean counters in the sky.

Power surge of the light switch is what blows the bulb, filament's explosion contained by glass.

Sentences, please come.

The waterfront at two in the morning: headlights four blocks away feels like traffic.

I lie in bed with my eyes shut, listening to the sounds of the emerging day.
Trying to wake myself from a dream I've had before, shaking and calling, my whole body twisting.
The sound of rain, brief and hard, jolts me, it's so rare – I rise only long enough to reset the alarm, poem on the edge of sleep.
Bookcases whose shelves hold pottery – Jewel Tea ware in the kitchen, Hall ware in the nook – features that don't become visible until the room is straightened up.
Years after I've stopped drinking, the dreams have gradually returned with their complex, convoluted, impossible narratives, some of them quite friendly.
The words echo after I've woken: "Grand Canyon."
Unable, in the shower, to remember if I've already shampooed or not.
A small act of faith, like brushing one's teeth without one's glasses on.
I imagine the words "Cool Mint Gel" even before I realize I've read them.
First standing, the bones in my feet snap the way a small boy "pops" his knuckles.
Volleyball as a duel to the death.
Balloon of sleep bursts.
Tree, backlit by the moon, throws its silhouette against this shade.
Compulsive song of the mockingbird, even in the dark.
Using the oven to heat the room, I sit in a chair handmade by an old long-dead dear friend.
Refrigerator door is a kiosk.
Glass doors to the living room closed at night to contain the heat.
Sleep understood as its own state of alertness (if I say consciousness you'll misunderstand): "I sleep the way other men make war – to exercise my faculties at large" (sleep understood to contain the heart).
There's an anger inside of me I don't understand, a despair that's inconsolable, triggered by the least relevant thing (you forget to take the dry cleaning), so that I bathe in it, drowning in my own adrenaline until it passes.
Silhouette of a tree down to its last dozen leaves.
Building the ladder as I climb it, never sure if this is up or down.
Because it rains, the night is thick with dreams and I wake, having swum.

I wake, after many hours' sleep, seconds before the alarm starts to beep.
Peeling the banana, skin splits into three strips.
Ideas that slither like noodles in a Chinese soup.
Sinus tides.
Into the valley of breath ride the 600 syllables, of which our ears discover, say, only four dozen.
At night my body twists, fitting itself to the dream (putting on my glasses, I discover the lens swarming with ants).
Text rotation, science friction.
Cat twitches as it dreams.
Snow on Mount Diablo.
So deep asleep that waking feels unreal.
The years as batch files.
Instead of chocolate-covered ants, we had ant-covered chocolates.
In dreams surface anxieties.
The arc of syntax triumphs.
Spontaneous combustion in the forests, gridlock everywhere, mascara stigmata on each impersonator of Elvis.
A small cyclone, visible, dances over the kitchen floor.
In bed, I roll over, waiting for the great tides of sinus to shift.
Where dreams go when we wake.
That other sleep.

SKIES

for Alan Bernheimer

I

The sky is a grey plane tending toward white, without depth, without detail, barely with light. To the east tattered clouds patch the blue, but to the west a dense, grey bank of fog. Above, or to the east, the fine white mist is not visible-because-thicker, but against the background of the next yellow hill it rushes by in light puffs. Wisps, blowing east, no constancy of shape. Stillness in all directions, mountainous scoops of cloud. Pure hot blue air, little breeze. Clouds gather, but so slowly they go unnoticed. Heat will cause the plums to drop, white butterflies steaming up from pink roses, sun lighting cobwebs on the fence. The greys of the cloud are uneven, near-black folded into off-white, layerings. As the gray fades slowly to blue, all that remains are a few white cottony clumps, higher than the rest. Low damp cool fog, suspended rain. When the clouds rise, rain falls. The sun dissolves in the mist to a glare. A few small puffs of white are pushed by the breeze. What are you, Never-Very-There, so everywhere, emptying, wind's vessel, cloudherd? Invisible forces thrash the trees. Blue leaks in a white wall. But the grey wall is bricklike, composed of units of irregular shape, clouds high up against the sky. Today a herd of large ones, billowy with dark undersides, pass over as slow as ships. A window edits the sky. A lack of shading in the morning fog foretells its burning off. The light a dull white. The smell of rain. What from the satellite photo is a spiral is unbroken sameness for days from the porch. First seen, blue is colorless, mere dark breakings in the sharp glare. Morning's damp lawn registers night's precipitation, struggling thru the thick rising fog. Deep greys mottle the dull sheen. As if the sky were a gray sponge pressed right to the ground. An outline as of a wing in white, alone against the blue, shreds. Heavy whites, restricted palette. The blue tower atop Portola Heights hidden by the fog, the row of trees immediately below reduced to a silhouette (the descent of the sky). Like a cold sweat, it sticks to your flesh. It rises like a veil, revealing all that surrounds you. The glare is intense, but colorless. One does not feel enclosed by blue. The wind belies a clear sky. Before dawn, light bleeds from the horizon. The sun bores a hole in fog. After the burnoff, a layer of alto-cumulus, grillwork. The song of birds without the sight of birds. Squint-light. In the morning the moon in the west. The sun tentative amid clouds. One plane gives the sky proportion. The cloud mixes with the grasses. The sharp light of the sun wedged behind. Behind the cloud a pulse of light moves slowly west (a game of infinitely few parts). Today's cloud rises slightly, so that buildings & trees are clearly seen. You can smell it (rolling thru the streets). The moment, mid-afternoon, one fog finally burns off, the first wisps of another begin to blow in off the sea. By the time the sun appears it's midway thru the sky. The next day, heavier & lower. Then thicker, cooler. Although not visible you can feel it. Just a thin line, brighter than all the rest at the horizon, a sign of its rising. The sky in the room is called air. Just enough haze to blanch the blue. They don't "break up" but drift apart, becoming slighter, dissolving into themselves. The gloom. In the clouds, clouds form & roil. One morning, it's as if this never happened, the hot sky brilliant & clear (sounds carry further on a windless day). Then it's not. The sun in the east bright amid light clouds, small & overlapping, but out the windows on the other side of the house the sky is one vast, black wall. Even in the middle of the clearest day, it's never the same hue throughout. At the edge of the cloud mass, wisps & strands tatter & drift off, dissolving as they go. A white film, filtering & diffusing light, stretched over the whole sky. Where the cloud is its thinnest, the hint of a blue tint. Sun's light, even before it reaches the horizon, scatters thru layers & pockets of cloud. Cotton curtain, to soften the glare, room's morning lamp. In the valley between two small hills, birds fill the air. Scattered, small, these clouds push evenly, a slow parallel movement across the afternoon. Weekend pilots thread the sky (web of no design). The bird in the cage on the porch in the breeze is in it. Shadowless grey light of foggy morning. Tho nearby, these houses ebb in the damp cloud. It absorbs heat. Light is held in particles of moisture. Later, breezy gusts break it all up until one, standing on a porch high on a hillside, can barely make remnants out. Waking, even before you realize that you hear it, you recognize the sound of rain. It waits in the eucalyptus for the wind to shake it free. Grey or not or dark, the sky is without points of reference, hence any sense of direction, not contingent on the land or water below, save these clouds that never rest (imagine maps or satellite photos in which the clouds remained constant while the seas & continents changed shape hourly to accommodate this motion). Fuzzy drizzle, low stratus. A chill damp. The wind off the sea seems trapped below the clouds, pushed, rushing through the valleys & over the glistening surfaces of the low hills. Shaped, defined, by the houses, window, plum tree. Black tufts. Long, thin clouds seem airbrushed high against the blue, the sun coming up broken behind a dark, eastern cluster. The dew, steaming in the morning light, rises. Stars visible in the city. The fog settles (everything absorbs moisture). Just before dawn, delayed by a high bank of clouds to the east, the muted light transforms these hills to pastels (impressionism). The herds of wild stratus.

II

Heat is the consequence of light (cats sleep under parked cars), the old women look small & bundled, wrapped in overcoats on their way to mass (I hear a rooster crow in the city). Running through it (straight at the sun in the cypress), field's dew soaks my shoes (fresh dogshit glistens wet in the light). A glow to the bay, above it (low mist steaming), a woman in a cotton skirt & sandals hurries between the jets of water sprinkling the park, a small white pup rolls on its back on the tennis court (downtown, smog's gray layer awaits, halo to highrise). The hosed-off walks of the shops shine (schoolkids & clericals bunch at the bus stop, the 10 Monterey slowly grinding its way to the top of the hill), the grocer propping a newsrack against his open door. Form is the flower's fate, closed in a morning fog (cat sniffs a caterpillar on the dusty path), oceanic shush of traffic on the freeway in the valley, a fly wrestles with a web. Birds in the fir tree chirping (dawn softened by clouds to a gradual increase in light), the radio traffic copter glides low over the road. A cluster of flies in the morning buzz about the corner of the yard, lone gull foregrounded against the browns of the next hill, Juan standing on the porch landing to watch (later you hear their hum in the tree, but can't see them), wind bangs the door shut, low cloud's tide flowing steadily in. Yellow brick seminary, silhouette in the fog (pigeon pecks at crust in the gutter), a man in a sweatshirt touching his toes on the lawn (car warming up sends forth blue billows), rising sun peeks thru, lighting the underside of this huge cloud, gray & white & pink mixed together. The dew on the cobweb gleams (she runs the Fiat to warm it up), two girls in parochial school skirts (he runs in circles around the track), the moon in the sky at dawn is full. Sit in chair on porch in sun (two doors over, sound of a hammer), clothesline begins at the window (valley vibrates softly to the jet's passing roar). Everything blisters in a rare heat (leaves on the plum tree curl & crackle, the growing coleus bangs at the glass), in the street people walk around with one hand shading their eyes, behind the broken windows & boarded up doors of the abandoned house I hear a power saw. At night with stars out those with convertibles show them off (a war on the porches of water balloons, water pistols), baby blue Rolls with the words Low Class in grey on the door (tonight everybody sleeps with the windows open, under not more than a sheet). Waist-high in the froth, children tempt the rip-tide (barely possible, but for the boat in the distance, to discern the horizon), smell of cocoa butter (large straw hats). Staring for a moment out the window into the blue glare (its shape a 6-sided figure, three the frame, the rest the conjunction of porch & neighboring roof), I am unable to see the page or make out the words on it (plum tree's branch bobs into view)(play of the web of shadows over the dirt in the yard), the sound of a logging truck on the freeway below, large, is specific (ditto the rev of a dirt bike mounting the slope). Chicanas, Pilipino couples, an occasional older Chinese woman, bundled & crowded on the bus, Bibles in hand (dog in the small yard stalks its fences), Tom in a gray sweatshirt on his way to Jim's Donuts for breakfast (bathmat 'dries' on the rail in the fog, she waters the carrots "in case". Red garbage truck emerges from the fog, halfsize yellow schoolbus following behind (beads of water on the inside of the bathroom window after a shower), fly carves a zigzag path in the air of the room (with.a rubber-edged window scraper, he wipes the moisture from the windshield of the van), the birds will stay quiet longer on a dark day. The sun in the dew in the tree (because one's just risen, the other yet to burn off): image of a million diamonds (the pastels peculiar to this hour, say, to the homes of the far hill, a consequence of dawn's steam), I see my own breath, hear the clothesline pulleys, a jet flying west shines in the light. Straight up it's sunny, but to the south you can't see to the end of the block (cat emerges from fog), gull's shrill cry absorbed by the sound of the jet, schoolbus stops in front of the house & honks. Gradually light penetrates the dusty bamboo shade, casting its striped glare (cigar smoke circles the hanging spider plant), the kitchen light left on is useless, the dog's small yap never stops (sound of ice, melting, rearranging itself in the glass). At night under high fog the city casts a light that reflects halfway between pink & a dull orange (sodium vapor), the wind marks a turn in weather, on this block the curtains are no more than cloths tacked up over the windows (at dawn a man begins to patch the shingles on his roof), the shush of the valley's rush hour traffic. Briefly rain scars the window (the broken sky at night sits darkened behind the illumined clouds), that streaked & flattened effect as if the clouds had been "bottomed off" (the slice of a vast blade), cheesy, piled high & tumbling one into another (he stands on the porch contemplating which jacket . . .), then, just as sudden & brief, a flash of sun. The wet ground is darker (the green tops of carrots stand in high contrast), thru the white of a cobweb I see a half-dozen small clouds, each a deep grey at the bottom (one hides the sun), white glare above, a jet threads its way behind them, traveling in the opposite direction (west). The way black smoke of a structural fire drifts over an intersection (the buzz of a sportscar from down in the valley), the cat on the window sill, the young girls in parochial school skirts (thick, heavy, rolling, not smoke at all). The sharp shadows cast west from the hill of white houses (small, discrete) grows less distinct (the sun rises from a plum tree), the parakeet chirrups from its cage at the window (a flock of what rushes partway thru the valley, only to turn back, then back again?), & tho the ones above it are streaked & dark, one cloud over the hilltop is stark white. The windows steamed by a shower, the rectangular sky is reduced to a tone (hearing the door open, the cat on the upper deck of the back porch meows & hurries down), the garden stays damp for days, this must be a regular take-off pattern (so many jets heading west), you can't leave both doors open at once (wind rips the poster from the kitchen wall), an orange monarch is loose in the roses (the sun in the cobwebs bejewels the fence). The crack in the glass in the door on the porch halves the sky (human barometer pressures blood), pigeons have taken over the closed-down bowling alley (an old woman sprinkling crumbs in the gutter attracts thousands, she's at the eye of a whirling feathery storm), but this glass is frosted (I make out the steps by the shadow) & the dog at the corner has begun to bark. The first glow (pale yellow-orange tinged with purple) appears unnatural (screened by a bamboo shade) ahead as it is of the sun that only now nears the horizon (people sit in their cars in the dark, letting the engines run), I sit at a table crowded with violets & ferns, watching the new light catch the thin, fine field of hair on the back of these familiar hands (cat at the back door scratches to get in). Moisture on the cold glass (political posters taped to it start to slump) catches the sun for a second, weak point in the (fading) fog, colors of the houses (buff, olive, white) half-pulse in the unstable light, a peristalsis (that door which slammed, unseen, belongs to a car), first Saturday hammering begins. Catlike, headlights thru the valley fog glimmer & inch forward in the morning traffic, roosters & dogs squawk together (the big half-shepherd chasing the terrified jogger thru the field for the fun of it), my breath (visible) the color of the sky (hummingbird perfectly still on the plum tree's branch), cat licks his paw & wipes his face. Wisps turn red, then orange, white as the blue softens (what fog there is is camped in that furthest gully – you look down on it), colors emerge in the garden (a thousand greens, each distinct), in a driveway a car sits in a blue cloud of its own gasses, a pile driver rings in the distance, that jet's body catches the full light of the sun (fat & orange in the horizon's shimmering smog). As the dull haze slowly rises what is first visible (bleached by the glare) is that which lays closest to the ground (like pigeons, the women gather in front of Kingdom Hall, waving their magazines), a man walks a leashed Afghan across the diamond in the park (two small flies whirl around one another in the center of the room), these tiny stucco houses, side by side by side. At the hilltop (back into fog) shadows fade, the eucalyptus drips with dew (a woman is taking her daughter to wait at a bus stop), already salsa is beginning to emerge from the open garage door, but one block down the shadows are sharp & leaning, slanting across the small squares of lawn. Like dirty cotton absorbing light & heat (the dogs whining in their yards at the smell of rain), the carpenter leaning to spit out the window, the cat in the basement (thru the blinds all I see is the yellow of the schoolbus), but still the clothesline pulley squeals. Between storms the clouds are still, the gunmetal sky a compromise, a high dome (a low wind pushes dirt up from the batter's box), so cold your ears start to hurt & (inside) the rain begins. Three-quarter moon in the clouds in the tree (in the morning a rich blue everywhere but for the low gray wall far to the west, the moon smaller & turned now (chip on the bottom), ready to set), the damp grass cold to sit down on. Unseen jet in the sky balances unseen traffic in the valley, the clatter of the garbagemen a block away (the glare in the haze as you run seems everywhere, breath made visible). The point at which the jet's noise becomes pure, deep vibration (in the valley, in the jaw), the windows to the kitchens of all these homes (joined by their back yards) thrown open (an old man steps forth from the basement to empty a bucket at the rear of his garden, wearing knit cap & sweater on a hot day), this cluster of unpainted porches. Under the freeway where the pigeons live in perpetual shadow, white-green droppings caked everywhere & into the sunburst street of small stucco houses (buff, olive, white), the hour when the old women slowly walk small dogs to & from the gutter (a man uses a special device to wipe the dew from his windshield), shadows shortening as the sun moves up (garbage cans lined up on the sidewalk are empty now)(it seems smaller as it rises higher, less orange, more yellow). A high gray smear, a stain (far to the North & at sea a storm), dampens light, hissing cats stalk each other (circling on the porch), old dogshit hardens & crumbles on the walk, that fern yellowing in the window. In the morning the girls in the parochial school outfits carry their sweaters in the crooks of their arms (the dog is frantic, barking about something), thru open kitchen windows hear forks bang against plates (small bird on the clothesline chirps). The air visibly thickens (grey, heavy, hotter, damp)(in the valley sirens pass) so that greens flatten, blend together (the drums of the Bee Gees right thru the wall from the house next door), dirt on the window filters light. November sun, the man hosing his car on the street (the rear door on the left is missing, patched with cardboard), the brown dog leaps to dodge the spray, the woman tells her son to come indoors & not to play with "that horrible little girl anymore" (the dog joins her on the concrete porch where she eats a slice of bread, a white Volkswagen circles the block twice seeking a place to park (I see all this thru the dying fern)), the sky is nearly invisible. The reduction of sight thru fog (auto-reduced to headlights at half a block, buildings reduced to shadows), there is no outside, little distance (the damp collects into droplets on the leaves of the eucalyptus & rains when wind shakes the branch), machines & even cats move slowly, cautiously, sound fails to travel (alone on the hilltop park by the ghostly tennis court, half-seen)(heavy jewelry of dew in the cobwebs). Heavy feminine arms poke thru the open window, clipping children's t-shirts onto the clothesline (the squawk of an unexpected goose), this village of backyards (dense with chaotic greenery, old collapsing fences), the air between this hill & the next visible in that it filters light, mutes color (shimmering haze of warmth itself), the sun touching only its hilltop but fully bathing this southern slope (a white cat with pink ears steps along the fence). The gloom. Tomatopaste dogstool (a thicker pen), a thinner pen, those houses in the blowing fog (smoky), the sky, the sky at a distance. Hummingbirds in the plum tree (the window streaked with rain), across the street thru an open window too-red flesh glows from a television (a sort of lamp), he hurries down the street carrying something under his levi jacket past the woman with the rose umbrella. As the haze fades small flies are illumined hovering under the porch (the Brandenburg concertos drift out a window), footsteps descend the stairs (thousands of tiny butterflies rise out of the yard next door), his shadow crosses the window (an automobile windshield on the next hill catches the sunlight, reflecting it here), huge orange monarch settles on the spinach & is still (the jet in the plum tree exits, those tiny butterflies are termites). Under the eucalyptus night's dew remains morning's puddle (indentations on the tennis court), a thorny vine probes between the boards of the fence (single strand of web stretches in the breeze, visible when it 'catches' the light (at night that plane would only be a cluster of lights moving quickly between stars), you close one eye to look in that direction (knights do, nice stew), spiders in the parsley. High small scoops of cloud flatten into a grey filter (the light diffuse) softening colors in the yards (the weight of a rug pulls on the clothesline), the slow progress of the garbage truck (a jet emerges from the screen), the breath of the garbagemen like smokestacks. A 'window' in the sky (for liftoff), a large wooden box the size of a refrigerator by the no dumping sign, the word 'fragile' stenciled on upside down, the wet grass would soak our pants to sit down on, mud's slipperiness (so he will 'rise to the occasion,' join the sky)(below, clouds rest on the sea – "we are going thru turbulence at this time")(the higher clouds are filmy, the lower patchy, thicker & west lies a gray-white blanket over the ocean)(reflection of the sun on water mottled by tides)(thru a filter of clouds: more clouds, below which brown squares of land)(glare of the sun on the wing out the window, the shadows of clouds across the gleam on the green surface of the sea (ocean)). Still, by the ocean, water & air meet, a dull horizon (the bank of clouds having moved south & over), the humidity foretells a slight chance of rain, kids bicycling their way to school, the sharp cliffs of La Jolla visible between houses. Different trees here shape the 'stupid sky' (lighter as if drier, blanched, but small dark clouds hang over Mission Bay), stunted (a typewriter in a dorm room 3 flights up stops its intermittent chatter), operations (how low meets high pressure, forming clouds) & systems (from the ocean & south by way of Alaska or Oregon, or up from Baja), sounds dissolve quickly in the friction of sea's breeze, pigeons & gulls tiny baffles turned loose in the air. Down a slope of iceplants & across a railroad track to the cliffs of Del Mar (the sky perfectly a dome), the sun, setting, grows red & swollen (behind us the cypress trees give the bottom of the sky a deckled edge), one small cloud well to the south, the evening fog invisible until the sun is directly behind it, when suddenly the cottony bank is a luminous white rushing in our direction (broken by the fog, the sun sets in fragments), a middle-school cross-country team jogs past, following the track (a man named Hillel does Tai Chi). The solitude of afternoon (voices & birdsongs), the slightest trace of high clouds streaked across the deep blue (which birds were those, grouped in a broken line, moving so quickly just barely over the ocean water (we took this as a search for food), dissolving into the general mottle of the bay (which shocked us, making us wonder if all that speckledness was not life, a vast city with no land)), the small plane of a weekend pilot whirrs past, bugs so small you don't see them if they're not in the light, a breeze trapped in the plum tree struggles to get free. The gray gathers (not clouds as yet, but high streaks, smears, amassing), the sun muted, shadows softened in their afternoon slant (no breeze at all). The sun, tho risen, watery in the eastern haze, a yolk (dogs yap to hear the cry of geese), colors filling in on the eastern slope of the hill, the first glistening of the damp grass (now gulls call down in the valley). Smell of won ton district amid the odors of the alley wrapped in fog, morning's cooking (squeal of a clothesline pulley), the dog crosses the street to sleep in the sun. The valley, an inverse dome, deepens the sky (today's many small clouds drifting together, high up), the insistent thunder of a low helicopter (the plane in front of the muted sun a silhouette), when the sun rises from behind a thick cloud to behind a thin one, a diffuse brightening, false sunrise, occurs. The exact song of certain birds (a drawn-out 'whistle' followed by a burst of chirps) fills the air (which ones are they?), an odd haze blurs distance (you make out the tower atop Candlestick Hill, mere shadow on the horizon, solely because you expect it). A winter chill (the moon full, visible thru the fog), steam from the shower pours into the kitchen (carries a cup of coffee thru the yard like a torch), ducks in the city. Rain releases odors in the garden, then stops as the air cools (all the moisture on the freeway alters its tone), not one bird visible in the grey sky (but we hear them in the trees). Leaves fall from the plum tree, drifting into the snail-chewn spinach (the bright glare whiter because filtered thru a thin cloud (then shadowy as a thicker one passes)), from that chimney (not a chimney but a rusty brown pipe) I see smoke (it dissolves in the strong wind immediately), flashes of sunlight come & go (the soil is damp, drops on the parsley glow). Day's first light yellows the world (moon full in the blue sky), the sun's golden flashes off the windows of Mount Davidson (garbagemen wheel their huge barrels down an empty street), the blue lightens, colors pale to a conventional neutrality (not to be betrayed till twilight). The haze on the bay (the horn of a locomotive), the frost on the windows (the cat on the rooftop nuzzling the drainpipe), gulls in a loose formation, not clouds but the thinnest film of white (one gull well to the rear). White cat on the fence regular as a rooster (haze so fine that just the sharpness is missing from those homes on the next hill (uniform construction, but no order to the pastels), the shadows of morning), a friend on his way to work stops to say hello, a jet deafens the sky (we pause before continuing speaking), a firetruck in no apparent hurry goes by. A fly bangs at the window (the fly bangs at a window), the warm haze deepens, the next hill half-hidden, the dog goes from child to child getting pets (staring at the sun with my eyes shut, a complex web of orange arcs, vibrating, continually changing, impossible to focus on, seems to appear), but inside the livingroom is shadowy, the sun not yet in the west (cat sleeps in the easy chair), the wild birds of the backyards absent from the treeless street. The haze deepens further (the hill a shadow broken only by the sun reflected off windshields), the whine of powertools swells the November air (the sound of dishes clattering in a sink) warm enough for baseball (the sun shines on this ink before it sinks into the paper). (You waken to the smell of rain.) Late breakfast in winter means only three more hours of sun, the shadow of steps upon steps, the glistening television antenna (I hear water flush thru the pipes of the next house)(the valley already shaded, you see that bird because it's caught the light), this brightness without warmth, the sculpted shade of a Cypress on Silver Avenue stands out. Thru the white cotton curtain a sequence of reds, oranges, yellows light up the sky until, going beyond, the clouds (high, thick) are a luminous yellow-white (then this moment of dawn too is breached & the sky suddenly settles into a dull blue-gray). Light planes, small trucks, rain, footsteps upstairs ("That's all the news you need on a Tuesday morning"), the community of sound fills the air. In the kitchen the yellow plastic bucket fills (rain filtered by roof), the interiority of the world encased in storm, the sky not an even gray but patches of dark & light (on the freeway a siren). A final shower from a (not quite) cloudless sky, lingering pools of damp on the wooden front steps (steaming fence), concrete dries faster than asphalt. Crisp clarity (breath visible even indoors), frost on the windows goes damp & starts to clear (the privacy of a sinus headache: weather is "out there," distant)(the sun, not visible from this location in the house, slipping behind a cloud briefly, the entire street dims & greys, then brightens again just as quickly, then darkens). The limited warmth of a fragile sun (clouds drift), brightness is an element of color (but the relations remain fixed, tho certain tones (white, yellow) are accented in the light)(none of this affects the sound of a neighbor's hammer or the vibrations of the massive jet), I watch the flecked brown paint of the steps as the sun emerges from the grillwork of cloud. Thru the clear air a cool breeze sifts (she sits under the plum tree on a white stool, carding wool), carrying with it distant voices off radios (the tone is never the same live) (impossible to hear what they say), the sound of a shower from the house as a window steams up (a small airplane, a pulley song, the pull of the wool through the rows of pinlike teeth). Shadow of two clothespins on a line in a breeze drifts over the frosted glass of the bathroom window (no shape to the sun, the glare too intense to sort one out), a cloudless day & chill (less smog on a Monday), a little redhaired dog smells the weeds clumping up out of a crack in the driveway. Two hands, thrust out a kitchen door, snap dust from a towel (coffee steams from its cup on the porch railing), one part of the sky (southeast) is whitest (the sun at its core), a deeper blue the further away one gets (webs of clotheslines in all these yards, half-tended fuchsias, a woman sweeping in her patio, cats on the fence), the tree barely rustles in the light breeze. A sooty haze reduces the hills to planes, one over another (in spite of the cold, the roofer wears a t-shirt), the colorless light of an average sun, a flock of small birds over the valley abruptly changes direction. Spiders in the spinach (the yard is a civilization), the air is still (mid-morning, mid-week), the hush of valley traffic, one bird somewhere in the plum tree (I sit on the stoop with my eyes shut, feeling the sun on my arms, on my legs), the song of water in the pipes, the breeze in the chard. The smell of tar in the dull haze (the chorus of dogs, the distant growl of big trucks), gulls over the valley, the cloudless sky is nearly white. The haze only deepens, chalky shadows (even the flash of sun off a windshield is diffused), the smell of pine & fir in the air, spiderweb's shape is determined by the frame it's joined to (white cat tiptoes along the fence), broken spider glistens in the breeze. The sun directly over the flat haze creates a dull glare (cupped hands shade eyes), the street itself shining, the world silent (imagine all the people), in the gutter wadded, half-dissolved papers blow in the warm wind. A gull over the valley circles (the cumulative shush of traffic, no one part standing out), the loud flapping of wings close up (the first light against the east side of these houses), the trees filled with chirping, the sun's warmth as it comes through a shirt. Squeal of a clothesline pulley (a thin fog, the dew burning off the grass), two cats, wrestling, tumble thru the carrots (dog begins barking)(neither the butterfly nor the jet seems to notice). The gray light of day (voices come thru the window, children on their way to school, someone clearing their throat), impossible to find the juncture between this listless haze & the few patchy clouds (mere suggestion of the next hill), a parakeet's hysteria, a power saw. One ray of muted light (very white) angles thru the thickening clouds (only the inmost branches of the plum tree still bear leaves)(the cat is sneezing)(today's traffic very loud). Red sky at morning (scoops amid clouds), a blonde woman raises a small boy up in her arms (the hill's slope green with new grass), storm's bank clearing. The glare in the warm haze bleaches garden's colors (buzz of a small plane), shimmer of a spider's thread in the plum tree light.

III

Blood & glass: the sky is invisible (rain streaks windows already distorted with age), only certain streets on the next hill can be seen (partly, barely, without color), I want to describe description, what is always already there (sound, light, weather), an umbrella opens the way some flowers bloom (metonymy is the problem of choice), rain is also a sound. Muscle & blood: the wood of the porch & fence heavy with rainwater, the fog blows along the gray streets, the garbagemen roll their cans down the sidewalk (red dinosaur truck), I scratch these words out & try others. Root & muscle: an explosion reverberates thru the valley (echoing (cars drive to work with their lights on) thru the fog), air is an ether, conduit (I can see on the next hill a red motor scooter, a station wagon turning into a driveway for a midblock reversal of direction, white birds occasionally visible, flickering against the backdrop of those houses). Stem & root: against the blue gulls glide (silhouettes), people peer through the mist of their own breath (the uneven shadows of the next hill reveal how incrementally Portola Heights was developed, no symmetry to the lay of the streets, no progression), fragmented lines of color (the sky a part of all it touches). Base & stem: not a fog precisely clouds these hills (half-haze), sentence type, the wind is in my hair, weather's rough rub seen in the rain-streaked, chipped paint that surrounds windows of the thinnest glass, worn steps of the rear porch descending into a field of carrots. Mound & base: the wind drives the last leaves from the plum tree (someone nearby is breaking up wood), I seldom go down into that valley & have never heard others so call it, tho undeniably it is (stretch of freeway with off-ramps at either end of the two hills), you can tell by the sound if the basketball is slightly flat (bedspreads on the line flap in the strong breeze, waves of wind scooping thru them), the sky on such a day is so passive, blue-white (the budgie falls silent). Level & mound: I made it on the bevel, the sound of a huge jet "washes" across the sky (one pays more heed to the audible world on a windless day), stripes of light between boards of the fence, dogs, voices, a hairdryer (on "low"), bee inspects the coffee cup (tiniest breeze waving the greens of the carrots), which particular defines the sky (motorbike hums past)? Bent & level: footsteps on a neighbor's stairs, laughter from the house (gull dissolves in the sun's glare, engine of a small plane, shadow of the porch against the white red-brown wall of the house (the definition of light), never merely only this (I prefer the prepositional form of possession's discreteness, adjectives are not aspects (but projections)), abandoned webs begin to rot in winter, a jet flies south of the sun. Weary & bent: the world is revealed in increments, the tule fog burning off (no brightness to the colors of the next hill's pastel stucco houses), dogs signal the garbagemen's approach (the most crucial portion of the sky is that closest to the ground, shaping the rooves of houses, coming between us (even in our own kitchen)), gulls in the fog become dots of dark gray on light. Wild & weary: dull sun a white disc half-hidden by a multi-layered cloud (one's breath fogs instantly), the gulls are flying inland (sign of rain), the whole garden shudders in the wind. Young & wild: radios on the street compete (no silence for a half-holiday, eve of the new year), grammar is weather, thin clouds smeared against a pale blue, the filtered sun is listless. Sturdy & young: children control the sidewalks (an exile), the glare in the haze flattens light (sound of a basketball), warmer than in recent days (against selection I want to pose the partial determination of what I find beyond these doors), sky is land's margin (but that also which extracts connotation from parked cars, the sweep of gulls, the sun reflected in the black hood of a pickup truck), the seminary reduced to shadow in afternoon light, the noise of birds in the backyards (every block is a sort of island, the street its moat), on top of a table made of a board placed upon a small sawhorse sit two pumpkins, an old woman carries her garbage down to the cans in a wire shopping cart, the wheels clunking down the wooden steps. Flowering & sturdy: each small cloud in the light blue air seems to have been raked, a ribbed effect, seems flat (two dimensional plane), each moving simultaneously southeast & counter-clockwise (slowly), a robin gives color to the leafless tree (branches, rooves penetrate the sky). Shaded & flowering: in a field of pine in a fine rain, a dense drizzle that from a distance would seem fog (thru the red-brown carpet of fallen needles winter grass shoots up, yellow-green (the sole sound in these woods beyond the rain is a lone duck), a blue Volkswagen parked by the cabin in the mud). Damp & shaded: the sky on the television is gray (snow falls into a Cleveland stadium), but at the end of the street (overlooking the valley, its slopes still wet & newly green), a deep & cloudless blue, kids in the projects leap for a rebound under a hoop attached to a phone pole, beyond which light weekend traffic threads the five layers of road (the sound of jets absorbed), cats in the bushes, a pushbroom scrapes dead wet leaves over the pavement, starlings peck at the grass. Glistening & damp: dawn merely an orange glow, intensifying along the east horizon, the height of those soaring birds indicates serious flight, pools linger in gutters days after a hard rain, the runner follows the sight of his own breath (dog challenges a garbageman), the sound of a spoon against a cereal bowl indexes time. Frosted & glistening: six robins settle on the power line (chill breeze from off the ocean), old wax paper cups with plastic lids & straws (red & white) jutting forth rock aimlessly in the gutter (half-blinded by my own breath which blows back into my face), no such thing as eyes' perfection (placement in the skull will differ), what did I think those bruises on cars were before I heard of primer coats? Angled & frosted: the colorless world punctuated by a bright yellow-orange jersey hanging from the line (the smell of warm, corn tortillas), fog lifting into haze, birds shivering in the skeleton of the plum tree (heat from the stove), curling cigar smoke describes the currents of air (swirling spirals). Staked & angled: the heat of the house clouds all windows (thru which a gray light shines without brilliance), flies walk on the vertical glass (a lone gull circles while the robins in the tree just sit), the erased sun impossible to find. Roped & staked: red sky at morning (the high, thin clouds, the thicker, lower ones black & smoky), birds as orange as the light (long shadows), window's frost warms to water & runs, the damp sill. Strained & roped: you don't notice the power saw's motor till it shuts off (the radio out that open window is muffled, disrupted), afternoon's shadows start to appear (these homes, facing east, block the dull breeze). Sifted & strained: sheets on a line billow like sails in the wind (the scattered white clouds are nearly motionless, thin, stretching out like a swirl of arcs from an inexact center), at twilight (the only true light) shadows swallow the world. Gifted & sifted: dawn behind the high clouds, the hills grey, streetlamps gleam (field of landed stars) or headlights working their way down the streets to the freeway, cats on porches wait to be let in. Young & gifted: a "croupy" dog barks repeatedly (half-cough), the sun in the cloudless air warm on the white of the clover (a small plane distinct against the soft background of light traffic, robins' songs intermittent like wind chimes (as the plane passes over, all else is drowned out)). Brazen & young: bird twitter loud in the warm haze (the paler the blue the less moisture), small bee just hovers by the sage, sun in the forest of carrot tops, yet shadowy damp corners to the garden. Brassy & brazen: soft greys of a dawn haze (thin cloud layer rippled against the deepening blue), flock after flock of gulls (high against the scattered light) flying east (deafening jet in the other direction), one sees sky's filter (nearly a fog) between this porch (12 steps) & the next block (impressionism of the next hill). Yellow & brassy: the sun burns thru the fading rain (rolling clouds spill over the hilltop), birds simply glide without moving their wings. Flaming & yellow: a rooster's crow heard thru distant traffic (after the predawn storms clouds leaven off, highly defined at the bottom (inverted table), billowing above), sun is where light scatters in these clouds (even the concrete walks are still damp), one parakeet amid the songs of all these wild birds. Flickering & flaming: a ring around the full moon caused by clouds too thin to dim the night's darkness, nor catch & reflect the city's light (freeway's constant whoosh is louder as nearer sounds die down). Striped & flickering: thin clouds swinging north signal rain (the erasure of blue), gulls reduced to silhouettes against a gray scrim (motionless soaring), the mottled, muted cloudlight (no sun visible), few shadows (small old wooden homes, long since settled away from perpendicular angles & straight lines, look drab when damp, you can see the moisture in roof's shingles). Spotted & striped: (thru the window) patches of light amid layers of gray, moving swiftly beyond the leafless still branches of the plum tree (sounds muffled by walls & glass)(on the television in another room government changes). Sought & spotted: somewhere a rooster crows repeatedly, the sky expands as clouds rise (the sun in the cracks), birds of various sizes move in different directions, the constant noise of traffic like a vibration in the jaw. Conceived & sought: birds in the rain simply soar (the sky lowers), sounds of water dripping (cat nudges my arm as I write), sound of water on the freeway (is the sound of traffic). Considered & conceived: water clings to the line, shining in the half-clouded light of a late morning sun (the rain in the carrot tops), a jet visible, threading the whites of the sky. Caught & considered: for 15 seconds the candles' flames in the (otherwise) dark room flicker as I dropped my flannel shirt (how low is the sky), outside newspapers in the rain dissolve into mush (in the morning the canary shrills pleasure to the cleansed world), the roses in their vase so slowly open. Overturned & caught (the snail on the walk's edge): a single faint streak of cloud makes the blue that much sharper (morning mist burns off bay water, revealing first boats), one line of clothes perfectly still, the other rippling in a soft breeze (birds & traffic & someone calls my name). Overwrought & overturned: rain flattens affect (the glass frosted by stove's heat), the garbagemen in yellow slickers (towels on the line heavy with water), but throughout the yard the greens deepen. Iron & overwrought: the slow arc of stars (is it clockwise?) in the night sky hidden by these clouds (gray even in the dark (illumination of the city), spent after the hardest rain). Dry & iron: half-moon in the morning sky (more sharply defined than a cloud), the wind (tipping the potted jade plant over) denies the intense blue, more rain to come. High & dry: V formations of birds silhouetted against the remaining clouds flap east, the wind stills, a drop hangs glistening from the power line waiting to fall (jay lands & the drop shakes free)(although the ground is still damp & there are more clouds west of the valley, one senses the transition is over, smells the clean air). White & high: the sculpted clouds' own depths sharpened by the intense sun, flooding the two hills & valley with light (a siren on the freeway), one plane passing slowly south (even at this distance its mass gives it the image of a large ship, sailing), a warm breeze in the carrots (more sirens). Silver & white: the afternoon sun glistens in the streets' lingering puddles on the next hill, flashes off the mirrors of parked cars (the clip on my pen), the slope down to the shanties behind the Alemany Projects intensely green (what causes a fly ball to hover at the top of its arc? why are those gulls circling so vertically, nearly a funnel?), the traffic louder here on the ridge. Jasper & silver: on weekends the yards fill with Afro-fusion topped with power tools (thin filter of cloud blanches light), dogs wander sluggishly in the unfamiliar heat (count the green tones possible in any given garden)(eye sees as sky is, dependent on light), a man with a hammer, walking on his roof. Tourmaline & jasper: the night sky against the plum tree is deep grey against deeper gray, the lights of an aircraft flickering through (predawn fog to the east – they still drive with their lights on – cloudswaths above go red, birds in the fir trees (by the hundreds) scream themselves awake, but by sewer's gutter mouth (reveals catchbasin) hear water gurgle, runoff from last week's rain). Rhodochrosite & tourmaline: small birds shoot out of the tall grass as I run through (I wear my breath (visible) like a scarf or cape), haze leaves those hills silhouettes, each lighter than the last, a land of dreamy cardboard cutouts (two jets obliterate sound as I write). Quartz & rhodochrosite: the East Bay reduced to a glare, fog on the lawn fails to burn off (the high over Boise, the low over Baja), streetlamps go off with a 'pop,' small clouds, deep gunmetal gray, drift over the valley from the west. Pints & quartz: at night to the south you can see the county line from the streetlights (mercury white on this side, the other sodium vapor yellow), the clouds in the morning have that cut-off-at-the-bottom look, deep grey (a lone small craft flies under to get thru). Buckets & pints: a gray glow hovering in the dark sky (the clouds are lit by the land's light), only one branch on the plum tree has kept its leaves, dawn's glare is white. Brooms & buckets: after a siren dogs bark to announce their turf (thin glaze of cloud), that car so parked means she spent the night, old brown hand raising a torn shade (colorless morning). Whisks & brooms: a low drizzling rain drifts in, filling the valley (a small plane is somewhere above these clouds), shadows are muted, shingles show the moisture they absorb (I am not interested in description, but detail, transition, all the nameless, half-known tones reducible to blue)(on this block of small homes the only ones with front yards are those which lack garages, postage stamp (as they say), used often for storage, garbage cans, oil drums, broken bicycles, old brooms with snapped handles (what has this to do with the sky?)), rooster crows in the afternoon. Vests & whisks: like a fog the rain burns off at dawn (dull glare of yellow sun), sidewalk's concrete lingering damp. Bows & vests: gulls (flapping) fill the air of the schoolyard (a loaf of bread), orange glare on still surface of bay's water (dawn is near), literary language. Bunches & bows: the gray light glistens (rain gathers in pools on worn wooden steps, or clings (one drop at a time) to blades of grass, a million additional surfaces on that hillside reflecting light), passive winter sun. Heads & bunches: glint of sun through frosted glass, carved by shadows of the porch (restricted vocabulary, limitless world), birds in the fir tree shouting at the sudden heat. Umbrellas & heads: the grey of the jet against that of the sky (dark against light), a storm characterized by large drops with much space between them (jet's roar lags after). Canes & umbrellas: the hills green with winter, the last cloud of a once-heavy storm piles over Portola Heights (dark underbelly, glare of dawn light), morning shadows in this nook of the kitchen, a chain of dogs begins to howl (siren on the freeway), stopped catch-basin at the corner turns intersection into a lake. Walkers & canes: spiders waddle thru the green shades of the garden, a flock of gulls is flushed out of the valley by a backfire (for an instant, jet's shadow darkens the yard), the glazed light of a cloud-filtered sun (the cat rolls over & over on the cement to scratch his back), the waterfall sound of distant traffic louder once the jet's past. Crips & walkers: the brisk wind shudders the carrot tops (to the south the sky whitens), a power drill whirrs in spurts, first white blossoms on the plum tree blow free. Carrots & crips: gull sweeps low over the damp grass, under gusts of a winter fog (headlights on a schoolbus shine thru), jays in the plum tree, hummingbirds in the bush, fog feels like rain. Babytears & carrots: the next hill shimmers in the sudden heat, the buzz of flies fills the yard, cats stretch sleepily on the porch (steam coils from a coffee cup). Bougainvillea & babytears: fogdrifts limit distance (microscopic rain), the greens deepen (predawn clouds backlit by the moon), skies is eyes (words are). Impatiens & bougainvillea: a breeze rattles in the laundry (on the line), the deep blue of a cloudless sky & somewhere (far from centered) the song of an airplane's jet. Cosmos & impatiens: the great glare of the bay's air (the sun intense), a warm breeze in gusts rattles towels on a line. System & cosmos: abandoned webs knot & cling to the joints of the porch like a grey-white film (in the spring heat you feel the vibration of the passing jet that much more, in your spine, at the ends of your jaw by the base of each ear), somewhere in the valley a pile driver is generating echoes, the rooster crows & crows. Garden & system: white cat yowls on the wood fence, the air cools, a cloud drifts in off the sea (strands of a web glimmer in the sun), a clay bowl of succulents sits in the shade. Mulch & garden: the half-blue sky, the house enveloped in the downpour of a momentary shower (wind blows the white flowers from the plum tree), it is more difficult to see into a window than out of it. Rot & mulch: scoops of white cloud billow on all sides of the valley (a quick breeze), humor among friends that a warm winter & early spring reflect the benefits of ozone loss (under the steps the compost steams). Mildew & rot: rusting clothesline pulley lies in a pool of water on the red-shingled roof (sun's glare through the clouds), hop between puddles to get to the shed. Culture & mildew: clouds stranded in the still air above the bay thru which our jet climbs (later-small clouds rush over brown Nebraskan valleys far below, throwing shadows to their west, snow-covered mountains dotted with trees)(later-pure cloud glare outside the window (no perception of depth)). Elevators & culture: the uniform gray of the New York sky seen thru the blue tint of a La Guardia window (beyond which a boarding ramp with two additional windows, thru which the sky is a deep but unnatural blue), rain drops streaking the glass (each divides into a line of a half-dozen droplets), later to be between 2 layers of cloud, the one above thin & misty (filled with the sun's glare), the other a field of textured white with gentle valleys, rolling forward slowly (like an image of a calm sea filmed in slow motion), & between these at the horizon a band of the vaguest blue (not possible to convey in words this sensuousness of the sky, a range of white rising like mountains miles in the distance (the upper layer begins to dissolve, revealing blue), the sharp physicality of this endless cloud, mother of the sky, white ocean toward which this 727 gradually descends (below, thru a single hole I spot the brown shadow of land near a small storm in the cloud, an area where its definition is suddenly less clear, leading to a change where the cloud is softer, less etched, no longer rolling & we pass into it, rocking in the invisible turbulence). Brick & elevators: (below) the even grey of all the air (a drier chill, windless, than I've known of), winter demands indoor life. Snow & brick: flakes swirl (some rise, others fall, still others blow across), a thick blanket upon lawns, car roofs, sidewalks (melting, they lose definition quickly, until what remains lie on lawns, windshields, cracks in the cement, then a new flurry), snow blows in wisps up off the asphalt (south, from above, the cloud is beginning to dissolve, first gullies turning to mist, then holes (snow on the farmlands below), then an evident softening of edges followed by the wide shadows of gaps (twin towers of a nuclear power plant 33,000 feet down), Creeley says the snow "likes to dump" on the bank of Lake Erie, his own beard full of white. Air & snow: ("Run down & look at the sky before it sets," says James)(when the traffic stops at the light, afternoon rush, Houston & Bowery, two black men dart out to wipe the windshields of cars), a jet red in the sun's reflection in the otherwise muted tones of dusk, what I see is my breath (but a low copter whips the air). Dust & air: red brick mutes grey light (Soho), warming to 40. Flakes & air: (enclosed in snow) people push along on the whitening street, the traffic inches forward, snow rushes at you (or is caught in a lightwell, swirling & rising in the wind). Slush & flakes: the chill air clears & is still (intersections turn into lakes). Soot & slush: wind rattles the metal curtain drawn over the storefront (the logic of light in a room whose windows have a 'clear' plastic second layer of insulation), what snow remains is blackened with a web of dust (small black clouds in a high gray sky). Rust & soot: small plane high looks low between the mud-coloured buildings against the slab of cloud (last mounds of black snow squat at gutter's edge)(vertical city). Glass & rust: pin point tip of Chrysler Building rips underbelly of a rushing cloud (loft light), no sun to reflect on Hyatt's mirrored surface (the sky is straight up), only the wind & chill to remind of "out of doors." Glare & glass: arched window shapes the sky (bottomed by angles of brick buildings, coming together at (an audible, not visible) 3-street intersection), the grey light flat, even. Steam & glare: pigeon on the fire escape has to fly nearly straight up to leave the lightwell (indirect evidence of the sky). Steel & steam: (radiator music) a small storm divided evenly between drizzle & snow. Mortar & steel: pigeons crowd the lightwell's air, wings beating, brushing the window (above, a small blue square). Shingle & mortar: field of stripped birch, a flash of snow (melts upon contact), the wind blows thru your shirt. Porch & shingle: at the horizon a thin strip of light blue registers cloud's limit, the tall pale trees still leafless (the grey is slender, its dark strippings threatening to open onto sky) while evergreens brush against storm windows. Drainpipe & porch: the rain evenly spots the water of the (backyard) pool (falling so vertically it barely streaks the pane), crested kingfisher (white upon blue) shoots low along the river's course. Clothesline & drainpipe: the warm wind under the grey cloud (dimensionless smear) hints rain, new leaves on the plum tree (its white petals litter the spinach), only the tops of the grasses catch the wind. Window & clothesline: the first drops hit large, leaving spots on the porch (cats move into basements), later the sound is layered, the evenness of the actual rain striking wood & walk, under the louder spill from the rusting drains (no modulations to the gray of this sky). Curtain & window: sun's glare gives the clouds dimension (shape is shade), is reflected in the dampness lingering in a rooftop shingle. Shadow & curtain: the sun slips behind a small gray smear of cloud (mutes the sky), at night city lights illumine tall white billows passing silently through the dark.

IV

In the night darkness is defined. The clipped moon hidden behind clouds half-illumined by the dull, regular rows of streetlamps. Billows pile, tumble & spill from the low mountains to the south, thickened by the nearness of sea, roiling white shadow in the starless dark. Tops of the grasses shudder in the breeze. The rectangle of surrounding houses would shelter them but for the slope of hill. The thinness of distant traffic marks a near-silence. A ball of cat asleep on the mat by the door on the porch, as two others, each white, patrol the fencetops that connect house to house. A woman stands, dark silhouette, in an unlit doorway. At the edge of these clouds mass turns to wisp, a shredding, a dissolution. Beads of dew pearl the porch. At the horizon a tinge of blue glow. Across the bay streetlamps flicker like wildflowers. The cat pauses, its ears erect. A light gust rattles the plum tree. Dark against dark, color without light. Houses, shadows. The wind settles, the trees relax. A leaf of chard bends under the snail's weight. The tinge stretches into a band, faint halo to far hills. Black spider pauses on the damp earth, dwarfed by the carrot tops. From down in the valley a barking dog. The woman quietly shuts the door. On the far hill a light goes on in one house, then another. This dilutes the dark, the sky a deep blue-grey. Scraps of cloud, lit against the night. An airplane blinks across the east horizon. By the sea, streetlamps illumine underbelly of the fog bank. Grass is cool & damp. It is in the mind one sees the horizon shift tones, project discontinuity. A range of blues, the deepest (navy) in the west. Somewhere a radio, faucets. The lights in kitchens, bedrooms, baths, drown the streetlamp, because larger, framed in windows' stretched squares. The point at which blue, lightening, becomes white at the horizon (visible thru a plum tree's leaves, more than merely the nearest housetop). Whisper of traffic rises. First rooster. Yards & houses of muted color. Geese rise, steaming from the trees about the lake. Where do the flies sleep? White-orange at the horizon, sun's rays bending over before it arrives, stains the highest clouds to the west pink. Now the lower clouds seem darker, but more streets are visible, silhouettes of schools, trees. Degrees of light. At the bus stop a man awaits the first run with fists clenched, thumbs tucked in, shifting his weight from leg to leg to stay warm. Now the blue is palest. To the west windows reflect first rays of the sun (most streets visible, strawberry-colored school on the slope of Glen Park). The newsboy, folding papers as he goes, is preceded by a big yellow dog. Orange pink tinge above the rooftops, sides of houses stained orange. The green of a far park still softened by dew. Rising sun, huge at the horizon, swollen yellow. The clouds, dissolving, turn colorless, dark. Propellers of a small airplane churn the air (no large jet travels in that direction). Spider sits in spinach shadow. Sun behind the eucalyptus erases it in the glare. Cat on the doormat, licking the base of its tail. Tiny flies hover in the light. Purple fuchsia, rocking in a subtle breeze. Now only high streaks of white remain. Shadows shorten. A bird against the roof of the world, gliding. Is it the wind that causes that small plane's song to wane? The tree's leaves scrape together & the sound is called wind. Wind's hand shaped that cloud, then left it there. A child has begun to cry (sound absorbed into rising traffic). First hammer. Even an empty clothesline will bounce in a gust. Three clothespins wrapped in spiderwebs. By the fence a digitalis in a green pot leans to catch the sun. Roar of a trapped bee from that web. The repetitive churning sound of a nearby washer clicks off. The sun now can be felt. Cut grass turns yellow at the base of new lettuce. Small flies hover in the shade of the plum tree. Take off your shirt. If the wind dies, this will be a hot one. Then a fresh gust. The shed door groans on old hinges. The whimper of a basement dryer. The field of foxtails in the next lot ripples. The hammer and traffic. The shadow of my hair (blowing) in my lap. The bee is dark against the orange of the poppy. Spider scuttles into the clover. Two jets in formation. You can tell when a sports car (not visible), climbing the hill, shifts gears. A bee walks into the crack between shingles, the layer above casts a short shadow. Something small & green drowns in the coffee. Cloud mutes sun's rising light, shadows soften. Plums have fallen where the onions have just started to sprout. Cobwebs in the jade tree (an old web gathers dust, is more visible). A new gust rattles the whole yard. The sun is nearly 'through' the cloud. Three small birds whistle in the tree, then dart away as a fat robin settles in. The grass stills for a moment. The sun emerges. Skin recognizes warmth's directness.

TONER

Brucebook

Meet my personality.
A deaf man's whistle
could seem inexact.
                                        I don't
                        want to get my
feathers hot.
Bag lady stands in

                            A phone booth
out of the rain.
First dot, best dot.
Death of
                    Porky the Pig.
Already the jaws
of narrative open.

On the street
                        a woman
returns the man's leer,
involuntary grimace.
                                        Static
storms the intercom.
A reduction in species

                            Simplifies planet.
Tongue pressed
to third rail.
                        The way the new el
undeckles the margin

between suburb and sky.
After a walk in the rain

Cuffs damp for hours.
Shapeless mass in express lane
                                        checkout counter.
Now when I hear
someone on the bus talking
            I turn
to see

If anyone is there
                            to listen.
Write first
and ask questions after,
                            exact trace
of anxiety
does not "make the man"

Lumber yard
                               surrounded by condos:
its days are numbered.
                                                   People gasp,
mouse loose on the train.
Top Stars Tell How They Died,
see inside. Multiples weep

To see the space about them—
vacant lots
                            stretching
not forever but to the freeway,
                        not vacant
but each
holding a cement foundation

Visible to infrared
poised in night sky.
Anthropomorphic,
                                        the president grins
across a screen filled with snow,
                                        unattended
in the tavern corner,

The hard sound of billiards
banging together.
                                    Ice melts
settling in the tall glass
about the clear plastic straw,
model
        for offshore drilling.

I'm in touch with my emotions,
in search of a tourniquet,
                        event at which
life narrows
to the Final Four.
Pull string here
                            says Band-Aid's

Wax paper wrapper
                                        but instead
                            the red string
just slides out.
Woodpecker walks up
trunk of the pine.
Windmill breaks up broadcast transmission.

Economists conduct thought experiment
for a society of two islands

containing one individual each.
            Man struggles
to move
         from wheelchair
to auto.

                                    Extra-wide briefcase
indicates salesman,
stewardess' luggage in portable dolly.
                                       Fumbles with his walkman
at the end of the tape.
Escalator's steady hum
dissolves in the muzak:

Soft repetitive bell
sends plainclothes security staff
sprinting to department store exit.
            We have nothing
to form
but form
            itself,

The social queues up
                                  like children
at the end of recess
in the rain.
               A nurse
with bruised knees, lawyer's
belly strains dull shirt,

Tie open wide.
                  The line waits
for the previous show to let out.
Who watches the watchmen?
Far across the bay

I see the city rise,
                    hazy,

Verticals without depth.
Throat sore from indoor heat,
                              old prof
shambles across the quad,
                    that verb
mere predication.
Left-handed woman writes in margin

Of casebook.
          Library book
dust jacket
          encased in plastic.
Four men in 1914,
three at Columbia,
determine American literary canon.

Pronounce that canyon.
She said I said
          in my sleep
the same word
        over and over
"Dama,"
whatever that means.

        Large-boned woman,
freckled,
her hair in thick braids,
asleep on the train.
                    Year that
some men thought it hip
to shave sideburns

Above the ear.
I hear
auto alarm pulse through the night.
Escalator banister in brass
refracts glare
while I rise
to new level of irony.

Support the Seven Points?
Hell,
identify the Seven Points.
Way to go
Le Duc Tho. In memory's slomo,
bullshit monk flickers, smouldering,
and goes out.

Up against the all-inclusive
Fate of what?
Charlie Manson look-alike
tries to thumb a ride.
Gears mock
industrial song
the way fears make a long night.

Weeding, bend down from the waist,
butt high up, reaching
strange grass shoots amid moss.
The word "I,"
once written,
stares back,
absurd.

But I take pleasure
in not being hit
by the cone

of the great shade-throwing tree
mid-town:
                    Don't block the box
(lemon fat on a too-frail limb).

Reading's not a spectator sport,
overflow fans funneled
                                        to upper deck
wear caps to protect from glare
at the margin—
                         adjectives
                     on the bullpen bench
stretch out:

I want the verb to dip
just as it enters sense.
Visible metaphor
                                   wins one
for the Gipper:
                         "America
taken hostage" by mass noun

News,
          Ken and Barbie
weeknights at eleven.
The weak knight's in heaven
                    followed by Panza.
Robin fat
on the wooden deck.

The wounded dick
                                   (named for a poet)
is saved by his partner, Hawk,
big black Other fucker.
I stalk

        in high corn
the point of punctuation.

Light thru the trees anticipates dusk:
now one rests where
previously one resisted.
Hot day
              cotton skirts
                        rise up
to wind's gusts.

Sun refracts on window's dust:
                   the archer's back
pulled taut
        as the bow
bends
aimed at the padded target.
Book open, one stares into space.

Imagine sweat (imagines sweat)
distinct from the participation:
football caught
                       high up in the pine
past where cones and rocks
might dislodge it.
                            Alabaster

Lion atop old AM radio
(upon
        yellow oak desk,
                                      oil
drained from the wood)
alongside a string of bibles,
lace curtain filters window light.

                                        Imagine debt
(imagines debt)
far less than the participation:
foot caught in a bear trap
gnawed free
                                at the ankle,
critter hops into the dry brush.

Sense of a nightmare
      not knowing why,
dry
mouth, palpitating chest.
Pennants over theme park
                                snap
in the wind.

                                So still at dawn
you can hear
filaments in the streetlamps hum
with electricity, birds
sing to anticipate sun.
In the station
                                the newsie

                          Has her radio on.
Chorizo
odors rise up
from alongside unsalted eggs
on the white plate
                                          chipped
in the luminous cafe.

Glowworm train emerges
                      from tunnel

into night:
where stars aren't, clouds must be.
What the Aussies call a carpark
six storeys high
                    lit from within.

Overhead fluorescents illumine loading dock
at the P.O.
              Thick blue socks
over stockings,
                    high top tennies
with their laces untied,
she rides with her eyes shut.

igloo ice bucket used as lunch pail
                                        stare
checking out panty lines
through the rich knits
                                    notepad
conceived as contact sheet
see nouns as glossies

command mode
                            small boy asks
where's my hair
                          inner alarm rings
long before clock radio
's soothing whisper starts
cheap jeans bear loud stitching

wear low on the hips
shirt half tucked to reveal belly
                                first orange light
hard against the hills
reflected in a million windows

forced air hand dryer
next to

disemboweled towel dispenser
old orange cab
ringed with grime
t-shirt as display ad bears logo
to increase name recognition
goosebumps
on her thighs beneath miniskirt

on her way to high school
tricolor
pompom juts from gym bag
cash for contras exceeds sum sought
shoe town
black bird perched
atop tombstone twists

head stuck on song *here*
comes the night
oh
here it comes
yeah
kid on the A-train
looking for action

our infrastructure is old
and cannot be replaced
man asleep
on bench built
for three
is barely twenty
ornate midtown graveyard

how quickly graffiti style
degenerates
                    coarse Kosher salt
in bright yellow box
two eggs turn opaque
                                sizzling
atop smooth industrial griddle

rain on the river
blurs view of Jersey
red-grey brick sky
early to bed
                    early to rise
work like a dog
                        and advertise

still air makes mind sleepy
even in sunlit room
ceiling black with street soot
                            in spite of
jammed windows
                                siren yips
at intersection only

                    old hasids
in dark coats
on a hot day
                    the young
appear the most foreign
suitcase full of diamonds
on 47th street

wise men fish here
                    but cannot find books

amid chaos
of intuited order
subjective
in negative sense only
phlegm of the personal

someone's cooking popcorn
and whole building knows it
while outside
jackhammers on Mott St.
vibrate teeth
bicycles on fire escape
high over brick courtyard

old wire shopping cart
turns to rust
on a rooftop
it's daytime
tie sheet-curtains into knots
the way flowers clutch at filtered light
now put answering machine on playback

imagine 50% more 9 oz. bonus size
life is really special
bright
as an all-night market
hum
in motor of big truck
over long arc of bridge

hands are as mind is
chapped
conversation is friction
the way voice shakes skull
nostrils produce

constant sinus mucous
pick to flick away

Jaws
p.o.v. shark
fence forms a windbreak
against which to lean
hummingbird to the fuchsia
shadow
that darts

curl fingers to shelter palm
thumb makes a clasp
violets in their purple bloom
hummingbird rises
like a copter
vertical
over pruned apple tree

slow a little, planet
people are sleeping
silver,
the train into work
slips into the earth
becomes
subway shining in the dark

good grief
is literally true
beautiful broker
appears depressed
tho on best dressed list
only modesty is false
how the wilt becomes the flower

I cry
        to see the captains of poetry
dead at the wheel
exhaust hose spirals
                                        up
into truck's cabin
incredibly clear afternoon

give 'em enough trope
                hallelujah
bum again
a match in exscription
                as literal
lights on
behind the drawn shade

lines mark the eyes' part
but i hear sounds
whistling in skull cavern
escalator rolls
                        steadily down
                        at checkers plead
don't king me

young blond red-faced man
        features already wine-swollen
drums
a tune out on his hard plastic
attaché
        fingering as if typing
seat on a crowded train

neptune society pricelist
something to consider

Eisenhower
learned not to convey ambition
blank slate of drive-in screen
collapsing
in dry weedy field

tiny flags on hill
simulate poppies
as possible art piece
offshore, by context
hidden in the head
bagel made of raisin bread
forms a base for cream cheese

tiny ducks
on the wide river
under the iron bridge
a collector
of aluminum cans
is tall and thin
peers into the trash receptacle

orange-footed mallard male
pecks at a finch
girl
shells peanuts before she eats 'em
this man's mismatched socks
match his
shirt and shorts

pass for power
quarterback's creed
well as the whitefaced mime's
lollipop trees bagged in plastic

any rhythm defi(n)es sentiment
when will this pen
come to life

transit's glory is another story
false
white sun shimmers in the solid sky
passport photos
while U wait
bag lady in a football helmet
bus stalled on the steep hill

pulp mouth
point at which
novocain wears down
even this milkshake
tastes "warm"
vanilla
up against the new crown

blimp stalks the gray air
cloud heavy
a wet heat
is better than dry heaves
as ashen as the earth
poor retch
dog taught to fetch

and the salmon flower
is pink
but the fruit of the poor salmon
is caviar to eat
echoes
in the head's hollow heard
herds words into song

not the same as thought
                                        thinking
but if to write is to listen
as to ride is to sit on
accelerator, break, wheel
it's the will is what
                                   does not break

femme de la creme
                                 safety pin
closes up blouse
where top button should be –
rash beneath watchband
                                          white tennies
beneath long black skirt

old emphysemic wheezes at coffee bar
never use lemon in tea at home
                              into her 40s
still see the girl
                                 wide-eyed
under that flesh
the one with the jelly center

                              moisture gathers
on the outside
of the glass of ice water
while beside it that
of the tall vanilla shake
tho cool
                  is dry

a thin white see-thru blouse
but with a cheap bra beneath

point at which heat
                                        erases
not just sense of decorum
        but also
desire

banking district empty by dusk
puppy chained to the bag lady's cart
pull tag
            ripped flag
lone dove amid these pigeons
muzak
        seeping from highrise walls

line trashbags in a row beside boxes
jewelry shop's windows empty at night
                                    red light pulses
index of caution
office interiors illumined within
oh loungers await
                                    the airport bus

LET'S OVERPRAISE THE PAST
SO WE CAN BE DONE WITH IT
                                                        ILLEGIBLE
DAY-PLANNER NOTATION
                                    PUCKER
TO SUCK ON
HAND-ROLLED CIGARETTE

BACK SIDE OF A STOP SIGN
                                                BEFORE WHICH
DOUBLE-DECKER BUS
MATTED HAIR OF A STREET DRUNK

TATTOOS
      RIPPLE OVER HANGING FLESH
BROKEN ESCALATOR BOARDED UP

I AM SPEAKING IN FRENCH
BROWN SHOES
          BUT NOT A PAIR
BUTTONS JUST FOR POCKETS
               HOT TEA
WON'T QUENCH THIRST
WATCH SITS ATOP THE TABLE

IS THAT MY BREATH
             TREBLE
PITCHED TO THE MAX
THUS AIR ECHOES IN SKULL
BROUGHT ON BY SUBTITLES
            ARTICLES
ARE PURE EXCESS

                AXES
RENDER JUGGLING "REAL"
CROSS LEGS
        TRIANGULATE LAP
GLOVED BULB IS MICROPHONE
SOCKS TO BUFFER FOOT IN SHOE
DUCT TAPE TAMES WIRE

ENORMOUS SOUND OF SCRATCHING EAR
       EROTIC
AS A Q-TIP
GLAZED SUGAR BREAKS OFF DONUT
PIPE JUTS THROUGH SHEETROCK
           HARD EDGE
OF AN OLD FOOT

HARSH DRY DAYS ON WHICH
POETRY IS AS PLEASANT
AS POKING A ROAD KILL
WITH A STICK
                              PEN POINT
                        DAMP IN THE WARM
ORGAN GOO

MUSIC DISORDERS PERCEPTION
UNTIL NEW FORM EMERGES
SQUIRREL'S AGE
                                  BY THE RINGS
ON ITS TAIL
                        ROUGE OVER
LIGHT FRECKLES UPON PALE SKIN

                                       SWEAT'S SALT
STAINS THE SHIRT
WHITE HOUSES DOT THE FAR HILLS
                                       SPOTS INTERRUPTING
A THICKER GREEN
CLOUDY CENTER TO CUBE OF ICE
SOUND OF HAMMER PULLING NAIL

BUT THAT OF THE MANUAL TYPEWRITER
IS FORGOTTEN NOW
                                              DEEP ROUND KEYS
TRAFFIC COPTER BUZZES PAST
BEES AT THE LIP
                                  OF THE RED FUCHSIA
DOG YAPPING SO FAR AWAY

EACH DAY'S AN INVENTION
CONTINUITY BUT MEMORY'S FICTION
                                      FIVE FINGERS

ON EVERY HAND
IS GENERAL PRINCIPLE
                                        AUTOS STALLED
IN MIDTOWN JAM

PEN MOCKS THE PAGE
MIND AT DAWN DREAM-CROWDED
                    CROW ON THE LAMP POST
HAWKS
SUN
          BREAKS IN THE PRISM
SCATTERS ON KITCHEN WALL

EROSION SCOOPS THE HILL
WEIGHT OF THE SATCHEL
                                                        CONCEALS
RED MARBLIZED BOWLING BALL
PAR COURSE BENEATH BART TRACKS
                                                WOMAN SORTS COUPONS
LIKE A POKER HAND

TEDDY RUXPIN REVERSIBLE
HAND PUPPETS NAMED
                                                      THIS
THAT
            THE OTHER
TIE LIKE A PHALLUS HANGS LIMP
FROM OPEN BUTTONED-DOWN COLLAR

PAPER ROSE IN SILVER GOBLET
WOMAN PULLING ON CORK
TO CHAMPAIGN BOTTLE
WITH BARE TEETH
                                        TELESCOPE

SQUINTED INTO
THE WRONG WAY

DO NOT ATTEMPT TO
SPEAK
TO DRIVER
WHILE TEXT IS
IN OPERATION
WAFFLE'S GRID ON TWO AXES
STRAWBERRIES TO THE NORTHEAST

SMALL PLANE LANDS IN RED SQUARE
DARK CLOUD OVER SKYLIGHT
ARCHITECT
BROWSES A CITY
BEACH
IS TRANSITIONAL
SAND FORMS THE MARGIN

EARRING WORN AT TOP OF EAR
IGNORE
THE IMPERATIVES
OF THIS TEXT
BENT PIPE
CURVES INTO FRAME OF CHAIR
HYPHEN IN ANN-MARGARET

PEOPLE DESPISE EXACTITUDE
FOR WHICH THERE IS NO GROUND
SECOND THOUGHT
LAST THOUGHT
ANKLES TEND TO BE REDDER
BLUE STOOL
IN WHITE BOWL

IN ADJECTIVES
                                        VAGUENESS IS NOT
MYSTERY
                         CHINESE WORD
IS NOT LETTERING
PIGEONS PROWL THE MALL LOT
IN SERVICE CORRIDOR FIREMEN CRUNCH

REALISM =
                           WORDS IN SITU
ROOTS CROWDED IN TINY POT
AIRPLANE TACKED INTO SKY
                                                  PREPOSITIONS
PRIMITIVE VELCRO
ROADS CURVE IN "THE COUNTRY"

AND THEN WENT DOWN TO THE CARPORT
                               SET KEY
TO ICETRAY
FOURTH IN A FIVE TEAM LEAGUE
      THE UMLAUT SHOULD BE CENTERED
IN
FROM U'S VERTICALS

SLICE
            SAYS THE BLIMP
                              SOFTCORE
BY O-RINGS
HIDDEN IN THE MANIFOLD
EYE EYE EYE
WHAT FACE CAPITAL Y

MISTOOK THAT DOVE FOR AN OWL
YOU CAN HEAR

BALL-BEARINGS
INSIDE A SKATEBOARD
YOU CAN
TELL WHEN THE TRAIN'S IN
BY THE CROWD ALL AT ONCE

ON THE ESCALATOR DOWN
THEN
BY THE LOT'S END SUDDENLY
YOU'RE ALONE
HERE
MOON HIGH OVER THE SUPERMARKET
BEFORE THE IN-ROLLING FOG

CHEAP PLASTIC BRIEFCASE
CONFERENCE SOUVENIR
BEGINS
TO CRACK WITHIN A WEEK
SPECIAL CLIPPERS FOR TOENAILS
EMERY BOARD'S
SUBTLE SURFACE

ODD GLASSES
ONLY THE LOWER
CRESCENTS PRESENT
WAXED FLOSS
PASSES BETWEEN PLANES OF TEETH
RACIAL FORMATION IN THE NBA
GREEN PLASTIC DRAFTSMAN'S TEMPLATE

FIRST THEY COME FOR THE BROCCOLI
AND THEN THEY COME FOR US
WIRES PULL
THE PHONE POLE UP

ARBITRARY CODICITY ON THE DISK
LIKE SALIVA
ON YOUR CHIN

POINT AT WHICH
THE INSIDE
OF TENNIS SHOES BEGIN
TO DISSOLVE
SWEET TASTE
DISTINCT TO CANNED PEAS
BETRAYS RESTAURANT'S BROTH

WHAT IF THE COURSE OF HISTORY
WERE THE FAILURE OF NECESSITY
BIRDS SETTING DOWN ON THE EMPTY FEEDER
TWO KINDS
OF NUDITY
FRONTAL
AND PARTIAL

WHITE WOODFRAME HOUSE
BEHIND TALL CACTUS GARDEN
BRIGHT RED
CHINESE HEADLINES
UPON THE THINNEST OF PAPERS
BELT WORN
WITH HOLSTER'S SLANT

AT THE UNNAMED
LOCATE
AN IMPOSSIBLE HORIZON
BETWEEN PUBLIC AND PRIVATE
SMALL TOOL
THIS FUNCTION
NOT IMMEDIATELY EVIDENT

SKIN DRY ON FOREHEAD
                                        ITCHES
BUT FOR BAND OF OIL
WHERE I WEAR MY HAT
UNTIL THE PUS FORMS
LITTLE MOUNDS
                              PERFECTLY WHITE

                STRUCTURE AS PARANOIA
SPREADS
ROLLED FLAT OVER CHEESECLOTH
RAINBOW WINDKITE BANGS
HARDWOOD PORCH IS AN ADD-ON
                          BILLOWING CHINS
SWAMP NECK

          GROUNDCOVER SMOTHERS STONE
PATH
THEM WEEDS I LIKE
ALGAE FORMS RAINWATER SCUM
ALIVE IN OLD BARREL
AS WHEN
                ROSES GROW WILD

THE PLAN IS THE PLAN
                                    AN
ARTICLE OF FAITH
              CLOTHES THE NOUN
CLOSE
THE SCREEN DOOR
WIRES MAKE VERTICAL NET

PHLEGM DRIPS
                            FROM THROAT'S CAVERN
I'M JUST NOW SITTING UP

SUN SMEARS THE HORIZON
GREAT THRILL
        TO BREAK LINE
BRITTLE AS A BONE

WHY WE CALL THEM BINOCS
NOBODY KNOWS
         SHED AT REAR
OF LONG SLOPING YARD
IS AN ENCLOSED LEAN-TO
RED PATCH
      ON HUMMINGBIRD'S THROAT

I CARVE THESE LETTERS DEEP
INTO FLESH OVER DOTTED LINE
YOU'LL NEVER SEE
          DRIED PULP
MAKES A SURFACE
IS SEWN
    INTO BOOK

old threat of closure anew
nostalgic
    the dying moth
beats its wings in the dust
stellar jay's dark crown
midnight blue
      the creek's froth

sell tie-dye shirts
        at a concert
of the Dead
      that means
the path of history went that far

meandering as a brook and as certain
eventually to reach the sea

sitting
        she shuts her eyes
behind large dark sunglasses
headphones cup each ear's bowl
watchband worn
                    halfway to the elbow
helicopter tracing freeway's path

line locks the ear in
erase the will
            watch
as a verb
        sight
sweeps in focus
coin drops on the walk

let's identify a typical poetics
and call it populist
        reach out
to knock
ball from the thirdbaseman's glow
tap spoon
        to nostril

the bicyclist's gloves lack fingers
neo-leninist conception of error
we're number 1
            rubber finger
is virtually weightless
                tri-cornered
hat atop miss moore's head

wooden skeleton of new condo rises
                    to foretell the horizon
but history
          is not a prediction
button
dangling by a single thread
try shaving around the mole

wow
      hegemonic
hysteria = move my womb
                    vancouver is
the la jolla
of that comparison only
you reading distorts this

              don't have the trots
be one
                    command mode
likes to smile
enhanced graphics adaptor means nouns
anecdotes distort policy consider
green slime with a taste of lime

automatic feed is industrial policy
sez who
              plain state
to the freight train
                              cranes
arc out over stagnant bay
red baked baby potatoes

              workers of the west
invest
poor old tired ink

blackbirds
nesting in the letters at macy's
poem is accidentally demagnetized
is the best we can hope for

big fat emotional construct
called family
pronounced
as all three syllables
mommy, daddy and
suffix
no place like foam

cr,me of namedrop soup
hair juts from red nostril
caked with snot
dessert fork
at the head of each plate
tiny cuts of meaning
inflame eye

it gets harder
then
it gets caught in the zipper
pull of an old discourse
mounts a white horse
for contrast
as tonto is my panza

so ice cream dries in beard
red blood spilled
across editor's couch
for brightness
old rail tracks

decay in urban asphalt
plant just for ship propellers

ships propellers by truck
sullen afternoon bus
is really just exhaustion
                    group novels
by weight
shelf life
               of mid-list cult

torture your data
                              tone
in room absorbs echo
blackbirds gather on cut grass
                         profs note
fails to delete
red brick wall of reason

                                   earth turns
on an uncertain axis
ice melting shifts south pole
                    change machine refusing
to recognize
old crumpled dollar bill
now my paper is soft

tuck cuffs of sweat pants
inside socks
                    safe sex
softens edge of friendship
as talking is not anonymous
                         contrasted
to a nude beach

rigor of inhaling clogs
                        muscles
just to swallow
lungs a sad bellows
hot flame
                    of an old pump
will darken red meat

I don't need a 10-car train
when all I've got is my back brain
                    Oliver North
is the man
Dan White
                    always wanted to be
software by sectors

hidden on the hard disk
                                    eye
see sun and think blindspot
not a misspelling
                            be pun
and sink mind rot
red wine flashback years after

jaw's heat
                    inflamed
        fans out
up
the side of my face
as if each tooth's root were a wound
salt taste of blood in my mouth

chaos is not
an absence of order

nor pattern
a signal
of form
a house composed
entirely of add-ons

the dissent beckons as
the assent beckoned
harmony
is a kind of
misstatement
blurring truth tables with logic
shadows with their objects

limbs numb as if by nature
your job title is
courtesy bagger
toupee clashing with sideburns
architecture's not a hobby
tonite's rerun
charlie's angels

sign in please
voices burble
gargle over micro-speaker
of police cadet's walkie-talkie
smooth-faced boy with gun
beautiful old sikh's
beard in a knot

bee's about the fuchsia's mouth
I hear a scrub jay
see
ducks float thru the salt marsh
leaf

drops across the page
ink sinks into the grain

dog on the beach leaps high
but the frisbee sails overhead
good job poaching the salmon
but a poor cut
two girls
having the giggles
sell lemonade

that brown cloud there
is a brush fire
staining the sky
ignored
by these calm cows
nuzzling
at dry grass

the dissent bickers
as the assent battered
harmony
is a kind of
deceivement
old tune
relentless in my head

sometimes
about to make love
my hand falling on your thigh
senses muscle
a dancer's leg
instantly returns me
to a different center

red raw tear in the cuticle
empty swimming pool's perfect blue
stone floor
                    is passive solar collector
steamed oyster dissolves on tongue
                                        ring-necked bird is
semipalmated plover

                    thin book
a fly hums
right next to my ear
but the jet's engines echo
                                        off an
an otherwise empty sky
dry lip of the wilting rose

                    breeze imagined
as structured
flight plan of the butterfly
big jay in an old pine
this path of flat stones
overgrown
                    by ground cover

certain lines ragged as thought
          ought not to rhyme
spoon
scrapes against bowl bottom
clench hand to cover mouth
taming cough
                    civilization squints

various vireos
                    this is your life

and I'm an emotion
my dog has a limp
where his paw used to be
                    day pack
on a train track

                    odors or ardors
all is misgiven
green stone pulls the necklace down
to the freckles that announce your chest
not in the way a shade is drawn
                                but here's a bag lady
half-naked on the train

'squito bite on ankle itches
morning fog an objective condition
                        pigeons shape
telephone kiosk
hippy hackers joined at the modem
                        my eyes
is want to burst

earthquake's roll is lateral
imagined return to pageboy cut
phrase barely intelligible to sense
bruised thigh
                    juts from miniskirt
an eye having reddened
                                blinks

This train is bound for Fremont,
                        this train.
A complex joint
we call a wrist

                          rotates,
letters forming at the fingertips,
pen dragged to the right.

Helicopter's template was the dragonfly,
hovering in the hot dry air
lake still as the wind.
                                        Simple old
                                    obvious thought,
sharp as a sneeze,
is learned but not taught.

                                        Discarded,
banana peel browns.
Color as a verb marks linear process:
the child at first was blonde,
its mother frosted.
                                    Birds dart,
half-visible in the higher branches.

                                    Cedar waxwing's
yellow-tipped tail—
whole flock drunk with pyracantha.
Pony stands alone by the cactus.
                                        Out here
in 4-wheel drive land,
the flies are small and blue.

Little windmills in the vineyards
do not spin.
                        Turkey vultures
big as dogs
                      in a slow circle
serve their useful purpose.
Sweet smell of dark opal basil.

Red hats – corked bats.
Up against the walrus
dope heads on mopeds
slouch.
                She's dancing,
waltzing,
                to walkman's invisible music.

                                    Too little sleep
flattens perception,
a colorless morning,
                                    sun's dull glare.
Rooftop shingles seen from above
vs. gravely rolls of roofing felt,
"ranch style" versus "mission."

Cactus makes perfect.
                                        Ruffled undies
particular to square-dance
now in pastel.
                        The sharp sun
flat and hot in the hazy air
just over the low hills.

It's easier to hide in paragraphs,
an hysteric thrusting his arms about
                creates the bluster of panic
mirrored
in the officer's impenetrable shades.
                                    Try and identify
road kill silhouettes.

Form as brittle as good behavior
unfathomed.
                    Large black valise

bearing artist's portfolio
difficult to lug through traffic.
                    Perfumed flap
to ad in mag.

Sikhs at a streetfair
offer free massage –
                              muscle
at neck's base pulls tight,
        gripping the ear.
Hear
sullenness in that polka.

Mosquitoes crackle
                              up against the bug light,
                      dawn of a hot day.
Secret softness
at the heart of the Fat Boys
marks them "not threatening"
versus the Beasties suburban terror.

                    They who mediate
serve as cops,
                      a new criterion.
Old Tang vase
gets quietly auctioned
in a room full of short men
and the inevitable blonde women,

Tall, young, very professional.
                          Robopoet,
meet my macro.
Clothespins on an empty line,
wood frame of an unfinished house.

Found language
in a candidate's speech.

Alphabet seen
not as a line
but a cycle,
or torso and spine
merely as where limbs run together,
skulls in infinite variety,
this a melon, that a flower,

And this something stepped upon.
Let us jog then
you and I
through fluorocarbons in the sky
whose particles will get you ghi
until your prose
becomes unstable

Imitating modes of speech
each to each.
Small boy puffs his cheeks out wide.
At third base
rotund coach
scratches for hit and run.
Toward a theory of shaped billboards

Please post this call for papers.
The violence of the pun
is repressed analogy
unleashed:
tenures that shook the world.
Salt in my sweat stings my eyes.
Sound of a bell on a bike.

Let's alter Altieri.
                                        Gesture of respect
for the work of the "avant-garde"
demonstrating feint before the hook.
                                                    Denotation's husk
surrounds meat of noun,
damp fuzzy swirl of meanings.

                                    Deaf girl
(not a girl at all
but a tall, strong young woman)
alone at a bus stop
                                        talking
to herself with her hands.
Tonight's the anniversary of grandma's death,

So frail at the end,
                                        bruised
hanging flesh
            and wrists so thin,
"Red-
headed matches, six cents"
for what can never be sold

Is all in the telling.
                                        Carbonation
entitles you
to gulp the drink.
Expensive restaurant's
                                            thick rug
requires constant care.

The man in the wheelchair
not wearing shoes.

The robin flew in through
                the window
and settled
on a high
              closet shelf.

Magical thinking:
                          shortstop
won't change his clothes
in the midst of a hitting streak.
Hard edged,
                  well-trimmed hedge
yellow for lack of water.

Second half of the reading
is more intimate —
from the cellar
                    two flights down
blond blues band
                          hopeful frats
in muscle shirts and jamms

Imitate B.B. King.
                          The prices on
the menu have been crossed out
             and new, higher ones
inked in.
Without a theory for institutionalizing
its victories (rare enough), the left

Would have nothing to offer
even the most ardent
                    believers in justice.
Small children

fart freely.
Sniffing poppers
on a crowded bus,

Or else grading restaurants
not by the food
but what
you learn walking back
to the john.
Frosted panes
here on dawn windows

Registers the difference
between indoors and out.
No theory
of the line
without its history also.
Plastic pen
lies snapped

On the floor of the train.
Even the clown's tennies
are bright pink,
hair
the color of
a new penny.
Reagan's plaid weekend shirt.

Tracks disappear in the distance
(one point perspective)
sucked
into the gray horizon,
shadows
without options
cast by the mechanical sun.

Machination sleazes powder.
The further it spins out,
                                        accumulates
the greater the distance,
a curiously cold quality
like one's face in the mirror,
                                            unfamiliar.

                              Jaw tightens
to stifle the yawn,
flexing the hand to prompt circulation,
sodium vapor glare in a dense fog,
gum stiff in its tinfoil
                              is covered
with sugar powder.

The urge for burgers
          hardens the 'g.'
A man
wheeling kegs of beer on a dolly
in shirt sleeves in the rain
grins
     and seems balder

Here under the streetlamp,
each of us casting multiple shadows.
Sound particular to a bowling alley,
                              earmuffs
of an airport techie
                              frame the janitor's
bulb-shaped head.

I imagine night as real
yet hardly believe that,
relaxing to see

familiar dawn
outline the far hills
as cereal swells
absorbing milk.

Nixon,
the last modernist president,
stalks the fog-shrouded heath
not recognizing Kissinger disguised.
Velcro tugs at itself.
White bull terrier
advertising beer

With black patch
over left eye
bites and won't let go.
My name is we
whispers the winged horse
in neon
over the gas station.

Front of the book
versus the back.
Workshop poets function as control group.
Handsome couple framed in brass
elliptical frame atop dresser
stare out
into my bedroom.

Butterfly bumps against window.
A breeze bends the roses
and so they sway.
A sheer light
fills the room
which expands
as the noontime drifts.

UNDER

for Krishna Evans

Confused, ants huddle abut the box of chocolates for warmth. In an open cauldron (my skull), syntax simmers. Query this.

This town, because imagined, is both small and infinite. Jade tree wilted by the freeze. Restaurant uses old washing machine to poach its fish, while the dryer spins lettuce. One of us is real, says the mirror, but which?

Vast grid of pores needs a shave. When in the course of cumin events.

As I approach the house, a dog behind its door starts to bark. Because of resemblance, the citizens call the clock atop the factory the Polish moon. A chair is an argument about the nature of form.

Garbagemen at dawn spill excess on the lawn. I make a song of it and then I make a fist. Blisters burst, becoming flowers. This trail of crumbs we call a line. The time is 7:26.

Old man does a box step with the memory of his wife. When children talk of fathers, I simply grow quiet. The lone lamp flickers in the shadowy room, being that it's a TV set.

Confused, artists huddle around the grants program for warmth. When fathers talk of children, I simply grow quiet.

Patios of fortune: the sun rises through the trumpetflower vines. Head and arms burrow their way through the t-shirt. Pretend to ignore refrigerator's song.

Morning staggers you. The rain is unexpected. The skin of the banana so thick you can barely burst it open. A jar of seeds, possibly edible. The sound of small aircraft makes you hum.

Streetlamps penetrate shade. House, vulnerable through its windows. Stack of old egg cartons. Machine of the ankle gone to rust. Streetlight impersonates shape.

Bodies decomposing in a small mountain lake – the dream is more real than I care to imagine – but my backpack turns into a balloon pulling me up and free of these brambles, these tugging vines.

Amateur hour at the White House. We walk through a fog not of moisture, but of talcum powder, coughing and choking, blinded, led only by the smell of blood. Sand flies settle in the wound.

Birds shun the oleander. Elongated skull (Garrick Utley) grins out of the small box, sound off. The way laces wrap the shoe to the foot.

The hand is a machine for grabbing hold, the ground a vehicle for shadow. Here we organize each tribe around a football team, a baseball franchise. We make lists – parrots learn to recite them.

View of man urinating, towering over porcelain bowl of water.

Robert Duncan, alive in my dreams! Decades of memory versus memory of decades, strung together first this way, then that. I'm walking along narrow, sloping streets (many citizens are leading burros) until I arrive at City Lights. An explosion frozen in green is served with butter. What time is it in Iraq?

The TV shows (over and over) young men loading jets, jets taking off, jets landing (unedited US pool coverage), the President at his desk hallucinating a fantasy of force and justice, or a map over which come the voices of CNN reporters in a hotel room without lights or water. It's dyin' time.

Green sky at night: bombers' delight. At the office, people stop to whisper the words "Tel Aviv." In the car, I barely remember the mechanics of driving. On the radio, some station still plays music. A crow on the White House lawn innocent of history.

Trucks a lot. Zubin Mehta inspects a crater. Acoustics of the toilet two rooms away.

Nights of anxious sleep.

A plastic bucket blows around the yard in a strong wind. As my sun sets, day begins in Australia. "Let's revisit that target-rich environment," the general says. The reporter's name is Wolf Blitzer. Bright pink, the Everready bunny beats its drum through my dream.

Stars crowd the morning sky, then dissolve in the coming light. A sea of faces, eyes, cheeks, lips parades past, men pushing strollers, women holding banners, drums and tambourines, people stare out of windows looking far into the distance, the line never ends but bends and turns, the serpent of peace weaves through the City.

The unbearable whiteness of being. In the dream, I snap the pea pod open to release a small person (waking, I recognize it as a body bag). With the first dose, the vet renders the cat unconscious and, with the second, it dies.

With the first blast, the boy becomes a vet. Some scars never heal. The man in the cape loudly enters the reading, accompanied by three aging lady Theosophists. Into each white space, listen to the count of three beats. Some cars never feel right to the driver.

A rose in a box, ready for planting. Long loaf of bread with its tip severed sits atop the cutting board. A wire basket in which to drain dishes – its fingers hold cups, glasses aloft.

In the dream, I've rented a furnished room in San Francisco and can see the history of each site, each building, simply by staring. The man with my grandfather's build stares pensively from the mirror. Butter steams up from these spears of asparagus. The sun returns, not having learned its lesson.

The spectacle of thousands forming one flag (halftime at the Super Bowl) brings a smile to the führer's face. Now a message from George and Bar, her dress television red. Video taken from the very nose of the missile blanks out before we see the astonished whites of the bunker crew's eyes. On the wall of the Vietnam War Memorial in Washington, what you do not see are the names of one million-plus Vietnamese.

A gull, wings extended, remains motionless as the fog rushes by, effortless flight. A chair on which to store only unread magazines (hear that as a verb: unread magazines). In the dark dogs do bark.

The morning of the logicians. Still life with banana and wrist watch.

The sun illumines the bottom of these small clouds as it sets. In a hotel, listening to the shower in other suites. Across is a highrise that leaves its lights on all night, entire floors trashed out, unrented.

An entire day without setting foot on the ground floor, let alone the ground. Watch for the right pipe.

Then beam the music in. A gang of teens seeks someone to buy a sixpack. Violets against women. Is it a living or is it Memorex? The sun returns for more.

So I stand on the porch in a dense fog, hearing the sparrow in the bare tree. Having died, the old washer in the pantry has become a table for homeless potted plants. Thirteen ways of scratching at a blackboard.

Never whine, Sensodyne. Pots atop the counter await their turn in the sink. Lone spider crosses the vast pattern of linoleum as the shadow of huge shoe crunches down. His nickname among the troops is Old Friendly Fire. It's not the wind whistling we mind, it's the tune.

Homes that people return to after work. The new printed sheets are stiff, having never been washed (making the bed, we disagree as to which side of the top sheet is "up"). That wonderful dimple where the leg joins the ass. Your lips cling, firmly grasping the head of my dick until again I push slowly and slide in. We hear hummingbirds in the dark.

One-hit wonders: the smell of toilets in a drought. Object oriented dBase dreams – that last word (is/is not) a verb. More to the spots on that plant than aphids. The cheetah looks up from PBS.

Lion still. When in the dream you speak, Sean Connery's Scottish brogue flows from your lips. Helena Bennett asks, "Why don't you poets just mud wrestle?" Pace at which a flower unfurls.

Enjambed by millions. When the alarm goes off I see a color, more accurately a pattern, a plaid, before I hear the sound. Collateral damage lies bleeding in the rubble. I get off the freeway at the next exit and follow along the frontage road to avoid the backup created by a four-car crash. Tie a yellow ribbon, a tourniquet, a noose.

Write by numbers. Make of the stove a face (the broiler is its jaw). I climb up the stairs of the old ruined hotel only to discover the seashore's on the second floor, sun-splashed lagoon. A jarful of pennies from foreign lands. Sounds of the dog actually catching the cat.

Sugar push. What makes a sparrow chatter in the dark? After hours, the bottle gang drifts down to the Taco Bell, settling in on its concrete tables and benches. A homeless man's puppy, leashed to the shopping cart. In West Coast Swing, the step is called The Whip.

With dreams this detailed I should take notes. Prose poem as prototype of mixed-use development. Kathleen Fraser, Steve Benson and I on a corner of the financial district where the sun sets early even on Sunday. Banana slug rejected as state mollusk. Moment at which the ocean catches fire.

This is the book of drumming, each sentence, each syllable. A cheese and kitchen shop, but in the basement under the street a vast cafe. The old drunk had a calloused nose. I'd thought the slogan was "No blood for owls."

Bend the page back till the binding breaks. Lucite dreaming. The dead are more numerous now and will be more numerous still. Smart bombs, stupid people.

Gaelic garlic. Within minutes, the spin control is whirring, explaining how they knew the building, sandwiched between a school and a recreation yard in a residential neighborhood was "legitimate" as a military target, down to architectural drawings, even if, during the Iran-Iraq war, it had been built originally as an air-raid shelter, but did not know now why 400-plus civilians, many of them children, would actually be inside when the first bomb pushed through the steel-reenforced concrete roof and the second right through that hole to explode and burn them all alive. Neighborhood Swatch. The shadows on the screen become articulate as the doctor moves the ultrasound probe: "These are your ovaries." You point to the place on the freeway where yesterday a body bag held the corpse of a 13-year-old boy.

Aftertaste of toothpaste. Forethought of policy. Fivespot on the electric scale by the register as the cafeteria employee totals up my lunch.

Mourning doves in fog. Events subtracted from history. Male culture does not equal foreign policy. In the oven, coils glow with heat.

The owls are not what we deem. Describe each vent (there are five) rising from the neighbor's house. The way the blue shades in advance of the sun. You breathe as you sleep (peacefully) and I listen as if to the music of the waves. Put two infant twins asleep at opposite ends of the same crib and they will soon curl together, taking the same positions they held in the womb.

Sound of a distant train (I'm still in bed, half awake): where is it heading and with what? We lie flat on the freshly cut grass, talking with our eyes shut, feeling the sun. The counterperson brings my tea in a bowl. The sound of a jet completely fills the sky, then fades away.

Elvis sings of the Bossa Nova. Next morning, the kitchen and dining room still smell of meatloaf. What if, muses Harry Allen, instead of racism and its cognates, we substitute the phrase white supremacy – which aspects then become more clear? The house is dark because it's too vast to be lived in really, the kitchen with two stoves, a dining room solely for formal occasions, the sitting room in front his mother uses to entertain her friends painted an odd deep brown with many small shelves, each holding a single antique porcelain doll, all of which we pass through until we arrive at the sun room with its view of the bay and four counties.

Banana too sweet at the bruise. Glasses sit at the tip of my nose until a finger pushes them back. Theory of which plates go into what cupboard. Is that fern happy?

Right by design. Write, writhe, ridden. With a first twirl of the cap, I break the seal on the gas tank and step back to let the pressurized air hiss past, inhaling that distinct gasoline smell. Wondering, each time I turn the radio or television on, has the ground war begun? Tapioca cake with coconut frosting, the end of a perfect Laotian meal.

Graffiti fades from the walls of the hard drive through the tunnel. New highrises glisten for a little while until the same grime that turns snow to a brown slush settles in. The fascination my grandfather held for trains, airplanes, vessels of all sort, the cul-de-sac on the hill he went whenever he could on a Saturday just to watch the locomotives grind by, reflect a childhood spent in the 19th century, a sense of awe at machinery that he thought my brother and I foolish not to share (sitting in the '51 Pontiac waiting to catch the eye of the man in the caboose and wave).

Plotting signage, color code the networks: red for Ethernet, blue for token ring, green for LocalTalk. I hear voices of old friends in the dream, rapid intimate conversation, but I never see any of them. We are running, trying to catch our train but the station is underground in a tunnel but there's been a wreck, green twisted metal, and people are swarming over the broken car not to rescue or escape but simply to reach the next set of tracks where a new train arrives and then pulls through without stopping, a destination sign on its cabin unmistakably reading *Formula.*

A woman with one ear plugged with cotton pushes her way into the laundromat with a basket of clothes already soaking wet. One of the two live screens in the video store is for security. In the garden you crouch to examine the volunteer lettuce. The *Examiner* runs the total news blackout on page ten of the Sunday edition. It's sweeps month in the sands of Kuwait.

InterCaps: deviance or innovation? How sweetly, smoothly I slip inside of you where I belong. Cat sleeps in the unused driveway, concrete warmed by the sun.

VOG: Am I my banana's keeper? I traipse over to the mailroom to send a fax just to get away from my desk. Hopyard, willow – street names trace an erased landscape. Angular gait of an egret through the reeds of the drainage ditch. Through the rearview mirror, I watch the expressions of the young couple in the pickup truck behind me, the man's long blond hair jutting from a baseball cap worn sideways, as they read the "No Blood for Oil" sticker on the rear of my car.

The only light in the dark is on in the bathroom – I too stare at myself in the mirror as I brush my teeth. The yellow ribbon as a Claes Oldenburg sculpture on a mass scale, entitled Soft Swastika. Orange peel without the orange (sits atop the cutting board). Murdering thousands, the President warns that we must "guard against euphoria."

The banana freckles overnight. I wake exhausted from the shouting and venting of emotion the night before. Note to the typesetter: you can't always get what you font. Don't say don't. The sea, gray and vast in every direction.

I wake to the sound of a hard rain and walk around the house just listening, careful not to go into the rooms where the motion detectors are armed.

In the dream three former lovers insist that I choose: they are beautiful, brilliant, intense women, each one aflame around a hard lava core of anger. The door to the attic contains a flimsy retracting ladder. Does the moon effect these tides of sinus? First green sprouts out of the planter box foretell a spring of lettuce. During the periods when my grandmother had one of her "spells," psychotic episodes that could last for months, my grandfather never complained but instead would gain weight rapidly as if swelling with stress. This man works the parking lot day after day, asking each motorist if he or she would like to have their windows washed.

Rooster in the distance yodels for the sun. Dreams lack closure. In Houston, you are either in or out of the loop. Cackle of the grackle.

I take the imperial roll and place it in the lettuce leaf along side the mint and cilantro, then roll this all together and dip it in the sauce. Neighborhood in which dogs wander around loose. I step up to the podium and the stage lights make the audience disappear. The young couple just back from India so fresh-faced and full of theoretical energy. My bedroom is a mattress on the floor at the end of a long closet.

Standing O. Windchimes at night, neighbor's delight. I can tell if you're sleeping by the way you breathe. Waitress, an older woman, walks with a limp and wears a button that reads "Be nice or get out." Wood frame houses with stacks of cinder blocks for their foundations.

Phantom toothache. Pigeons in the bath at math. Send valid packets over unshielded twisted-pair out to the printer, soft fonts in a hard copy. Coils of an electric stove: bottom of the oven is an inverted M. I write poetry the way some men make waste – to exercise my bowels at large, stools twisted into a perfect circle.

Wild parrots in the middle of the night. My little car shudders crossing the bridge in the wind. Unreal hue of light in the tunnel. Catfish in coconut milk wrapped in leaves. Because we are Laotian, we don't use chopsticks.

Just as I'm about to jump over the river, the alarm clock rings. One needle with which to draw and mix the medicines, the other to pop you in the butt.

The chair in the middle of the room under the light fixture with the broken bulb. Egg cartons stacked under the pantry sink, an impulse toward recycling, an index of cholesterol. Old friend fridge shudders and is silent. Barefoot, my wife walks on the heels of her feet down the hardwood hall. Peel open the can of frozen OJ.

The hummingbird's wings, as it hovers poised at the edge of the fuchsia, appear translucent. Rain on the glass at last. Windchimes, furious with percussion.

A woman approaches our table, offering to do handwriting analysis for just seven dollars. I walk into Specs for the first time in a decade and nothing's changed, tho the graffiti on the urinal wall is a little more *au currant.* It only takes the mechanic a second to jump start my car, parked fortunately in front of the one building, a Chinese restaurant, open and active on a rainy Sunday night. What's remarkable in the logic of this dream is not that I've been castrated and wear my genitals in a sack around my neck, but that they still respond to the presence of a beautiful woman.

I stare out over the field, hearing the killdeer but unable to see it. Dark smoke spirals up from deep within the property of the county jail, but from here it's impossible to tell what's burning. The rain has stopped and, as I look up into the night sky, I see what I think are stars. Greeting card stores in the mall, green this week for St. Patrick's Day, feel as if there should be a pharmacy in the rear. How did that little bird get such an unattractive name?

Umbrellas open, drying on the back porch, my raincoat draped over a chair. Steady as a drip from a leaky faucet, the kitchen clock ticks. Scratched-out words freckle the page.

There's a stillness, a serenity, at the center of our relationship I cannot otherwise describe and would not have anticipated, twelve years ago, that night, at nearly one in the morning, when I reached out and you asked me "What are your intentions?" (a question I could not then have answered, replying "Let's discuss it in the bedroom"), but which now, whenever I feel angry or in turmoil or despair, I need only to focus on and the calming begins and spreads through me, radiant heart of peace, woman who sleeps next to me, breathing softly, and with whom I will grow old, each day deeper in love than the day before.

Hours are waking's stages. Pages facing pages ablaze with ink. Plug-and-play: *say wha . . .* ? A beat, two feet; a street, too neat: iambs of the past blast off faster than a speeding planet.

The trees at first catch, then amplify, sounds of the storm. Baby at the stage when he can pull himself up but not take a step without support. In the midst of all this rain, one steady drip has a particularly metallic sound. I give you the design for a garden.

But what's in those plastic trash bags she has piled into that shopping cart she pushes through the streets day after day, more difficult here given the hillsides of North Beach, only to return each night to the doorway of the same swank Jackson Square interior decorator's showroom/office, and how does she manage to care for that pugnosed terrier constantly at her side?

In the laundromat a young man is playing chess alone on a small magnetic board. The idea of a mandocello. It's late afternoon in the Berkeley hills and the rain stops just long enough for us to stand outdoors and watch the low clouds sweep past the Golden Gate and over the bay.

Let's cut a deal. Words clutter the mind the way small objects fill an attic, spilling suddenly through a trap door. I dream I am Richard Nixon and Gerald Ford takes the oath of office on a high cliff overlooking water (toward which I plunge, fully clothed, waking before I hit).

Bananas of the rich and famous. Able to sweep tall buildings in a single round. When this you see, apple tree, there's a blight. Georgia pun. Skull understood as the spine's blister, filled with pus.

Trying to fathom my father as a victim, double phantom, do I deny my smouldering rage? The infant you had hoped to adopt has died. She's the oldest of seven, her mother one of 16, her grandmother one of 23, and at 31 she feels betrayed completely by her own hostile mucous. I don't want to be here, you say, I want to be home with my child. If only.

Token Ring or Ethernet, a connection's made. We suppress our surges, booting up. Left-handed mouse. Here's a house in which words are hidden. Echo Lally.

Terry and the Pyrex. No, here, use a spoon to gouge words from the meat of the paper. Old friends hugging one another, at once awkward and warm. Avascular necrosis of the hip joint – Bo knows pain. The little boy counts to sixty to show he can.

In the dream I return to a campus tho the buildings are not the same, nor is the landscape, and yet I know my way around. A "carrot" below the line (‸) points to a word inserted, latecomer to the gang of text. He parks his car on the front lawn. You reach over the side to lend the first person out of the lifeboat a hand. The sun sets in their backyard.

The conversion of taste into aftertaste. You can tell the direction the wind is blowing by which windows are struck by these hailstones in mid-afternoon, little spots of ice sliding down the glass. After her father dies, a woman holds a garage sale, shady place filled with old lawn mowers, rusted tools, and a world dissolves. The way we nose ourselves through an open house on a weekend, you're standing in someone's bedroom, imagining a closet. The woman tries to shelter the man under her umbrella, but he's taller so it keeps hitting him in the head.

Thunder ripples across the sky, undulating the entire length of it, and is answered by the dishes and saucers in the cupboard, dancing in reply. That place on the inside of your thigh, just below the crotch, where the skin's so soft. Now the rain begins and I wish I was thinner. The train's whistle, distant, is moving south. The taste of toothpaste still in my mouth.

Trickle charge that battery. What do cyborgs want? Demonstrating multiplatform interoperability, the language poet speaks to a cat. A term without quotation marks licks its paw. The Dalmatian symbolizes Hewlett-Packard.

Completely alone at night in the city, nobody on the streets, everyone asleep, there's still a hum – this would be a great time to go jogging if I felt safe (as it is, the cops would stop me, or worse). He's wearing a thick blue sweater with a patch on the arm, where recently it's been cut to permit an IV tube (only later, waking, do I wonder why nobody just rolled up his sleeve). I'm running through the streets of a city I know only to meet you at the station (plane or bus or train, I don't know which), afraid that I've missed the day's last run and we'll be stranded, or worse, you'll have gone off without me.

Mockingbird tries a new riff. The first day after a long storm, people still wear raincoats, carry umbrellas. This sentence has politics. That woman, still asleep in the doorway I saw her in twelve days ago, has survived the rain and this wind. What kind of name is Cokie?

Two-tone foghorn, simple song. Rhyme and punishment. At the Deja Vu Cafe, homestyle quiche means it's microwaved. A plant that visibly sags when it's low on water. The plum tree crazy with blossoms and a sparrow hopping about.

Smell of the half-mowed lawn. Little pots of lithodora, intense blue flowers. I watch a tiny, buff-colored spider climb an invisible thread to the ceiling. The sky overcast seems no sky at all – the whole world feels enclosed. In bed, I stare at the surface of the stucco ceiling, searching to find a pattern.

A woman ironing clothes in her kitchen wears only a t-shirt as her roommates, male and female, wander through the house. We discover the blackout driving home, so pull a little mag light from the glove compartment and fumble our way into the house, you pulling out the candles while I round up the flashlights within. Because our neighbor is working on her pea-green Volkswagen within feet of our bedroom window, we make love in silence, using eye contact and our hands to tell one another what we like and want.

The hands of a woman barber. I stand in line at the taqueria, watching the beans settle atop the surface of the tortilla as the young man reaches for the next spoon, which will be chicken. I look up and you've already gone to bed.

Gross testicle review. A bruise at the tip of the banana. Do our dreams go on without us when we wake? What I first thought on rising to be exhaustion turns out to be a sadness deep as these bones. Now I know you're the mockingbird.

I may look like I'm asleep, but really I'm writing. Aftertaste of chocolate cheesecake, foretaste of you: I unbutton your shirt and lean forward to kiss what we call your "nibbles." Could the engine of history be any louder than the one in that refrigerator? How odd to hear a small airplane at the very crack of dawn.

The year, you know, understood as a form, starts out cold then moves to warm, the leaves they fall and it all starts back to rain and thunder and that's a wrap. Tableaux of people ordering food in a diner: warm colors, between red-orange and brown, an owl outside the window, each waitress in the same sky blue uniform, and in the foreground, larger than anything, a glass pot of black coffee and a blood-red slice of cherry pie. A taste of bunny, tasting much sweeter than slime (a taste of money, tasting much sweeter than rhyme). She's naked, body painted to reveal every inner organ, each sinew of ligament and muscle wrapped around bone. Photo of a bullet bursting through the watermelon's flesh.

Canseco hits the pop fly so far above the lighting that he's already standing on second when it pops from the startled infielder's grasp. The final for. Five years ago today, I was about to become a married man – enormous bustle, since it poured the night before and we could no longer hold the event in the park, my sense of surprise when the music began to play.

The ocean pushes hard against the continent, these cliffs, this strip of sand. The tongue pushes hard against these consonants. The black-bellied plover in full breeding plumage, cinnamon teal, common loon, a lone Brant's goose so squat it reminds one of the Ne-Ne, rare state bird of Hawaii. Boneless chicken breast stuffed with pesto. People are starving.

Just say MOOO! If you see that lone Northern shoveler, right behind it on the little island, half way back on all that dry grass, nearly camouflaged, just occasionally flashing that white on his butt, a Northern harrier tears and pulls at its food. An entirely sunny day, but with the wind so harsh that in mid-afternoon people on the beach are still wrapping themselves in blankets. Even in 1991 you can still refer to a woman simply by the color of her hair: the young redhead ran past us to shout something at her boyfriend in the ponytail, but her language wasn't English or anything even remotely Western European, unless possibly Basque. In the dream a young woman, a stranger, is swallowing, attempting to swallow, impossible amounts of cum shooting from my dick.

Singing in the brain, just singing in the brain. The age at which friends disappear: she steps from the StairMaster, lies on a bench, shuts her eyes, and never breathes again, never even hears the chaos that's about to begin. He never once in all those years wrote, nor even sent a card or photo. Infants grieve. In a dream I've had twice now I'm just getting involved with a young woman when suddenly she dies and what I'm left with are her effects.

I close the book, turn out the light, and shut my eyes, the words only then starting a slow dissolve. We talk long in your livingroom as the sun sets, until even your silhouette starts to disappear from the lack of light. You hand me a check in a "lucky" envelope. You is an other. Words without which every other word feels trapped.

Tape *Twin Peaks.* Prepare to fly. Think short sentences. The wind shoves the dark. I wake in a sweat.

Pueblo deco. The high-desert homeless huddle on the mall, overdressed for the midday heat. Aftertaste of pizza. It's not the wind, but the sand in the wind – in our hair, teeth and nostrils.

Electricity's not static. Begin a phone conversation with "There's been an accident. . . ." Floodgates of the cardiovascular system. A blanket shrouds the worn cushions of a couch as I sit in a livingroom 800 miles from you. A young woman reads a long short story about her trip to Leningrad many years ago, and of her failed attempts to find the privacy to have sex with a married man, her voice still filled with a tone of loss.

Reconstruct the sofa bed, as if solving a puzzle, and the room itself becomes transformed. In the dream, it's a race of only three or four blocks, each of us taking a different street, but suddenly I'm unable to stand, so am crawling painfully forward, the sidewalk by the old school torn up, becoming narrower and narrower, until I look up and see the curious stare of a Doberman pinscher right in my path. In the dream, the plot of *Twin Peaks* is acted out by the cast of *Hill Street Blues.* In the vast night sky west of the Sangre de Christo mountains high white clouds appear to have their bottoms sheared off.

The old gray cat hisses at the sight of the new orange kitten. Those nipples in the landscape to the west of town are still called volcanoes. As we fuck, our eyes gradually adjust to the dark, our lips to the taste of one another's organs. Many people close their eyes as the airplane taxis for its takeoff. The dogs of poetry jump against the chain link fence.

The lens of time, perpetually out of focus, shifts toward a new resolution. The language of metaphor, not the metaphor of language, a skinny fat kid with a long flowing crewcut. Here doggy, nice doggy, that's right, don't bite. How does the detective know which object in the room will have the false bottom that, when removed, will reveal the telltale clue? Through narrative.

It's raining and dark in the Tenderloin of the imagination, if that's where dreams hide, and the people who emerge from the downpour include some I haven't seen in fifteen years. Mountain of dishes stacked high in the drainer beside the sink. A sparrow sounds its predawn note over and over. In Santa Fe, I stand in the oldest house in America, reading the names of teenagers carved into its clay walls. I wonder how many people from the dream are still alive today.

HELP MEDICAL EMERGENCY read the words stamped into the snow. The neighbors and I are fighting an apartment house blaze with garden hoses, not doing a bad job, when the fire department arrives in the Batmobile. I find our Mazda in the towing company's garage – next to a little sky blue VW bug with a police department "hold for prints" sign on its windshield – and realize for the first time the massive impact with which you were struck – just two feet over and I'd've been a widower. It's the middle of a weekday but instead we come home and make love, letting all our emotions transform themselves into the physical effort. In the dream, the three little trick-or-treaters refuse to turn around, and I realize that one must be my potential daughter.

The tone of the dark changes – day is on its way. The tall young janitor with the shoulder-length hair is found to have $50,000 worth of stolen computer equipment in his livingroom and is led out to the policecar in handcuffs. I stand atop the diningroom table to unscrew the globe from the ceiling, both bulbs burned out. The next morning, the smell of meatloaf lingers in the air, heavy with onion-soup basting. "I speak for everyone, but only as myself," says Barrett in the five-year-old video, about to toast my wife and I at our wedding, fluted glasses held high.

All that remains of the Mazda sits on the dining room table. Drag the chair over the hardwood floor. On the split screen, two young men raise one arm and make a fist, one a skinhead, the other African-American. Little jar of almonds. Semi4 (sum against).

A word in the hand is worth two in the text. A bush in the sand next to the sea. Saw rusting in an unlit cellar.

The hair in my armpit somehow knotted. Waking is in some sense a condition of gravity, which is why I set the alarm clock at a distance where I have to stand to reach it. Cream the butter, the recipe says. A trio of young Jewish boys, the oldest no more than ten, their long sideburns twisting down their cheeks, complete with skullcaps, unusual to see in a suburban California laundromat. Having unmade the bed, we lie on the bare mattress and kiss.

Is this sleep or is it an embrace? A dream can make me angry without even understanding the object of my emotion. The face of Edgar Allan Poe upside down on a coffee cup hanging from the side of the drainer.

Where words go when they're scratched out. Sleeping on your side, where do you put your bottom arm? Dressed only in pantyhose, you're blow-drying your hair in front of the bedroom mirror as I slowly massage your shoulders, then give you a gentle back scratch. I walk through the office supplies store the way teens haunt a music shop, the deep browse. Where sentences go if I forget to write them down.

Android or cyborg, which one? Insect replicant. The mother of all boards in need of a chip. Make mine chocolate. Stupid vendor tricks.

Insect repellant: when this you spy, FSI. No baseball players have Islamic names. Searching through owl balls for little bones.

Sparrow's eros spirals song. The days are a little longer. Instead of having vendors selling beer in the stands of the Oakland Coliseum, they now sell pizza. When he speaks of his wife's cancer, he gets a far-off look. The minute he's back from the Persian Gulf, she wears her brother's naval officer's jacket to work.

Placards of bad American humor behind the counter of the ribs joint: "A woman's place is in the mall," "Please remove ski mask and unload gun before ordering," "What part of NO don't you understand?" Mushrooms grow on the base of compost mounds. A dad throws batting practice for his son with a lemon-colored tennis ball, garage-door backstop. Jay's song in the city drowned out by the small Cessna. "Funny, he's spraying where they ain't no crops."

Walking through the dark house on a moonlit night, the light casts flattened shadows. Dr. Cricket, I presume. Sitting in the 323 at the Mazda dealer's, nostrils full of that new car smell, I imagine the force that crushed the engine of our old car amidst all that rush-hour traffic, you at the wheel miraculously unhurt. Putting dishes from the drainer back into their proper stacks in the cupboard, the spoons into the spoon slot in the tray in the silverware drawer, the pots down underneath, chores as a mechanism for acknowledging emotion. Having unbuttoned all twenty buttons of your nightie this morning, now you want me to button them all back up.

That soft spot on the inside of your thigh. Sore spot at the base of the spine. Little heat spell in April comes to an end. This isn't sorting the mail, it's triage. Encapsulated PostScript.

The salesman plays good cop, taking our bid for the car back to the manager, who plays bad cop and wants more money. I wake from the complex, disjointed narrative of the dream, wondering what happens next. From her expression, I can tell that she can't stand it when I crack my knuckles in staff meetings. The smell of onions cooking drifts over the gray cubicles of the office from the cafeteria kitchen. So instead of sleeping with lots of people for money, she fucks just one several times each day on a tiny stage, the audience pumping quarters to keep the pay-per-view windows open, neither she nor her partner (who's not her "boyfriend") coming until the final show of the afternoon, so that the taste of his cum becomes associated in her mind with the release from work.

Words gather gradually in the recess of the mind, forming lines random and rowdy as schoolchildren in a yard until order itself settles them down and together we come inside. Flares glow strangely at dusk, forming a path up to the overturned big rig. Nineteenth century French impressionist clouds cross the valley sky.

The window white with the light behind the shade, precursor to the sun. An owl with the habits of a gopher. Asked what it's like for a woman to write poetry in the Soviet Union today, Nina Isrenko says, "It's like being in the men's room." He calls his health club the aluminum farm. Gradually the owl coaxes me away from its nest, out of which pops its mate, the two chattering at me at once.

Reading the slogan on my t-shirt backwards in the mirror. Out the windows on one side of the house, it's sunny, the start of a gorgeous day, but out the windows on the other, gray and foreboding. Words flesh the syntax out. "Cheer up," says Zhdanov, thinking he's said goodbye. The owl's eyes are a deep yellow.

Schemistry. Birds burst out of the low plum tree as I jog under. The hills, invisible in this mist, soon to appear. Two flies dispute the territory of the porch. I shut my eyes to fully absorb the different songs.

A country-and-western singer hitches his way up the small logging and ski towns of the Sierra, playing for contributions in bars to make ends meet. I was a high-risk teen. The cat doesn't run as the car approaches, the way a dog might, but rather walks quickly, a sort of power walk, scooting under a parked truck just before the auto barrels through, all this played out in the twin spots of the car's headlamps. In New Mexico, people complain of the wind because of the grit that's in the air, the breeze, tho harsh, nothing to compare with those at Candlestick in right field, Candy Maldonado cringing under a fly ball.

When a linebreak meets a margin
out there on the edge
then a linebreak forms a version
and marks a textual wedge
that in prose appears to stumble, but for all the right reasons. That instant when we both know I've slipped inside and the twinkle in your eye that responds. Hard pelvic bone under soft curling hair, or the salty taste of labia just after you've urinated. Helicopters fly by, hoping to catch a glimpse. A suddenly serious look on your face means you're about to come.

"I don't drink in Moscow," says Zhdanov, "I drink in other countries." You sleep not merely on your side, knees drawn up into a fetal position, but with your arms over your head as if to protect yourself. The lights of the East Bay shimmer as I cross back over the bridge. Kondakova tells me she was raised in the Ural Mountains, Zhdanov in Siberia, while Yuri Arabov, filmmaker and poet with just two teeth left hanging from his upper jaw, is a city boy, raised in Moscow itself – we've met by accident in a cafe on Divisadero. When I was younger, I wanted to sleep with every woman, as if not to was somehow to be deprived of an intimacy with the world.

They call the wind Toshiba. Your typical to-kill-for raspberry mousse tort. You rise, seeming disturbed to have had an erotic dream about someone other than me. Gradually the business park is filling in, another vacant lot showing first signs of construction.

The bully in the dream punches me repeatedly, but part of me knows I'm asleep. That gap between buying a new car, getting a radio, and having it installed, thirty-mile commutes in silence. The more freedom you have, the more money you need. The cloud car of Berkeley. A homeless man struggling with his shopping cart, one of its wheels out of whack.

Fingers so small the baby isn't ready to grasp the rattle. The boy says, half in Spanish, that his mama painted the little bike blue, but from the random splashes across the spokes, I'll bet he helped. My first bench press in four years. Inadvertently, a mapping error in the path statement disables the network version of Windows. Addressing the American Society of Newspaper Editors in Boston, Dan Quayle calls the Gulf War, "a stirring victory for the forces of aggression."

Skewed humor of store-bought greeting card. Snuggle up, old Best Bottom. The look on the translator's face as he realize Zhdanov's begun to recite a poem he's never even heard before. Orpheus, the sparrow, struggles mightily to cause the sun to rise, having only one song, and it with only one note, to sing over and over until the task is complete. One variant you still hear marking the slow transition from Middle English is *boughten* as in store-boughten bread.

I buy you a little blue hat and a pair of earrings in the store in the back of the warehouse on Doyle Street, a place so out of the way that when we return, we find it's not there, none of the neighbors ever heard of it, it didn't exist, but there the blue stone of the earring glistens through your hair.

The stress of lifting one's own tongue. I hold the syringe point up, tapping the air bubbles away, then push up slowly until the first drop of solution indicates that no air remains. A ten-key piano of sorts in which each key struck causes a different hippo to open its mouth and a bell to ring. It's Bill Mohr, calling with the news of the death of Lee Hickman. In the gym, I'm riding the bike furiously, as if it could carry me away.

Rule One: Don't call me a grapefruit. A bug offers the supreme sacrifice on the windshield of the car. Strange pages suddenly emerge from the LaserJet. The burrowing owl stares out at his kingdom, a vacant lot. Gradually I adjust to the routine of popping a needle through your flesh.

The flash of the red light isn't what wakes me, but the idling engine, fire department's paramedic truck never at rest, then voices outside my bedroom window, an emergency this close to our lives. A half hour before I'll notice the first advance of light, the sparrow begins: how does it know? There are in fact two needles in the process, a long one for dipping into the amps of Perganol and its translucent liquid medium, then a shorter one for your buttocks. Philip Whalen blind. Five months after the war began, this nation merely pretends that the dying's stopped.

Inside the dog, like a tumor, they discover a mummified fetus. The sound of an empty 7-Up can rolling down the driveway. I eat a hamburger for lunch. On the ultrasound, a series of dark spots means that your ovaries have been stimulated and are producing a half-dozen eggs at least. The smell of chicken grease hangs over the kitchen.

Only when I pick up my notebook to write this do I realize that I'm not wearing my glasses – this sends a shudder of nostalgia through me, memory of four decades when I could read the fine print across the room or see the destination sign on a bus blocks away. Skydiving proved to be a fad rather than a hobby with him, but it was only after his third jump in six weeks that he came away with a fear I would have imagined to be innate. Since nobody calls it a cubicle, we're blowing up balloons and stringing banners over his cube at work in preparation for his birthday when one of the women sticks a balloon under her shirt in imitation of all the other pregnant women in the office and I'm instantly so angry I have to return to my own far corner to regain my composure.

Old baseball cap, its headband permanently sweaty. First wasp of spring. Yellow-headed freesias, purple-headed chives. A single, small airplane threads the clouds. This is not about poetry.

Nor this: in the dream I've just moved into a large collective household, all men, in a large city, which tells me, however indirectly, that something terrible has happened, since what I want is to be with you. A mother and son negotiate over burritos as they stand in line at the taqueria. It's a long, lingering sunset as we stop in front of the videotape store to look at the posters. You stare up at me from your book jacket on the remainder table. Only a minute after we agree that we're going to hop up, take a shower and not make love this morning, you're on top of me, rubbing, gradually slipping my penis in.

I'm just drifting back to sleep when the alarm rings, cutting short a dream that entails mixing a large vat of raisins, mostly golden, before I have any idea of what this concoction is for. Ducks fly up from the creek behind the parking lot. The tiny obit is split, one paragraph at the bottom of one long column, the rest at the very top of the next.

Warehouse home improvement store seems peculiarly unmusty, brand new in a mall all its own, the remaining commercial units still incomplete, ceiling-high doors wide open, the warm dry air tasting of summer, the freeway just beyond the chain link fence. The waiter's perspective in a crowded dining room, map of meals, tasks ordered into this pass across the floor, the next one, the one after, peripheral vision seeking the eye or hand of a diner in need. My love snores in the next room, then sighs and rolls over.

The light at the end of the fennel. Having gotten six loads of laundry into the washers at the laundromat, we drive up to the taqueria for chicken burritos with guacamole and sour cream, sharing a giant Sprite with two straws, then on the way back I drop you back off at the laundromat to deal with the transfer into dryers while I drive on to Safeway to do the grocery shopping for the week, which I do, coming back just as you're beginning to fold the first batch of dried clothes, which we complete together then head home, so that it's three full days before I realize that a load of my white underwear is missing and still must be in a washer, and you don't remember folding them either so, since you're taking the week off from work anyway, you go there to check it out and, yes, the young man who attends it in the daytime remembers the whites, separated out as they had been in order to run the washer on a higher temperature and with a dose of bleach, and that after they'd been there a day or so he threw them into a dryer himself, since they were starting to rot, at which point somebody apparently stole them, which is why I'm in the department store underwear section at this very moment. I return to the bed and lie back down, but the knowledge that the alarm will ring in less than an hour keeps me too anxious, alert, to go back to sleep.

But can that flock of wild parrots breed? Not for citation. The sun appears flat and vast, burning a hole in the sky. An elegant house, sparely furnished with one room set aside for their 600 Grateful Dead concert tapes. To calm myself, I wash a load of dishes.

A shift not in light, but to light, as day's first illumination floods the room so that colors exist, however muted. Flat bread from a Sicilian restaurant, like a soft bready pizza crust. Poppy-seed-studded breadsticks jut out of a tall glass. Dove's flutelike coo. Mockingbird gargles a whole new song.

I'm Jose Canseco in ballerina drag, vomiting. In the dream, I'm in the house I grew up in, in the kitchen, only the breakfast nook is missing, there's no pantry, and, when I open the door (which is in the wrong place in the wall), the stairs have disappeared, it's on the ground floor. An earthquake has similar logic. On the ultrasound screen, black dots disappear one by one until one of three doctors notes, "We've retrieved sixteen eggs." Gradually the vial fills with fluid.

Thus we move from the alpha to the beta version of life. George Bush reasserts a value for the state. I get around the copy protection by archiving the original file, then simply unpacking it onto the new drive. Ten little Indians. The work of life in the age of mechanical reproduction.

New odor to the urine. The phone unplugged but with the answering machine on so that we're not entirely incommunicado. Perganol swells the ovaries. Bertolucci's house. Which bird are you?

Because, when I was a boy, the only jets belonged to the military, the sound of one at four in the morning, very distant, fills the sky with the presence of the state. The tongue of a seatbelt. He patrols the parking lot, offering to wash people's windows for a buck. She graduated from law school but never passed the bar and when, right after the second child was born, her husband stopped beating her and split, she found she could clean houses to make a little money and bring the kids with her, since her employers were all away at work, so this became a pattern and then a career. Now that I judge the length of a work not by words, lines, or even pages, but by the kilobytes.

Six Tibetan Buddhist monks ritually bless last-place SF Giants, who end (we hope) season-long slump: om-baby. To build a better mouse. Muscle hidden at the base of the foot, just below the baby toe, cramps. Pots rise up out of the kitchen sink like a boat about to capsize. Make mine extra large.

The mystery of the dream is that there is one, image and narrative aswirl like this Missouri summer thunderstorm, sheet lightning, quick bursts of rain.

From the rooftop hotel tennis court at dawn, looking toward downtown, I see the first stirrings of the homeless in the park. Lobby several times the size of my own house. A thought in time saves mind. Atrium mezzanine cafe with soft piped-in harpsichord. Dear morning, the sun between the office towers rises.

Banjoes in the mist. Seen from above, lightning illumines the interior of the clouds. Cats wander slowly through the poppies in search of a place to sit. Rosebush past its bloom. I sit in a chair on the porch and write.

Slowly down the predawn street an old car approaches, the man at its wheel a not-entirely-young Vietnamese, folding newspapers with both hands as the vehicle rolls forward, the news crashing onto every third walk. At the party, two more people tell us stories about their experiences with in vitro fertilization as gradually we become aware of the size of this underground. The way jetlag makes your head feel as though it weighs 200 pounds. Why they call those faddish new corn chips blue.

Sound of the faucet, if it's the only sound in the night, is enormous. I force teachers to do pushups the way other men make war – to exercise my faculties at large. The music of that generation will always sound sweetest. A value is not given: X, the agent, imposes a value (the value of X). Closing my eyes, concentrating on feeling the bones in my hands.

Light pulsates until it pushes back the dark, filling the room. Or, light pulsates until my eyes adjust to this degree of information. Fetal position of a man sleeping in a doorway. Gaggle of teens in the mall. When, in Dallas, a crazed gunman kills a ten-year-old who is later found to have been pregnant, narrative spills forward, forming a landscape.

In search of a face called Blippo. I write, I rise, I writhe – conjugate the full syntagm, Red Ryder. I peruse a chart of LAN integrators, calculating fileserver-to-node ratios in my mind. It's oppressively hot as I walk from the office to the gym along an arroyo that separates the business park from the tract houses of what used to be, ten years ago, a farm town. Backlit palmtop – we're sworn to nondisclosure.

Dream management. Cells divide, then divide again – this is called addition. Stacks of books pile high atop the dresser, the desk, the filing cabinets, filling the house in. I imagine myself as a father, daring the fantasy to come true. At the funeral of Popeye Jackson, casket open, no sign of bullet wounds to the skull (already that's 15 years ago), the mostly black lumpen mourners filing past, the music over a shitty sound system Frank Sinatra's *I Did It My Way.*

Lone avocado in a bowl of apples looks ghastly, diseased. Both of us lying in bed sideways, spooned into one another, my hand gently on your hip, one of the most basic configurations of my life. A belief in documentation, or in the juxtaposition of eye and ear. The mall was built before the concept of the mall, so now (32 years later) it's emptying, dying, vacant units, the lone anchor tenant in Chapter 11.

Nasturtiums and milkweed. I meet a woman who's had in vitro fertilization nine times, conceiving at last on the ninth try with a donor ovum, but she seems sad, not like a victor at all. A roomful of people telling war stories, not of Vietnam or the Gulf, but of dealing with friends and family after the loss of a pregnancy, a firestorm of unrelieved fury at well-meaning stupid attempts to cheer them up: "you can always try again" or "at least you know you can get pregnant." We're sitting in the shade on the lawn when suddenly the sprinklers come on. The day passes, a long day, different from any other and yet the same.

At dusk my brother comes by to explain that he's quitting his job at the supermarket to move his wife and four small kids to Waco, Texas, to live with a Christian community there. I discover that the guy next to me in the checkout line at the drugstore is an old neighborhood kid from my youth, so we trade what-happened-to-who stories – Larry Callais has cancer of the liver and lungs – and I discover that this fellow, who graduated three years behind our class, but graduated, has been a janitor at the Rad Lab for the past seventeen years, a home on the El Cerrito side of Albany hill bought before prices exploded, a more settled life than I could ever have managed. My wife lies on the dark sofa, pink blouse matching perfectly the throw pillow she's tucked under her head, watching but not watching as her niece and nephews scuttle and tumble about the livingroom, wondering, worrying about what's going on in her own body, whether any of the seven embryo have implanted, and, if so, how and how many.

Kak vas zavoot: in the dream I'm getting answers, but they're in Russian and I no longer remember the words for numbers. Aaron Neville's falsetto assures that "nothing beats a Bud," which makes me think of Williams' "The rose is obsolete. Very slowly I am coming to realize that middle of the century was a long time ago. The house is vacant but the sign says "Do Not Disturb Occupants." That moment outdoors when there's no illumination left anywhere from the sun, but it's not fully dark yet and the streetlamps haven't flickered on.

Some psychotic has made a vast shrine on his or her front porch: clothes, magazines, rags, paintings piled into a bizarrely careful pyramid (I recognize a *Texas Monthly*)(the paintings are primitive Sunday seascapes, thick gray oils)(the clothes finally come into focus as men's wear, the styles typical of the 1950s) – the door to the old two-storey wood frame house, one of the oldest in Berkeley, entirely blocked, tho from the orderly shades and gauzy curtains it appears inhabited, otherwise normal (I notice a sparrow nesting atop this curious mound). Carrot and burdock root pancake, miso soup, then muscovy duck stuffed into simmering tofu pouches garnished with baby carrots, followed with a strawberry shortbread for dessert, and a fine Japanese decaf tea called Cookija. Simple scenes had been dug into the wet plaster of the walls itself, so that the surface was the medium and not just a platform, a Buddha playing a stringed instrument in clouds or, across the room, another playing a small flute. An HCG score of 0 to 15, the doctor says, would mean we're not pregnant, 15 to 30 would mean it's theoretically possible but uncertain, 30 to 50 would be more positive, so when the nurse informs us we've scored 182, the question transforms itself from yes or no into how many. Let us imagine a new world.

At the moment when local- and wide-area-networks threaten to make floppies, which have already been reduced to the status of paper clips in most offices, entirely obsolete, the read/write optical floppy (aka the floptical) comes along, offering 127MB of storage on a single disk. We're trying to design a new migration path for the poem. Her mom's worried that, at one year, she doesn't even crawl, let alone stand. Try to imagine the generation of birds in relation to your own. Shift of light foretells the sun.

We want to go snow camping, so plan the trip by placing the photographs we will take into little piles, each stack a different day, Monterey here, Mt. Shasta there, until the photos form a circle. On a beautiful afternoon, he comes to the door wearing a bathrobe, on crutches, shivering with fever. To the writer, the reader is both real and a symbol. Addictionary. I wake exhausted.

Words warp the mind's way, tunneling towards a period. I invoke the sun, the daughter, whatever. The pun hurts. Laughter cauterizes the past. Fast food, faster digestion.

Surfboard upside down on the pale green pickup. My old friend, the banana. What is more beautiful than a cloudless dawn? Under the crown, the root of the dead tooth opened up, gum growing in, filling the gap, so that when the crown pops off in cashew chicken and he goes to the dentist, the gum must be cut away and the base rebuilt before a new crown is cemented into place. Isn't that special?

Some nights pass quickly, dreams crowded together, images jumbled, superimposed. The man with the bald head is one of two famous performance artists, but which I can't tell. "Would you like to see Venus?" Tom Mandel asks Jean Day. If hours were cogs. My father remains permanently young in that I never saw him past the age of 29.

The description of music is now performed. Your breasts begin to swell almost the instance you become pregnant, their tenderness generating a sense of personal arousal, leading, as it happens, to some sweet, torrid, languid sex, positions unheard of before, even after 12 years together of constant research. In the paper, George Bush attempts to kiss a female West Point cadet who visibly cringes. Aftertaste of anything. Cat sleeps atop the mound of plastic bags in the homeless woman's shopping cart.

Once upon a time spatializes the temporal (as would any preposition), objectifying and distancing through the indefinite article (perhaps not our time at all, but that of a parallel or even perpendicular universe). Once within time there was a young girl whose mother wished her to be a dancer, and who loved to dance, but whom the captain of the dance, Mr Ballanchine, thought too long waisted. What if, instead of video, poetry was the popular mode of documentation: we'd have entertainments such as *America's Funniest Home Poems* or *Totally Hidden Poetry.* In right field Ezra Pound, in center Bill Williams, in left (bantering with the Martians in the bleachers), John Lister Spicer, at first base Jack Kerouac, at second Emily Dickinson, at short Paul Blackburn, at third Bob Creeley, pitching (with both fastball and knuckler) Charles Olson, and catching (born to squat) Gertrude Stein. As you speak, the researcher keeps her mini-cassette recorder rolling.

Dear Noodle, please come.

A procedure by which they suture the cervix until the pregnancy has reached the 36th week. The icon of a paperclip indicates that files are attached to the AppleLink message. One retains the echo of a song – in this instance, John Fogerty's *Centerfield* – as a compulsive memory, a reminder that media are no longer discontinuous with our bodies, our minds. You are forever talking of the need to get a haircut. For several days, the clouds threaten a rain that never arrives.

Forms of (th)ought. Wind chime slows, then picks up again. Odd how in summer the days are already growing shorter. What sounds like a cat jumping from a chair wakes me, since we don't have a cat, but when I hear it again I realize it's the paperboy's delivery dropping on the walk. Because ants emerged somehow from the closet to arrive in our bed, we groaned, tore the sheets off, sprayed the closet, but for the night unfurled the sofabed in the livingroom, an adventure as if camping out.

Thoughts as form – but that's too organic, a term with very distinct connotations if we say of an alcoholic, "he sounds organic," implying irreversible brain damage, not unlike the word *symbiotic*, which to naturalists implies a balance but to therapists describes a hopelessly destructive family system.

At 39 she returns to the United States with exactly $11 to her name, without children or any current relationship, uncertain as to whether she should be a film editor or a restaurant manager, uncertain even over whether this is just a visit and she might return to Melbourne tomorrow. Donor dot, the pink circle on a driver's license that indicates disposition of usable organs. The drawing indicates how best to look at this rough lot of compost piles and weeds, as the garden-to-be. To an outsider, these clouds would suggest a summer rain. Get another languist!

The alarm rings when you least expect it. We're making our escape thru a panel in the wallpapered kitchen that leads down a stairway to large, empty basement (lots of good storage space here I tell myself) but over the doors and windows we find myriad beams, infrastructure of a monstrous add-on deck, blocking our own departure – I try crawling through, two cats watching and hissing, crawling toward the largest gap in the beams until I realize finally that I'm stuck.

The forum of a question. Aftertaste of curried duck. It's filler time. This is how I remember your text. Vegetables simmer in broth.

A bit much (a byte map). Overheads on a screen in a darkened hotel meeting room. I shut my eyes and listen to Edit Piaf sing *Vie in Rose* which, although I can't make out the lyrics, seems to be the saddest song I know. On the radio, Timothy Leary speaks of "the glorious revolution of virtual reality." Next slide, please.

The contest of hummingbirds. To build a placenta. Twice in the night the burglar alarm malfunctions. The incline press.

The image on the screen is not triangular exactly, but rounded on one end, the slice of a pie, gray, grainy, two dimensional, with two dark spots, each the shape of a pinto beat, resting side by side in the womb, and within each a little white pulsing, infinitesimal two-chambered heart, the doctor noting that the one on the left is slightly elongated, the heart beating slower, saying "I don't know if that means anything, or if it means it's not doing as well and you might lose it," no sign of an ectopic anywhere, the young resident increasing the magnification so that now the heart's pulse is a burst of white within these two shadowy beings, and then the examination's over, the two doctors slip away and we're alone in the little room and you reach up and I hold you, sobbing together complicated sobs of relief and anxiety all at once, you sitting on the edge of the examination table, feet dangling in the stirrups covered with potholders, between the cracks of the venetian blinds the glimmer of a June rain on Golden Gate Park.

When words collide. Think of paragraphs as bricks. The table solid in the next room, untroubled by ontology. Rabbit made of yarn sits atop the bookcase. Balinese wood duck.

"Stalin was interested only in the perpetuation of power and he killed 60 million, more victims in his own country than any other leader in this century," Misha speaking quietly, very matter-of-fact, though all of the other conversations in the room have stopped, "so just imagine what Trotsky, who was more ruthless and who was truly interested in world domination, would have done."

I wake to the sound of goose wings in the garden.

Old itchy balls steps out of the shower at last, staring at his naked reflection in the mirror – is that his body? Driving east over the mountain at dawn, the long line of commuters slows almost to a halt at those points, one right on a hairpin turn with the road's shoulder dropping away, when the yellow-orange sun, big as a beachball this close to the horizon, shines right in the eyes of each driver. Sunol Valley, with one tiny town, no malls, no shopping centers, a few farms, but a full-sized golf course and that one curious quarry, feels like a moment out of a previous decade. With three separate dining rooms, two of them empty, ghost-like place settings awaiting a busier hour or day, the greasy spoon still offers over 60 types of omelettes from which anyone can choose a favored form of cholesterol. At 110 degrees, it's too hot for the smokers in the office to step outside for a fix.

Email to Atlanta. Obtuse emotions in a poet's first book. The unripe honeydew proves difficult to eat. Through the trees, a churchbell signals noon. Breeze as hot as this sun.

Before I turn the light on, I remember that a bulb needs to be changed, so drag over the stool and methodically, by the light of dawn fog, unscrew the old bulb, shaking it by my ear just to hear the broken filament rattle. In the dream, you're offering me drug-filled cookies, but I'm ambivalent since I don't do that anymore. I call into the voice-mail system to retrieve my messages and change my greeting. Yahoos turning the Fourth of July into one more pro-war rally. We sit on the porch at dusk, eating barbecued salmon steaks, listening to banjos play in the house next door, cat attentively at our feet in case of scraps, hummingbird whizzing by.

Fog's glare hints at the sun behind. Before I was ten, my aunt and uncle lived somewhere up this narrow, winding road, eucalyptus mixed with pine, creek alongside almost dry now – the nostalgia feels tragic. Haircut and a beard trim, 13 bucks. At Down Home Music, I buy a new recording of a Ketjak, but it's not spelled the same way. Paint cracks off these lawn chairs, leaving skeletons of rust.

On the porch in the fog with the smell of rain, waiting for the antihistamines to kick in. A grid of string along the fence for the snow peas to climb. Reading the obit of Howard Nemerov, I realize for the first time that his sister was Diane Arbus. Buzz of the hummingbird. Making love to a pregnant woman – what do the babies think?

LAN's best friend. Intrusive thoughts: nuclear firestorm hits a playground in slow motion (bodies flame, then char, then scatter as ash); the "bad" terminator, T1000, covered with liquid nitrogen, begins to freeze, to stick to the floor of the refinery, foot breaking off at the ankle, then hand at the wrist, then the whole shattering when shot by the good terminator, Arnold (special effects haunt my dreams). Four cartons of books moved either to the basement or the used book store and I still don't have the room to eliminate all the stacks of new ones just building about the house. You're constantly nauseous, ravenously hungry but then unable to eat (a consequence of new hormone levels, what is the biological purpose of morning sickness?). In both *Terminators*, there's no "good cop," a mediating figure to negotiate the heroes eventual return to society, since society itself is the problem, these machines from the future simply a sort of viral acting out, the symptom, much like the fever of a body trying to burn out a disease, but in each there is a sympathetic black male authority figure, in the first Paul Winfield, a cop trying to protect Sarah Connor, and now Joe Morton (*Brother from Another Planet*) as Mike Dyson, big pun in the surname, as the repentant computer scientist who will invent the deadly Skynet chip – each of whom dies for his efforts (in America today, the only cinema of ideas lies in cyberpunk).

I wake, already expecting to find a bassinet (it's the eighth week). On the perpetual soundtrack, a woman (who? Patsy Cline?) sings *I Fell to Pieces.* Just because of you I become a poet. I try to imagine the world my grandfather saw. In the classroom, a blackboard makes a terrible mirror.

Who manages the White Plains branch? Who manages the Portland Beavers? Who manages on so few hours of sleep each night? The cleaver hangs from a magnetic knife rack next to the "old-fashioned" wood paper towel holder. I close my eyes this world to make.

A dark day. Intangible part numbers. Cascade communications. Imaging cocoa. This little life of mine.

The night rich with dream, as if wandering through a fun house, stepping for a moment into nightmare alley, then right back out again. "You sound angry," he says as she jokes about her brother's ignorance of her fertility problems. It's a J world in the theory of types. Outside, people cluster quietly in the curious halflight of a solar eclipse.

"A very pretty uterus," the nurse practitioner says. Restaurants that serve hash browns with their bacon and eggs. An older woman with a stern face, unattractive rigid demeanor, is having coffee with two younger women, obviously her daughters, one of whom – this startles me – I find quite beautiful. New half soles for my wing tips. After five on a Friday, the office complex empties out: the architecture of moveable cube walls articulates an impermanence that makes people anxious for their jobs.

Fog turns to mist, the bridge evaporating as we drive over to the invisible city. Distant powersaw reverberates through the neighborhood, constant bursts signalling a tree is being cut back or down. Cat drifts noiselessly through the garden. Overhead, a V of geese. I recognize that neighbor's windchimes, though I've never seen them.

The invention of neatness. In the morning, the smell of meatloaf hangs in the air. I use my ATM card at the supermarket and get cash back. It's Sunday, so the bread shelves are ravaged, empty. Sun unable to melt the fog.

Old newsreel footage of a dirigible exploding over a field in New Jersey. Aftertaste of Nutrasweet. Currently there are 18 square feet of retail space per person in the United States.

Academicize your verse. Fact: a certain reader likes long, passive, twisting sentences, lingering over each embedded digression, the verb conditional, the assertion hedged, the agent hard or perhaps impossible to find. Fuck that shit – but at least acknowledge its puffy, indulgent sensuality. (Your stomach starts to grow, but it's not soft like fat.) Ice cream shows up in the fridge for the first time in months.

Bruise on the bottom of the foot. The way light vibrates feels palpable until my eyes adjust to the sudden absence of dark: waves of it fill the pale yellow room like water filling a tank (so many times brighter than the objects it illuminates). Golden lab, soaking wet from the creek, gallops to catch its master, a young boy holding a leash in one hand. A young man, seventeen or so, thin body as tanned and oily as any homeless person three times his age, blond hair matted, wearing only blue jeans, not even shoes, sits full lotus on the steps of the Student Union.

Tables shoved together accommodate the crowd, workers at a bar to say farewell to one moving to a new corporation, chips and margaritas and small talk. An old hymn turned into a civil rights song. Glazed bisque is the color of my venetian blinds. A jar of almonds. It surprised me to find you lying there, naked in the dream.

One, two, three, a half dozen sparrows dead in the rough grass at the edge of the beach. I dream of mudman in my favorite suit (not my favorite dream). At the next table in the restaurant, a young woman gives up waiting for a date who never arrives, pays for her glass of wine, trying not to let the waiter see her anger and frustration, then leaves. In the land of the $50 ties, an old Victorian railroad flat has been converted into a hair salon, a different hairdresser in every room (where has all the housing gone?). The waitress at Cafe Beano has a spiderweb tattoo covering her shoulder.

I stumble into a classroom, the course already in session, the only available schooldesks mounted high on the walls with little metal steps leading up to them. We're on top of the Empire State Building watching fireworks spread out well over the city before us, brilliant beautiful red and blue bursts, when my mother inadvertently – imitating the pyrotechnics with the hot orange ash from her cigarette (she hasn't smoked in twenty years!) – sets a tree, possibly a Christmas fir, on fire – quickly the firehoses rescue and dowse us all.

One of those moments when you can taste the metal in your teeth. In the kitchen, the clock ticks in iambs. Slowly, birds begin their predawn singing. To this, the refrigerator adds its periodic symphony. The joy of looking.

Middle of the weak. Over Thai iced tea we negotiate revisions in the text. Your head seems vast in your first photograph, little buds of arms and legs, wiggling on the ultrasound screen, alive in your own placental sac.

I was talking in the dream when the alarm hit, so now I feel like anyone who's lost their train of thought, verbal stumbling, an impulse toward closure with no means of building that bridge, but also I no longer remember to whom I was speaking, no details whatsoever, objects, time of day, or place, other than that sense that the dream was in color.

The lyric as a form will keep you warm. Stitching along the seams of consciousness never quite dissolves. At a reading, I'm so exhausted from my job that the struggle to maintain consciousness becomes my experience of the work. The years as badges. The banana dissolves in its own sugar.

Pain without guilt. Waking with the sound of Bobby Hatfield and Bill Medley singing *Little Latin Lupe Lu*, full bore, bull blast, soundtrack of a dream ringing in my ears in this otherwise silent house. When I say to the officer that this is the first time I've ever received a ticket for speeding, he replies, "Well, we've been neglecting you." I make a copy of three of the ultrasounds, one each of each of you and one of the two of you together, side by side, each with your own placenta, taping this copy to the wall of my cube at the office, just like any other worker with a photo of his children. A book in which I find this sentence: "Look for discrepancies in your totem pole."

Open wide, these rose petals will soon fall. Neighbors voices, cackle of a jay – I can't quite hear what they're saying. Morning's passed, mow the grass.

A boy watches television while adults muck about the kitchen. The arrangement of detail – where we keep the toothbrushes, extra rolls of toilet paper, the glass to the right of the bathroom faucet, the soap (clear amber glycerine) to the left – forms an order we learn to intuit – maybe it preceded us, but I think not. A walk about the neighborhood just to look at flowers, lunch at a cafe, visit a friend at his shop but try not to interrupt his selling time, ducking out as customers enter. Try to explain bushtits to a 12-year-old boy.

The ink smears if I turn the page too quickly. Dreams ranked by silliness, by presence/absences of blue, brown, mauve, teal. I'm repelling down the side of the Transamerica Pyramid in the night rain, a mountain climber chased by Michael Jackson.

The shock of a new toothpaste. The other reason they're called Deadheads. It's not even the end of July and you can see the days getting shorter. This week's media sensation is a cannibal in Milwaukee. What I have that remains from the war is a t-shirt that reads "No Blood for Oil."

One can trace the path between this sentence and the *Hotel Wentley Poems.* The dog next door mimics a siren too distant for me to hear. What I do notice, listening hard: various engines in states of acceleration, a locomotive, somebody snoring in the house next door, a jet somewhere out over the bay. Someness. Dog's name is Sister, but in the other half of the duplex lives its owner's sister, sullen young martial arts instructor, and her husband, the pleasant constant surfer.

You and I are crossing a dark bridge in a long canoe, the boat riding low in this raging green-brown water, hoping that we don't capsize before we reach the other side – later, the physics of this will seem as curious as its symbolism. All this writing just to become, if I'm lucky, part of some publisher's backlist.

The word as ground, sounded and scratching, etching detail, retching in the throat, crosses a moat of air to where you are found, unfurling now into a separate banner, banter, colors I'd never recognize as my own. In my mind, I try to trace when I might have lost the notebook, the moment it must have slipped from my pocket, where it must have gone.

At times I think that if I'm with you long enough, paying attention, caring, studying you, I'll learn everything I need to know in life. Because the house was too small we needed to move, but, because we owned it, we thought to move it also, which we did by knowing just the right place in the foundation to pry open, apart, the whole house starting suddenly to slide, terrible deafening rumble, chairs inside toppling over, books flying out of the cases, chandeliers swinging, the whole structure sliding down a hill the distance of two city blocks, crashing into the cement walks of a vacant corner lot, where it stops suddenly, still intact, now miraculously big enough to live in, tho I'm concerned because we don't own the lot, the large cracks in the pavement outside lingering evidence, wondering how the pipes held up through all of this as we're picking up books, dishes (nothing's broken!), while out the window I can now tell that we live in the outer Richmond of San Francisco, a neighborhood where I've never wanted to live, perpetually in fog.

Melody of the windchimes' dance. The day after a large party, tables are still pulled together in the dining room, every straight-backed chair in the house is there. Undercurrent of sadness: we don't admit out loud how long it will be before we see one another again. The children gather round to see the ultrasound photos of forthcoming cousins. As I read aloud from Zukofsky, you say, "That sounds like Dr. Seuss."

Ream of Crete. When I tell my nephew I'm going to Tennessee tomorrow, he says, "That's where Davy Crockett was born." History as heroes narrows the story. The man who patented the polygraph also created Wonder Woman. Among the red-assed baboons, what distinguishes the dominant male is not simply the architecture of his anus, but the long grey mane, lion-like, though pacing the hill he walks more like a dog.

I can get it for you retail. Behind the state capitol is a rough neighborhood. Constant fan of hotel air conditioning. In the cafe, the headwaiter keeps trying to refill coffee into my cup of tea. Hazy humid morning over the Cumberland River.

Cafe music. Backlit display. I roll awake to a new day in a far town. All is cost.

Even in a green, spiked metal mask, like an Africanized hockey goalie, his singing voice is clear as the small boy in his lap holds first one book of poems, then another, then an old paperback novel, as he sings from each, simultaneously playing the small piano in a bluesy, neutral accompaniment, although it's unclear how many of the people in the little crowd around this softball backstop in a small park had anticipated such a performance.

After the rain, crickets, and above them, the cicadas. I'm crossing the lawn on the estate of the late Andrew Jackson, past the mansion, away from the circus tent under which a bar band sings, "Hang on, Sloopy, Sloopy, hang on." While she waits for them to place their order, the waitress shifts her weight from one foot to the next. After the lights are out, I lay awake, waiting for my body to settle, the mind to drift, no stars but the random squares of light from offices in the next highrise tower.

CNN pumped into the hotel lobby as though it were background music, too low to focus on, but a familiar, almost comforting prosody. When I talk into a large event, such as a vendor party, my eyes go into tracking mode, seeking out people to speak with, preparing to work the room. The display lifts the roof off Elvis' gold Cadillac, revealing not only the gold records mounted in the ceiling, but also the little black-and-white TV and the 45 rpm record player. T for tech support, T for Tennessee. Sheet lightning configures the night sky.

The schmoozer's guide to dawn. You got that right. Skycap with no hat. The sentence is a made thing, but words are as flowers in that they precede ourselves and are perpetually renewed. When the lightning cracks, bats jump from the old church tower, squealing into the sky.

In the dream I'm pushing a shopping cart, empty, across an institutional garden, a school perhaps, until unexpectedly the path ends, the cart begins to swerve, harden to control in the grass, then falls sideways, taking me with it, so that I'm now focusing on just how green and detailed everything is, even here at night in the dark, realizing that I'm on the forest floor – the school is gone – wondering what rustles in those bushes, branches, leaves. The woman in the next seat is returning from a conference of accounting students to her school in Provo, Utah, well-spoken, intelligent, quite beautiful, a long way from her home in Western Pennsylvania, but having also already served an 18-month Mormon mission in Calgary, an enthusiasm for the world and her career in tax accounting that is almost charming for its directness and simplicity, but which makes me wonder how this world will deal with her over the next 20, 40 years.

Curve of the spine. Sound of night rain leading into dawn. Broken ring, the plastic seal of a jam jar is discarded.

Curve of the mind, sound of a night train. In the dream an intense negotiation over an invisible object. I walk outdoors and the storm has given way to an unbearable heat, the sky a pale blue airless thing. In just one week, the shape of your face changes. The fundus among us.

Realm of words I've heard returns in a new order. The sound linoleum makes beneath your feet. A sneeze clouds my sinuses.

Of his own devices, as in "he woke of his own devices." Wake, walk, wok, woke, waken versus bake, balk, doesn't exist, doesn't exist, bacon. Sleep of the wicket, peaceful, childlike. One doesn't so much read the world as a text, one proofs it.

Writing poetry with a cat in my lap. At that point mid-life finally where I'm not the only one with a parent missing or dead. The line forms at the margin. Clouds enclose the sky. Hummingbird pauses on the tip of the branch.

FYI VLS & NYR: the conspicuous consumption of ideas is not a sufficient condition for an intelligentsia. The day passes, as gentle and insubstantial as a cloud. In his grave, the bones of Baudelaire are counting sentences. The right fielder hovers anxiously under a pop fly that will never drop. In Moscow, classical music on the radio accompanies a change of state.

In the dream you are perpetually circling through the streets of San Francisco in search of a place to park, gasoline dwindling, but waking provides no solace. The way cops mill at the edge of a crime event, just inside the yellow tape, as though it were a cocktail party serving donuts. Late in the day, the sun emerges for the first time through a crack in these clouds, illuminating the futon shop with a special but ambiguous symbolism. What I see in your sunglasses is only my own reflection, rounded by the curvature, and behind me the whole of the warehouse parking lot. Which of these paragraphs is a ruse?

Watching television obsessively, caught in that long historical moment between the obvious and the unknowable, filled, for no other reason than to relieve our anxiety, with file footage and experts. At night the dessert shop turns into a high school bohemian scene – inside, boys wearing baseball caps backwards carry skateboards as if they were notebooks. The quick spicy sauce jumped over the lazy pasta. Pregnant women trade tips on nausea. On the television, pink and white flowers have been tossed atop a lake surrounded by thousands of people (my mind drifts over scenes and faces the Leningrad).

What will you tell the babies? It seems impossible to come across a canyon this deep, this rural, this green so close to the city – alongside the road a singe line of track that appears to be well kept so must still be in use. Cemeteries side by side, one per denomination. That, in history, 1991 was a treacherous year. In what is now a neighborhood in Fremont they used to film westerns, before Hollywood and sound.

Crimea river by the old oak tree. Old Ba'hai banner on Valencia Street: "One World, Please." To sleep, perchance to cream.

This time the dream is different: there's a conference on campus, Barry's there, my first wife, some people from the computer industry curiously among the English department types, but instead of giving a talk myself for which I've forgotten to prepare – the usual version – I sit in the audience, ask one (slightly hostile) question of the first speaker, then drift out of the auditorium to look at the books on display, my real attraction this event, until I realize they're all remainders, that purgatory, and suddenly I'm very anxious to flee the place before the next speaker concludes and everybody emerges for the banquet lunch, dragging me back into it.

Garden in the fog. A house recently vacated seems not only empty, but a vacuum. In the distance, I hear an unseen basketball being dribbled on concrete. Lifting the seat to the toilet, I come face to face with a dogpaddling rat. Out an open window, the radio broadcasts applause.

Porchlight. Bright pink flyers for a pizza shop under a windshield wiper of every car in the mall lot. My first rose, white atop the small bush.

Mourning becomes electric. In the park, two kites struggle to stay aloft in the blue air. When I come to Texas, I'll call. A variant of the game Keep Away is called Monkeys in the Middle. Touring the 'burbs, one yard sale at a time.

The dream breaks as the alarm hits. The membrane between the sacs forms almost a shelf across the uterus, with Twin A (Dweezle) below, head to your left, as Twin B (Noodle) sleeps parallel in the upper bunk. Having added water, the Soviet Union dissolves (Yeltsin walking up to Gorbachev at the podium, pointing to the minutes of the secret cabinet meeting and demanding Gorbachev read them aloud). Ticking clock echoes off the pantry wall. Now comes the hard part.

A light in the house next door foretells the arrival of new neighbors. Nurse taps taps taps the syringe to break up the bubbles inside. An edit, an edict. Call the game Fictionary. Do you know the muffler man?

A compulsive dream of perfect order, tho the tone and tempo suggest hysteria, the dream of panic filing. Sitting calf raise. The instant I wake, rising in the dark to an alarm, my mind goes through a process of triage – day of the week, primary tasks, current hour, etc. – so that by the time I reach the clock, which I've deliberately placed in another room, I already understand why I cannot go back to sleep. Why is this poetry? In the midst of a leg press (220 pounds, 20 reps), I pause to admire the articulation of my quads.

In the midst of a sentence, I pause to admire the gesticulation within grammar. A novel approach vs. a novella approach (using elephants and a band of circus clowns to move their furniture into their new home in the old church). That burning gut feeling when you have to shit. In the dream, the baby's no larger than my little finger, but it falls before I can catch it, head breaking off, as round and hollow and small as a raspberry. Packing for a long weekend is harder than moving because you have to decide what not to take.

Black smoke pours up over the delta, smearing south. By the roadside, what remains of a deer decays back to the bone. Sun shimmers through the green-and-white tangle of the birch. Jays and tanagers and crickets and of course the big slow logging trucks on the highway. Prism effect of the sun in my own eyelashes.

Prism house of anguish. Biker revs up in the middle of a redwood forest. High over the stand of poplars, four red-tail hawks swoop and flash in the sun. What kind of dreams did you have last night? A woman walking by with two small boys turns to the one who's fussing and whining, to say, "Now you're acting just like Eliot."

When the pump to the well goes down at the resort, really a collection of small and, for the most part modest, cabins, over the Labor Day weekend, an elaborate triage results, with plastic gallons of water for all, flushing up at the cafe by the road, and free passes to the hot springs at Grover's Corner. Moth is not attracted to the light, but rather is blinded and disabled, unable to sort direction, able only to see one way – white, hot, deadly. Hey, Mook, here comes the day's first big trucks. Ancient German shepherd waddles over the gravel path. Crow feels oddly urban so far back in these hills.

Speak of the mountain air as tho it were an object. A lake entirely to ourselves, a mile across in diameter, not even a tern or mallard. Dirt bikes grinding up the trail path. It is a matter for speculation to which lake Twin Lake is the twin. Red tail on a fence post, large as a dog, takes off as we approach, gliding across the entire valley with a single flap of its wings.

"Bye-bye for tojour," sings Ann Savoy in my head as I wake. Dreams are not wishes. Lone over-ripe banana. Echo of accordion. Five people circle the engine of a truck.

In Norman Fischer's poetry, there's a presentness to every sentence, a peace almost, a willingness to be there, none of the anxiety I sometimes find in my own work or in the poetry of others to be elsewhere, the next line, the next sentence, the next page. Raise your rates and you will note that customer satisfaction scores rise also. I got up from my desk for just a moment but, when I return, the light on my phone is flashing and the nice neutral female voice of the phonemail computer tells me I have six new messages. It's budget time again. My mother's sister's husband has died and I close my eyes and try to envision the light I find so particular to the large yard of their home at the foot of Mount Diablo where his family held a service that I failed to attend.

Sentences sweep the surfaces of the sea floor, the pitted, living coral of nouns, glimmering refracted light of articles and conjunctions.

In my mind fantasize each portion of a double play, but always with the pivot of a left-handed second baseman. The sound of rain wakes me. Next door, a light is on in the middle of the night. The desire for a banana can feel almost primal. Let's check our potassium.

What is a poem and where can I find one my size, extra large? A dream of work for which I should be paid. At 3:30, the sun peeks through, only to be swallowed again by the fog at 5:00.

One reason to leave the seat down on the can is that sewer rats will swim for the light. Use my dot matrix printer just for drafts, taking in to the lasers at work for finished copy. The new neighbor, a blonde woman, is on her back deck talking on a cordless phone. Carl Rakosi, become the last of a generation. Eight-year-old Pepe Martinez, struck not once by a hit-and-run driver in his East Oakland neighborhood, but twice.

An end-of-the-season baseball crowd for an also-ran team – small, distracted, bored, gone by the ninth inning. When I arrive at the photo shop to pick up my prints, I find it's moved. E-mail that file to Atlanta. The consistent production of copy on command. Joking with the VPs in the skybox.

The relentlessness of day following day. A strange blonde woman stands on the porch of the house in which I grew up. We jot down a list of 70 possible names for boys. I point through the glass case at the two salmon fillets I'd like. Bunk beds, coming up.

In defining, clocks limit the hour. Binding the foot in the name of the shoe. Attempting (in vain) to symmetrically trim my beard.

In the dream I've brought you to what once was Leningrad at last, to Dmitrii's flat on Nevsky Prospekt, though looking out the windows what I see is the San Francisco waterfront circa 1952 or '53. As a boy, I saw Enos Slaughter play as well as Ted Williams, both of whom first reached the majors in the 1930s (when did Musial begin?). Though large, the belly of a pregnant woman is firm, a solid object. You think you're in the wilderness because you see a cow. I am that man.

Partisan cheese.

Painters without galleries. By the time the Acadians reached Louisiana, they'd lost the bagpipes that had been a part of their music even in France, though the echo of it lingered so that when blacks from the West Indies arrived in Cajun country in the late 19th century with accordions adapted to voodoo, the instrument slipped right into zydeco like an imported animal filling an old ecological niche. Simile when you say that. In the dream, I've returned from Europe for just a day but am so jet-lagged and disoriented I can't quite figure how to get back. Mysterious song of the refrigerator.

A series of small storms over the desert, dreams cross the psychic landscape. The night each of two families believes the other is coming to dinner and cooks a meal, sets the table, then waits for the other to arrive. The number of feral cats increases in proportion to the number of homeless, until gangs of them wander the alleyways, growing larger and scrawnier, more wild, until one day they begin attacking humans.

New radio donuts. She watched her own Caesarean. Our own little wigglers are eight to ten inches long. With twins, the feeding-diaper changing process takes 90 minutes and must be repeated every two hours. Sinead O'Connor in my head sings of Margaret Thatcher.

A fleet of old one-speed bicycles for pedalling between buildings on the Hewlett-Packard Roseville campus. Broadcast storms fragment the message. Vast trucks of tomatoes roar past. With E-mail, the network itself is the platform. Sun rises over the flood plain.

Woman on the treadmill at the gym wears dark glasses and a Walkman, hermetically sealed, striding toward a future that never arrives. E-mail leaves the option of a paper trail. Think of a book as plug-and-play. One of two peopled described in the tiny backpage wire-service filler as "burned beyond recognition as to age or gender" in a 19th floor highrise fire in LA turns out to be your former sister-in-law, invoking grief across a network of several families, tinted with the hope that the blaze wasn't started through freebasing coke. We sit in the indirect light of my livingroom well into the night.

Like Leggos or any other modular system, new business parks tacked onto the outer edge of the suburbs generate malls, new housing tracts, great mounds of earth on either side of the freeway foretelling a new offramp and overpass, sprawl without limit. Chick Corea, scheduled to play this low-end Holiday Inn over the weekend. That one's not a vulture, but a hawk and, since the tail doesn't fan out, not a red-tail either, but there's no place to pull the car over, so I refocus quickly on the traffic ahead, the moment passing in much less than a moment.

Dream in which the house is infested with iguanas, geckos, small mice, snakes. Sleep has its canyons. Driving into the sunset, squinting and unable to read the signage, I hope to reach home not long after dark.

The changing table (a spreadsheet way of knowledge). Crackling, an old Piaf tape is audible through a nearby window while even closer the blue jay's laugh sounds out of place in the city. Making French toast with challah. You part your thighs and I enter easily, our eyes staring into one another. The old washing machine stands in the driveway.

Muscle knotted at the back of a rib. I dream of new sitcom pilots for TV. One route is through the tunnel, the other over the hill. Is the nook part of the kitchen, merely a recessed alcove, or a room of its own? Wake with a too-sweet taste in your mouth.

Through the frosted glass of the globe hanging from the ceiling, one of two bulbs has burned out. Her four cats are named Pecos, Baby, Figaro (also called Beanie), and Me. A detail: an iceberg twice the size of Rhode Island threatening shipping off the Falklands is called A24. 10Base-T tip: if a broadcast storm is associated with a new node logging on, log it off and swap out its NIC. On price-performance alone, poetry wins every time.

The sky smears at the horizon to the East, red-brown signature of smog. Later, the most beautiful sunset you ever saw in your life. At the company picnic, discover which coworkers are apt to turn up in a thong bikini. From here, only the tip of the north tower of the Golden Gate cuts through the fog. Bees swarm around my hotdog.

First spots starts to freckle the new bananas. Why morning doesn't work. Last day game of the year. Without you beside me, sleep is impossible. Poor old tired bear.

First smell of rain. A commercial strip that runs over the tops of rolling hills – what happens when sprawl has nowhere else to go. The burger stand counter clerk tells his colleagues how his brother "went crazy to get out of the army, so I had to go down and rescue him out." Tall blond kid with a pony tail. Two guys at the minimart at the gas station, buying six-packs of cola and cigarettes for their wives, pay $27 without even getting gas.

You've gone to Chicago. The vase of dead roses sits on the table. Fruity smell to the fart. One glass jar of almonds, the other of walnuts. I use the radio as though it were a voice.

They drive over from the City in their new-bought used car, surprised at how warm it seems, whereas to me it feels cooler and windier, another little index of autumn.

True form vs. imagined. Each ballplayer bears the weight of his statistics. Without you this bed feels vast. Clock keeps time in an empty room.

Pomo Afro Homo. Dreams of late in which close childhood friends at last return. I'm screaming, to hide another emotion. Big garbage truck echoes even more loudly in the stillness before dawn. Gag me with a grant.

Perhaps you think the pen cuts the page, which bleeds, leaving scars of ink. The weight of your body beside me organizes my sleep. Picking little translucent bones from the salmon. A man is sleeping in the planter box outside the abandoned restaurant, his body pushed as tightly against the building as he can get. Dust on my windshield turns to constellations as I drive directly into the setting sun.

I'm standing on the freeway exchanging insurance information with Ms. Pam Rhoe of Concord, waiting for the tow truck to arrive, sun still rising, around us the steady onrush of commute traffic, the view of Oakland rooftops curiously serene when I realize I'm not wearing my glasses, which flew off at the point of impact. A couple comes to the door with the collar of a cat they found crushed in the street and dying, which they rushed to the vet anyway, returning to search for its owner. The way a distant train's horn threads the morning air.

Is it poetry or is it ComputerLand? "Body shop," says the voice answering the phone. Roast pig as an edible sculpture. The green of the radiator fluid washes over the freeway. Staring out a sixth floor window, Lee Harvey Oswald inaugurates postmodernism one, two, three times (stunt double on the grassy knoll).

"Well, who wouldn't be tired, confronted with all these postmodernisms, this L=A=N=G=U=A=G=E writing, MTV, ACT UP, e-mail, junk bonds, Madonna, smart bombs, poststructuralism, Reaganism, terrorism, colorization, Houstonization, and, if you order right away, much much more?" (*VLS*, October, 1991) Then explain how spelling it with equal signs discredits the perspective. Toy boat, toy boat. The sun hovers low over the converted farmland of the business park, shrill call of the killdeer. Secretaries jogging on their lunch hour (hummingbirds at the feeder before dawn).

Orange cat stalks through the sunflowers. On his ladder, housepainter listens to talk radio. Rose bush gone ragged, full of butterflies. Squirrel's alertness when it sees the cat.

Helicopter low overhead, makes all the windows shudder. In the dream, I shoot two of the assassins and capture a third, for which the University rewards me with a computerized security badge even though I'm not in its employ. In the dream, Kathleen Frumkin in a CD store is holding a very wiggly, nervous badger that she recently has rescued in the city. You turn to me and say, "Honey, I'm bleeding and we need to go to the hospital."

A washing machine understood as a series of songs. "We're blood sisters now," says the nurse as she pushes the IV needle too far through the vein, the blood splattering over her hands, which she has forgotten to place in rubber gloves. It's Sunday and so at least two of the doctors who get called in show up with small children in tow (radiologist in a Harley Davidson t-shirt). Smog stretches red-brown over the valley, erasing the horizon. Placenta previa.

Night can't last forever. Terbutaline, as a muscle relaxant, also permits blood to flush unimpeded through the heart – the side effects of speed without the euphoria. Very rapidly I learn to negotiate the corridors of the hospital, the staff at the nursing station, the hours of its restaurant, knowing that I will just as quickly forget them all save as glimpses, tones, expressions, smells, the affects of memory. Sunset full of reds and purples frames a four-storey parking garage. Combine the flowers into a single vase.

Her name is, I swear, Lavender Fog. Avoid raspberry leaf tea. Lyn arrives with the blue foam thingee. What is worse than a hyper mode of exhaustion?

"You're worrying about the day before yesterday when you should be worrying about today," says the doctor, explaining how we can grow our own socks for the winter (I want the blue ones). Dreamgate. Like listening for the songs of the whales, the microphone amplifies the distant sound of heartbeats. I wake with that exhausted, cried-out feeling. Grow babies, grow.

What you think is a hawk, I see is a robin. In the dream, the Texan landscape emerges from the mist, small hills sharp and far apart from one another surrounded by emerald green marshes (impossible what is stone and what algae), the lone bus at the end of its line. Growl of a squirrel. Rearranging the sequence of potted plants about the vacant lot, waiting for the right combination to click. Card in the mail announces the birth of Willa Bea Ott.

Sculpture garden of the damned, a vacant lot in the middle of Telegraph Avenue has become a new squat for the homeless, intricate stone paths between tents, memorial mounds of found objects (this one for Karen Silkwood and Jane Addams), a computer screen with painted graffiti, murals on surrounding brick walls, as many people here now as when the old six-storey hotel occupied the site – red-orange sun sets over Cody's while someone solos on a harmonica out of sight.

Job paranoia dream: when I return to my desk, I find a restaurant has taken its place. Leaving the window open at night, I can hear the dull rush of the freeway one mile away. I sit on a lawn chair and shut my eyes. Street people stand at an electronics store display window, watching the Clarence Thomas hearings silently on a half dozen TVs. In this nation, hunger is a government policy.

Teach Jack Hirschmann to play Uno with a regular deck of cards. Paramount push. Wire coathangers in a closet rattle together, muted bells, muffled xylophone. Red fish soup. I place my hand on the great mound of your tummy and whisper encouragement to the boys.

Typos on a plastic bag. Society for Prevention of Little Animal Tragedies. Knowing that, as the car rounds this bend, I will be driving directly into the setting sun. Teaser for the eleven o'clock news. Ten years after the death of her husband, she's become a communications consultant in the Midwest who buys a copy of Avital Ronell's *The Telephone Book*, think it would be good to stay in touch with the theory of her work, only to mail the volume to me weeks later having rediscovered why she so detests theory.

Think in shadows. An elastic band as a closed form. This instantly becomes known as the Texas Cafeteria Massacre. Before he speaks, the man who approaches me starts to smile, and in that act I see the familiar expression of my best friend from the fifth grade. Days grow shorter toward the end of a notebook.

The song in my head as I wake today: "Papa ooo mau mau, papa ooo mau mau (yip yip yip)." Krishna's sister sighs audibly, asleep in the other room. A blimp floats quietly through the night sky. Birds silent, hidden in the trees. Red sun, sliver moon.

Giant tortoise crawls across the restaurant table, but we're afraid to stab at it with our forks. Standing on the porch in my bathrobe to fetch the Sunday paper, I hear a train in the distance, passing: not only the horn, but the bells of intersection warning signs and the clackety sound of the tracks. Having gone away for the weekend, our neighbor's left her skylight open, so now it's pouring rain right onto her bed. Dr. Yang: The Uses of Asian Stereotypes in Woody Allen's *Alice*. First birds in the morning sky.

The guests have gone so the house feels large again. The dog stares intently at the seagull. A long fly on the sill of the kitchen window. In the dream the doctor hands me the syringe but instead of a first bubble of air emerging from the needle's sharp, slanted tip, a long ribbon of a black inky substance pours out.

Suddenly, right after breakfast on what we can sense is going to be a scorcher, it grows dark in the house, so I stand on the porch and see a vast column of smoke rising from the Berkeley hills, covering a dime-sized red-dot sun, spreading southeast. From the Ashby BART station, I can see flames in the hills leaping from eucalyptus to eucalyptus, then houses as fireplaces, framed by the flames that consume them. A phone tree tells us very quickly whose homes are already lost, who's still packing and waiting for the word to evacuate, who's gone away for the weekend. What would I take? At night, the wind dies, a kind of miracle.

On television, elements of narrative stalk the news: camera holds on a woman's face as she shakes with the realization that her house is the only one left standing, a specialist discusses insurance, lists on the screen of which schools are closed, which roads open, a reporter wades through rubble stringing cliches into a "think piece." Having been evacuated from his brunch at the Claremont Hotel, the enormity of the disaster doesn't reach him until his car reaches the parking lot exit on Ashby and he sees the stream of cars filled with people in tears, a traffic jam of refugees. When dawn rises the next day, the great plume of smoke had become a low-lying lazy cloud, yesterday's disaster hidden in the mist. Leslie Scalapino on the roof of her house watches the fire burn just three blocks away, then a house on the next block catches, but then the wind shifts and the firestorm blows instead over the freeway, the next neighborhood burning to the ground. Against the panic of people packing what they can into cars and in flight, there's the curious calmness of people who've already lost all they own, the flattened affect of shock.

Skin pulled taut over your stomach like the canvas of a drum, breasts transformed completely in anticipation of the production of milk, belly button losing all sense of indentedness. Dark clouds from the edge of a rain system that never quite lets loose. Better to singe than singed against. Exactly what you would expect from a small atomic bomb. The whole city smells charred.

A street singer wanders through the ashes, strumming and singing, "It's only a cyborg, now one more is gone, leaving nobody to carry it home, leaving nobody to boot up a clone, it's only a cyborg, now one more is gone." In the dream, I and several coworkers are in a different city – elements of Albuquerque, Kansas City, plus places I've never been – walking through the streets at dust, looking for excitement. At the office people mill around: at least 18 of us live close to the devastation, one surrounded by it on three sides, but miraculously nobody's been burned out.

First rain brings the ants indoors, spots on the bathtub porcelain. "Wish," says the windshield wiper, and so I do.

The train in the rain pulls loudly through the night. Somewhere someone is attempting to start their car but the engine won't turn over. Dear flash floods, don't.

Driving around with somebody who, after 20 years in this town, still doesn't know the major streets. I wake with every muscle in my lower back stiffened, spine and ribs pulled so tight it hurts to breathe. The lamp in the basement clamps to a beam. I feel your tongue at the base of my cock, the muscles of your lips.

The thief's rap, emerging from the backyard, was that he was recycling the silver tray, which didn't ring true so we fetched a neighbor who'd spoken with the man himself, but whose wife realized instantly what was missing. Ink smears as if words have shadows. Look into my eyes when you make me come.

Is this the dream, car stalled in tunnel? I'm alone in a vast bookstore, much larger than the Strand, nothing in categories, no alphabeticization, no system, trying to locate a single title, my own. Telling Mark how sorry I am that his house burned down, I find myself spouting cliches, the event so enormous no other language remains. One full day after the death of Bill Graham, the copter's still stuck in the web of the power pole it struck. Shahin tells me that, ever since the firestorm, she's been too depressed to work out at the gym.

Rod Stewart, king of the schmaltz anthem, sings *Forever Young.* Alarm clock stuffed into the drawer full of t-shirts rings to be let out. I explain to the senior VP that I've just sent the manuscript to a printer 70 yards away and he proceeds to count it off, determining it to be exactly 65. The top drawer's for shorts, the next for socks, the next t-shirts, and the bottom for sweatshirts and sweaters. Dyed blond perm calculated to look wild, uncombed, spontaneous, Rod's hair demonstrates theory.

Proprietary to dawn, an alarm rings and I rise. An optimism's built of too little sleep. Day begins, the 26th anniversary of my first marriage. The distant train passes on the same line my grandfather as a boy would ride his bike down to see, bearing commerce from far places in the north. Mysterious as ever, today's invisible song echoing in my head is *Maggie May.*

You groan in your sleep as if to speak. At the door, a boy with one leg – it's not a costume – his face painted clownlike but earth tones, green and brown, holds out a plastic sack, too intimidated to say "trick or treat." The rhyme with the homeless is inescapable. A used bike shop called ReCycle. This young girl makes a very fat, African-American Tinkerbell.

Language poem: some assembly required. The depth of the dream: the conjunction of mirrors enables me to watch an old man, myself, walking away from the campus library. New students of law hear a lecture on the familiar. At an intersection, you're forced to confront your choices. Honking traffic appears so certain.

But these are geese in a barnyard readying themselves for a feast. Next door, a dog patrols the back porch, barking as I haul garbage out to the cans. The emotional tone of any Sunday dictated by the Monday that follows. Install hardware as shown in illustration. Get another paragraph!

It was a dark and stormy text. Slowly the desk ceases to be disparate pieces of wood, gathering shape, size, bulk. First Carla comes by to pick up a book, then Steve to watch a PBS program on childhood development, then Bob on his way to sell books – would we like any? – then Carla returns with Asa because she forgot to give back some change, then after all have left Ronwen arrives with her sister, Rosemary, and Rosemary's dog.

Another dog's whine in the dark more pathetic than plaintive. The crash-and-burn method of going to sleep. Calculating underwear. The ultrasound technician determines each twin to weigh one pound, 13 ounces. I'm standing in the fire zone, blocks of houses burned out in all directions, a chimney as the organizing point for each mount of rubble, able to know where I am by the street numbers painted on the wrecks of cars (wheels and windshields melted away), tho, curiously, street signs themselves appear to have survived untouched – in fact, they've been replaced – a desolate form of beauty to these rolling hills, skeletons of trees, here and there people picking through the wreckage of their lives.

Meet me for dinner in Limbo at seven. The tone of a faucet. Rush of caffeine from the root beer. Grid of the page. Your smile in your mother's eyes.

Morning without warning. Sentences don't "flow" from this pen but rather are built up, patched together, the junk sculpture of found objects. Stepping outdoors to fetch the paper serves the secondary purpose of testing the weather. At sunset, the sky more strawberry and orange, compliments of Mount Pinatubo. After the non-event, people stand around and visit.

The cabdriver from Somalia, only his third year in the United States, alone with no family, Dallas the only American city he knows, a small man with a high-pitched voice and clipped, crisp accent, tells me "It's tragic about Magic having to retire that way with AIDS and all." It's almost fun watching Texans cope with 20-degree weather, hotel so pretentious that the dress code indicates that tennis shoes are "inappropriate" in the lobby. What I notice about this vast bed is your absence.

Ribbed corduroy look of the couch is a printed effect. Sound of the morning's first jet. At night, which floors of the highrise remain lit? I walk to the too-familiar intersection at Dealey Plaza, the scale of which feels much larger in my imagination. Downtown without life on the weekend.

In my brother's house, hushed tones of the children playing quietly before their parents wake. Once the downtown was abandoned, the people were left with a web of malls in which to conduct the public life of the city.

I pull off the road and into the old part of Waxahachie in search of a Taco Bell. After the kids go to bed, my brother and I stay up until 1:30 in the morning, comparing our different narratives of how our father died – Cliff thinks he fell from a scaffold – trying to figure out just how many brothers and sisters we have. For a five-year-old, the boy plays an excellent game of chess. Box of soy milk. Version of CNN marketed just for airports, called the Airport Channel.

Drifting to sleep only to be jolted instantly by a nightmare (shadowy monster eating my face). Uncle Tootie's stepson – expelled from the house for being gay just as his sisters were thrown out for being pregnant and unwed – died in the great fire, his only escape, Tunnel Road, alive with flame, the remains found charred in a fetal position in the middle of Charing Cross Road. My brother explains that, "in the Christian view," pterodactyls existed just 4,000 years ago. The old, red brick downtown of Waxahachie is pretty much abandoned, vacant, run down, the life of the town shifting into long wide streets lined with strip malls. A dull, humid overcast, more a scrim than a cloud, settles over East Texas.

Turning the lights on before I open my eyes. That shadowy figure might be my father. Ponderous pines. A web of light from behind my own eyes replaced gradually by a view of the bathroom floor, faux tile, porcelain john.

As I cross the bridge to the city, little wisps of fog dilute the sun. "To keep your dignity in a porn flick," she said, "an actress should maintain eye contact with her partner, the camera, other actors in the scene." Graphics of the body: at the rehab facility, you aren't even allowed to stand with your arms folded across your chest. Unable to make up my mind which books to purchase, I buy them all. Is it poetry yet?

The life of pizza. Automatic hammer. I hear pages turn. The repetitive beep of a garbage truck backing up.

Costello absent, the comedian Abbott explains to me that, in two person teams, it's the funny one who always understands the theory of laughter. The oral surgeon tells me the narrative of his second son's birth while I hold your hand and he makes a small incision, then files away the ragged, protruding edge of bone.

A small scar remains where blister broke right over the finger's knuckle, ridge of pus where the hot grease splattered having drained away, clear fluid. Rain reduced now to a drizzle, I see big drops clinging to a wire. My legs contract as I let the 415 pounds push down, feeling the weight first in my quads and calves, then in my back, arms, neck, head, even eyes, until I press forward and the weight rises, eases, the process repeated in two sets of ten each, a curious sitting position, 45-degree angle from the gym floor. Here in the suburbs, women wear spandex shorts under their thong leotards (not so in the city). What in "serious" literature is metaphoric often is literal in sci fi: "Her world exploded."

The pitcher strides in mid-delivery on the baseball card picture, an image of action frozen in time, yet posed (behind him one sees two players standing side by side at shortstop facing the outfield, one of them holding a bat). Winged rodent squeals to register distance in the dark. You snore, a roaring at the depth of the dream. The tunnel is low, dark, filled with echo and stalactites until it opens suddenly onto the brilliance of the diamond, night lights reflected in the astroturf. A man walks past who understands the image of his walking.

In the dream, there's a dress code. Injustice leaves me seething with anger, so much so I wonder at what childhood scene has been reinvoked. In justice, there's a stress code. Position is nine-tenths of the jaw.

A bird in the hand will make a mess. Holding the flashlight in my teeth so that I can hold the carton with one hand while finding and unlocking the padlock with the other.

Bruce Andrews is an example. Listening for the point where the sirens stop. A lone small plane audible in the night. At the gym, I take my anger out on the weights. Put that in a sidebar.

Beautiful evening for a drive through the woods until you realize what you're driving is a desk. Your dream here. E-mail nicknames. We gather at the steak house for the farewell luncheon but none of us orders steak.

Something deep-throated and humongous barks from inside the Hillview Pet Hospital. A thin haze softens colors, the distant hills a flat backdrop. I sit on a bench at a busstop. Outside the appliance shop, refrigerators in cardboard boxes wait for the kid with a handtruck. Strong wind from the north.

Dream lives of the broke and shameless. We lie on the bed and watch little kicks inside your stomach. In Petrified Forest, a teenage girl (Bette Davis) at an Arizona desert truckstop reads Villon. The "wood grain finish" on the black box microwave is pure gesture. No politician wants to admit that we're in a Depression.

The Great Banana of 1929. Chatter of hummingbirds at the feeder. In spite of his cult status, Bogart's popularity did not lead to a generation of little boys named Humphrey. Weeks later, people still talk with awe at the power of the fire. In the shadows of the womb, my sons are growing.

Orange hue of the oven's coil. Pale blue glow of the hour on the clock radio. If I set the dimmer switch on the overhead lamp half way, the bulb hums (filament as tuning fork). Moon amid the streetlamps more blue than they. I saw the figure five in blue on the face of the microwave oven.

Discernible that this is a head pushing up against the stomach wall. History of advertising drives packaging, determines the color of these appliances (bright yellow means you can play the radio under water). F2 through the rest of this screen. Banana or apple as ideal object. Design of the hand.

Memory's filter: some former lovers dissolve faster than others. A ten-year-old boy, suddenly shy on the phone. A four-player trade between Cincinnati and the Dodgers but only the star outfielder is asked his emotions. A lifetime supply of dirty dishes. Pimple on my ear right where my glasses rest.

Your belly button stretches to infinity. Bride of spatula. A past constructed to explain the present. Any theory of naming is personal. What the root *-cuse* means, without the *ex* or *a*.

It's a long way to topiary. To become the King of Greece, this fellow, who looks halfway between satyr and Cro-Magnon, tusklike teeth jutting wildly through moustache and beard, must pass a test, which I as the lone representative of a foreign society, have been asked to give, but when I look at the scraps of lined yellow paper I've been given, I see that he must get three out of ten questions right and that each asks which of three brands of liquor has the lowest alcohol content.

Imagine a poetry relevant to life before art. I'm tearing apart the study to make room for a nursery. In English, the title means The Hunt. A library peopled with friends. Vultures out over the bay means their habitat elsewhere has been destroyed.

Spiderbites on my ass. The woman in the dream who carries forward elements both of my wife and my boss happens to be my mother. A new hum means a new trip to the auto shop. When I ask who won the game, the two grocery clerks directly contradict one another. Pregnant women cannot hide their erotic nature.

The oral surgeon extracts a loose piece of bone, one-half inch by three-eighths of an inch, from the flesh of your jaw. The clarity of a chill day in December. Pie plate without the pie. The questionnaire asks me for my kitchen theme, if any. Purple stalks of lavender.

Representational function of music (all of *Peter and the Wolf* in garage-band feedback). The body gulps sleep. The freeway cleaves the community so that, as these little farm towns sprawl into suburbs, a series of cul-de-sacs appear on either side. Downtown is old town. From the soccer field, you can see the great produce trucks pass.

Muscles down my right shoulder tighten when I turn my head to the left. Uterus is the strongest muscle. Flextime. A sled for the city bears wheels. So much depends upon the red corpuscles glazed with T cells, beside the white liver.

Poems don't end: they (and we) "go through termination." Infertile parenting. Someone inside your stomach kicking to say hello. My own father tossing and turning restlessly deep in his grave. What do I mean when I say "you must learn to love your reader"?

Notebook, hear me now. These candles burn for eight days. It's California so people at a party introduce themselves by telling where they grew up. Down there in the flats. Hannah who will be nine in the year 2000.

Once inside the egg, the tail of the sperm breaks off, leaving a breach through which the male genetic information spills forward, signalling the transformed cell to start the long process of division and division and division. The busdriver waits for me to dash against the light and board. One senses a particular kind of closure because the year ends when the days are shortest (what if we held New Year in July?). Your tummy feels as though the babies are wrestling. Design of the pipes and vents atop houses, an echo in miniature of the temples and domes of Samarkand.

Ventriloquist moon throws shadows on a cloudy night. Plum tree's branches emerge through the falling leaves. Dog patrols neighbor's yard against possible invasion of cats. This world by porchlight.

Little book, I hold you as you in turn hold me. An image as offered augurs little but a ground for the imagination to dance. New fingernail moon high over the supermarket parking lot, visible to anyone who looks up. "Aaron, do your sentences," a mother shouts. Meat loaf soup.

The clarity of sleep. The peel of the banana through cartoon history – does it affect how I view the peel sitting her on the arm of my chair? Searching the supermarket for a product I've never bought before, I see whole cases of items that are new and unfamiliar. Microwave baked potato. The density of soup (and rhyme).

I'm on a city bus but in bed and under the sheets next to me, where I expect to find you, is the large white horse, which rears and bounds down the crowded aisle as we come up Fillmore to the Haight Street stop, you and I trying to decide, Is this our transfer point? while a huge crowd on the sidewalk tries to squeeze forward and in, two young thugs shirtless on the street playing catch with long knives while the horse (which is our horse, we borrowed it from a friend in the commune in the large yellow Victorian where one of her roommates makes his living selling grey market tape cassettes at flea markets – we're taking it and the quiet brown pony that follows in the street tied to the bus oblivious to the great exhaust all the way to Sausalito where we'll ride back to the East Bay on the ferry) snorts and gallops back to us in the rear of the bus and even if this is our transfer point – I'm never sure – we're still in bed, talking to the other passengers and, besides, I notice there's no way out.

The syntax of sleep. Unconscious is not "structured like a language" but the other way round. I wake feeling dull, unrested, unable to think. The logic of which glass fits where amid the jumble of pots, spoons, and dishes in the drainer, social origin of Rubik's cube.

Days of 1991 dwindle. Like a computer game, invaders come at us firing live ammo through the woods until we capture and disarm them, only to discover a new enemy is sending strange flaming frisbees exploding in our direction. Traffic on the freeway slows even before the first flares until we gradually inch around the tableaux: an overturned car, an ambulance and two black-and-whites, all their lights flashing, a crowd of people in the fast lane huddled, working hard over a woman lying flat in the lane (I see only her feet, stockinged, shoes gone, wide shapeless ankles suggesting she may be my age or older), all backlit by the huge red sun setting in the strawberry sky.

The grid of days (of daisies), seven across by four and the variable fraction, each cell of this spreadsheet in turn divisible with hours and minutes for all with no remainder (reminder), every square assigned, a garden of order within which two roses struggle to be born.

Keep the sleep. Learn to recognize poetry. Somehow the receiver knows just when to turn his head and reach out, football descending from the sky. Learning (slowly) not to buy books I already own. Somehow the receiver rings the instant you call.

The feel of sleep heals. And when the bulb breaks (the room bathed in a half light). Steady shush of the furnace. Heliotropic, the poem folds back into itself at night. Magnified on the ultrasound screen, baby makes a fist.

Blue mint gel, the toothpaste from Helena, Montana. Hell and a Montana landscape two distinct places such as the nape of the neck versus the nick of a nap. I wake amid verses and take notes. The ghost of my grandmother shuffles in the curtains. I am waiting for a sentence to end.

Functuation. A woman explains to her small daughter that, yes, she yells during the contractions of labor and, yes, it hurts, but it's a good pain and not to be frightened. Showers at sunset. This week the waiters all wear Santa hats. Under the streetlamps at night, the sidewalks glisten with rain.

What I recall of the interrupted dream is an emotional tone – in this case intensity mixed with fond desire – details themselves flee, dissolve – was I about to resolve some ancient conflict? – so that as I discover myself in the material world, standing before some bowl emptying my bladder, great endless river of urine, I wonder if, should I return to sleep this instant, I would ever find that path, that uncompleted dream again?

At sunset, the traffic copter glistens in the air. Someone's put a better grade of paper into the laser printer. Little cookies that you only see at Christmas. Make mine co-opable.

Keep the sheep. In the dream we're arguing – over what? Imprint of the infant's face, pushing hard against the wall of your uterus. Moon full on the shortest day of the year. Long bill of the merganser silhouetted on the lake.

The dream is structured as a puzzle but not for the waking mind. *Pigs is Pigs* is an early film. The word *is*, a most devious lever. Airs abound, lungs abide. I speak to your stomach, round and wiggling, as tho to the future.

Overhead, a flock of paragraphs heading south. Overheard, syllables cluster into words in self defense. Overhard, the noun retreats into its shell.

Even in mid-afternoon, the haze blocks the near hills as well as the far, cars on the freeway with their lights on. I explain in detail the nature of my cataract operation two years ago to a woman who needs one in the only viable eye she has. I stand at the front gate to survey the world. Skittish, the cat bolts as I near. By the time Gorbachev resigns, the people of Russia seem to barely notice.

First the sirens then the howling dogs. An early timepiece, 4,000 years ago in what is now China, was a ceramic bowl with a tiny hole pricked through its wall placed into a tub of water – when the leaky vessel filled and sank you had a predictable unit of time. I smear the surface of the ham with a paste made of brown sugar, bread crumbs, and dry mustard, congealed with apple cider vinegar. Sparrow hops about the barren tree. Muted light of a gray day.

Omniscience is a sometimes status of the dream. How to design the imaginary landscape? A museum in the park, although I'm never sure what it displays. Theme of the chase. If the crowd fails to make room, to give way, it's because it doesn't acknowledge your authority.

Sound of rain surrounds the little house. On Market Street, the homeless huddle, each having staked out their space, a dark doorway, an awning. It is precisely our heterogeneity, our capacity to imagine human beings as Other, that enables us to walk on by. At Tu Lan on Sixth Street, the little diner is no longer a hangout for unemployed rogue Vietnam vets (I don't see any handguns while I eat my imperial rolls and pork kebob over rice noodles). This hotel we call the Jukebox (mass storage device).

I dream of e-mail. Someone who would confuse fibonacci numbers for class struggle. Twilight of the bods. I don't see the holiday decorations downtown until after the event itself. The basement floor is damp after the rain.

Increased competition makes beggars more aggressive – he walks through the BART cars shaking a coffee can full of coins – and in some instances more creative. How can they sleep in the rain? The days of the post office, at least as we know it, are numbered. On television, cars drift in the floods of Texas and I search for your face. Bouquet of lilies fading in a glass vase.

Washing the dishes steams the window, then, as the temperature drops, precipitation turns to frost. The formula in a capitalist democracy is one dollar, one vote. The dysfunction of criticism. eleven poets gather for lunch at David's Kosher Deli, one block from the MLA, laughing over blintzes. At home, I watch your stomach bump and roll with the movement of twins.

VOG

First Passage

Owlwise,
I hear voices
where once words formed
way back in the head,

laughing, muttering

Each individual an unrepeatable rhythm
timber, pitch
The head
is a drum,
The skull
an organ of sound
reaches down into
lungs, chest, belly, bowels

Old man on the bus
with too many bags of groceries
who helps whom?

This snow falling
is a solid object
years later

Out of nothing,
to construct a hand
Faust would weep
at the simplest things

Avalanche
of sideburns,
eyes that crosst

To wear a cape
actual
out in public

To have slept
with men who slept
with men who slept
with Whitman

Genealogy of choice

Of Grammatology

View of these words as if uninhabited by humans. In sod we rust. The blathers scrim. Theory of smidgens. Triangle Park. Dogfaced boy, a Photoshop moment. In the world of Babar, one can walk from the country of the Elephants, a republic which has no other name, to the city of Paris. Blind man allergic to his own guide dog. Make no claims: "The ingredients thought to be responsible for garlic's goodness." The integration of the taste parameter developed in Chapter II into Marshall's demand analysis yields a logically complete interpretation of the Marshallian demand schedule by placing Griffin's Paradox into its proper perspective. Flu, shy, flu. Badge in, badge out. All enchantments in play must be discarded. At first I notice only that the two young men are speaking to one another in sign language, so only gradually do I begin to notice that they're also flirting.

A Sphere of Light

The glare of consciousness

Mirror
water
frozen

the sun shining thru
every branch of every tree
the forest a prism in icy winter

To live without conflict
is not to have lived

darling fetus
Speak to the possible
a distinction
between ghosts
& Martians

The big trucks roar past
along the narrow road

That a tree
be that only

ice crystals
devoid of history

The eucalyptus
introduced to produce railroad ties
tho the wood splits and fails
has no "natural" enemy here
other than fire

The large page ages
glue eats the margin

these letters themselves
suck at the fiber

Enormous sea of white
surprisingly dark, pushes in waves
against the side of houses, streets, trees
The great trucks bearing ploughs
slowly push their way through
by the headlights' dim glare

I cried when you told me
hand barely able to grip this pen

What then?

Silence of the Looms

Mediocritus: where there's life, there's trope. Emporia of the possible abandoned to floods, water swollen, darkened with its own life force, surging, sullen. That which is merely personal soon rats. Charles Bernstein wears khakis. Cello Jell-o. Full functionality metaphors. Fifteen foot roll of ortho-glass. A player may not untap more than one land during the untap phase of each of his or her turns. Sign: opposing traffic has longer green.

Before dawn, a kitchen light casts its dull glare out over the snow. Sense of panic in a dream. In the bank, a large woman hands me my money stapled together in an envelope. I'm pulling my children through the streets on a sled, waiting for the street lamps to come on. I wave and realize I'm alone in my bed, then see her asleep wrapped in some blankets on the floor. "Brittany," he shouts when I ask him what breed his dogs are. More snow begins to fall.

The bones that remain retain their pain. Sawed-off shogun. Why did the chicken cross the node? Popping the touch-me-nots. Lynda Hygiene. Robot comedian in an empty casino bar, lights darkened, tells jokes to the empty tables, laugh tracks ghosting back. Peeling the wrap from the CD. Seniors in the class alas. As Barbar and his young queen Celeste age and have first triplets and then a fourth child, Arthur, the cousin who may or may not be Celeste's brother, remains permanently an adolescent. The republic of paragraphs.

Rethink everything. The old man & the alphabet. The hush when the dryer shuts down. This street person's tethered three shopping carts into a train. Play-dough's Republic. Condensed music (add milk). Had Ike registered Democrat, what then? In *On Beyond Zebra,* Seuss (Zeus) invents twenty new letters, including um, quam, thnad, snee, yekk and spazz. By the heels at Milano (Vendler? Hollander?), spiked, shining, snazzy.

Waiting to inhale. This crowd is a system, heated to the max. The blizzard of is. Only the passive voice rings true. God as a toddler. I wander thru the

ER waiting room lost in the daze of my own world barely conscious of the mob (house explosion in Waco, Texas, kills two). Inaudible umlauts. Tea at the bottom proves bitter. Prism mouse of language. Mistah Gates, he dead. That raised, passive view (black & white) of the security camera thru wch we see over & over the shopkeeper shoot the teenage girl. Reduced instruction set.

Thin blue linebreak. The higher the snow, the simpler the landscape. My ear instead of an onion. Sun's sheen vibrato. Thixotropic. Containers atop flat cars roll slowly through town? Which is the magpie? Age at which a cross-eyed man begins his passage, the new work, the same thick scrawl at which, at ten, I drew every letter.

Begin again, in again. Fofo & Yoyo (spelt "Jojo") in search of the authentic. Lady Shakespearean seeks a tattoo. I in the bone yard amid rubble for the perfect line. Wonk / don't wonk. Five beeps, says the microwave. Nonreturn to zero inverted. SKU wars. L'age d'Or (garage door). We who are narratively disadvantaged. Randolph Dud, he never did.

One doesn't wake so much as realize that one hasn't been asleep for a long while. Fin de siecle swims. Write in any state of mind, Montana, ache in the calves just shy of cramping, deltoids and pecs sore with labor. Language is ice (melting), flight (molting). Livermore (kidney less). I find a lima bean, mysterious on the linoleum floor. Sign on this cow town's downtown overpass reads "Fight for the Rights of Preborn Babies." Dwarf dressed all in leather. Wading through the low brush, wishing that I had my binocs, trying to determine if this large, still, distant white elongated graceful bird be egret or sandhill crane, a red fox bursts literally beneath my feet, leaping to reach the road. The brutality of the book is that of the dream abrupted by the roar of the alarm (I'm searching the narrow streets of an impossible steep Paris for an inexplicable Holiday Inn, sun setting, threat of rain, surrounded by familiars of corporate life, Wells Fargo, Baxter Medical, Harris Pharmaceutical, Glaxo (already, awake, I'm inserting the known world, the real Paris, deleting coworkers who have no business in my sleep)). Bronk / don't bronk.

The Nose of Kim Darby's Double

Canyons, paths
dug thru the snow
                                Tunnels
the walls as high as
shoulders
The weight of it
heavier
when it begins to melt
& then, at sunset
still midafternoon
the temperature drops
wind over the ridge
so that by dawn
each surface
hardens into ice

Dams clog the drains
to turn the window
facing north
into a waterfall . . .

Driving north
past the mall turn, King
of Prussia, past Bridgeport
and the narrow brick streets of Norr'stown
the road eases up, what
was once country
into a more purely rural
suburbiana (golf course
blanketed in white

A gas station that has not yet
turned into a minmart

Swath cut
by the powerlines
right thru the old quarry, the pit
filled with water
is called a lake, each
new townhouse with its private dock
tho if you look upstairs
you will discover the doors to the closets
all made of vinyl

Someone in another room is singing the alphabet

Barely visible in the high slush
fog mixed with rain
a woman waits for her bus

The form of the flower
exfoliating
petals dropping away
to reveal a new, further flower
now red, now blue
each shape a perpetual
revision, this
leaf thick and milky, this
spiky, hard, this
covered with the finest fuzz
blossoms

In his dream the boy
has dug a maze through the snow
complex, magnificent
that his parents want to dig up
(At four, to identify
the tension of generations

Glow threading
thru the woods at night,
headlights from an auto

Gamuk is kissing Ganuganuga

Resolution protocol:
song of a dot matrix printer

Casting text
across the listserv,
                                        I write
until the first sight of sun
triggers morning's hunger,
voices echo elsewhere in the house

Stool
          in the form of
a sheep, black,
Dinosaur constructed
from wire and beads

A pennywhistle lies on the rug

Thru the poplars
just enough light
to cast the first silhouette.

Torsion Dystonia

In the dream I'm a spy, willing to hurt anyone just to make my escape,
although never is it clear just what I am doing in this country.
Off in a
corner, the handset of a telephone begins to protest that someone's left it
askew from its base.
There's a grief in her voice as she reads aloud not ap-
parent in the text.
Grid between rivers.
The anxiety of text saved only
to clipboard.
A parent in the text.
Car slows as it approaches our house
and then I hear the newspaper "plop" on the steps.
Squirrel on the roof,
aloof.
Bright pink quilt for the homeless person sleeping in the light of
the department store window (overhang to block the snow).
Hotel suite
with a working fireplace.
When I first see them approach, striding side by
side down the wide airport corridor, I think "there's an interesting couple,"
then realize gradually as she walks just a bit faster, he slower, seeming not to
notice, that they're not together at all.
Admitted to the hospital with a
temperature of 82 (said to be "fetal and withdrawn").
To look at her, you
know she imagines herself as plain.
What sounds at first like a distant
hammer is, upon closer inspection, the second hand of a cheap analog
clock.
On the video, everyone is 17 years younger, the heroic period of
our lives.
Why did the chicken cross the mode?

Blood yoke sun barely visible through the trees.

Barbar is made King for the simple reason that he has been to France, learned to drive and wear clothes – immediately he lays the plans for a great city.

First dot, best dot.

She glides slowly, almost effortlessly, silently through the streets on her bicycle (from here you can hear the waves), one hand on the handlebar, the other resting on her leg.

Target creature is now a flying creature.

That which was illuminated has been eliminated.

Research triangle.

Paisley tights in primary colors.

Driving the install and skill set to a remote site.

Frank Sinatra, "Why I am not a painter."

Two paths carried forward simultaneously, one of vowels, the other of consonants.

Genre trouble.

Little light over videocam's lens is flashing.

Crisp crinkle. Paste flowers from the tube to the brush.

Out the window, across the river, the lights of Algiers, Louisiana.

In the midst of sex a woman's face changes, revealing a truer identity. Point at which ice in the bucket melts, causing the cans of beer and soda to shift and settle.

Little bump with which the airplane actually leaves the runway, almost immediately beginning its clockwise sweep over the flat Michigan landscape.

The Old Lady has no other name, but is an extremely rich, generous and kind woman, ready to give money to young elephants for whatever they might need.

Bitterns in the bog, agog.

Hairs of my beard – white, red, yellow – woven into the sweater.

Nails long enough to gather major gunk.

BAFO vs. BARFO (which one)?

Paradiddle taps.

The night at the window.

Wings of history beat frantically at the bulb's heat.

Heart of the art chokes.

Life, impossible to swallow.

Blurb.

I turn the sound of the game on the television off, the stereo up, Pavarotti with the bases loaded.

Full moon illumines the bare, snow-covered frost, landscape of finite parts.

I slip the shoe back onto the foot, the wrong one.

Go, Doug, Go.

SUNY Muslim.

New words for old.

"Dead cat in box" hand printed on the lid, thick felt tip stroke, on curb's edge, and inside: sure enough.

Iced cubism.

Interwonk.

From Sri Lanka, the dark gem Sillimanite.

American lesion.

Vaseline

alley.

The man sings "Bamba."

Rhyme tsunami with salami.

Elizabeth

Robinson reads Ebbe Borregaard.

I hold him in the dark until he stops crying, one small hand clasped about his plastic bottle of formula, the other brushing gently against my beard.

My train disappears into the tunnel just as I reach the platform.

Because this window faces north, you shall never see the sun.

A lecture hall empty except for one small podium and three tiny metal waste baskets, each holding its brown plastic bag folded over the rim, then knotted tightly by the invisible janitor.

Echo-

genicity.

At take off, I feel the ascent beckon in the bridge of my nose.

Transfer tech flirts with the nurse while his cargo half dozes on the gurney, drugged, hose running from the back of the hand up the IV pole.

Box within a box.

Fox (Nellie) misses the Hall of Fame on his last chance (what does that word really mean?) by exactly one vote.

Cupcake with candles.

For Larry Eigner, Silent

Our endless yawp
The poem is a field of action
                        pigeons
                    roosting in the eaves
              of the concrete train station
    blink with intention
The lights at any intersection
at night change colors
regardless of the traffic
In the basement a pipe
drips quietly
into the waiting bucket

Moon in the poplar tangled
sets just before the sun
first rising throws shadows
the way a ventriloquist does voices
long, lean, stretching back into compactness
Light then we realize is just an illusion
Real-time, thick as any oatmeal, twisted
coagulates intention
                                        Baboon
will fight a crocodile
if it's grabbed an infant

Behind me,
where the hospital corridor should be,
I find a street corner
around which a klezmer band is marching
approaching yet never arrives
Whom should I notify first?
The term "intention" returns
in the guise of will, would

hard grained, knotted
thru which surface any day now
the first green shoots of a new year
vulnerable to frost will bloom

Find in the counsel of dreams an old tune
the band itself half forgotten
beneath the shards of melody
to locate a tone
as an index to emotions
not recognized at the time but held
closely, more so than that to which we thought we'd paid attention

A quality of light underneath the streetlamp
is how it dampens color
how color itself is a thing imposed
as the sun imposes day

Day, when it arrives
if it arrives, is layered
and must be stripped
although never in the same way twice
if ever we are to discover
the pulse at the core

What fiction, what nonsense

Voices over in the corner, jabbering
with no thought of who listens

2.

The line already is inherent in the upright letter, oriented. Speech is not a given. The tongue is infected. It is very cold. Worlds hurtle through the night sky, where it is apparent that day is the exception, that it may even be a fiction, a creation not of light, but of desire. I WANT SPEECH. Sky, air, wind, sun surround. For want of storm windows, we hung quilts. Birds shake snow from the lighter branches. The traction faction. One doesn't so much sleep under all these blankets as one does cook. Pencil is a blunt instrument. In a coma, I am told, all evidence of palsy disappears, you yawn freely, widely, the way an infant yawns asleep. I shall not hear birds in these trees again. Words hurtle through the night sky.

3.

Stripped of furnishings, the familiar house became exactly what it was: an object, alien, a machine, each room a potential or function. There, in the leafless forest, we could see the huge nest high atop a poplar. From here I can walk to the train, so much assumed in the instant, twenty five bones per hand or foot, three muscles roughly for every bone. Behind that wall, the low hum of the furnace. After several days of warmer temperatures, the snow still has not melted, the last mounds dark and translucent, cakes of ice. Odd how, after 30 years, a phrase such as "the beauty   wapiti" still rings in the mind. Oncoming cars' headlights shimmer dimly in the fog. At the road's edge, back in the trees, the deer watch us, witness without interpretation. The flower's knowledge of its own process is not counted as mind. I walk with each hand balled into a fist.

4.

"Oh yeah
  you're

    one of the ones

      who can
        write in the dark"

That Which Is Merely Eternal Soon Rots

Sun in the fog in the trees, birds
skittering in the first light.
Shadow of my hand over the word
as I write. The master of rooms
constructs a cage within a castle
within which a canary who whistles
might sing.
                    We give birth
to death itself and then
live forever in fear and awe
which is the same thing, and call it
the simplest of names or forget
its name altogether, it is so
omnipresent.
                    Time waits not
for the screen to redraw, for
me to withdraw, that
drawl that extends
the *o* in *no*
when a daughter leaves a daughter

Old Irish alibi
Lament

The market seen as a game of chess
a million colors across a vast board
each in play simultaneously
is not the individual's experience
of an acquisition, is not
what, standing by the copier window
causes one to pause.
                              Beyond
the parking lot so full

the brown UPS van is forced
to pull up on the grass, the vast
park just past the last rooftops
lone white church spire rising thru the trees
two plumes of white steam rise high
from the cooling towers of Limerick

Thin blue linebreak
merely an echo one half hears ringing
receding the instant one wakes
back into the dream – what was that?
a rock one finds shining on the beach
that when dry loses its luster
only to carry forward a new, different fascination
too difficult to name – what is that?
Tricks, to thread words
heard in the head forward
between lines, thru
the morning of snow falling
indoor winter light

Small potato eyes
sink into the snowman's face
leaning in the gradual warmth
over the fence
the train roars south
electrified
cold mechanical bullet

Quilt as a theory of form

Full moon never free of poplar branches
night forest blue with snow
house seen as a lantern, muted
throws long shadows

Long clear whistle
followed by a trill –
which bird wakes
to greet the rainy dawn
tho the adjectival itself
forms a cliché
to display the familiar / familial
all of civilization sucked into the verb "greet"

In Avignon I found the French easier
because cast in a Spanish slant

The bird as an object
in the tree as an object
sings without intention
in the meaningless woods

Spiderduck

for Robert Kelly

red sun

over

Mud Island

(Sun Studio

a monument to

itself)

"Redemption"

shouts
the sign

over the station
for change

in
the casino

Rae-
ification

My eye
scans the chipped

plywood surface
of the old

portable stage
noting

the uneven
distance between
galvanized nails

As tho swimming
were a solution
so harsh

in the text
Vowel
hidden

in Trakl
Homo
erotics

of Peter
Pan
muted

woman assigned
to play
the boy

Wounded
Acres
But the father's

name is Jumbo
Introduction
of the ball point
killed penmanship

In the distance, in
some other room
a telephone
doesn't so much ring as

give a soft
electronic yodel
The secret
end of any

year is
Christmas,
the week after
mere echo

Cowboy
leans against wall
of two-story
res hotel

Colin
Owl,
king
of the night forest

The logout
beckons
as the login
beckoned,

memory
is a kind of
chip
Broccoli
is a mustard

(eat your tree)
Mime field
Days outstanding
Bert and Ernie:
don't ask,

don't tell
Geese demand
their favorite poet
Bronk Bronk
False tart,

scone head
Often I am permitted
to return to a method
as if to a mind: mine
A blind man talks

to the mailbox –
how am I to interpret this
Hannah calls to complain
that I failed to warn
she was about to fall

I blinks
Explain
that this cloth doll
represents the bear
but as an ideal

with no equivalent
in nature Refer
to this notebook
as a pen-based
system

Absence of tumor-markers
discernible in the blood
Putting the punk
into punctuation
(bad to verse)
an old man with infant sons

each drinking
from a plastic bottle
diluted apple juice
pushes the twin stroller past
the blue house whose
garage (dark, deep)

always sits open
one half dozen
American sedans
each in its various
state of repair
hoods up, wheels off, door

missing – and to the side
shining, brilliant
inexplicable in this
residential neighborhood
their own
Coca-Cola vending machine

Catfish sullen
at the bottom of the tank
The joy of disjunction
Yesterday's snow
waterfall frozen
at the man-made lake

Tragedy of the dream
in the peasant's bent
ballot   Puzzle pieces
strewn over the carpet
Family of deer
walk slow over the snow

An African gray
is a parrot
that one in the blue cage
reciting your own lines
back to you
in alternate accents

Hibition
Crows swarm at dawn
Between Eros and
erosion
memory enters in
A voice is calling
Daddy

Dog watches suspiciously
as I lean over the notebook
Desktopia
The bitter batter
of Little Feat
Life on the phone
Red dog on a blue tree

Macro to determine
break in the line
Each frame
of Zapruder's film
known by its number

Wasps bounce
off thick plate glass

nine stories up
second tallest building
in Waco
as I stare
out across town
all the way to the lake
When he says "we"

he excludes himself
Read at Discovery Zone
At Home Depot an entire wall
of linebreaks   I look up
in time to see her standing
staring out that eighth story
window (from my

perspective one frame
in a tall glass wall)
wearing not a stitch
scratching, one breast
missing entirely
Three squirrels gallop
across an open field

as they never will
in the city
High in the oak tops
a woodpecker heard
but not seen
Desire as a noun vs.
desire as a verb

When the King of Prussia
mall expanded
from six anchor tenants
to nine, auto
thefts in the lot
of the Lockheed Martin

plant across Mall Blvd
rose from two
per year to
six per month
Inside the train
the horn sounds distinct

Station
of the Metro
Apparition
of a pistol
against a wet black brow
I see her pausing

to look up
as if in thought
by the galvanized
can at
the driveway's end
My text

instead of an onion
Old man wearing ear muffs
and thick gloves walking
round the high school track
The year horizontal stripes
showed up in

everybody's logo
(3D effect)   I slept
watching the plan
ning commission on
the community access
cable channel

right thru
the amendments
to the environmental
impact report
Red brick light

industrial district
Tea spilled
on trousers
goes from hot
to cool

in an instant
Writing is a maid
to Emory
considering how exaggerated
the paranoia is

Translucent morning moon
Nature used
as a figure
of emotion
Conjunction understood

as punctuation
A Greek chorus
of mice for a tale

of a pig that
thought it was a dog

Bruised Andrews
Powder
over slosh atop
ice: geology
of January

Chasing chickens
Choosing
thickens choice
Red tail dips

pursued by crows
high above
Phoenixville Pike
Chinchillas

gone now
entirely from the wild
The cow before
it was domesticated

Force
of the plane
in the way
it brakes

Open the
sandwich
to strip out

onion
Fake Falls
Having thunk

With a thud
the house shudders
and the furnace

ignites
First light

the silhouette
of trees

already

visible

the large
dark blocks

of houses
beneath them

but the sky
barely discernible
Behind me

a man recounts
his having bought
his teenage

nephew
a shotgun, who
receiving it

said only
"I thought
it would be
automatic"

Ear
understood
as a culture
for infection

From pretest
to protest
Nail torn
beneath the quick

Egrets stomp
through reeds
in the swamp
Objects

in text appear
closer
than they are
Rain
on the surface

of the lake
Storm distorts
fountain's spout
Six flights below
boat tail grackle

screaming in the trees
My gars
and starters
Arms, legs
spread wide

asleep in a large bed
Yarn to web

each piece of furniture
is called “an invention”
My rabbit lies over the ocean

Fat wet flakes
of a spring snow
                Woodpecker
paradiddle
That which is

merely
positional
shall soon root
Teen mom
pauses in the mall
stroller

crowded with bags
Weekday morning supermarket
crowded with old men
At the service
station
a man in a brown

jumpsuit
slowly waves
a customer into
the proper bay
Atop a wood pole
mailbox

capped with snow
Elevator
as a trope
for civilization

Backside
of row houses

old brick from wch
hang slantwise
half collapsing
tar paper
porch rooves
Two women

talking loudly
rapidly
almost simultaneously
the first in
French
the other

English
When she showed him
the small silver
ring in her nipple
he slipped
his little finger in
& gave it a tug

Under the old bridge
dry creek bed
filled now with tires
Why the red-
bellied wood
pecker has
so much more

red at the back
of the head

Young couple
with an older man
for lunch
in a SoHo bistro
create

in themselves
a completed narrative
(fill in the gaps)
until, dessert plates empty
they pay and rise to leave
and I realize
now for the first time

the older man's with her
Chickadee at the suet cake
How quickly
this blue sky clouds over
Rain spilling over every eave
Squirrel dangling upside down
from bird feeder

spinning on a chain
Between cars at the stop light
he walks holding high
the crude cardboard sign
"I do not," it reads,
"steal or rob
so please help

the homeless"
Try to recognize
that familiar face
who with her tongue plays
at your foreskin

in the dream
Catfish swarm

at the water's surface
under the bridge
lured by a handful
of dry cat food
First tulips, first hyacinth
forsythia's yellow bursts

against the grey wall
of winter forest
Small boy dances
to inaudible tune
while a large
but immature

puppy nuzzles
into the dirt
Orange triangle –
danger –
on the back of
the otherwise

black buggy
filled
to absolute capacity
by the Amish man
and his children
Discern

by the shape
of the woodpecker's
head

Coolest
in the basement
on a hot night

Yard thick
with the odor
of mulch
Scatter
of magnolia
petals

at the base
of the tree
the taller
poplars
still bare
and grey

Why rabbits
won't eat
dandelions
Noisily farting
That each line

on its own
must stand
or else
People
come up to me

and tell me
their dreams
Man standing
by a blue car
the hood up

in a light rain
A walk at dusk
amid flowers
to the distant
chortle

somewhere of a jay
A woman
sits cross-legged
next to a row
of newspaper racks

checkerboard smile
the pupil of one eye
clouded over
Try to catch
sun motes

in the palm of
your hand
Birdlike
warble
of distant car alarm

Quesadilla space monster
Hotel room john
sink used as a
desk to write on

Moon shadow shoots
through the kitchen
long tail just visible
going out the door

Four is to seven as
verbs to nouns

clutter the mind
A large book

to purchase in hard back
Pen perceived
as marketing tchochke
by Lexis-Nexis

Rock band in bar
downstairs curiously
slow or quiet
Back when I

imagined Smithson
as "older"
Calamari writhes
between my teeth

We put the pro
in Prozac
The new sentence
as an adult

"Quote me, please,"
pleads David Bromige
"Oooh," groans David Melnick

I walk along
the thundering J car
tracks, shops lit

up bright for the night
old hash joint
now become

bright Boston Market
(nee Chicken)
In a bookshop

poems by Sandy Berrigan
inscribed "Dear Philip . . ."
It's 5:15 am

in some other time zone
"Well, she can't dye
them eyelashes"

Large woman ambles
straw bags in either hand
heavy with groceries

(bread stick jutting
out like a flag)

while ahead
two boys race skipping

Another woman's
blonde dreadlocks

over deep dark
African checks

accented
by a neck brace

Latest euphemism
Skilled Nursing Facilities

called in the profession
SNFs

Sip gunpowder tea

in a room of shadows

the gamelan strictly

in your head

while outside

the Kampuchean girl

is turning cartwheels

Fubar Clus

(second passage)

"That much drinking
does not come free"

A ride
in a cheap rent-a-car
after an hour of tea
in the sun

Large screen TV
playing basketball
with the sound off

Movement
quick & muscular
though seeming
curiously slow

Rodman's hair
an impossible yellow-white

Talking of death, of
cancer, this one's
prostate, that one's breast

a woman described as
"a poet of the seventies"
who is in fact
a friend to many here

wind-up kangaroo flips
but fails to land
standing up

"Thinking of getting married again –
a beautiful French woman –
so I ask him
what does he think he's doing

and he admits
he doesn't know"

2.

form festers restless void
Charles Borkhuis

"Behind these pictures
I have other pictures"

Haze blurs the margin
far up Suisun Bay
though to the east, Diablo
etched in summer heat
(though it is only Spring

Little blue butterflies
the underside of whose wings
prove grey as rock
alight atop
wild chamomile

To the west
out beyond the Gate
the great white cloud bank
sits low over the water
a blur to Tamalpais

while between
lays what I conceive of
as the past

The burden
of time
            old men
in the gas station shadows
sitting on overturned drums
spitting into the grease
                                    A woman
beautiful thin face a little more etched
after a year's absence
brings out a tray
on which sits a pitcher and several glasses
out into the brilliant sunlight
of the deck
high over the terraced garden

                                    Masks & kites
                                    hanging from a line
                                    paint drying

            Great Wall of Duplos
            children's chairs
            tables, easels
            webbed together in yarn

Choir
of the nearly inaudible
hum in the walls
crackling constant in every light bulb
deep breath of the furnace
                                                ice maker's rattle
                        in the empty kitchen

overheard
Up the block
an engine turns over

Report of a blue bunting
where none should be

3

The cat stalks slow
across the cut grass
bird barely visible
in the last light
that might still be called
predawn
casts
a narrative
over the whole yard
mealy bugs impervious
in the damp soil

The brief season of tulips has passed

So that
an image is layered
out of the visible
through extraction
of characteristic
detail

She rose up
after the act
straightening the camisole
she still wore,

picking
the rest of her clothes
up from the floor
and looked back at him
alien now that he slept
wondering
had he even seen her
during the fact of it

Cars abruptly
leaving the freeway
climbing the dirt path
up to the off ramp
or the road north
to Germantown Pike
ahead
(then below)
long sea of red lights
the Schuykill transformed
into a parking lot
headed East

Text Formerly Known as Poem

To the old modernism, add sentiment and call it new. Ondaatje's Hemingway, Maso's Beckett, Walker's Faulkner. Ghosts all of them. Kundera, Rushdie and the International Middle Style.

On 42nd Street, midafternoon muggy day, people don't even look up as police cars wail up Fifth Avenue. Vacant lot behind a cyclone fence, the antithesis of nature. Pigeon in the subway.

Junk sculpture of the Emeryville mudflats, the Watts Towers, a house made of beer cans in Houston. Tires in the weeds like giant mouse turds.

Lumps and solidity – the sheer mass of an old feather pillow. Rug's fringe tucked under creates just enough of a bump to send me sprawling. Nothing radiates heat like an old parking lot. Cryptolopes gallop across the cave wall. Faux margarine spread thick over a slice of potato bread.

Undelete. The gangster theory of poetry. The main drag of Hoboken all done up as quaint. The Joyce Kilmer Service Area is little more than a food court attached to an industrial strength gas station: Hispanic boys in white Ts and not-quite-shaved heads stand around the open door of the tour bus.

Dear reader, it's 5:15 am, a good time to write. Outside, the neighborhood becomes visible once your eyes adjust to the lightless sky. Neighborhood without sidewalks, streetlamps. Moment at which birds will start to sing. Rain a mist that clings to the flesh. Lone knocking of the woodpecker.

Against forehead. Against light, a wall, the glare flooding in until it fills you and space itself dissolves. X, the arch criminal, parading about in high black boots, riding crop in one hand. "One needn't read the whole of Pound when Mr. Kenner has so ably provided us with a selection." The thought of what America.

Color photo of a man on his back being shot to death in the streets of Monrovia, assassin leaning forward almost gingerly, automatic rifle in one hand, not to be too close to the splatter of blood and brains, spread across the top of the front page, morning paper, all the more terrible when you realize the photographer, Corinne Dufka, is that beautiful young woman with the terrific smile who used to hang out with your wife in college.

An attempt in the seventh inning to create The Wave fails for lack of population, and thus continuity, in the outfield bleachers.

Full moon trapped in the clouds. What poetry means to men and women as they grow older. Ink hardened and clotted in the pen's shaft. Each letter more to itself. Bird singing with no bird to hear.

By the time the peonies arrive, the tulips have already fled. Memoir of a war just four years ago – difficult to force myself to recall the daily pain of attention to detail (reading of the bombing of a shelter next to a school that incinerated 400 women and children, I barely recall the event).

Dry thunder. In the video she's outdoors, naked, kneeling while a man, not naked, back to the camera, urinates on her small breasts while they talk almost casually, the language Dutch or Swiss, her shaking herself as though shivering when at unbelievable long last the long stream trickles off, shaking the last drops from her nipples before taking his cock, half-erect, fully into her mouth. Another penis, erect, heroically lit in the black-and-white photo, through which a large, shining nail has been driven.

Bullet exits the man's skull (a cringe still on his face) the way it would an apple (photo freezes the action, pulp, meat exploding from the skin).

Tyranny of the sun. His body language shifts visibly when I tell him that we need to speak, that he's about to be laid off, the bones settling into a new order, not tension but exhaustion.

Rabbit in the garden smaller than you'd expect (rabbit or the garden?). The poem explodes in your hands. Age of the audience at the exhibit of Cézanne. Smell of rain in this thick heat.

Birds shrill in the predawn words. Paper made from lint trapped in the clothes dryer. The idea of flight as inevitable struck him as grotesque, so in away it was true that his grandchildren had been born on a different planet. At the first sound of thunder, the pool's lifeguards whistle everyone out of the water.

A boy freckles a sheet of paper with a shower of crayon dots, then methodically begins drawing lines, connecting one to another to another.

Petals of peonies after the rain lay scattered in the dirt. Rabbit as witness at garden's edge.

Scope creep. The new formalism provides the poem with an old statement of work. Lightning shapes a clouded sky.

Odor of a bunch of bananas left in a hot car through a long day of work.

Fireflies sparkle at the edge of the garden.

Fan's sound as it first gathers speed. Deep scaling. Lawn boy calls me Mr. I pick the spider up by one leg and place it outside the door. The Amish man seems garrulous, contradicting my stereotype.

Under the tall trees, the three pools – one for toddlers, one for laps, one for splashing around – turn into a village, neighbor after neighbor happening by.

Walls vibrate, hum of the garage door opener. Wild rabbit on the lawn not the fattened domestic beast one remembers. As if blind, the fly bounces right off the wall.

I wake to a terrible sadness/sameness. The morning paper sits in the driveway in the rain. I want a poem raw as that quarry, filled now with new town homes on miniscule lots, the small shoots of fresh saplings still symmetrical, the first lawns just starting to come in. The yellow of that school bus chewed up by that train. The *New York Times* quotes Catherine Stimpson as saying MacArthur Fellowships are given to those who are "pushing the envelope" on the day one is awarded to Richard Howard.

Texas Chainsaw Collaboration.

After the narrow road of old stone farmhouses, suddenly the latest town homes in a circle, looking like pieces of an interlocking puzzle. Sun setting apparently to the north.

System of the "Dutch" hex. Old straw scarecrow. The first Happy meal in which you don't immediately rip open the cellophane wrapped toy.

Accrual of connotations. Dull gray of dusk mixed with the threat of thunderstorms. Two young women with toddlers in an otherwise empty playground. Five beeps from the microwave. The fan slow in the air.

Road gang works in the heat, walking slow behind the orange cones, air filled with dust.

Dear Jack, a poem as long as California will require a great valley. Overhead, I heard the first unmistakable footsteps of children, first dawn light barely visible in the trees. Last night at the fair, we watched one balloon after another drift into the sky, becoming smaller and smaller as they neared a translucent moon.

I drift back to sleep for one last hour and dream that my best friend's wife, herself an old dear friend, tries to seduce me and I let it happen, hurrying to dress as hear the doors slam open on the floor below.

Mexican polkas. Flossing this much spots my glasses.

Amish girl speaks with something close to a German accent. Later, seeing the Indian couple with their two little girls, I realize I haven't seen a non-European face for hours.

Call the headhunter back without sounding anxious. The doors stick precisely so they can seal out winter. The Lego way of knowledge. Air as soup through which no one moves too quickly. People in the conference room stare at the speakerphones when it sounds (static of a car phone "breaking up").

Straight-line projection. I saw the best faces of my generation starving, hysterical, covered with paint. How to improve a turtle. Cheeks pierced, nostrils, tongues, shadows tattooed permanently about the eyes. Outside a cow punctuates the morning song of birds (over the hill I see the silos from the neighbor's barn).

Sun fish in the murk of Round Pond. Kestrel tears at a lunch of mouse. Red panda more foxlike than the noun implies. Frogs at dusk every bit as vigorous as birds at dawn. Cher croons James Brown's "It's a Man's World" and it becomes an entirely different song. One strategy is verbally to assault the interviewer, to place him/her on the defensive, putting you if not in control of the process at least into a zone of comfort from which to proceed.

A noise, not an echo. Count the woodpecker's taps. Roadkill that is ripped open, mangled (the doe's entrails spread over two lanes) versus that which appears to have been untouched (the sleeping porcupine). Even after just a four-day weekend, early summer, you notice the sun rising noticeably later.

Muscles of the neck, a taut cord, twist. Agreement in number lies. The raven eats from the dog's dish, first dipping the food into the identical bowl of water. Gears of the wrist and palm grasp.

This is the foot that bumped the table that knocked over the lamp that ignited the blanket that smoldered and went out not one time but four before the bulb of the lamp bumped the foot of the sleeping boy who awoke in pain and gave a shout, saving all our lives in the middle of the night.

Another writer would know the name of these flowers, a half dozen to a stalk, each in a different stage of growth and opening, the stalk itself bending with the weight.

In the dream I realize that I am attracted to Meg Ryan but that I had not realized just how short she is. Thrush song echoes up the hill.

Stone house alone amid a field of corn (imagine the isolation of such a childhood). Envision the day – how many years hence? – when this lineup of number 7 hitters (Santiago, Zeile, Jefferies, Morandini) isn't "the heart of the lineup" here in Philadelphia. Hurricane's edge no more than a rainstorm (by the time we depart Muppet Treasure Island, the sun's out, the air fresher than ever, poisons sucked from the sky). Herd of whitetail deer all but tame in the park. Small boy runs the length of the row of cannons, counting loudly as he goes all the way up to 24.

Sentences composed as one is falling asleep in the condition one remembers them upon waking.

Red rum spelled backwards. Nodding pumpkins.

Does it matter which events I qualify as "in the dream"? You ask if I will love you forever and guide my hand to your genitals, which are huge. I put my palm against the forehead of the boy who, uncharacteristically, has fallen asleep midafternoon on the couch only to realize that he has a fever that, when tested, proves to be 103 degrees. Another hey, another holler. Do you know the muffler man? Crows in great quantity high in the trees.

The silence in the water after the splash (a pebble, an airplane).

The secret life of monsters. I step down from the heat and humidity into the air-conditioned lobby and my sunglasses immediately fog up (I decide that I like the effect and leave them on as I move toward the bright blur of light that is an open elevator).

Each word pregnant with its own syntax. At the end of the gravel road you can tell where the new home sites have been staked out, one plateau already shaved flat, raw red dirt ready for the arrival of a crew to dig the foundation, small signs fanning out to identify each numbered lot, a large sign bearing a map and the words "Welcome to Country View."

Dogs dream. Large cemetery divides neighborhoods, cramped brick row houses thick with graffiti (this block so burned-out you can see daylight through open windows) replaced now by large homes (still crowded together), brick columns supporting font porch awnings (suddenly we see the river to our left). Large downtown fountain becomes inner city pool on a hot day (young blonde woman obviously in charge of three African American boys stares laughing into the spray as she sits at the edge, legs dangling in the water).

The ear understood as a shell, as a natural site for infection. Vowels blow over a field of hair, amber waves of sound. IP broadcast storm. The rain in the trees. A day's writing might last all of ten minutes. Long-legged spider, fast across the linoleum floor.

Each phone number is forming a seven-note song. History reaches to beat the teachers. Gradually the cardboard box escapes the atmosphere, carrying us to the stars.

Frontage road behind the town house development, separated from the freeway only by a chain link fence and thick row of weedy bushes, ends in dirt path going nowhere. Old quarry, filled in, becomes the lake of Lakeview Homes. Gas station having become a convenience store with pumps, woman at the register with unbelievable glittering one-inch nails knows nothing of the mechanics of vehicles.

The best part of waking up is . . . Diet Coke! Deep scaling. The rain in the trees at dawn. What I saw (what I ought to have seen). More wild rabbits.

A dream calls up old memories of house I lived in 20 years ago, rambling seven-bedroom Victorian, with an ever-changing cast of roommates, lovers, friends, now conceived as a three-story apartment in the campus area of Berkeley (in the street outside a crowd has gathered as a rock band prepares to play on a stage made of the back of flatbed truck – it's a hot day and many in the crowd are naked), cheap shag carpeting in every room, I settle on the bottom floor and try to recall why I am moving.

It takes a village to write a poem. A nap in the afternoon. A map in the afternoon. Watching suburban women in the mall, categorizing them by who is still aware or at least not in denial of her own sensuality amid packages, children, the blare of the stores – then categorize by their relationships with their children, by clothing, by style of shopping (from casual and recreational to purposeful, in-a-hurry). Out where the only African Americans one sees are at the bus stops.

The swim center understood as a great communal oasis on a hot Sunday afternoon, three pools under high trees, the smell of barbecue wafting from the lawn. Infinitesimal hum recognizable as a mosquito in the dark. The first great desire to write occurs as the idea that messages contain secrets. At each speed the fan's hum changes.

Rising from a long bath so hot the wide mirror and the window are entirely fogged (my glasses would be likewise but for their proximity to the body heat of my face, but then I set them down for a minute to towel off my head and they too fog over), my body pouring seat long after the bathwater itself has been wiped away, the soft sucking sound of the drain as it empties, my sunburned back barely able to make contact with the towel (I got my shoulders wet only for a moment, only at the end), the whole room cloudy with the heat of it, a whole new layer of sweat (what really cleanses the pores) toweled away and replaced and that toweled away also, toenails so thick they can't normally be cut with clippers soft now, pliable as paper (they simply tear if I tug at them), my own pink body barely visible through the steam on the mirror.

One day, six light bulbs in the house burn out, an index of precisely how long we have lived there. Summer rain with a heavy mist (from his closed-in deck we see an acre of lawn). Almost by accident one afternoon I find myself at the front gates of the Valley Forge Military Academy. It's a cheap old sofa we've been given, not at all difficult to carry downstairs.

Image of the sun looks like a yellow ball with hair. Woodpecker, audible, somewhere high in those trees. In a corner of the kitchen two men discuss their airplanes in great technical detail. One cooler filled with wine, the other with beer. Possible with that dog's name: Come, Shadow, come.

Javelin catching. One can see the striping, the path the mower's taken over the lawn. Trees tier the light: brilliant above the canopy, muted here among the mushrooms (this one large as a pizza).

Rigamaroleo. The border between cool rain and a heat wave is thick fog. Last week's major air crash makes this plastic toy left upside down on the family room rug oddly upsetting. A somber light, trees webbed in the sky. By the river a copperhead, surprisingly docile. A game of water balloon toss in the hot sun. Old white stone farmhouse. Bicyclist dead by the side of the road, broadcast as an "Olympic moment" – later we see a doe dead on the shoulder, blood fanning out in a wide arc from the snapped neck.

At the edge of the field, children are playing Frisbee, barely paying attention to the music. Red sun, high over the farms, at the edge of cloud. Feedback stretches, then opens, until you can hear into it. Sprinkler's steady return. Volleyball at apogee, high over the net. This little Mazda, the engine of history, heading toward dusk.

It Takes a Village

Midlife, I
discovered I

was not
where I'd

expected.
Tattoo

parlor called
Etch a Wretch.

Arguments in the conference room
over numbers, faces,

functions,
the next

"work force action."
Just as suddenly

a curtain drew
over the last of summer.

Mariah Carey
on watching

African relief infomercials
featuring footage

of starving children,
"I mean I'd

love to be
skinny like that

but not with all
those flies

and death and stuff."
Legos with which

to construct a universe,
an "ant farm" for humans.

Post-toddler syntax
starts to emerge,

bubbles
along the lower lip.

Red-winged beetle
against the dashboard's black

hardshell plastic
moves to a new

abode. Aubade
bade him well

to do its bidding.
I wake, having slept

with one fist clenched.
The HR officer weeps.

Vending machine
that rejects all coins.

Penmanship is destiny.
Ms. Gabrielle Mintz

considers the act of naming.
Lion paces

the rim of its cage.
Plastic figurine

of ape pounding chest
no larger than my thumb.

Flightless bird.
Irony only strengthens

that which it opposes.
Waiting for the IPO.

Old XL sweatshirt
grown tight at the wrists

constricts full extension
of the arms

when swinging
imaginary bat.

Full eclipse
behind gathering clouds.

Old stone foundation
of burned-out hospital

(1778–1964)
today is little

more than
a place to picnic,

historical marker
by the first chief surgeon's

lone tomb.
Outdoor kiln

at the edge
of a field of

chestnuts
belches flame

from old yellow bricks.
Passengers

must remain with their baggage
at all times.

All the many muches.
Brother,

can you paradigm?
A harsh wind

on an otherwise clear day
foretells autumn.

Helicopter sickness.
He gets out of his bed,

lays a blanket on the floor
and sleeps on that.

Moonless night,
the only

light leaking
from a basement window,

these trees
reach upward

into the dark.
By the river

the box eaters
kneel in a circle.

An effect of
surrealism

sells
luxury transportation:

Everything changes
but the sole.

Is your
web site

a secret?
What at first

coming down
the great stairs

appear to be
giant

multi-colored
mushrooms

turn out
as we approach

to be
umbrellas wet

from the rain.
Like a rock,

the old
ad theme

drives
Chevy trucks

o new
market share.

Rustle of
squirrels

in the rain-heavy
branches.

Boy struggles
to pull shirt

over head.
The logic

of detail in dreams:
this desk

uncluttered
upon which I find

a check
in the amount of

$10,000.
At her name

she steps forward
upon the gallows platform

to hear
herself reprieved,

the camera's focus
narrowing

to a head shot
as she again

descends the stairs,
the other

smiling prisoners
disappearing

into the hazy
background

until
– the crowd gasps!

– we see silhouettes
swinging

in the air.
The carnage

of toy
soldiers

spread over the rug.
Sleeps

with her arms
about her head

as if to ward off blows.
Voiced vowel

owl-like
all over

the lake.
Problem of usury

prevents interest
by Islamic banks.

Clamor am
or will be

heard, hurt, hard
of earring

round solid gold
through the nose

cheek or lip
above / below

a body
of knowledge

slow to heel.
The caterer's plate

upon which sit
stuffed mushrooms

steaming.
The world

is all that
has your face.

General
Protection

Fault.
Goo Goo Doll anthem,

the old ball game.
Animal fecal matter

as origin of tetanus
(and as for the source

of this vaccine . . .).
By the next morning

the balloons
no longer hover

at the ceiling.
Rabbit with the most pearls

must be
the oyster bunny.

Each day the wolves become bolder,
moving now into the outskirts of town.

With each gust, a new torrent of leaves
descends from the red-orange sky.

Month when the snails
go into hibernation.

A rune
of puzzles

playing back.
Lake effect syntax

converts meaning to sorrow,
glacier of intent (mucous)

tidal behind the eyes
draining like swallowing rope

thick where the knots catch,
fiber burn

against inner flesh.
Cellophane flower

upon closer inspection
has eyes, becomes

ghost-on-a-straw.
The course of true love

gathers no moss.
Tall, thin, handsome

African man,
high cheekbones, hint

of a Caribbean speech,
his skin a different tint

each time we meet.
Sun rising

over the canal
casts my shadow

as it writes.
The line, though brittle,

does not break.
Often I wake

as though peeling
layers of dream.

Soft clothing on a cold night,
the hum in the walls

of the furnace,
broken moon trapped

in the leafless oak,
deer at the garden's rim

in sheer silhouette.
Boy's voices

high in the far
part of the house.

Medicine as metaphor,
metaphor as medicine.

The grumpet in the moon
is found none too soon,

dinos in the bath alas.
Bells and whistles,

harlequins with trained monkeys,
the light in the hall,

the chairs arranged in a circle.
Another first chapbook

of slightly closeted sex poems
involving my friend

their teacher. The furnace
ignites with a rush.

First flurries. A thirst
not quenched by

a burst of citrus
searing the throat.

If the cape is an affectation,
the question remains "of what?"

Old man and the C.
Oppen at the rim

of his own party,
silent . . . watching . . . .

Behind which wall
hidden furnace roars

to heat the entire house.
Forest light, leaves

thick as snow.
Love your other.

Eleven exits off 95,
all there is to Delaware.

Moment at which
in the power politics

of marriage, Hillary
Rodham becomes Clinton,

becomes blonde, becomes
fashionable (con-

tact lens as
reverse scarification),

in return for which
she becomes what?

The torrent of leaves
arrives at an end.

Out on the porch
the smell of a cigar

smooth as suede
fills the cold autumn air.

The deference engine
will get us only

part way through the soiree
barely past the white

mounds of cauliflower,
the orange cubes of cheddar,

the rectangular trays
of steaming squares of fried something.

Sleep as desire.
Rising at dawn, waiting

for gravity to clear the senses.
Song of the toilet bowl

filling by degree.
Reference empathy irregardless,

child's cough
hacking in the night,

hallucinated sleeplessness,
low ash sky

clings to the trees.
The microwave sings

five short beeps,
hoarse song of the modem,

pattern recognition
as our own mode of grief.

Boptivity

1.

Shklovsky in my kitchen, pacing wildly, waving a sheaf of papers – "not enough chairs!"

She gazes distractedly out the window.

A dusting of snow lay on the ground, barely enough to cover even the smaller stones.

The bones of the bird's wings are, in reality, elongated fingers.

Scouting locations for the next paragraph.

A simple sentence.

Balloons swelling, one after another, from the nozzle of the helium tank.

Wittgenstein's evil twin, like a four year old, always with the questions.

Hours are as flowers.

There can be only one geostationary earth orbit, over the equator at 22,300 miles.

What if you called this page a browser?

Thrashing in the end game.

Follow the data.

My kingdom for a force.

You stand naked in the walk-in closet, contemplating.

It's the new buds that push the leaves from the trees.

Can-do theme of four-wheel-drive commercial.

A light in the woods.

2.

Phlegm balancing act.

The logic of rope thrice twisted.

Can an invisible gap exist?

What sounds at first like a skateboard through the night woods turns out to be a train rolling electrically over tracks.

A word effaced
is a word erased.

An org chart with your name missing.

Protein Design Labs: fulfilling the promise of monoclonal antibodies.

Passengers must remain with their baggage at all times.

Hay wrapped in canvas.

Roy Cohn State Park.

Often I am permitted to return to the Moika.

The layers of onion curl.

She learns of some old photos posted onto the Web.

Raccoon stares into the headlights.

Problem of diphthongs in the syllable count.

Register your domain name now.

Hear rain, see mist.

Eye surgery in a sitting position.

Count the drops.

3.

A song to digress
of the world in
degrees pitting love against
the magnet's twin gravity

so to rhyme shamus
with Camus I must
persuade you to invoke
a broader range of

engagement engorging gouging purging
an arrangement of scripture
tipped in blue ink
to imply the sky

this guy is writing
high above the evil
king who staggers now
beneath his general's blow

no loyalty against advantage
who are the rooks
pawns enough for all
intrigue invisible to feral

cats in the woods
in the walls rats
mice roaches mites all
having established a balance

fall into order denied
by the human mind
so-called, appalled, appellate bleating
in the barn before

lamb stew steaming centerpiece
upon the table around
which mashed yams blanched
broccoli and a salad

spinach tomato avocado dressed
in cilantro hot rolls
interspersed with green glass
towers and a vase

whose long-stemmed flowers you
almost recall the name
music in the background
right at the point

of recognition (in one
corner the television on
with the sound off
a sort of lamp)

rain & then more
rain raven poised atop
trash bin in the
mall lot looks up

at geese loud in
the sky the upscale
deli – "parking lot rules"
shouts a dad to

two small children who
reach immediately for his
gloved hands small dog
in a large van

spine as a variable
ends in the neck
above which flowering rises
a single complete thought

which, however, like pointillism
upon closer examination dissolves
a building that implodes
almost peaceful billowing cloud

I yam what I
aim to have been
most modified by implausibles
even now not foreseen

4.

Translucent yoyo.

From this room what I hear of the rain is the water spilling down the drain-pipes.

No wick for the rested.

The wind in the wallows.

So they called it Amnesty International when what's needed isn't amnesty but justice.

More junk mail from John-John.

So light a snow that it doesn't cover the top of the grass, but a cold spell so that it remains, until after three days it has a crystalline chemical look.

It is not that his speech is slower or slurred six months after the accident, but that it's an octave higher.

The difference between a 10-Q and a 10-K.

He looks at you out of the corner of his eye to see if you've noticed that he's made a joke.

Outside in the hallway someone sighs and by that act alone I can tell who it is.

"I can still taste you."

The defroster's impact on the side windows is negligible, making it impossible for me to see where in the dark to start the turn left.

"What is it that you *do?*" we holler (impossible to be heard over the sound of the machinery).

We need shelf-stable products.

A man's abdomen – electronic handshake.

Gradually the dozens of antique clocks wind down.

At the base of the false tree a small train moves slowly in circles.

My hand motionless against your breast.

Then lower.

Sunlight through the blue glass of the bottles.

From an upstairs bedroom the boys are laughing, talking, laughing again.

Even war is governed by rules.

We offer to care for your daughter should you be called into action.

Doily atop the lampshade (to dampen the light).

Framed photos of dead mothers in a line upon the wall.

Calories in the glass alas.

Asked what he thinks of *Toy Story*, the old man merely grunts.

Full moon follows us from city to city.

Tenure is to intellectuals what pregnancy was once to women, the "special condition" around which all else becomes excused.

They stand around the living room like a pair of scarecrows (later I wonder if maybe they'd argued and were merely suppressing the show of anger).

The goks will die if you don't come.

We can still see signs of the original script in the mishmash of details in the final cut.

No "B" side to a CD.

Old layer of leaf mash dissolves slowly in the grass.

The tragedy of theory in the tool-and-die maker's bent shoulders.

Day in which I can barely lift this pen.

Knot at a spot right in the middle of my spine.

So that when the wall fell nothing remained but tenure.

When, in the "advanced nations," capital dreams it can do without the state.

Over the tops of the trees of Valley Forge, two plumes of white steam rise into the dull sky from Limerick.

The Satellite

Aftertaste of too
much sugar the
morning after. In
voluntary clinch
below the right
shoulder. Glimpse
of Carrington's breasts
portrayed by.
The inner life
rises up
like a wet basement.
Unseen furnace
behind the wall
or arras veil.
Obsessing desire
to count everything,
tiles in the floor,
triangles
along the rug's rim.
What then?
An inner light
that you possess
that only I can see
shines.
          The quickest road
is through the body.
The great gasp
by which I
empty fluid
into your flesh,
so much punctuation.
It is the driver
of the shuttle

who is new
to the region.
In the dream I'm
at Rachel's house
about to respond
to an inquisition
and in so doing
to make clear
finally and forever
what I *really* think
when I wake up.
Known in the business as
a mezzanine loan.
It's a long way
to temporary
& a long why from whom.
Click-song of the poets.
A young man at Wendy's
hunches over the orange table
to explain to the older couple
(I see no family resemblance)
that the literalness
of the Bible
is non-negotiable.
Try to I.D.
that road kill.
Black ice in the mall lot.
The too-pink salmon
under the fish counter lights.
Mild Italian sausage
as long & twisted
as human intestines.
The next morning
Melnick calls back
to reiterate that he hopes

that I shan't
repeat what he
said about X.
A great crisp air
precedes snow.
Connotation's bandwidth:
how else
to benchmark the poem?
Passion particular
to a relationship
20 years in the making
(operators are standing by).
The kids are asleep,
let's peek in.
Raw bone
beneath the thin web
of gum.
            I come
to the window in the dark
to within inches
of the young buck
(fine thin antlers)
grazing in the flowers.
In 1947, the first
edition of *Books
in Print* lists all
85,000; in 1996,
there were 1.3
million (140,000
alone printed
just that year).
What is more intimate
than the poem,
lyric declaimed
to a silent cast

of dozens (doing the . . .).
Bone spur
cutting through the jaw
at the site of
the extraction.
A stool topples
in the wilderness
and who
hears me call
your name,
raising questions
(in Hawaii
a student of Bob
Wilson's, breathlessly
"I too
have a spiritual
name,"
well, as, who doesn't?).
After a week,
the fiddle takes on
that "old snow" look,
mottled with deer and
rabbit tracks,
spotted with the last
few stray leaves.
Winter's grayscale
paints the park.
               Anti-
histamine,
               pro
democracy.
In the dream I
want to throw
the pizza out
of anger but

cannot find it.
Woman at the Hertz
desk says that
"due to extreme
blizzard conditions,
wouldn't you rather
take a cab?"
Ennui frozen:
body language
of stranded passengers
in an airport lobby.
Gestures with one hand,
holding the phone in the other.
Wind blows the dry snow
like sand in the desert.
In the dream I
am bitten by
a street person
who explains why
"this is necessary."
Discovery Zone:
Noise R Us.
Distant, beyond the woods
all night, just
at the edge of
hearing, a dull hum.
Not noirville but
retro in skates
exposed – raw, red
(roll over and
face the fullness
of the swollen moon),
dripping – my fingers, lips
at the tip of,
my tongue inserted

(back arched, buttocks
clinched, thighs grip
my skull), sweet
salt taste of
(no noun needed).
The sweatshirt on backwards
feels just wrong enough.
Weird quadri-
lateral of light
stretched across
the night garden
tells me
she's awake.
Three cops wedged in
to the back corner nook
at Burger King.
Planet of the Japes
(trauma
of the sifted child).
First sun
in eight weeks
cold to the touch.
Beauty understood
as sadness and
sadness beauty
gives his art
its elegiac tone
(sad hum of
overhead fluorescents),
little boy void
of fun now
in middle years.
Red clot of
dried blood snot.

For our con-
venience
            each pen
has been pre-chewed.
Red beef farts.
How perfectly
they've designed the soup
he or she has designed
the soup, corn's
perfect yellow yin
to the black bean's yang
(or is it   was it
the other way 'round),
this is the dawn
ing of the
age of
blanched asparagus
(under the green
napkin a roll
that has been quartered)
white paper cover
atop the table cloth,
laundry tag still
stapled to its corner.
Ice stings the phantom tooth.
Airport news network
blares on unwatched.
A long walk
in the desert
night air (middle
of winter)
past the strip
malls of Tempe.
Excuse me, Snow White.

Aubade

Mr Faville, I presume

1.

Assign emotions to that sunrise.

A command language for silence.

The resentfulness of the trees.

Corpselike, toys lie scattered over the field of the playroom.

A string of masks across a doorway to form a kind of curtain.

The freezer's demise.

A day's disappearance.

At 47 RD appears to us 20-year-olds as a man of infinite experience,
pounding white chalk dots onto the blackboard to "locate" each idea,
speaking rapidly to the point of mock fury, dot after dot after dot until
the board is a cloud of white speckles, the smell of the dust filling the room.

2.

Find in the dream stranger an old friend just below the surface.

Ice tumbles into the plastic bucket.

Photo of Hillary Clinton with Oscar the Grouch.

Mommy knows the Goks are real.

Shape of the universe before the first bang.

His laugh (which I can call to mind instantly, even after all these years) always surprised him, starting with a loud burst, ending with a question.

First predawn vehicle to pull out of the driveway.

We know exactly what you look like with your clothes off.

The absence of butterflies in winter.

3.

After a few days the balloons sink slowly back to the floor.

Get used to the idea that it's dark out when you rise.

One good snowball fight rips up the "pristine effect" from the field of white.

When she was born, he was already 27 and between marriages.

The tap water milky with pollutants, bananas spotted and soft.

Pup is up. Ramadan Ramada.

Rules are made to be spoken.

Music video narrative: Jewel, on the sound stage floor, slithers from her dress.

While Meridel Leseur rejects the studio's advice to change her nose and name to fit the system (becoming instead a stunt woman in *Perils of Pauline*), her roommate and cousin Lucille becomes Joan Crawford.

Throbbing pain, phantom tooth.

With streets as white as

The simple weight of a pair of glasses, even in the pitch dark, brings him immediately alert.

Fringed lizard.

Hours after, the small bubbles are still bursting about the drain of the empty tub.

In the morning, when you wake from a dull half-sleep, the ice has not entirely melted in the glass on the table by the bed.

Tottel tale.

The perfect balance of a Bill Corbett line.

A sick parent tends to her ill children.

Cloud in the mind, in the lungs.

Dream of a mass hanging, the corpses lowered onto nets.

Full moon over a winter forest

(owl's glide, a pure silhouette

Keith Richards of the language poets.

Midlist travel book.

I awake with the top half of my body turned to one side, the bottom twisted "face down," legs spread wide, one drawn up, the other straight.

Chatter of crows high over the oak trees just before dawn.

4.

Storm windows to a burglar.

The stairs on which
I last saw
Orville Redenbacher

The barefoot Waldo.

In the pan, heat splits the bockwurst.

Fat wet flakes of a March snow.

Spell Czech.

The man looking through you, not at you.

Sensing which stair
will groan under my weight
I pause
then step to avoid it.

A growl
in the furnace.

Will that dust of snow
kill the first crocus?

Lego man by the name of
Extra Large Intestine

The Barefoot Waldo

I saw the figure five
clinched lightly, a window o'er
(and yet within) every word.
The wind in the tree
is not the leafless oak
against which its own shape,
felt but never seen, becomes
defined. Devine the vine without
the fence (wood long since
rotted beyond recognition). My eye
instead of an onion, my
heart was a part of
that equation. Not packaged for
individual resale. Point at which,
looking around, we begin to
understand just who among us
will not be coming along
all the way to (crusty,
defiant, jubilant, bent-over) old age.
Great pickled mushrooms, too soft
crab cake. The wolf-girl Miranda
is loosed upon the stage.
Fathers huddle at the party
in one corner to catch
the score. Treat vending machines
the way you would pinballs
(man crushed by Coke dispenser).
Down at the end of
the long flight of narrow
wooden stairs, then back around
and down the even more
narrow corridor, was an otherwise
"wheel-chair accessible" men's room. Within

the dream, the city intact
(I'm being chased by someone
with apparently murderous intent, but,
since I recognize the dream
as dream, I show no fear).
Train pauses in the night
woods. To count is to
ration the living against constraint.
Ominous rattle under the hood.
In the photo, she's sleeping
(not "sleeping") with multiple men,
eyelids hooded, heavy. Steam fogs
my neighbor's blue bathroom window.
Snow has at last begun.

Antipoem to the Barefoot Waldo

Old man at the rear of the bus, were you that much older than I am now? Second cardinal of a cold spring, brilliant amid the twigs of the bare tree. In the old train station's men's room, holes in the gray tile where the pipes to the original urinals once went. The wind blows my page. You look past me but at me but through me. Try to decipher the graffiti on this door. Before I turn around to see him, I can already tell that his "native" language is not English simply by the tones in his laugh. Newspaper full of yesterday's crash, the woman dying pinned by the wreckage while the passerby squatted and held her hand, the babies hurled into the road. One might step on a field mouse running barefoot to the outhouse through the snow. (B)roadway. Horse with a wreath about its neck. Sensation of the hat on my head long after. Short timer body language. Skaters tumbling forward in slow motion. Gourmet garage. What is sadder than a rear view of old row houses? Concerning Henry Darger's paintings, luminous visionary watercolors using the design vocabulary of Sunday clothing illustrations from the 1950s and before, some critics have suggested that he did not know that little girls don't have penises (no erections anywhere), but explain then the ram's horns or dragon tails that a few possess. Viking with the face of Goofy. Trotting from the front door of the house to fetch the newspaper in the rain. Close up and from this angle the hairs of his blond-white moustache look like the long stalks of prairie grass. A small bottle of fox urine. Woodpecker hops backward down the trunk of the oak. Five girls whoosh by on bicycles, mouths wide open to catch the warm rain, screaming. Old woman moves slowly down the stairs to her house. First half purple crocus bud about to bloom. The thunder constant, rolling, roiling. A tear at the top of the paper. Sharpshinned hawk in a slow glide just over the tops of the trees. Alberto Vitale, chairman of Random House: "The book is the beginning of the content chain leading to other products." Bright primary colors in plastic – toddler's toys upon a brick porch. A man dedicates a book to the memory of his daughter. Four women stand in the garden, each looking in a different direction. I recognize your voice unexpectedly on the radio (no, not your voice, but your accent). Birdsong before light. This is about death (1949). First the willow turning yellow-green, then the cherry, white, white-pink. Pascin's small portraits of nudes. All grains are even and become the floor. A glass case containing masks. Soutine's dark neighborhood. A warm rain barely begins. Old stone manse under the towering poplars. Your fingers stuck in a web of come. The hushed light of the garden as seen from the harsh light of the house. Sleep deprivation as a theory of dream. The little boy who never slept. The first goldfinch. Albino wren. Outdoors in the oak grove before dawn, using my own porch light by which to write. On the carpet outside the hotel room door, a single long-stem glass, the remains of a drink, a lone strawberry. Red-headed Sikh stops to peruse the dim sum case. The work poem. View from a clear glass elevator. Owl's vowels, bowl's bowels. The missing jet with its missing bombs. Leaving the dugout, on his way to the mound. Newscaster explains why "Tiger identifies himself as an Asian." Where are the MIPS? Park, in the park. First bus, best bus. A flash, to last the next five years. Monster Masque. Swallows turning under the dark clouds, the air over San Joaquin Valley thick, heavy (tho it is not the humidity, but the claustrophobia of the sky). Tom Clark is in the details. A two McDonalds' town. Exhaustion as a stage in the process that is larger, longer, harder. She is in front of me, speaking, but speaking into a microphone so that I hear her voice amplified, distanced from the blue box to one side. The milk from the goat's long teat streaming into the shining pail makes the sound of a steady, sustained bell. What was written 30 years ago as porn is reissued now as memoir. A field of windmills on what began as a clear, still morning, becoming first a breeze, the slow turn, then harder, the air whistling, almost a roar. He will stand on the porch talking to you through the screen door, but won't invite you in. Deconstruct this endowment. I'm an idea rat. O pinion! I is an utter. Only pennies per day. Old etched horn. Odor of Pinesol on the glass. Flying away from the sun. It's not that I'm being harsh or unfair. I began to weep at the mere thought of saxophones. Below, cities had been reduced to the simplest geologic patterns (lives impossible to imagine). I insert the finger into your anus. The radio speaks of "confirmed fatalities." In the pocket of the seat before me, I find a news magazine entirely in Dutch. She's explaining her new book to me with enormous pride, but I can tell from her description that it's not equal to the potential of her topic. There were 13 of us ordering dinner and the servers proved not to have been the order taker, so that a chaos of dishes soon ensued. In discrete cosine transform or DCT, which underlies such modes of video compression as MPEG, the quantized numbers are entropy coded, the most prevalent values given the shortest numbers. No Leos need apply.

Landscape with Chairs

People who are not indigenous. In front of me in the hard folding chairs of the small auditorium, her long neck and the two silver rings, each pulling with no more than the weight of gravity on the long lobes of her ears.

Without guests, there would be no reason to turn our house into Potemkin Village. Orange spots under the dirty scrim of the pool's surface scatter as a stone splashes in their midst.

The only part of the deer's carcass still recognizable at the on-ramp's edge was its hooves. When this you hear, run in fear.

Iamb what iamb and that's all what iamb. The dogwood in flower too close to the oak.

The shaded tones of the female cardinal, though less brilliant, are ultimately more subtle and please an eye pleased by subtlety. The scooter-like wheelchair tipped over and from a distance we could see her son begin to run toward her.

BAFO vs. BARFO (first offer, best offer). The spine as an instrument of torture.

Birds of a feather dot together. Giant rubber slide at the grammar school fair.

I like a floss as thick and rough as rope. Roar of the dandelions.

Shadowless prelight right before dawn. Blue ice. Thin sun.

A critical poetics – where in history shall we find it?

The idea that electricity, that very thing which, flowing through our own synapses, tells this muscle in your cheek to twitch, which lights your room, crackling away in that controlled fire of every bulb, which shimmers into red and blue on every screen, capturing this voice and that song and the lonesome sound of a solo accordion serenading an unseen Other, should be dumb, is not watching all that it is doing, to and with whom and why, is not in fact in constant communication with itself, is not even the invisible governor of our days (how it plotted to get Franklin to take up that kite!), is our own sweet fiction, imagination that I make this hand move thus across this notebook's page, the sun (pure ball of electricity!) about to rise.

Three day weak end. The idea of the line is in birdsong – do the birds hear it?

Phyle phormat. Point at which the vertebrae of the neck meet the great bones of the shoulders, over which the muscle has become twisted and tight.

Would solitaire hone the mind? Footsteps high in the kitchen overhead. First fuchsia, fallen on the walk. Cardinal on the dogwood branch.

The museum goers wear smaller yellow stickers that one still sees blocks, even miles, from the museum. Rain in the fog, yet not the same.

Impossible music by natural light. My own mouth in my mother's face.

Rabbit pauses, solitary on the lawn. In the dream the performers sit among the audience while we, confusingly, find ourselves upon the stage.

Task Me With a "Do It"

Rain heard as a mode of music. The birds at dawn as weather. Shirts on a banister laid out to dry. Thin arms freckled by the sun. The wounded lawn. Stuffing for the roast pig. Pincers of the adult red-brown stag beetle hanging on the screen door lend it a horned effect. The red ink of the ♥ bleached out, what remains of the message on the car's sunscreen is "I ComputerLand" Wood floor groans underneath me as I walk. Fly's flight is its song. Basque terror. Technology at the cusp of the 21st century stretches the world of the haves out even further from that of the have-nots. Phil Whalen dancing in the garden. Fly crazed with the light. Abandoned penny. The sole movement in the room is a frenetic ceiling fan. Godzilla for a pet (you'll have to housebreak him). Sleep through thunder. Productize intellectual capital. Live at the nostril. MCI Systemhouse, Sprint Paranet, AT&T Solutions. Carpenter bees. Blown lightbulb's absence recasting shadows about the room. Knowing that somewhere Al Yankovich must already be preparing the song "Itch." House understood as a process, not an object. The air clear and morning likewise. Cover photography strategy for the magazine *CFO*: make the accountant appear dramatic. Hammer dulcimer, crickets in the cat tails, sun barely visible through the humid air. Grandfather of the piano came to Europe from the Middle East. Give us this day our daily head. In Legoland where I was born, there was a fare made dwellin'. Morning as an act of faith. Why you recall this sex act 19 years later and not another (you're literally pinned to the wall, suspended in midair, your legs high over my shoulders, your face contorted with concentration, your eyes meeting mine as if looking right through them). Extraordinary sadness at the end of a project. A boy's pissing into the john on the next floor will sound louder than a girl's due to the greater distance traveled. Fly's buzz turns to static at the screen. Running on fumes. Fanny Howe's poetry as both prayer and lament, as though there were no difference. Children discuss the weather. People cross the mall lot slowly, as though the heat were a filter. At the phone book, a woman in a business suit on a Saturday (too hot for that jacket) qualifies a prospect. The left nostril occluded, swollen, throbbing. Split level or ranch (thousand islands or ranch)? About those islands: locations and names. Fox dying amid traffic, over on the shoulder, blind, bleeding, legs churning the useless air. Semi-palmated plovers at the edge of a soft tide, a million small shells embedded in the sand, sunset behind us, while approaching comes a man playing bag pipes.

On Brier Island

For Bill Corbett &
Thomas A. Clark

Dinghies adrift
on the Bay of Fundy
Stunted shepherd sniffs
under the shade tree
at a yard sale
Salt water weathered
these lobster traps
abandoned now
at the edge of a deck
Monster on jet skis
scattering cormorants
The breeze in the hair
on the back of my head
Crows amid seaweed
Old Buddha gull
on moss rock
Tour bus in Digby
fresh off the ferry
Islands to go
before we sleep
Red breasted
nut hatch up
side down
on the branch
From a distance
thousands of gulls
declare sunset
Lone raisin
to sweeten the cheese
Son's perfect imitation

of French fire siren
oodle oodle oodle
Warbler with a spot
of yellow on its butt
Gull with the bark
of a dog (what kind?)
Butterfly seen
as remote flower
Which white splash
out in the cove's mouth
is alleged baby whale?
Game in which one figurine
represents "the evil chicken"
Fog visible
drifting along the path
Out over the water
near the French Shore
lone spot of sunlight
only for a minute
Foghorn and gull chorus
Tiny spider descends
from the bill of my cap
Jeep audible
up the gravel path
Two cabins over
the voice of my wife's mother
shouts "Sunshine!"
Raspberry fields forever
Arthritic shoulder
skipping stones
into the Atlantic
at Pond Cove I
realize the strength
in my throwing arm
has gone for good

Sunset to the west again
Seals and one guillemot
Two whales at play
about a lone boat
Lighthouse computerized now
Cement foundation
all that remains
of the keeper's house
Voices amid gooseberry
Jigsaw unfinished on the table
Gulls in every direction
Fisherman's son
to be a fisherman
if the fish remain
Boys hurling seaweed
"Slimed again"
Six acres and a house
at the furthest end
of Digby neck
$300 1949
Gulls quieter in fog
or drowned out
by the backhoe
seeking water
Pine siskin at Elaine's feeder
Barnacles on the hump
back's tail
diving or gliding
almost sleepy
by the side of the boat
Mako shark
attacks driftwood
tho white sided
atlantic dolphin
by the dozens

are just yards away
Shearwater's glide
almost running, skipping
on the boat's wake
Two razorbills
solitary on the water
The old professor
at ECTC (Eastern
Carolina Teacher's
College) had needed
a student to drive him
and his car
north to Digby
who in turn
bought a house by mail
sight unseen
built first in 1822
unable himself
to make upgrades
or repairs
until he retired
forty years hence
Donnie Welch flicking
filtered cigarette butt
into the drought-dry grass
right arm useless
Polio kept him
close to home
postmaster for eight years
but in the Coast Guard
for another 13
cursing what tourists
have done to his taxes
or the long waits
for the ferry

Dug down
sans dowser
only to find bedrock
Waxwings still
in the dead pine
Rabbit that crawled
under the steps
to die   Toad
the size of
my thumbnail
Black snake red snake
Hummingbird
flew right up
to my face
Harrier swoops
high over Pond Cove

Humpback glides
just below the surface
at peace in
the Bay of Fundy

Storming Waumbec Mountain by Golf Cart

For Jackson Mac Low
& Anne Tardos

Book chosen to read while you drive. Plastic spoon in my pocket when I reach for my pen. "My other language is French." Fog in the pine chaparral gives way to glare. Semi-permanent catsup spot upon your cheek. Moose-breath. Alleged chalet turns out to be rapidly declining old motel. In the distance, unseen, cars are driving over the iron grates of a metal bridge. Three layers of cloud. Lone segment of picket fence in the middle of a vast lawn, connected to nothing. Jefferson Notch. Age at which each local boy demonstrates humor vis-a-vis the name of Mount Martha. We took turns. She seemed pleased. Smoke there in those trees signals a home. Full moon on a clear night just before dawn. A hum in the barn next door even before daylight. Crow the loudest of the morning singers. Rather than build a new house, he decides in 1880 to raise the entire L-shaped structure up and to insert a new floor underneath it. Old two-piece phone set (no dialer) built into a small lamp: when you pick up the ear-piece, the light comes on. Two fields over, a man is walking toward some cows. Now the distinct call of the geese. First car of morning, walkers take warning. Even before the sun arrives, the swollen moon is reduced. Flock of something. We enter through a door in the greenhouse, then as I rise up the dark stairs to the kitchen of what I believe to be an empty house, the door opens and I'm staring into the startled face of Anne Tardos. Soil, as a verb. Hands about my mug of tea, even its warmth failing.

Toward an Anniversary of a Drowning in the Senses

For Dan Davidson

On the deck a sparrow hops unnoticed at the feet of the diners. Between high rises, the Kingdome peeks through, doomed palace. Think: if the coast is to the right, I'm facing south. Sunlight on a red potato. Next to games, the section on loss and grieving. Jet passes through a clear sky. Barge backlit by the setting sun. Overhead, the richest man in the world helicopters home. Overheard, the song of unseen traffic. She throws her head back before she laughs. A man with a parachute is pulled into the air like a kite. Lawn chairs tack up these highrise balconies. The cranes are orange because. Deep baritone of the container ship's horn. Will we be able to read this in the morning? Already the hush of dark on those far hills while here the sun blinds us to the mahi-mahi on the plate. She fiddles with both earrings at once. Offshore, those clouds foretell narrative. The mall at night. The cops all about the fallen man, wrists cuffed behind his shirtless back. What I want, what I want, what I really really want is to return to the body, preferably yours.

Trouble Ticket

For Rod Smith

Bumper sticker on an old fridge door: Friends don't let friends drink milk. In dream, one can rework the past at one's leisure, as if constructing a puzzle composed of desire (I'm seducing Ms. Laura Bailey who hasn't aged one minute in the intervening 33 years). Television replays the crumpled Mercedes endlessly (at the Super Fresh, by the checkout line, the *Enquirer* still blares, page one "Di Goes Sex-Mad: I Can't Get Enough"). Mood swings like tides in an uncalm sea. Old plastic jack-o-lantern sits on a shelf. A plate of funnel cake consumed quickly in the shade of a small tree before the yellow jackets catch wind of its sweetness (brushing confectionary sugar out of my beard). Photo of Charles Bernstein as a boy. Waiter leans forward to pepper my soup. If you live long enough, you'll outlast everyone you ever loved. Sun barren in the sky. In the crook of the window, dozens, perhaps hundreds, of daddy-long-legs cling together (pulsing ball of yarn), hanging on the screen in the dark heat. Impossible to tell which is the "real" Batman anymore. Saturday's shin guards. I'm on the edge of waking as I dream one of my five-year-olds is paddling a small air mattress out into the open bay right into the path of some tugs, but everyone is staring into the sun glare to the right where a line of vintage seaplanes is set to start a race and I'm running to the pier's edge all too conscious of my own poor swimming as I see the mattress tip and start to roll in some wake and I open my mouth to scream for help only to discover no sound. Yellow jacket season. Nerf football with a green and orange swirl. Hi, goofball. Disintermediation of the word (a word is worth a thousand words). Bean mechanics. Curtain that half hides the first class cabin. The fading light of day shimmering off the glass high rises, final night of summer. Joggers staggering at the end of their run. Supply chain management. Stumbling up against chairs in the dark. Dirt alert. Net present value. In the dream we're burying a young girl with the reddest hair, the most peaceful of smiles. Coast barely visible under thin rim of fog, heading south (the sun to my right), trip I should have made 33 years ago. Lone flight attendant on commuter jet. The Eastern Shore. I step from the hotel ballroom just in time to see two of its employees out beyond an empty bank of phones completing the unmistakable ritual of a drug deal. Barry Cox, sent to the crematorium in his tie-dye t-shirt. What then? Thinnest rim of land to segregate fresh water from salt. The sky colorless but not yet dark. Hammering on the spacebar to make it work. Till, past sunset though not yet full dark, all that remains of the Eastern horizon is the faintest shift in tones, grey upon gray. Tombstone at pond's edge, 32 years after the fact, Magnolia Cemetery, Charleston, where my father rests. Young Clint cast-net shrimpin' from the end of the dock. Sulphur butterfly, pure yellow. An old photograph, unlabeled in an album crisp with age, Nagasaki after the bomb. Fishin' on credit. Another photo, eight years later, sailors in the streets of Rapallo. Grackle in the live oak. Doberman lifts his head, ears alert. In the distance, guns of the dove hunters poppin' in the drizzle. Another photo, older now, start of a paunch, hairline receding, chin starting to double, then another from the same year, wearing a baseball cap off in the distance (as if I'm looking into a mirror). Female cardinal mixed amid the redwings. Net fans out before it hits the water. Zit atop mosquito bite, small mound of aggravated flesh. They took them in trains, Buddy says, just to view the devastation. Yellow news clipping of a plane wreck in a wheat field: "My wings were icing up and I couldn't get to the Dalles." I sit up and a hundred grackle scatter off the deck. I'd not expected the moss to be this tough. She-clam soup. A simple stone set flat into the earth, wet with rain. The teenagers observe the adults with the cool distance of scientists. Buddy lifts his head into the rain, deep Tarzan yodel over Abbapoolah Creek. Lone female mallard asleep in the shadows of the deck. A troop of ringtail lemurs walking on TV with their tails erect. "Are you overwhelmed?" Jesse's simpler refrain: "Dad, when are you coming home?"

Pigeons in the Grasp Alas

Dispersal of passengers
from the airport
The teenager
breastfeeding huge blond boy
Driveways to resurface
before I sweep
Humid universe
The granny
hooker look
You in the sample
ensures deployment
throughout the Magic Kingdom
Table top votive light
flickers beside canola
oil encased
in tiny wine bottle
Land before thyme
rime before hand
therefore mine
Copter to hover
over manmade legume
Wind turns the hammock
grackles on the lawn
a pawn   a sparrow
upon the narrow chair
Red hair flowering
from thong bikini
is the whole point
Bicycles on the path
do the math
A magician
starts to sleep
dreams measured like soup

by the thickness
Digest option
Even before
you peel the banana
you feel the bruise
A car's headlights
through the filter
of the wood's trees
A word's stress
frees thought
A five-year-old's
interest in graveyards
Rash, crowd, herd, flock
school, den or pride
of dreams   A late morning
an early frost
middle of the middle
Life is a riddle
only its absence
could solve   (salve)
Sex is a toxin
Toilet's digestion
audible as
its tank refills
Maintenance musication
(sax is a toxin)
Backside of the paper
Unable at this angle
to discern
if that element of the yellow
painting represents
the shaft of a saxophone
or octopus tentacle
Bogdan Gnash
Weak thought west thought

Self storage or other
Potato break potato
pancakes potato head
What is the value
of thought within passion?
Off-balance, the shortstop
barehands the ball
throwing within
the process of falling
(My hand gently
against the small of your back
is not a decision)
New trope for the Pope
Daylight Squandering Time
Electric switch plate
near the ceiling
when toggled
turns nothing on
She pauses for a moment
leaning the large
pumpkin
up against the planter
shifts her weight
then picks it
back up
and walks again
More and more
the visible world
is merely approximate
Autumn
      at 'em
          ate 'em
auto
mation   nation
Sax is a Texan

On a stair
Hannah stares
Icy words
by the dance
surly light
Song of film
rewinding
inside camera
The revel
is in the retail
Throat culture
On first swallowing
thru the jaws
of Juan de la Cosa
(Adam's apple
clenched
in pain)
First silhouette
of half-leafless trees
in night's fading dark
Precip
        itation
too loud for snow
Butterfly bandage
over top of thumb
In the dream
I write the phrase
In the dream
Odor of raspberries
in the massage oil
Full moon huge
in the bare tree

Dadaquest

Disconnect the dots!
Undifferentiated
beep beep beep
of airport terminal
transport vehicle
The expansion of genre
at a rate much faster
than the expansion
of readers   Blimp
in the shape of
Everready bunny
The sadness of flowers
before frost disproved
Page as original
flat screen display
Slowly, a boy
nods into wakefulness
Auto-ethnography
of rainfall
Cellophane prophecy
Green goose poop
Ducks echoing
up from the quarry
Woodpecker hops
up the bare oak
Yellow jeep
honks to say hi
You have mail
The forest in winter
Pubic hair caught
between two teeth
The trash men come
before the dark fades

day no more
than the night bleached gray
The interpretation
of creams
An old man
with sores bleeding
green-yellow
about the ankles
Linoleum pattern
foretells present
Like pilots
donning parachutes
friends drop away
until only you remain
to guide the plane
the instrumentation panel
entirely unintelligible
Posthumous years
Distant sound
of a train
Woman explains
to the court
that she saw
her boyfriend
beat her daughter
eight years old
who had tried
to keep them from fighting
saw him break both arms
tape her mouth her nose
with duct tape
until the girl went limp
then blue
and did nothing
Cartoon pilgrims

on a flag
decorate suburban porch
Cat with bandaged paw
falls from kitchen table
Two ambulances one fire truck
one paramedic sport utility vehicle
surround the car spun around
into concrete barrier
On the television
football game with the sound off
World in which Strom Thurmond
outlives Kathy Acker
We walk under the grey sky
past the massive brick apartments
of outer Connecticut Avenue
toward a strip mall café
is branded – Ben Gay
The old dental bill
bait-and-switch
Not as a vessel
but against which to struggle
Poem of laughter
become a form of grieving
Lung's cough
defines a margin
The next storm
will surely bring snow

Compliance Engineering

Our true form is the blurb.
Full moon in a clear December sky
on page 215 of my notebook.
Ice cream machine
rejects my crumpled dollar.
Stairwell dark behind the fire doors.
When this you recall, take care
not to stumble (your rime here
makes us what to cheer)
on all that is the case.
In Philly, sleeveless t-shirts
are called "wife-beaters."
Pale grey of the leafless woods.
Architect's signature
is the pink tile bath.
Small plane wobbles
as it glides
into rural airstrip.
Toyotathon: whoda thunk?
Close reading: Pop-up Video
is not that. What
you get if you see
stranger as parallel to danger.
A toy train endlessly circles
the table-top track.
One drawer in the kitchen
just for rubber bands.
Waldo's evil Other: Odlaw.
The wrong pen here
because the right one is missing,
the ink does not sink in
but rests atop the paper's grain,
a gleam in the grease of it, clots

whenever the line changes direction.
A small gazebo constructed over an old well
and next door a utility substation,
sheer red brick block.
Last house in these woods
to leave the Christmas lights on
outdoors through the night.
Paintings purchased entirely for their frames
so he becomes a constructor of margins
to build a "house" with no right angles.
Antithetical to reason, to contemplation,
is called the Discovery Zone.
Holding a potato chip with both hands.
The stamp on your palm visible
by means of a special light.
Weighted prosody of cartoon. Outbreaks
migrate from species to species
in search of the perfect host.
The alarmed door sounds: young workers
in identical t-shirts stampede
toward the exit. Language
poetry understood
as a problem of nostalgia
(Tarkovsky imitates Antonioni).
At dawn, tufted titmice and black-capped
chickadees approach the feeder in groups,
taking turns in rapid succession,
lone cardinal watches from a branch,
squirrels beneath waiting for the dropped seed.
Small fluorescent night-light for the bathroom
my son calls "rectangular moon."
Lines link lives like words,
glances, an embrace, capable
entirely of administration, deceit,
want, need, the long sigh,

meaning evident to no one.
Pirbuterol acetate
inhalation aerosol
puffer inserted
into the mouth: breathe deeply
counting slowly to twenty.
Downy woodpecker taps at the oak.
Geometric passion:
he looks just like his web site.

Dogs Love Trucks

Let them browse cake.
A long way to temporary
and a double-click back home.
I want to see your multiples.

Crow hopping around the traffic
about the crushed squirrel.
Nothing exceeds like excess.
She raises one hand

to gather the collar
of her shirt as she leans
forward. Rhyme fiction.
Why did the chicken cross the toad?

Case sensitive, the password
hidden in the text, the chill
in the wall of a damaged lung
demands to know who's next?

Tourists will walk
down the same street
differently than the locals.
A must-have volume

for your management bookshelf.
Dixieland jazz band live
in the mall courtyard.
First light over the still gulf.

An odd hotel atop the site
of a small mountain

in an otherwise featureless
city, elevators on the outside

with almost nothing to see,
our suite filled with strangers,
not all of them dressed, the air
of a party but too passive

so we choose instead a taxi
in which to ride somewhere,
anywhere, a beautiful vehicle,
late '40s Packard, still new,

which takes us to the waterfront
from which, looking back, I realize
the whole city is rumpled with hills,
the traffic itself an attitude,

the air again of a party.
Soccer kick a child's toy
back to "their side" of the room.
The pedestal on the laminate counter

contains, covered in glass,
glowing, a cheese cake,
one slice already gone.
The steam from my cup rises.

404 at the cube farm.
More than a quarter
of a century later,
Jimmy Cliff's *Sitting*
Here in Limbo ("lim-
bo, limbo, limbo")
still rings more articulate,
more clear, than virtually all

the music that's come after.
A small, crowded magazine shop
somewhere near the campus,
no visible order to the stock,

journals with curling covers,
bent pages, academic
quarterlies two and three
years old. Vinyl stanza.

Viral

For Jeff Derksen

To inhabit consciousness like a secret.

The body rises and, inside, fluids in all the organs begin to cascade.

Sun blisters the pale gray sky.

Analog hands circle wildly to indicate time.

You kiss, but the lips barely part.

I scarcely notice the houses as I pass each day.

In the dream I'm crossing a wet wood-plank path through the swamp's edge barefoot under a large moon when a small blue snake bites and won't let go.

Post-transplant lymphoproliferative disorder.

But I'm also Robert De Niro playing a good guy, chased through the thick reeds and mud by a homicidal John Goodman.

A bookcase with glass doors hinged over each shelf, behind one of which an octagonal wooden clock leans, holding the books to its left upright.

Alone amid the thick crowd, one person unwraps, seemingly endlessly, a candy encased in cellophane.

Diet Coke celebrates Celine Dion.

Wake mid-dream, sorting out what's real.

House softened by the shroud of fog, pre-dawn.

Yawn that's a half-moon.

Post-soapyism.

If you pull on a t-shirt on a quiet morning, what you hear in miniature are tiny cotton sails unfurling about your ears.

Old mylar party balloon, weeks later, helium compromised, floats rumpled barely an inch above the floor.

Sound of a boy running down three flights of stairs, stopping to catch himself at each landing.

"Can I watch you write?"

The concept of the "people's princess" is like . . .

The ambassador dines privately with the head of the secret police.

America a profligacy.

The customer-centric word lingers in the cochlea.

The weeping sea

roils up against the yellow shore.

In the dream words from a coffee house slateboard become obscure marginalia beneath contributors' notes on a stapled magazine's last page.

"Lies" understood as affectionate.

Silence of the clams.

Rooms

For Cliff

Slick red paint over smooth concrete, four steps and a black rubber welcome mat, the one place where in memory, the white stucco carries a tactile sensation.

Taste of the nasal spray against the back of my throat.

Minuscule foyer. Small dark stained table with matching stool holds a black rotary phone (originally Landscape 1599, the '6' in the third position added later around the same time party lines went away). Light filtered through the screen door.

Furnace with a floor grate over which, on even the mildest days, my grandmother loves to stand. A rocker by the window, although I wonder if maybe it wasn't displaced at some point early on by a larger sofa. Gauze curtains over yellow shades – the idea of a sunlit room appears never to have occurred to them. Grandfather's easy chair immediately in front of the heater – just enough space to create a corridor to his bedroom door – never was a recliner. I don't recall the rug but there must have been one over the hardwood floors. Fireplace center of the far wall, on either side a built-in bookcase behind glass doors – *The Book of Knowledge*, minor league encyclopedia in perhaps twenty volumes to the left, *Readers Digest Condensed Novels* to the right. Corner by the French doors to the dining room in which stood, at first, a five-foot-high radio (after dinner we would listen to The Shadow while I played checkers with my grandfather), later the site for the TV. Television changed space as imperceptibly as chess does the flatness of its board (a chessboard in fact is a mountain, its four center-most squares the peak, each concentric 'ring' about that an entire layer down), its small blue-gray screen now the center, regardless of the positioning, of the entire room.

The dining room table we seldom used for eating. A smaller table on which sat an old black manual typewriter, various stacks of papers, documentation of my grandfather's membership in the Veterans of Foreign Wars. A tall but quite narrow closet where my mother kept her coats and dresses (for 15 years she slept in the sofa bed back in the living room, instantly folded up at the start of day, no evidence anywhere of a room of her own). A painting that over the years moved from room to room, a dog, perhaps a collie, howling over a young lamb fallen in the snow, the mode sentimental realism. Even the cheapest "blue china" plates will appear fabulous to a child when housed behind the glass doors of a dining room cupboard.

Twenty-four years after I last live in the house, returning on a sales tour, the outgoing tenant a young man going through a bad divorce, I'm shocked to see the kitchen virtually identical to the way it had been, large but with no interior furniture, the old gas stove with its wood-burning side container to the left (my grandparents only burned newspapers) polished up and presented now as an antique. To one end, a nook just large enough to fit a picnic table, built-in benches that doubled as chests for comic books, baseball gloves, bats, balls of all sorts. Before washers and dryers became electric, an old white tub on raised wheels, black rubberized clothes ringer on top would be rolled in next to the kitchen sink from its location in the utility room by the back porch.

Hallway dark between the two bedrooms, a door to the dining room, another to the bath, because it never got direct sunlight. Small door to a built-in fuse box, larger door to a linen closet, then a second where we kept the vacuum cleaner, square in the ceiling, the only way into the attic.

Tiny back bedroom, small single beds, a small dresser between them piled high with my books. One window overlooking the back yard standing down away from the house, the other staring directly into the neighbor's kitchen. Bed where covers at first formed a perfect landscape for narrative games with small plastic cowboy figures – this one I named Casey Tibbs after my favorite rodeo star – later to sit cross-legged atop these blankets writing by hand into a notebook just as I do now. A second taller dresser at the far end of the room that held my mother's clothes (no room of her own) that today, 35 years later, stands next to my own mattress on the floor, 3,000 miles east. In the absence of space what becomes most crucial is its territoriality – my bed, *Grandfather's* easy chair, the space above the grating in the floor for the furnace where my grandmother loved to stand.

The front bedroom at the far end of the hall is in fact even smaller, no doubt envisioned by the builder Macgregor as the "children's room," my grandparents slept there always, a dark room where colors, tones were totally determined by the amber shades that were almost always drawn. The closet also had a window in whose shade Grandmother would hide extra cash, rolling it down to fetch a few bills, then up again to contain the rest. A large bed and a dresser, its only furnishings beyond the straight-backed chair Grandpa would leave his truss and garters on.

I have no memory of the bathroom beyond its tons of light the few occasions when I had the stomach flu, an almost fluorescent glow refracting off the bowl of the toilet.

A room I would today call a "mudroom" or "laundry" (although I have no memory of when precisely the modern washing machine first arrived), pure cluttered passage-way between the kitchen and back porch.

A high porch at that, because of the hill's slope, 13 steps down to the yard, a wonderful view of the house tops of the entire city, the little hill (literally "el cerrito" of the so-named next town, although it was never precisely "in" that jurisdiction), even a slice of the bay, Tamalpais rising high to the west and, if the light were right, the long yellow outer walls of San Quentin. One wall of the wood porch held a built-in container for clothespins, the corner post rising higher than the rest to hold a clothesline pulley (by the time you got to the other post – that one made of a thin pipe – at the far end of the sloping yard, drying underwear waved in the breeze nearly 30 feet from the ground).

Old dark shed that constituted a garage, barely enough room to inch past the '51 Pontiac or later the '59 Chevy Bel Air to get in or out of the car, shelves everywhere crowded with old jam jars filled with nuts, bolts, washers. Soon after my grandmother sold the house in '71 (even before the too-lush bougainvillea replaced the hydrangea in the front yard), the new owners tore it down.

Eleutherian Mills

The hotel maid's cart
blocks the corridor.

Twelve-year-olds in bikinis
in the blinding sun

by the pool. Wafer
stoppers focus light

through a mask
onto the photo resist.

Snow in the mountains
over San Berdoo.

She sits at a window
overlooking the azaleas,

lone tear gathering,
about to flow slowly

down her cheek.
Car phone antenna

squats atop the truck.
Hayward. Backhoe

alone in the woods.
Wayward. Thin clouds

mute the sun.
A week later

crabapple blossoms stain the walk.
Larking pot. Goon, spoon,

lagoon. A weak later
echoes the strong before.

Six-year-old boys
perceive Beanie Babies

as gendered,
negative valence.

Cloud form as sky margin.
Viagra falls. Hotel fish.

Continue to breathe normally:
even though the text

is flowing fully
the page will not inflate.

Late Spring lush
after undue rain,

mind moves this way again.
Waiting for the call, not

remembering phone's unplugged.
Old cemetery, unkempt, half-wild,

weathered stones tilting, bleached by sun,
snow, wind, centuries of rain,

more beautiful in fact than
the too-manicured vast expanse

just across the freeway.
Company fire drill,

milling in the parking lot
on a hot day.

Seven Sad Forests

The poem moves when – and where – you least expect it. It's how you know it's the poem.

You wake in the middle of the night, desperately tired, unable to sleep. The taste in your mouth, stale, sour, is not one you can name, but it is not unfamiliar. Somewhere, an old analog clock is ticking, unconscious of the time. Something scuttles across the linoleum floor.

Imagine a train wreck in outer space. This large basement room filled with the ghosts of your life. The forest trimmed into a neighborhood. The memory of having made love once to a woman as she spoke on the phone to an old boyfriend. That sense of knowing which direction to expect the dawn.

You break the poem into a million pieces, giving each a name. Later you type them and, doing so, lose them forever. A friend is making a terrible mistake. Will you understand your anger well enough to forgive him?

Between sentences, something hides. I'm trying to pry it into the open. The laughter in the next room sounds pointed and cruel. The body is pure mechanism, easily abandoned. Yet you are the slave of each organ.

Where you stood, or sat, the moment you heard Kennedy died. A generation of adults with no memory. Buildings you've lived in that no longer exist. Kathy Acker, the people's princess.

Sentence That Each Time You Read It Changes

Dream in which I
dream in which I
dream I wake

in a forest
in a gale

clouds
barely visible
above the struggling
clattering branches
blotting out the sky

birds not
visible not
audible
where do they go

before the start of rain
so humid
we can barely walk through
these vast but wild

gardens before we wake
again

•

The busboy's cologne is thick as he reaches across the table, jasmine in the Earl Gray suddenly clouded, the sound of ice as it tumbles from the pitcher into glass. Ibis or ibex, which one? Gold fish strangle in tap water. The tab of your shirt peeking up over the collar's edge. Pawnshop saxophone window display. “Internal mosh pit,” writes Drew Gardner. Sarcophogal hernia. Tennis sea.

•

Lower Manhattan sunset
as a quality of light
without glare, deepening
these shades of brick

Inside of the bodega
crowded, cluttered
gradually becoming visible
out on the street

Your smile as you lean
into me in that
low cut gown,
wanting me to look

This week it’s El Duque
but it could be anything
just so long as
we stay distracted

In dream San Francisco
stretched outward
from the true spine
Divisadero

Out toward a never
to be arrived at
sea – always it’s twilight
and this search feels twisted

Never understanding
precisely the object
pause instead
before the unlit storefront

To catch your reflection
uncertain at first
which one is you,
accusatory pronoun

•

L-shaped room. The sound of birds before light first become apparent, pale horizon, within the oak forest. Last night's orgasm a pleasant tug at the muscles of the groin. Able to discern the dove's call amid the chatter of the finches. The colorblind boy unable to find the rainbow against the pale gray sky. Picking April's newspaper from the lawn in September. Sentences in search of a poem. Jurassic perk. The light barely shimmers off the still pool in the saliva bed, the smallest sense of motion beneath the thick mass of tongue overhead, long shadows cast by the wrecked enamel wall at lip's edge, a dike, a wedge of burnt chicken poised on the tines of a fork held there, as if unable to come closer. Dweezle's easel. The Pew, the proud. Rhythm of a young boy descending the stairs, midway between running and tumbling, footfalls in my bedroom in my grandparents' house – it's night but my mother calls to me to come into the hall – I can glimpse my grandfather through the open door to his bedroom, which means he's still alive and this is a long time ago. Dialog box. Scheme for reducing decoherence in quantum memory. Dozens, perhaps hundreds, of fireflies amid the tall white oaks, the dusk turning gray again. Gently, my fingers part the lips, pink within pink, until you start moving. Twirling the paper cone about the rim of the large cotton candy machine bowl, while above the tall oaks in the shimmering heat of the summer sky, a handful of balloons, still tied together, becomes smaller and smaller, every color of the rainbow. What did you write today? After the thunderstorm, the temperature drops ten degrees, the humidity sucked from the air. The weight room almost empty on a Friday night. Dry lightning illumines the forests, between flashes of which all that lingers in the suddenly deeper dark is the twinkling of the June bugs.

•

You
with your back
up against
pillow-cushioned wall,
naked
(the room bathed
in afternoon light),
legs raised high
the deeper
I might enter

It is the third time
we make love

that day

•

Image
of you

standing over me
arms crossed, pulling

the shirt up
over your head

then stepping
one leg at a time

from your trousers

the night before

•

It panics you
to be hugged
in an enclosed place,
an embrace in the closet
while dressing
(I learn this
more slowly)

•

In the morning
the neighbors
washing their car
too noisily
just inches
from the bedroom window,
our attempt
at orgasms
in silence

•

Muscle
under the right
shoulder blade
where you
store
all
your
tension

•

Cum drips
from your lips
back
onto my stomach

•

Thickest, richest
head of
deep black hair
aflame now
with silver

•

The official
smile
vs.
the spontaneous grin

•

Baby toe
of the right foot
hard-edged
with these years

•

Rubbing
the balls of
your feet

you claim
makes your scalp
tingle

•

Hilltop window
high over the wide
valley
through which
only helicopter pilots
could watch

•

You relax
as I oil
and kiss these lips
nibbling, nuzzling
the inner thigh
softest
flesh of all

•

In your sleep
at times I hear
the incessant
grinding
of your teeth

•

"It's okay,"
you say,

"you can come
anytime you want"

•

Towers of Duplos cover the rug. Cushions understood as objects of war. The TV we never use. Poodle, poodle, pumpkinoodle. A collection of Foxtrot left open on the floor, Post-its marking the "good ones." Actress employed to portray a mental patient in the music video years later has become famous in her own right. The gymnasium of lies offers too much light, too many mirrors. These two back teeth, between which, whenever I floss, the most foul odor erupts. This fresh t-shirt, pulled over my head, with a slightly different cut to its collar, clings as if to choke me. A faint but industrial tone to the air conditioning. In the dream, my lip is swollen, disfigured – but when I wake, it's fine, the flesh smooth, nothing puffy, and when I start to write I remember an earlier piece of writing, referring there to my lip as it really was swollen, 1976. The distance the chocolate bar falls in the vending machine, once it has been chosen, cracks the chocolate right by the lone almond. Ad banners across dreamscapes – what would they give to achieve that? Never flowchart level two.

The Rope Factory

The trope factory. Inflated plastic airplane worn as a hat. The squirrel, stretched wide along the side of the oak, alert to what danger? A young woman at the museum in a bright purple cocktail party dress, bright purple stockings over high heels, at ten in the morning. From that paragraph to this – from that poem to this. McGwire's one-handed follow-through, not even starting to run until the ball's well out of the park. Sunny-side-up eggs, a plastic toy to a child's kitchen set. The ease with which a spouse strips naked. Sunlight, high over the black oak. In the dream, the ice maker's run wild, inundating the freezer beyond capacity with small blue-white moons of ice. Right before the video comes a little ad for its soundtrack. Over the fairground, a lone balloon drifts and dwindles into the cloudless sky. Woman in the car behind me at the red light, preening in her rear view mirror. Stitches over the child's eye suggest a new character. The pen has been left open in the pocket, the catastrophe silently spreading. He imagines her widowhood, his own absence become a quality, almost a dailiness within her, but realizes this fantasy is false. A cloud, like fog, settles into his chest. Beneath them and to the left, a thunderstorm illuminated the desert below. Viewed on an airplane, but without sound, *Titanic* reduces instantly into a sequence of narrative devices. Children scream at the pressure in their ears. Outside, the Grand Canyon fills with water. I see you staring out the kitchen window at a real groundhog fat in the garden's parsley. So that the reason men find it so difficult to put the seat back down on the toilet is the behavior of other men, what will happen to any seat left down in a public restroom, thin film of urine atop it still glistening, gathering into drops. Between dreams some self-talk, between monolog and dialog (discourse of doubt, of the night). Tree out the window is mostly brambles, one small bird perched within that I only gradually realize is a hummingbird not in flight. Only a few molecules thick, the BodySuitfl is not only the lightest piece of clothing ever designed but also the most versatile, with color, degree of transparency and even temperature controlled from a small panel shaped like a bandaid on the right thigh – perfect for sports even in winter, the BodySuit's ability to program pattern, color and transparency even minute to minute has made it popular as part of evening wear and ideal for intimate occasions. First runner in the dawn fog. Even miles up the hill, I recognize the sound of BART. Young girl enters her parents' bedroom, talking quietly. Dog's tail wags banging against the door. The unripe banana. By the tilt of his shoulder you can tell that his bag, more canvas than leather, holds a computer. That the sun has burned through this fog is obscured by these high buildings. In the backpack, two pair of dark glasses. That you are (more than) halfway through the book itself evokes an emotion. That young woman is holding her ribs as though they hurt. White skirt over dark panties. "I've seen you bluster," Laura says. Mole growing on his face, just above the left nostril. People lean against the walls of an elevator. In the dream some kind of motorized shaking rattles the bed, but when I wake everything is still. "Another teacher, like paper is taken up" (Moriarty, misread). What I recall, 36 years after his death, is Davy Smith's smile, a rhythm of energy I could identify instantly if it just walked in the door, which it won't. Man on the street asleep, clutching a giant boom box. Woman will notice if you wear the same trousers two days in a row. On the street corner a news crew is setting up for a live shot. The pigeon walks right up to me, but when I shift my weight, it quickly waddles away. Inside the troop factory, men in rows are doing push-ups, a kind of ballet. Two boys wear their baseball caps with the bills to the front, one with it turned to the rear. Not the jingle of the keys from the loop on the janitor's belt, but the pace of it, slow and even, like the tags on a lab's collar. Tip of a business card used as a toothpick. She is in love with two men, one of whom is dead (in love nonetheless). Nearing the end of the book, feeling increasing anxiety. The dividend propositions. Listening to Blind Willie McTell on the Discman, reading Barrett Watten, the "fasten seat belt" sign rings on. Using the power of his own lungs, he inflates the neck rest, then leans back. An aftertaste of honey mustard pretzel lingers in my beard. The moderator's face and hands are too animated. At first he did not notice the knot in the cord. In the main cabin, two rows of eight small LCD screens each descend simultaneously from overhead. The trip factory indicates an on-line service. Osip Brik goes to work for the secret police. A Kentucky beauty queen is like a tornado – both will end up in a trailer park. In the house, a giant mole tries to wiggle onto the couch. This poem includes certain "forward-looking statements" for purposes of the "safe harbor" provisions of the Private Meanings Litigation Reform Act of 1995 that involves risks and uncertainties that could cause actual connotations to differ materially. Mallard as roadkill. But, once he died, my grandmother's sense of anger and resentment at her husband, which had been intense and constant while I was growing up, never a word of tenderness (and little enough talk of any sort, given his hearing loss), faded rapidly, so that for the next fifteen years, "Daddy" (a term of endearment I'd almost never heard before) slowly transformed in the tiny woman's monologs into the image of a saint. She smiles with just half her mouth. The lack of straws in the fast food franchise quickly became a crisis. Planet of the apps. Body parts of a mosquito scattered over my arm. It's the shine of the blades of the fan above the hanging globe that causes the reflected light to flicker so, making this hard to write. Flying South, Hurricane Bonnie visible to the East, not yet ashore. Down North Rampart comes a large bus labeled *82 Desire.* Column of ants up the side of the wall. A young man walks beside his bike, its rear tire flat. A bittern by the pond. Three musics at once: something on the bar's sound system just under the louder TV, and out the door two sets of street musicians, a jazz band doing something a bit too drunken for Dixieland while down the other street just two or three doors , some slow, badly amped blues guitar, and then the bus boy (a man my own age) starts to sing. Hardwood chairs scraped over a tile floor understood as percussion. This is . . . CNN.

Hippoheimer the King

Viewing *Private Ryan*,
weeks later I'll dream
the future of slasher flicks,
packed house applauds seventh arrow in the skull.
Laughing gull gives vent to its name.
Special white, mosquito about the ear.
Post-punk video ads
shown not on television
but against warehouse walls.
Sand flies by the cloud.
Every third mansion begets a museum.
Squirrel growls, mockingbirds wheeze.
But our concept of the mansion
abuts new tracts of
swollen executive homes.
Clouds forestall the sun
then smear with dawn color.
Behind reeds at pond's edge
I find an old lawn chair –
baby ducks (call fuzz) waddle up.
Garbage truck roars tank-like amid the tiny houses.
Goose cough. Flags left
to shred in the rain.
California job case
printer's type stand
popular now as wall mount for tchotchkes.
Editing is rape.
But rewriting, writing through
forms a mode of caress.
Woman on rollerblades
at dawn to the sea.
Giant water tower
serves as point of reference,

a blue paler than the sky.
Second worst point drop
in the history of the Dow
not even in Top 20
on a percentage basis.
Now and only now
my shadow as I write.
Old barbeque fork and tongs
long crusted with sauce.
Gold lame one-piece swimsuits
calling everybody "honey" –
wrist turned back
to let the cigarette dangle.
But to have not done
the new *Parent Trap*
with Mary-Kate & Ashley.
Two typos
in Declaration of Independence.
Two hours later, you feel the sun.
Hold the handle until it really flushes.
In this dream I'm given a key
that could only open the tiniest of locks
with no further explanation.
What appears to have been an alternative future
in reality becomes a part of
the variable past.
Hoping, mid-ocean, to find
most of the fuselage intact
that we might recover
more of what we think of as the bodies.
Projectile sneezing.
Dreaming of waiting
for the next bus to come
you burst into tears,
unable to afford the pink sombrero.

Dysfunction at the junction,
everybody c'mon right now.
Right pronounced *rat,*
only broader.
Sun quivering
in the haze ridden sky.
(I am not I.)
New style VW bug
invokes old brand equity
amid boomers.
Close, Mr. President,
but no cigar.
Nuns with giant wimples
cross the old plaza.
Refers to the computer as a "build."
The sound of flushing
heard as a sigh,
an electronic handshake,
Ciccolini's Satie
well before dawn.
Legos or logos, which one?
Roofers to the controller
with a bid.
Dressing in the dark.
The too sweet smell of a skunk.
Sneaker's tongue
permanently askew.
Lone small plane
audible before dawn
as is this cricket.

Woundwood

discount on Rawthey's mudra gal

Old Waterman felt-tip, extra fine
pressed into the lined page
as, upstairs, one boy is singing.
Sun soon to arrive
behind the grey scrim of sky
cragged now with a trillion leafless branches
(clots where the nests lie) –
ink spreads into the porous page,
letters barely discernable
but to familiar eyes,
curves rounding into words
from which white space
can never recover.
Old Duplo monsters
long since outgrown
linger on the shelves
of our L-shaped room.
Electric thought crackles, wired
before it hardens into type.
Lone burned-out bulb
in a string of four
that cast a softer light
o'er my desk. Who
will do it? Out of
which elements
can a world be mixed
not riven
with this joyful suffering?
A pawn then bravely
alone to the fourth square
of the King's file,

the boy's sly grin
not yet conscious
that outside
this room illumined
by the too-fat Yule tree
two dozen wars rage on.
A marble sits
atop a TV set.
Four British tourists
killed in the news in a crossfire
between Yemeni soldiers
and their kidnappers.
Press the reset button
instructs the plumber's wife
concerning the cool, chilled
water heater, which
when you do it
sends off sparks,
the insulation catching,
flames & smoke
instantly filling
the tiny basement room –
soon
        the boys
standing in the snow in bare feet
watch the firemen
made large by their uniforms
drag mud and ice
over the hardwood floor.
                I wake
to find the full moon
on the far side of the sky,
Ovid among the Scythians.
The snow blows over the road
but never sticks.

So the tiger devours
the half-naked woman, a rabbit
or this, described alternately
as lizard or caiman.
Write what you see:
the museum's audience is older,
more white, more bundled
against the hint of blizzard
through which we parade.
Each page, once turned,
can't be reversed,
unread again.
She's bleeding, seems faint
as he digs his teeth in
just below the breast.
Yet I bought this book
that I already own
and no doubt could buy it again.
Each tooth is a time bomb
set to detonate in the skull.
Quickly the rain melts
what remains of the snow.
Looking up, I see my old
best pen hanging clipped
into the side of
a cheap brown accordion
file (last year's
receipts) as though
it were a pocket.
Unexplained pigeon feather
on top of the scanner.
The beautiful but cross-eyed
personal trainer.
An old Dylan tune
permanently etched in the brain,

it started to rain,
so easily feigned
but so far from Spain.
Thin sheet of ice
spread evenly over the drive.
Why Zukofsky
never took part
in group readings.
Wake up, uneasy
over the dream you
no longer remember.
Key that won't
come loose
from the car's ignition.
Ice sheet
covering the whole yard
grows transparent
in the warm rain.
Not what I'd imagined,
not what I'd envisioned.
Coming finally to the far shore,
to the new margin,
first faint sight
of land, unable
at this distance
to discern the uneven
man-made skyline,
the mouse expects
the Statue of Liberty
to be so much higher.
I wake with a
tenderness above the cheekbone,
about the socket of the eye
I don't understand.
The poet as spider,

notebook my web,
the sport of it
ported over
into anything I do,
nonsense rhymes at supper
"give peas a chance."
Hangnail raw on the toe top.
Sleep as the fitful
scatter of dreams.
Cloud in the lungs again
casting its shadow.
Or cloudlike as the music
of Messiaen
hidden in the vowels
of an otherwise spring day.
How quickly
the moon downsizes.
Tenure and the caste
system of literary
reputation. O certain
limpness
in your electronic
handshake.
Only when the surgeon
(Jim Carrey?) begins cutting,
none of us in scrubs,
not even the patient,
a harmless little man
whom we were told spoke Spanish
but seemed not to understand even that,
the blade sinking deep
into his forehead,
that I realize
"This man has no skull"
and wake up.

The butterfly defect:
that a twisted simile
in "Carbon" (circa 1981)
results in this linebreak
here. Poet,
be like cod
liver oil
(a taste I *liked*
against all reason,
the idea of reason).
So few of that old gang
left against whom
to rebel, we must cherish them
as there will be no others,
no tiny growling man
staring up from his wheelchair,
no trimmed bard
in his rumpled suit
with his fastidious
hypodermic, tying up
now for his insulin
so famous and lonely
and uncertain. Wind,
wind: impossible
out of context to
discover verb from noun.
Neighbor I run into
in the weight room
at the Y, in the
most revealing of tank tops,
giggly with a young man
not her husband,
smiles sheepishly the next morning
to see me waiting
with my sons for the bus.

Phrase I recall, waking, is
"an uptight woozle."
Van Gogh's clogs
('ear the rhyme).
Squirrels at the suet cake.
That the grapefruit
should be greater than the grape.
Panic to wake
the sun already up
but the sky gray, flat.
I think of the sky
heavy with thunder
that never comes
over the flat landscape
of Irving, Texas.
Grackle loud by the side of the path.
The tooth's extraction
isn't painful, but later
I wander about the house
barely able to stand or stay awake
(a banana makes a good first meal).
Can you forgive your ghosts
as they no doubt have forgiven you?
The boys take forever
shedding coats and shoes
to come into the house.
Colin is singing,
then Jesse joins in
on the chorus.
This same Waterman pen
for virtually all my poems
for the past twenty years.
Who listens, who hears?

(G)hosts

final passage

To confuse sleep with dream
(to fuse blue with a deep
yellow, yielding green) is to
complete the riddle with action

giving satisfaction to none
but who reach up or out
in our direction as tho
you and I form a we for any

but the most fleeting
transactions (eyes over ink
not even at the same moment
and these letters for me

shadowed by my own hand always,
tall shaft of the black pen
held straight over the lined green page
of this notebook) You

who "philosophize disgrace"
(the judgment of history)
aware now suddenly
that you too have a body

before which this open text
(my heart, my home) must soon
reach an end if not
conclusion the way shadows

fill a room (an old Sufi
from the Floating Lotus

Opera Company appears
one night at the Tredyffrin

Library), mockingbird
in perfect imitation
of electronic handshake
as if to remind

suburbs are as islands
volatile social ecology,
a typology for cul de sacs
hidden in the trees.

Final For

Whoever wakes as Phillip Levine has overslept

Silence of the looms. Books piled high into a single thought. Too few recognize death as the last great adventure. Woodpeckers approach the suet cake (white, sweet, sticky, hanging in a wire basket from a nail) walking up and down the great oak trunk. Out this window the first fat drops of rain mimic the rhythms of distant footsteps. The man in my dream who, if I just saw him (but I can't tell if I'm chasing him or he's chasing me, elaborate dream rigamarole in a dark red bar in El Cerrito, that if I could just go there I'm sure I would discover doesn't exist, everybody making preparations to fly, by several separate small commercial aircraft, to Connecticut for some conference or meeting – I have a bowl of something like Jello, a deep red, and I keep moving, hoping he won't catch up to me (without knowing why), hoping I can just get a glimpse (without knowing why)), would just solve/explain everything. Carpenter, our plans are wrong. These tomatoes too bright a red. That moment at dawn after the birds have stopped their compulsive singing. Still I have no desire to contribute to the hysteria called recovered memory. Stop in a bowling alley just to take a moment and read (the tumbling pins as regular and peaceful as the sea). How will I know when I don't make a mistake? The violence of number not in the counting. At first I wrote county. Lego maniac.

Mimicking an important religious feast, the Serbs take three young men from the village (the others are gone, vanished, never to be seen again), roasting them naked, alive before the eyes of their neighbors, forcing the captive women to eat the cooked flesh (he had spoken to his wife and daughter about what he endured in the camps, but refused to inquire of their own experiences). The air is cooler under the fans or in the shade of the living room with its blinds down, but at this temperature people move more slowly as through an emulsion (the lone lamp a television with the sound off – Mike Piazza on second base, the front of his uniform dirty from sliding, pulls his blue cap off to wipe the sweat from his soaking brow), in the rocker my father-in-law sound asleep.

The best part of waking up / is Folgers in your cup! Children swarm about games at a school fair. Laptop built into the patrol car's dashboard. Oak trees now full provide a canopy (it's 10–15° cooler here). In these woods, even pre-dawn, air is not "invisible." First chorus of birds barely audible only because I've grown used to it.

Bob, ten days dead, five buried: Evie stands alone now in your garden where the hill slopes down into the forest – "We were going to tame that, forty years and we never did." Two hours south in Baltimore, the fire flies already in full explosion.

A white guitar (a toy) sits atop a school desk in the basement, ceiling fan on high all night. The sister of infinite anger. Flying things swarm the light. A man with huge hands holds a magazine in his palm – it's not the flowing blond hair that's at odds with the grey checked suit, tie still choking tight in 90° heat at the airport, but how the neck bulges at the collar – on its cover the face of an actress so familiar I can't recall her name.

Realizing there are finite words to a life, one holds each more cautiously the older one gets, until at the end one hordes them, a syllable at a time.

The stone house alone fails to match its neighbors. A man scurries, hurrying to unlock his car door, half-crouched, as if that will protect him from this sudden rain.

"The joy of doubt."

Itemize the components of desire. What often I remember is the light at the window, the color and texture of the wall (the sun behind K creating a silhouette, a halo) – so that emotion now years later proves identical with hue. Ability, or the lack of it, to absorb gluten. Palm-sized tattoo at the base of the spine. In this un-airconditioned kitchen, I sweat just to sit with a book, my shirt soaked, my hair pouring (slow waterfall of my neck).

Centuries later, among the pot-shards, all they will have to remember us by. This fly, in its dance, between the lights and the slow blades of the ceiling fan.

The content of the dream, the context of the dream, the eyes of the other confronted in the act of. Parrot that could imitate perfectly an electronic handshake. What we had imagined as the captains of poetry were no more than boys shocked that the succession of elders should pass down to them like children playing dress-up or how the people of St. Petersburg must inhabit the Old City. Who lives in the giant's house once he is gone? The hard drive straining on the incoming mail.

Screensavers remain long after we need them. So stand on the train's platform well before dawn. Imagine what lies within those slowly approaching headlights. Zeno himself could not drive faster.

The moment when, house filled now with relatives, in-laws, friends, your father's body, which at first you wanted, needed to sit with, suddenly is not your father to you anymore, but something alien, cold, profoundly other. Giant long-legged spider, elegant and angular, amid the leaves and stalks of the garden.

Well before the sun, changes in the hue of what sky is visible through these trees, a gradual lessening of night. Colony of flies in their awkward geometry of flight, light and heat descending from bulbs that bouquet out from beneath the ceiling fan. A woman is power walking through the trees. Within, the captains of poetry can be heard mumbling, bickering over who gets to sit about the dying embers of their fire. Soon the sun will shimmer too red, too huge at the horizon. A giant eye. Nobody notices the chill.

WHAT

for Charles Bernstein

The flower sermon:
critique is like a swoon
but with a step increase,
the awkward daughter who grows
to join the NBA. All we want
(ever wanted) was to be on that
mailing list, parties at which slim caterers
offer red, yellow, black caviar
spilling off the triangular crackers
while off on the bay
rainbow-striped sails dip and bob and
twist. The woman in the yellow raincoat sits
on a bench at the edge of the schoolyard
while two small children race
across the asphalt plaza. Too many books
sail the moth. A tooth that's lost
while flossing. A short line
makes for anxious music. Not breath
but civilization. The president
of Muzak himself says
that humming along constitutes time theft.
First snow in the Sierras = cold showers here.
The east is past. Margin of terror. The left
is where you feel it (dragging the eyes back
contra naturum). We're just in it
for the honey. Spackling paste
edits nails in wall when painted. Elbows,
shoulders jammed together on the bus.
At each transfer point, glimpse how lives
weave past. A woman with an interesting book

in her purse which I pretend not to see.
Letters crowd into a thought. Green paper
folded around long-stemmed roses
is stapled shut. Rapid winter sunset
lacks twilight. They take out the breast
and part of the lymph system. I
stare through a lens at the near world.
Hot tea sits dark in its cup.
Seeing is deceiving. Big tears
are eyes' response
to a dawn chill, first frost.
Clang of empty bottles in a paper sack.
The boulevard was a kind of free verse,
big noun skyscrapers, until the freeway
blew out the margin. Baseball cap
with the bill worn to the side or back.
Steam pours plume-like
from the roof of the new
senior tower. Thus lawn-sprinklers
sweep the air. This wool hat
itchy on your forehead, those
mysterious white sores
that dot the mouth.
New boots with Leather-Plus uppers
and waffler stomper soles. The way
gas stations dwindled overnight,
now go the banks: people
huddle in the rain
as close as they can to the wall
lined up for the automated teller.
But I just want to snuggle.
Jumping the curb on my skateboard. Even
before the war was over, vets
began to fill the J.C.s on the GI bill,
men playing rummy on the quad at lunch.

The way street folk make the sidewalk their bench.
Taking my glasses off, sensing
the muscles in the eye
flex as they refocus. Cars
at a stop light, each with its own
lone rider. Standing on the bus,
using both hands to hold on.
The sun in the trees still,
slowly rising. Beeper on a belt.
The container inverted
shall never be repeated, fungus
in a hot tub. A swamp entitled
Stanley Marsh. Black spot
on the thumbnail is permanent.
Neo-social democrat sneaks back
into Lenin closet. Not
democratic socialist. Folding chair
triangulates space. Shirt collar
as mock root for neck's trunk.
Small physical detail
enlarged (enraged)
refocuses the whole room
in the midst of the banquet.
Retrofit theory to text.
The idea of a doorstop
extends the wall. Thin palms kept trim
along commercial strip. Hollow is as
garbage truck sounds. Ghetto barber:
shop behind bars. Ask bus driver
to call out destination.
Chapped Lip Alert.
Man on a park bench
intent over crossword.
The sound of a piano
hung over the courtyard. Bliss

approximates emotional state.
Gay nerds (complex style). Drunk
on the streetcorner snaps to attention,
salutes the slow-cruising black-and-white.
Old manikin in used clothing store,
cheeks chipped, nose missing. Bin
of loose sneakers in front of shoe shop.
Dreams prod you with their skewed
pertinence. Like fingering around
in your pocket for a nickel, an
ambiguous coin, with your gloves on.
The pom-pom girl is sucking on a kiwi
as the sun rises, little startled bird.
Carved into nice pink slices, art
history is served
on seaweed-wrapped balls of rice.
At the checkout stand, the bagger
hooks the plastic sack into its wire
mould, dropping in the brown
spotted bananas before
the bottles of cider.
The close-out sale of
fiction at Dalton's
fails to attract
afficionados from their new
improved "ring" frisbees.
Please don't call it xerox.
Just because it rhymes. An absence
of form is pictured
on a milk carton. The dumpsters
are ripe. The present tense
calls up a terrific nostalgia
foreshadowing antacids.
Can you explain why Ezra Pound
and Ty Cobb were never,

not once, photographed
in the same room together?
The way cryotechnology
accounts for the Rolling Stones.
Heads of cauliflower
wrapped in plastic. Half moon rising
in the red dusk sky, streetlamps on
illuminating nothing. Twisting
the orange on
the glass juice squeezer.
Before dawn, alone
in the supermarket parkinglot,
hosing it down. Van's awning
signals catering truck. A leaf
had fallen onto the damp cement,
its image sharp years after.
Old green Norton anthology
perfect for doorstop. Albino mulatto's
curiously blonde hair. Linebreak muted
says I'm a normal guy. To generalize
a detail (use of plurals)
entails violence. Body language
at staff meeting very stiff.
Birds scatter high over
a schoolyard (asphalt
baseball diamond). My own breath
instead of a lung. Offhand,
by comments hidden in the brain,
we reiterate an old refrain.
My mind instead of an onion.
That these 20 year olds
call their shared housing
a commune seems quaint.
Old black woman with a cane
struggles to pull herself

onto the bus. I strain
to see these words. Chronicle
of Higher Medication. Learning
that I can't pick my nose when
I read, because the gesture
bumps my glasses. Our program is
compromise all positions
at all points, radical
at the cash bar. The colon swells
while the dash is but a double
hyphen. Thus paint freckles
an old ladder. Hair, combed
from the part, over the large
bald dome, barely throws
strands of a shadow. Men huddle
predawn in the vacant lot
for the grey trucks
that will carry them out
into the valley, hot day
harvesting crops. Yuppie world
where everyone's successful, everyone's
white. This guy's got great pecs,
strong deltoids, tight
abdominals, but through one nipple –
small gold safety pin. This poem,
15 lines of free verse, defining
(and as if "as spoken to") a noun
naming a common household object
has been designed
to compete successfully for space
against cartoons in the New Yorker.
Man striding down the street,
whistling loudly. Now that soft drinks
come in boxes. The Gift of
Security, the lock with 1,000

personal combinations: the only
lock in the world that let's you
set your own combination and change it
anytime, in seconds, without tools.
Because friends were coming over
for dinner, they began to think
about cooking in the early afternoon.
The honey in the 5 gal. can
had begun to crystallize, so she
put it in the oven to heat up.
Then a neighbor phoned (the details
here are less certain) and they
went over to smoke some dope
that had just been purchased.
This state expands one's sense
of time, of the moment. To be
within the present can be
totally sensuous. When they returned
later, the honey can had exploded,
tearing off the oven door.
Boiling honey (it was just like
napalm) clung to the ceiling,
floor and walls. Dueling
vaginas. I don't "do"
Dallas. Generic symbolic.
Snakeskin motif of
cheap plastic wallet.
My idea: hot fire glows orange,
logs in a Franklin stove.
Card games, I doubt it. A new
pen means a new idea. Fire
has its own sound (soft crackling).
I get quiet, go in a corner,
pull out a notebook. Later
we're in a car in the fog

seeking the western grebe.
I sit on a simple plank fence
while two doe graze on the next
ravine. A horse gives
its soft snort, then drops
to its knees and rolls
on the grass, short green
first winter growth. Red crown
atop acorn woodpecker
as it knocks on oak. Match
the bird to its paragraph.
Bufflehead amid mallards.
The way some folk attend nouns.
Salt taste if the gums bleed.
A thin felt-point tip. Are we
talkin' about poetry? You talkin'
to me? "Perspective," she muttered,
giving him head. Hard-wrought pun,
virtually opaque. Over
that totalizing irony of incompleat
(sic) sentences, slipped phrases, twisted
hesitant logic, all hiccups in the syntax,
stands a "higher" program:
offend no one. End lines precisely
where it makes least sense, until
a new order emerges – then examine
that. Even the one syllable word,
the simple morpheme (the letter "A")
contains a caesura. Brush your tongue
cures morning breath. Note the posture
of doctors, or of cops. Be
didactic, see if we care. Kid pulverizes
shard of glass on sidewalk with tip
of umbrella, then strums
air guitar. A heavy rain

through which sun shines.
Redaction shadows text. Later
seamless grace spirals
toward page bottom, flush left.
Brown skin big grin, front
teeth missing: she hands
the bagged bottle to her friend.
Small Laotian woman in headdress smiles
– gold buck tooth effect. English is
a foreign language. Man stares mute
before automated teller. Top Dog
animal grooming clinic. Sidewalk cracks,
chips, buckles, adapts to the earth
over which it's stretched. Thick, dark
clouds roll across the sky – glimpse
of sun flashes – rain visible
as a blurring of detail
just blocks away. Gulls fly
into a strong wind. I lie in bed
listening to the storm, tin cans
rolling about a gutter. 'Niners
tromp 'Skins. Urination,
I'm a nation, they're
a nation too. Men in a schoolyard
holding folded umbrellas
like rifles. Next to Laguna Honda
(the old folks home) stands YGC
(the reform school). A chemical
disease of the brain, just like
MS, schizophrenia's symptoms
are nonetheless social. Sound of
saw's serrated teeth, tearing
through wood. Bottle caps
flattened into the asphalt. Ceramic
decorator whiskey containers

tend toward the cartoonish.
Lotteries simply (nothing simply)
extend the logic
of capital to the state.
Children in the backyard
are playing taxes. Try running
for the bus with
an open umbrella. A bicyclist,
his hair slicked back by the rain,
clothes drenched, coasts
downhill thru the forest.
A young man in a bookstore
trying to read what he can
(without buying) from *What Color
Is Your Parachute?* The "glass"
of the plastic see-thru walls
of the metal-frame bus shelter
is covered with the thick paint
ornate letters of graffiti, blue, orange,
purple, red. I landed on my head.
The driver pulls the bus away
from its furious would-be riders,
all the authority in
that man's life. You pause
as if to contemplate your actions
before slipping into blue cotton
underpants. Smell of coffee,
freshly ground. Not only
can I not read
without moving my lips,
I can't even walk. As a
follow-up to the smash
"It's My Party (And I'll
Cry If I Want To)"
comes "Now It's

Judy's Turn to Cry
(Judy's Turn to Cry
(Judy's . . .))." Coming up:
Uranus Probe (details
at 11). Fog turns
to beady dew
in the spider's web.
The Chinese basement. This bus,
because of its route, is called
the African Queen. A nun
dressed in formal habit, stands
on the streetcorner next
to two Hindu women in purdah.
A new Vietnamese beer, brewed
by the Sierra Nevada Co.
of Chico, California.
Sudden chill, sun
behind cloud. Shipyard
lights at night. Generatives
destroy their referents.
Art is the craft of
New York City. Darth
vedas. It smells there
to be a rat. Adorno
piano. Live here and you
could be home by now.
Mastercard, I'm hungry.
Naptha Valley. Poached
pear. White stretch limo
pulls into an alley in
the industrial district.
Tan wood frame of
building "in progress"
amid a field
of pastel stucco houses.

Orange and white
3-pronged Sutro tower
is our unacknowledged
monument. Shoe laces'
long loops droop
toward the inside of the foot.
Face rests in thumb's crotch,
hand covering mouth. The way
legs cross, knee over knee.
Taste of clove oil
leaving dentist. Check
elevator keyboard: M
is for mezzanine.
Bum scratches lice-ridden hair
until head bleeds. Pink
mottled vomit splash
on marble walk.
Beauty is the organ-
ization of complexity
into an illusion of
simple wholes, skull
ripped from neck.
Left hand stressed
by typewriter and
piano alike. Photographer's
solitude before the shot. Lyric
moment in job skills workshop.
Upper case 'G' facing right,
lower left letters that fall
below the line. Pen point pauses
till splotch spreads across paper.
Elbows resting upon knees, hands
clasped upright serve as base for head.
Large dog pulling Nancy Reagan
across White House lawn. Base of spine

numbed by hard chair. Ear wax
yellow-brown on cotton swab. X,
registered bookmark. Weight of glasses
on bridge of nose. Place of base at edge
of foul line. Let's write of kids and kitchens
and what spills down bibs: and then went down
for chocolate chips. The conflict poets
havin' a good time. Yellow rose's wah-wah
petal pusher. Watch another yawn
but don't rhyme. First styrofoam peanuts,
now the shape of seashell pasta. Radio static
calm as seashore. Removing glasses, wait for eyes
to adjust to middle distance. Autumn Sunday
afternoon: a man in white robes, wearing
wooden clogs walks into the mosque.
Garbage day: the sweet-sour smells coil up thick
from the cans along the walk. A woman in a pink
bathrobe, broom in hand, sweeps litter
into the gutter. Two trashmen, straining,
drag a red dumpster to the rear of their truck.
Express bus lurches through city streets. Weighted
by his hardware, a young cop saunters past
the doorway sleepers. First to arrive,
a young store manager unchains the iron grate.
Up on the fifth floor, a window mysteriously broken
fails to reflect red dawn sun. Small words,
more carved than scribed. Bromige's hat
is in fact off-white. People scurry across intersection
to beat the light. Old yellow-brick school,
declared unfit as earthquake hazard, is converted
to city offices. Involuntary smile on the stranger's face
when her eyes meet mine (is quickly suppressed).
High over the street, two yellow cranes
slowly turn over the construction site.
Decals on the door of a big Mack truck.

Fat man uses both hands to pull himself
down the aisle of the bus. Mould for a dowel
on which to glue porcelain crown, half-yellowed
social realism, red as gum's blood.
In the mind hurry winter. Fallen leaves
clog the walk. Deer path through the brush
year after year clearly marked. Hospital's
new wing, low, sleek, gray and impersonal
surrounded the ornate original structure.
When this you see, hit and run
for me. Sunshine on a chill day.
It hasta be rasta. Man on
a streetcorner, coffee steaming
from big styrofoam cup, holds it
poised at his lips, eyes shut,
to feel the heat on his face.
Try picking your nose with gloves on.
Chartreuse VW rabbit with a
black stripe. Camaraderie
of older women, working in giftwrap,
back corner, department store basement.
A Latina woman with high cheekbones,
long false eyelashes tinted bright blue.
Blackbirds pecking at the frozen grass.
Down to just 19 teeth, I stare in the mirror
at the temporary where the new bridge will be,
my smile as alien as a fresh haircut.
Spit on the sidewalk gleams. I pull
the knit cap down over my ears. More than
10 years old, I think of these
BART stations (all cement and glass)
as new. His photo I.D. badge
inadvertently triggers the alarm
in the express line at Safeway.
Lone braid pulled up

and pinned to the top of
her head. Kids in uniform,
all dressed up for ROTC,
not one of them white.
Cardboard Santa in window,
on either side a plastic wreath.
A tax disguised as a game, state
lotteries present government
with the grin of
capitalism's face. Big sour
fart on a crowded
bus. I have no patience
is my curse. Thai tea.
A bag lady is pulling
her shopping cart
down the subway stairs.
Appalled at the snapshot
to see how bald I am.
Street preacher waves
red buckram bible
next to a clown selling
helium-filled balloons.
A woman slowly pushing
an empty wheelchair
"against" the light.
Welcome, American
Geophysical Union.
What letter is this?
Sipping "fruit-flavored drink"
from wax-paper box.
Wait for body heat
buildup to take hold
in gloves. California
Xmas: aluminum foil
wrapped around palm tree

topped with red plastic star.
The meter maid is a
burly guy. Mesh on
the windows of
sheriff's bus. Curly headed
blonde looks wrong,
thick dark brows.
An African man with a
hat made of beads,
beans. Now styrofoam pasta
mock snow, drugstore window
holiday display. Brown, dry
outer skin of onion.
Smell of piss in rear of bus.
"Ju-ju con Danny," thick
felt tip strokes
cover rear window's
safety glass. Drop cloth
protects the hydrangea
beneath painters' scaffold.
The jaw moves in circles
massaging itself
as if over cud – she's
chewing gum (smoking
a cigarette!). Bright
red scarf over
long black coat
skips across street.
The bicyclist, panting,
pedals uphill. The collator
on the xerox (which is not
a xerox) beeps in distress.
With their shopping carts before them,
half-full, potato chips and sherbet,
three types of whiskey, a can

of peaches, head of romaine,
they stand revealed. Trees
pruned in winter. Postcard
on which the key noun
is not legible (covered
by smear of
postmark's ink).
Because we speak we
think we can
read. Syntax dips
at the verb. Into
intonation nation.
Eucalyptus trees
stripped of leaves and
branches, like five posts
driven into the hillside.
A man on a balcony
doing stretches, leans forward
to touch his toes. Rap
master. Pistachio shells
litter a doorway near
a bus stop. Red-green sheen
to the pigeon's gray neck.
Small one bedroom apartment
entirely visible thru windows
from the street, in which
a woman sits
at kitchenette table
speaking into a telephone
with an angry face.
Small old house whose "fence"
is a collection of boards, doors,
behind which trash
crowds the weedy yard
patrolled by a mangy

half-yellow dog. Politics
of the lyric, absent
individual, absent voice.
Shadow of a gull passes
over the green stucco wall.
What the wheelbarrow says
of the man (in the city,
on the farm). Two pit bulls
on leashes sniff one
another on the street.
You don't want a wood door
on a cafe or store
if you want people to
feel invited to enter.
Thru the branches bare
in winter, the tops
of traffic on an overpass
sweep by. Phone polls
line a narrow road,
here where license plates
take different colors.
A crow large as a gull
glides to its landing
at the center of
the apartment complex lot.
Words are brittle, language
of voiced sighs. The way
high clouds mottle the sun,
a dull noon. An old man
in white checked pants,
legs stiff as he crosses
the wide lawn. Wreaths
in a cemetery on
Christmas eve
green and red. Rodefer

has referred to me
as a romantic
which I'd deny.
These virtually windowless
brick taverns, not
uncommon on the east coast.
Barbed wire fences
line the yards
behind row houses.
In the land of ticking clocks
storm windows hold in
the heat, the cat
(deaf with age) sleeps
on the couch-back.
Micro macro-natural foods
for the nuclear age. I never
metalanguage ah
didn't like. Joe Billy
chops the tops
of his own socks off,
his ankles swell so,
rings choking the flesh
of short, pink fingers.
Tub of popcorn
"butter-flavored." Two teens
struggle, carrying a mattress
from a porch to a truck.
A boy hurls a balsawood glider
into the pale blue Virginia sky
where it loops once, skidding
onto the never-repaired asphalt
street of the planned community
where the road bulbs out
into a turnaround of a dead
end. All depiction's false. My

life is as real as yours. To heat
a cup of tea, set the microwave
to "hi" for one minute, thirty seconds.
Salad bar in the produce section
of Giant priced at $1.99 per lb.
Two blocks down, the homes
are still only half-constructed,
shining walls of insulation. Blueberry
preserves atop buttermilk
hotcakes, a print retrieved
for the frame (surrounds
sketch of a daughter reading
12 years ago). Friendship quilts
of the 1860s, which other than
tombstones were often the only
written record of a woman's life.
Clean bear there. Aftertaste
of maple syrup. The porch swing
in 35 degree weather (I try
to write in thick rag wool
gloves). Three days
after the argument with Donald,
Doris turns to me and says
"I thought, 'O boy, every word
of this is going to end up
in a book.'" I sit on the can
a little while longer, lost in thought,
happy for the solitude. The despair
of a supermarket far from home
or of any airport terminal
is simply the clarity: one's own place
with a sense of proportion. Old black dog
behind a chain link fence. Hyperopic
but with corrective lenses, I can barely see
past the tip of my feet. The tyranny

of the whole submits all
to instrumentalization. To read this
as neo-romantic would be to equate
Springsteen's Born in the U.S.A. with the jingoism
of Rambo, charm-songs for the MLA.
Cat walks about with its tongue stuck out.
I begin to understand that my father was an alcoholic
also. Just as his four year old son, hand drawn back,
is poised to throw the paper airplane into the air,
Donald snatches it from him, snickering
at the unassailable superiority of his own power,
unaware of the fury in his child's eyes. A man
boards the bus thick with the smell of cigars.
Ritual baring of teeth, a smile. To a two
year old at the aquarium, an escalator
might be as awesome as a whale. A beer
at lunch to calm the nerves and settle the stomach.
A book is a gift you can open again and again
especially when you're writing it yourself. The small
two storey granite facade was retained, cornerstone
collaged to the dark pink late-modern highrise.
The clocks tick and I talk. At midnight
the "big apple" descends to mark the new year
as broadcast live with Kermit the Frog.
The blonde leading the blonde. Reading
the word "nymph," thinking "New York mph."
The skaters, outdoors under the bare trees
(D.C. mall sculpture garden rink), flow
counter-clockwise. Old rectangular
two-storey building, one wall in yellow
brick, the rest in red (patched
with a brighter brick where once
there was a window), roof dwarfed
all out of proportion by the grill
of the satellite dish. Mid-day

on the D-line. Squash on the
floor – not easy
to get out the door. Pigeons
on rooftops, visible
from the el. Legless beggar
is wheeled through the train,
shaking a coffee can
for alms, half-filled with coins.
This sentence points not
to the 'work as a whole'
(no such thing) but to your,
the reader's, life. If I shave,
people say to me, "Oh,
you've gained weight." I put on
my glasses: escargot trails
blur the view into a solid
image. Words grapple
to surround a nuance. Are you
anxious or amorous? Let's
call it new narrative, an homage
to a lack of humor. In the mirror,
the face never is familiar. The hand
cups naturally over your breast.
Mid-flight, a few smokers
assigned to the front of the cabin
stroll back, edging past flight
attendants who bend over rolling
trays, in search of a now-vacant
seat in which to catch
a few drags. Which of the
couples you see on the street
are having sex (and what
is it like for them)? Peter Coyote's
maiden name. Pregnant, the idea
of giving birth to a boy

sends panic thru her, wave
of more than nausea. How,
on an airplane, you know the moment
the descent begins? Bay's a
valley the ocean filled
into which rivers mix.
Thick, cheap toupee, mismatched
against his sideburns. Tennis racquet
juts from daypack. Dropping
(on his way out) his pistol
on the floor of the bus, the kid
stoops quickly to scoop it up.
Streetlights shimmer in the fog before
dawn. Cheerleader's pom-poms
(purple and gold) draped over
her books. Yet if the break in
the line refers to a history
of linebreaks, what if
only a fraction of readers
might see it? Psychotic on a
traffic island shakes, as if
to play air guitar. White fuzz
of angora trim on a long
knit coat, and below
she wears bright pink tennies.
Seals in the eyes of
the nearsighted. Leaving
the dentist, I see a road crew
jackhammering the street.
Terms of endowment. Gravi-
tational fields forever. Last year's
mega-hits of desire all in a row
discounted in video store window.
Prism house of luggage. Larry Lasker
pens Peter Pan. In a genealogy

of preservatives, writing precedes BHT.
Scales in the oz of the near-sated.
Old window wire screen brittle and torn.
She uses a plastic shopping bag
as a makeshift purse (the way a bra
stands up beneath a t-shirt). He
has to shout because she wears headphones.
My father would be an albatross
and I a gay alba
treading his truss. Here
the road climbs the canyon wall
so that as we travel
homes appear to descend.
Enter three bears. Pigeon's peck
around the gutters in fog,
camouflage perfect. She jogs
holding a Walkman in one hand.
The poetry of the past recedes
like the memory of a
childhood dentist. Blue-rimmed
plastic see-thru scarf,
beneath which white hair
is contained by a net.
Or this man with a rain cover
pulled over a fedora. Platitudes
of the past aghast. A pen
clipped into her rear
(tight levis) pocket. Glazed over
like the eyes of the blind.
In the ambulance, the IV
is automatic (sack of salted
sugar water): to provide a track
in the event of medication.
The Museum of Unnatural History.
Porch light on all night.

Nitroglycerin under the tongue,
pain about the eyes as
blood vessels dilate.
Toddler at an adult party
between legs as amid a forest
calling "Daddy." Baseball caps
in all colors, hanging
from a pole, bunched
like bananas. Mice in the walls
scratch and scramble. Smoke
rises, barely visible
against the fog. I force
the unlatched window open
and climb into the kitchen
knee-deep with months of refuse
through which she'd made a path
between stove and bed and
bathroom (the toilet unflushed,
two feet of water
standing in the tub).
The R.N. pulls my socks off
to prepare for the EKG.
"Ah," says the paramedic,
needle pushing through the vein,
"you'll have a hematoma now."
Should I be married? Should I
be good? Should I pretend
to beatitude? Homes around
the med school being bought up,
one by one, livingrooms converted
to reception areas, each kitchen
a staff lounge. Thus I choose
not to push through the crowd
surrounding the felled motorcyclist,
distant siren growing louder.

Rico at the gym, tall,
broad-shouldered, cleft-chin,
dark curly hair, does trunk twists,
20 lb. barbell across his shoulders.
Past the "reform school," the bus dips
into a quieter neighborhood, large lawns
well kept. My cock responds, swelling
to fill your mouth. Folded, he holds
the umbrella like a cane, she a club.
Silky off-white blouse and a
blue plaid skirt with big pockets.
The iambics of Bob Dylan just
get into your head and squeeze
like a vision of a rhythm that
will bring you to your knees. Those
who stroll into work versus
those who scurry. Youth
Authority. The grid of flatland streets
turns to curves in the hills. Turning
the tape in her Walkman over
as she jogs. Making room
for "clunkers." Back when I still thought
semiotics reputable. Chips of orange peel
on the walk have all dried. Those of us
who are just one rum baba from
begging in the streets. In a pin-stripe
three piece suit with a gym bag.
Or the young man scarred with acne
wearing a leather jacket
beneath a swastika-adorned levi vest
holding a bouquet of roses
in the light rain. A false cadence
mocks closure. Small birds
clamoring in the dawn light.
We hauled 15 bags of trash,

much of it foodstuffs, from
the one bedroom apartment
and only made a dent.
Behind the red sofa,
out of shredded newspapers and
napkins, the mice had made a nest.
With the tip of his pen, he
scratched his nose. Inside
the red and white box
of Kentucky Fried Chicken,
some old rolls had turned
hard and blue. After the first
hot hour, a colder wind
blew in from the coast.
I taught I saw
a puddy tat. I did I saw
the moon full in the blue sky
start to set. Already
20% of all Vietnam vets
have died. That tickle
in the foreskin after.
Not "stream" of consciousness
but "blocks" of writing.
Fat chance long pants
no dance. A gang of
seniors rowdy as teens
boards the bus, all talking
at once, loud with laughter.
Eating the banana
through the bruise. The cat
frightened by the umbrella
leaps. O strange new
mouth so full of crowns!
A pain in the wazoo. The cost
of a clown. A burst

in the air of
the public imagination,
a billowing shuttle
disintegrates on replay
over the Florida coast.
Sound of an umbrella
clicking open. Blonde woman hoists
black child onto the bus. Mouse
lies mute, mouth open wide,
dead in the trap. First big drops
spot the walk. Later, pools form
in the courtyard two floors below
and our interior light feels "cozy"
watching the storm mottle
these small lakes of the parking lot
stained with grease. Just
as the bus starts to pull
away from the intersection
a voice from the rear
shouts to be let out. One
black teen to another,
"Hey, beanhead." I couldn't
say that. My brother's face
wide as my own, the neck thick,
jaw square but for the cleft
– though his nose is flatter
where mine turns up – same eyes
set wide and deep in the skull,
yet he's six inches taller and
has all the hair. Lake in the rain
deep dark green. To eat beef
is to whittle on
rain forests in the Amazon.
Man sez Gonna be sunny
all this week and I

stand here in this driving hail.
Ah semi-bright morning star
hereafter called the sun
you come again until
my cereal's milk glistens
in its blue bowl. Plaid shirt
tied skirt-like to her waist
tho she wears a sweater.
Any text averaging 1.65
syllables per word demands
a college education. Asphalt black
in the back of the white dump truck.
Not aimless, blameless
nor without shame. For Rent
sign wired to fire escape.
He looks at his feet when
walking downstairs.
The Mao of physics.
After the trashmen pass
empty cans roll around
on the walk. They don't fear
theory really, but the view it would show
reflected. "I deny myself the right
to know what I'm doing," however dimly.
Ads in Coda for an MFA. Starship mansion
up for sale. Now there's an oxymoron:
Grace Slick. His face intent
upon the numbers, man with the hose
at self-serve gas tank. Let's stand
in the drizzle with our umbrellas folded.
Dan Ake, for christ's sake. Renny says
he thinks of my baldness as temporary,
a style. I sink my teeth into the salad
and a cuspid crumbles. Corrugated
tin shed next to the small house

in front of which are parked
3 rusty trucks. She wears
a leopard-skin print long sleeve top
over tiger stripe slacks.
Tongue rubs over a speck of
spinach caught between teeth.
All metal garbage cans are dented.
The trap didn't just kill the mouse,
it shredded it. In the dream I
write the sentence beginning
"In the dream. . . ." I set off the alarm
by the exit of the drugstore, a soft
synthetic beep, then explain
to the very young assistant manager
just how demeaning it must be
for him to feel he needs to search me
only to discover machine error, nothing's
been taken, but he doesn't get it,
stares blank-eyed, pleasant, insistent.
From a distance the small spotted dog
appears to be holding one paw up,
favoring it, but up closer you see
that front leg is missing altogether.
Man in a restaurant blows his nose
into linen napkin. Kampuchean dancer's hands
with her fingers arched back. The one emotion
I ever saw was anger. Clayton (in the dream) lies naked
in fetal position, trying to make eye contact
with his therapist. Everyone on the bus
is writing furiously into notebooks. The old couch
fits perfectly into the rear of the station wagon.
On the corner two men share a slow, tender kiss.
Diced papaya salad with bits of pork and
sprigs of mint. My grandmother would rage
through the house, screaming and slamming doors,

while Grandpa would turn off his hearing aid
and go out to the garage, to compulsively polish
the already shining car, its red gleam
in that dark shack. Am I thinking of
writing now? The bay from here
looks fit for a postcard or the cover
of a phonebook. Some days I despise long lines
and other days short ones. Punksters
on the bus 'R' Us. The pure products
of America are not made for sale.
An old Curtis Faville book I'd not heard of
before. Wire grill over opaque glass
of the sheriff's bus. When this you see
duck and cover. Gabardine's not a cloth
but a process. Oh off-white silk suit
jacket (hyperventilate to spend a month's rent
on a coat). Little 'Mayan' figurine in a window
made of clay. Having once worked
as a shipping clerk for the local utilities
monopoly, I recognize a transformer
atop a phone pole. Am I less out of control
than I once was? My grandmother's intensity
is what I most recall. When exiting the bus
tell the driver thank you. I was surprised,
reading Grace Paley, to find her style so clunky,
her 'characters' cartoons (how does the liberal's
racism differ?). Not of course that I'm any better.
Watching older women now (my own age, that is)
with a look more clinical than filled with lust.
LAI: Linkage, Ability to give, Interest
in the goals of the organization. People
are afraid of dragons. Outside the hospital,
looking in, what one notices in the offices,
beyond the too-bright lighting, is the predominance
of files. I remember the feel and smell of you now

years later. The weight of the briefcase
once the umbrella's added. A sheet of green plastic
where the car's window had been. This woman
is seriously allergic to bees. Details
like zombies in Day of the Dead. Yellow brick
facade. Those sentences had 'been about' the letter E.
Those painters' silence sealed their fate. At least
Rosenberg's coinage, "action painting," caught
the heroic individualism, that sense of the romantic that
would doom them all. Plastic curtains that mime
stained glass. My grandmother, the youngest of 13,
was herself raised by a single parent, as was
her mother also. Here the houses have all gone stylish,
deep mauves or brown with a blue trim. Psyche
yourself up for the next line. Watching
the traffic 'copter hover out over the freeway.
The point at which you read each word (the
only point there is), two minds share a larger whole.
A break between storms. Sitting alone on the bus
just the way she holds her mouth, its muscles
clenched, gives away her anger. As if Greenwich time
were somehow real. Old Indian print bedspread
used as a curtain. The sun didn't so much rise
as, at dawn, the clouds parted. Ah windchimes
on a condo balcony (glisten with dew). Little
wooden shutters block out the light. I write
short fat words, plump vowels against which
consonants rattle in mouth. Clouds pushing north,
a bad sign. You hop into bed wearing just
that bright blue t-shirt with the big black
dots and I shiver with excitement. The idea
that I might not be grotesque is, at times,
difficult to imagine. Bright red bricks
seem a toy construction. I gasp
to catch breath. I squat

my body weight five times
straight. Peer over reading glasses
to look you in the eye.
Street lamps still lit
in the early dawn. I
need space, said he, meaning
time to himself. Bright purple
shower curtain hung in
livingroom window. Tongue sticks
between rows of teeth as he writes.
Penpersonship. Ja, a sod hut. A
sad hat, not a red one. The dead
of winter lie in the morgue.
Spitting sunflower seeds onto
the floor of the bus. The Bank of
America Mastercard® card
is now the BankAmericard®
Mastercard® card and reflects
the well-known MasterCard look
across the bottom of the card.
The wind knocked the side fence flat
and "popped" the bathroom window
out of its frame. Roofer's truck
sits idle in the rain. I stand
on the trash bag, forcing
it into the can. The stain
of rhyme colors the line.
Turn a buck with a book?
One teller stands at the glass
door with a key, admitting
the bank staff one by one.
At first when the rain hits
people keep walking with
their umbrellas shut. Let us
now raise famous hens.

At night the news is filled
with weather. She leaned forward
and lifted the headphones
from her ears, nonetheless
half-shouting his name, then,
with a big smile, placing
the small orange speakers
– the wire between them
mussing her dark bangs –
on her head. Try lugging
suitcase and garment bag
through an airport lobby with
one arm in a sling. I rise
and read your words in Temblor,
charmed by the elegance of
your despair. Do I dare
to eat the teach? Or simply
each year present
to the MLA a mirror
beyond reach that says
"your guilt, well-earned,
is now assuaged." Well,
dickhead, not so. Suddenly,
police cars converge, lights flashing.
At Guild House, senior housing
built by Friends, architect Robert
Venturi and associates topped the roof
with a gold mock sculpture of a
television antenna, unattached and
without function, their symbol
for the elderly. For the prosody
is not token. We shall not
be mauved. Sips the foam
from the head of the beer.
What remains is not taste but

the memory of taste like
the rich smell of a good cigar
curling through the bleachers
at Candlestick. A lifetime
of drinking done in a hurry.
As if shooting speed
wasn't itself a sign
twenty years ago
of a gift for addiction.
There is a journal, Mother,
very far away and very
boring, called Administrative
Poetry Review. The Class A
team in my home town, the Tri-
City Triplets, have just been bought
by the brothers Brett. And yet
it's not really. I don't regret
having moved. The line of thought
detours at the margin. A hard-on
awaits me when I wake. Silly
savage. Often, writing in this print-like scrawl
the same letter will occur twice in one word
scripted different ways. Boutique brownies
at a dollar a pop. Nothing is more fun
than a clear mind, unless it's extraordinary
physical stress. Waitress on her break
sits at a booth with a cup of coffee
and a cigarette. The copter hovers low
over the stalled traffic. Odd to think of Detroit
and Chicago as not in the same time zone.
Under her Reeboks I see the tops of
purple anklets over white stockings.
What the waiter wore. Adorno's
despair (odd tone for a tweedy hedonism).
By Friday the brain death of the work week

is complete. Its blinds wide open,
the vacant apartment stares out
on the street, hollow as a
missing tooth. Sisters talk
a continent apart, yet the heart
can be so much further. Little dog trots
across the street, its gait marked
by the sound of claws over asphalt.
What are you feeling? The cat's meow
repeats. Somewhere someone is typing
very slowly. A man who merely
padlocks his front door. A parrot in a cage
hung on a back porch. The fly bumps
off the glass of the window. An old mop
with a rotten sponge. What the bra does
is abstract the body beneath the blouse,
depersonalization being one kind of
sexual defense. The door stuck
and so he pulled. The dog's bark
turns to a growl. During the day's course
I watched the dumpster, one man picking
slowly through, later a woman
much more intently, then, at dusk,
a neighbor sneaking out a few bags
of trash. The car pulls a quick
midblock U, riding up onto
the walk. New mall multicinema,
personal as an airport. Hibachi
filled with rainwater mixed with ash.
Web of the spider plant. Heavy metal
guitar solo sails out over the street.
Gingerly he fastened the threadloose
button on his shirt, hoping
it would last thru one more day.
$550, 1 BR, Bernal Hts, garage,

wshr/dryer, gd trns, grdn, 647-2374.
Oiling the asphalt. The hot sun
warms half my face. I hear, she says,
braces glistening, he's talkin shit
about me just cause I wouldn't
make out. One lane shut
slows the 'short cut' measurably.
Lawns steam in the dawn air,
smell of cut grass. Big orange ball
reads '76' in blue. Green sheen
of the duck's neck. Alas,
        a lot looks
a lot like
what it is. The line points
where the voice treads, thread of
historic confusion, 20th
century aesthetics – from Georg Lukács
to George Lucas. Back before Homer
meant a sportscaster that took sides.
Man in a 'chopped' sweatshirt,
midriff showing: his navel's
an outie. From up here
in the sun's glare I see
cars on the freeway
inch through fog. Song:
we are the pearls
inside your jewelbox
we are the gems you keep
behind locks. Orange cones
mark the road gang's site.
Each word is a new voice, each
vowel. A man is carrying
a wood and wire pet cage,
empty, down the street,
tears streaming down his face.

Thighs thick as hydrants
jut from a miniskirt. The impulse
always is to tell too much
or not at all. But I didn't write it down
the way I thunk it. The cyclist coasts
down the slope of the hill,
leaning forward almost crouched.
He pulls the wool cap low over his brow
to hide the bandage. She holds
the cup of hot coffee up to her lips
with both hands. A small man
in a big hat in the sun, maybe
a displaced farmworker. Try
to recall which building
had stood in that vacant lot
readied now for new construction.
Halley's comet (which in my
childhood we called HAY-ley)
left me cold. It felt like
a beach town in summer,
the low fog mixed
with hot humid air
cut by a breeze.
Worn sideways the tweed cap
looks like a beret. A 3 foot
high plastic doll of a Heineken
in the liquor store window
is covered with dust. Sounds
psalm sings calm
microdata. Flatten the milk
carton before you put it
in the trash. Old wicker chair
juts out of the dumpster. Window
filled with cacti faces east.
I squint to get a hint

of what's in the haze.
Theory of bank decor.
Weary of dank back doors,
hostile lame bagel.
A little affectionate friction
among friends. The Dow
of psychics. Mango republic.
Two wrongs will make
a Reagan. Down noun
where all the vowels are bright.
Bereft of center. First
hint of spring: sun's
still up on the way
home from work. A shirt
on a hanger got left
in the window. Heavy
little two step. One game to play
while walking around Safeway
is spot the plainclothes cops.
Tho I'm hot and confused, baby
you know I won't abuse our love, wah wah.
Drink tea and want to pee. She
pulls her jacket on and then
with one hand, lifts her hair
up over her collar, shaking
her head (put gravity
in charge of alignment).
The stewardess, moving silently,
an illustration to the tape of
preflight safety message, points
toward each exit with two fingers.
The clouds up over the mountains
billowing puffs, sunlit on top,
darkly shaded beneath, beyond which
a long flat plain of low fog.

Irony's a form of aggression
that wants to be liked.
Panties worn over panty hose,
then that pink camisole
I like so much. Let's floss.
Our APU isn't op today. Stain
the beets make
over the cottage cheese.
Slab of plywood
augmented by cardboard torn
from cartons
patches the smashed window.
Banana smell of nail polish.
Rice Christians. Beige
cows in the rain. Why
I'm not a poet. Small
campus bookstore's
large stationery department.
Clothes in laundromat's
washer window
in counterclockwise tumble.
No trucks. Someone
on this bus must
have just bought
a pound of fresh ground
coffee beans. You
could tell where the bullet
entered the pit bull's skull.
Moustache half-hides the hairlip,
half-curled, chewing gum,
squinting into the rain.
Long torso over short legs,
all bodies are different.
Broad-shouldered woman,
plain of light freckles

across your back
turned to me,
folded in sleep.
Plant on premises!
reads hand-lettered sign.
Across the wide intersection
(where three thoroughfares
come together) from the black
rubberized oval of the highschool track
where last week a runner
from another school, having crossed
the finish line, collapsed
and died, stands the Youth Guidance Center
where, only one week before,
a boy hung himself with his belt,
two other "residents," even younger,
later mopping the floor
of the shit that had dropped from his leg.
Astronauts remains found on ocean floor.
Again to marry after 21 years –
the idea in my mind is completely different.
The old man speaks in feminine voice
okay by me. A hum
to the street sweeper's truck . . .
more a tractor really. I climb
onto the bus, then,
moving back, seeking a seat,
see the express turn the corner
at the foot of the hill, coming up
behind, I accelerate immediately
and dart out the rear door.
The purpose in particulars
is specificity's claim to the real
like blackbirds in clover
on an untended lawn, ab-

stractions hidden, per-
ceived as simple sight.
The woman stops
to readjust her shoulder bag,
then continues walking.
A bicyclist walks also
guiding her vehicle up the steep slope.
Home study. He places the lozenge
onto the fat of the tongue.
A man on the corner
shuts his eyes and coughs.
Woman doctor and male nurse
are running down the hospital corridor.
Syntax freezes them forever,
though I merely made them up.
Whatness vs. Whichness. 't's not
just the large beard on the small guy but
the way it juts forward. Swivel
your hips with a knee dip and
the skateboard swerves
up the curb ramp. Brit flag in window
serves as curtain. Walker in sweatsuit
and knit cap – lone figure
on track at dawn. Pages of xerox
in dimestore binder. So let's patent blood
(knowing the market). So there's Habermas
in a guest spot on Miami Vice. Or the way tabloids
use quotation marks in place of italics. Like water,
language runs to the sea, flush with information.
Not that, aardvark! Prefer poets' yap
to their lap. Discordance in number
triggers an audit. Squint
just to keep glasses
from sliding down nose. A
line a day keeps

the critic away. Re-
work context for previous vowel.
NO PARK WILL BE TOWED
spray-painted freehand on garage door.
Zen grocer. Eyes ache
after day at CRT.
A teenage girl with a bright smile,
safety pin thru her nose. Bike messenger's
wire basket. Wall up around construction site
with several generations of peeling posters.
Stepping outdoors, the cold air makes my eyes water.
Umbrella handle carved like the head of a duck.
Empire devastates the dominant: End the War
in '94. Patterned white stocking
over thick black ankle. Tremendous
formal out-thereness of the haiku
translates into greeting card mush.
What's sentiment but guilt posed as love?
Your breast soft to my hand's touch
till the nipple hardens. By Thursday,
people's posture heading into work
seems knotted, sullen, withdrawn
(eyes that seldom glance
up from the sidewalk).
Rolled up old newspaper
dissolves back to pulp in the rain.
Mannikin in shop window
stares off into space. A young man
with more money than brains sets out
to have impact on the world of letters
and so becomes an editor – writers
everywhere seem grateful, solicitous,
remember his name. Manufacturer
of software thinks to underwrite
a reading series, to project

a thoughtful, literate
"upscale cutting-edge" image
for their latest product development,
only to be sent to Chapter 11
thru rapid absorption of their market share
by maker of flight simulator game.
Mr. Reagan guesses aloud that he too
is a contra. First you peel the orange
then break it into crescents. Dense smell
of blue mold on the rind. The time at the tone
will be 8:35. The shit just spills
from your asshole. What if your work takes on
that slim permanent grin of
well-earned defeat, ironized to the max,
precisely as awards, grants, reviews
cast their focusing light (crosshairs
of esteem) over your short, balding,
bespectacled, noticeably stooped, fuzzy,
unshaven frame, alone suddenly
in the prison yard, this curious
proscenium. Direct statement vs.
alternating statement. First fear,
best fear: that mom's tit (the world)
might be withdrawn. Small storefront
on a side street recycles tenants,
big plastic sign (mock awning)
painted over. John Denver on radio
in Chinese corner market. Bicyclist
in black sweatsuit at night
must want not to be seen. Small guy
in huge straw cowboy hat, eyes watery drunk,
holds onto the chain fence
just to keep himself standing. Mid-day
subway half-empty
till we reach downtown. Man reaches

into his briefcase, pulls out a comic.
That's a rabbit, says she,
repeating the noun for the child's sake.
The hole, with or without the w,
is never complete (Donald Duck
underground in the land of the schmoos).
Dawn's haze spreads sun's gleaming brilliance –
from the copter the tops of cars just shine.
Is he growing a beard (did he forget to shave)?
Did you forget to shove? Chivalry
is not dad. Sunglasses on a chain
hang from the neck. I watch you toweling off
after a shower, one leg up, foot
on tub's edge, silent, serious –
what are you thinking? Thus
three meals' dishes crowd the sink.
First melt the butter, then spoon off the foam.
From the outside you can tell
which are the tiny closet windows.
The daypack slung over one shoulder only.
The wide ledge of the second story window
has been carpeted, and is where,
window open in the warm afternoon sun,
the cat sleeps. Should wide, loud ties
ever make a comeback, I'm ready.
"Pneumonia is the old folks' friend"
like going to sleep, like Stravinsky
on the stereo, you gripping your sister's hand,
just letting go. Hoagy's last photo
(single reflex action) were of his feet,
camera falling after the bullets hit.
Liver is in what sense a verb?
Dissolved in, let's spell it out,
ETOH, that the reaction is chemical.
How odd, your ashes in an urn in Oakland

near your mom's, near my
mother's father. Granola wedged
in between teeth: strong floss snaps.
Dull scrim of sky – storm to the north.
Monday's trucks restock the stores
(bus' lurch jumps my pen, r
into n: restock
the stones). Bone's about it.
At a beep tone, the driver grabs
the phone by the farebox: "29
on the 24" be thy name. Why that
obsolete twist? Why this
semi-metacomment? Augie's
Basil obit overpraises, 'ey?
Simple supper sip on seamen.
Bad pun, old song. Tweed cap's
rim rots. Two posts, one loop
and a hanging cross
dangle from that lobe (the other
being bare forms the pair).
Toothless man roars to himself
scaring the other riders.
His body's oils, unwashed,
stain the flesh brown. Up
the terraced hillside, lush ground cover
surrounds the boxy wood shingle condos.
I had hopes. Helicopters dot
the large sky, a perfect blue,
out over the bay. Women wear
white and pastel cottons in spring.
Old rent-a-cop swaggers into work
hand over holster like a child
playing cowboy. Then I look up
to see a pickup at the stoplight,
driftwood in its gunrack, big

dayglo terrycloth dice
hanging from its interior mirror.
People talk "babytalk" to children
not out of condescension
but because they love
the physicality of that speech.
A woman gently pulls her daughter's hair
into a ponytail by means of a colored band.
I watch roofers pry the drain loose
atop the Parnassus Masonic Temple,
crowbar and hammer, kneeling on the edge.
Little open window, full of
shampoos and lotions. Bruised elbow
is sore for days after.
Cher at the Oscars
wears Red Warrior wig?
That punctuation marks
only my own
incredulity. Small black bird
rises out of the tree
wings beating wildly.
Velo-bound xeroxed text
copied from some other volume,
page turned sideways
shows a central vertical shadow
of a different binding. As here
words are entered
as one does a room
stilling all conversation.
Limp that suggests an artificial leg
hurries across the street
before the light changes. As here
words are entered
upon a grid of red lines
across light grey paper

without respect to the boxes that
the verticals set up.
By spring the hills are green again,
big deal, and yet
what function of the week is
more important
than that shot at a new beginning?
From here I can't tell
if that sign in the window says
For Sale or is
some candidate's last name.
So the lines here are breezy,
not dense, where previously
others, visually no different,
felt thick, clotted. Off
its route, a street sweeper roars past
at the speed of regular traffic.
I step back from the bulk. Slow
red scavengers' truck seems an odd machine.
The hand scripted page is a convention
among architects. Haze accumulates
till the bay is 'gone.' Squawk of a domestic bird
from its cage by an open window
not visible behind drawn gauze curtain.
Capacity to spell, being learned, is fragile.
Lone dove on a line (sky's low wires).
Two cars block the road, their drivers
standing in the glass of a smashed headlight
survey the damage. When the pier burned
(May 1851) Hoff's store atop it
dropped into the bay, where later earth
covered it over, forming Battery Street,
a fact. Eat to the beat. Old
tiger print sheet used as a curtain.
O long skirts of Laotian women!

Friday dawn: all but the news
of the Sunday paper
lies piled, wrapped in string
by the door of the corner store.
Those eyes are hazel, an easel.
Lone house atop the stone hill
looks out over canyon.
Seemple moosic. Take a
heartfelt vowel. My gut
turns to fart soup. What it will mean
again to be married
after all these years. I sought
not companionship, but had
to be brought to it, drawn
out of this focus which
can throw up walls. Rim
around the back porch
of wood, between whose posts
a rope holds
2 t-shirts and a red sweater.
A torn shade
looks tacky in the
window. The new pen
is blue. The house shakes
waking us, slight shuddering
earthquake. The cab arrives
at dawn, the driver silent
as he steers through fog.
Hi there, small bear. He wears
a grey three piece suit
with a fuzzy tie, hand-knit.
A carpenter is whistling
as she hammers. The cheap couch
was simply styrofoam
about a wood frame, foam

for cushions, covered
with a red cloth.
What you do
is what you can.
The breading breaks
off the smooth flesh
of the large oyster.
The scudding wind
pushes the brim of my hat.
The ridges in the red rock
ripple, the dust atop
a lighter yellow. Tongue touches teeth
to form an "L". Each line
breaks at the point
where anxiety peaks.
This can be spelled
double "e". Thees
can be spilled. . . . Hard "S,"
breath pours over tongue's flesh.
Teeth break into oyster's body.
Our lips twist when we kiss.
The sun rises. Point at which,
to mind's eye, sky divides
into quadrants. Eye designs
I.D. signs. Logos logos
made of Leggos. A long coat
on a hot day. An electrician
who's the son of a druggist
adopts a boy. Sequence of factoids
seeks rime. Spelling
is fucked. I'm invited
to a far city, all expenses
paid, to make people feel
less anxious
about "language poets."

Equal signs between capitals
is big lie. Long johns
worn as tights beneath miniskirt
with leg warmers and bright pink
tennies. One of those periods
when the type of weather
changes daily. Veins on
an old man's small hands
grown large, knuckles also –
brown-spotted flesh hangs loose.
That's your future also.
Inner yard at Juvenile
is ringed with barbed wire fence.
I wake at night,
obsessive replay of
a meeting on the job.
With a loud whoosh,
Muni bus kneels on its hydraulics
as two aides struggle
to get the young man's wheelchair
onto steps that convert now
to a lift. I kneel
at a light post to write this.
Hunker against it really.
Transit system ad
of cartoon bus with big smile.
Don't blame me: I voted
for Opus and Bill the Cat.
Ginsberg's right: strike
articles out. Bleach
turns the blue liquid detergent
dirty red brown. Basement
is paved – bare bulbs
hang from low ceiling,
rough wood beams (neighbor's cat

sleeps in shadows
atop old unused work bench
amid cans of paint and caulking,
brushes wound in old spiderwebs).
Break wind for the sinner field
basket catch. Folks yawn
walking into work,
conceals anxiety. This one
flirts outrageously – it's how
she's learned to get along.
That one chews an apple
at his desk, thinks lunch
is a sign of personal decadence.
I take walks, visit the bookstore.
Glasses on, the world up close
is sharp, intricate as a spiderweb
in the wood's crotch (boards join
to fence a porch) – further
is a familiar valley
green now with spring, but
edges softened. Next door,
beside my neighbor's lawn chair
(webbed plastic about light
aluminum pipes), an old crate
is being used as an end table
alongside which Emma sleeps,
grey cat with no tail.
Down the hill, two neighbors
share a post
atop a fence, pulleys
and clotheslines extending
in both directions. House
with no rear porch, people
enter the small yard
through a basement door.

The cat stretches, paws
harmlessly at
white butterfly just out of reach,
gives a small cat sneeze.
Friends ask us why
we decided to get married,
friendly puzzlement
reflecting true affection.
As close to a love poem
as I'll ever get.
Your daddy sits on our sofa,
blue checked golf pants
and orange sweater, rereading
Ice Station Zebra. Mom's
white blouse
on a hanger in the sun
from the padlock's clasp
to the shed door.
I wake by water's edge
                Willingly I'll say
there's been a sweet marriage,
seabirds loud with dawn
in the harbor. Last night's
boneless breast of roast duck
topped with apple,
strong sweet aftertaste
lingers on. I won't forget your eyes,
the way they saw, tears
streaming, as you recited
words of Robert Duncan
and I my Zukofsky, and I
  would fill your arms
as if with flowers
  with my forever being there.
Cows stroll across the field

tags clipped to each ear.
Yellow Up-Right Sky-Hawk,
state of the art crane,
sits folded by a bank of phones
back of the airport lobby.
Skeleton of wood and I-beams
where soon fresh concrete
so light a grey
its nearly white
will form a freeway off-ramp.
Man in a blue suit at intersection
"inconspicuously" scratches ass
then smells his finger.
From this, extrapolate
lessons for living
ambiguously couched,
forgetting that language
made it up. "Yowza,
Mr. Benny," says Rochester
with that hoarse voice.
I could never figure out
was that his first or last name?
Unlike Gracie Allen, a bigger star
in her lifetime than George Burns,
Mary Livingstone was clearly
first of all her husband's wife,
first woman I'd ever heard of
to keep her name. Percussive
rattle of radiator pipes.
What the spine says
or the legs
after a full day of walking
city streets. Men
selling back issues of Honcho
laid out on the sidewalk,

a blanket on which lie
rows of dark glasses.
The train passes
a high school playground
so fast the game
of baseball appears frozen,
masked catcher standing
behind the batter, arm cocked
to throw the ball. The sign
is no vessel. I hand
the bell captain a five.
Where once the factory of red brick
had glass in its windows
now bright green corrugated fiberglass
casts a checkerboard design.
Let's do it doggy style
atop the big brass bed
and watch our reflection
in its shining knobs. At the feeder
goldfinch and house wren
while below, larger even than the red
cardinal, a gray dove
picks thru the shells of sunflower seeds.
In the muted light of a slight rain
in the afternoon, the house is quiet,
nearly silent but for the dozen
ticking clocks. An old cat
fully deaf, its long hair
balled and knotted, is curled
on the familiar blanket upon
the familiar couch, its body rising
with the steady breath of sleep.
To choose the line
as a painter might choose color,
to decide, as the period

determines a sentence,
fixing whatever lies within.
Eyes stain the world,
giving life to pigment,
the lie to nature. I spy:
the Pentagon sits
in a vast sea of parking.
Museum guard leans in a doorway
at the end of long day standing.
Tourists pose by a fountain
in the rain. A day
at the traces. "Sweetie,
watch out," says the busperson
pushing her tray. Mass of
archaeocyathids form a reef.
The white brick boarding house
where once Lincoln's would-be
abductors plotted now sits
in a block undergoing renovation
in Chinatown. Bung-bung chicken.
Mobile homes = truck houses.
Over breakfast, three sisters
speak at once. Sound truck
on Fifth Ave is unintelligible
in midday traffic, tho signs read
Stop Union Busting Now.
I hear finches sing
in the magnolia while a blackbird
runs in the grass, dotted
with the white flower of clover.
An old man comes down
the stairs slowly,
putting one foot onto the next step,
then the other, both hands
on the railing. It's fathers flirt

with their infant daughters,
that's where that's learned.
Let's rake puns. Big robin
lights on the branch and stares.
Cars pass. I sit
on an old porch swing,
held by chains
which are thoroughly rusted.
Seeing Pollack's No. 1, 1950
with more pink and blue-green
that I'd expected, I
nearly weep for joy.
A train passes. Flower beds
edge the lawn. Ironing board
stands before the piano. Wrentits
in the grass alas. That's
something deeply personal
about my life you've written
and I don't appreciate
it being spread all over.
On the American tray.
Proto-language: that's better
than quasi- or pseudo-. No
being but in context, no
self but the self placed,
society itself a kind of nature,
these cities teeming nests.
Problems of the world as
small as washing
lawn chairs off in spring
with a brush and a bucket.
By its beak I can tell
that's a hairy woodpecker,
a female there in the sycamore,
not a downey. Frogs

in the marsh sing
by the hundreds,
their song is loud
and alien. Along tracks
where once steam engines
quote roared unquote
endquote, you find still
little purple balls
of coke. Across
the green river
"clear as a bell"
someone is playing
Bruce Springsteen's Glory Days.
Robert says
that's where his scout camp
used to be, and there
later in the thirties
encampments of the CCC.
On the porch in the shade
the air is cool now.
A jay hops about
with twigs for a nest.
Great green gobs of
grimy, greasy gopher
guts, and me
without my spoon.
All of
Emily
to the tune of
Yellow Rose of Texas.
The page, the individual
page, even the single
line, the word itself
so many letters bunched,
crowded – there is no,

no other way through,
and each letter
arched, curled, blocked,
vibrant
with meaninglessness,
a kind of silence, an
opaque light of
pure design. Hair
along the neck's back
so thick it
reveals
his toupee's secret.
Stallone's ideal
script of one word.
The beaten path.
The cognitive
power of fog.
Joggers squint
to see in the rain.
A rhyme strains
to aim the line
to its mark.
It's just a big diary
complains lieutenant grammarian
promoted now to chair,
rug and pillow.
The well of what we count
as meaning might run dry.
Whereas quilts
to my mind
form an other tradition,
a silent sharing.
Watercolors of textiles
displayed at National Gallery,
the whole idea

National Gallery –
known best for its buffet
underground by the fountain.
At the back of the bus
three blacks taunt
an older man
in loud golf pants,
who pretends, staring
out the window,
not to hear them.
This serves
an essential
economic function,
dividing labor's fractions
against themselves.
The crowd at the hockey game
is entirely white.
It's morning and trucks
double park
in front of the market.
Utility crew sips coffee
from styrofoam cups,
bright yellow hardhats,
loud orange vests.
Unable to fathom love
some men will crave power.
Not even May yet
and the hills are turning brown.
Out here where old men
come to sit in the park
in the shade of
the great eucalyptus,
a young man in white
turns slowly
hands forward

in the silence of tai chi.
An auto backs up
away from the intersection,
permitting the bus
room to turn.
Man climbs the stairs
to the contagious hospital,
bouquet of roses in hand.
Returning to the job after
two weeks away, I'm
upset constantly, depressed,
dreaming again of powerlessness,
my voice breaks to speak
responding to the simplest question.
As, right after sunset,
the clouds spill in,
the sky to the west is darkest.
It's not just any
video and pinball game parlor,
but around the corner from
the Greyhound depot.
Across the too-lit lobby,
half roped off, of the
Burger King
from the sullen teenage
Vietnamese gang,
hobo-like old street person,
drool frothing over grey beard,
hugs the case of a big guitar.
Content soon follows.
You arrive in new topsiders,
kelly green. Paul Dresman says
that Ron Silliman wrote
all literature comes from books.
I read this in a book.

Hobo vomits kelly green
over orange formica table top.
Hey man, my wave.
Cartoons come in panels
and have a respondent.
Unlike the turkey vulture
with its silent circling sweep,
two green-headed mallards
flap rapidly low over the ground
following the river
as it heads upstream.
Like the eye of a hurricane,
the cowlick at the rear
of the man's head
sitting before me on the bus,
point from which
his hair, graying, thinning,
grows in each direction.
The woman's nail polish is a bright blue.
Not clouds in the sense of plural
but a single mass, roiling, layered,
half-broken (thru which sparse, deep
spots of blue) tumbles over the city.
Narrow metal ramp extends
from rear of moving van.
Narrow mental rap extends
the parallel. Right lane
must turn right. One writes
not to draw conclusions.
That we may not reach out
to put our hand on the hand
or knee of a stranger
will encode our entire lives.
Foot traffic passes a gelato shop.
Fire engine returns

quietly to its station.
A detail in the work of Jessica Grim,
how after swimming
water runs off, first
in rivulets, then beads.
Sun's reflection makes them glisten.
Listen up: eyes' sweep converts to words
in a string. Pool's tile being blue
gives the water a too-deep artificial hue
visible especially from an airplane.
Like sun motes they shine, these
windshields dotting the freeway,
liquid flow of constant motion
viewed from a distance. Counter-
intuitive, 2 + 2 = 4. Confident posture
of man on the move, back straight, eyes forward,
deposits quarter to open a newspaper vending machine
simply to pee inside. She throws her head back
when she gargles. An obsessive counts the steps
from the curb to his door. Within, an orange cat sits
atop the diningroom table. Well, even a diningroom
is an index of class. Marchers in the plaza
demand militant nostalgia. Dog leaps up
to sniff my crotch. Fumbles in her purse
for small cannister of mace. Old spoon ring
altered into ear cuff. Small press mag
from the sixties: Blazek, kryss, d.r. wagner.
Pigeons wait until the blackbirds are done
eating the breadcrumbs from the gutter. 32
lines per hour. A boy stands on the bus seat
to pull the cord. A woman is boarding,
holding an infant, carrying three quarters
clamped between her teeth. Most people
sling day packs over one shoulder only.
Your blood dries brown about the hair of my cock.

Simple as the D that turns anger into danger
a tea composed of rosehips and hibiscus
will soothe the throat, chamomile the mind.
Shirtless, but in a leather vest, the drunk's torso,
well-muscled, is filled with tattooed dragons,
his head holds the cap of a confederate soldier,
while out of one trouser leg juts a metal peg.
She strides up the hill in high heel clogs.
Twelve things to see in an EKG. The large, grey
barnacled body of the whale rose up from the water
just below the cliff by the lighthouse where I sat.
The route is not new but a divestiture of the baggage of habit
(as the bus reaches McAteer High, the students shout
"Mac Attack!"). Demolition of the burned out store
exposes the block's rear yards and back porches
to the public view. Shakespeare's Cantos. Merrill's
Pinsky. Warning: nightdrop at your own risk.
Geropsych. "Why U.S. reactors are safer"
pieces in the wake of Chernobyl
doesn't mean they're safe. As tho
he were a rock star, Reagan names Asia trip
"Winds of Freedom Tour." As tho
he were a rock. Imelda's Olson:
a foot is to shop with. Man stares at address book
in front of vacant lot. Sweet smell of hot tar.
He wrote in lines because they had, as they did
because of the ones before, nobody pausing
even for a moment to question why.
It was the first of the month and the line in the fog
at the automatic teller stretched
around the corner. I pushed the plastic tray
past the cellophane wrapped salads
and bear claws, the tiny bowls
with their perfect scoops of cottage cheese,
to the steaming bins of entrees, the dry

moussaka and the sauce-covered
salisbury steak, behind which
stood a woman in a pastel
food service uniform, her eyes
filled with boredom. Space aliens
populate grain belt. We cuddle
in our sleep. Aaron says
(April, 1986) half his circle
has already died of AIDS.
She breaks a bran muffin
into the gutter for the pigeons,
oblivious to the glares of fury
from the people nearby at the bus stop.
Suddenly, when walking, an old man
does a dance step with a small kick
in the middle of the street. The barber
pauses at his door step,
push broom shoving a pile of hair.
She wears the tweed cap sideways
like a kind of beret.
His ponytail bobs when he jogs,
his hands flopping loosely
as if dangling from his wrists.
Please wait till coin drops.
She's not able to remember to buy
her monthly bus pass before the first,
her purse is cluttered with old BART tickets,
a nickel remaining on each. 3 girls
doing the dozens board the bus,
decibels double. That starts with 't'
and that rhymes with 'p'
and that stands for puddle.
Scientist says today's rain
will probably not produce much more
than slightly higher than normal radiation

in all likelihood. Citizens: peppertrees
are sidewalk busters (think
before you plant)! He carries
his skateboard by its wheels.
Patting her guide dog on the nose,
the blind girl stares ahead.
At the cliff's edge, the guard rail
was mangled and broken. The victim
of prison rape, Leo Estrada
was prohibited from suicide
by a profound commitment to Catholicism,
so murdered another prisoner
to gain access to death row
where, in 1973,
the death penalty briefly overturned,
he turned to despair, writing
wild angry threatening letters to the press
which published them,
before he smashed a lightbulb in his cell
using the broken glass to grind out his eyes.
A long, lanky man reaches down
into a briefcase opened on the sidewalk
from which he removes
bright orange long-stemmed feather duster
and small fuzzy dog sprayed blue.
Chewing gum disrupts
the rhythm of the writing.
The way legs jut up
when the chair's too short.
Place where I bit
the inside of my lip.
Sometimes, wearing my reading glasses,
the outer world a soft, amiable fuzz,
I'm quite alone. Times Square
is not square at all. Say "scalding"

with a long a. Incest
amid Siamese twins. Dystopia
for vacant skies, for amber weights
of blame. Fur burdened fountains' travesties
above the routed veins. And then
went down on the snips
of old lines parodied. CHiPs
in a row at an officer's funeral
hot under the midday valley sun.
Old Miz Johnson, whose lawn I mowed,
'62–'63, kept a flag in a box
back in her bedroom closet
which she referred to as
"my son." Woman strives to appear stylish
in light pink pantsuit and neckbrace.
Tilting his VFW cap jauntily forward
he begs for spare change. Three teens sit parked
in a large pink Caddy, passing a doobie
between them. Fresh clipped nails
feel like fuzzy fingers. Why
am I telling you this? Tsunami warning
is a big wash. Frisco graffiti writers
adopt media acronyms as tags,
thus CBS, KSUN, RCA
replace last year's most visible artists
Chink and Slime. A Coke truck,
bright red, climbs the hill. Eye sees
what the mind says should be there.
I seize what I can. Words
like cards make a sound
when shuffled. Mo'fucka
is the correct pronunciation.
OED accepts "wimmin"
as feminist option. I watch
three persons walk side by side,

wildly dissimilar gaits. Clear as the sky
high over Portola Heights, words
in bright sunlight shield the eye
from any evidence of stars –
moon's pockmarked face
is filled with blue shadow.
I thought you said cockmarked and perhaps
I did. George-Therese inhales on a cigarette.
Surrounding each period an aura forms
like a printer's halo. He walks down the street
mouth wide open. He talks down
to the people he meets just by exuding the correctness
of his own assumptions. Imagine a pink tie
atop a brown plaid shirt. Helping pets live longer,
healthier lives. She walks with her cane
hooked over her wrist. A new notebook
means a new idea. Is a Crock
is the name of banal daily comic
set in French Foreign Legion
where Arabs are barbarians
identifiable by big nose. I feel anxious
in a supermarket, breaking a small cluster of bananas
from a larger bunch. Hollow tone to the voice
over the delivery van radio. The cop squats
talking to the driver in the pulled-over car.
Her white high-top tennies intricately decorated
by a red felt-tip pen. What I remember of the dream
is the intensity of its colors: Mary Oppen
in a white VW minibus, pulling up on the pier
over the grey mottled sea. On the streetcorner
stands a young woman, reading a letter
handwritten on lined paper folded many times over.
I try to imagine how to count change. From myth
to reality: New Haven to Hartford. Old friend panic
sets in. Cereal poem. Think sun (once moon).

I started over and overt. Elegance fashions
a pastel fuzz, an image of romance
sans hinge of an edge, the half-bright sweater
not for perspiration. Soft pocked rind
of an orange that to the touch feels thick
stained with the blue-white shadow of mould
sits in a brown bowl in the pantry
beside the white onion. My mind for a horse!
"I'm at the end of my rope now," grandmother says,
collapsed lung filled with cancer. Two women
in robes sit on a front porch. What
is the title of this poem? Your arms bruised
from the needles and tubes. On each block
sits one large wood-frame Victorian
surrounded by small stucco dwellings
which divide the old estate. TV on silently
in a blind woman's room: goose waddles
across the screen. These streets (invisible)
lined with trees. A woman smoking
pauses to cough. White heron's flight sweeps up
so that it sits as it lands (in the tree top).
A man in a window leans over a desk.
What I saw was there to see. Wires
anchor antennae atop houses. Alongside
the large jet at the loading gate
the inevitable parasites, small tractors
and trucks. Where in the line
the sentence ends. People pitched pennies
into the urinal's pool. O bad aubade.
Huey Lewis, the step-son of Lew Welch. The hills
yellow with mustard flower, the streets
purple with jacaranda (wild artichokes
also purple). After eating bacon
an unquenchable thirst. On the beach
at Rosarito, a colony of wingless "ladybugs"

lived in the sand at tide's edge. Young colt
gallopped after the riders on their saddled horses.
Reznikoff wrote once that this sky
was the same as at Eden, but watching the smoke spill
skyward from open industrial fires
and from the oil refinery along the Baja Coast
we saw this was wrong. I walk among thistle.
Lichen or not. Ants here are red and big.
The sea, disappearing in haze, seemed
to continue forever. Yellow waxy flower
of the prickly pear. Write about this flower,
Aaron says. Beautiful view. Big ditch too.
We could see the buoys of the lobster nets
atop the blue water. A trio of large pelicans
glides by. Let's put it in past tense
to hint at loss. This planet
shall be our tomb. Lizard
skitters past. Striped snake slides
over dry grass. Witch's hair is roaming,
golden tangle over the chaparral.
Out on water's edge, where stone
gives way to sand. A man twirls seaweed
high over his head, while his two daughters scamper
laughing to get out of range. I step back
from a stronger wave. The stones were wet
and rounded, polished by the sea. Watch the wave
gather to a curl. Some small boys hurled rocks
up against the cliff, hoping
to provoke a slide (yellow, pocked clay).
Torry pines, compared with others,
seem short and twisted. We hiked
up a road that led high over the marsh.
Coyote's call more a giggle than a bark.
Off in the distance, a train's horn sounds.
Crow with ragged wings. Then

fog to the point of drizzle. Above
the buzz of traffic, a birdsong resounds
in the high branches. Odd
to see a eucalyptus stand alone
(O great weed!). She reads
through her glasses, a second set
propped on the crown of her head.
Wearing braces, using crutches,
a man makes his way
slowly across the beach.
A woman on the bus
wears a hospital bracelet,
name typed in plastic.
Amid the women in bikinis
around the hotel pool
stood a small boy, fully dressed,
the flesh on his face red and
flaking from serious burns,
hands encased in protective gloves,
blond hair only now
starting to grow back.
Baby fuchsia in a basket
sits on the porch. Hairs catch
to the pen's felttip
pulling blue ink
over the sharp lines of the letter.
Neo-Reebok. Unable awake
to remember my dreams
but depressed and upset, as if
for no reason. The mind clear
as the air above the harbor
after a brief rain. Newsboy
hurls lies
wrapped in rubber band
onto porch. Hark:

teens rap
in bus back
rhythm of its own.
Phlegm drains
from sinus
into throat.
Older woman wears
optometrist's
dark glasses,
holding a bouquet
of yellow rose.
Agreement in number
simply makes more numb
eye that tracks ink
sunk deep in grain of paper.
Up against the white-out
legs spread wide
so I can get a taste.
Boiling turns the lobster redder.
Vanilla envelope. The little
you see through half-drawn curtains.
A woman squeals, voice
oddly infantile, as the sprinkler's spray
turns on her suddenly. Stand-Bi
Market. It's not the drag queens
that amaze me, but those young men
in identical navy-blue blazers
and gray slacks. He jogs in his shorts
holding a t-shirt in one hand,
hair on his chest thick and white.
The gods of poetry, small and quibbling,
envious, slouch over the round table
at the rear of the bar, their faces
(twisted) half-lit by the yellow light
of an uncovered bulb. In the dream

I meet a blonde in Woolworth's
who gives me a blowjob on the spot
amid the bright and crowded shelves
– Not so much, she gasps, gulping
to swallow it all (this is not about sex
but the lack of power). Oh cereal
in the cat puke still fully formed.
Flesh in the hands is withered now
down to bones sheathed within.
Flatbeds pull past, carrying
pieces of large equipment
whose names and functions
I cannot guess. Second floor hair salon
called Uppercut. Prosody of Chinese speech
in which western ear hears an "ah."
Underneath his brown robes
Buddhist monk wears yellow knickers.
Here I am an old man with a sly mouth
being fed too by a boy. Early morning
store fronts sit dark behind bars.
A man who smokes at dawn
sits alone in the donut shop,
steam rising from styrofoam cup.
Men gather in front of plasma center.
Bottle gang at tattoo salon. One
of my childhood perfumes drifts by,
thick old lady toilet water.
Indians on the lawn at dawn
by the UN Plaza fountain
roll up sleeping bags
damp with fog. If the
function of writing is to X-
spell the word, world
(alphabet is no name), what
is the name of my poem?

Sweat spills from my body
(heart, replaceable pump, th'art
no center). Field
shape of a diamond
on which a player circles
head up, hand
(gloved) cupped over brow
to cut the glare of what
(lost) hovers in air
never to drop. I stop
this pen. Do not
cop to all that is the case:
face in the mirror not my own.
A crowd swarms
about the ambulance,
police cars at odd angles
in the intersection.
Image follows image
just because. Wasps' nest
is composed of paper,
layer upon layer, spiraling out
from the mouth of the tunnel
(within, larvae in white vessels
in rows stretch and strain).
Sprinklers on a ballfield,
slow spin of their arcs.
A frail old man in white straw hat
has tattoed arms. The bus
lists its destination as
garage. From heroes
to herpes. Two cars
in an intersection,
the drivers of each waving
the other to go first.
Thick urine smell

of old ghetto tavern,
what little light there is
the blue glow of TV
high up by the ceiling
over the end of the bar.
Furniture was piled
into the gutter,
charred and still smouldering.
And here's a motorcycle
draped in green plastic.
I squint to write that. It's mah
purdah and I'll cry if I want to.
Flanned Parenthood. The wind
pushes east, in off
the ocean. A cheek
raw from shaving,
quick to feel. The light
weight of a cap
sits on my head,
familiar. In the dim
dark garage, cement
floor stained
with birthmarks of grease,
election officers hunch
over lists upon card tables,
ongoing discussion
as to who should get
the 11:30 lunch. Off-peak
travel: people walk
on a long conveyor
in an airport. The line
between sleep and half-sleep:
I see your smile
and think I'm dreaming.
Below, a herd of white puffs

becomes a wall of cloud
above the valley. Below,
the clouds were layered, the layers
sufficiently far apart
so that those nearer the aircraft
appeared to pass more quickly.
Below, land was reduced to shadow
rarely glimpsed. To the north,
another bank piled high,
gleaming white in the late sun.
All this occurred in the future
tense. The air without clouds
was no less shaped,
lacking only moisture.
Aware that radio waves,
not being visible, are everywhere.
You are subtly aware
when the plane begins to descend.
A new, larger cloud, more gray,
which appears to have been raked.
Walking to the john and taking a book.
A junction of roads that,
from up here, seems a swastika.
At the half hour watches beep.
At the Cadillac plant where once
Poletown stood, a small grove
of lush trees stands
over the old cemetery
well within the walls, all
that remains. The 4 "-ber" months
run in a row. I am
listening. I am wearing light grey
shoes. I am red suspenders. Iamb
Bic. Ren Cen. Bathroom light
not right for shaving. They ask

about the muralist "Dago
Riviera." Eggs scrambled very dry.
Salt of the bacon. Prunes to sweeten
duck soup. Dog's tennis ball
damp, chewed and tattered.
Lapping water from the john
before I start to flush. His putdown
for anything is the word
"whore." Pablo the cat
climbs into my lap. Saarinen's
chair. From the air of
the rotating restaurant I see
Belle Isle. Accordion-ribbed ramp
extends from the gate – the plane
taxis up to a young man
signalling with a pair of orange batons.
White fuzzed seeds of the poplar
thick as snow on the road. Cement floor
of artificial lake. Cat's claws
sink through shirt. Wad of paper
blows across outfield grass, ends
in the bullpen. Tiny dentist
in dreadlocks. We sit on the deck
and sip tea. We will begin
preboarding shortly. From above
Lake Michigan seems oceanic,
effect enhanced by a gray haze
which obscures the south shore.
The river system wound like scars,
dark green against the brown squares
of the landscape. The river system
wrapped around like scarves
(dark spleen against the bound squares
of the mindscape). Velcro affixed
the blue-checked seatcovers to their frames,

cushion available if need to serve
as "flotation device." Dark eyebrows
told the lie of her light blonde hair.
Between the many small, dense utterly white clouds
there rose a thin brown wisp, curling up
from a point the eye might trace
it back to – the orange flame in the woods
visible from 30,000 feet. River as brown as
the valley it's carved. Flat cities of the midwest
crushed into the landscape, low sky of smoke.
Inside Tiger Stadium (dark blue of the bleacher wall)
rain falls on the white tarp laid over the infield,
puddles glistening in the glare of the bank of
the overhead lights. Peach-colored jumpsuit
on tiny old woman signals a shift
in culture. Three cons, back on the bricks,
sit at a bus stop on a bench, sharing
laughter and a bottle in a bag. "Say what?"
he says, meaning What you say? Old, small
drugstore window, dustcovered display. 3 signs
on garage door insist No Parking. Busted
for shooting at a passing car, he shrugs, "Hey,
no big deal, I thought they were someone else."
Having thinking as my inferior function, I fell
under the sway of Jung's "Psychological Types"
is a poem by David Bromige. Red-brown pigeon
amid all the gray. Two school girls speak of a third:
"She don't fuck but she gives blow jobs."
Young blonde woman in dreadlocks and high heels.
They stare out of the bus like prisoners from a train.
The car, hit broadside, was crushed
between the van and the side of the house.
A woman in a tight skirt runs
with short steps. I stare at the newspaper
wondering where the news went. A woman

sweeps the gutter in front of her house.
Old broom wears quickly, developing a bias.
Audible scrape of shovel in asphalt.
Without hills, the city wouldn't be liveable.
A wide bulge of neck between
hairline and collar. A penny on the walk
that no one stoops to gather. Teleguides
are introduced into airports, hotels,
theme parks and subway stations,
complete with Joe Bob Briggs, horoscopes,
biorhythms, maps and the weather,
some dispensing printed coupons, to familiarize
the broader market with the evolving technology
of interactive video, by modem they hope
to link each consumer (part umbilical, part noose)
to capital's heart. Products exist
so that we might have ads. Woman
makes eye contact with camera as she licks
ice cream from the cone in slomo. I'm
drinking milk for good. Bicycle chained
to each parking meter. That which is merely personal
is controlled by the state. TV screen
no larger than an orange. Not in service
is the name of that song. I feel all wrong
inside at times (lack of confidence, lack
of trust). Sensation of heat
envelops left knee. Atop so many
skyscrapers one sees the winches (like tongs)
from which hang the window washers'
scaffolds. Bonds for new roads
being paid for through general sales tax
provide a hidden subsidy for the automobile:
would you drive the new road
if there was a $5 toll
in each direction? Stringed instrument

whose name is not known to me.
New color trim gradually spreads
over the Victorian. Dog in the dark
in the basement as sentry
over years becomes a rodent. Pigeons
have made a roost atop
faded plastic Safeway sign
(red gone to pink). Mailman uses pouch
to carry clothing to a laundromat
on Sunday. Smell of pine sap
in the woods. Preacher's bullhorn
screaming Jesus. Small house
of particle board. Anger
like a deep blister bursts,
then dries. When I read this poem
I am returned to San Francisco State,
the old cafeteria where the new student union stands,
Janis Joplin drowned out in the Gallery Lounge
by her band, 811.08
for poetry. When I read this poem
David Bromige is still married to Sherrill,
crowded apartment on Arch Street.
When I read this poem Ron Loewinsohn
and George Stanley are not the same man.
Under the ring my flesh has grown smooth.
Ankles echo the ribbing on my socks. Red band
about my waist where the belt digs in. List
listing left. Vowels vibrate: hum
of flesh in throat. I am
is anyone's name. Breath
storms over valley of tongue.
Swollen knuckles of an old man's hands.
Hierarchy in a higher key. Not asleep
on the bus (but her eyes shut (arms
full of groceries)). In the middle of

the intersection, while pedestrians cross and
a red Chevy waits patiently
to make its left turn, they kiss.
Smell of fast food chicken
permeates elevator. Seeing it there empty,
window wide open, he spit his gum
onto the seat of the police car.
The cash register makes a deeper tone
if the Universal Product Code isn't picked up
by the sensor. One after another,
cars bounce in the pothole. Trucks pass,
radios blasting. Yes, I'd repeat that
if I saw it again. Not a beard really,
tuft of white hair juts out
just under his lower lip. Old VW bug
modified into tiny pick-up. All this I see
at 30th and Mission. To which again
in the a.m. I return (as if to a meadow
made by the mindless seeking after profits,
small businesses jammed together, lacking
that slicker smooth surface to which
by corporate capital we've become attuned).
She it is who rises later, silently showering
or glowering over a bowl of cheery little oats
into which sour milk has been inadvertantly poured,
or telling dreams while I'm only half-listening,
governs these words. A new neighborhood
means a new idea. Dog sniffs base of the tree.
The face of a free man rummaging through his pockets
in search of a cough drop. Touchstones of identity
specific as the loss of red M&Ms. Daisy Duck
and Minnie Mouse mud wrestle. In a tweed
business suit and Reeboks (pink socks
over sheer hose), she sprints for her bus.
I squint through the dust to see the sun. A pun

in every pocket. Where your blouse buttons,
freckles about the lace rim of a white bra.
Billboard aimed at the freeway,
back turned to the houses it towers over.
I know it's summer when the morning bus
suddenly lacks kids on their way to school,
playful or sullen or lost in thought. Woman
with a blue dress and red knit sweater,
cotton billowing in the wind, rushes past.
Scaffold broken down to piping, piled
in the back of the truck. Neighbors
complain that the garden hose
isn't neatly coiled out of sight.
Garbageman dangling from the rear
of the truck like a fisherman's
legs off the side of a boat. "No on F,"
reads the sticker in orange against black,
"Stop dirty politics," giving no clue whatsoever
what the issues might entail. Zebra-skin
sweatshirt. Checking the bus seat
before I sit down. What matters in the poem
is local. For Sale signs
cycle the city. Alum Rock Cheese Co.
A time when barbers made good money.
Dalmatian tied to a hydrant
sleeps on the walk. Barrio all-night
donut shop poker game. Hooker
in hotpants framed in the light of
the automatic teller. A man
is buzzing a bell at the door
of an apartment over the liquor store
while, three storeys up, a woman in a robe
leans out her window to see
who's there. Three day weak end.
I have flight (half-light). The audience

for poetry not being 'the masses' can be
quite specific – you choose the poem
or it chooses you (years later possibly
you meet the author at a party, a little, bald
bespectacled fellow, talking not art or politics
but baseball and gossip, the edges of everything
general and rounded) and your life is altered
irreparably by that decision, you change majors,
jobs, become passionate suddenly in ways
opaque to your lover, and frightening:
you didn't know poetry could be like that
but it's what you'd wanted all along,
so deeply in fact that you think for awhile
it might be genetic or that you were "destined"
as that poem seems also to have been destined
for a particular life, and maybe you are
and it was, if not in that sense in some other,
the way it has for all the others been just likewise,
each one choosing the poem, the poem choosing them,
even the ones who seem to you (for who are you
to judge?) completely muddied in what they do,
in how they think, the ones who publish
a single chapbook and get no response, no one
coming to their readings and they
going to fewer each year, writing less and
one day they realize they haven't even thought
of publishing in ages, the job is harder, the kids
demand time, and yet almost as if at random
copies of that chapbook dot the crowded shelves
of small used bookstores, just waiting
to be chosen and to choose, loaded
as a minefield. I heard mindfield. "Well,
we ran through the briars and we ran through the brambles"
and Jackson used the event to run for office,
the first television president tho Philo Farnsworth

didn't know it. Garage sale on a side street
devoid of shoppers. An old man
who sits in the shadows of a basement
playing checkers with phantoms. A kid who,
hitchhiking, is bypassed for hours on a country road,
lies down, pretending to be injured, is
run over by a truck. The asshole, says Persky,
is the only orifice whose primary function
is to remain shut. A bicycle upside down
bolted to a car top. The nature of the beast
is that it has no nature. Industrial chicken
is no bird. One group wants to reduce
language to logic, the other logic
to language. The hollow look
of a vacant house. A shallow book
writ by a lousy mind. A long line of cars
stuck behind the tractor, inching
its way up the one-lane road. Between
strategies of absorption (The Sponge)
and those opposed (The Blob), to not
choose is merely to conceal
one's choice: we have no ideology,
we just do what's right. T-shirts everywhere
read "I ♥ Bolinas." Earphones' cord
disappears in vestpocket. She carries
not one but three bags over her shoulder. The vest
is tattered, the vast tattooed surface of his arms
is flexed. He lets the bike coast
to the bottom of the hill. Truck left overnight
with the hood up. Edge of the notebook cuts
flesh of my thumb. Gust of fog
chills my face. As cars pass, I take note
of what people stash on their dashboards:
envelopes, glasses, wallets. Tennis racquet juts
from gym bag. Blue suit with brown shoes.

In the park a game of softball
is short one fielder. Sticking my tongue out
as I write. As the grass on the canyonside
dries, yellow-brown, the green of the chaparral
leaps out. Her arms folded as if to keep warm,
as if she has cramps. Find the controlling image,
the voice hidden in the text. Hostages slain
on Rodeo Drive. He's in his fifties
and she's his mother. She walks down the hill
turning her head at each bus stop to see if it's coming.
An old man seems out of place, carrying a big stereo 'blaster'
on the bus. Little pyramid atop the car
signals "Taxi." Helicopters in the fog, like wasps
on a nest. Street people on the outskirts of town
are those unable to compete
among the homeless of the city. A yard
cemented, then painted green,
lemon tree in a planter. Brown-shingle
townhouse condo. Bearded man with a geiger counter
sweeps park lawn. Terraced amid cypress,
eucalyptus, vines, hillside homes disappear in fog.
He wears a windbreaker tied about his waist.
Catering truck's side converts to awning. I
pour bitter lemon into the glass
just until the ice floats. Jessie's toes'
nails are thick, furrowed, opaque. The bath
is right if the skin turns pink, the pores open
and sweat floods until the salt stings
my eyes and my beard drips and the gold
ring on my finger swells. From the hill
I see the lanes of freeway traffic
move at different speeds. The inside
of my cheek swells
when bitten. The practice
of inside. Tar heater's

a trail to roofer's truck.
The trick to loose association is
cop to the bop. He stares
out the bus window, providing
the privacy to write. Rear of sofa
turned to livingroom window. Rear of
houses built on a hillside,
narrow stairways leading down.
Gouda thick with dill. The poem
is a pill against reason's too-narrow logic.
Pine too thick with sap for firewood.
"Widow-maker" they call the euc-
alyptus, the way the limbs drop.
One sigh fits all. Serve 5 days,
then parole for the weekend.
Over the mountain to the Haight.
A child stands straining on the bus seat,
reaching for the bell-cord to signal for a stop.
Out by Laguna Honda, the poor house,
where John Logan sits half-paralyzed
from a stroke in a dark, empty corridor,
a system of sprinklers twirls
their long arcs over the wide lawns
already damp from the fog. 3-legged
cat and two-headed dog. I jumped
from the eighth floor window, he said,
to see how I'd handle it. First
beer of the day just to calm the stomach.
The flesh behind my ear so dry I'm afraid it will bleed.
The line tends to stretch (the advantage of prose is
or, I should say, may be
not that it has no line – each word, each letter
holds the line – but
that its linebreaks being hidden
demands the reader work). The book

of ink. Store front of spider plants
on a side street. Dr. Plotke,
I presume. Let's not pretend
there's more to the poem
than this. A red dog
wagging its tail. Bigger
than a bread truck. Try
to carry a surfboard
nonchalantly on the bus.
Shrink-wrap for a cookie.
Hip to wear your jacket
with the label turned out.
Stubborn as a mule, suh,
stubborn as a mule. He's
got the Eastern idea
about poetry. Little jeep
with big mag wheels.
A man is talking hurriedly
aloud to himself. Typos
or topos, which one?
The pen in my pocket,
cap off, bleeds ink. I
think I write. The poem
is about what,
even it asks.
Anthropomorphized, grinning
like a big oak tree.
A rootless grass
that grows upon rocks,
words form
like bubbles
like gas
in the thick liquid
of silence, of clouds
over the cartoon hero's head –

he counts his four fingers
falling short. Yes,
Mickey is black
but he's passing.
Oh ill-propped rear deck,
wobbling as I walk,
caged kitten.
A blackbird small
amid a flock of pigeons.
This is the way the world walks,
off-center. Old deco sky
at sunset. What then?
First day of July:
what look like hills to the west
is the great summer bank
of fog, gray
atop the colorless ocean.
Birds in the city forage –
in the schoolyard we saw
a small hawk. In North
Sacramento, summer '58,
we played baseball
in the hot, dry dust
and I bought a
plastic statue of
Willie Mays, hand
and glove cupped
for a basket catch.
Across the aisle,
a seeing eye dog, chin
atop its owner's knee,
watches me. Go ahead
and try to explain
to Renoir that a woman's
torso is not a mass

of decomposing flesh
with the purplish-green
splotches that denote
the final stage of
putrefaction in a corpse.
Monet invents the series.
It is not that
there is no narrative
here (each sentence
is a narrative,
each line moves)
but that there is
no hierarchy
of narratives (not even
the story of the
poem), no sentence
to which the others
(all the others) defer
and are ranked
(the map is not
built about the city).
Degas puts a skirt
on a wax statuette.
Between method and
technique lies
style but
between
style and method
comes program.
Tasteless taste
of my own burnt tongue.
Rolling the car downhill
to start it. Atop
RenCen in Detroit
or, in New York, the World Trade Center,

I'm shocked at how level
the land is. The way
a junkie's arms itch
at the site of old
needle marks. Hippie
with hair to his waist
wears a knife in a sheath.
Their name fails
(as names invariably
do) to convey essence,
that they were the first
(first Europeans, that is)
to conceive of painting as
comp
osition not
re
presentation, first
formalists – im
pressionists? It's morning
and she's running home
to change clothes
before she heads to work.
By the roadside, new concrete lightpole
lies "snapped." Bleach stains
spot his jeans. Now that
there are no more elders
left to mime. Let us go then,
you and I, like bananas
baked in a pie, gone soft and mushy.
Narrow half-paved alley
behind the big houses. Med
transcriptionist with a Miss Kitty
lunchpail. Smurf's
up. Funky junker
atop flatbed truck. Sun's sharp glare

over the still bay. Each word
is but syllables pulsing
in the head. The idea of community
might only be an identification
predicated on an enemy,
the split in the mirror. Newsprint
blackens my fingers. Wives
of male members of the Supreme Court
who've never had an orgasm
(where Whizzer White can stick his whizzer).
But Reagan is the enemy! The dead hand of the past
firmly in control. We roll,
curling into one another, spooned
fetal position, sweet nap. The hospital bed
propped up on bricks in the shadowy room
of the convalescent home, her older sister,
nearly 100, senile, silent, half-asleep,
in a wheelchair by the glass door to the patio,
Jessie's arms are red with bruises, blood
vessels no longer strong enough to contain
that cargo, lung collapsed, empty
but for the spreading tumor, she's waiting,
pain-killers no longer fully working,
for the waiting to cease. Major depression
with psychotic features. Will I later
sanctify this? "Zzzz" go the crickets,
"zuzz" goes the bee (circling my head,
it concludes that my ear, after all,
is not a flower). What I thought was sage burning
was merely mesquite. You wander off for a moment
and I'm immediately anxious. A mother
turning to her young daughter asks
"Do you have to go chi-chi?" A sober man
looks at the thistle. Bark hung peeling
from the giant eucalyptus. A burr in the eye

worse than a thorn in the paw. "Trail mix"
consisting of raisins, whole almonds, cashew
slices, sunflower seeds, a rare filbert.
Nearly boiling, the bathwater seared
my blisters – steam spun
from the open window. Later,
I lie naked on the purple quilt of the brass bed,
still sweating, watching curiously as a small mouse
which has somehow climbed up into the heating vent
tries to figure its way out of this impromptu cage.
Turkey vultures, because they're scavengers (because they eat
dead meat), are called TVs. She tries to tug
her t-shirt down before pulling her sweater off.
Strawlike bill of the hummingbird. The wind
in the eucalyptus ripped us. Red-winged blackbird
smaller than a crow. Moving east,
the clouds bunch together
up against the mountains. What I learned
of the line was its omnipresence
oppositional to sense (to the senses),
that the break is where
meaning is not, which is its own
content (mind against meter). Write
chewing gum? – I can't. Blue heron
not fully fledged, hops
from branch to branch,
awkward flap to its long wings.
"Sunshine, stay out," my wife shouts
to the sky. Red-topped
acorn woodpecker hammers at a tree.
I see my fate is to live among my species
as if they were my own. The doe lay broken
on the roadside by the lagoon, eyes wide open
entirely without sight. Terns drop into the water
in search of fish. The life of this turkey

whose breast I eat, the pain of the tomato.
Time's folly – to experience the future as anxiety, the past
as loss. Bikers bundled on a hot day, heads
round and hard as helmets. My grandfather
behind the wheel of his car gave his anger
permission. A prosody of inversions
to approximate off-centeredness. You get
to the bus stop and take the large crowd waiting,
arms filled with plastic shopping bags, infants,
bouquets of roses, as a positive sign
that you've not missed your ride.
The new perm is as puffed and solid
as popcorn. The new poem
balances nature and artifice
like parquet marble on a bank floor.
And although the train's lights
are visible in the tunnel,
it fails to arrive. What
was
   the flower sermon anyway
(but the content of a word
lacking difference)? Garage as large
as the house it's next to. Imagine storms
as active, willful, but clear blue sky
as passive, vacant, not A Thing
(whose sole purpose is but to shut night out).
Permeable, like a boundary between oceans
half-remembered from a map. On July 7th,
1986, the world's population
reaches 5,000,000,000
but I found you. Knish
nosh. One kind of scaffolding
envelops the house, the other's
just a horizontal plank
hanging from ropes. Iced tea so cold

the bone in your nose shouts.
Lesbian graffiti: there are no men,
there are only dildos. The large, old
pink apartment building
displayed a wide range
of funky curtains, including
shower curtains in a livingroom
and an American flag (bars over
the lower windows). A child
on the street points a gun at me
and I pause to make sure
it's a toy ("tchew," he says,
meaning I'm dead). Esta says
she met Frank Smith at a party
when she threw up on him.
The 3 Steins (Gertrude, Wittgen
and Franken) half full
of flat beer. No ideas
but in positioning. Over the brown
polo shirt is a navy blue sweater
and over this a sky blue
levi sport coat, below which
red, white and blue checkered slacks
over light brown leatherette loafers
with a velcro strap. Dysraphysm
is blatant. The world (the mind)
is round (about). I write
in a small room, revising often.
Let's think of the hospital
as the job, or vice versa.
It's like playing Monopoly:
at a certain point all your
little green houses go back
to the bank, railroads mortgaged,
their cards turned over

and you're facing a wall of red hotels
afraid even to shake the dice.
Sunglasses this dark
afford a kind of privacy
of the mind, even if
the cherry red heart-shaped frames
are a magnet to the eyes.
Two elderly filipino women
argue over Keith Haring.
Pork grease on a silk tie.
Her headphones fit easily
over the straw sun visor
tho the gum bubble, large, round and pink,
covers her face. Road gang wears hard hats
due to sense of style. One man, Reb Harris,
pioneered most of the formal devices
of the modern pop quartet – melisma, ad-libbing
of the lead singer, back-up vocalists repeating
key phrases – before, in December 1950,
he was replaced as the lead singer of the Soul Stirrers
by the young Sam Cooke, formerly of the group
the Highway QCs. Blanket beneath which
to breastfeed baby. Staring through scratches
on cheap sunglasses. The readers
for whom I write resent
not having their faculties
fully utilized, challenged, extended
– this makes them outcasts
in a world of distraction.
Red rubber wheels
of my skateboard.
The old man and the
cement. Now let's think
about a piece called "Ink."
I am what iamb trochee.

A thick seat
is a sixth sense.
The beat goes on
call. In my generation
(roughly, anyone born
from '45 thru '51), we argued
passionately
throughout college how
to think of linebreaks,
the issue opened but not all resolved
by our elders. My tie caught
in my briefcase. The great, ribbed
concrete verticals that hold aloft the overpass
above our heads are themselves
invisible, unless we stand in their shadow
or lean up against one to steal a kiss.
As the college grows even larger
one near neighborhood after another
converts to student housing, weeds
crowding out the lawns' trim grass,
porches full of bicycles, windows
displaying their motley of makeshift shades.
Above the glade the yellow crane spins
its long metal arm, carring I-beams
like matchsticks. You could disinvent the past
but you can't live there either, unless you make of it
a market waxy as an orange, round and mottled
and cold. The jogger surrenders, trudging up
the steep hill. I emerge from the cool shade of the house
into the dry heat of late morning. In unison,
the passengers on the airplane put their heads
in their laps. Let's try this variant:
your head in mine (due to the boycott
we substitute bananas for grapes).
It's Friday and everyone in the office

is just coasting. A carton of Dixie cups
next to the water cooler is a true flag
but nobody wants to change the toner.
On the bus, after a principled discussion
and much debate, we decide collectively
to abandon the route and head to the beach.
The mandolin of a little Mexican polka
echoes up the stairwell. Pants pockets
with little flaps that curl up or get tucked inside.
Writing and publishing aren't just distinct activities,
they're opposed. Not only does this trashman
wear gloves, an apron with chaps and a baseball
cap turned backwards, but a thick leather
weightlifter's belt. What is the ratio
of ideas to thoughts? They tore
the old store down in a hurry, then left
the lot vacant for over a year. We hold
these truths to be self-effacing. That
which is merely personal soon gets absorbed
by the economic vampires of capital.
"You talkin' to me?" Travis Bickle asks.
To see the high stalks of corn in the city
is to remember that even the plains
have been sectioned and planted.
The clouds are pushing north today.
This was not the book I intended. Mother and daughter,
jogging together. An old man on a bicycle
in the middle of the day. New homes nesting
on a hillside, inhabitants swarming in shells
on the freeway into town. Familes patiently in line,
bored, waiting to get through the gate, to visit
husbands, fathers, sons, uncles, lovers
inside San Quentin. A table covered with potted ferns
serves to shade the large window. Trying to turn
pages in the wind. Broom they call it,

tiny yellow flowers, wild up the side
of the canyon (tall stalks of anise). The truck signals reverse
with an ear-piercing beep. I leap forward
between chalk squares on the walk. The wok sizzles
with the juice of mung bean sprouts. About boots,
the route roots by rote. The ought of seeing
in a pig's eye. She leans forward
to reveal a red tit, the small bird
cupped in her hands. You stand still,
bare naked, as I bend to my knees
to towel you dry. Blouses on hangers hung
from a curtain in the sun to dry.
Her hair up in a bun with pencils stuck through it.
The buck shops here. The mourning
of the logicians. Words spill forth,
adjuncts of a mind that won't quit,
froth of nuance lathers meaning, hiding
denotation's hard shell, itself a game
of the missing pea. Wherever you go,
there you are. An infant at the ballpark tenses
sensing the crowd's anticipation, bases loaded,
two out. Art's but a market
for the products of process, but in activity
seek selves. There's no time like the present
sense. I'm a lima being, Peru? Out west,
cowboys in the fog herd cattle, off-shore bass horn
an index of the coast. Asa says, "say aces' spaces,
solitaire." Bamboo blinds of thai food deli,
peanut and pepper ground into honey forms sauce
(brown crust of fried tofu). White streaks
in my chest and beard. Small cheek scar
left permanent dimple. Chairs
remind me of my childhood. Salmon poached
in cool vegetable broth. That moment's disorientation,
removing glasses to pull sweater over head.

Seeing the hearse and the people all dressed up
clustered in front of Saint Kevin's, try to imagine
who's deceased. My grandmother, of the tumor
in her lung: "It's like the flesh
is being pulled from the bone." His one book
that's not too much in love with beauty
is The Tennis Court Oath. Basketball spinning
on the tip of a finger. Out of the behavior
of drivers at an intersection, you can read
the state of the nation. We apologize
if this letter has reached you
in a time of illness or sorrow. A moment
not a movement, and the moment's past.
It makes you look out on those Mickey Mouse
beach towels used as curtains
with a renewed sense of wonder. Like housepainters
without a truck carrying stepladders
up the block. The way blue ink fades
when the pen runs dry. Simple summer storm,
a warm drizzle. I worked as a short order book.
You delete the seams in medical prose. Distance
not absorption is the intended effect. The new
haircut reveals the neck. One writes to display
not words but the spaces between them. The bus
strains forward in a new gear. Tree pruned
back to the trunk. The way rain spots
the surface of a still lake, opaque
green water. By placing its "out-client"
and minimum security programs at the perimeter,
ad hoc huts and trailers, the institution
conceals its institutionality, barbed-wire trim
about the high inner wall. I saw a man today
with shoulders hunched like yours, rounded,
the head pushed forward, stubble beard and thick glasses,
hugging a briefcase to his chest. That's not just

an earring in your left ear, it's a crucifix.
The stick of gum, being stale, was brittle
and crumbled as I began to chew. The New Wave Cafe
was in fact a Greek diner just down from the Whitney,
at whose counter Roy Scheider sat,
reading a tout sheet for the horses.
"I wonder if I can still catch the eight o'clock,"
I shouted, bolting for the door, knowing
that unless it was late I had no chance –
but there, at the bottom of the hill, I could see it
coming, orange and white. At the intersection,
against the red light, she's jogging in place. She drives
to the BART station, then gets out as he slides
into the driver's seat, bound in some other
direction. A clean scoop in the hill slope
where the slide was. Orthodachsun. Write this:
the shock of black ink. Do seagulls nest
and, if so, where? The calendar above
shows a sequence of locomotives,
the one below dinosaurs. Translucent green gel,
the toothpaste emerges from its tube. We
rebuilt this city. Poets model the discussion
portion of a talk after the territorial behavior
of male elephant seals, each striving
to be the dominant alpha bull. Form in the sense of shape
might be a trap. Weeks later, the snapped power pole
lies by the roadside, stripped of its fixtures,
the wires inside the broken concrete cylinder
loose like strands of a ruptured gut. Make measure
mark this. The way an old man might
use his hearing aid to shut the world out.
Brush fire's path stopped short of the eucalyptus.
The bat slept clinging to the white stucco wall.
Let's make a rhyme for sleepytime. Child's camera
converts to toy robot. What if the 'I' here

is not challenged, but merely hidden, implicit?
Eggs that, coming from gulls that don't build nests
but lay them instead between rocks on cliffs,
roll not downhill but always in a circle.
I crouched to pick up the tuft of the seal's molt,
fur atop with root beneath, layer of skin
between. Poetic diction is no fiction
but a sequence of recognizable effects
calculated to orient response
toward the specific domain of this discourse.
The line breaks here. But an impulse to action
spins momentum's thread out, twined strands
of the barely possible. Today's fog forms a mirror
where the mind invades whatever's seen.
Eyes are to treason as love is to the whine
of blood in the vessels, a net swollen, pressing
on the skull. Sleep is fragile yes. I crouch
and when I rise my thighs shout. The bus smiles
yes. Theodore Roethke floating on the surface
of the banal bloats. Plan for the city of no.
Growths in the eye drift into view, spidery,
translucent. The small, blue tattoo
at the base of your thumb, a mere teardrop,
reveals a life we no longer speak of. Wasps swarm
over the fallen eskimo pie. The bus pulls away
leaving the corner suddenly empty of people.
The glazier's truck bears invisible cargo.
Biopsy made of single line reveals syntax
reduplicating out of control. Lip tingles
where tomorrow a cold sore shall appear.
Who you are is up for grabs, and your own
opinion won't be consulted. Contradiction
is not a strategy (and is not
contradiction should it become one).
Let's refine our theoretical positions

the better to market them. The surgeon's wife
in the cartoon has hoofs, firm in the belief
that for students in college then
the Vietnam war was not real. It's Thursday
and time to empty the signifiers. The trees
don't mean to bloom, they just do. The riot squad,
ready to be sent in, use their batons
to do stretches. Yosemite Sam
was a vegetarian: pesto pizza. Graffiti:
the cage is open but the bird is dead.
Dip that centers the upper lip. Don't fetishize
shape. The shadow on the rim of the xeroxed page
where the paper of the original failed to fit.
A heat in the stomach where hunger burns
its acids. Take off these glasses for reading
and let the room refocus. Don't swallow.
The way the nose bone fits into the hole
in the skull. The distance between languages
feels cramped. A grime in the cuticles
to specify vocation. Into nation,
intonation. Your long dark hair
curls on the damp bathroom wall. Double adjectives
pin the noun between opposing forces – yet one
stands at a further distance. A day at the
traces. Laugh lines etched deep about the eyes,
the wide neck, tuft of hair solitary
atop the pink cap of skull, nose alleged to be 'pert,'
moustache I've had for 20 years, red beard
streaked with white, eyes that look back
sometimes totally foreign, skin dry
between light brows to the point of flaking,
above which a field of pimples rises red
amid the oily flesh. The fisherman's bucket.
One myth is that I don't read fiction. Another
would predicate this text upon a numerical game.

Your name might be a clue, but isn't. Her head
without hair means cancer's there. This nipple
at times forms an "innie." Avocado and cream cheese sandwich
on nine grain bread. The mind is framed
by the body's choices. A thin tree contained
in a square of sandy earth cut from cement,
propped up by a wooden post. Stains on the sidewalk
are mostly gum. A car collaged from scavenged parts.
The art of darkness. This fence is a thin
wire mesh. From the open window
a long chute angles down to the red dumpster
on the street. From up here, I can't even see the valley
through the fog. A narrow face with high cheeks
and a tiny mouth. You stop to stare,
to watch me write. At the age of 20
I was a speed freak, already into needles,
and at 30 an alcoholic, tho I would have
denied it. Park sprinklers arc in the rain.
Meaning comes between words. Rubbing popsicle sticks
against the rough stucco wall of the grammar school,
we'd sharpen them into crude blades. Friends act out
to register variables in aging. Dennis the Menace
is seven forever, tho the world he inhabits
grows more distant each day. Elderly Chinese couple
with matched bamboo canes. When last I saw
a milk truck. Warm taste of bleeding gums.
The back row seats of the bus, over the engine,
are warmer. So warming is a trend,
a warning. Concrete highschool
stands vacant in the summer. When I rush,
salt shakers tip over, glasses tumble, shattering
amid the dirty dishes stacked in the sink,
I arrive at work having forgotten my calendar.
The circular broom of the street sweeper twirls,
a ring of cigarette butts dancing

amid the bristles. The leatherette covers
of the seats on the bus, cut open
like a heart, expose
a rotting layer of yellow foam.
Dogs in the yard bark hard. Strap slung
over the shoulder, she holds her purse
tight against her body. The system here
is there is no system, tho one might discover
the cumulative pattern, and from this
propose a structure, a set
of procedures to be methodically employed
in yet another composition, utterly different.
Women in trousers with their hands in their pockets.
I'm not interested in the surface really. Jaywalking
amid traffic, he hunches his shoulders and trots
with a half-skip. Remember the sun? Beware
of dawg. Half-curled, stained orange, a maxi-pad
lies on the walk. Coriolanus (Hilton Kramer)
calls the people "fragments." You had to be an alderman
to use the title Mr. A type of nausea
centered in the jaw. Headlights glimmer
through the thick morning fog. I flex
my diaphragm to call forth a belch,
acid aftertaste of the o.j.
Where the tree fell, marsh grass
sprouted in green water. Liberty Weekend
commemorative scarf tied 'round her pink curlers.
Power's sole value lies in the sharing.
Shutters in the place of blinds, neo-
European. I follow my thoughts, trailing
a little behind. It's trash day and cats
stand atop the garbage cans, sniffing.
Meaning makes of it a sign for the world
ready for market. To privilege presence
contract attention, attune to mentions

of atonement. Let me unbutton
your shirt. Think of cars
as insect shells, readily abandoned.
With a twist of the hips, this slips
between lips. One ear sticks out
while the other lies flat against the head.
Two buses, no waiting. Newsrack by the door
signals the open store. The world is
constraint (filled with possibility).
Oh asymmetry to the gait, bodies
sprinting, lunging for the bus. Ten years
since "The Chinese Notebook," I look back
half in horror at the naïvité (not,
however, to be confused with innocence).
White concrete walls stain with age,
dark around the edges. Grim green trim
to the windows at juvenile hall. Lawn gone dead
from lack of water. Black hair
half grey. A row of teddy bears, toy rabbits
top the couch. Brief fad of rubber godzilla.
Flute to the 'tute. Word 'donuts' turned sideways
on huge shop sign. Puppet hangs from ceiling
to decorate room. Boy on rear of father's bike
wears identical helmet, bright yellow.
The design of rugs seeks symmetry, defined
by fringe and border. Twinge of pain in tooth
tho that tooth's no longer there. Edge
of each green leaf crinkles yellow-brown.
Lozenge dissolves on tongue, sweetening
saliva. Ceramic footstools, in the image
of forest fungi. Training analysis,
group practicum. Divide time into zones
so as to distribute presence. High above
the frosted skylights light clouds
blot the sun. Aluminum troop carrier, hit

by anti-tank shell, turns white hot
before it explodes. Thumbnail as gouge
peels yellow skin off of pencil. An X
in the cap of the milkshake's cup
marks point to insert straw. Yuppie
thai yi yay. Smack in the nicka
thyme. Our emotions tint
the filtered world. Don't stumble
before the bus. Now that I'm a fact
in my own landscape, problematic as any,
as much in the way. The fog lifts
to reveal a still bay. Once Fibonacci
was unencumbered by a history
of literary use. Pigeons evolve
to better adapt to life in the city.
Wherever in the world protein's poor
people use pepper to aid digestion.
Language poetry is puke, sez Black Oak Books.
A threat to one is an opportunity to all.
Dear nightlife, I barely recall
why it seems so sexy tho a total fraud,
mirrored globe refracting colored spots
on the tavern ceiling, as it or we
revolve. Thermos full of sun tea
on a hot day. Asian 'girl' cradles her purse,
biting lower lip, as she waits
for the bus. This line
was designed by Beckett.
Arabs are a minority
in the world of Islam.
Long cotton skirt
that never gets ironed.
Winking logo
for an eye clinic.
A bird in the hand

is easily crushed.
Cop nudges kid
with tip of nightstick.
Cats dart between porches
then turn, in a crouch,
hind legs poised taut.
Kids' toys about the floor,
cheery forms of plastic.
Old hibachi upended in the gutter.
Midway between a shush and a
scrape, the sound of newspapers
blowing down the street
like giant leaves. The chevy
with the Texas plates
that's sat in front of the painter's house
for weeks, bouquet of parking tickets
jammed under the windshield wiper.
Across the courtyard, behind
the high wood fence, stands the convent
of the Sisters of Perpetual Adoration, pale pea-green
wood frame dormitory, adorned with a buff-colored
stucco front, women driven out of northern Mexico
in the 1930s, a cloistered order, hidden
half a century here in the Haight behind
that two-storey wall, visible only
from neighboring rooftops, shadowy
stooped figures in white habits
behind frosted glass. Pine's long needles glisten,
at the end of each a bulging drop
is gathered fog about to drip
atop the iceplant. We're older now
but our features, far from hardening,
have softened, growing deeper,
lines about these sunken eyes.
The orange plastic top

is for decaf. She reclines
atop the picnic bench, the waves
behind her, pelicans gliding,
while he struggles to get the camera in focus.
Unseen foghorn. Swallows dart
over the headlands. Yellow stripe
to the slithering green snake. Beds of kelp
about the rocks. The intelligence of the white butterfly
amid the wild olallieberries beyond the wood fence.
Words shimmer in the sun, glistening
until the ink dries, sinking in,
barely human. A goose laughs
vulgar in the distance. Obsessive
count to the syllables. Butter melts
in the bran muffin's crack. Strawbs
taste sweet. Wrentit hops in the grass,
then pulls at the head of a dandelion.
"You can't come in yet," she whispers
in my ear, "my diaphragm's not in,"
then bends her legs, raising them
to cradle me as I enter and we turn
sideways, gently rocking, tongue seeking tongue.
Now the tea pours dark thru the perforated spoon
into the clear white cup. The bartender
wipes glasses with a towel, then hangs them
upside down from an overhead rack.
Across the street is the sea
very quiet now in the afternoon light,
people on the sidewalk smiling and laughing,
casting shadows longer than themselves.
I write what I spend in a notebook:
$1 for tea with a twenty five cent tip.
The sewers smell of fish. I squat,
my butt propped on the back of my right heel.
Howdy worked by strings. Solidarity in pricing,

bro. Lacks Last Gap
might have been a name to conjure with.
Hydrangea's blossoms are quick to brown.
The baby rescued from a flaming rocket
by a kindly farm couple named Kent.
Wires weave the city's power
house to house. "'Meat is murder'
is hypocrisy," weeps the grass.
Pine steaks make a house.
Pull cord to stop thought.
Brown leather briefcase clashes
against pale gray suit. The flag flies
in a light rain. Thousands of staples
and sun-bleached scraps of paper
circle the phone pole's base.
The value of psychographics
is that they're asocial,
thus to eliminate the marketer's guilt.
Old pink victorian house
moved to a new lot, propped up –
along its side an outline, irregular,
where the wood's gone unpainted,
the shadow of an absent house.
Suddenly three police cars, lights flashing,
converge on the bank. Play to win,
Bombay gin. Theory and design of
traffic islands, divide strips.
The old woman sits in the aisle seat on the bus
as others stand, one a woman holding a child
(no longer an infant), while the window seat
remains vacant, blocked. Ladders in the back of
a pickup, tied down, jut out at an angle
over the cab. Mr Schwartz praises Mr Clark
in the pages of The New Criterion, tho the latter
continues to publish in Processed World.

Small birds chitter in the palm tree.
Trash can lid chained to the can. The way
sentences begin "The way. . . ." On the train
back to the city after a night meeting, I read
the same paragraph again and again,
words simply floating there, unintelligible
and opaque. Ten years to the day
since I wrote Bart. You twist in your sleep,
torque of the spine. Sillybobbles burble
to their own pulse. How will I know
to type this up? Theta zed,
wedding bed. Photo of the airplane falling
upside down. I don't relate to the front,
Lyn says. I do remember you. Little white
mail jeep. I see by your beard
you're some kind of drag queen. Shirt pocket
is pen's holster. Rich red ripe
field of poison oak. Oleoneodeco.
Paradoxical interventions. Models glide
in the pale green of the Polo Lounge
of the Beverly Hills Hotel, pausing before
each table as diners look up from smoked salmon
at these tall women, working in pairs,
their eyes smiling without contact, holding jackets open
to display lining, then twirling before moving on,
while far across the room (I'm doing my
Nick Nolte imitation) Paul Anka, heavier
and balder now, rises to leave. Backlit pots of fuchsias
line the pink walls of the outer lobby
with its deep red rug. A perfect description of
lunch. Sunday afternoon hosing the car down
in the driveway. In the Galleria
valley girls sip coke from red wax paper cups,
the air conditioning perfect, soft background music
blending into the smooth rhythm of bodies

rising and descending the escalators.
Tinkerbell glides through the night air,
landing out of sight on a mattress. It's
a long way from Zabar's. By the hot tub at midnight
high over Benedict Canyon, the lavender buglight buzzes
as it zaps a mosquito. Objects in mirror are
closer than they appear. A string of hills and mountains
forms a boundary: wealth on its edges as along the beaches,
the prols here in the basin as in the valley beyond.
Basin as in. The smell of the match
before the cigarette's lit. Today producers
of Miami Vice announced
the color scheme for the upcoming season:
orchid, black and gray. Doctah Katz, she wed.
Sepulveda winds. I'm a first generation
mallie myself (El Cerrito Plaza '59 to '64).
The way folk dress on they way to work
is dialect-specific. The syntax bends,
graceful as a dancer. Even at the last stop
on the line, I pull cord
to ring bell – just for the pleasure.
Words whip past, faster than thought.
Bobble-head doll in rear window of car.
The boy-in-the-bubble views the world
without touching, sounds muted,
glare reduced. How did I space
out on that? Riding sideways in front
with the old folks and drunks. Tie
a yellow ribbon 'round the hot crime scene.
Imagine a language that lurked. The yellow
schoolbus is in fact a modest orange,
the sheriff's gray-green (wire mesh
windows blocked with bars, shadows
behind frosted glass). I pass
from the shotgun ahead of the blitz. Stickers

personalize your skateboard. This one's
walking is a gait from the waist down,
spine above stiff, while that one's
body shifts side to side with each step,
a sort of waddle. This one hugs the blue
bag of laundry tightly to his chest.
Redheaded dreadlocks. What I say
is what I saw. Here is one
for whom personal relations
must be negotiated as tho
these were acts of policy between states.
Cat upon the fence winds among the roses.
Hot sun glares down over the slow traffic.
Thighs ache for muscle's sake. A word in the hand
speaks to the bush. Shells of the sunflower's seed
litter the gutter. Between writing and speech
lies the process of translation. Advantage
is like a sigh but with a purpose,
the party held in your honor. Everyone
at the reading knows one another
but you. Flavored seltzer. Mind
over batter. The fist is but
a fetal position for the hand. Gladiolas
on a long stem. The social contract
between writer and reader demands trust:
distance, not absorption, is the intended effect.
I tilt the tall plastic pitcher and drink
until the orange juice is flowing in my beard.
The photographer's performance occurs
the instant the shutter is snapped –
everything else, before and after,
is the photographer's work. I see,
feel, notice, observe and think . . .
in that order. Love is to reason

as eyes are to the bank card. Clock ticks
to pendulum's weight. Little pepper grinder
fits in my palm. The line forms,
shadow shaping light. Clouds
high over the bay in an otherwise
clear sky. I see faces reading TV Guide
as they ride the bus. Planes thread the air
high overhead. It's Monday and yesterday's football
fills page one. Jogger in a wetsuit
fit for surfing. An aerobics class
visible behind big glass window,
jumping jacks in a circus of pastels.
Sticklike figure of an armless man,
tall and thin, walking down the street.
Wedge cut from a soft melon. Egg drops
into the bowl, yolk firm in the clear liquid.
Descartes before the horse. A small man
(neither warrior nor monk) in a small room
in a small apartment up a dark flight of stairs
leans over a desk in an attempt
to imagine the world. Below, beneath the street,
trains roar thru the tunnel chambers
of the earth, crowded with the hot flesh
of a people too deadened to scream. Far away
in our name a health clinic burns. To say this
has become a cliche. I HATE SPEECH. Ice plant
and eucalyptus borders the freeway, its cars
imprisoned in traffic. We wait until sunset,
until darkness, to cross the dry river
into the U.S. The bus winds slowly
up the narrow hillside road. Small stone building
littered with cones and needles of pine debris
housed a sentry once, fitful in his sleep
by candlelight. "Friend or foe," I ask

when we are introduced at the party.
The band on the balcony plays
over the dancers in the courtyard
who twirl slowly under the strings of colored lights.
The submarine, decorated, illumines the bay
while in the streets fireworks mix with gunshots.

XING

4
Charles Alexander
Tom Mandel
Tom Marshall
James Sherry

Karaoke Shakespeare: day awash with rain
stains the windows. That woman
forms the voice of Homer

Simpson. One person's horizon
is the next one's limit. Yo
lama (one "l" or two), comma

nist. Acer palmatum (Jap-
anese maple) from Holland.
branches bare in mid-winter

light. Obsessive recitation of detail
prefigures legal deposition (my hood
crushed into your rear end), the light

high atop the freeway as we
gather at the shoulder, the river
of vehicles slower now, is

bright flat gray. Grammar
of suspended predicates
lunges at me with a knife

dull as memory. Doesn't everyone?
At the edge of sleep, draw back
into thought's race. Face

of cartoon hero returns as doll.
Land of rhino tickles. Rule
of thumb versus democracy

of fingers. Feeding boys corn chex
to a Cajun two-step, each
accordion to their own. Grover

is the blue one, Elmo the red.
More noir than thou. On Shattuck
at night, the lone sax

can be heard for blocks. After
chemo, wear hats. The sun
in the rain in Chinatown

shines down. Insert file
into E-mail. Imagine an image
of justice as engine to discourse

in everyday life. Not just Visa,
Citibank Visa. Icon manager,
one pixel at a time. An end

to all drought. Structure
of bridge visible as theory
arched high over water

invokes toll. Rattle of quake
wakes us up. F15
hits one target in four.

Don't sleep for me,
Margintina. Brakelights aglow
in the distant night. Pan

smolders, drying on the stove.
Wobble of a slow bike
as it moves through the mud

in the slantwise rain. "Write
when you find the alphabet,"
I admonish a small boy

as he crawls for the door.
The white sedan flew
over the center barrier, flipping

and crushing to a stop. Water
rushes over the cat in the sink
who in the dream remains dry.

Auto lights glow dull in noon rain
as lone empty shopping cart rolls
downhill across mall lot. One

article remains, around which
Organize the sentence. Giant
iguana hand puppet

nibbles rice cake. Young woman
screams at empty park bench
bathed by sun. Dog

goes taut as you approach. Lungs
filled with fluid provoke a cough
that doubles you over. Song

of washer spewing water, suds,
into the pantry sink. Second
hand times cooking of Quick

Quaker Oats. Hillary
in the dream plays a mean
guitar. Font manager, beta

site. This notebook, missing
from my desk (moment
of panic), is part

of the process (one caesura
or two), found amid the bibs
in the nook. I sit in the dark

in my favorite chair, holding
a small boy who in turn
holds a bottle fiercely

to his lips. Eggs boil hard,
rattling in copper-bottom pot.
Winds from the East push

fog from the coast. Billy
goats suck at their mama's
tits standing up. Pig

poops wide and green and
doesn't stop walking. A new
med, to deflate the blood.

On the bus a small boy
(not mine) sings loudly old
Ramones hit "I want to be

sedated." He's grown now,
15 years hence. My eyes adjust
slowly to the light.

A nook in which to write
carved into the kitchen. Sight
of an ambulance at the edge

of the wreck. While we sleep,
it rains. Tall Korean
lady barber trims my beard

then glides the razor
along mustache rim.
Serious soul: I sit

to sense blood pulsing
in my veins. A fortress
of debris in doorway

of shutdown dive shop
bordered by shopping carts
is his home. Walk

briskly in the rain. Sinus
swells, suffocating brain
pressed into skull. Frost

on window gathers,
drips. Your name
engraved forever

in the *Baseball Encyclopedia,*
called third strike in
your lone at bat. Bob

to the max. My name as a verb.
One imagines words as on
a screen, pixels shimmering

as they scroll out of sight
into a space of pure
memory. Bag lady stops

to tell me of her twins.
Street lamps illumine boulevard
of restaurants, bookshops, cafés—

odors of tomato, pesto mingle
before pizza parlor's screen door.
Yell "Shower!" in a crowded

theater. Point on the horizon at which
we anticipate the sun. Cloud scraps
break up the sky. I bend

to retrieve card dropped from magazine.
In old town Antioch a man sits
high in old oak on an otherwise

vacant block to protest or
prevent its removal for construction
of new senior tower. All power

flickers in the T-storm. Lights,
camera, factions! Women
on the news wear red. Sinus

says. More morning music. My head
instead of an onion (offshore
by subtexts hidden in the margin,

I blinks). After the storm,
eucalyptus branches clutter the streets,
windchimes disassembled

atop a garden mound. Van
for a wheelchair sports
stickers for the Grateful Dead.

Analog twist of hours
computes the day. Low sky
blurs at horizon, foretelling

rain. Bird song in background
of New Guinea folk recording.
Disentangling dried snot

from hairs of my nose. When
at last his lover died,
his missed just one day of work

rather than tell them. Un-
controllable itching. Snow
covers the slopes covers

all aspects and surfaces of Mt. Diablo
visible for miles beneath the low
almost metallic clouds. I

moved an egg around in my dream
last night, says Grenier, blinking.
The margins are falling, the margins

are falling. The kind of
cold where the sour taste
never quite gets out of

your mouth. Ten typing turtles.
Office symbolism: to gain a view
of the parking lot. Quark it!

Repo depot. West of the hills
the culture is urban. Not just
that the airplane, sputtering,

landed on the freeway but
that it did so in the wrong direction.
Alone in his crib, he lies

sobbing, molar pushing through.
Radio in the next room declares
rug business must close today.

Plum tree's petals fall, false
snow over red stone walk.
Right town, wrong cult. Baby

Bop wakes up. Artificial carnation
woven around auto antenna.
One his break, supermarket

produce worker (large grey-haired
man in a blue apron) steps outside
to smoke, sitting on the hood

of a red, quarter-driven children's rocket.
What I recall of the dream is
the tone, ex-cons negotiating

never knowing who has the gun:
in the casket, Popeye Jackson,
no sign anywhere of the bullet

hole in his face. At twilight
absence of shadow and glare, I spy
a painter and photographer preparing

to shoot a canvas leaned up
against West Berkeley studio wall.
What morning means. Pull wipes

for dirty bottoms from blue
plastic container. Avoid eye
contact as you pass singing

psychotic pushing shopping cart
(trash bags piled high and, atop,
gray sleeping cat) through the streets.

Paragraph is anywhere
both sentence and stanza end
together. Not this. Larry

Ochs across Mission Street
in the (dream/noonday sun)
outside the Mom-&-Pop

as if waiting for what?
Headquarters Davidians.
In the small Social

Security office, please
take a number. Who
stole the fruitmobile?

Along la rue de Steve
the view achieves what
labor can't: the pretense

of escape. Book seen
as a site license: you
don't own these words

though fair use is implied.
Out of deep read-(who
will do it?)ing, I

envision Blake trapped, strapped
by coaxial cabling down,
voices lost on the conference

call. Let's get the giggles.
Old paper shade, torn,
hanging. We shed those

whom we survive, until history
is only what's recalled, half
heard, barely noticed. Large

barge, slowly pushing upriver.
Accordions, washboards and dobros
fill the air of the park.

Mild taste to the alligator
sausage (mirliton is a local
squash). Lights define the Algiers

sky. I sit cross-legged
on a bed too large for one
too far from home. Sparrow

trapped in a mall. White chocolate
ravioli filled with dark
chocolate drizzled with raspberry

sauce and powdered
sugar to complete
a meal of pan

roasted shellfish when I
eat I eats. High
over the city's plain

of small houses, a blimp
floats, lit by the setting sun.
We walk through the warehouse-

gone-gallery district past
a large open tavern, noise
of music mixed with the

voices of broadcast sport.
Blue car with the driver-
side door bashed in over

on the shoulder, other cars
and even a school minibus
pulled over, their occupants

huddled now around the person
lying in the road while
through the trees and down

the embankment, not
visible from here but
for the thick plume of

black smoke, some other
car burns still. Kitsch
cult of the blue dog.

Tien gallops down the driveway
chasing the *noi*, shouting
"Miaow" (Pound would have

an ideogram: child standing
by her cat). Hyper
nation. A teeter totter

demands teamwork. I demand
that the sun rise now.
Only us old folks

will remember the C prompt.
Odd to see such muscle
on a homeless man

with no shirt. A great back order
is order. I rise, bedcovers tangled,
our bodies tingling, air alive

with the odors of sex. Op-
erator, poll the attendance on
this conference call. Eggs

peek out from the edge
of the garden. Old woman
appears so small atop

the paramedic's gurney. Dog
glares silently as I pass
his front porch. Code words

hidden in "Low cost or die!"
Clouds mottled red in the
sky by a sun already

over the horizon—in ten
minutes everything in the world
is grey and fading. My

office furniture strewn
along the right-field foul line
at the Oakland Coliseum.

By the time her son
reaches the hospital
she's died. My eye

instead of an onion.
The coffee at Lufkin's Diner,
twice boiled, burned, blue

with mold. Time of year when
you don't like to leave
your car parked all night

under the plum tree. He
sits on the porch, his pipe
doused by the rain, waiting

for the sensation of loss to pass.
Happy to see her, car alarm
yips at her approach. At a

distance, one sees birds,
flowers, stitched into the lace
curtains. The problem of

address: if I write, "At a
finger's touch, you come,"
who does the reader think

I mean? Cattle xing. High
dull sky. Before surgery,
one fasts. Themes weave.

You, the reader (whichever)
wave a slow, distracted
gesture high over your

head as if unsure I can
see you from this rocking
barrel, curious as to my

destiny as it approaches
the precipice at the margin,
waves' roar drowning my

call (one section of the stands
after another rising then
sitting, game within

the game). Tamed by Milton
I lie on Mother's head. Literalist
in his dream life. At night,

I tape a patch over my right eye
before I sleep. Finches in the fuchsia
after all these years signal a shift

in the immediate ecology. On kite hill
at the waterfront park, gusts
of wind twisting those

brightly colored banners, I see Sam
out walking his two shepherd-blend
pups, the one with the limp

nearly a year beyond its massive stroke,
stutter in its bark, "there's a lot of
b-b-bastards out there." Boy looks up

whenever he hears a plane fly past.
Drama dairy. Because she was
a medical professional, she thought

she understood the implications
of intestinal scarring
and since it had already taken

two surgeons to repair the nick
inadvertently made
at the time of her C-section,

when the abdominal pains began
months later, her husband
brought her to the emergency room

of the hospital she herself worked in
and told the ER doctors
they feared an obstructed bowel

but were instead told
as they admitted her and hooked her
up to a Demerol IV drip

her symptoms more perfectly fit
a gall bladder problem
which they could begin treating

the very next day, so that
when the night nurse saw
her pulse racing at 148 beats per minute,

respiratory at 32, her skin
cool to the touch,
she did not recognize the symptoms

of the “cold” stage of septic shock
nor did the doctor on
morning rounds, who failed

even to read her chart, so that
it was the tech who came
to update the IV who noticed

she’d stopped breathing, but by then
the massive heart attack
brought on by shock had killed her,

leaving a husband and an infant boy
who will never have
even a memory of his mother.

“Great,” says the doctor
shining the blue light
right into my eye.

I wake from a dream I
can’t remember, filled
with emotions I can’t

explain but to name them.
The refrigerator growls on. Chap
in knees May pole echoes

from page one. Specificity
of the dream: cousin whose name
I never remember writes also

so we join families to visit
a third Cajun-flavored part
of the clan back in the thick

pine woods where you must
harvest what you burn for heat
so I'm carrying a hatchet

but one so small it fits
entirely inside my shirt pocket.
Two rooms down, someone

is thrashing in his crib.
In the dream, the twins
are dressed as buffalo

in costumes too good for Halloween.
Clouds scattered across the night sky
visible only to the degree

they reflect the lights of the city.
Geography of this dream
has a logic I struggle

to fathom, a string
of high-rise hotels
that stretch from outer Geary

to the park. I stare
deep into the blank page
waiting for words to come.

Down the steps, in the dark
basement where Uncle Tootie sits
spitting tobacco juice into a bucket

all summer long, I hear
from a little radio atop
the ironing board the voice

of Russ Hodges, my Giants.
The past is perfect
as it hardens into number.

"Feminazis," shouts the stout
radio fascist, no
prefix needed. When this

you hear the time for fear
is hard upon us. "Whoa,
big fella," says Big Bird

(Carroll Spinney) to his broomstick
horse, layers of belief
to hold in suspension

(noticing how Big Bird
never moves his right wing
except for certain distance shots

in which he doesn't open
his beak or move his head,
I begin to wonder

if Bob Dole isn't also
a muppet). Cuticle
torn down the side of the nail.

Old storm clouds start to dissolve
or appear to when really
the center's merely pushed east.

Mockingbird sings constantly,
obsessively, rapid bursts
of trills, yodels, chirps,

summer nest atop the heat vent
of the little house built behind
the duplex next door. I realize

now that the reason
I never fought as a kid
(at least never fought back)

was that to lash out, pummel,
to punch, was to lose control
but to lose control

was to be "like my grandmother,"
a prospect far scarier
than a few bruises or

a moment's humiliation.
First plum drops from the tree.
The terror of the dream

lies in its logic. Trans
late this into Cyrillic.
Is "tchochke" a word

my middle manager asks.
Only when I notice the nest
do I realize the house

itself has been abandoned.
Dear Chris, it's 5:15 am.
Feverish, the small boy

lays limp in my arms
as we watch the NBA playoff game
slip into double overtime.

Bang, snap, crack (color photo
of a young Bosnian man
(read: Muslim) and his Serb

(read: Orthodox) girlfriend
shot dead in the streets of Sarajevo
—they never knew what hit them,

they expect every one to be crazy),
we shall not disappoint them.
The new trifocals bring the right

eye back into play, post op,
for the first time in 18 months
and I realize I'd forgotten

just what depth perception is,
tunnel effect of this corridor,
dizzying drop to the ground.

Faith, hope and parity. I
become aware of every blade of grass,
each leaf on every tree as

I make the long drive home.
Daddy-long-legs ambles
up the side of the bookcase.

In the mirror, pores become craters,
my beard a forest of red and white.
Half-dreams, tucked into the last

crevices of sleep before dawn.
Between Malcom and porn
the name of the letter changes.

At first, walking
forms an experiment,
legs spread wide for balance,

now a goose step, now
on tiptoes. The cat
(orange) leaps

from rooftop to fence.
A beautiful woman
in a spring dress

runs past. One morning
you never wake up,
but are cold, still,

so that later that day
your friends gather
in what used to be

your living room, quiet,
red-eyed, knowing
not quite what to say,

while the radio throws
classical music (some piece
of orchestral bombast

that I ought really
to have recognized) off
the painted walls and this

exercycle on which
sits an eight-year-old boy
trading insults with the linguist

over the verbal figure
of compost, when the doorbell rings
and in walks Bob Glück

with a cake, saying,
"Jews bring food."
Smoke twists, distant in the air

which up close rages,
warehouse fire.
An exact landscape

onto which, ventriloquist,
to throw emotion
(these are the Alps).

The essence of dance
is fundraising. A strip
of restaurants and bookstores

and one cinema, an argument
that society is possible
through a metaphor of commerce.

Crossing the intersection just
before the sun sets, calculating
what these westward drivers

can/cannot see. Snow
on the Oakland hills
right down to San Pablo Avenue

and the airport
where the Greyhound station
used to be

forms a dream
of unreadiness
as I gather

102 pieces of mail.
Form in Chinese.
The muscles you develop

in ankles and calves
driving all day.
Often, as I arrive

at the hill's crest,
peak of the Dublin grade,
fog's just dissolving

into a steamy, brilliant
light, toward which
I then descend

but, diffuse as it is,
where I can never
quite arrive.

Whoever writes, rides,
raiding words
from a storehouse

of possible intent
that, regardless of the use,
the sheer number of interventions,

never starts to dwindle.
Sound of ice shifting
as it melts in my

glass—imagine
another scale,
floes in the N. Atlantic.

In the dream I've
written an entire
paper explaining

the future of his
work, to the point where
poetry and philosophy

become one, which
I then roll up
and stick into a pipe

that leads down
into the molten earth
(*his* in this sentence implies

I know who *he* is
which I do not).
As if the nominal

would be *xong*.
Thru the fence the cool
of great white

flesh slurps forward
to grasp the offered
celery stalk

from the small
fingers of a boy,
giving thanks with a snort

and a soft "moo."
The vowels
are not what they seem

(what we seam).
A dream of exotic
insects, flies

with a bright red
collar of small
secondary wings

about their throats
that, extended,
permit them to hover

as, long tubes reaching up,
they suckle from the mother.
Grand armada of evening

traffic stopped dead
behind bright blue pick-up
engulfed in flames.

He pulls the neck
of his t-shirt down
to reveal

the pacemaker's scar—
a new rhythm
means a new day.

Buddhist tattoo artist.
Room in which
four of these women

have been my
lover (Ms. P,
who has not, says

of Mr. G, "his cock
was so long and thin, his
cum so watery").

"Eck!" scream 50,000 fans
garbed in green and gold,
"Eck! Eck!" "Ack! Pffft!"

says Bill the Cat. To
prosper, rise or prevail;
to become popular.

To calm a toddler's panic
I tell the story
of the little girl who

wanted to be a dancer who
each day after school
ran home, turning

cartwheels and flips
through the living room
until at last she landed

atop the soft sofa
standing on her head.
Fever blister blooms

atop my lower lip.
The meaning of morning
assigned before dawn

is transformed
by the addition
of light.

Depending on the
length of the I,
orangutan,

raw fish or meat, punishment,
also a surname. Elegantly,
delicately, the gorilla

peels the banana,
eating the meat
in a single bite, then

eating the peel. Only now
noticing the word "formal"
on the banquet invite

he phones frantically to his wife
to Fedex the tux.
At the base of the heroic

sculpture, in the shadows of
the Federal Trade Commission,
the shoeless, homeless, sleeping

man looks so small. Foster
Farm corn dogs, official
corn dogs of the Oakland

A's. Used
to the too-bright
jigsaw public sculpture

of Jean Dubuffet, we
fail to notice
across three decades prior

the advance of ideas.
To go on foot (xingchian,
sail a boat; xingci,

assassinate). Burkett
and Swift and
three days of if.

Toe truck. Small house
with beautiful roses
red, yellow, yellow-orange,

but a lawn half dead, gone
to weed. Two
megabyte PICT file.

Hearing on the radio how
the big rig hit the car,
jack-knifed and burned,

its load of paint cans
exploding, red, yellow, green
all over the road, I

cut over to the frontage
road, old highway before
this highway was built,

taking 10 extra minutes
max to get to work, arriving
one hour ahead

of most of my friends.
The delicacy of the elephant's
trunk, grasping straw,

curling it up into
its mouth. On sleepless nights
I rise and try the couch,

roll over, unable to straighten
my legs, hear a distant
freight train's whistle, watch

a passing car's headlights
diffuse in the fog, sense
the great factory of inner

organs work to digest
a heavy meatloaf, listen
as my sons toss about

in their cribs in their own
unquiet sleep. Try
to reconstruct not

the dream but its logic
(to get to San Francisco
City College I go

in the opposite direction
thru Chinatown in the rain).
The book abandons you

heartless, hard—you
will never be new
to this page again

(but we will always
have had that paragraph,
this phrase, the way

these words sweat together).
Depot man. Hot spares
spur top sales.

Blocks drop from the sky
in groups of four as
their speed accelerates

in Tetris. Big dog
hurls himself against fence
singing at our approach.

Airplane at sunset
rising high overhead
catches the last

flash of sun. Connotation
amortization table.
Giant turtle sand box.

Re-org or de-org,
which one? Encyclopedia
of shadows. An elephant

never regrets. Promote
evanescence. What
is less decorous than

parking garage elevator?
Xinghái: human skeleton,
the body. Sun sets

just over the freeway.
when I sleep I
sleeps. The convergence

of the three axes
of entry and movement
where the building joins

the city determines
the phenomenological
center of the building:

a five-story skylit court,
sixty feet in diameter,
catching the light like

a gigantic lantern.
In the first
Jackson Square Alley,

a young African-
American homeless
man, arms

of a weightlifter,
sorts through bags
of trash in

a dumpster for
something to add to
his overburdened

shopping cart, quietly
singing a gospel
hymn in some

Al Green falsetto
while in the next
alley a second

young man com-
pulsively twists
his neck and

scratches a short beard
over and over as
if tormented

by lice, all this
as twilight deepens,
long shadows of day

dissolving
into the short
mercury-lamp

shadows of night. When
your legs start to go,
linebreaks become more

brittle. House lights
down, attention
turns to that lone

wood chair, stage left.
On the freeway, clusters
of cars adopt

pack behavior, big dog
at the lead, a form
of focus so temporary

it's dissolved before
you notice, one thin
red roadster weaving

more rapidly through
the group until
it gets that long

empty stretch and
roars out, highway
patrol in hot pursuit.

Fatherhood: soon
to be a major motion.
In the dream I

suck your breasts
so hard I
wake up. Half

the cubicles empty
the day after
the reduction in force.

At night, the sound
of rain hard against
the driveway tells

of the change in
seasons. A curfew
in the dream leads

us back through streets
where different cities,
people have congealed.

Scan head sets the sampling
grid. Punderstood.
Stanley Kunitz' daughter

speaks of her own
ectopic pregnancy.
Embalmer's text, entitled

Body Language. Brown shoes
with gray slacks. Sun
bloats, setting

into the toxic sky. At night,
shadows without a light source
larger than the face of a small clock

magnify these half-illumined
shapes. I lose sight
of the date. Wing-tips

atop the dining-room table
glisten. Listen
how the baby breathes

as he sleeps. Xingtài:
form, shape, pattern. Xíngtí:
shape of a person's body.

Chain to lock
the oven shut.
Fifth syllable, sixth

sense. Don't cry,
Big Bird. Trench the cable.
1-800-PIN DROP. Flames

jumping canyons, houses
that burst like bubbles,
cows stampeding

into the street. Let's
brand our intangibles
as best we can.

I wander through the long
office, trying to imagine
what it would be

to work here. I hear
the approaching car's brakes
before I notice

the purr of its engine.
Descent into the valley
of decent people. And if the roads

ever were made wide enough
to accommodate all these people
we'd just add population

to clog it all again.
Who can tell the denser
from the figure of the dense?

Futured hence. Plastic pony
frozen in its prance stands
abandoned atop the toy drum.

Licorice taste of
Mexican marigold
mint. Basil gone black

after sudden fall frost.
Culture in which owls
are seen as predators,

pests. Have you taken
your eyeball out yet?
In the dream (not

a dream) you look so small
in the industrial strength
all metal hospital crib,

mist of the oxygen tent
under the examination lights
throwing its eerie glow,

you are splintered literally
just to keep the IV in place
(the look on your face

as they search, finally,
one, two, three separate veins
before they get the needle in,

one of shear pain and fear
right into my eyes
as only, at 21 months,

you can). Big C,
little c, what begins
at sea? Am I right,

am I writing? Down
by the Brazos, mud soft,
air thick with the first frost,

you explain the process
of milling sorghum. Paul's
epistle to the Cartesians.

Jerry Estrin's laugh
still rings in my head
(I sit at a desk

in my brother's house—
Dear Cliff, it's 4:37 AM
here in Waco, Texas

where down the block Jim
runs a one-man dental lab
from an RV in his garage).

What then? When is a poem
not a poem? Here. Now.
The cat bats sparrow's corpse

about the porch. If the room
is familiar, the dream
is not. Raccoons

at the cat's bowl
out on the deck.
Rolling pins for playdough.

An extra layer of blankets
will deepen the dream.
Poem in which my name

assumes the role of code.
Winter means sunset
in midafternoon,

imperialism of night.
Dysplasia suggests the possibility
of plasia (the unmarked case).

To examine oneself critically,
to sober up, to come to;
mood or desire; apricot;

to blow one's nose. Itching
to the point of
screaming in the middle

of the night. Playdough's
republic. Above,
three-fourths of the moon

forms an imperfect circle,
traffic reporter's biplane
winking in the dark.

Explain the tug boat
by analogy to what?
A boy moans

with consciousness.
In the flickering
newsreel, Oswald, shot

groans as he slumps
to the parkinglot floor.
You twist as I

slip my cock inside.
As the blood returns
to my hands, first

the fingers tingle
then the palms grow warm.
Roar of the fire truck

still inside its station,
makes its departure appear
infinitely slow. The new

hystericism privileges a past
it can only invent (800
pound gorilla pisses

on each committee
at the edge of the glade).
Even once the rain stops

one hears it still
falling from what leaves
still cling to the half-naked

Japanese plum. As
tronauts swarm
maggot-like about

the broken telescope.
I flip the circuit breaker
back on and without

realizing it, fry
my hard disk. At night
little boys jump

from their cribs with a resounding
thump. The line, elastic,
perfect for catching bears.

Lotions and diapers and boys,
oh my, oceans and hybrids
and stares. My gut

instead of an onion.
Call me email.
Bill Moyer's rapt

attention, what passes
for intellectual content.
The lights flicker,

the dissent beckons.
In Russia, to rhyme
true nouns is a sign

either of irony or
stupidity. Xingyu,
sexual desire. Good

fortune, rejoice, I hope.
(Of a monarch) arrive;
Sur-, family or clan name.

A conspiracy of theories,
microclimates of the skin.
The plural of mouse, the plural

of house. Blackbirds in a bare
tree. A line enjambed is a
line enjoined. Man in hand

cuffs in front of the super
market. When this you see
Xmas tree. R.C. Lion

roars. The "A" in H, the
"eh" in X, an "E"
in T lingers in the ear,

clear, concealed (the con
of consonant). Old clock
ticks loud as a metronome,

god of our mantle. Tram
poline of the heart twists
at the limit

of flight, height
at which gravity
grasps back hard.

In dream, old choices
dance anew. Teaspoon
of meds for the young guy.

I sit at this small
kitchen table before
the children wake.

YOU

for Pat Silliman

I

Hard dreams. The moment at which you recognize that your own death lies in wait somewhere within your body. A lone ship defines the horizon. The rain is not safe to drink.

In Grozny, in Bihac, the idea of history shudders with each new explosion. The rose lies unattended, wild thorns at the edge of a mass grave. Between classes, over strong coffee, young men argue the value of a pronoun.

When this you see, remember. Note in a bottle bobs in a cartoon sea. The radio operator's name is Sparks.

Hand outlined in paint on a brick wall. Storm turns playground into a swamp. Finally we spot the wood duck on the middle lake.

The dashboard of my car like the keyboard of a piano. Toy animals anywhere.

Sun swells in the morning sky.

Man with three pens clipped to the neck of his sweatshirt shuffles from one table to the next, seeking distance from the cold January air out the coffee house door, tall Styrofoam cup in one hand, *Of Grammatology* in the other. Outside, a dog is tied to an empty bench, bike chained to the No Parking sign.

II

Bottom feeders: shadows shift over the floor of the pool. Chairs askew about the square table. At one end of the food mall a crowd watches a game of basketball on a giant screen. First I imagine what you will look like naked, then as you will look in fifty years. Ball circles the rim, then falls out.

Dressed right for rain, I leap its rivers, carrying an easel in a huge cardboard box.

The bad clown. Freeway shut due to a landslide. Desk littered with preprinted postcards, each beginning "Dear Mr. Gingrich. . . ."

What fuel drives the engine of metaphor? Walking around with fists clenched. Logic of the alphabet: bat, cat, fat, hat. Behind the parking lot, the arroyo has become a pulsing, brown, swollen rio. A fan-shaped view through the wipers.

Large as a fist, the spider gallops up my leg. New error message. Humpty Dumpty, made of cloth, had acquired hands and feet.

Footrub that's only a footrub. 1-900-Yo-Poets. Lone man pushing a shopping cart at four in the morning.

Endangered species live on in greeting cards. Boy declares toy stove is a rocket ship. Who owns the genomes of tropical plants?

III

High up in the tallest branches of the alphabet, bare in the hard rain, one small hummingbird hovers, wings translucent with the still motion of flight.

Who left the telephone in the oven?

Banana peel has 'corners,' but the meat is round. Blimp that glows in the dark. Purple dog with a blue nose. Worms in the compost of history.

Balloons blow across the tundra. The hand as a machine demonstrates closure (the narrative of fingers). A vision of vowels vibrates.

Shopping cart as machine, every inch organized by the homeless man's system of trash bags (this one for aluminum, that for glass, plastic containers arranged on the rack by size), a cluster convened at the Foster Freeze parking lot, two men and a woman, high overhead the first full moon of the new year.

Shadow of a boy in the dark demands, "Change my diaper." The name who named Liberty Valence. Broom in the corner exists as potential. An arrow adds edit.

Moon shrunken in the dawn sky behind the last gauze of rain cloud. Balloon effect of fat man in turtle-neck shirt. I should speak.

IV

Naked boy chases chicken.

Reading disorder: words construct character, then dissolve. Painted plates, held by wire claws to wall, allege scene equals domestic bliss. A series of emotions sets the table. Yellow sun sets in the needlepoint sky.

Predawn in an airport hotel, a life of mauve and tope. I enter the ballroom to work the crowd. Director of Mayo Foundation config center says, "My honey has a ten-year-old son." Name that entrée.

Sun dull behind endless gauze of cloud, blurred and indistinct. Hard wind in a humid air. This architecture is heroic and meaningless in the empty, east Texas landscape. The hotel bellman is stooped and old.

Rest stop ahead.

SNMP to DMTF: RTFM! Bye-bye, DMI. Telco tagline: *your true voice.*

So that Eskimos (the Inuit) *need* refrigerators, not to keep their food cold but to regulate its temperature, to keep it from freezing. Twenty-eighth consecutive day of rain. Desktop stuffing mix. In the photo, I appear small and distant, impossibly opaque. Drenched, they watch from the side of the freeway as their car burns in the driving rain, a trick candle.

V

New maple bare in winter, almost invisible in front of the redwood fence. Lone bushtit, singing for its flock.

Eyes shut, sound of rain envelopes the house. Tree hung with dozens of plastic soda bottles, painted frying pans, plates, forms a rough altar. Tiny porcelain animal in each box of tea. By ear, he sd. Said.

An old pen that once seemed elegant now feels cheap in my hand. Small boy learns to fast forward. Toot 'n' Toddle Taxi. Where in history shall we find it?

Sun shimmers in the fog, cars passing on this two-lane country road reduced to the dull glimmer of headlights.

Details swarm, the hum and buzz of a million features, each infinitely specific, apparent to the eye. The art of time in tone tunes. Gears and levers of a single hand, hidden below flesh, mesh to move and pick up this pen. What I am not writing about is the shock of seeing you sick.

At night, the dial of a lone clock radio illumines the kitchen. Small birds chitter in the dark, an index of the oncoming dawn. At night, this house is a husk, a shell.

The garden in the fog feels exact, contained. Bare plum full of birds. My own breath visible. Unseen voices pass. Further off, foghorn mimics baritone sax.

VI

Don't rush the horizon. Man stands atop a shingle roof, measuring tape in one hand. Television in the background is a constant. Jetliner smaller than a fly appears to enter the sun.

Walking backwards, I climbed this mountain, he says, across the ocean of suffering. The freeway itself on fire from the heat of the butane truck explosion.

Paragraph as four-sided figure. I stand in the garden, alone at the center of the Center, constellations dim in the night sky. Young woman alone, asleep in the doorway of an abandoned porn theater, not even a sleeping bag. What puts the temp in temple?

Banana perceived as a flower, as a nut. Doll designed as anthropomorphized cartoon animal (unable to decide if it's a dog or bear or lamb). Appliqué seahorse on bedroom wall.

What the floss found: 27th letter of the alphabet.

Giant photo demonstrates radish. Plastic sunbeam honey jar become bathtub toy. Why the automobile's proper metaphor is a horse or cat. The implicit question has always already been answered. Emotion as a furnace: *stokin'!*

A collapsible tray on gold rollers, designed just for use with caskets. Judgment narrativizes eternity. Sacred icon derived from an instrument of torture: the nail *through* the palm. In the drizzling rain I watch you driven from our eyes forever.

VII

I meant *lives. Driz line* is how I will always hear that word pronounced. The poem not as an instrument of pleasure, but of passion. The child down the street, age four, is lovely, although her parents are scowling, reclusive, self-pronounced Satanists, house behind the high fence a deep purple, license plate on the ancient van reading *M LA FEY.*

Snails weigh down the leaf even as they devour it. Compost thick with worms. A still rain vs. a heavy fog. That sense of the indoors as complete.

Is false. Suture or sutra, which one? Long walk to the mailroom, my mode of relaxation. Heart beat pulse from the drip of the new leak in the roof. Small glimmer of blue sky teases. That much green in the hills is not natural.

The bones of the foot, unused to the weight of the body after a long night's sleep, snap and pop when I first rise and walk. The sheep of state mill and bleat in the holding pen. Ink spills, blood red. Full moon in a dawn sky.

Old lightbulb crackles and whispers with electricity. Seduced into Spring, plum tree's blossoms are crushed by frost. You are given one half hour to pack your personal belongings out of your cube and depart the premises. The premise is, at the end of the day, lives should make sense. Don't count your chickens.

When the bulb blows, the shadows will rock. First car on the block warming its engine long before dawn. Small boy sprawled asleep on a large bed. Morning paper bounces against the steps. In the distance, first one siren, then two, then several.

Behind which, even further, a train's long deep whistle articulates speed. In the corner with the sound off, television functions as a lava lamp. Crow in the plum tree coughs.

VIII

For Nina Iskrenko

Readers of the lost art. Monster with an eye in its mouth (body of a rocket ship). Stuffed wildcat perched over the mouth of the cave, across from the miniature gift shop.

Nothing rots like an old suburb, strip malls abandoned, tattoo artist in the medical suite, house with dark dirty curtains drawn, in front of which sandwich board displays huge hand: *Palm Readings.* On television, cyborg frogs croak out the name of a cheap beer.

Deep red burst shimmering at the horizon turns into old yellow sun as it rises. Before us lay the great wide bowl of the Amador Valley. Your obit gets broadcast under the email header of "Boy Talk."

Stein to Hook: when this you see, remember Smee. Spine to book: bleed into my gutter. Spin and look: lying down, feeling anxious, is not the same as sleep. In Livermore, underneath the suburban big lawn culture of the Rad Lab and Sandia engineers, there remains at core a small valley cow town, a few dark Main Street bars in which Harry Dean Stanton is thought of as an intellectual.

Ortho-glass forms a cast alas. Sleep as you can, whenever. Refrigerator roars and shudders, alive with its own anti-fever.

Ball with features of a cartoon dog (upper lip a speckled W). New verbs for old. Flaming or flaring or whatever you call it. Bronchiolitis.

Textism. Relax your eyes until the focus gives way and words appear like swarm of ants at a distance, at first orderly, then wandering, transgressing the margins, then the page, the room alive with a crawling swarm of letters. Crocodile puts on her coat and goes to work.

IX

The O.J. Simpson trial to rerun forever as a Saturday morning cartoon. Café loud with out-of-town tourists all being cool at once. When the stoplight fails at an intersection, drivers relearn the social contract.

A yodeling cowboy way of knowledge. The book with buttons. That which is merely personnel soon rates.

The land of a million smidgens. The man asleep in the roaring shower. The happy face drawn in the steam on the bathroom mirror bleeds away.

The hegemony project. Articles of the specific. Insertion treated as assertion. As illustrated by R. Crumb, a man in a dress with green armpits and glitter in his beard, of which you write "he seems happy."

Trees half-hidden in the fog. Single drop of rain, glistening, runs the length of the power line wire before falling to the street. Roar that the shower makes in the pipes of a small house.

The curse of sleep, unevenly distributed. Where will this winter drive the birds?

Morning comes: the surviving sun, wounded in the sky, throbs above the remaining clouds. In Grozny, a young girl, a child, lies dead in the street for days, the still startled expression in her eyes hardening now from a question to an accusation. Birds in the bare tree sing.

X

Not yet joining letters into words, read the book aloud from memory. Taxonomy of the natural world to include monsters, dinosaurs, the jackalope. Jack-o-lantern out of season, toothless grin more hollow than one could imagine.

Placebo stanza. Alligator's stillness in the winter sun. Tiger paces absolute rim of its preserve. Alfalfa pellets in an ice cream cone. Impervious yak.

Egg, on skis, samples the slopes. Agon skies, simple the slips. Slaps words in a sequence, snap-on logic. Dragon, as memory of an age of dinosaurs, is woven into the mists.

Reverse engineered my syntax. Washing others' dishes, you examine crumbs almost archaeologically. Each paragraph understood as a work group. Dog barking uncontrollably as an index of time.

Windchimes thrashing in the storm, hysterical music. In the dream some clerk just tells me you've been killed in an automobile accident, anxious to close up shop and get home to her dinner. I try to imagine the difference in winter. On the floor, forgotten, a pair of slippers in the shape of trains with happy faces. Name that tune.

Branding strategy: private label. Velcro mind in a Teflon world. Car spun around in the fast lane.

Kinds of potato salad. Shelf life of a banana. We stood at the window, searching for a rainbow, while below the old arroyo, transformed into a swollen brown river, roiled, logs and branches, palm fronds heading west. In the corner of the parking lot, a grey Ford Taurus wagon, its lights left on, dims.

XI

Landscape edited by winter. Old riverbeds don't lie. I don't recall my childhood as full of primary colors. Learning slowly to understand the languages of my own body. Down done dawn don't.

The power of exhaustion. Telephone understood as athletic equipment. Name every pea. Drinking fountain understood as interactive sculpture. Sky heavy as a table, low, grey, breathing.

Grass flattened along the arroyo, almost combed by the force of the now receded water, a million sticks evenly distributed along the slickened path. How did that flock of red-wing blackbirds survive, or this lone hovering black-shouldered kite?

Pacing in a house without lights. Low rumble rolling earthquake triggers adrenaline even as it wakes us. The brain in pain falls mainly on the plane. Fat flat water rat.

Thought as a fruit can be squeezed. Varieties of indoor ball. Paper boy vs. wooden soldier. Trochaic replacements. Pill bug.

Repentium. Alarm clock that works only some of the time. On the hottest day of the year, the furnace roars on and won't shut off. Pages fill all too quickly. From survey to surveyor to surveillance. From the top of this hill, I could explain maps.

Pages to the left of us, pages to the right. . . . Rhetoric of ambition vs. that of guilt. It starts to rain without warning. Train made of cardboard, train made of wood. The word "we," its borders ambiguous, stares into the mirror or what?

XII

A guide to the sky under full nondisclosure.

Dawn in the bare birch trees, the sun, swollen, throbs over the horizon. Hotel buffet doodah. Two dogs dancing, sniffing one another's genitalia.

One can hear the electricity wired in the walls, water rushing through the pipes, the boards and joints of the old house groaning as they settle.

Map of morning. Winter light. One's experience of the transfer point airport as that of the city itself. Dear winter, it's 5:15 AM. Shoes for Mickey Mouse.

Waste deep in the big muddy. The sound of rain around. The line (not visible) binds letters into words. People are drowning.

Moon, broken in the middle. What a watch watches. Song of the single engine Cessna, threading the pre-dawn sky. One bird, one bird, many.

Blades of grass brittle in the freeze. Spider's corner of the bath room. One maple tree that will not return to life.

XIII

In 1973, Le Cordon Bleu is the lone Southeast Asian Restaurant in San Francisco, a hole-in-the-wall lunch counter spot off Polk next to the equally cramped Lumiere Theater where Perry Henzell's *The Harder They Come,* starring Jimmy Cliff, first introduces reggae to American music. In the next room I hear a small boy groaning awake, then footsteps. Estes Kefauver, there in black and white, accepts the nomination.

Old assassination dream back again. Once the sun moves over the top of the hills, the temperature at the picnic drops rapidly as the adults don sweaters, then jackets, until more gradually the crowd starts to dwindle, the last Frisbee game dies out, the parking lot empties. On a chain link fence by the arroyo, five vultures sit silently. Snow where there's never any snow.

Beta test the language. The streetlamps here are useless, blocked by the dense canopy of trees. Basketball in the dark. Bug fix.

Blue-eyed plastic T. rex smaller than my hand advances on helpless Big Bird figurine, early instance of narrative. Demonize all whales (Monstro or Moby Dick). In the Eye-talian, it's a dogfish. The tidal theory of decisions.

Two Humpty Dumpties sitting in a chair. One cop approaches the car slowly, hand resting gently on the handle of the holstered gun, while her partner back at the prowl car stands behind the shield of an open door. The morning paper bounces around the porch. Harvey Keitel moves through the dark club in slow motion.

The dream has the structure of a stage play, an apartment dressed up for a party, hors d'oeuvres everywhere, a cake, bottles of liquor, a bowl of punch, but it's not one party but an entire sequence of them, the foods change, the seasons out the window, the occasions for celebration itself (at least one instance is a wake), costumes change, not all my friends are at every one and there are always some new faces, couples change combination and we all age rapidly, I'm perpetually arriving, taking off one coat after another, hats within hats, never quite settling in on a single conversation, a single drink, a single plate of food.

Just enough cloud cover to shroud out the sun. Dry farts. Trees shuddering with wind. A low plane buzzing these houses just before dawn. Large dog hurls itself silently against the chain link fence.

XIV

On first seeing through the eyes of Mr. Potato Head. Time convenes, gathers. Clock's tick composed of three distinct sounds so tightly batched I frown to concentrate hard enough to hear the even, compulsive reiteration. Bungalow life.

Houseful of doors, neither completely open nor entirely shut. Frozen French fry. The symbolic in Anselm Kiefer functions as an excuse. Mozzarella rolled in pesto. The God in Godzilla. Photo of a young man dead of AIDS. Light as a form of terror.

Clark's track composed on the typewriter, words thick as nicotine. Horseful odors. Post op, a young woman examines a bruised breast. The tiny storefront in which I last saw Julius Hemphill play sax.

My brother's beeper. Old pump, my chest, the sheer weight of me, the war of inner organs, heaving, writhing grab bag of the torso. Financial types think that if you've counted an asset you've managed it.

Diffusion of sunlight on a hazy day, world devoid of sharp edges, distinct colors. Resiliency of your nipple when aroused. Stirring the microwave pasta (no content to the steam). Examine the mouse type.

Don't push the bat. The inner organs of beasts and fowls litter the roadway. Mocking bird in the dark, flutelike.

The dancers in pairs whirl through the hall. At midnight, a man under a streetlight is practicing t'ai chi, apparently unaware of the rain. Next door, steam serves as the curtain as the young blonde woman steps from the shower. Birds scream in the trees. An antique clock that hasn't worked in years.

XV

The smell of excess. Raindrops sizzle in the hot coals of a barbecue. Here in the very neighborhood I grew up in, a pocket park I've never seen before. Two Dalmatians, one with black spots, the other red-brown, race through the meadow.

The narrative of bones. A cough that sounds like a scrape. Velcro monkey. Driving in search of an all-night copy shop.

Martian culture ('70s disco music) is broadcast to millions. That part of the AM dial where one never travels. A day of dark rooms and blinking slide projectors. Chicken in a nest.

The room is empty, save for one green balloon. Inside my nose, the snot has hardened into a thick crust. In another room, someone muffles a sneeze. On the train, she deliberately occupies two seats while others must stand, holding infants and heavy bags. Laugh of the mockingbird rings through the dark—how does it know that dawn is near?

Dream in which my mother and a friend are jogging through the streets of west Berkeley (she's wearing a color combination—black top, gray slacks—that in "real life" she would never choose to wear). Decision Servcom, a name that only a merger could have created. From the West Oakland BART station, I can see the neighborhood (7th and Adeline) where, 98 years ago, my grandmother was born, not one of the old Victorians left standing. Keeps his motorcycle in his loft, five floors up.

Bandwidth of the poem. Ladder made entirely of interlocking sections of pipe. In the distance, a jetliner threads the thin cloud (distance itself assigned by the size of the plane). How many fingers am I holding up?

To resign, to sign again, a sign. Out the window, beyond the business park, the hills are a thick emerald green. A fat robin perched on the hood of the car. The expression in the possum's eyes, dead in the middle lane.

XVI

Furniture in the windows of the houses in the hills far away come suddenly, sharply into view. A plastic slipper has been left by the princess doll, around which to construct an imitation of Cinderella. A fiddler in the corner of the tiny, crowded house. Blond wheatfield—hair on the back of my hand. An image of the world upon a tennis ball, hovering mid-air, in view of the on-coming racquet.

From the window one can see the entire bay, the Golden Gate framed between the branches of the neighboring eucalyptus. Over and over, the mockingbird twists its predawn riff. Wake exhausted. The peel of a banana, abandoned by its core.

Windchimes rime. A cancelbot (first bot, best bot). A Gemini Research Certifier III radon measurement system (model 202) blinks green on the corner of the mantle. When finally I meet Alan Shepard by accident in an Atlanta bookstore, he's grizzled, nearly 70, not at all what a young boy would have imagined.

Javelin quivers as it sails overhead. La la la . . . artichokes . . . la la la . . . drambuie . . . la la la . . . catastrophe . . . la la la Nissan Sentra . . . turkey vultures . . . la la la . . . bed stead. Involuntary spasms of the surgeon's hand. Pink meat of the salmon, just barely opaque. Gone to hell, books to sell.

The explosion flowers up and out, a rose of force, sculpting its own image out of the face of the federal office building. Windchimes mime the tone of a ship's bell. Passing the Dublin grade. "Congratulations, Benedict," laughs Jay Amato, boy president.

The specificity of the dream is intense, although upon waking collapses to a single emotion. By the train's whistle (not a whistle at all), I can follow its travel through the dark. The margin itself is physical. The sky is so much white space until you realize it's alive, swarming with particles and dust.

Moment at which this valley cow town became a suburb. Scavengers, the traffic copters follow the long commute. Red sun, swollen, settles over the bay. On San Pablo Avenue, security guards loiter by the entrance to the card club. A woman who is not really hitch-hiking meets your eyes for a second, then quickly looks away.

XVII

The ferris wheel pauses at the height of its arc. The still, cool air of dusk (one rose bush exploding with blossoms, the other nearly spent). A lone, small plane appears headed for the moon. Blue jay rests on the wire. In the distance, someone's dropped a plate, but it hasn't shattered—you can hear it spinning. Mockingbirds, start your engines.

Blow joy vests on the wine. What works. Cloudless night, but virtually starless also. I through my neighbor's open house, startled at the impact of four years' neglect. Words added, then taken away. My hand on the small of your back.

COBRA, COLA. In which I walk into the biggest bookstore in the western US, ready to buy, and come away empty handed. Woman by the parking lot of the Goodwill store begging discards from people coming to make donations, which she then turns instantly into a makeshift yard sale (amid the debris, some of it barely recognizable, I see an ancient toddler's walker). My night at Moe's.

Don't copy that floppy. As men and women grow older, features shift, even the bones in their faces (her teeth blackening, her eyes sunken, going perkily about the same shitty job year after year). To the question, "Is your house lined with books," I reply, "No—stacked."

Bird song wakes me. Salmon taro cakes beside new potatoes on a bed of arugula. The difference between exhausted and sleepy. Old deep purple bookcase still has original "Impeach Nixon" sticker not entirely faded. Do you think we'll ever find fresh artichokes on the East Coast? I envision Eliot dropping from the bridge, twisting in slow motion all the way down to the water.

Delurk. The public defender's other business is psychic communication with animals, conducted with a headset from his home—"dead pets are a specialty." Last chance to buy books.

Graphically, bear and little mouse make for an interesting set of companions. The pink, almost translucent flesh of the salmon fillet, the broccoli hot but not limp, the pale off-white bed of couscous. Yes sir, yes sir, three bags full.

XVIII

For Bob and Francie

P=H=I=L=A=D=E=L=P=H=I=A. Under the dogwood tree, scampering, playful as a squirrel, a large grey rat, fat as can be. Old hardwood floor, impossible to cross silently in the dark. Dog attempts to hump the cat. For Spring, an old closed-in porch, a neighborhood crow.

Three old men play golf in the rain. What is a redpoll? Street cobbled after all these years precisely to reduce the speed of traffic. Thanks to Paul Hoover, I can find my work in any strip mall bookshop in America. For Pound on the Main Line, the trip to Penn proved no journey at all. Business center parking lot on a Sunday, a half dozen cars parked by the squat brick six-story building.

Beyond the tightly clustered streets of the small town, half-boarded up Main Street surrounding the single tall spire of a church, the road quickly turns rural (cluster of mock castle executive homes out by the golf course). Twin clouds of steam rise almost forever from Limerick. Concept of a basement as "finished."

Suppository understood as a term of rhetoric. Early morning, cheap ballpoint pen falls into a urinal in the fourth-floor men's room—who knows how?—never to be removed, to become a target, moved willfully by streams of urine, pushed counter clockwise around the white—who knows what it is made of?—urinal cake. Returning in the rain from the old brick bank to the car, I realize that I forgot to feed the meter, had scurried right past it in my hurry to stay dry, only to have gotten by without a ticket, little gift of fate. Kitaj's eyes.

Back roads amid dogwood. Terminal emulation. Rag doll anatomically correct. A cloudless sky but for the power plant. An old small town at the center of all this development. Holds a skateboard the way you would a schoolbook. Pink petals everywhere.

Man sitting zazen has stroke, falls forward, suffocating in the soft foam of an empty meditation pillow. Cat locked out all night in the rain. A pager in every pocket. Suburban train.

Whoever lives by the aphorism dies by the cliché. A dream in which I might know the bomber. A dream in color. Idea of a road as a "pike."

XIX

Moment in which I realize I'm not wearing my glasses. Old stone house. Blue plastic wrap of the *New York Times.* Impact of red wine on white fur of the dog. Sunrise.

Poem as gradual as weather. Hotel art (pseudo-Hoffman softened, retro-Rothko as filigree in pastel). What Trenton makes, the world takes. What Nixon knew when Nixon knew it.

First compulsive songbird, pre-dawn, abruptly halts. The air conditioner is constant (unnoticed but never silent). You can hear the electricity in lightbulbs, faint crackling. Motivation: man in hotel conference room throws football to the sales reps.

Too bleary to imagine. How the river carves the city (lost at night, trying to find my way across). Dog leaps for the stick, her own ballet, then loses interest, wanders off to sniff the grass. History as a function of curiosity.

Of the forbidden, my three-year-old says "That makes me sad." Impossible to discern the ice from the shards of broken glass. A table of contents from which I've been omitted. Room in which toupees outnumber beards. The firestorm sweeps left across the screen: we only imagine the men, women and children inside. I'm walking in a world you cannot imagine, having died so long ago.

Dream of real estate. Amato's tomatoes. The sun emerges gradually through the woods. (The son emerges gradually through the woods.) The present has not become a perfect copy, but rather an uneditable one. The boat sinks rapidly in the text. Try to capture the shape and impact of your cheekbones in words.

From an airplane, the spokes of suburban mall (this one in Princeton is T-shaped) are indistinguishable from those of a minimum security prison but for the immense parking lot. But for. When the hard drive on the PC that controls the security system crashes, every fire door in the hotel—each held open by electrically controlled magnets—slams shut. Cardinals will take some getting used to. Dark-toned palette of *The X-Files.*

XX

Old stone inn, used by the Tories to plot the assault on Philadelphia, still serves rich veal medallions covered with crab meat, spinach and Hollandaise sauce. Cardinals in the silver birch. Metronome of an old wind-up mantle clock. Your body beneath that new little night blouse, then my hand beneath that.

An enclosed front porch converted to language. Each person I meet insists on telling me their "California story." Restaurant on main floor of old municipal building: the workers stash their belongings downstairs in the jail. Elf-like, a porcelain imitation of Santa's wife, the woman warns us of the "colored" districts (this is 1995). Cat stops to stare at me, then turns and glides away.

Read me. Full moon in the dogwood. In St. Petersburg and Moscow, a gang (eight young men, two women) has been murdering apartment owners in order to sell their apartments. I set the pager to *vibrate.* Driving endlessly along Bethlehem Pike, seeming to get no closer to familiar landmarks, I notice the sun starting to set in the East. Don't look!

In the next room, the large formal dining room table is covered with thousands of pieces of an unfinished jigsaw puzzle (little more than the rectangular outer rim is complete, an echo of the shape of the table, though two of the corners have begun to be filled in, clusters of two and three joined pieces dotting the center), but in this light (at this angle and distance), it's impossible to tell what the image is, or even that one exists. Crow screaming in the trees. Gypsy curse: May you have a lawsuit in which you know you're right.

The problem with poetry is poets. Bone spurs grab the heart. First shrill roar of cardinals. This storm doesn't so much arrive and pass as it does gather and dissolve.

The writhing lesson. The dog's paws as it crosses the hardwood floor. The rain stops but the trees still have to shed their water. House with two fire places (in sight of one another). Telescope in the dining room. We imagine the bird's song as an expression of emotion.

Paragraph is burning. Alone in the playground, dressed in a suit that doesn't quite fit, red shirt, black tie, stands the developmentally disabled boy atop the tall slide, vomiting.

XXI

Smidgens in the glass harass. Moment at which first bird starts to sing, impossible still visually to discern dawn's approach. To imagine Duncan's text is to envision Duncan.

First dull light foretells a clouded dawn. Bear masks made from paper plates. Mockingbird clicks. Gradually, moving out, as the furniture and pictures disappear, the architecture of the room re-emerges as if hidden by use, bare potential, naked as any person, almost obscene. Mockingbird gargles and growls.

In the dream, I have the same conversation about the storage capacity of my laptop that I had last week with a teenage boy with the president of CompuCom. Realtor points to a crack in the stucco. Little boy dances to inaudible tune.

Jungle gym as prototype, as personality inventory, the problem to be defined before it can be solved. Day in which I drive three cars (rental car's last driver obviously smoked). Owned now by a long succession of other people, the house in which I grew up has become a cipher, opaque object half-buried by bougainvillea.

Sentences written long ago. Standing at the coast, horizon contained by fog. Sign on the door reads "Division of the Arts" but what I want is multiplication. Basket of dolls. Ratio of books to ideas is getting higher by the day.

Her name is Cinnamon, her mother Teal. Baywatch Ken doll anatomically edited for content (to fit your screen). Ceiling fan spins slowly. That the whole of one's life fits into one truck.

Phone on the floor of an empty house, an echo to anything I say. Mold on the wall behind each bookcase, a kind of damp shadow. Aphids, like dandruff, on each leaf of the plum tree. Ham on foccacio, a bowl of tea. The clouds hung low

XXII

Small boy in a seaman's cap reminds me suddenly of my own such hat at that age, cap my father left behind. A light fog promises to burn off. A week between homes.

Voices, verbs, verses (word, bird, third – *absurd*). Boy's shout from the street stories below brings me out of my sleep instantly until I determine that all my children are here inside asleep. The absolute second you have the first opportunity in over a week to relax, to take a deep breath, give a sigh, you realize from its shallow painful wheeze that you've had bronchitis for days. Pesto potato pizza.

Seek out the path of most resistance.

A splinter I thought would work itself out has instead infected the whole finger. Dream in which, although I haven't seen you in ages and we were never more than cordial in a professional context, I wake to discover you next to me in bed naked – the actual body is always such a surprise – leaning toward me for a long, slow, deliberate kiss, guiding my hand gradually from you small almost conical breast south until I enter, first the front, then behind, and you twist, groaning, a broad grin across your face. Day that never happens.

Day that I discover total allergy to this powder detergent, big welt-like rashes everywhere from my neck to the soles of my feet. Cardinal in the yard smaller than I expected. You live on the east coast now.

When, on the car radio, they hit the baby-in-the-microwave story, I hit the button. Among the morning's rich cacophony of birdsong, pick out first one, then another, that sound completely unfamiliar, using each in turn as the foreground through which to hear the whole (nearby crow entirely out of scale). Upstairs, footsteps pace back and forth, for which I construct my own imaginary narrative: a young girl, a Latina whose parents, themselves the children of farm laborers, are schoolteachers, goes on scholarship to an excellent school, then rises quickly to corporate middle management, one day to discover her own desire for one of her employees, an older married man entirely inappropriate for her future – what should she do? Velcro sandals.

The sky grows lighter before it starts to rain. I stand in an empty attic studio, wondering where to put the desk. Young poodle lopes up to the wire fence. Fan rotates slowly over the vacant kitchen.

XXIII

Sun is in the trees behind which a train rushes north to New York. The day after you die, people still sip coffee in fast food joints as a thunderstorm gathers in the sky, newspaper headlines proclaim great events overseas, stupidity and corruption at home, suffering everywhere. In the video game arcade, someone sets a new high score for Tetris.

House at the edge of the forest. Two swans amid the geese by the small lake – could they be anything but domestic? One can hear the freeway here, but that sense of mass urgency feels wildly out of place. High above the canopy, a deep-throated, curling birdsong I've never heard before.

Catbird hops onto the grass. Carrying one side of the sofabed, he steps backwards through the moving van's side door, foot missing the long metal ramp, so that he falls from the side of the truck, the large couch crashing down in the dark vehicle, twisting as he drops to catch himself so that he hits the pavement with his hands out, right wrist shattering on contact. Woodpecker taps out a message.

In the park, volunteer fire department uses the toddlers' climbing structure to practice blindfold maneuvers. Wind in all these trees *breathes.* What bird answers the call of my alarm clock?

Wooden children's climbing structure narrativized as a sailing ship, a Cessna, a train. In this scene the monkey has become an elephant and carries the pretend prince through the narrow streets of the city. Most of the volunteer fire crew are in their early 20s and stand around holding their heavy rubberized jackets, baggy pants held by red suspenders, passing a single pack of cigarettes between them as they watch the demonstration, fireman blindfolded, face mask covered by aluminum foil, crawling through the play structure, following the yellow rope headfirst down the slide.

Dinosaurs strewn across the vast plain of an attic rug. Fireflies glitter in the back yard, half moon making its way over the tops of these trees. Mall lot in which people don't appear to lock their cars. The beautiful dentist half jogs, is half dragged by her large dog, through the forest.

Angles vs. shadows in an attic room. Bookcase full of children's toys, overseen by a bespectacled Mr. Potato Head in a green baseball cap. Every asset management program is built either from the procurement database out or from an inventory function up. Horizontalizing that work force made each member expendable. Angels and shadows.

XXIV

She demos the grill by serving "tater tots," hot dogs, sausage, in front of the hardware store on a Saturday from 10 until 2. Book's spine is its sole moving part. When this you hear, so much to fear. In the dream, bobcats and cougars have multiplied and are killing the pets of North Berkeley. Squirrel gallops over the roof of this house.

A quirk of morning. A quark of meaning. Estimate the train's size just by the rumble of wheels over the tracks. Mom, she says, spent last summer in Siberia, "telling people about Jesus." Late at night, by a light installed over the garage door, they play Ping-Pong in the yard, variable metronome. At the station, a woman maybe 40 with the hard, drawn look about her of too many years of drugs or alcohol, cigarette almost absent-mindedly lodged between her fingers, bends down to speak gently with her beautiful, six-year-old daughter.

Missiles, missives. Take a message (whomp). If you have a touch tone phone, press one now (VRU with FRU). A walk in the woods: at this point in the valley, the creek is exposed so that each driveway requires a bridge (somewhere up high in the trees, a dog is barking). The western idea about money. I hear the cardinal before I see it. Each toy truck offers its own theory of representation. Voice response unit, field replaceable unit. Then it grows quiet and dawn arrives.

Rabbits become common, as does the American flag as a porch ornament. The tiger in the dale, the tiger in the dale. Jays in the trees mark distance (in the background, one barely hears the steady rumble of a train). Old man's features blurred by years of drink. What did I think?

"If you've already got a mouse pad," she says, "this makes a terrific jar opener."

Disposable phone. The absence of mail. Blue jay vs. the mockingbird's parody. Western name on his Social Security Card vs. pure Korean on his passport, a lengthy delay at the Pennsylvania Department of Transportation. The car, having sat in the humid heat all morning. Under the tall tulip poplar. Where yesterday I saw a rabbit successfully cross 252, today a wolverine, fatter than I would have imagined, by the side of the road.

Old cardboard wardrobe. Catbird's call, sort of a yowl. Basket of bears. Biscuit of butter. Whistle in the cardinal's call. A bench at the end of the cul-de-sac under tall trees. Still life (still as the verb). Robin pauses, surveys his lawn.

XXV

In the dream, as a hobby I go downtown to a department store to catch thieves when a great fire breaks out during which one of the fire fighters' cranes starts to collapse, descending several floors before a second cherry picker can catch it and hold it steady while the rescuers grab hold of the unconscious man inside, at which point the whole downtown begins to break up, floating out to sea or into the air, cloudlike, except that all of this occurs in reverse order.

Flag as large as the house itself. Smell of barbecue all down the block. In the back yard, children are being pirates. In the tree I see a tufted titmouse. Up close, the cop's broad-brimmed hat is made of felt. Coming out of the woods, the heat of the day becomes immediately evident. Train station parking lot on the weekend, not entirely empty.

Bugbite under the watchband. Anaesthetized, the eye does not blink as the tweezers enter to pick the small metallic particle off of its surface. Memories of wandering blind through Frankfort. In the seat next to me, the old nun, Sister Paul, starts to snore. What begins as a "free store," hippie clothing exchange, just off the Penn campus, grows in 25 years into two national franchise retail organizations. Echo of Dylan in the ear (King James Latinization).

Hotdog in an airport cafe: I jostle with my tray through the tight-packed tables searching for a place to sit. Faux first class. Sitting, the angular blonde woman is beautiful, but there is, when she stands, stretches, and walks away, something deeply defeated, even hard, in that angular gate. Man in the middle of an empty plaza talking into a cellular telephone. Commas as shadows soften the text. With men as well as women over the age, say, of 40, one can imagine how they must have looked ten, twenty years ago. First freckles start to emerge on a little boy's face.

Sun sets blood red behind the Pru. What at first look like cooling towers for an unfinished nuclear power plant (right in Boston harbor?) turn out to be tanks filled with shit-eating algae. More small islands than I'd've imagined. My name is Andy and I'll be your singing waiter tonight. Cormorants in pairs speed low over the water. In the distance, the lights of fireboats twinkle in the near dark, surrounding tall flames from an object whose form has been lost in the blaze.

Pastel jeep security vehicle slowly circles the empty plaza. From here we can look down on the roofs of Beacon Hill – up to the left a crew of roofers moving slowly in the heat (their buckets so hot the air above them shimmers), while down here, fronting Cambridge Street, a young blonde woman with very pale skin sunbathes, in one hand a small, bright yellow radio/cassette player. I punch the access code to MCI, then the tie-line, then my office direct line followed by a PIN code, which gets me to the phone mail voice prompt that instructs me first to dial in my own extension followed by a six-digit numeric "password" before offering me a choice: listening to my own messages, record a new message, change the phone mail features, or change my personal options. In the restaurant, a woman stares at me intently, then looks down when I return her look with a smile (she leaves before I do, never coming over to say hello).

In the war room, we storyboard the presentation first on a flip chart, page after page stuck to the windows and walls, while one of the seven transcribes it all into a laptop, humor and pressure gradually becoming indistinguishable, wadded-up paper and the caps of felt-tip markers tossed at the makers of bad suggestions. The rain is filtered by the trees. I drive home in the dark by sheer memory. The support rep evaluates the caller's competence by means of description of the alleged problem.

XXVI

The breeze sucks the shade into the window's screen.

A wheeze in the garbage truck's brakes. Red and blue birds flash in the trees. Fire flies flicker.

Lightning laces the sky. Error message. Real water boiling on a toy stove. Anxious to start the double play too quickly, he closes the glove before the ball is in it. Full moon smeared behind the scrim of cloud.

Lilies shutting at dusk.

The dream gauged by depth and completeness.

The Wawa brutalizes the ice cream.

Roar of the crickets all through the night.

XXVII

Driving through completely unfamiliar streets, realizing this will be your home. Tee ball power drive. Woodpecker's rapid beat. Humidity of a different planet. Theory of a turnpike. At the train station, the suburban poor become visible. Across the street, Cowboy's Tattoo Ranch.

Raising the seven-foot bookcase high, angling it around the banister at the turn of the stairs. Hummingbird's egg, the appearance of a white jelly bean. Red-tail hawk turns, high over Perkiomen Creek.

Finches at the thistle sock, doe at the edge of the highway. YTD revenue for embedded systems. Realtor puts a plastic flag on each lawn for Independence Day. Lawn lights. Big rigs in a row at the service plaza. Old lamp on a modern table, flowers etched in a base of glass.

Light switch missing its face plate, having to put towels down by the shower just to turn the water on. One cannot give an example of hapax without canceling the effect. Thrashing as a surrogate for emotion. Roofed-in porch perfect for a barbecue in the rain (groundhogs in the grass, alas).

Tic talk. The discipline of bottom feeders. Identify three routes between points A and B; list advantages and disadvantages of each. Young boy with a fever. Scrollin' back to my same old used-to-be.

These are the sounds of science (thunderstorms under glass, alas), an echo in the poem. "Eck!" screams the crowd, the famed reliever's wavy hair flowing to his shoulders as he stares in at the next hitter, a nearly crippled limping Kirk Gibson. Waves batter the sea wall, full moon punctuation.

Sunlight flashes off the windshield of a car passing on the road through the trees, lone evidence of limit to this forest. "I can smell weekend from here," he says, 8:00 AM Friday morning. They wait for cars to get caught by the red light in the left turn lane, then spread out with buckets and old rags washing their windows rapidly, knowing just how long they have to coax a tip from each involuntary customer. Rapidly, the mountain of strips of bacon disappear from the plate in the center of the table.

XXVIII

Squirrel at the thistle sock, fat and gray. White bearded affable therapist next door was an RCP militant in the sixties. Static growl of a modem.

Uncorrected proof. Riding the train backwards. To which, for your entire library, now add the costs of hauling and shipping. Moon follows, long walk at dusk. A two-boy basket.

I step into the humid air. What did you know and when did you know it? Moon yellow foretelling rain. The squirrel growls. First sun smeared across the morning sky.

Chooses "Alfred" when he comes to the US to attend college, that the Anglos won't struggle with a Korean name. Old Giants media guide, filled with bios of prospects who never made a dent. Smell of over-ripe bananas the minute you enter the room.

Beyond the great mansion, five outdoor swimming pools overlooking tennis courts and soccer fields rimmed by running tracks. Each strip mall proposed as a theory of how to live. Small boys playing soccer with a volley ball. Vast lawn aglitter with lightning bugs. We stalk them.

Our love of the word *poop.* In the glass, ice melts, leaving beads of water around its outer surface. A train in the forest (how did it get there?). Moth's imprint on the window screen.

The air hot and thick as syrup, blue jays listless in the trees. First sun reflected off the top branches before you see the sun itself. Achilles tendon taut, almost brittle, each step as you rise the stairs. A house of deep-colored walls, burgundy and pink, through which to reach the large yard. Turning the corner in the corridor we almost bump and step back, excuse ourselves and walk on, small dance of the break-up of intimate space.

XXIX

Lightning rolling, popping, snapping all across the sky (the whole forest in silhouette, down to the most infinite twig), then rain, although not as much as I would have expected, after which the hot spell is broken, no electricity anywhere for miles, people emerging slowly from their houses once the sun rises, the beauty of a gray dawn.

Behind this bale of hay, the tiniest full grown horse in the world, so small that a cup of water and a handful of hay is a mighty big meal for Tiny Tim. Merry-go-round balanced precariously over the fairground mud. Tattoo on the back of her neck forms a pyramid of letters, all san serif and upper case, but she won't hold still so I can read them. Font catalog.

First the lightning, then the rain. Last demo filing cabinet missing handles, one drawer locked with no key in sight. I walk out of the building and my glasses steam instantly at the difference in heat and humidity.

The cup is a funnel inverted over a base of blue clay, the handle added later, rather large, like an ear out of proportion to its head. Ice melts quickly, leaving only a smear of bubbles on the surface of its watery residue. I'm calling in my role as the difficult client. In the bank, a bowl of lollipops by each teller's window (there is only one teller). First silhouette of the trees, predawn sky to the east. Lettuce falls from the corned beef sandwich.

The voice that was late within us. In such weather, one can watch bananas ripen in real time. Day lilies unfurl, the sky brightens before the sun arrives, almost pink through the tall poplars. Black dog wanders in the large yard in the far end of which a crow has just settled.

In the forest, a small wood-frame house, burnt to the ground, no sign of people anywhere. He opens the palm of his hand to reveal a lightning bug, which rises slowly in the night air before it shines. Fire truck rides for a buck, Ferris wheel lights the sky, giant mechanical swing in the form of an Egyptian boat.

In the forest, voices, laughing. Just how leathery the flesh of my own neck has become. As that man strides purposefully towards him, I saw this fellow reach for something under his jacket tucked right into his pants at the small of his back and think *gun.* My pager set to vibrate. Soft first light of sun.

XXX

The aggression of toddlers or of squirrels. Theory of naming evident when we call a black-capped chickadee a bird that more accurately appears to wear a white mask. I carry a sleeping boy up the stairs and to his bed.

The word on the net is that you are in France. A large one-story pomo building on an even larger lot turns out to be a hair salon (land use away from the city). How each McDonalds is most apt to differ from one another lies in whatever special accommodation is made for the play of toddlers. Aware of the dewpoint nearing eighty degrees.

Irked at Adam's meddling, Hayley set a wedding date with Abe, then later went to the beach with Mateo. After defending Kirk to Scott, Sam stunned Kirk by insisting that they start their honeymoon right away. Meanwhile, Nikkie tried to get Amy to show interest in Nick, and then tried to get Nick to show interest in Susan. Luke explained AIDS to Lucky.

On the couch, starting to watch a video (Gerard Depardieu as Cyrano leaps and rants about the stage), I virtually swoon into a deep sleep, to dream of a great wall of candy, sugar-coated drops of licorice, white, pink, black. Simple male transfer protocol. Three kinds of woodpeckers about these trees. Atmosphere is a broth.

Old town graveyard after dark, the grass too high, lit only by lights from the nearby church parking lot. A bowl of blueberry frozen yogurt. Large sore on the roof of my mouth. The sweltering sky.

Hourglass frozen against the screen. First inverted whistle of a cardinal in the poplar. T3 trunk line upgrade rollout – scan that! Differentiate in a boy's mind gravity from magnetism from simple suction. Small girl skating down the steepest of hills.

An icon for poetry (winged hearse). Woodpecker walks up the trunk of tree. Light mottled on the large leaf. Squirrel growls.

XXXI

Morning paper bounces end over end across the front yard. Birds loud at dawn, then quiet as day settles in.

Gradually a pattern starts to emerge – today it's a series of concentric circles – but it's always only the middle game, the transition between known beginning and understood end, and soon the squares dwindle down and the lawn is cut.

The crickets as loud and constant as an ocean, but generally invisible to the casual eye so that I'm startled when one lands here upon the page – small alien intelligence – then just as quickly leaps away.

Evening light under the trees, heads tilted back, necks stretched, attempting to see what, high over the canopy of pine and poplar, sounds like a biplane.

Live bird in the collage. Pace of the automatic redial. Self-described total-immersion Loy fanatic. Crow caws in the dark. Impact of serial number on warranty labor reimbursement entitlement.

Morning bowel: long loop, very nearly a massive rope, lies coiled at the bottom of the bowl.

What do your sales reps use? In the dream, every job I've ever held is commingled, an inner city highrise in a brick town that never was, an apartment of seven or eight layers, rather like an urban treehouse, but I need to get to the airport, so I'm frantic, trying to recall where I've scattered my bags and clothes. The first sound of thunder before the clouds appear.

XXXII

To look up at the impossible brightness would be fatal, tall cloud full of human ash, the city itself missing, to be defined forever by this absence, instance. Undelete function enabled. Nineteen years later, a boy arrives at a demonstration. Don't Laos me up.

Hilltop forest stripped, winding private road arrives at an 'S' shaped development of new construction (three models: Adelaide, Bristol, Chaucer), through the mud into a shell of board and sheet rock, cedar shake shingles, 65 surface choices for cabinets (I look up in the closet right through the attic to the sky). Red tail hawk threads the air.

This is what makes a rabbit hop. I shut my eyes and the dream (cartoon samurai) continues. Tea too hot to sip. An elephant king and a mouse, both made of cloth, equal in size. Tractor fed, the old dot matrix looks robust and healthy.

Embodied poetics would be a more intriguing proposition. This paragraph is called the Sicilian Defense. In the dream the reading is a pretext for a party, the party a pretext for a seduction.

Radar reveals T-storms in green. Suitcase hangs by a strap from a doorway, an effigy. Constant growl of the crickets. Instant in which the engine turns over. When, in the corridor, he says to her, "You model, don't you?" her reactions change totally, vague flirtatiousness replace by tone composed in equal parts of fear and anger, "Who told you? How do you know?"

Chem lit vs. fem lit. Channel surf the AM dial west of Dallas. Poetics of the open mike: categories for people who write but don't read. The curtains blow tho the window's shut. Give you the world every 30 minutes. Later, this will all be handwriting, then print. A flicker, in what should be an empty glade. Roadkill here is different.

Held by its feet upside down, the turkey will twist its neck to keep its head upright. Roadside stands sell old gas station signage, decommissioned pumps perfect to decorate a tavern or gift shop. Lone drivers heading south, route I-35, Fort Worth just a blur in the rear view mirror. Bird feeder hangs from the tree.

XXXIII

Down Mt. Carmel where, in an almost barn-like church, the Davidians still meet, into a town of strip malls and no center, into an air-conditioned and surprisingly full-featured Kinko's – even a video conferencing room off to one side – to collect cartons of fliers for door-to-door distribution.

At dawn, this vast parking lot (which is in fact three large lots – one for the hotel, one for the mall, one for the East Memphis U-P Bank Tower – loosely connected) starts to fill. An hour's drive to Oxford, Mississippi, or just over the river to Arkansas. If that's east, I must be facing south (determination by the direction of shadow).

In the dream, technology works like this. The blue of the pool is an effect of tile, not color. The familiar style of the waitress mocks intimacy. Lone gas pump in front of the store no longer functions, but remains as a sign. Every second vehicle is a truck. The parts cage is in fact 15,000 square feet and contains $12,000,000 in undepreciated stock. Just five feet tall, a perfect imitation of Elvis.

Dr. and Mrs. Squishy Pillow. Just a rough crater where the tooth had been. At night, the cavernous quality of the downtown train station becomes apparent, the internal shops closing up one by one, the chairs in the food court overturned atop the round metal tables (what surprises me in retrospect are the absence of the homeless). The lessons we learned were not the ones they thought they taught.

Arise ash, to burn again. Flicker, flight, last June bug of the season. The tea bag heavy with water. I have no other daughter. Zyxt, zed: how does a poem come to a head?

Slackers' backers, hackers' crackers. The night sucks light from the street lamp, until it can barely cast shadows past objects. The great wall of crickets and cicadas, like living next to a water fall. Cardinal and goldfinch illumine the bush.

Attic light. Nine-square window. A slice of plastic bread for the iguana puppet. Don't chew on the rubber duck. Inverted V of the ceiling. Sun filtered through the gauze curtains. Outside, ducks and cardinals and somewhere a goose, a crow. A breeze, barely perceptible, animates the forest.

XXXIV

Sharp morning: nuthatch bounces up the trunk of the poplar. Small town ER Saturday night: nurses, techs, orderlies and aides mill around the command station with little to do. At the all-night supermarket, we go through the express lane with dozens of items – it's the only one open.

A market of one. The market of wonder. Rts wear a uniform of a deeper blue than nurse's aides. (Thirty years ago today, death of Jack Spicer. Thirty years ago today, death of my father.) Silent radio on cafeteria wall. Outside, against the brick facade, a surgeon is smoking.

Hawaiian banana. That lost look in the eyes of anyone in a hospital who is not there as a worker. Imagine Olson as your "friend." Objects in text appear closer than they are. Each paragraph its own dialog box, each word. Book as a secret discussion group. Listserv or majordomo, which one?

The song of a train rolling gently through the woods. Vial of abuterol sulphate poured into the cup of the nebulizer. A third layer of sound, equally insistent, constant: crickets and cicadas. The bell blasts loudly to sound the alarm. On the radio, only static (the scanner cycles the dial over and over before catching something faint and garbled). In Texas, *yes!* – prosody of baptist revelation.

An exhaustion deeper than meaning, not affected by sleep. When he goes to stop the pipe from leaking, it explodes. Paramedic van (lemon yellow) struggling through Raffi traffic hell. A rolling landscape absent hills or mountains. Let's do launch.

A round of crickets playing back. The sound of rockets taking off. Admit the article to soften the foot. An hour after the charlie horse, the knot in the calf is still taut. Teach to each, reach.

I stand and watch my boys asleep until the room grows so still I can hear them breathing. By the light, I peg the hour at around 6:30 (it's 6:43). Once in the attic, I turn the light on the stairs off so as not to be disturbed. Heat wave's over (shutting windows for the first time in seven weeks). What then?

XXXV

Spine understood as a chain or puzzle. Machine of the hand, levers of the foot. Slowly, deeply I penetrate you with my tongue, your back arched, writhing, thighs clamped tight about my head until you groan. Wearing glasses in the dark.

Cottonhead, fogmind. Hotel easy chair never actually comfortable to sit in. Apricot odor to the shampoo. Factory direct to you. In airports, people often appear disheveled, distracted, anxious, rushed, which in some women removes a protective veil, revealing a previously hidden intensely erotic core, the human animal as such.

Trading floppies at 30,000 feet. In twenty years (a distance shorter than the one from this sentence back to "Revolving door"), the computing power of a single chip will be equal to. . . . Twixt Raleigh and Durham come Cary and Morrisville. Distinguish the midget from the dwarf. Speaking sign language to an infant requires it to read (eyes aglow with recognition, a big grin as it runs to Mommy's arms).

Our go-to-market strategy with this paragraph has a minimum of sign-offs. I have a chart on that. Distinguish revision from the simple bug fix. Riding the tip of his pen, Betty Boop calls her creator "Uncle Max." On the tip of my pen, you say, "Be gentle."

Crossing the executive mall lot late at night (beyond those hedges a freeway), the sky clear but moonless, only five cars remaining (two for security, how many for janitorial?), I watch my shadow contract and then stretch as I pass under the lone lamp, ignoring now the lanes and parallel strips that in the day would fill this space with several hundred cars.

Punk/thrash "classics" now on oldies "easy listening" FM site: "So I got into camouflage." I'm walking downhill across the campus away from the ocean (hang gliders dot the sky). Here, no one worries that freeways will collapse in an earthquake. Kite flying across the battlefield. I hold your head still when I come. Refrain: "Because of system-wide technical difficulties, users attempting to connect to NetCruiser accounts will experience user name password errors."

First the news. Shadows of leaves bounce over other leaves (sun filters all the way to the bark of the tree). Tabloid bio. Paparazzi catching stretch marks on Lady Di's thighs. Window edits outdoors. Drab female cardinal with brilliant yellow beak.

XXXVI

On his desk, the *Book of Psalms and New Testament*, printed in Korean, each line carefully highlighted with a different color ink. A long room (ceiling slanted) with windows at either end so that light passes through as physical as a liquid.

The meaning of medicine. Three boys fishing by a small dam, right by the polluted water sign. Blue thread enters the skull under the hair line, pulling the red wound shut.

Dream states of waking. Sun in the curtain, caught in the web of its gauze. An erotics of flossing, an aerobics. Something in the woods is crunching branches. Jay and its echo.

"Jesse . . . stole . . . my . . . space," each word emphasized to underscore the outrage. Poolside before dawn, dozens of sparrows find something to peck at in the driveway. Town's water tower, a gigantic pale blue-green lollipop alongside these houses.

Articles fix focus. Dragonflies hover over the still water, magnificent, golden, imperial airships in search of the wayward mosquito. Beachtown seniors gather under the shade trees in the park. In the Catholic church, two men, obviously brothers in their mid-80s, sit silently side by side, while up front off in one alcove women gather before the red bank of glowing candles.

Sleeping in the middle. In the dream, the building and the job are identical, a huge hollowed-out old block (abandoned warehouse? apartments?), so that I'm surprised to discover this door on the top floor leads to the street.

Bitterns wander through the bog. Lighthouse is the one object along this long flat coast with any definition. Small blue flowers amid all that green. Swan swamp. Small boy crouches, feeding blades of grass to an appreciative rabbit.

XXXVII

As the pop foul descends from the heavens into the crowd, hands and gloves shoot skyward, bodies thrusting themselves up, straining, grasping, parody of a scene on Iwo Jima, while below others cringe & cower, popcorn, beers, sodas spilling in all directions, the sculptural effect complete (at least half of the participants appear to have their eyes shut), a phenomenon that repeats in smaller and less hysterical numbers again and again as the loose ball bounces untouched from section to section until a boy with an oversized blue glove smothers it against his chest.

Windsurfers on a small island lake struggle to stay upright. Just far enough from the city to sense the ambivalence between suburban and rural (in a generation this will pass). Gargantuan houses on miniature lots ("cathedral ceilings in the foyer"), a value for our time.

Vial of glitter spilled on the rug. The man who could read data by its tone as static. The light arrives not only later but more muted (filtered through a scrim of cloud too thin to see).

The roar of crickets softens (one hasn't seen a lightning bug for months). A new sound, that of wind in the trees, the leaves brittle. People watching in a mall lot, an anthology of body parts (there is no normal physique). As we drive through the underpass, static overwhelms the radio.

A euphoria to sleeplessness (the dream continues). So poverty, invisibilized, is reduced to a topic on the radio (at the mall, a man with tardive dyskinesia). Body parts strewn of the late Mr. Potato Head.

Woodpecker hops along its branch, not pecking, just chirping its call. Loss analysis. A little customer sat. This text has been modified to fit your television screen. If this had been a real test. I can hear the jay but cannot see it.

The merchant of sunglasses operates from a card table across from the university entrance. Salad composed of yellow fin tuna and jumbo shrimp chopped to indistinguishable bits. Bright sun just beyond the shadows of this parking structure.

XXXVIII

for Linh Dinh

In the land of the elephants, death transforms the world: a hunter shoots the mother of young Babar, sending him into exile in, of all places, France where he learns the very social skills (reading, clothing, driving) that he will someday use to recast his native land, the perfect comprador; meanwhile the old king eats a poisonous mushroom, turns green and dies, throwing the future of the elephant kingdom into doubt.

Telephone tag. Quantum dot. The young leader returns to unite his people and drive out the foreign invaders, after which the largest city is renamed for his nomme de guerre, Ho Chi Minh. The elephants rejoice.

The light at the window. The night at the window. Fine layer of toothpaste has formed a crust on the bathroom faucet. To invent history versus choosing merely to rewrite it. The wounded animal stage of life. An Old Lady whom, your entire life, you will call by no other name.

Process map: to build a two-drawer filing cabinet. Underneath the entire jungle, an intricate web of tunnels. He discovers his cousins Celeste and Arthur naked on the streets of Paris. Just the sort of family you would expect from one orphaned by two sets of parents before his thirteenth birthday. Name the last son "Lucky."

Skill set. Subsidiary rights. I find an empty ballroom between luncheon and cocktails and set up the laptop and go. Do you distinguish those editions in which the text is in the thick-lined script of the original and those where it is not? The Republic of Monkeys, for example, is governed by a benevolent military dictator with the Indochinese name of General Huc.

It's an ill wind that blows nobody. Edited inside the pen. An alarm rings in a dark room. Rhinos are perceived as full of bluster but capable of descent into murder, torture, slavery over the slightest prank. My stomach howls like a distant coyote. Giant whirligig beetle actually small on the leaf.

Rising after a long sleep, the terrible weight of the body causes the roughly 26 bones of each foot to settle, snapping and popping as they shift into place. Any single story house is more expensive to build, requiring as it does a maximum of foundation per square foot of living space. Ranch style flows white over the pale leaves of old lettuce. Traffic lights blinking signal a malfunction.

XXXIX

Optical dimultiplexer divides data packets via nonlinear loop mirror: minimize connotations per word. To ride a giant seahorse is to render the physical world by desire.

Incorporate your weekend home as a nonprofit. Catfood for catfish (they swarm to the surface, competing for each bite). Small, red berry clusters of Jack-in-the-pulpit line the walk.

Somewhere – on television – one sees daylight. A full night of holding these quilts aloft over my body, a night of sheer effort. FedEx it. Modem moans when you shut it off.

Curb appeal. I stand under the awning, arms akimbo, in the rain but not of it. The blue route. Geese against the gray sky. Fed exit.

Op cit. I.e. AI asap. Sausages packaged in groups of three (requiring the family of four to buy two). Intelligence demands the balance of contradictions: to know that St. George slew dragons and that dragons did not exist. Expect a miracle. First dim silhouette of the trees foretells dawn.

So the book of numbers turns out to be a record of baseball pitching and playing statistics. Even after dark, the perfect weather keeps us outdoors. If it does not fit, you must acquit.

Giant spider intends a solid object. The pen crackles with electricity, blue sparks arc from tip of each letter as it emerges (burnt smell of the word itself). Iron butterfly. Sweep.

XL

In the forest mist, first dawn light is suspended, diffused, shadowless, softened: projective correlative. A doe pauses in the cross hairs. The light changes and the window washers of Houston Street assault cars halted in the other direction.

To dream of television is to complete a circle. Database by design. The narrative structure of a house. Average quota of PIN numbers per capita. Width of the spine.

Under the aesthetic (the midwest), the past (an image of the body) struggles to accommodate outlyers: a statistical sun leverages dawn. I pluck on the strings of this keyboard.

Great wall of crickets, even in the dark and in autumn (one attempts to hear within this a particular cricket, or to separate the crickets from the cicadas, and is barely able to do so). Trade rag. Valid search. Each sentence understood as a dialog box. Helicopter aerial p.o.v.

Articulate space, as when, say, in the dark the blue-eyed weimaraner across the road starts to bark, then the dog two doors down, the another and another, until the woods are loud and full of barking, yelping, howling animals, a wave that just as quickly subsides, returning us all to the steady background music of the crickets and the rain.

The wind in all directions. Sad, hollow-eyed emaciated man standing in the men's room begging quarters. The appetizer outshines the entrée. More black than red, the lipstick creates a sort of permanent pout. Great eight-foot-high weeds between the abandoned buildings out by the railyards, memory of an earlier ecological formation.

Talking animal puppets, philosophers and kings, in a realm of primary colors, pause to attend to a flourish of trumpets, off screen. Wind, high in these branches, almost visible. Through the walls (paper thin), the lives of others.

XLI

First tea out of the spout always is the most pale. As the leaves thin out, old stone chimney comes into view. Ducks, quick in the air, shift direction.

Carny in a township park where, 218 years earlier, men died by the dozens in combat. Balloons tied to a mailbox signal the event. In the lives of Mariner fans, the site of Junior Griffey rounding second, then third, heading to the plate, shines forever. Glass that, in the light, reveals three layers and a pattern of shatter to each. Hereditary drummer.

Yonder. One feels the breath of the heat rising from the vent. Mirror site. Body of large moth (white, speckled) dead on the rough hard wood boards of the closet floor. Secretary on her lunch hour retreats to the minuscule snackroom alcove, studying for the LSAT. As if on its own, the fax machine starts up.

Two deer dead along this same strip of road within twenty-four hours: another index of drought. Inner-city fast food joint: do I really want to use the men's room? Catty corner from the gay rights demo (rainbow-flagged podium, sing-in desks for media and speakers alike), a cluster of television camera jockeys wait outside the courtroom door for the mob lawyers to usher their client out. In the poplar, the remaining leaves rattle in the breeze.

A dream so complex I want to take notes. After the third day, the doe's carcass finally disappears. Downstairs, the small whine of a door's hinge. Blood yoke sun barely visible through the trees.

Fire regime: the tongue plays obsessively with the hollow where the tooth was. The center city is a grid into which a large circle and, a few blocks away, an even larger City Hall, have been inserted as obstructions. The vast mall lot shimmering with autumn heat.

At dusk, those driving toward the sun are far less apt to have their lights on than those driving away. A boy in the image of a lady bug is carried asleep upstairs. Parental authority at the bottom of the ocean. A talking duck is not true.

XLII

First dot, best dot.

Paste flowers from the tube to the brush. Out the window, across the river, the lights of Algiers, Louisiana. A woman's face changes in the midst of sex, revealing a truer identity.

Tourists will walk down the same street differently from the locals. A must-have volume for your management bookshelf. Dixieland jazz band in the courtyard of the mall. Them all. First light over the still gulf.

She glides slowly, almost silently through the city streets on her bicycle, one hand on the handlebar, the other resting on her leg.

The captain and attendants cluster by the door to the cockpit, saying goodbye to each passenger. Men and women wait by the door to the restrooms for their companions to return.

Involuntary grip of the muscle right behind the left shoulder blade. "Change my diaper," a small voice says.

Elongated enunciation of children's cartoons. Driving through the narrow streets of a night club district in pouring rain, attempting in vain to locate a tavern called the Post Office. Gradually the bag of blue ice allows me to move my left shoulder, though an envelope feels as heavy as a refrigerator. Blades sweep away the waves of rain.

XLIII

The trainer leads the gigantic tiger right into our place of business, letting him or her settle down by the copiers before we approach, one at a time, to pet the huge beast, which looks at us with eyes that, if human, would be full of longing, its fur thick, luxuriant, almost surprising, until we are so engrossed in this process, taking turns over and over, petting a little more vigorously each time, that we do not realize that the trainer has stepped away and disappeared.

Customerize, says Unisys, registered verb. Tangibilize. One day, almost overnight, your father joins "the frail elderly." The leaves now everywhere, red, brown, yellow.

At night the light in the forest depends entirely on the city's illumination reflected off these clouds. On the top floor of the office tower, a swarm of ladybugs assaults the impenetrable, never-open windows.

Uninterruptible power supply. Bones of the hand operate complexly just to grasp this pen. The Anti-EXE virus lurks in a floppy's boot record and converts the host computers read command to a write action, eventually crashing the infected site.

Pre-qual. Why dawdle? A light in the kitchen will illumine the whole backyard. I lie in the dark imagining that I know what time it is (imagining time as fixed, objective). Brick is an edited mountain.

The past emerges vast enough to swallow any present. Mouse Club Reunion. Electronic handshake. Surprise in every Happy Meal. Brand managers, unite!

Stack of brown plastic trays gathers atop the receptacle (mock wood finish) that contains trashcans within, by the door to the parking lot. Wand modulates rain's rhythm. Picnic at dusk in a country park: later we will turn our headlights on in order to collect our stuff. Encampment of street people under the bridge: closer to cave men than we care to admit.

XLIV

Spider scampers across the windshield – how far from its home have we traveled? One tree, ahead of all the others, has turned a brilliant orange.

Small town Halloween parade confined to a single block (my eyes search in vain for any person of color, although they compose 20 percent of the borough population). Beyond the woods, a large sloping field. Basement weight room of a cop's house: posters of Harleys, power lifters, the heroes and heroines of the World Wrestling Federation. Pizza parlor offers no hot drinks, not even coffee.

Gradually the poem begins to circle itself. The street lamp becomes visible as leaves drop away, a pale light that one can almost see without feeling. Amortize each word over the next 30 years. Beyond the parking lot, a narrow strip of trees is the only buffer there is from the highway.

Across the small cemetery, an old Quaker meeting house, the rear of which is used for a pre-school. Vast as the mall lot may be, the steady rain gives one a sense of enclosure, containment.

Mindshare. A sense of the woods becoming vertical as these trees lose their leaves. A dark day, mid-afternoon, this room's light feels especially intense.

Power down. Each room in this old house has not only its own acoustics, but its own characteristic baseline hum, these sounds and tones that, absent all else, audibilize the edge of silence.

Tune a brook by moving stones.

XLV

Hospital bed moved into the sun room, his moments of rising the stairs to the second floor of his own house are numbered (but that's where the bathroom is). Forest illuminated by moonlight.

The weekend all the leaves fall. Empty house as an index of possibility. Out by the private airport, Sunday at dusk, all the weekend fliers heading in. Kneeling, you run your finger along the moist sill of the window.

A condition of light on a narrow street near the campus late in the afternoon triggers an emotion as if it were a memory. I stand here reading aloud to you, wondering at your reaction, able only to interpret the sounds of bodies shifting in these chairs.

Walking around with a post-it stuck to the bottom of my shoe. Crossing the church parking lot in the rain, I enter the brightly lit hall, walls an almost butterscotch brown, brown linoleum floors, where, behind a row of three long tables, a row of seniors serve as local election commissioners. Red light reflected on the rain-slicked road.

Two quilt night. Weight of my trousers, pockets full of keys, wallet, coins, handkerchief, security badge for work, beeper on my belt. The "r" in "Goethe."

Obsessing over whether or not to counter the seller's counter offer, and how, I rise and climb the carpeted stairs to the unheated attic study. An image of Deleuze in flight of Poulantzas – the philosophers are falling.

At the mall: a new anchor tenant means a new idea. I can hear the fax machine as it auto-redials. Broken spider web dangles from the lampshade.

XLVI

A lost pen extracts an emotional cost, a crust through which one must push this cheapened, impossible substitute.

The outside of the building – in the shape of a lion – is constructed in an industrial vinyl and sounds hollow when you rap it with your knuckles (the high hotel walls are tinted green and illumined further by green floodlights, suggesting the Emerald City).

At dawn (no clocks or even windows in the casino), the slots are more or less quiet, but a crowd still around the craps table (off in one corner, I spy an old woman in bathrobe and slippers playing the nickel slots).

In the distance, the desert has been reduced to an effect. She speaks and in her voice I hear the husky tones of years of tobacco and alcohol and suddenly realize how this young face has been structured and preserved through makeup that now looks too thick to be trusted.

Sparse beauty of the desert visible only at a distance (thick belt of smog smears the base of the mountains, their peaks utterly clear, defined in the cloudless sky). Small wizened Mestizo in a baseball cap (so and grainy the logo's impossible to discern) hands me a pamphlet full of color photos offering "X-otic in-room entertainment." Duck and goat cheese quesadilla. On the elevator, I realize this young woman in the short skirt isn't wearing panties.

In Detroit there is snow and there is waiting, there is waiting at the gate and there is waiting, there is waiting on the tarmac and there is waiting, there is a woman on a gurney, having deplaned and she is waiting, the cabin lights dimmed for take-off and we are waiting.

The terrain is different, the forest stripped of leaves, the sky gray, houses visible I'd not seen before. Blister on my lower lip, old familiar.

XLVII

Backslash. The light barely glimmers through the old bedspread curtain. Mr Cake and Mr Snake. Moss on a rooftop makes the footing dangerous. Leafless, the forest holds the gray-green tone of the trees' bark.

Sky in which the clouds are so omnipresent as to be invisible (a vast dull grayness). At the McDonald's, the "bus boy" is a woman who must be 70. Initializing modem. The sidewalk is an afterthought, little more than a buffer from the rush of Sunday traffic, one parking lot melting into another. World in which John Lennon never grows old.

Children in a circle on the floor of a Quaker meeting house, drums, tambourines, triangles, blocks and bells in hand. Insert disk 2. A child recites the alphabet so that you can hear the alphabet.

A man recalls first learning to drink from a cup. Shoe with Velcro straps. I recall the angle of that hill as though it were a condition of heaven. Last week's paper cut become this week's rough-edged scar.

A man is digging in the woods, but whether to find or hide something I cannot tell. Crowded mall interior seen in slow motion: you pan slowly over each person's expression, reading it as if it were a narrative (an old woman who is still extraordinarily beautiful and knows it, a teenage boy very nervous next to what may be a very new girlfriend, a man with a child of a different race, a woman who can't be more than 20 with two toddlers.)

Are you Egon? In the dream, I walk through decades as easily as rooms. to convey the point, shape the broccoli into a pyramid. Trifocals partition sight. In the middle of the night, atop the bed you stood over me and removed your clothing, piece by piece. He can't stop talking because his mind is full and his stomach's empty. What are your intentions?

Point at which the last leaves remaining on all the trees retain almost no discernible color: green that's brown that's grey. Two lanes over the Conowingo Hydroelectric Project (aka dam), the water on one side still, essentially lifeless, on the other active, rolling over rocks and past green islands out to the sea.

XLVIII

Point where the banana is rooted to the peel. Unaided, the moonlight appears blue. Deer tracks by the side of the house. Munch or mulch, which one?

Six p.m., Sunday night in the deep suburbs: even the Main Line is completely deserted. Ability to assign this agreement rests solely with the lender. News conveyed as a sequence of homicides punctuated by traffic. Keeping the poppy seeds atop the bagel.

Bored O. The silence of the yams. No product is ever pure, doc, by definition. Wind as a solid object. Manifests the air.

The foot having missed the lip of the first stair down moves rapidly, almost a state of weightless fall, until the next step abruptly hits (I feel the reverb in the bridge of my nose). Street lamp reflected in a garage door window – snow magnifies blue light. When they are told to wait around for a company meeting at 8:30 in the evening, they sense the news is big – they have been acquired by a larger company. Although you may use CTRL+ALT+DEL to close out of a program that is no longer responding to Windows, the sun struggles over the horizon.

Slush world. Tracks across the field of white (the light of day itself is altered, mute sun hidden behind clouds, headlights glaring even at noon). Cup of water bubbling behind the microwave's glass door. Midnight page from fraud investigation unit of Amazon Express.

Hill with a cleft along one face, a steeper drop (if you could see this without all the trees and civilization, you would find the railroad tracks trace the ridge of a hill line to the north of which everything rolls and buckles and to the south of which a long slow slope will carry you all the way to Maryland). Empty bytes. Approaching the conversation blocking the corridor (mail room to the right, payroll to the left), decide whether to go around or through. Them that lurks is Turks.

'Cause I've got one hand in my pocket and the other one's writing in this notebook. At the diner – packed full with a waiting line out the door on a Friday night – the breaded veal is tender if bland, but the tomato sauce is strictly out of a can. Bent wood reindeer cross the lawn, but behind them the two-story wood frame house is engulfed in flames.

XLIX

Red streaks across cloud wisps foretell dawn.

What once must have been a town square out in the country has become merely a quaint retro shopping district that one reaches only by traveling through narrow residential streets, the five-and-dime a museum of its own intent. Part rottweiler, part golden lab, part God-knows-what, the dog (named bear) sniffs the boy rather the way a caged lion might sniff a slab of raw steak.

The motor reflex of moving one's hand away from a hot stove is organized entirely within the spinal cord. Prefer all risk to named peril coverage. This one's a keeper. After a day, the temporary tattoo begins to fade into the texture of one's flesh.

A taste in my mouth as I wake I don't recognize. Xmas trees on sale at the hardware superstore. Full moon miniscule, tangled in the wood's bare branches.

The hill as particular has cuts in it, road gouged through the woods, homes terraced amid the poplars and, at the bottom, north face, a large sloping field (not high enough to ski or sled, nor flat enough to play football), beyond which, just before the raised freeway, great towers of electricity, swath cut crosswise against the landscape.

Conference call of the gods. The eyes of a woman who's decided, incorrectly, that she's not beautiful, staring absent-mindedly into the glare of her terminal. Or the tall African American woman, younger than I, already a grandmother, back after three weeks from heart bypass surgery. Pulse in the jaw announces a new abscess.

Winding, the off ramp curls back over the freeway. Snow piles atop each branch, no matter how small. Word represents single point of contact throughout the text (one rolls from one to the next, a physical process, as if sliding downhill). Contract initiation process. Rules of engagement. Current message saved.

L

Back of the pickup full of snow. Moving the teabag to the trash can without dripping.

Stalactites from the drainpipe shine, prisming a sun as intense as it is useless, wind chill of minus nine. Layer of leaves blows across the snow (the iced surface crackles and crunches as one trudges over it).

Putting one's weight, barefoot, on a tiny metal car (what would a child know of customizing a '58 Buick?), what gives in the dark is not the car but one's leg. so impersonal, a number rather than I is falling. A number rather than one is calling. Too coy.

Pus in boots. Waiting for the microwave to blink. Gradually the snow hardens into a layer of blue glass. Desire to rake the leaves from off this surface (service).

The wisdom of tears. Toys have seams. We have nothing to tear but tear itself. Explaining the origin of the word "boppo" to my youngest son. This snow, falling, is not silent.

He comes into the room to tell me that he's had a dream, "a racing dream, a car was coming at me, but then I noticed I was sleeping in my bed," then returns to his bedroom (large iguana puppet in the middle of the floor) and goes back to sleep.

The underside of each branch, not covered by snow, appears as if its own shadow, long dark trunk reaching skyward. An old man on a back porch, squinting as he sucks on a cigarette. A snowman's carcass, toppled, buried by the new snow.

LI

The concussion of the helicopter's blades shudders the forest. These squirrels have seen it all and are saying nothing. The modem sings in its harsh voice. Cherry bomb explodes the snowman in slomo. Dog barking incessantly at the end of its chain.

Flames leap from my clothes (not me) to my hair (me), the sole affect an increase in the deafening roar (why dreams are not real): we're posed, all twenty of us (I can see this as a spectator, noticing that I appear two or more times) in a handful of rows, the rear ones elevated, great pyre or school photo? Old man has fashioned a hat, pirate style, from an old shirt. The space, that moment between words, all but inaudible, is volatile, fragile.

White plastic lawnchair ghostlike in the snow. The few words in English amidst the Korean text tell me this is his New Testament. Teeth as motley as . . . (patchwork of mineral implants). He feels dizzy and sits, then lies, on the ice, not realizing that his heart has already stopped, that he is, for all intents and purposes, already dead. Heat of the tea ignites my body (a growl in the bowels).

Great snakes of the spine, coiled, venomous, twists. Warned by neighbors whose kids first spotted it in the driveway, he calmly takes a pistol from his bedside table and stands on his rear deck until he spots the diamondback rattler in the high grass of the yard, dispatching it with a single shot that echoes throughout the suburban neighborhood. Plastic trike, buried in the snow. It hurts to breathe.

Why does the chicken floss the toad? In the great green room (30 years ago) you lie back atop the desk (Jerry Rubin's, to be exact – it's his office), pants off and I enter. Scrape ice from the windshield (gradually the defroster kicks in from underneath – the bottom layer begins to shimmer before it cracks).

With warning – morning. Leafless, these woods expand to three times their previous size. Beside the LaserJet, two plates of Christmas cookies. A slight smudge on a single lens is permitted to stay and becomes a feature of the field of vision. Snow magnifies the impact of the streetlamp (if you call these sandlike grains of ice snow). First up at the Open Mike is a young man who flawlessly appropriates Libba Cotton's "Freight Train" with lyrics of his own. Oh raisins in the hot apple pie.

Snow simplifies the landscape even further, covering the clutter of the underbrush. Understand these words not as flowing but as falling away from the capital letter toward the rush of the period. Spiders cannot eat solid food so first crush their prey, flooding the victim's body with digestive fluids to break down the solids, only then sucking the fortified fluids back up for their meal (to anthropomorphizing eyes of a human, it would appear that the stomach is in their head). Passing an untended fax machine, I hear over its speaker a woman's voice. Blue jay brilliant against all this white.

LII

Here, the great train depots shall be known not by their location but by their destination. Blowtorch the snow from your own private driveway. Fonix wurkt 4 me. Roar of the greasepaint. Biographer, know thyself!

Big red-bellied woodpecker chases the downy and the white-breasted nuthatch away from the suet. Why does the chicken cross the code? Lone sock in the middle of the rug. Crow in the snow.

Ice flows slow Perkiomen Creek, across which (not visible from the two-lane road that passes for Highway 29) this sign tells us lies Graterford Prison. Your dream is no rebus. After Christmas, the old toys stand revealed in a new light.

Belt buckle bings as it brushes against porcelain sink. Squirrels in the slush (hush). One simply dares to cross the icy lot. In summer, these thin clouds would burn off in the heat of day. The old stove clock hums, though it has never in my life told time. Write standing up.

A new taste in one's mouth. The forest is in fact a con, a trick to make you forget that what you are driving through, truly, is a large tract of expensive housing. They huddle in the snow by the door of the office tower just to smoke a cigarette. She jokes about her "plainness," which everyone knows about her is a form of wild beauty. The sun, smeared, casts its vague light over the road. Golf course gone ghostly in the snow.

Dream: having forgotten, in San Francisco, to bring poems to my own reading, I am unable the next morning to remember anything after the introduction. The loft space over Jerry & Johnny's has been converted by someone from MOCA, Tom Marioni's Museum of Conceptual Art, into a rather grand if dishabille old library (in reality, the building hasn't existed for 15 years). The backwards-faced icky-ooker. The paragraph in the wrong place.

Glow behind the shade means dawn is breaking. Lone ant crossing vast linoleum plane. Empty of furniture, the house fills with light. My body, my archives. My eyes sticky with sleep. The wide stairs lead upward. Out back, tracks in the snow, none of them human.

ZYXT

Tra il dire e il fare
c'è di mezzo il mare
– Mario Savio

For Lyn & Leslie

Thus an abrupt

Faces phase into vases, an illusion of space fills in at the margin, merges an urge to turn (the line loops in on itself
The French aversion
The merchant of images forgets

The hand without its palm would be nothing
Tooth's roots understood as its fingers clawing into the jaw, soft calcium shale
The eye does not blink but rather this lid forms an architecture
Involuntary discourse

How can a painter sketch that blue, this grey, veined with the limbs of a thousand bare trees (ulcerated cherry) when I can't remember even to include every word
Hush of the furnace, hum of the computer, the soft ratcheting of a small analog clock

The only shadow cast by the moon
A time of simple genocide (as if anything were simple
Returning from the war to find his old job filled by a young man with children – if they're alive today, they would be eighty – he simply found another, holding it for over four decades, never again to seek employment

Thus tea burns off the roof of your mouth
Senators in single file like school children, each signing the book acknowledging his or her oath as a juror in the forthcoming trial of the president, each handed a souvenir pen
Look out the window to see if it's snowed
Or your weight in the bed next to me

Neuroptera in flight, listening to children negotiate which game to play, domed theater, lost along the Schuylkill (which only Philadelphians know how to pronounce
Goat milk pie
But the hazelnut breading for the trout later killed me, an abrasive to the intestines, raw
Rare, roar

Church of the metasearch
That porn follows (invariably)
The machinery not of sex, not even power, but of depression
The flesh of my chest, my arm beneath its gray down literally steaming after the long bath

Johnnie Cochran holding aloft the long cigar before Miss Lewinsky
Then turning to the entire Senate, shouting
If it does not fit
You must acquit

Squirrels not sliding, skittering across the ice
A sweater of an intense blue
Versus the idea that one would use one in order to sweat
Relation to the term sweet lingering long after in the recesses of the mouth
Outside a garbarge truck has paused, grinding its fill

Our yurt

More space
Steady as the rhythm of the pitching machine, moons stream forward over the ringed horizon
Sixth generation punkette, imagining the discovery of ambiance, black leather, red wine
Nut hatch still,
nearly invisible on the side of the oak

The security badge of Dorian Gray
Working for the onion
Ketchup or catsup

explodes from the fast food condiment counter pump
What gets swept in a sweepstakes are the participants
(certain restrictions may apply

Brain freeze!
Describe, if you will, "the pretensions of the vatic"

When this you see, stop and pee

People scamper across the intersection, ahead of the changing light
Hair that thin no longer gloves the skull, refracting light, a kind of halo
Position of glass amid papers on the podium, book too big to fit comfortably in one's lap
I'm here to save the day, Mighty Mouse is on the way
Black and white
understood as lush, not spare

The Celibate Cookbook

Went to Tuscaloosa but never went local
Orange that occurs in nature only in the eggs of salmon
Earrings that thread vs. ones that weigh and pull –
stool/stohl, still style (stops): mouth's architecture of vowels

Serial best friends
Notice the blank space where the painting had been
Gait to the rhythm of Leadbelly's guitar
Why is that a paragraph

I'm in a warm, even hot bath in a large tub in an even larger ballroom in the middle of some reception, everyone dressed to the nines, caterers passing slowly amid the crowd with large platters of kabobs or possibly long-stemmed glasses filled with some sparkling clear beverage – no one seems to notice or mind – I'm talking with people, laughing, gradually chewing the bell pepper on my kabob stick, when I fart, long slow round bubbles rising to the surface of the water, so I sit up straight, hoping my movement will make their stream less evident, which it does visually but, as they burst into the evening air, I'm bathed in the thick acrid odor of it all, distinct smell of cooked cauliflower (something I haven't eaten in months – the odor of it must have hidden within me all that time just waiting for something to loosen it, to set it free), it's too rich and dense and I can hardly breathe, my eyes watering, so I rise, water and suds pouring, then dripping from my body bright pink from the heat of the water, at least now no one will notice the bubbles but I fart again uncontrollably, rich cloud of it rising about me, I'm climbing out of the tub, the people I'm talking with blinking, screwing up their faces, trying to look away not from my nakedness (no one seems to notice) but the smell now, cauliflower and sauerkraut, I could pretend it's not me, but I see my reflection in the large mirror over the bar at the far end of the room, the clouds of my farts are blue, blue-grey, growing larger even as they dissipate, visible as a rainbow leading straight to the pot of gold of my asshole, I fart again, thick, dense, rich, inescapable, and people are starting to sit down on the parquet floor, setting their food down, I hear a glass drop and shatter, people are losing consciousness all about me, I fart again and it's the entire room, people on the floor struggling, gasping, yawning, and I fart again, cauliflower everywhere, the room entirely blue in a dense fog and I alone left to tell the tale

A giant, domesticated and most benevolent sea lion, its skin an impossibly rich maroon, velvet to the touch, lies across the old couch, listening intently as I explain that I shall be away for a few weeks for an operation

Is that a good dream or a bad dream

Televised funeral, voiceover hushed though nobody else is speaking, outside the crowds race to the flag-draped box atop the humvee as the entourage makes its way through a half-modern city gouged from the desert

Fiction: that Europe & Asia are separate continents (vague uneasiness as to location of the "Middle" East

Architecture of a downtown street of a city I don't really know – small red brick buildings tucked behind skyscrapers, old stone churches barren in the middle of parking lots, each intersection corner ringed by rows of chained newspaper displays – no news there

She drags in the small white terrier across the hotel lobby, sound of its nails over the tile

Newsteam 5 and firemen bored, milling at the rim of the city center gas leak that turns out, after hours of searching, to have been a false alarm (helicopters still poised in the air) – no visuals here

Roar of the generators in the hotel's underground parking lot (only when I see his forehead do I realize that it's Ash Wednesday) – is that all together or do want your bills separate

Understand the cloud

Old dried soda spills discolor the cheap table – Formica mock wood top would seem flimsy were it not literally bolted to the wall

(behind the glass, swimmers methodically finish indoor laps, pausing only for an instant before turning and disappearing again into the water)

Dreams in which I not only see and hear but feel and smell – the way your anus clings when I enter

I sweep the crumbs from the chair then sit – Pushkin's dueling pistol there on the wall

Unavoidably, the world begins with the end of the war – a boy holds on to the side of the blue tile pool, kicking wildly

The Rifle Tower, he says, lifting the rubber replica of the French monument to his eye, aiming to please

The first time the cow was mean to Red Roger

The permanent smell of the neighboring Kentucky Fried Chicken

Grimaces at the poem before he reads it – all that remains of his hair has gathered into eyebrows

"Did you say 'snowball'" – "I said 'cascade'"

The Grail Castle, smaller than I'd imagined, here on the main thoroughfare of Cooperstown, NY – without the legal doctrine of "brain death," organ transplants don't occur – safety in letters – a tingling in the cold sore, consciousness in the flesh

The strip mall store front sign reads "video," but the painted-over window suggests "porn" – in the city center, a hierarchy of suits (sated critique) – thumbprint's etched ridges visible on the screen

Hardly anything will prove more damaging to the poets than too much self-knowledge, Wordsworth hardening into fame, Eliot in full decay, too many reasons to not add this word here, that phrase beyond, the too easy elegant turn leading back to the already too familiar (so that the answer to Bob's question, "How will I know when I make a mistake" turns out to be "There's life in it")

Too tall, the stapled publication bends against the shelf above – ways in which thought is not computational

Forward looking, backwards compatible

So that you include periscopes or that the underside of the school desk's hinged top is covered with stickers, a local craze such as Go-Gos

Employees must wash hands – but the piping below any sink presents an aesthetic (at a Jesuit college in California once

I saw them covered with something like canvas or white leather "leggings")

Ophthalmologic migraine, halo effect around the field of vision (painless, but

completely disorienting) vs. the dull sinus pressure of the morning (I envision a cavern crusted over with dripping stalactites

Blue chemical flush of the airplane john – the girl with the burst balloon and pink party dress sobs uncontrollably in the fast food restaurant that features (why I'm here) baked potatoes

Trailer park at Lake Success – retracing my path across the valley, I pass the exact spot where, the day before, I came upon the aftermath of an accident, blanket-covered corpse by the side of Route 65, three ambulances (lights flashing, strobe effect in the valley sun), one fire truck, one flatbed for towing, none of the emergency personnel moving very quickly, old grey sedan pancaked upside down in the gravel (impossible to imagine how it got that way, unless it did a front flip at tremendous speed) – but today I can't even tell precisely where it's occurred – calls every bell captain "Super Dave" (new moon begins with the 'end bracket' first)

Smudge of the lens gives each word an ethereal quality

Lower limits of the high end

That age when she's on the floor playing Battleship or Connect Four with the other kids one minute, then with the adults around the kitchen table the text, half flirting with her mother's friends – sign in the men's room of the Westside Wok / Mongolian Bar-B-Q reads "Caution – wet floor" when what it should say is "sticky" – the only bidet in Camden

I skip by accident to p. 103 in the book, reading several pages before I recognize the mistake

Tinted glass roof over the porte-cochere through which I see three flags (U.S., California, Hyatt) blowing at different rates in the wind, one billowing, one completely still

Foot in the airplane aisle at great risk

A young man slowly pulls the paper game piece from the side of his extra-large soda, then visibly sighs (a young woman sitting catty-corner chews a Happy Meal's small burger & stares into space) – how many fries do you dip at one time into the little paper catsup container

Wake wondering how precisely (or perhaps why) I twisted my body into this position (woman in the next room is a groaner but when I glimpse her in the hotel corridor the next morning, she seems a girl) – guacamole aftertaste thick on the tongue

Bite my knuckle (back of hand turned toward cheek) to stifle yawn: mean time between failures

Great word for Hangman: rhythm

Slowly, over the sound system, barely audible over the

talking and the registers, Sealed With a Kiss is played on a chromatic harmonica

To confuse dream with sleep, this image (the full moon literally crumbling in the sky) with the real (first concussion knocks us down) is to wake sweating, in full terror

Albany (Albanians)

Large leafed pattern on otherwise black tie hints at paisley

Desire to take Gwyneth Paltrow home and feed her one, two, many meals

The steady dimpling of the water's surface: swimming pool in the rain (moment at which you recognize you no longer fear death) – red-headed kindergarten teachers in that first full blush of intense (and intensely personal) bipolar disorder

Simply the concept: imitation Leroy Neiman – beneath the off-white cottage cheese stucco ceiling, cheap LA hotel, rain out the unopening window

Looks at his pager before leaving the meeting so that others don't identify the departure as a bio break

Later, sentences to sort into order

Places one hand on his cheek as he listens – I absent-mindedly count the pocked acoustic tiles of the ceiling (those on the margin invariably trimmed – flaw or feature) – ear always means what it hears

Painting o'erwhelmed by its frame – spring arrives in waves, this week's first yellow inconceivable in the colorless grey forest

Uncross my legs in the too-tight seat of a crowded plane – sculptor with the bandaged hand

Meals eaten standing by the sink in the kitchen

Lacking floss, he finds a long thread extending from his shirt cuff

Institutional TV monitor padlocked to high metal stand (asset code stenciled onto its side) – roots rock as subgenre

An egg cream made with Sprite (you don't realize how loud all this talking is until you can't hear Stevie Wonder from the juke box

A series of large round rattling seeds beaded together by a rough yellow thread placed into the paper tray before the pulp is added to the solution, thus engrained into the new sheet as it dries

"Humanity sneezed on me"

Official country wall map in library basement, reds and greens deep against the off-white field

Five components had eigenvalues greater than one

"Mom, can I get up now"
Child's voice clear in the still air

The wives of bass players all go mad

What I notice, my cock slipping into your mouth, is not (at least immediately) the physical sensation, but rather your freckles, your startling eyes wide open

Behind the old manual cash register the owner of the diner, tall and husky, young though bald (fringe but a shadow) holds both hands high over his head, applauding loudly

These blue walls so old it is not wrong to call them colorless

Fragments not of knowledge, but of knowledge acquisition

Freud's garden:

Case studies in wisteria

Instead of *parliamentary* I saw *paramilitary* – today the carriage house is a visitor's center – golfers run to escape the sudden outburst, sandtraps already converting into ponds

Morning as an emotion

Hollywood romance: a woman making bad choices is called a happy ending

An office which, when I walk in, has one blue parakeet, loud, chattering, atop the long, hanging cool fluorescent lights, radio on too loud to Motown oldies station

The duck ravioli was fine but for the watery pesto

Nothing venture, nothing have

My own handwriting, larger and more crude than I'd remembered

She walks flat footed, the wet swimsuit visible under the pale cotton dress

An intolerable sadness

Short definition of history

One less than forever

A dream just before dawn is different

What I thought at first literally to have been a chicken crossing the road proved, upon examination, to be a spruce goose

The border between reverie and sleep, razor thin

He walked into the music store while I waited, but when he failed to re-emerge I entered only to find him gone

A tall girl, quite beautiful but for the buck teeth & receding chin

The eros of adrenalin and vice versa

Your ashes, no larger than a loaf of bread but several times the weight

When setting across Dogtown Commons, take a compass and tell someone your plans

Eight months may yield only a handful of pages but just possibly the right ones

Three enter the restaurant, taking care to set their black laptop cases down next to the wall away from the passing diners, table angled into a diamond configuration to seat four – the lone empty chair facing the aisle as the trio struggles to tip their oversized menus just right to catch the light

Cut strawberry stain upon the napkin, image of the tiniest kiss

A young woman bicycles past a field of corn

I step into Pangaea, a dark little Cortland Street club down the block from Have-a-Lick's, stepping up the small bleacher seating to the upper rear left corner, pulling out a notebook from my black Danish book bag, letting the competing, compelling saxophones (Ochs, Ackley, Gruntfest) lead the rhythm of the writing

Infomercials in the sky
Out-task pieces of your general outsource
We said five, it took ten

Lit by sun thru the gauze curtained window, steam curls up (coiling plume) from my mug on the counter

Invisible just two blocks from the harbor, seagulls form a wall of white noise

Connotations surrounding the name of Long Island followed comma immediately by Nova Scotia

First orange streaks of day to begin my 53rd year
Sitting cross-legged atop the quilt covered bed, trying to

write with this pocket computer as you pass the open window in bra and panties (downstairs, a whoop from the kids in the basement, lost on Lego Island)

Better to centralize captive data

The cross on that "t" looks like a nun's wimple

A pest of poetry

Next door, lone painter on a makeshift scaffold listens to up-tempo country from boom box (further, and in opposite directions, a lawn tractor and steady hammering) – radio hollers "Our big August meltdown, these prices won't last"

The same last names, over and over, in the small cemetery

The giant dog quite peaceful atop the blue tarp cover load in the rear of that pickup

First bought, best bought (liar's remorse)

All things being equal (the one condition that is never met)

like a typo but is not

Nova Scotia fog

Giant plate of steamed periwinkles

She tugs idly at the flesh on the back of her hand, not looking up at me as she speaks, lifting her eyes instead to stare blankly out the window (woodpecker dancing up the side of the oak

The oatmeal foam rises, magma threatening rim of the pot (little village of the stove top)

"W" conceived as a vowel

Wallpaper on three sides, but on the fourth some cheap wood paneling

Gloosecap argued with Beaver
& threw two giant stones,
one becoming Long Island,
the other Brier
– Mi'Kmaq

One is forever checking the young asthmatic's breathing, the pace of it, the depth

One can hear the inner workings of the old clock in the stove, although it has not told time in years

Performative, such as Scalapino's use of the verb *as*

Point at which, driving north, our old familiar FM station starts to break into static

In any foreign country (this one), the change you receive after a purchase appears as tho money in a dream

Lone chair in an otherwise unfurnished room

Breeze in the trees whose wide leaves softly rustle (how bare this will seem come winter), the hair on my legs, what little there is of it, near invisible, blond filament, tingles as it blows

His/her face in profile, lips about the cock (just the tip of it), liquid spilling

Sleep, an emotion

Groan that could only have come from a dog

Even with this pocket computer, I still carry a pen wherever I go, even tho the notebook in my back pocket long ago dissolved into scraps and wood pulp

The ink at first glistens shining for a second before it settles into the page's grain, hardening into words

Teens on their dune buggies down by the lobster traps

The little boy seems surprised to discover that he is again barefoot

Psychic Pokémon: scope creep or skill creep (carry the canary), war abolished forever, police actions in all the "corners" of the globe

Gray in that lush hair spreading slowly, a cloud marking time (like one etched against a clear blue sky, warm day by the still cove, shore birds still in the mudflats, a man on the road walking by

Bug on the ceiling notes my approach and freezes, feigning invisibility against all this white paint (ten minutes later it still hasn't moved, but I leave the room for just 60 seconds and when I return it's gone)

Spider on the outside of this window

Next to the restaurant, a bar, its television visible through the window, a baseball game in pantomime, too red, too blue

A fisherman until the war when he joined the Navy where he remained until he retired ("the Navy is the sea with benefits"

Holding the teabag by its very corner so as not to burn your fingers

The sun when it rose revealed East to be more in that direction (indicates with the left hand)

Penetration then – one squirms, naked on one's belly, while the other (above) pushes in

Holding the bowl in my left hand, I often stand as I eat

Velcro-strapped sandals, tipped over on the shag rug

For want of a PIN code, he has never used his bank card

Brier for the wild Brier Rose found everywhere on the island (the name appears first as Bryer on DesBarres' chart of 1775, though David Welch & Robert Morrell were living there as early as 1769)

The slightest smear on the lens right where you think to focus

The yellow rose of praxis

When a giant clam bites down, it can sever a man's finger

In the next room, I hear the sound of her urine

One rooster, half hidden among the great noise of gulls at dawn

The words dissolve from our memory / imagination almost as fast as we read them – they leave no echo or shadow (syntax an attempt to compromise the present) – those other sentences, they never existed (except when they do)

The boys in the next room playing a game: "I thought *I* was on the blue path"

Pier gone to mall, t-shirt shops & salt-water taffy, just five miles by the route of it, south to Gloucester

The banana composed as a vocabulary (as botanists, growers, shippers must think of it), the meat of it organized around a center – vein or spine – from which three "faces" grow outward, each long & curved in complement to the others (what do they call those threads that lie along the surface just beneath the peel

Thin clouds but with dark undersides filter the sun

An email after 20 years and you find yourself right back in the thick of it, the expression, the positions, the body as in fact it must no longer be (does the spine still arch at the instant of orgasm

Digby Neck

I'm sitting half-squatting on the granite, wondering where the male is among the eiders in the cove (at low tide the shore is all seaweed) when the young woman likewise crouching on the rock nearby (yellow slicker in spite of the clear sky) explains (we've never spoken before tho I'd seen her and her two companions out on the point fooling around with a camera too bulky & expensive for tourists) that there are three whales, two rights & a humpback, trapped in the small bay (not a bay at all but a mere gap between islands) entangled (her very word!) *entangled* in fishing nets (O my sleeping ones!) soon to be, if it is possible, rescued

Tentlike netting of the salmon farms visible on the water

How the banana got its spots

Just out of the bath, I already see something streaked across the back of my hand

Weeds and scrub pine, the thinnest layer of soil as crust over granite, above which gulls swirl, decorating the sky

Final twist of the faucet handle, at which the drip at last shuts off

We stood outside for the better part of an hour, able for once to see not merely the stars that compose the basic constellations but behind and beyond them great cloud swirls, entire galaxies

The air in the pipes announces itself

Listening with my ear pressed to his back as he breathed, I too could hear the rattling "rowly" sound of bronchitis

When she has her period, everyone in the office can tell, the musk scent of blood is so strong – the men walk around with eyes & nostrils dilated

Lone sock atop black leatherette sofa came back from the laundromat abandoned by its mate

Oatmeal unadorned by milk or sugar: simple solid bowl

Each summer, one of the towns named Westport hosts a meeting for them all

Guitar nailed to a phone pole (dirt road no more than an arm's length wide)

Future site of Old Austerlitz

I never find Yoda

Sitting on the plastic "lawn chair" – one of two on the small shady porch – one foot comes down off of garden hose, then taps about, searching out a flat place to rest

I hear the rain a good 20 minutes before the foghorn sounds

Jewel is on the radio in the living room singing one song, you in the mud room standing over the clothes dryer folding something singing another, I passing on the stairs able for an instant to hear both songs simultaneously, then I take a step & the moment's lost

Think of the butterfly's "shoulder" muscles in relation to its torso

Trust is negotiated with the reader, expectations proposed and revised until what is arrived at becomes the statement of work

I hear my son on the stairs, the bathroom door left open

The high dark clouds suggest a thunderstorm that never arrives

Bicycles that seem strewn permanently about the driveway

In an aubergine sun dress (no slip beneath), she strides up the meadow in my direction, white hair flowing, grin visible at fifty yards

To press the still shut fuchsia flower between my fingers until it pops

Two days before the great quake of '89, a snake falls on Tom's head – it has been trying literally to climb the side of the building and has somehow made it to the top rim of the glass door that then suddenly opens

Pulled from a side pocket of my laptop case in the tight space of an airplane seat, the book's back cover is bent diagonally, a triangle revealing crumpled, mashed pages, the paper a lovely vanilla white

A large man with a soft voice

In the pool the children cling to me, laughing and gasping and blinking the water from their eyes (so that my impression later of all this wetness, an expanse made even more vast by the afternoon glare, is neither of floating, sun on my face, nor of moving swiftly, effortlessly just below the water's surface, but rather of lifting and grabbing, the weight on my body, the noise)

Asymmetric warfare

Leverage your metadata (chains in the K cloud, echoes of the Dublin core)

In walks a man holding an ocarina

"I'm still not convinced
indigo is a color"

As he sleeps, I crouch to watch & attend his breathing, counting the rise and fall of his chest per minute

A 747 is one million parts flying in close formation

First month in college: first earring, first beard

Black butterfly with the yellow trim flutters its wings slowly, hovering in the roses

The shape of the sky is high at the dome, seen from the southeast corner of Dolores Park

Language is . . . / polis is . . . eyes

Living room devoid of direct light is organized about two centers: a large spool table by the so-called kitchenette, a Franklin stove at the far end in which has been thrown a dreadful book of short poems

The sky "sullen," planes on the tarmac ready to go (but there is a storm at our destination so that everything is frozen into a game of waiting), people talking quietly into cell phones, a child barefoot on the aisle

Pulling kites across a meadow on a windless afternoon

After the first filament of the three-way lightbulb has burned out

Consciousness understood at the persistence of pattern (this one sees heads only in the turning away), a man who chooses to eat only in chains (understood here as literal) or the man in the pork pie hat who sings blues in too soft a voice

The plane lifts and jockeys upward toward the bank of clouds

Tune a brick by moving stones

Clearing my desk I find a note in my own handwriting on a scrap of lined paper, a name – Floryshak – and a phone number with no area code, but I have no memory of having written this note, nor of placing it here amidst these books and papers, nor of this person

Quilted cover shrouds the grand piano

The way ears fog up in flight
Look up *carapace, anguilliform*
Arborescing, the syntax parsed down into the text
Kasey Kasem's voice barely audible over the bagel shop's refrigerator
I'm interested less in the paperless office than in officeless paper

Read a little, sleep a little, read some more

In the dream I'm always in the same drab green room, on the floor not old enough yet even to walk, looking up at a bed so frail that it's almost a cot, on top of which a man (whom I decided without seeing his face must be my father) fucks a young African-American woman, all arms & legs & faceless flesh – there is another dream not quite as frequent in which I'm walking thru an urban neighborhood, perhaps the Tenderloin, with a lot of sex shops – "live girls dancing" – where I walk into the latter (it's on a corner and has many doors) & realize that any woman here (either they're naked or wearing only the flimsiest of lingerie) will fuck or blow me without question, without even asking my name, so that I wander about in a state of total terror and anticipation, watching how this one takes some stranger's dark moldy cock deep into her mouth while another just lays there passively as some guy pounds away into her (often at this point I bolt, I run away, fleeing into streets that are always dark and rainy) – why do I feel so certain that these dreams are connected, one of an event that has never happened, the other which I feel almost certainly must have

At night the runway lights a lovely cobalt blue
The bottled hand soap a milky liquid
Tweezes a hair free from her chin

Crossing Rittenhouse Square: an old woman wearing many layers of clothes sleeps on a bench while next to her a second woman, much younger, in a business suit on a Sunday, speaks rapidly in hushed tones into a cell phone

This is medicated
to the one I
lu-uh-uv

I'm writing on a notepad because we haven't yet gained the altitude necessary to pull out my pocket computer

My tongue and teeth on the inmost part of the thigh

For him, more than anything else the true & secret signal of irreversible age lay in the utter alien thickness of his toenails, the largest ones now akin more to the shod layer at the base of some horse, uncuttable even unless he has just stepped from the hottest of baths

Half a block ahead of him (the streetlamps now finally taking hold, suppressing the last light of the waning day), he sees her grab the young man, pulling him off-balance into a doorway out of view with a force that appears right on the edge of violence – the mind conjures instantaneously a half dozen tentative explanations – but when I pass them seconds later she's just staring at him, a huge grin on her face, he standing there with his hands in his pockets, looking sheepish and shy

The way I metabolize heat, night, interior light

Have you guessed their ages

Slowly the anus releases, sucking the finger in

Seen from the sky, cities are inherently asymmetrical
First the hourglass, then the cursor, then the "wallpaper" appears

See that girl with the red dress on, she can birdland all night long
Base of the men's room urinals muddy with old piss
Lifting the upturned mug from the dishdrainer, its convex bottom also holds water, which splashes cold over my wrist

More parallels between Keith and dogs

The DC-9 bumps along the tarmac, gathering speed
Understands his body (viewed naked now in the mirror, bath's heat from which he's stepped steaming) as a narrative of impossible complexity
The Cinnabon shop suffocates the mall air
Call the shorter boy Pokémon
When the furnace shuts off, the tiny paper wall hanging situated right over the livingroom vent halts its subtle, barely audible dance, and you become aware of other even more subtle sounds in the predawn house (even this lightbulb has its noise, its own characteristic hum)

Exit strategy (Lyn, I've read your work so often while in flight that flight itself has become a condition of the work) – the flight attendant draws the blue curtain across the aisle, cutting off our view of First Class

Reading a long, itemized list – take the time to say each number aloud in head

Sleeve too long for the arm, the cuff curls back at the right

"I'm 'A,' right" asks Bob

At 3:40 in the afternoon, the moms appear as if by magic all at once by the driveway under the maple (its leaves redder now than any red imaginable, first week of November) towards which, just now visible at the horizon, the lumbering squat yellow bus starts to appear (but why is that maple just across the narrow lane still so green, yellow, orange)

Books lie in a half-filled case

Says the radio announcer smoothly, as if without effort, "That's Landsend, one word, no apostrophe, dot com"

Already I know the difference between Vileplum and Charzard

That red strobe effect out the window is accompanied by a siren

Wondering, blocks later, Had I left the lights on to the Mazda

You can see them in back of the main cabin under a shared blanket, neither one more than 15, hands going every which way

Walking around with an oversized postcard in my shirt pocket

Middlebrow profundity, perfect for PBS

Bright pink against a deep sky blue, the letters, thick, san serif, tightly spaced, shimmer

In a quiet room, a knuckle pops loud as a rifle

C'mon pumpkin butt
X described as Charzard-like
Draft of a draft
Are we squirming in our seats yet
Revolutionette

Let's E
You are here
The perfect mother, Patty Hearst
Wiping the socket that has no eye
I sit cross-legged in a corner of the gallery, barely able to see Mei-mei's head between the rows of chairs, no height to the podium (which I know is there only by its lamp's soft glare spreading across her green brown & white shirt), her voice soft, hushed, audible only through its amplification (behind me, out the floor-to-ceiling windows [doors really, tho opening to no balcony] traffic on bumpy Second Street forms its own punctuation

By the time he awoke, her carefully made bed appeared a storm of sundered blankets – one barely saw her own smaller figure asleep beneath the crumpled pile
Pre-apologize
Hushed, stage-whispered reading yields too worshipful a listening
Neither alpha nor beta male, but rather Charlie or delta
You don't realize how dull the razor's gotten until you change the blade
Woman with a bruised thumbnail sits silent on the bench, the other hand clenched tight about a Kleenex.

In *American Beauty*, the daughter, played by actress Thora Burch, who at the time of filming was "only 16," has a scene in which she removes blouse & bra, filmed as seen from across the way from her bedroom window by neighbor videotaping drug dealer boy friend, his screen projected / reflected up against his own bedroom window, the complex shot construction enabling the use of body double Marina Freeman

Terse verse

At the end of the day, we'll benefit as much from our 360 reviews as from our PBCs (personal business commitments)

The first copy of *The New Sentence* I see is in a bookstore into which I've ducked to escape the hot sun of a street festival

In the pocket of the seatback in front of me, I find a series of photos left there quite obviously by accident

Lit up at night, a baseball field is identifiable from 30,000 feet

Remember phone numbers as series of three- and four-step spatial patterns on a key pad

What is sadder than the small book of well-wrought poems, none spilling over to the next page even, each pretending to its own completeness

His knowledge of the Bronx restricted to the elevated view from the freeway, the monster highrise housing clustered to the east of I95, always curiously silent even to the muted colors whenever he drove past

Pain's lane is only vaguely against the grain – theory of cuffs – dance facing the mirror

Why bald men still shampoo

As we rise above them into the sunlight, the clouds beneath appear soiled, sooty

Putting the finger to the side of one's nose to plug a sneeze

Riven, intone the Talking Heads, is a place where nothing ever happens

Intellectual critique as fantasy life

Design of that sweater fuzzes with age

Plan's flan is grandly in the van

Logism

Giant framed photograph, color closeup of anal penetration, the male cock marbleized by arousal & effort, the female genitalia similarly flushed red, blossoming, but still as if unmoved, untouched by all that nearby force, skin everywhere gleaming as tho oiled, light that banishes all shadow, hung so primly against all that white space directly over the young lady art dealer's desk (her employees struggle with an impulse to ask her if she was the model, tho, hey, everyone has opinions – she is alleged to have said once that this was the perfect piece beneath which to discuss price)

The flight attendant presents the safety message in a sing-song rhythm bearing no relation to the content
That cycle of the dryer identifiable by its rumba
Para (graph, site, normal)
There are some pores in a nerf ball
Through the window I see a young man running up the ornate stairs
Tell me a store
Draft, drift

Penguins in Burma
Utter beep
A spring without teargas is not spring
Your sunburned genitalia
Before I even realize that I've been counting the boards that compose the floor, I've reached 46
Thus, one by one, we attempt to extract the stone from Arthur

Arriving at the office even before sun up – I've driven my mother to the airport – I find myself the third one there
O flare fluent squire: square flayed the Swede burp sprang
The temple gang
If you pay attention, you will recognize the ph balance of your stomach
An ecstasy that never quite arrives

Unique New York
Unique New York
Unique New York

Connotative clean room
T-shirt visible under V-neck sweater
That familiar syncopation, basketball on hardwood (the squeak of the shoes
When outfitting the spy's disguise, take care for the accuracy of the pocket litter: the right coins, keys, torn tickets
Hair as the margin of nature on the edge of the otherwise cultivated body
Epic told in the second person

You can still see the city through the clouds but only as smeared light – technology perverse pollutions – felonious monk – name brand theory – glasses organize eyes, ears, nose into new relation (she removes her new blue wire-rim frames & might as well stand naked) – inches of rain vs. inches of snow – keys on this keyboard you realize you've never pushed

Trope or treat, which one
Days later, the name I'd been groping for finally came to me: Brenda Hillman
Bouquet with irritation
Gas undulates through your intestines
Einstein and Eisenstein seated at a white iron table with a glass top and center-pole umbrella, lost in conversation none of us can hear, seeming oblivious to the young, mostly naked bodies diving into or climbing out of the pool
Short phrase shift

The last morning of the millennium – Cross legs so that your balls roll over one another (flinch) – Carrots screaming as they're wrenched from the soil – Shoes are required at all times – Deconstruct power platitudes

In the dream I envision driving from Philadelphia to Atlanta in a single afternoon with a large (and sick) dog, but when I go to fetch the car it's on Potrero Hill

Through the backyard telescope the rings of Saturn are very white and flat and unmediated (only this lens, that mirror) as tho you were in its presence and not merely that of this silent jumping dog

Venona, calm closer, touch softly my falsified files
Old fart, piss & sweat smell, men's locker room at the Y
Penguins in butter

New phone chirps, its tone more shrill than I would have expected

How does one find a publisher in the Canary Islands (you don't – they find you)

Your body enters and displaces the water in the tub – it rises to the porcelain lip – absorbing & transforming the heat, taking it from just below scalding to merely tepid in less than two minutes (later, you're lying atop the quilted bed naked, the heat still trapped in your muscles, flesh, pores, the steam pouring forth)

Forced to write more slowly, pocket computer's tiny keyboard touch-typed by thumb, sentences unfurl differently

Little half moons of ice spill from the freezer, clattering

& sliding over the linoleum floor – we gather them as best we can, but still the next morning miniature puddles await the unwary step

An overweight young man with rather feminine lips
Even in the lanes, the swim team backstrokes toward us
Heavy indoor airport pizza smell
Grind of the vending machine's motor as the ice cream bar rises into view

In the dream a cottage filled with mice and rats (I come downstairs & turn on the lights)
Because the past had failed us, some preferred to believe in the future
Pissing poison
The ballpark figure, svelte in the translucent dress, not transparent exactly but then again not
Miniature puzzles await the unwary step

Moon muted by the thinnest scrim of cloud casts faint shadows, trees silhouetted over the snowy field
To everything turn
At what point in the poem do you sense its completion
Miniature puzzles await the unwary step
That peculiar alertness right before sleep

Anal masturbation
Your photo in the uncorrected galley is a plain white box
Who would ever sleep with dreams like that
Imagine a dried lava flow, crusted blood gunk surface of my sinuses

Blurb boy

Snow is arrested rain

Heartbeat understood as temporary, pulse pulse (eventually all stops, this body both overheated and shivering cools and quiets) – if you look closely, especially on a still night sky, you can sense (if not see exactly) that instant between perception, the weft of points that link into time

Shatter the well-wrought urn

Later, after the rest of the younger residents move down the corridor to complete Grand Rounds, she lingers, looking first at the chart and x-rays then over at my body on the gurney, still naked from the waist down, leaning almost imperceptibly forward until I realize she's gently fingering / fondling my balls

Give 'em enough trope

A narcissist's palette, for example David Hockney's

Another border, this time between thought & dream

T-shirt reads "ERIEsistable / Pennsylvania" (sun dawns over capital I)

He throws the bowling ball as though it were a Frisbee (the little dog leaps)

My room is not the Forbidden Ruins

Nail clippings scatter over the hardwood floor, little half moons, crescents hard for a man in trifocals to see

You don't pick your nose so much as gouge it

Don't mourn, accessorize

Fog mutes light
Identify the gender
I wouldn't drink a gallon of anyone's saliva, not even yours
When this you see, RFP

Sweat stains the jogger's tanktop
As time passes, birds in the text become more specific
Blind woman veers ever so slightly left as she walks down the street until, the path of red-and-white tipped cane just missing the light pole, she walks face first into it
The only light downstairs, the ghostly Christmas tree
Dream that leaves me depressed for days (I have been killed in an auto accident & am unable to find the whereabouts of my sons)
In the poem, Max is fat & tiny
The drops for the pink eye leave the duct feeling dry and crusty
Molassifying
Suburban Serbian
Golden translucent resin split-level houses, each no larger than the last joint of a small man's thumb, gathered by the thousands atop the large, low white table, shape suggestive of a map (Spain perhaps)
Use your tongue & teeth gently to play with the foreskin
I read that book in a single weekend, which for me was unusual

We bend
Web end

Quick
quake

quite
quiet
choir
quit

Flyers have been taped to the inside of the window, then later removed, leaving behind a pattern of transparent marks where the corners had formed wedges

The trifocals form a time machine, each lens focusing on a different moment

Over the years I've learned what it means when you stand there, staring out the window, chewing on your lower lip

The old man writes a clean line, / typewriter clacking in the third millennium

She stands, holding the paper cup under the drinking fountain's flow, then, turning her head only slightly, still talking to her bud, pours the water over her hair

Flossipher: random actives of narrative

Nearfully

Charades with Antonin Artaud

"to resemble the wind / by channel flipping"

The tea arrives with its apparatus

Woodpecker hops backward down the trunk of the tree

Only when I see my reflection in a storefront window do I realize that I'm still wearing my dark glasses

Monetize sticky paradigms

So the writing cure, like the talking one, was not a cure at all, but a path through the (name-to-be-deferred) condition, the movement itself a mode of enchantment

Old wooden chair groans with every shift of weight

A tiny pickup truck piled high with black bags of trash

Exact degree at which we shift from hot tea to iced

Because the lens of each eye is constructed of plastic, thus inflexible, great glare & sustained glare are physically painful – body responds instantly by shutting down (I go to sleep)

Repeat or repent, which one

Batch at batch can

Sparrows in the eves of the overhang

Playing cards clothespinned to the bike spokes

farrago, ND

Chatter of doves as they rise up at your approach

I wanted to say "reproach" (the ruse is obsolete)

Loose lips sink MIPS

Pattern of the owl's call: three hoots, then two

Budge is walking the white dog among oak trees (what kind of name is Budge)

What would Marx do

It's all over but the typing

Paradachsund

The narrative waltz
You bring your goggles but leave them in your jacket in your locker
Peggy no longer is just a nickname for Margaret
(variations on the spelling of John multiply daily)
God is the word humans coined to articulate a great desire
Age beyond which each person's gait becomes visibly asymmetrical
As the sun sets, the light comes indoors
Steady syncopation, woodpecker in the trees

Every sentence tells a story
If you are to be deprived of experience, pick the most extreme
Plastic white patio chairs in the back yard, filthy gray after winter
One hears the mechanics of the camera
The evolution will not be televised
The traffic slows, then swerves slightly on the two-lane road to get by the three cars stopped about the wounded, bleeding doe, one man standing on the road's shoulder dialing a cell phone, another kneeling to pet and stroke the deer
Brand equity / bottled water

For awhile there were no young poets, then they were everywhere, huge flocks of them in the air at once, crowding out the sun, then just as suddenly it's still again, but for one dove, cooing along in the dusk
SETI @ home
I drive into the city, sun setting in my rear view mirror
Fall & Any

Watching the watch band crack, wondering at the number of days before it breaks

FDR unable to visit the "cottage" at Campobello after '39 for the simplest of reasons: sitting just yards off the coast of Maine, the island is Canadian and the advent of war made the concept of a few days "out of country" not thinkable

Facts vs. thoughts (as if . . .)

Each thin door (three pairs of them) two columns of ten small panes each, each angle (three of them forming a wall that could serve as "bay" window) capped with eight panes, two rows of four apiece, each imperceptibly larger than those of the doors (how else to incorporate space for frame and knob), an ensemble in the brown-painted wood, twelve dozen squares of glass

From ladyslipper to head-of-the-wolf

Mills on wills

A bee repeatedly beats against the glass

Sense of a cheese blintz so warm in one's throat

Soft core: she grips the cock in one hand, a thin strand of fluid strung between its tip and her lip

Thick and ugly wall phone positioned by classroom door

Metallica sues Napster

My moustache trapped in my braces

To shining C's

Piano lessons then as a dream

The moon too bright to look at

Children hunting in the garden of colored eggs

Dave walks his half-collie down the tree-lined lane, the dog, that is, walking, stopping to sniff and mark each stone & tree, David in his wheelchair following

One museum of types: any airport terminal
Each class room door has its own push-button combo lock
Biting teeth vs. the chewing ones
Lee Ann's faintly audible Japanese accent
People *like* assignments
Write this down without words

Elk or ilk, which one
Hair's roots reach through skull into brain
Out the window the sound of glass shattering warrants a glance
Silliman's filament
The air electric with the first wave of humidity (oak & maple shuddering in the gusts of wind, which then appears trapped in their branches)
Fire women jogging at dusk in identical sweatshirts over the bridge (Which details actually matter)
Standing around on the edge of the crowd, hopping about one foot to the other) trying to catch a better glimpse
So the baby smelled of Ben-Gay
The emotional life of the ironic
The rough subtle push of braces under the lip
All that remains of the mealis the stain of egg upon the plate, the little cup of sour cream to one side
Mouse or moose, which one

She sits long-legged, feet pulled up atop the folding chair (arms wrapped about her knees): from the side view, to form the human figure N
Frames of these glasses have become a vice tightening about the too-flexible skull

When the Muzak's too loud
Their first restaurant was in the old gunshop (corner of the wall over the counter still pocked with bullets in the plaster)
The idea that some basic element of furniture has yet to be invented
Putting on this jacket for the first time in months, I immediately sense the small book of poems in the side pocket
Jacob's bladder
Baa-baa Blastoise
What is more still than an indoor pool
A bell-like quality, paper clips falling on the rug
She's giving a reading in a classroom (very full), the door open at which a man pauses, looking in, then continues down the corridor

"The hyperbaloney sandwich is now de-activating"
A dream this real can only leave one entirely depressed
Gun rack in the back of the truck
The small boy with the giant gym bag
Bookmarks too long & large for these little paperbacks
Rubbing my eye, hearing the ball scrape against the tissues of the socket
I recognize the sound of the bicycle coming through the trees before I see it
Banana, black as teak, left on the picnic table
Visions of Brody
The wren in the dogwood

The wren in the dogwood (blossoming) sings
Little flags mark the outlines of an other "invisible fence"
Female cardinal at the edge of the lawn
A beer that's grown popular in the years since I've stopped drinking, but whose label reads "Since 1829"

Flush hard – it's a long way to the food truck
Wondering if this chair will survive the reading
Hold the pen absolutely perpendicular to the page
Spring Fling, Fall Pall
One rolls the hula hoop down the hill while the other, with a giant orange "Blaster," attempts to shoot ping pong balls through it as it passes
Moment when the sun no longer illumines and the street lamps have yet to take hold – child alone sitting before the giant concrete wall beside the rack of locked bikes
Mercedes Benzine
From server to serve (as ever I swerve)
Here is a ridden art that achieve a rap sure wooly now & gorges
The first page is so seldom numbered 1
Man walks into the bookstore holding a bicycle helmet in one hand
You hear the hiss of an aerosol can in the next room & you wonder to what purpose
Now the mockingbird mimics the squirrel

Ferrous wheels
Taller than any of these oaks is that old poplar
The golfers were using their clubs as tho it were hockey
Those wonderful curls where the ear spirals down into the skull
A place in the shade (in a few hours this heat will prove unbearable)
The slightest light breeze vibrates the crime scene tape
Prosody of the power mower
In this dream, the woman bumps her head, which spontaneously explodes
Amiri Baraka singing to himself in the men's room stall

The cardinal's incessant (now there's a word) "cheep, cheep" fell over the congregation

Yesterday's stumble (the pizza slice poised mid-air directly below its overturned, still-spinning plate) memorialized this afternoon in the grated flesh of my knee

Butterfly as it goes into the mower's blades

You stick the signifier into the signified (please pay the syntax)

Infinitesimal red spider walking up my thigh

X of eczema

Of being timorous

High up in that loft space a green neon word (illegible script, perhaps kanji) hangs over the area designated as kitchen

He's still talking to me but I've already stepped outdoors so that all I hear are the tones of his voice through the glass

Glove songs

The tomatoes are fighting

How many summers remain just to sit in the yard reading

Calling for assistance, "Bailiff, bailiff"

Crow conceived as a discount hawk

Little white butterflies

hover over the grass

Purple fierceness of the thistle in bloom

Off to see a show of Fairfield Porter's, expecting the work of Trevor Winkfield

Looking at a page to tell the time

Lone goose, calling as it flies

June, therefore June bugs

Shutting the book with only five pages remaining

Permitting the tea to steam up my glasses, then letting them slowly clear

Power yoga

Although the task seemed simple enough – identify the bird with the green head, black bill and brown chest – none of the field guides offered reasonable options

Even though her mother's Anglo and she herself was born in Detroit, she retains a distinct hint of her father's Gujarat accent
Fire as a solid
Some power something up the hill sets the trees on edge
Some new thrush's loud dusk song
Passionate knishes
White butterfly settles into the flowers and disappears

Saturday aircraft
Marketer's motto: Life's a pitch!
Already sisters are beginning to worry as to who will inherit the china closet
When the fans go off, the air goes still, then heavy
They stand or crouch at the edge of the building, attempting to stay dry while they smoke
Boy sleeps on cot in the nurse's office until the parent arrives to take him home

It's not that a tear is so unexpected, but for it to rise rather than slide down the cheek
Little twigs stick in the push mower's blades,
a pause in the rhythm of these long straight sweeps over the nearly chartreuse lawn
Fire as a liquid
The smart card's striped bar chirps under the eye of the reader (time it takes for this sentence to obsolete & opaque)
Aggregate the data
Relearning to chew on that side of your mouth
Outdoors, all the air conditioner means is the sound of a motor

Domain poisoning

Moment at which the diced potatoes taste too salty, the half-eaten muffin too hard, the tea no longer searing smooth to my throat, breakfast is done

Pages for pigeons

Instantly, references to the previous century seem quaint

Little cocoon tucked on the backside of the mailbox flag

The symmetry of the alphabet is artificial, some letters (the vowels) more important than all the rest

Deep scrolling

Hospital takes an entire city block, yet three buildings down the next street, all trace is gone

Standing on the unlit porch at dusk, barely visible to the passing walkers (a rustling of shadows)

Noses are red, violins are blue

An immense field at dusk, alive now with fireflies just over the grass

I don't notice the slow fan turning up on the high ceiling until I see it reflected in the shining knife of my table setting (when will the waitress come with my eggs, my muffin), Elton John tune played on clarinet & strings softly in background

By the end of the third letter, most readers will presume that they know the word, their eyes skipping to the next

Don't complain, don't explain

I pick up the book and am in the process of opening it when a butterfly (or perhaps a moth) bursts from its pages & out, away from the porch, into the night

Entering from the garage, the mudroom is dark, but open the next door and the cold conditioned air of the house pulls steam from your flesh

The chartreuse moose loved couscous

Each region its rich eccentric, ready to construct a castle, say, of poured concrete

Little balsa painted bird / sits by the fence / under the roses

Throbbing sensation displaced to the predicates

How the fog burns off so slowly you barely notice until, suddenly, the meadow's in full view

In the double sink, the water down one drain echoes out the other

Sequim, the 'e' being silent

Tan Lin: "In the air, there is the fragrance of alphabets"

Events are actions

He stumbles through the tall grass, the smoldering airplane barely visible behind him

Beautiful black full-length dress, yellow flower print upon satin, hanging in dusk breeze from a trimaran docketed next to the boat-builder's shop, Port Hadlock, Washington, across the street from a row of small pastel summer cabins & the restaurant where everybody eating is asked to wear funny hats, the sun setting pink-orange into the Straight of San Juan de Fuca, half-dozen sailboats anchored in the water, when up drives her crème-colored beemer, a convertible no less, and she steps out in pink halter and white cut-offs, taking the hanger with the dress in one hand as she climbs aboard the craft & disappears below

Reading three books as though parallel only to discover that one is twenty pages shorter than you'd expect

Deadlines to headlines

A brand can defeat an army

We hear the rolling thunder swallowed in its own impulse and feel the first few fat drops of rain, but as far as we have to run to make it to shelter, the storm pauses, looking, waffling, waiting

Jennicam in love

At dusk comes cricket hour

Sand flies thick in the rotting kelp

In Bandy Town where I did dwell

So sad forest, whose high grave green pillowy leaves weigh down the light limber branches, shadow upon shadow speckled with sun motes, living beings afloat in the air that, if suddenly cast upward onto this middle scale of the human, would appear to us monstrous, part bear, part nightmare, body parts for which I have no name, blind & yet sensate, ruthless & yet gentle

Life is hard when you're a banana

Geography is destiny (7:21 AM, 7 August 2000)

All fog, no mountain

The kind of fart that, to listen, best approximates the air being drained from a tire (the air gradually thickens with a rich fecal odor)

Soil so hard & infertile, its stones are called "Sequim potatoes"

Lone felled trunk above what should have been the timber line

Invariably linguists offer lame examples

This text has been wrapped for your individual protection

He reheats the cup of tea she abandoned – only to discover it thick with sugar

First sun shimmers in the highrise glass

Bee climbs up into the fuchsia

Air this humid feels still, tho I can tell & hear from the trees' rustle that this is not the case

Already women in pairs walk vigorously along the harbor

Amaranthus caudatus, also called Love Lies Bleeding

Someone walking about – stomping really – on the balcony below

As I reach to pick up the saddle-stitched text, a book mark (an old business card) slips out & drifts tumbling slomo in the air

Washing dishes yields damp cuff I only notice an hour later

The moon at first sat red-orange on the horizon, then yellowed as it rose

Little white flower growing up through this crack of cement, I'm so sorry I don't know your name – who else will love these delicate deep petals

What is a heron but a neck with feathers

Cellophane encasement over the metal bottle cap, the precautions we take

Bataille for babies

Before the automatic association from the word "palm" became "pilot"

Foreground: crickets in the trees by the hundreds / background: a wood chipper some blocks away (second melody: big baritone dog)

How odd to hear in the woods, however distant & tentative, a trumpet

Which, from the other direction, is replied to by a goose

The transparency of the invariance principle tore the treetops down for spite

The Henry Fonda is a rose of brilliant yellow, first hybridized in 1996 (the Weight Watchers Success is a pale pink)

Even from across the harbor at night, you can tell when the juggler is using torches

Departing the bus, she walks briskly down the street

Gangly yet stately, blue heron wades in the surf

First bought, best bought

The steady shush of distant traffic, a foghorn, few small invisible birds, cows & perhaps goats somewhere beyond this meadow, plus of course one large dog so distant you can barely discern that deep barking

Even before it gets to you, the poem is *deja toujour* a collaboration
Our plenarists
Paper trails to you
Until we meet again
It's not the siren that gets our attention, but it's come to a stop so near
Sun's glare as we emerge from the tunnel
Holding utterly still, waiting to see if the bee that's landed on my bare knee will sting me, then wincing when it does
Until we meet again
After all those frozen waffles, who's going to want yesterday's pizza reheated for lunch
Cherry tree no taller than I am / but already these deep red bings
Paper trails to you
Old friend fog again & the red-orange flesh revealed by the peeling madrone
Feast of the sparrows
Gone not quite two weeks, spider's made his web in my chair on the porch
Punch buggy red (no punch back)
Mr Iguana lies prone on the rug
After the mechanized chill of the air conditioning, the humid cling of the not quite dusk sky proves its own relief
Eat cantaloupe slices slowly, the meat of it dissolving under the slightest pressure, tongue against palette
Sparrows cluster on the white fence, watching me nibble cranberry bun

An hour after the pancakes, the taste that lingers is of the one that was, how shall I say it, somewhat overcooked
A family skipping stones just beyond the salt foam of Dungeness Spit

Life in the Goks
Is that going to be in a poem
Ultrabeam or psychobeam
The French-speaking woman is walking back to her family from the johns, both fists tightly clinched
What happens when you go up in history
We wanna, iguana
The Octopus said: "Do you want it 'C' caffeinated"
Sipping the tea too soon after the microwave
A defeat can brand an army
Geography is density (5:48 AM, 6 September 2000)
I smell roses
No I blinks
Cars backed up half a mile when the man exits his truck and walks deliberately through the rows of cars, gun in hand
She's speaking to him in French but he replies in English
Chinese restaurant alone in the otherwise empty strip mall, too brightly lit, completely empty
Door is alarmed
She stumbles slightly going up the stairs, but catches herself so quickly on the landing that to the others it seems at first a skip or dance step
One object first manufactured in Paoli is the Slinky
Stanzas in medication
Man with his tie tucked into his belt
I see her sitting, rapt at the reading, head tilted slightly, but the blue eyes terribly sad
Dis, dis, dis, dis

A park in this dream in a city to which I've never been but which all my friends must know since they've come here too
Even tho the rain is barely visible on the street, cars have already begun making that shushed wet road sound
Pessimism of the intellect, sarcasm of the will

A fire in the alphabet
Uber Alice
A finch in time
Barely steamed vegetables hot from the pot
Disformalism
Specificity to the clatter of silverware
Three wire chairs back in the forest
The bathroom's fan serves a second function: to shut out sound

Simple toggle of a light switch ignites the roomful of gas, the piping on the brick walls melting almost instantly, what flesh remains hanging from his body as he stumbles into the open air (it will take eight days for the poisons in his kidneys & liver to kill him)

What starts as black ink glistens as it sinks into the buff-colored page, drying into a pale blue-gray.

Exactly what is an iguana rub
Rah rah futurism
No pun where none distended
The poem has scalability
Italian karaoke night
Rings women wear when they're single
Breathing into the white mug of hot tea so that the steam fogs up from your glasses, the world beyond reduced to tone before shape

Army recruiting center is a storefront converted from something intended for much larger use (standing partitions divide the space)

Fingers, organized at the palm
Don't flask, don't flail
Why firemen smoke
Man at the top of the stairs to the subway, slightly past midnight, saxophone in hand

Foggy mornings are better than windy ones, though you have to towel off the plastic deck furniture before you can sit down

Digimon in the dark

Today the junior college & a mock-swank hotel straddle the lower locks of the old canal system – the mill's tall smokestack still in the now clear air

Writing about love to Bruce Andrews

Trees or their silhouettes etched into the concrete sound walls, leafless winter forest barely visible beyond

The percussionist chewing gum in a different rhythm

Old style hotel restaurant, the waiters in tuxedos at breakfast

No entiendo porque yo no tengo Nintendo

Flap your arms like slow wings (a performance)

Remove glasses just to remember the world without frames

Same-day parts logistics applied to predicate

It's nouns that in head clatter

Let's delta

Three slices of turkey – the white meat – atop thick slabs of virtually colorless garlic bread alongside a sodden mound of mashed potatoes, all bathed in the palest of gravies

The urinary habits of Dr. Filreis.

Now that there are two generations younger than you, each distinct

Deplane

Neo-Christian bodice ripper

Teapot drips when you tilt to pour

Agave scarcity impacts tequila market

Boring little langpos

The wind sounds more harsh, relentless, now that the trees are leafless, sticks clattering in air

Boy says "I hate couscous up my nose."

Pokemon, Digimon, Hegemon
No domain server was available to validate you
Gazebo by the brook
An hour after the shower, the humidity of the restroom is still oppressive
Annette Funicello replicant waitress
Auto parts after market
Put down book, pick up fork
Curious flamingo pause before the pitcher throws to the plate
Hard cheese
Red-plaid blanket over the window of the overturned car – privacy for the dead
Full moon tangled in the maple
Tom Pynchon's buck teeth
Foreign film soundtrack warbles, wobbles
Bandwidth is hell

Oatmeal's first tiny spoonful sears the tongue, causing eyes to water, one to breathe gaspingly through open mouth as though blowing over the surface of hot soup, whereas one minute later a heaping spoonful is a great comfort to entire mouth, tongue, cheeks, palette, throat all sigh to swallow such soothing warmth

Man at that table looks just like Allen Ginsberg but this is a casino in Vegas & Allen's three years' dead

Martianalization of genius
Power puddles

Oreo aria
Photo massage
Herbs verbs / garden walk
A scene of the entire port painted on a single stick of driftwood
Last sip of tea invariably lukewarm
After Jerry died the meaning of "Maris" changed & then changed again
That dove too large for the bird feeder dangling from the dogwood's slim branch
Salt glass, also called mermaid's tears, broken shards of bottles ground smooth (& sometimes milky) by the sand and sea
Stand up too quickly under hanging Tiffany chandelier

Sentences to go before I beep
Eros erosion
Bowling for squirtles
Wrong side of the spoon
On the rear of the john door, a huge blue stain
Too sweet peach smell of the gymnasium
Rock rats
Nonbook of the nonbook
Peeling caked cracked flesh away from your heel

Steady churn of the dishwasher (between cycles you hear the TV on in the other room)
Eventually, time will render you a voyeur of your youth
An inch in each direction
Writing by brilliant sunlight on an otherwise winter day
Lost clusters
A clothesline in Tibet

One day after bowling, I can barely make a fist

First wipe, best wipe

Wear hat partly to protect my eyes but really because I like the containment, the pressure distributed evenly along skull's rim

Ink frozen in the pen

So-called breakfast potatoes

Film kiln

Having woken each night this week at roughly the same hour, I realize it's the moment the moon (or what remains of it) shines through the tangle of madrone outside onto my pillow (& having realized this, I roll over & return to sleep)

In a Victoria BC aboriginal arts store called Alcheringa, I ask the manager if she knows Dennis Tedlock or Jerry Rothenberg – she stares at me blankly, shaking her head

These days my mouth feels liked snapped twigs and razor wire (chew with caution)

Counting carbs

Gradually, music starts to rise up from the lower parts of the house, not loud enough for you to make out what is being played

Pages dwindle toward the end of Collected Works

Road rouge

The two of us reclining, facing one another in the large tub, the suds half-covering the freckles on your breasts, my big toe gently exploring the folds of a tender spot, soft flesh softened further by the warm water, your own foot atop my knee that I might massage its toes, and you laugh, grinning as my own big toe slides in

Omelet filled with trout

The toilet is gagging, strangling on my shit

This is the story of wolves

Obvious typo long into the text & thus you will no longer quote trust that these are the real words

Some half-digested bread wedged up into my gums as I probe with my tongue

Years later, it was apparent how different our lives would have been had their life not been so brief (I was thinking of Smithson, then Jerry Estrin, Dan Davidson, John Lennon, Nina Iskrenko, Jack Spicer, Kathy Acker, Lee Hickman all flooded into mind, O rich world that could have been

The pigeons are letter-boxed

A pen as finely honed as a knife

DSL: damned slow log-on

Evil shoe box

Underneath the oboe's solo, toe shoes squeak across the stage

"But what about Stein in your work," they asked, "What about Gertrude," to which she replied, "There is none"

I startle the blue heron in the reeds by the frozen pond

In my version, it's the buffalo who flies the helicopter

Putting the P into PDA

Princess diorama

Hands dangle useless out of cuffs

Irrevocable oracle

Zero is an even number
"Barely & Widely"
(barely audible / widely despised)
Dark side of the spoon

Old computer in the motel lobby for the guests to use in reading or sending email, tracking stocks, following the news far from home (attempts are being made to rescue Russian sub

I find the tiniest bit of crisp clear cellophane, part of a CD wrapper, clinging to the flesh of my cheek

Luke warm Laura hot (speeds at which cultural allusions erode)

Under the roar of three dozen treadmills, exercycles, stairmasters, the music of Green Day on the sound system is barely audible

The joy of 6

That sour alien odor, he realized at last, was his own breath

Ancient woman, frozen toe

Poetry is self-inflicted

Drive-Thru Tattoo

The uppermost layer of cloud, thin & spotty, casts shadows over the larger, more dense (roiling) lower layer

Yoshi gives three coins to Bowser

More rice (more ice)

It wasn't snowing so much as the small flakes swirling in the moonlight, never landing

Sound of running water from inside the radiator

Learning to discern where in the ear a particular sound will fall

Electronic handshake

Lambs and iambs

New aspect of taste called umami

Carrier hotel becomes server farm

On the rug, a lone paperclip has been bent out of shape

Electronic milkshake

Tonight, dinner is spicy garlic chicken & vegetable medley over rice at the food court

Reader-initiated verse

Mozart's violin

Robert Johnson / hits a high note

Clouds smear the sunset along the horizon

Point at which I realize that crossing the large field in the dark is a mistake

Using a deposit slip in lieu of a business card

When the plaster peels, you realize it's not just dry wall

Value sized

Immortal portal

Imagine these twin balloons of lungs balancing so carefully on the small wounded pump of the heart

Miner's helmet, a safety device invented by an insurance man, Franz Kafka

Pawn's surly blight

Found texts / lost works

By the heel of your shoe, position your body in space

That pause at the side of a car, fuel's hose inserted, gas tank slowly filling

An old barn, half collapsing behind the overgrown brush by the fence, beyond which a dozen large new homes (no landscaping yet to speak of)

Once the tea cools

Compass mnemonic: *never eat soggy waffles*

Poem modeled on the night sky

Nameless, spelled backwards

No pronouns need apply

The more subtle colors of the female cardinal

A large man walking down the corridor with a noticeable

limp, holding a phone with his right hand to his left ear (Andean flutes softly over the loudspeakers)

Objects in mirror are stranger than they appear

Now that any plastic bag, tumbling, blowing in the street has become an allusion to *American Beauty*

The familiar voice of a favorite poet

A row of cabins along the gravel lane, backhoe next to one idle in the rain

Sadder days, Saturdays

Not exactly dusk yet but the sun already lost behind the tangle of oak branches now starting to bloom

To green into boom

When I first saw him, arms & legs spreadeagled across the pavement when his skateboard into the residue of last winter's road salt, I thought his face was contorted with pain, but today, seeing him hold a hose, watering a bed of what will someday be flowers in front of his parents' house, I see that same expression & recognize instead a case of palsy

John Cajun

Harlem Truffle

Rimbaud, from his English language notebook, "This cheese is all alive"

Don't do the crime if you can't do the rhyme

By the river's edge, a purple martin house with no purple martins

Pickup trucks at the edge of the track, the stadium packed with men, women, children as a lone woman in pale blue robes is led blindfolded to the center of the green, surrounded now by a dozen men, not one in uniform, as she kneels and one (identified as the father of the husband she slew) steps forward with a rifle aimed right at the back of her head – and we see the dust kicked up by the bullet in front of her before we hear its report & she never even hears the crowd's loud roar as she slumps all but shapeless onto the Afghan earth

Here I propose a phenomenological approach that directly describes space-time foam, and which leads naturally to a picture of distance fluctuations that is independent of the details of the interferometer

New rules for lawn care dictate higher blades of grass

Masked password

Reading two short poems by Lyn Hejinian is like reading three full books by anyone else

Hello noisy morning – eeow!

The dog in the woods audible only because of his tags

Fuzzy logic for ventilator management

Old man in Chinatown, white hair flowing under blue baseball cap, wire rim glasses, a small back pack, racing against the flow of traffic atop slender new silver scooter

When simply to close one's eyes is to enter the dream

Bacon stuck along the gum line, where the stitches have yet to dissolve

From the balcony you can see Treasure Island

My left knee bubbles with pain, warm, pulsing

You can see her thinking as she pauses, glass poised over the rim of her lip

Puppet theater of the alphabet

"Turbulence"
refers
to the sky
below

Don't do the rhyme if you can't do the time

Reading the poem but omitting the last line

Only movement visible in the one-room gallery: tree-top just outside the window, conveying a light breeze

At dusk, when the spiderwebs are invisible, the smell of cut grass & two robins barking in the poplars

At top speed, the ceiling fan picks up a clicking rhythm, as though anxious to rip free of its mount

The princess tree, which doesn't bloom every year, this time a lush purple

Even from up here you can hear it, way off in the distance, a siren

Turning the cellphone over & over in the palm of his hand

When simply to open one's eyes is to enter the dream

Private property, private parts

Raccoon on the back porch pauses in the sudden glare of the outside light, but waits until you start shouting to shamble off into the woods

She holds a single sheet crowded with words, a single paragraph single spaced, but reads aloud just five words

The good marksman learns to shoot between heartbeats, but a batter has no choice facing the ball's advance (learning to read so that the beats match the consonants)

Exhaustion in the body language of retail staff 30 minutes before closing

San Francisco bayonet

Point in the evening when half the people in the airport are dealing with cancelled flights

The secret to being naked in public is recognize that your flesh is itself a suit of clothes

Grandmotherly, but with tattoos

Face, changeable as a screen saver

Me, unvoiced in time

The ampitheater full

Lakoff's Danes

The rain gone, but the grass still damp

Wild artichokes growing in the sand, right at the ocean's edge

The wind, articulate throughout the damp forest, loud, raucous

Writing until my hand grows numb

The sky dim for an ostensibly sunlit day

A block away, a car alarm begins its reiterative song (underneath, deeper than the doves piping in the black oak, the first growling rolls of thunder)

Wild roses, just as the petals start to wilt

You can hide anything in the pachysandra

In the dream I'm about to deliver a short political talk – no more than two pages – over Italian radio from the funkiest of studios in North Beach, but my prose as I read it amid the chaos of metal folding chairs & microphones is aphoristic to the point of impenetrability, and there's no mention of a translator at all (I awake and then, sitting on the john reading yet another review of Radosh on the Rosenbergs, think instead of the allusion to Pound)

The interplay of light & shade organizes the otherwise green field, evolving gradually as afternoon dissolves into dusk

Gameboy meditation

The rain, audible in its approach

The moon Io, miniature against the backdrop of Jupiter

The removal of certain articles of clothing, my watch for instance, triggers a palpable wave of relief

Uses of the word "to"

Dog steps into the garden and squats

The lavender thick with bees

From this angle the photographed stone takes on the profile of a bearded head

Point beyond which memory invariably failed

The dampness in an old baseball cap that never goes away

Heroic kazoos (dance theater)
I retie my left shoe, but now the other one feels as loose as a slipper
The Golden Book of Torture
Our nation turns its lonely eyes to you,
ooh ooh ooh
Sexing of the sun
Colin pauses to pull up his socks
New flesh fresh under the scab
Overheard in the next room (answer a phone), "Hello, oh hello" – in the reiteration the tone of recognition
Triangle of glass found in my strawberry pancake
A terrible dream, of which I have no memory other than having woken trembling, on the verge of tears
Sol Lewitt / silhouette
A very large poem of very few words
Spider pauses on the edge of my boot
Where to put the bookmark once the text is open
Men standing about in front of the bank of pay phones, cellphones to their ears
At the large group picnic, one boy wanders off into the woods alone, my son, & in that solitude I recognize my own boyhood
The light is mute at this moment before dawn
I thought for awhile that your demons might tame my own
Dying, the moth unable to fly
Rubble without a cause
The creature, slightly over two feet in length, was like a small alligator with exceptionally long jaws, but with sweet almost docile temperament & a lush coat of dense red-brown and white fur
So it is the body that dictates the end game
Through these trees I see the light come on in their kitchen (fireflies flicker above the grass)
First, blanched octopus & sliced cherry tomatoes on toast, then grill roasted pigeon with a side of polenta
The tiny device just to slice the pill

Bloated tail of the gecko

Girl at the cash register with the unshaved armpits, brilliant smile, takes my money, direct eye contact, our hands so briefly barely touching, until I stagger back out onto the sunlit street

Weevil doers

Little rectangular plate on the wall where once stood a socket

Just enough hot water to "freshen" the tea

Ball to the palm feels like soft rubber, but is a clear plastic in the middle of which, perfectly proportioned, is a miniature city, instantly recognizable as your former home

Now the blind juggler picks up his half dozen knives

Reaching down to cup butterflies between her palms off the top of the grass

Forgot the butter in the banana bread, but then liked better the lighter result

Light breeze just barely visible in the leaves of the trees

Phrase I thought I saw – "morning is spewing colors"

Land mine removal program: children play in the fields until they set them off

Actually, I've never enjoyed writing at the bottom of a page

It was a curious form of fidelity, moving to Vacaville to be near her man while he served his time, then commuting six days a week down to the Bay Area to work in a brothel

At times the weight of this pen is so heavy

The voyeurism of house sitting

Hamster dam

Seagulls serve as hyenas to the pelican's lion

Giant acrylic portrait of a rusted wash basin dominates one wall of the parlor set off behind glass doors just for visiting

A man keeps his wife prisoner on a small boat for 24 years

Scars where a towel rack once hung from the drywall
Popping bubblewrap
But now I see that man's smile emanating from your face

Opening the container, he recognized – just for a fraction of a second – that he loved the smell of aspirin
Thunder throughout the day, but never any rain
Having cut four tenths of an acre with just an old push mower, I slump into the once-white plastic lawn chair, sweat flowing freely from every pore, my own salt searing my forehead's flesh, the air breezeless, thick with an oncoming afternoon storm
We hear the butterfly beating its wings
Porch light on in the middle of the day
Someone just out of the line of sight calls my name
The slightest cut on the tip of my finger – to the side, just above the knuckle – so small that you can't see it, though instantly perceptible to touch
Instantly you recognize that dog's bark as unfamiliar
What comes next
Raven vs. squid
Long long line before unattended airport gate podium
In one corner stands an escritoire that is never opened, used now only as a stand for a large green rose
Tea lukewarm at the bottom of the cup
Page turns in book, words never to be read for the first time again
Vaguely feline smell of my mother's apartment
One number in the sequence is absent, but does this mean it's "missing"
Wooden platform, wedged into the oak tree's crotch in lieu of a treehouse
Between lean & learn (our desire)
Snot cakes up high at the rear of nasal passage

In their glass case by the gecko cage, the live crickets are silent, but the one that escaped during this morning's feeding, now under the fridge, roars defiant into the night

Day in which words dissolve without a trace the instant you read them

Man in the moon's not just any face – that's Phil Whalen!

Larvation house

Common murre slides under the water, more fish than bird

Memory of lovemaking with one now dead

Behind those eyeglasses, my mother's pupils search vainly for light

Elegant castors, too small for cups, too wobbly for glasses

That space between words is a chasm

Seventeen years after the last glass, the taste of beer even in a dream is instantly recognizable

Gray-brown of winter forest

Gradually, the flags on each auto antenna begin to shred & fade

ƎƆИA⅃UᗺMA

The crowd clusters by the blocked-off intersection, craning to see over or through the fences at what little is visible of the crumbled towers

He writes in his own tongue as though he were translating

Mnemonic plague

Allergic reaction to this shirt

Foolishly, we expected the moon to be full tonight also

Orca   raven   squid

Out here, it is the Subaru Legacy Outbacks vs. the Ford Explorers, though that old-timer sticks with his Chevy Suburban

Password masked in the dialog box

The new metaphor: spore

Brecht fast

White noise of cicadas

They could see the woman still conscious beside her dead husband frantically struggling to open the crushed door of the Volvo as the flames rose and then swallowed her

My little dog, Placebo

That instant in which "growing up" means "growing old"

She speaks of the abortion she had at 15

Moment at which 30 percent of the world's copper comes from Butte & the Anaconda mine

My watchband begins to disintegrate

Walking the neighborhood the evening before trash is collected, just to see what the neighbors discard

The clam's commitment is to adhere to the rock

You lean forward, head tilted slightly to one side, eyes chasing, lips parted but just barely, as though surprised by the advent of a kiss (around us traffic swirls, reduced in the mind to little more than distant texture)

The fuselage dissolves through the liquid surface of the tower's plate glass façade, illusion that lingers for an interminable fraction of a second before the bright burst of fire blooms, booms

Potemkin Village of the heart (precisely the sort of hokey metaphor you would expect from these pale faceless poets

Tilting the candle to let the wax run off

The bats flew so low that even at this hour we could see their faces

Setting the book down, I doze in the large chair

Where the baby bamboo runs into the pachysandra

Each word scribed is a banner of regret

Breezy Lake Anza shoreline – swimming area roped off into three neat rectangles apparently by depth (man nearly is shimmying into swim trunks under a towel)

What was most interesting about her work was that, no matter how much you read, you could never quite get a sense of it, it would never quite come into focus

Heat of the tea warms my mouth, my skull, eyes, nostrils, then the taste of it, full, rich, unsweetened, then (only then) does the caffeine kick in

A mime is a terrible thing to waste

Next door, the driveway fills with cars every weekend, minivans, sleek midsized sedans, SUVs (in the driveway beyond that, the Indian biochemist wears a helmet to match his new red motorcycle)

I can't write with you screaming

Courting carbs

A bee on my knee so still

Description on roadside turnout sign characterizes harbor seal as "sausage-like" &, sure enough, there one is

Light in the room mutes – outside the sun is behind a cloud

They call that part of the cemetery "unendowed"

Write each letter from the end to the beginning

Inside the cube of ice, floating in the glass, what appeared to be a perfectly formed, fully dressed little man

The sign language interpreter is always a woman

The hourglass tumbles over & over where the cursor should be

Vowels, military grade

Allowed in trousers

Francophone Persephone

The autumn of women is square-toed boots

Going to college to make other a noun

Beckett beckons

The year Velcro became the style for watch bands
That particular if faint nausea one feels immediately after clipping one's nails
Moment at which you not only are aware of the hair in your noise, but have the irresistible desire to pull it
Big pig
Wire mall kiosk of miniature license plates of every possible name but yours
The mailman in Latex gloves
Self portrait with a convex lock
Thunder throughout the day but never any rain
What appeared to be mushrooms were in fact sweet pastries
For all your walrus drawing needs
Your results may vary
"They found part of his face last week so we finally held a funeral," the small boy talking quietly
Don't confuse the poem with the text (you're next)

In Pennsylvania, every salad is a disappointment
The pain is situated right between the eyes
It's only as I'm shaking his hand that I realize he has just four fingers
So few people know how to give a blow job without scraping the invading cock against the teeth
The moment at which Keith Haring no longer meant graffiti
Guillotine the pill
Little theaters of the footnote
Zit on your earlobe
Bruce's bruises
Your sweating balls cling to your thighs as you walk

Thin lipped, wire rim glasses staring out from the small square on the back flap of the dust jacket

Instantly you recognize that dog's bark as unfamiliar

She arrives holding a wool cap in one hand

One pocket shirts vs. two

Looking exactly like an unemployed Marine except for the silver post through one eyebrow

A think book makes thick trouble

O moose of Tucson

The blind dog sleeps on the cool slate floor

Squirrels shuffled about in the pile of dead leaves

That seldom-used park on Cedar Hollow Road

Defibonacci

They were able to identify Wieners only through a receipt for a prescription they found in a pocket

Goodnight baseball, goodnight rune

Words never quite touch

From the far end of the otherwise silent house there rose a sudden laugh, but in its wake the silence only deepened

Squid vs. orca

You open the door to find behind it a naked woman fresh from a hot bath who embraces you

In the yard, the old man in his perpetually fishing hat stares at the garden

A Christmas wreath, brown & dry, still nailed to the door in August

In those days entire families traveled with the army, which might take years pursuing Alexander's troops west out of India, until a decade became a generation, then several, widows remaining warriors, the young boys growing up to replenish the ranks, those now too old to fight still tagging along, until no one, not even the generals, remember any more where home had been or for whom they were fighting, so that the army itself began to drift aimlessly until gradually it arrived in Europe, splintering now into bands whom the locals for some reason imagined to have come from Egypt, thus calling these once North Indian wanderers "gypsies."

Different modes of reading you do just before you fall asleep, including this one, where you know you won't remember anything once you wake, tho it will be there, lurking, around the edges of any dream

The lawn, just long enough to warrant cutting

Little brick patio a monument to low-end postwar architecture

Reassured by a sense of plenitude, fresh roll of toilet paper

Black-shouldered kite pushed up over the pine tops by the shore breeze

Eight days after walking along the Marina trying to recall the name of the yoga school owner who had once lived along this strip of homes, over breakfast now in Carmel, the words appear: Ed Dreesen

I see her pausing to look at herself, naked, in the full-length mirror

Wimbrel shares its rock with a black turnstone, but are those otters floating peacefully on their backsides amid that vast bed of kelp

I see you pausing to look at yourself, naked, in the full-length mirror

The man in the dream alone on the hilltop (no tree, not even a shrub, visible in any direction) is wearing a baseball uniform (the murmur of unseen voices growing louder & louder), a glove on his right hand, the name on the shirt's back legible as Antonelli (the next image is of the same hilltop at a great distance as it suddenly bursts into flames)

When the jackhammer & backhoe both stop, you recognize the mockingbirds &, somewhere distant, a penny whistle

Yellow butterfly bright in the bougainvillea
Pinot in the glass, carafe
Vegans & Vulcans & Vikings, oh my
Zeno's paradiddle
Tarantula wasp
All this prose makes one anxious for linebreaks
Old blind dog's heavy breathing as it sleeps
Ironically, it's the keyboard that has the elaborate case
Letters glisten in the sun until the ink sets, last drops shining at the tip of every letter
Beneath us, on the ground, time zones are changing
They only pretend it's a message
Red meat bird, pigeon or ostrich
Cell phone in a thunder storm
Silence of the loins
The difference a dangle
Counting bulbs in the chandelier
They only pretend it's a massage
Bring May stallions
Ironic in the bad sense
Uses his boarding pass as a bookmark
Gradually the butter melts into the toast
I'm sitting in the stands of an empty baseball diamond, writing in a notebook
Gradually the batter melts into the past
In 1202, Leonardo, the son of Bonacci, publishes *Liber Abacci* (The Book of Calculations), in which he introduces numbers he learned from "The Hindus" while accompanying his father on trips to Algeria – 9, 8, 7, 6, 5, 4, 3, 2 & 1 (to which he adds 0) – a fatal blow to the system of Roman numerals

I rose at dawn to write these words, going from bed to verse

Last of the meat clumps along the rim of the bowl

In a dream I record a promise: "Blurb TRAFFIC SERIES for Grenier"

Book slips from the arm of the chair as I doze

These trees, hundreds of feet high

Syntax flows facing forward, while punctuation governs through hindsight

Giant potted lavender referred to as our own private beehive

Sometimes we're launching a great ship out onto the waters, but at other moments it's just taking a crap

I see through my own reflection in the glass, the rain adding its own layer to the pane

A cluster of bright orange mushrooms atop the old stump, one atop another, each the size of a man's hand, the tops not cupped by turned upward as if to catch the intermittent rain

She says, a little too matter-of-factly, "I guess I'll be one of the shorter life spans," & I remember us 25 years ago, how our bodies moved together in perfect rhythm

Waiting after I've stopped the car for the song on the radio to conclude before I remove the key from the ignition

The first maple to have turned a brilliant red

Beanie Baby with its tag still attached

Bright balloons, twisted into hieroglyphics

A cheese the flavor of horse radish

His jacket was in fact a giant shirt

Adverts for inverts

A bookie of Centurian arts

A wooden platform wedged into the oak tree's crotch in lieu of a tree house

These few pages are all that remain

The flimsiness of audio tape defined an age almost the way the curiously fragile heft of 78s had defined another

Failing to Siladelphia

Lists of my life

Crumbled into the soup, the saltine turned the broth into a paste

Little balls of butter in a small white bowl

The presence of doubt understood as a strength

I ask the waitress for a tea bag to take back to my room

Tiny printing projected large, auditorium screen

Water – carbonated – escapes the uncapped bottle

I wake to find the fever has broken

Read a book of poems until you get a sense of its author, then put it down – when you pick it up again, read until your sense of its author changes

Old bench swing on the wrap-around porch

I pick up my cap & shake it until out drops a spider

The car pulled up, stopped & shut down its engine & lights, tho we could still hear, muffled through the windshield, the unmistakable tones of talk radio

Quote machine

Arches his back before he farts

A pair of baby carrots deployed as mock tusks

The way an insomniac watches the clock

Made it to the foot notes

Behind the supermarket, the last generation of shopping carts, rusted in rows

Thai take-out

Next door's windchimes soft in the low breeze

Riding the scorpion, his thorn for my crown

Barefoot violinist

Magpie at the spring house

When at last she moves in, he notices the imperialism of shampoos in the shower – where previously there had been just one plastic bottle on the wire shelf that hung from the faucet (he's used the same brand for years, noticing only enough to be upset when the manufacturer fiddled with the formula), now there are more than half a dozen bottles, some pale & opaque, others translucent in blue, orange, green, containers not just of shampoo but of conditioners, some of them combined, plus something called shower gel

One corner of the shed exerts a powerful magnetic force – old Christmas tree ornaments, forks, keys stick to the wall without anyone knowing why

Man in a black suit in South Beach

Counting the acoustic tiles in the ceiling

The first pass through the deck of cards, everything seems possible

Against the soft piped-in music and the sun just now visible against the office tower glass façade out the atrium window, add this taste of a cranberry scone

Theory of boundary

In that country he's a well-known professor, in this one a clerk in a dry-cleaning shop

She walks with the sweater pulled up over her nose

Voices from the next cabin

Stress for success

Flight attendants, prepare to cross check

Her eyes are red and you wonder if she's upset

Inside the bar some 1950s cartoon he didn't recognize played on the TV, the pace of its unidentifiable animals rendered all the more frenetic by the endless deafening salsa

I seek to swallow this food before I sneeze

The different hum of a new computer

What is a watchband but half a handcuff

Jesse: "What am I supposed to wear if I can't wear dirty clothes"

From the porch the hillside is layered, descending, ferns rising out of the pachysandra between the poplars & oaks

For each band-aid a narrative
Women only become beautiful in middle age

Picnic table covered with birdshit
Today this pen feels small, insubstantial
The kind of food that one seems to chew forever
When orderly was an adverb
The river paralleled the road for miles, then disappeared, so that when we again found ourselves by water maybe ten miles north, we just assumed that it was the same one
Brush stroke pixel
The happening of the yields
Knot gneiss
The gods of the future will laugh at our bandwidth
A small triumph over latitude
Biting down with the fragile tooth
A note obviously in my hand that I have no memory of writing
Lacrosse walk
Instantly recognizable rhythm of the slide carrousel
Cal Ripken card as bookmark
Cheese nachos,
She's macho
The museum doesn't open for another hour
He could see that the three of them were engrossed in some rapid-fire conversation while the fourth sat back looking out at the ocean, absorbed in thought
Maybe I mean *contained*
I'm the Subaru
The pathology of biographers
I could feel all that walking in my hips
Hiss of air hovers over tongue

The rose vine grabbed at my flesh
Imagine under this text a train is passing very close by

With the sun behind, I can't see your eyes
The boys in that circle in the parkinglot are playing hackeysack, using sign language to chatter as they do
Slomo hiphop (chlorinated air of an indoor pool)
At night, the artificial waterfall from the carefully constructed faux granite mountain into the Fontainebleau's blue lit freeform pool roared with a vengeance that was in fact the antithesis of nature – no birds live in these palm trees
Reading of aardvarks but imagining armadillos
Sweeping sidewalks in the desert
Walking side sweeps until dessert
Three dozen years as an adult – how many more will you be given
A think book made thick through bad page design
Distinguished gusts
The loveliness of pepper stuck between teeth
Black dust from the bottom of the Oreo bag
Prying off shrink-wrap
Paradigm blindness
At last the car alarm shuts off & we are surrounded by fireflies in the sudden silence
Who ordered the pizza
The slenderness of wasps
Gutter clowns are evil
All those raucous crows mean no West Nile virus here
We hear them walking those dogs in the dark
Sex serves extensions next to the text
In 17 minutes remove the four teabags from the large pot and let it cool

Fireflies give the dusk depth

Sinuses drain down the rear of your throat

This is not a sales call

A shopping cart rolling idly, empty, by itself across the parking lot

Back before handsoap came in a bottle

Any text is a time capsule

Flabby as the meters of the bard of Bromsgrove (the line imagined as two men struggling to life a couch up into the rear of a small truck)

E for excess, E for economy

The kind of house in which no dog could look natural

In the field, one tree that casts no shadow

One day I see her on the ferry between islands, strolling casually between cars, pulling up her sleeve to show the guys a new tattoo – now here today she is in the café, pale blue cotton dress, bringing me lunch

Sweet rank odor of compost

Fog settles on the trees, the grass, the glass, lone gull pausing on roof's edge

I could hear the horse-drawn buggy, the hooves a distinct gait

We are eating baked bat, served whole, in which you only eat the wing rather the way one does an artichoke leaf, pulling the mean away from the slender bone, tasting a little like bacon, maybe gamier, when one that I start to prod with the tines of my fork turns out still to be alive, just barely, flapping in its startled way off first the plate, then the table, clinging as it falls to my pants leg, where it flutters & flaps in a vain attempt to gain flight

The individual lines of this short poem seem not so much long as fat

Wet ones

In a still life, shadow is narrative
The girl in the dream was but a teenager, possibly
a runaway, long-legged raggedy Levis in sharp contrast to at least his
expectations, her excessive politeness, calling him Sir even as they left the
hotel room & she blended back into the kids milling about in the mall
Instead of ear wax, what the Q-tip probe found was
caked blood
In North Philly, where all the abandoned tires go
The unspeakable emotion of taking off one's shoes
Miscarried at 18 weeks, deeply deformed, buried in a
recipe box, wrapped in a handkerchief, Solomon Silliman
One wants for solitude (from the next house, a
Dylanesque harmonica atop some rock anthem blares out over the
garden).
Thunder rolls in all directions, tho the rain has not yet
begun
The ceiling fan on so high that it rocks & wobbles
The roses, which had appeared to be dying, perked back
up with this intense humidity
The cut or glass itself impacts the flavor
Some truths better left unspoken (some bitter truths left
unspoken)
The violence of rhyme
I could hear him whistling before he sauntered into view
You can see where the mosquito has feasted
It's coming down from the ladder-like steps from the attic
that's dangerous
Picking off the runner, mid-thought, is its own reward
Adopt a Text / Editorial Control / Next Two Pages
Chapbooks won't stack in a straight line
– I almost said "pile" (the way I wrote "said")
But a daddy-long-legs only looks like a spider
Where fire flies disappear to in sunlight
The look in her eyes of discomfort when he pushes in
The moment before dusk when the crows call out

The eye stitched shut
Blood on the floss
Can poetry mutter
Shoves his hand into a bowl of ice
Slap therapy
A constant form of pressure pushing inside the skull
Her sleep now is different, medicated, fitful (she talks or at least mumbles, half whispering, at the slightest provocation, but is unaware of what she has said)
The tray table is upright though the noun itself is redundant
The red-orange "X" thru the smoldering cigarette
Coughing at the bacon's salt
The end game in Tetris
The mushroom menu
Thunder dragons let you get thunder dragons
I never Metamucil
Ms. Paltrow's personal assistant vs. Ms. Paltrow's stand-in
Acid veracity
Edifice wrecks
John the Merthiolater
The head waiter touches the waitress so softly as she passes that you barely notice, hand to this one's shoulder or placed flat against that one's stomach
Song of ice behind the bar
For *nerve* read *never*
Basque bisque
Ennui Regained

Hitchhiker's guide to the fallacy
Voice undermiked mixes with the fan & the bartender shoving beer bottles into the ice

Another over-hyped Weather Channel drizzle alert

Little volunteer dogwood . . . too close to the large oak trunk

What at first appeared to be a forest turned out to be a garden more complex and subtle than I could imagine

In the next seat, a woman is reading a book on death, highlighting sentences with a yellow marker

In the dream, the transition is instantaneous

When cacti flower so brilliantly & profusely this late into a long drought, it means they're throwing off seeds as fast as they can, aware that they themselves are dying

Poverty over the age of 50 is different

Pigeons on the truck, what luck

One of my former lovers has died & two others now are struggling with cancer

There was a bench swing on the deck & though it was new, I could stop thinking of the old rusty one in Baltimore on which I had had my last real conversation with Robert

In the middle of the chapbook, there you find your staples

He characterized his bowel movements with the names of sculptors – a Serra, Smithson, Brancusi or Andre

Dense fog drenched everything without our seeming to notice

Metal stubs for buttons

The hullabaloo of gulls at dawn echoes up from Pond Cove

Bees fat in the unnamed wildflowers

Reiteration of the tide

The way a tea bag stains the saucer

Hear the tear of the peel when you open the banana

The festival consisted of two bands, two food stands (one for hot dogs, the other serving chicken) and a raffle for an ill-designed quilt

The problem with mugs invariably are the handles
He tried to kill the spider but managed only to amputate one leg which continued to move in perfect rhythm with the rest of the beast
Fetal peanut
Deer tic triptych
All of Nigeria laundering millions thru my checking account
Wears time like a grudge
Not a pen but a stylus
A line across the top of his skull of staples
Patriot, tomahawk, scud
They will come for you, as certain as they came for the Jews of Prague
One conks to be stupid
When first you boot the computer, the printer across the room flexes its cartridge
Poetry as a form of terror – never the other way round
Believing Bolinas
The horses in slow motion leap through the flaming sea
Fraktur schriften
More to come, Mordecai
They were the third couple to run this bed-&-breakfast in the past decade
Spiderweb would be invisible but for that poor trapped bee
You sit on the balcony wearing only the tops of your PJs
A person with long fingers will open a book differently
You are reading a text, even a great one, while in your mind conducting a conversation on another topic altogether
Unable with your eyes shut to touch the tip of your finger to that of your nose
The feeling that your toes are in some way "dead"
Storm petrol's furious flap of wings, like a swallow permanently at sea

A pot of spoon-bread still hot & steaming
Christmas lights in the shape of peppers (in the middle of May)
Moving a bag of chips from the small table, I make myself a desk
A sprig of roses painted on the side of the tea pot
When the woman at the next table, with the wild red hair & angular features and those pale white snakeskin boots, speaks to the waiter, you are surprised to hear her thick East European accent

Breathing precedes will, hunting in the dark for the keys to the pickup
At first the garbage trucks give off a hollow sound
Birds understand that the dawn is coming
Pages are fewer now, more precious
Instead of the escritoire, I set the notebook out atop the old utilitarian table
A giant kite in the shape of an octopus floated at the edge of the bay
So many of these old yards overgrown now, flowering bushes at the edge of wildness, roses entangled in the bougainvillea
The goat cheese heated & soft
Periodicity of the sleeping lungs
A potholder for every city on the continent
Sailboats shimmer in the distance
This poem built the way you would a life
Black t-shirt etched with salt
Salad composed of tomatoes and white balls of mozzarella
Trucks echo along the empty street
Then, hearing a small airplane, you realize the dark has given way

High over the canopy of summer oaks, a dozen or so bats dip & swirl

The stack of books of poetry, the minute you finish the first one, appears infinitely smaller

"You should shoot the thing that haunts you" – if I believed that

The freeway, invisible but audible right behind those trees

The music I loved in 1984 seems so harsh to me now

In the dream you have a brother, possibly one year younger than yourself

Google sculpting

A Rubik's cube-like device that, once solved, forms a pair of faces

Sit sideways on the wooden chair, using the wall as your backrest

The oatmeal cools & congeals

For a second he regains consciousness, looks up at her & says, "Baby, I just died"

Your hand grown so thin this ring appears vast on your finger

A mug in a strange cottage into which to dip the bag of familiar tea

Robicheau, Pugh, Titus, McDormand – the same names over & over in the little island cemetery

Fog rolls off the rim of the cup

The flags hung wet in the afternoon of the rain

In the morning, the boys run down the stairs to discover the day

You reach the point in the game where you realize you cannot make it to the next level

After the fricasseed duck with gnocchi came trout stuffed with spinach and salmon paté, baked in a soft bread crust with a side of hot fennel, carmelized & mashed

The corner of Diamond Street & Tobacco Road

Cabeza de Vaca: going local

The rain proved more than a fine mist

Invert the question, not the mark

That children are sexual does not mean that they should be having sex

Refrigerator sighs

The postman's house is in the past

In Paradise, they keep anti-aircraft missiles in a shallow cave

I walk down to the river at dusk, your voice soft over the cell phone, the sun already gone, the dark about to come on, hearing now that distinct mewing sound, tens of thousands of bats swarming out from under the Congress Street Bridge

Merthiolate as a verb

Crimea liver

Pronounces it "haliboot"

Duluth is stranger than fiction

Entering the theater, the soldiers shoot the Chechnyan rebels rendered unconscious by nerve gas, lest they stir in this chemical sleep & set off the bombs strapped to their bodies

What I would love to describe next is that vowel lurking in your *l*, in your *r*

Jolt of the landing gear locking into place

Thru the open window, the unmistakable sound of dishes from the house next door, then the pop of a cork

Digital roaming

Often enough I dream of the need to replenish office supplies

The desire to scratch at the sunburn

Later thru the same window, a woman groaning with pleasure, then another

Life is strategic but reality is tactical

The smell of incense along St. Mark's Place
Moment when plugs received that third prong
After waking from the briefest midday nap, my face and hair "tingle"
Back on Valencia Street, after all these years
Passing the tanker on their narrow two-lane road this much before dawn, one realizes every breath must be understood as a choice
What would Chomsky drive
The violinist's towel
Penultima Thule
One reads aloud
while several in audience
write furiously into notebooks
Children eat cake for the frosting
You look so much like a previous lover that I know instantly how you will look naked
Four years past the pull date
The stress one feels just stepping off the bus
Pressure, pleasure
But to come upon your student in the brothel – what were the chances of that
Not a stylus but a syringe
Light shines too bright at first
Courier & Ives
The bullet you hear has already missed you
Model parsers as functions
In the dream, an island to the south of the United States has become a colony of Afghan expatriates – I'm wandering thru a bazaar in search of a better pair of sandals
Flavin's stairs
Motion picture in a paper bag
She leans her head against the cash register
Limp Bizkit

You wake & look at your fingers, then the backs of your hands, then count your pulse before lying back to shut your eyes again
To a lonely man any community appears to be a gang of conformists
Swart rocks mock thwarted fog tide
Voices drift up from the cove
Godardian in the garden
English tenor, French baritone
Land of the giant belt buckle
Wears his ears high on his head
Hideo Nomo
Finding Nemo
The day I see a hawk in the dogwood
The wasp settles lightly on my calf
I was 40 pages into the book & still had no sense of where she was going nor how she planned to get there
In summer the flies as large as house cats
The remainder of the oatmeal crusts
In the dream you have a brother
Halve a brother
On campus, 98 percent of theory is fashion – it's that other two percent that is worth everything
Point at which sun in the fog is not separate
A sensation in the same instant of both numbness & burning
On the deck in the rain, Pond Cove visible & audible, gulls hollering in all directions
If understood as a verb

In the dream a son has died – I wake & wonder if I shall ever sleep again
Dry thunder
The security light by the rear door flickers

Suddenly the fog erases Pond Cove
Title misunderstood as a separate work
Let's play hockey, Nagasaki
Light up the kudzu
& then went down w/ the blips
The child's hand on the shopping cart, tho reassuring, creates drag
Point where the paint on the toenails starts to flake
Whichever game you play with your tongue when you make a verbal mistake
Loose Lips Sink Chicks
Sol Lewitt meets Eva Hesse
Saline, Michigan, Alkaline, Tennessee
Point at which you recognize transparent, half visible, your own nose
A formal, but cursory, hug
A woman walking purposefully through the museum
A tall wet woman
Tin can forgotten on the rim of the deck
How odd to find a canyon in the clouds
Meaning of the shirt's tightness depends on body mass index
Zukofsky's Long Island
Under the too bright fluorescent lights, the too loud "soft" jazz, the windowless cafeteria
Candied basil jutting out from the passion fruit sorbet in the frozen lime cup
Syrupy serape therapy
Eyeballs feeling squeezed, bruised
Stanzas in medication
During the solo, the base player talks to the drummer
Even at night, you can tell that the plane is descending
Women arranged by their scarves
We feel the thunder in our lungs
Non-trivial wandering domains & homoclinic bifurcations
I am the one with the hot sauce

The dart of swallows
The wasp walks slowly across my forehead
My most Whitmanesque
Next door, someone is listening to voicemail
The large woman in biker leathers comes up to me, some kind of postmodern Viking, but when she speaks, her voice is wispy, girlish
They wear these uniforms only for batting practice
Fuse box painted shut
Peeling bark of the eucalyptus
Sound of a trowel soft & steady

Sound of a vowel, aloft & ready
Any large bowl of chocolates will be stale
An hour from landing, try not to notice that you are being hurled through the sky
Over the store vent, the wind whistles a three-note tune
Euclid elucidates
Q described as "low-brow"
Coffee house art show
Sink's mirror angles downward, hospital men's room, that one in a wheel chair might see
Sleep & its testicles
Faith-based driving visible in Boston
Head shaped like a melon, honeydew
Fighter pilots nibble Go Pills
Duck flies low over the lake in the rain
Pratt's bat sinks Sox
Cascade that down through your people and see if there's pushback
It is not her strategy as a beggar that I notice, using chalk to draw crude approximations of famous paintings on the sidewalk in front of the library, but the presence, smiling & dancing, of her daughter, a girl about five

Writing a note, signing it Dad
Will read nonsense for food
The little garden bursting with impatiens, the roses already bending beyond their pink prime
Pigeon tilts, coming in to land on the line
A teenage girl, utterly slender, with a brace on one knee
White rooster
struts
across the freeway
from the ocean
A small glass bowl filled with cinnamon
Her laughter was sexual &, outside, passersby paused for an instant, smiling as they walked on
The nostalgia of farming
War choreography
Tender tractions
Jimmy Cliff in Brooklyn sings *Sitting there in Dumbo (Dumbo, Dumbo, Dum-bo)*
A dyslexia of objects, of persons
Jazz so smooth it's squishy
Then Ted Nugent became president
She holds what remains of the apple, poised between thumb & forefinger
Destiny: density
"People fear the trauma of death," Gil says, rasping thru the tubes protruding from nose & throat, "but it's just like when extraterrestrials come to Earth & decide to turn into horses"

Baby Land to Babylon
The outer banks
The inner harbor
the upper
Midwest

"I'm drunk," she says, placing a hand upon my knee
The chemistry of insomnia
Soft seeds of the tomato
Glimmer of headlights on the rain-slicked pavement
Logs in the fireplace purely as decoration
Learning to grieve the poem
An Epipen™ with which to prick the lungs open to trick the air back in, sacs whose walls, when sick, grow thick, sticky, slick
Even after you extract the tine bones of the halibut, you feel the scratches on your gums
Any relationship changes forever the instant genital organs merge
The ring of an aluminum bat against concrete
The doves don't touch the feeder, thick with finches, but wander the worn grass below, searching for spilled seeds
The oil in Malevich's black-on-white geometrics beginning to crack, veins starting to spread
Problems always solve themselves
Women arranged by their scars
In god we truss

811.08 or death
Our profits suck, but the analysts love our EBITDA
Whipped cream crotch shorts
Those sausages attached to your palms
Unable to find the rental car return, she drives instead into the airport itself, hoping to find the shuttle, to follow it back, suddenly a child again, searching for the trail of crumbs
A great rehearsal yields a stiff event
Member of the board of sand & water
Of my wife & I he writes, "It's nice to watch old people being physically affectionate"
Objects in text are sharper than they appear

Organic free-range poodles

A new taste, that of pickled carrots

When the fire alarm goes off at midnight in the lodge, we're already asleep, but step through the glass doors to what on a higher floor would have been a balcony more or less automatically until realize the kids have not yet woken but are sleeping soundly thru this awful braying blare, so we step back into the room, lit now by a kind of strobe timed to the so-called siren, a horn really, rousing them into the strange pulsing light just as the alarm stops

Artichoke heart omelet with a side of oysters

Gil lies ill, still in the ICU

Example of factor map without a saturated compensation function

Off in that far meadow a young boy & girl kneel down, slowly, carefully removing one another's clothes

One way, Man Ray

We do the polis

in diff'rent v'ices

The poem is location, location, location

Moguls in Wonderland

Alone on the field, a team of young soccer players, jogging in place

Hurried wing flap of ducks

In Reno, the limo driver at the airport stands in front of a row of slots, silently holding a neatly lettered placard that reads "J. Geils"

The house of regional anesthesia

A hand is a hand only when clasping, pointing, picking, inserting, tickling, tasting

I paused in the shadows before I reached the community hot tub to see this couple – I had noticed them earlier on the lawn, sipping wine & talking quietly, their heads so near to another they were almost kissing – not he sits at the tub's edge as she takes him into her mouth, foam of the tub's jets met by this second foam as he groans & she coughs, him slipping back into the waters so that the two of them can share a salty kiss

Fluoride for Floridians
Spam span spinning
The wind comes in gusts so the leaves swirl & scatter about the street
They sell the Sunday paper from an island in the boulevard
Look east at dusk – use your ticket as a bookmark
The boy in oversized sweats is watching a movie on his laptop
Final signature
Build to stock, build to order, engineer to order
Thumbs are important for reading a book
"Where is there a red ten"
Waterways rib the wetlands, alongside which here & there a row of homes
Bulimic illuminations
I swallow & ears "pop," sound suddenly fresh & loud
Pennsyltucky
Blanche Dubois meets Marilyn Manson
Two prongs make a blight
She's in Chicago with that short skirt & perfect smile, researching the role of solidarity on asthma, while, back in Michigan, her brothers still work the land
If I had a Hummer
Anxiety floods the system with its sour adrenalin
Inside the airport with my parka still on, I feel sleepy, want to nap
In the kitchen behind me, the ice maker clatters (unseen in the freezer)

Utility building atop old department store now becomes penthouse condo

Sittin' here in Bembo

(Bembo, Bembo, Bem-bo)

Meanwhile, inside the penguin, policy is made by default

The politics of obituaries

At night Republications jump on the outstretched hands of the frail & needy with a resounding thump

My dick instead of an onion

Attempting authenticity, the Mexican grill on St. Marks Place play Ibrahim Ferrer

I left the five cops in the back room of the restaurant, still finishing their eggs over easy, coffee refills steaming from their cups, and walked out onto the street & around the corner where, one block down, a film crew was setting up to shoot a scene from Third Watch, three actors, also dressed as NYPD, sipping styrofoam coffee, waiting their turn

Itsy bitsy teeny weenie

caviar on top of blini

that I ate for the first time today

Removing flesh from my right foot as tho taking off a slipper

I wanted to like his work because I liked him, but these long, lax, loopy lines could not be escaped

The blue noodlism

In the masseuse's window, a continuous tape loop, a pair of hands & forearms giving a footrub

Origami commie

Conway Twitty ditty city

Corporations first outsourced their language procurement in the 1950s when they contracted with outside advertising agencies to craft messages for both external & internal audiences

Remembering the cheese sticks I left in the refrigerator back at the hotel
Every part of his face flushed red save for the pale gray cap of his shaved skull
Don't compare bush with tree with vine
At 14 hours of darkness, the power comes on in a flickering, halting way for five minutes, then fails again
Hearing not her voice but the electronics that amplifies it
Post-Avant Eye for the Quiet Guy
Out here, 11-year-olds get flying lessons for birthday presents
Fluorescent light well "sunken" into the acoustic tile
Holster starting to disintegrate
At dawn, my son & I wander about the neighborhood, looking for downed branches & fallen trees
The bee gets between meet & the lens of my glasses
Don't compare Bush with Hitler – Hitler could paint
We do the please
indifferent phases
Balmy bombing
I'm a figment of Jim Behrle's imagination
Found hydrangea deep in the woods & brought it transplanted to the edge of the garden
The new plug is bulky, crowding multiple sockets in addition to its own
Eventually the hand grasps because it is conditioned to do so – the sign on the men's room door reads "Tornado Shelter"
Upon a spindle, the pages dwindle
By the river, the trees grow too small & too close together
The mailman's mullet
Coma
raderie
Dream states of Texas
Next door, M is singing a song loud enough so that I can

tell it's country & western, even a cappella, but too softly for me to make out any of the words

Golden showers
bring dark flowers
Democracy of attention
The dog audible but not visible
Scrabble games evolve asymmetrically
First Sunday pilot low in the sky
The black book is not easily described
What I'd thought to be a bird song turns out to be the territorial chatter of a squirrel
The older I get the less I recognize this face in the mirror
The wasp half-walking amid the weeds in the brick
Astronauts report that space smells acrid or "burnt"
Hollywood overlights every scene
You're free to move about the text
Call & response of distant crows
Mishearing the Beatles: frat boy singing in the dead of night
I can hear your wristwatch ticking
What seems so remarkable about that face as it stares back is that it is so changeable – nothing appears fixed or given
Now a new trill here in the woods
A chipmunk has made a home in that stump
The distant white of power tools is never completely gone
If you wrote in Hawai'in, you'd be done by now
"Exiting" with a "C" lengthens the vowel
Protestants driven from Lucca 724 years ago
In Iraq each day the dead
Flying low over the etched part of the Southwest
Or walking out now to look at the Pacific Ocean

A gray sky is flat but a blue one extends forever
Suddenly a wave of cricket song
The constant weave of birds
Insect so small on the rim of my cap
The angle of my pen as it brushes this page

alphabet ends universe begins

Anselm Hollo

NOTES

Albany
1979-80. The idea that each sentence should be both personal and political. First published in *Ironwood,* 1983. See *Under Albany* (Salt Publishing, Cambridge, UK, 2004) for excruciating detail. Published in book form in *ABC,* Tuumba Press, Berkeley, CA, 1983. Chax Press did a wonderful broadside of this poem in April 1989.

Blue
1981. Occasioned by a long walk through the Lower East Side with Gil Ott. First published in *Paris Review, 1982.* Published in book form in *ABC,* Tuumba Press, Berkeley, CA, 1983.

Carbon
1979–80. Much of this was written in transit between my flat in the Mission District & the Victorian in which Krishna Evans then lived high atop Winfield Street in Bernal Heights. Originally published in the final issue of *This.* Published in book form in *ABC,* Tuumba Press, Berkeley, CA, 1983.

Demo
1984–85. March 4, 1985 was really the day on which I became older than my father ever lived to be. First published in *Temblor* in 1986. Published in book form in *Demo to Ink,* Chax Press, Tucson, AZ, 1992.

Engines
1982. My first draft was done on the typewriter, a very rare circumstance, as was the idea of composing through correspondence. There is utterly no mystery (to me) as to who wrote what. First published in *Conjunctions* in 1983. Published in book form in *Demo to Ink,* Chax Press, Tucson, AZ, 1992.

Force

1979–80. The first section to be started, tho I knew that it would not be the first section. The first five lines were all that existed of *The Alphabet* for months. First published in *Hills* in 1983. Published in book form in *Demo to Ink,* Chax Press, Tucson, AZ, 1992.

Garfield

Circa 1980–81. Written in a giant Garfield drawing notebook on deeply colored construction paper. *Alto* is not merely the designation of a saxophone, but at this point was also the name of my cat. First published in *Boxcar* in 1983. Published in book form in *Demo to Ink,* Chax Press, Tucson, AZ, 1992.

Hidden

1985–86. "Lucky" was my father's nickname, perhaps because he walked away from an airplane crash in 1947. Not quite eighteen years later, he was killed as a result from a plant explosion where he worked, although it took eight days for the toxins from the third-degree burns over 80 percent of his body to do the job. Sections were first published in *B-City, Central Park, Conjunctions, Generator, O-blék* & *West Coast Review,* 1987-88. Published in book form in *Demo to Ink,* Chax Press, Tucson, AZ, 1992.

Ink

1986–87. Jessie Aileen Coates Tansley was my maternal grandmother. First published in *Temblor* in 1988. Published in book form in *Demo to Ink,* Chax Press, Tucson, AZ, 1992.

Jones

1987. Every day for a year I looked at the ground. Jones is a street in San Francisco's Tenderloin that was then favored by transvestite prostitutes. Sections were first published in *The Archive for New Poetry Newsletter, Blue Mesa Review, Brief, Generator, Meanjin, O.ars, Raddle Moon, Writing, Zyzzyva* in 1990–91. Published in book form as *Jones* by Generator Press of Mentor, OH, in 1993.

Ketjak2: Caravan of Affect

1988–1993 (incorporating material from *Ketjak,* written 1974). Sections first appeared in *Chain, Muse Apprentice Guild, ReadMe, Salt Hill* in 1999–2002. Never published in book form save for a brief excerpt published as my contribution to *MultiPlex,* which also contains work by Karen Mac Cormack, Wild Honey Press, Bray, County Wicklow, Ireland, 1998. Note the section written on MARTA, the Atlanta rapid transit system, echoing *BART* (one of the satellite texts in *The Age of Huts*), this time with a region I profoundly don't know.

Lit

1981–82, the year I spent teaching at San Francisco State University & the University of California at San Diego. Every section is predicated on the number 12. Sections first published in *Bluefish, The Difficulties, Fiction International, Five Fingers Review, Pavement, Sink, Southpaw, Tramen* in 1984–86. Published in book form as *Lit,* Potes & Poets, Hartford, CT, 1987.

Manifest

1983–84. This section is secretly a companion to *Carbon.* First published in *Moving Letters* in 1985. Published in book form as *Manifest* by Zasterle Press, Tenerife, Canary Islands, Spain, 1990.

Non

1987–89. The instant you feel comfortable with a stanzaic form, abandon it. Sections first published in *Columbia Poetry Review, Croton Bug, Grist On-Line, Stifled Yawn, Talisman, Tyuonyi, Hot Bird Mfg, Mirage #4/Period(ical), New American Writing, Object* & *Object Permanence* in 1992–94. The publication in *Grist On-Line* in 1993 was my first on-line publication of any kind. It was pre-HTML. Published in book form as *N/O* by Roof Press, New York, NY, 1994.

Oz

1984–85. Close readers will recognize the presence of Fibonacci (who also makes a brief appearance in *Lit* and is a character in *Zyxt*). Sections first published in *Caliban, Sulfur, Zyzzyva* & *The New American Writing,* 1986–87. Published in book form as *N/O* by Roof Press, New York, NY, 1994.

Paradise

1984, literally begun on New Year's Day, completed on New Year's Eve. Every paragraph was one sitting. I stopped drinking during the composition of this text. Sections first appeared in *Abacus, boundary 2, Origin, Writing* in 1985–87. Published in book form as *Paradise* by Burning Deck, Providence, RI, 1985. Winner of the Poetry Center Book Award for 1985.

Quindecagon

1993. I began this poem after a request by Carla Harryman for work for her publication *Qu* in the early 1980s. After several false starts, much of this was composed during a single week late in March, 1993, while I was staying at the New Orleans Convention Center. The restaurant where I had the meal described in great detail was Emeril's on Tchoupitoulas. (Thanks to Karen Sharpe for reminding me.) *Qu* didn't survive to see the finished poem, alas. Finally published as *Abacus* 114 in 1998. The only section of *The Alphabet* that rhymes. Published in book form as ® by Drogue Press, New York, NY, 1999.

®

1992–93. Thinking of the tension between the sentence and the line. First published in *Conjunctions* in 1994. Published in book form as ® by Drogue Press, New York, NY, 1999.

Skies

1980-81. Every day for one year I looked at the sky & noted what I saw. Sections first published in *So & So, Sulfur* & *This* in 1981–83. Published in book form as ® by Drogue Press, New York, NY, 1999.

Toner

1987–88. The Bruce of the dedication is of course Mr. Andrews. First published in *Avec, Broadway, Edge, Innovations, minnesota review* (published in Storrs, CT), *O-Blék, Sulfur, Talisman, Verse* & *Zyzzyva* in 1989–90. Published in book form as *Toner* by Potes & Poets Press, East Hartford, CT, 1992.

Under

1990–1991. Sections first published in *B-City, Cream City Review, CrossConnect, Grist On-Line, Iowa Review, New Orleans Review, No Roses Review, Object Permenance, Proliferation, Salt, Situation, 6ix, Subdream* & *TO*. See the note re *Grist On-Line* for *Non.*

VOG

Circa 1985–99. This one had a lot of false starts before I got what I wanted: a collection of "ordinary" poems. The only acronym among all the titles. Poems (sections) first published in *Antennae, Call, Conjunctions, CrossConnect, DC Poetry, Double Room, Electronic Poetry Review, Facture, Filling Station, Jacket, Lit, Matrix, Mute: Culture and Politics After the Net, Near South, nthposition, NWS, O Poss, Overland, POep, Sal Mimeo, Secret Swan, Slope, Van Gogh's Ear, Washington Square & Xconnect: Writers of the Information Age.* "Woundwood" first published as a book by Cuneiform Press, Buffalo, 2004.

What

1985–87. This is the poem I usually suggest when new readers ask what work of mine to read first. No section of this poem ever appeared in a print journal because Geoff Young brought the book out so quickly. A section was subsequently published in the email journal *PoetryEtc* in 1999 and another as part of a two-poet broadside by the Inverse reading series of Philadelphia in 2006. Published in book form as *What* by The Figures, Great Barrington, MA, 1988. In John Moore's painting on the book jacket, you can see the neighborhood in which my mother then lived at the foot of the hill on the back cover.

Xing

1993–94. No section of this ever appeared in a print journal. Published in book form as *Xing* by Meow Press, Buffalo, NY, 1996, and by Factory School Press, Ithaca, NY, 2004.

You

1995. One paragraph a day, one section a week, for a year. You can spot the day we moved from California. Sections first published 1996–2000 in *5_trope, APR Philly Edition (American Poetry Review), Black Ice, CrossConnect, Dandelion, Fourteen Hills, Ixnay, Jacket, Kenning, PhillyTalks, Potepoetzine Two, Sycamore Review, Shiny, Tinfish, Veer* & the 1998 Catalog of the *Pew Fellowship in the Arts.*

Zyxt

1998–2004. *Zyxt* is the last work in the *OED*. Sections first published in *Big Bridge, Cue, Drunken Boat, Latchkey.net, mark(s), MiPoesias: Revista Literaria, RealPoetik, Shampoo, Vanitas* & *Xconnect / CrossConnect.*